DATE DUE FOR RETURN

THE CHARACTERS
OF THEOPHRASTUS

———

HERODES, CERCIDAS, AND THE
GREEK CHOLIAMBIC POETS
(EXCEPT CALLIMACHUS AND BABRIUS)

THE
CHARACTERS
OF
THEOPHRASTUS

NEWLY EDITED AND TRANSLATED

BY

J. M. EDMONDS

SOMETIME FELLOW OF JESUS COLLEGE
AND LECTURER IN THE UNIVERSITY OF CAMBRIDGE

CAMBRIDGE, MASSACHUSETTS
HARVARD UNIVERSITY PRESS
LONDON
WILLIAM HEINEMANN LTD
MCMLXI

First printed 1929
Reprinted 1946, 1953, 1961

Printed in Great Britain

CONTENTS

PREFACE

THE *Characters* of Theophrastus are a good wine that needs no bush, but it has been bottled anew, and new bottles may need a word of recommendation. The mere existence of an early English translation such as Healey's would hardly justify an archaistic rendering, but the Character, in the hands of Hall, Overbury, and Earle, has become a native *genre*, and that, I think, is enough to make such a rendering the most palatable. And this style of translation, taunts of 'Wardour Street' notwithstanding, has a great advantage. Greek, being itself simple, goes best into a simple style of English ; and in the seventeenth century it was still easy to put things simply without making them bald. A simple translation into our modern dialect, if it is to rise above Translator's English, is always difficult and often unattainable.

In preparing the text I have discarded much of my earlier work, in the belief, shared no doubt by many scholars, that the discovery of papyrus fragments of ancient Greek books has shifted the editor's bearings from Constantinople to Alexandria. With the 'doctrine of the normal line,' exploded by A. C. Clark, went much critical lumber, and the dust is only just beginning to clear. The peculiar character of this text, with its recurring καί and its natural toleration of displacement, makes it an excellent *corpus vile* to experiment on. It would be too much to hope that my readers will come away from my Introduction as confident as I am that our MSS. go back to an 11-letter line archetype, but I cannot help feeling that there is a plausibility in the emendations I have based upon my hypothesis which is not to be found in the others.

My thanks are due to F. C. Burkitt, A. C. Clark, A. B. Cook, A. E. Housman, A. S. Hunt, and R. D. Hicks, for generous help of various kinds; I gratefully acknowledge my indebtedness to the labours of D. Bassi, W. Crönert, O. Immisch, O. Navarre, and G. Pasquali; I would thank Isaac Casaubon if I could and if I dared.

J. M. EDMONDS.

CAMBRIDGE,
15th July 1927.

PREFACE TO THE FIRST REPRINT

BESIDES a few minor corrections this edition contains three more important changes, θεαινῶν for θεᾷ at XVI. 11 and two truer renderings in XXV. In II, IV, V, and X there are new references to the *Comic Fragments*. Some of these changes are due to my friend Mr. F. H. Sandbach.

J. M. E.

CAMBRIDGE,
16th February 1944.

THE CHARACTERS

OF

THEOPHRASTUS

INTRODUCTION

I. The Book and its Author

LIKE other unique products of the human spirit, this great little book has aroused much speculation among those who not knowing how a thing is done must needs find out why. Some measure of re-editing it certainly underwent in after life—mending rather than emending, or the thin disguise of the name Alexander would not have been maintained after the necessity for it—political apparently—had ceased.[a] The first editor was in all probability the author. That Theophrastus collected and edited these pieces himself substantially in the order in which we have them, is suggested by certain signs of artistic development which we may observe in comparing the earlier as a whole with the later. First, the earlier characters are generally the sketchier, not more carelessly drawn but less completely coloured. No. I is any (Athenian) dissembler, and his dissemblings manifold and anywhere (Athenian). Dissembling is a sepia-wash. With the exception of VIII, the Newsmaker, of whom presently, the same is true,

---

[a] xxiii. 3; for editing in the Peripatetic School *cf.* Lycon's will (died 225), Diog. Laert. v. 73, and Arcesilaus' unpopular revision of Crantor's works, *ibid.* iv. 32, *cf.* vii. 34; and see Barthélemy-St. Hilaire's Dissertation prefixed to his translation of the Aristotelian *Problems*, Paris, 1891.

more or less, of all the Characters till we come to
XXIII. They, too, are sepia-washes or, at the most,
tinted drawings. Pretentiousness, however, has
fewer and larger parts ; and Cowardice, its next-door
neighbour but one, though it is one of the longest,
contains only two scenes. These are water-colours ;
and of the last eight Characters no less than five are
of this kind. Secondly, there is development in the
smaller matters of style. If we divide the book into
three equal parts, (a), (b), and (c), we find that though
δεινός appears equally in all, οἶος is preceded by
τοιόσδε instead of τοιοῦτος not at all in (a), once in
(b), three times in (c) ; that the qualifying phrase
ὡς ὅρῳ λαβεῖν, or the like, occurs four times in (a),
twice in (b), not at all in (c) ; that the word ἀμέλει
occurs four times in (a), four times in (b), and eight
in (c) ; and that the construction ὥστε-and-infinitive
occurs four times in (a), once in (b), not at all in (c) ;
whereas ἵνα or ὅπως final occurs twice in (a), five
times in (b), eleven times in (c). And it may well
mean something that the average number of lines to
the section in modern texts is two in the first half of
the book and two and a half in the second. The
general effect of which these minutiae are the outward
signs is that the reader somehow feels as he proceeds
that what was Anyman in the earlier parts of the
book comes to be Somebody in the later. None,
probably, of the Characters is really an individual
masquerading as a type, yet when we read of the
Pretentious Man, the Coward, the Oligarch, or the
Friend of Rascals, we feel what we do not feel of the
earlier Characters, that Theophrastus' contemporaries
must have said ' That is meant for so-and-so.' And
another thing shows the artist. A mere philosopher

would have arranged his types scientifically. The Garrulous man, the Loquacious, the Newsmaker, the Backbiter, and still more Penuriousness, Parsimoniousness, and Meanness, should properly be presented in groups. The artist is more likely to arrange his sketches either in the order in which he drew them or as he thinks will be most pleasing to his public. Which brings us back to the Newsmaker. This Character, though it is numbered VIII, belongs in form to the later part of the book; and it is exceptional in another way. For here Theophrastus breaks his 'rule of the infinitive'[a] by no fewer than five indicatives; the only other instances are halfway through the book, the two potential optatives at the end of XV. Now it is agreed that VIII must have been written after XXIII, because in the former Antipater is dead and in the latter still alive. It is only a matter of a few months, but there it is. We have seen that, apart from Newsmaking, there are clear traces of a trend. Then why this exception? The reason, like that of the disguising of Alexander's name in XXIII, is very likely political. It may perhaps be connected with the dedication[b] of the book to the adviser of Eurydice, wife of the imbecile king Arrhidaeus, whose rival the four-year-old son of Alexander is made by the Newsmaker—so absurdly as it would seem to the contemporary Athenian reader, and also, let us hope, to Polycles[c]—to defeat Casander who was then in favour at Athens. However the exception may be explained, exception it is.

[a] With οἷος.
[b] If that is genuine, see pp. 37-9, and add that Diogenes' lists of the works of both Aristotle and Theophrastus contain letters; there was one from T. to Casander.   [c] See p. 36.

The pieces are arranged as none but the author would arrange them, and therefore the publication of the book, as a whole, is the author's.

From the order he has adopted we may gather that the object of his book was not primarily scientific. For according to Diogenes Laertius[a] one of Theophrastus' famous sayings was 'As soon trust an unbridled horse as an ill-arranged disquisition,' and his extant botanical books are the work of a great classifier. For whom then, apart from Polycles, were these Characters written? Like other works of their author they served perhaps, as a part of 'poetic,' to fill a gap in the Aristotelian *corpus* of human knowledge.[b] They seem to have originated a Peripatetic *genre*.[c] But what capital after-dinner recitations[d] they would make! First the definition with its suggestion of the game of εἰκασίαι or 'likenesses'—'I say,' says the tipsy Alcibiades, 'that Socrates is very like those Silenuses that you see set out in the statuaries' shops'—and then its so convincing justification in a string of humorously and gently sarcastic examples, extending often to little scenes—the Unconscionable man at the butcher's, the Coward at sea; and the touch which makes the whole world kin—' and this done he will away home and tell his wife what a great success he has had.' They may indeed have been, as the use of the word ἀμέλει implies,[e] answers to 'dinner-table questions,' συμποσιακαὶ ἐρωτήσεις, like the dialectic questions addressed

[a] *Lives of the Philosophers*, v. 2, ed. Hicks, L.C.L.
[b] *Cf.* Rostagni, *Riv. di Filol.* xlviii. 417 f.
[c] Heracleides Ponticus (?), Lycon, Ariston, Satyrus; *cf.* now Pasquali, *Rass. di Ling. e Lett. class.*, 1918, pp. 7 f.
[d] *Cf.* Plat. *Sym.* 215 c, *Rep.* 487 E, *Meno* 80 c, and *Rhet. Gr.* viii. 789 W.   [e] *Cf.* xiii. n. 1.

6

INTRODUCTION

by Stilpo to Eucleides at the table of Ptolemy I., and the 'inquiries over the wine-cup,' ἐπικυλικεῖοι ἐξηγήσεις so much resented by Arcesilaus.[a] Perhaps they were composed for the monthly dinners of the Peripatetic thiasos for which Aristotle wrote his *Mess-rules*,[b] and which were the original scene of his *Dinner - Table Problems*,[c] a collection which was doubtless the prototype of the *Convivial Questions* of Plutarch and the *Doctors at Dinner* of Athenaeus, not to mention the *Symposiacs* of Didymus. For a Peripatetic book written in light vein we may compare Theophrastus' contemporary Heracleides of Pontus. At the end of Diogenes' list of his works [d] we read 'Some of these are composed in comic style (κωμικῶς πέπλακεν), for instance the tracts *On Pleasure* and *On Temperance*, others in the style of tragedy (τραγικῶς), for instance *Those in Hades*, *On Piety*, and *On Authority*. And he has a sort of intermediate conversational type for dialogue between philosophers, generals, and statesmen.' Unfortunately we do not know to which group Heracleides' *Characters* belonged, nor whether their title betokens a similar book to this.[e]

Whether the companion volume of 'good' characters apparently referred to in Theophrastus' preface was ever written, is not certain. But Diogenes' list of his works contains two mentions of *Characters*, one of which *may* refer to the 'good' volume and one

---

[a] Diog. L. ii. 111-2, 118, iv. 42.
[b] νόμοι συσσιτικοί Diog. L. v. 26, συμποτικοί Ath. v. 2, 186 b, cf. i. 3 f.
[c] συσσιτικὰ προβλήματα Hesych., cf. Plut. Q. Conv. 6 prol., Macr. Sat. vii. 3. 23.   [d] v. 88.
[e] It may have been a rhetorical work like Antisthenes' Περὶ λέξεως ἢ περὶ χαρακτήρων Diog. L. vi. 15.

7

to the 'bad'; a clearer indication is the passage where Eustathius speaks of Theophrastus' Brave man in contrast with his Coward.[a] The 'good' characters the dinner-table would not perhaps find so amusing; yet not all amusement is laughable nor were all ῥήσεις comic.[b] To write a book to serve, as it would seem,[c] two such diverse purposes, would need an uncommon but happily not unexampled nature, that which combines philosopher, teacher, artist, and wit. Readers of his delightful *Letters* will think perhaps of the late Walter Raleigh. Readers of Athenaeus [d] will remember the account he takes from Hermippus, who wrote about fifty years after our author's death: ' At a regular hour Theophrastus used to appear in the Garden spruce and gay, and taking his seat proceed to his discourse, indulging as he went along in every pose and gesture imaginable; he once mimicked an epicure by putting out his tongue and licking his lips.' Add to this his saying,[e] ' The most expensive thing is time,' his pedagogic contrast of a lecture-audience (πανήγυρις) with a class (συνέδριον), and his calling somebody σχολαστικός, ' a pedant,' and you have a portrait to prefix to Diogenes' great list of his works.[f]

The *Characters* were a new thing, but even new

[a] *Il.* 931. 21.   [b] *Cf.* Ar. *Nub.* 1371, Ephipp. 16 K.

[c] Jebb is very sound here: ' The difficulty [in supposing the object of the book philosophic] is, not that the descriptions are amusing, but that they are written as if their principal aim was to amuse,' p. 13 (29).

[d] i. 21 a, quoting doubtless from H.'s *On Theophrastus*, Diog. L. ii. 55.

[e] For these passages see Diog. v. 36 f. and add vi. 90.

[f] 490 ' volumes' as against Aristotle's 535 (=' nearly 400 works,' Diog. L. v. 34); but of course many were in size mere pamphlets, as is shown by the totals of the lines.

8

things have origins, and, though this book's resemblance to its forbears is slight, it is unmistakable.
Passages like Herodotus' description of the Despot [a]
are doubtless in the direct line; and though the
Oligarchical man of Plato's *Republic* [b] is almost as far
removed from that of Theophrastus as Theophrastus'
Flatterer from Menander's, certain parts of the
Nicomachean Ethics show a near affinity. I translate
a well-known passage: [c] 'Such then is the μεγαλο-
πρεπής or Magnificent man. The *excessive* nature
corresponding to the *mean* in him, that of the
βάναυσος or Vulgar, shows its excess in extravagant
expenditure. For the Vulgar man spends much on
small things and seeks distinction in wrong ways,
entertaining his club, for instance, as if it were a
wedding-party, and, when he stages a comedy, in-
troducing purple in the Megarian style where the
Chorus enters. His object in all such actions will be,
not to win honour but to display his wealth and
cause a sensation, spending little where he should
spend much, and much where little. The μικρο-
πρεπής or Shabby-minded man will always show the
corresponding *defect* and, after he has spent a fortune
on a thing, lose honour in a mere detail of it, always
stopping to consider what is the cheapest way and
bewailing even that, and exaggerating the importance of everything he does.' There is humour here,
but it is incidental. The humour of the *Characters*
is essential. In Aristotle the examples are a means
of expression, in Theophrastus they are the thing
said. In Aristotle the teacher predominates, in
Theophrastus the man of letters. Plato, here as
always, is as much one as the other.

[a] iii. 80.   [b] 553 A.   [c] iv. 1123 a 6.

THEOPHRASTUS

I add an outline of our author's life. Theophrastus, whose true name was Tyrtamus, was born, like Sappho, at Eresus in Lesbos, probably about the year 370 B.C. His father was a fuller. He was twice instrumental in expelling tyrants from his native town, and the democracy of Eresus, overthrown about 357, was restored before 334. It was perhaps therefore partly for political reasons that he first went to Athens. Anyhow he sat at the feet of Plato and, before his death, left him for Aristotle. It is probable that when, on Plato's death in 347, Aristotle withdrew, first to Assus, then to Mytilene, and thence to Stageira to educate the young Alexander, Theophrastus spent some time in Lesbos and then joined his master in Chalcidice, to return with him to Athens when, in 335, Alexander became king. When Aristotle retired in the year of Alexander's death, 323, to Chalcis, Theophrastus succeeded him as head of the Peripatetic School. As many as two thousand pupils, it is said, attended his lectures. One of these was the comic poet Menander, who brought out his first play a year after the final triumph of Macedon at Crannon, 321. The *Characters* were written in 319. In 307 Theophrastus shared the banishment of all philosophers under the decree proposed by one Sophocles, returning on its repeal the following year. When he died, in or about 287, all Athens followed him to his grave in the Garden where he had taught. His will, which is given by Diogenes, is an historical document of the greatest interest. We gain from it among other things a clear notion of the Garden which was the undoubted ancestor of the modern college.

INTRODUCTION

II. The Text

The manuscripts of the *Characters* arrange themselves into groups containing respectively :

    (1) I–XV : A and B and the class *E*
    (2) XVI–XXX : V
    (3) I–XXI : M
    (4) I–XXIII : the class *D*
    (5) I–XXVIII : the class *C*

A is Parisinus (Fontebl. Reg.) 2977 membr. saec. xi,
B is Parisinus (Med. Reg.) 1983 membr. saec. xi ineunt.,
V is Vaticanus gr. 110 chart. saec. xiii vel xiv,
M is Epitome Monacensis gr. 505 chart. saec. xv.[a]

The mss of classes *C*, *D*, and *E*, none of which is older than the xiiith century, are described, with the above, by Immisch, who has done more for the text of the *Characters* than any scholar since Casaubon.

The text is peculiarly liable to loss and dislocation owing to two circumstances, the unusual number of sentences beginning with καί, and the unusually disconnected nature of the subject matter. The first invites *parablepsia* ($\pi\beta\lambda$), the second toleration of displacement. (*Hence the length of the critical notes in this edition.*)

Next to the contents of the mss, the most valuable datum for constructing a *stemma* has, as I think rightly, been thought to be the position of certain

---

   [a] Besides these there are papyrus-fragments : (1) *Oxyrh. Pap.* 699 cent. iii, Epitome of xxv. 6 and xxvi. 1-2 ; (2) Philodemus περὶ Κακιῶν *Herc. Vol. Coll. Tert.* col. vi-vii, text of Char. v. 2-end.

neighbouring passages of *Char.* XXX. V has these in what is clearly their true position, all other mss at the end of XI. Of this there can be three explanations : (1) V represents half of a different recension in two books ; or (2) the ancient recension from which all our mss have come had the passage in both places ; [a] or else (3) the half-book (β), from which V's ancestor (*v*) was copied, had, or rather came to have, at or near the end certain loose portions which alone, or rather some of which alone, eventually survived and were inserted in the other half (α) before the ancestors of the other mss (*m*, *a*, *b*, etc.) were made.[b] Of these alternatives the first is rendered unlikely by the title of V, ἀπὸ τῶν τοῦ Θεοφράστου χαρακτήρων ιϛ′ χαρακτὴρ δεισιδαιμονίας, and its having no index, which show that the scribe of V knew that he was copying a fragment ; and the second is not likely in so short a work (*but see below*, p. 30). All the other large displacements probably took place in the earlier antiquity. Compare the history of the library of Theophrastus in Strabo, xiii. 54. One displacement, at any rate, is shared by the Philodemus citation (*Pap. Herc.* 1457).

A third datum has not hitherto been taken sufficiently into consideration, that furnished by the omissions, the repetitions, the transpositions, and the minor displacements. The great majority of

[a] *Cf.* the Urbinas of Theophr. *Hist. Plant.* ix. 8. 1 f ; and the Aristotelian *Problems*, of which 14 out of 896 are identical repetitions (Prantl *ap.* St.-Hilaire, *op. cit.*).

[b] More accurately, the Archetype was divided into *p* and *q*, *p* with full index, *q* with none ; from *p* came α with half the index ; the other half-index was freshly compiled and added either to *q* after *v* was made, or to an intermediate ms β, ancestor of all exemplars containing any of XVI–XXX.

these can, I think, be most easily accounted for on the following theory :

(a) *That all existing mss except the papyrus fragments come from a papyrus-roll without compendia* [a] *which had 11-12 letters to the line and a column of the unusually short average length of* 12½ *lines* [b] *;*

(b) *That this exemplar was purposely divided into two halves, either so that it could be copied by two scribes at once, or because of the awkwardness of this* format *;*

(c) *That this exemplar was copied not only in contents but to some extent in form by the ancestors of all our mss (except the papyri).*

(d) *That the edition to which this archetype (Arch.) and its more immediate descendants belonged was made from an earlier exemplar (Pre-Arch.) which had about* 18 *letters to the line.* [c]

I take first the chief evidence for these conclusions in order, and then the indications that the supposed *format* of Arch., though apparently unusual, is possible :

(a) i. *Evidence for the* 11-12 *letter line in Arch. and its immediate descendants* (I star the instances where πβλ seems to be involved, underlining the letters concerned, and adding within brackets the number of letters in each line) :

[a] Except such ancient devices as the stroke over the penultimate letter indicating N.

[b] Or, allowing ½ a line per col. for paragraphing, say 13.

[c] I can hardly expect my critics to write out the whole book, as I have done, in (plausible) 12-14 line columns of (plausible) 11-12 letter (rarely 9 or 13) lines with an eye to the possible causes of gaps, etc., but if they would—!

13

V :   repetition, in XXII 5-6, of   -τοῦ ἀποτιθέναι (13)
κἀὶ τὰ παιδία (11)

after   δεινὸς δὲ μὴ (10)
πέμψαι εἰς διδα- (13)
σκάλου ὅταν ᾖ (12)

repetition,* in XXVI 3, of   ἀμέλει δὲ δει- (11)
νὸς τοῖς τοιού- (12)
τοις τῶν ὀλί- (10)
γων χρήσασθαι (12)

after   ἐπίστασθαι (10)

C D^a :   omission,* in XVI 4, of   ἱερῷον εὐθὺς (12)

after   ἱερὸν ἐνταῦθα (12)

transposition,* in XVI 9, of ἐλθεῖν between
οὔτ' ἐπὶ νεκρὸν (12)

and   οὔτ' ἐπὶ λεχὼ (10)

omission, in XXI 8, of   ἐν τοῖς μύωψι (11)

transposition, in XXVIII 2, of φασὶν
after ἐν τῇ πατρίδι (12)
εὐγενεῖς εἶναι (13)

A :   transposition,* in III 6, of   μήτε σχολὴν (10)

and μήτε σπουδήν (11)

anticipation,* in XII 9, of   καὶ ἀναλίσκον- (12)
τας

after   μεμαθηκότας (11)
instead of after καὶ θύοντας (10)

10 lines below.[b]

A B e^c :   omission, in Proem § 4, of   τὸν λόγον ἀπὸ (11)
D :   repetition, in IX 7, of   κριθὰς ποτὲ δὲ (12)
omission, in XV 10, of   καὶ οὔτε ᾆσαι (12)

---

[a] After XXIII C alone.
[b] Of respectively 10, 9, 9, 10, 12, 11, 11, 12, 10, 10 letters.
[c] c, d, e indicate one or more mss, but not all, of the classes C, D, E.

14

INTRODUCTION

M : loss,* in XI. 1, of $\qquad$ $\dot{\epsilon}\pi\iota\phi\alpha\nu\dot{\eta}s$ $\kappa\alpha\dot{\iota}$ **(11)**
before $\overline{\epsilon}\pi o\nu\epsilon\dot{\iota}\delta\iota\sigma\tau os$ (12)

These give an average length to the line of $11\frac{1}{3}$ letters.

ii. *Evidence for the column of an average length of 12-13 ll. in Arch.*[a] (this depends, of course, on the acceptance of the 11-12 letter line): The latter part of XXX[b]—the eventually saved loose part (β_3) of the second half (β) of Arch.—gives the best example. It may be divided into nine columns thus, if we assign to the margin of Arch. words which there is good reason to suppose (*see critical notes*) were there and not in the text :

(1) $\kappa\alpha\dot{\iota}$ $o\dot{\iota}\nu o\pi\omega\lambda\hat{\omega}\nu$—$\theta\epsilon\alpha\tau\rho\hat{\omega}\nu\alpha\iota$ (marg. $\dot{\epsilon}\pi\dot{\iota}$ $\theta\dot{\epsilon}\alpha\tau\rho o\nu$) 11 ll.
(2) $\overline{\kappa\alpha\dot{\iota}}$ $\dot{\alpha}\pi o\delta\eta\overline{\mu\hat{\omega}\nu}$—$\phi o\rho\tau\dot{\iota}o\nu$ (marg. $\dot{\epsilon}\pi\iota\theta\epsilon\hat{\iota}\nu\alpha\iota$) 11 ll.
(3) $\bar{\eta}$ $\delta\dot{\upsilon}\nu\alpha\tau\alpha\iota$—$\beta\alpha\lambda\alpha\nu\epsilon\dot{\iota}\omega$ $\kappa\alpha\dot{\iota}$ (marg. $\ddot{\alpha}\lambda\lambda\omega\nu$ and $\pi\alpha\rho\dot{\epsilon}\chi\epsilon\iota\nu$) 11 ll.
(4) $\epsilon\dot{\iota}\pi\dot{\omega}\nu$ $\sigma\alpha\pi\rho\dot{o}\nu$—'$E\rho\mu\hat{\eta}s$ (marg. $\dot{\epsilon}\pi\rho\dot{\iota}\omega$ and $\dot{\upsilon}\pi\dot{o}$ $\tau\hat{\omega}\nu$ $o\dot{\iota}\kappa\epsilon\tau\hat{\omega}\nu$) 12 ll.
(5) $\kappa\alpha\dot{\iota}$ $\dot{\iota}\mu\dot{\alpha}\tau\iota o\nu$—$\mu\epsilon\tau\rho\epsilon\hat{\iota}\nu$ $\alpha\dot{\upsilon}$- (marg. $\tau\dot{o}\nu$) 13 ll.
(6) -$\tau\dot{o}s$ $\tau o\hat{\iota}s$ $\ddot{\epsilon}\nu\delta o\nu$—$\dot{\alpha}\pi o\delta o\hat{\upsilon}\nu\alpha\iota$ $\kappa\alpha\dot{\iota}$ (marg. $\sigma\phi\dot{o}\delta\rho\alpha$ $\delta\dot{\epsilon}$ $\dot{\alpha}\pi o\psi\hat{\omega}\nu$) 13 ll.
(7) $\tau\hat{\omega}\nu$ $\upsilon\dot{\iota}\hat{\omega}\nu$ $\delta\dot{\epsilon}$- -$\mu\dot{\alpha}\tau\alpha$ $\delta\iota\dot{\alpha}$ $\tau\dot{o}$ 14 ll.
(8) $\theta\epsilon\dot{\alpha}s$ $\epsilon\dot{\iota}\nu\alpha\iota$- -$\rho\dot{\iota}\zeta o\nu\tau os$ $\kappa\alpha\dot{\iota}$ 14 ll.
(9) $\phi\rho\dot{\alpha}\tau o\rho\alpha s$- -$\delta\epsilon s$ $\mu\dot{\eta}$ $\lambda\dot{\alpha}\beta\omega\sigma\iota$ 14 ll.

Of these nine columns M, or rather *m*, lost col. 1, probably by $\pi\beta\lambda$ between the top lines ; all mss but V lost, probably owing to mutilation entire or partial, the first 8 ll. of col. 5 and the whole of cols. 7 and 8. The average length, then, of the column in this part of the roll was just under $12\frac{1}{2}$ lines. Now, as the tendency of papyrus is to tear vertically, and *C* stops at XXVIII, Char. XXIX probably began a new column. If so, between XXIX init. and XXX § 5, Arch. had (with two titles) 3 columns of 12, and 6

---

[a] Allowance for possible paragraphing would slightly raise the average length of the columns, and perhaps tend to equalize them ; contrast cols. (1) and (7) below.
[b] Disregarding the last part of all, §§ 17-20 (β_4).

15

of 13 ll. Again, as the roll was cut in two between XV and XVI, it is reasonable to suppose that XVI began a new column (this would doubtless be originally due to the planning-out of the *format* of the edition). It is interesting, then, to note that if we take 12 ll. as the content of XVI col. 1, the column ends with an unelided ἀπό (before ἱεροῦ); that if we take 13, 13, 13, 12 as the length of cols. 2-5, cols. 3-5 may have been lost from *m* by πβλ between καὶ ἐὰν ἴδῃ and κἂν (καὶ ἐὰν) γλαῦκες. Again, if β₃ ended with the end of a column and the ultimately legible parts of it were copied and the copy inserted after Char. XI, Char. XII would seem to have begun with the top of a column ; and if we give this column 14 lines, we can account for *m*'s displacement of

$$\text{ἀσχολουμένῳ} \quad (12)$$
$$\text{προσελθὼν ἀνα-} \quad (12)$$
$$\text{κοινοῦσθαι.}$$

Lastly, if cols. 2, 3, and 4 of XII contained 14, 12, and 12 lines respectively, M's omission of

$$(\S\ 7) \quad \underline{\text{καὶ ἐκ μακρᾶς}} \quad (11)$$

down to (but not including)

$$(\S\ 12) \quad \underline{\text{καὶ μαστιγου-}} \quad (11)$$
$$\underline{\text{μένου}}$$

is due to the omission of two whole columns through πβλ (of the scribe of *m*) between the top lines of cols. 3 and 5.

(b) *That the halving of Arch. was designed* is clear from the equality of the division I-XV, XVI-XXX.

(c) *Arch. was copied to some extent in form* as well as in contents by the ancestors of all our mss (except, of course, the papyri). In some this identity seems to have included columns as well as lines, in others it was a matter of lines only. Both lines and columns apparently remained unchanged in both *v* and *m* throughout. The rest show evidence of the 11-12 letter line, but not of the 12-13 line column except in β₃, where they naturally coincide with *m*. (This

16

perhaps indicates that *v* and *m* retained the roll-form while the ancestors of the rest were codices even in the first generation from Arch.)

i. *Columns*: Apart from instances already given under (a) ii, M omits passages of about 12 or 24 lines, apparently by πβλ of its ancestor *m*, in

II 4 f* : between καί and καί   (12 ll.)
IX 5 f* : between καί and καί   (14 ll.)
X 2 f* : between οἶος and οἶος   (12 and 13 ll.)
XXI 8 f* : between καί πομπεύσας   (12 ll.)
                    δὲ

and   καί κυναρίου   (11 ll.)
            δὲ   (11 ll.).

The evidence for V is given above under (a) ii.

ii. *Lines*: The 11-letter line is indicated above under (a) i for the common ancestor of A, B, and some of the E class (*abe*); for the C class and the D class; for the common ancestor of C and D (*cd*); for the common ancestor of A B (*ab*); as well as for *v* and *m*.

(d) *Evidence for a line of* 17-18 *letters in the Pre-Archetype* : This, naturally, is rather less definite.

Proem § 4 * : τὸν λόγον · σοῦ δὲ παρα-   (17)
                    κολουθῆσαί τε ὀρθῶς   (17)
                    καὶ εἰδῆσαι εἰ ὀρθῶς   (17)
                    λέγω.

The first ὀρθῶς clearly comes from the second.   Comparing Aesch. i. 116 ὑμᾶς βουλοίμην ἂν οἷς ἐγὼ μέλλω λέγειν προσ-έχειν τὸν νοῦν καὶ παρακολουθεῖν εὐμαθῶς, we see that it has in all probability ousted εὐμαθῶς.

III 5 * : displacement of

                    καὶ ἐὰν ὑπομένῃ τις   (17)
                    αὐτὸν μὴ ἀφίστασθαι   (17)

before καὶ ὡς Βοηδρομιῶνος (17)
μέν ἐστι τὰ μυστήρια (17)
Πυανοψιῶνος δὲ τὰ Ἀπα- (18)
τούρια Ποσιδεῶνος δὲ (18)
τὰ κᾱτ' ἀγροὺς Διονύσια (19).

IV 13 * : displacement of

καὶ ἐν βαλανείῳ δὲ (16)
ᾱσαι· καὶ εἰς τὰ ὑποδή- (18)
ματα δὲ ἥλους ἐγκροῦσαι (20)

before καὶ τῆς αὐτῆς ὁδοῦ παρι- (19)
ῶν κομίσασθαι παρ' Ἀρ- (17)
χίου τοὺς ταρίχους· (16).

The average, taken from these three cases, is 17½ letters to
the line.

XIII 5 : All mss except M (and some of the *C* class
which give καταλιπεῖν 4 ll. of Arch. too late) omit

τὴν ὁδὸν καταλιπὼν (16).

This probably stood in the margin of Arch., having been
omitted by the first hand. As *D* omits it, it was apparently
adscript in *cd* also (*see below*).

IV 9 * : ABe's omission of 19 letters, καὶ κόψαντος τὴν
θύραν, is most easily explained by its having stood in the
margin of Arch., whose first hand had omitted it by πβλ
either between τὴν ὀλύραν (M. Schmidt) and τὴν θύραν, or
between τὴν θύραν (already corrupted from τὴν ὀλύραν) and
τὴν θύραν. Pre-Arch. then had

ἐμβαλεῖν τὴν ὀλύραν· (17) or τὴν θύραν· (16)
καὶ κόψαντος τὴν θύραν (19).

XI 5 : It now looks as if we might explain ABe's omission of

περιμεῖναι κελεῦσαι (18)

in the same way, though without πβλ.

I now give reasons for supposing (e) that this
format was possible, (f) that the *format* of an ancient
or medieval book was sometimes perpetuated.

INTRODUCTION

(e) *That this* format *was possible* :

i. *Letters to the line* : In *Oxyrh. Papp.* 1093 and 1182, mid-2nd cent. B.C., by the same hand, containing parts of Dem. *contra Boeot.* and *Fals. Leg.*, the average length of the line in cols. iv and xiii of the one is 11·35 and 9·83 letters respectively, and in col. x of the other 10·31. That this length was not exceptional appears from A. C. Clark, *Descent of MSS*, p. 44. (The columns of these fragments vary between 33 and 36, and 28 and 31 lines, respectively.)

ii. *Lines to the column* : *Hibeh Pap.* 13, Hippias (?) *On Music*, 3rd cent. B.C., has 17 ll., the palimpsest of Cic. *de Repub.*, and Harl. 5041 (Theological Tracts) of cent. vii (*cf.* Clark) have respectively 15 and 14.

iii. *Short line and short column combined* : *Ryl. Pap.* 28, Περὶ Παλμῶν Μαντική, cent. iv papyrus codex, has 13-18 letters to the line and 13-17 ll. to the page; *Oxyrh. Pap.* 1779, *Psalm* i in Greek, cent. iv papyrus codex, has as few as 7-12 letters to the line and 8-9 lines to the page; *Oxyrh. Pap.* 1782 *Didache*, cent. iv vellum codex, has, in fol. 1, 8-11 letters to the line and 7-8 ll. to the page, and in fol. 2, 8-14 letters to the line and 8 ll. to the page; and *Oxyrh. Pap.* 1010, *Ezra* in Greek, cent. iv vellum codex, has 10-11 letters to the line, and 12 ll. to the page.

It is clear then that, apart from the Περὶ Παλμῶν Μαντική, parallels to the short line and to the short column existed in Pagan literature, and that Christian books afford early examples of the combination of the two *in short works*. It should be noted, however, that the closest parallels are codices.

(f) *Perpetuation of a particular* format :

Here I may refer the reader to A. C. Clark, *Descent of MSS*, pp. 41 and 405 f. In the latter passage he shows good reason for supposing that the close similarity of lineation observed in Plato, *Parm.* between B, cent. ix, and D, cent. xii, passed through an intermediate exemplar. The Aarau Fragments of Juvenal, cent. x-xi, tally page for page with the Pithoeanus, cent. ix.[a] A fixed *format* for the

[a] *Hermes*, xv. pp. 437 f. ; I am indebted to Professor A. E. Housman for this reference.

19

editions of the Academic and Peripatetic books in the Alexandrian Library is probably [a] indicated by the line-totals ascribed by Diogenes Laertius to Speusippus, Xenocrates, Aristotle, and Theophrastus himself. We may compare the end of Josephus, *Ant.* ἐπὶ τούτοις δὲ καταπαύσω τὴν ἀρχαιολογίαν, βίβλοις μὲν εἴκοσι περιειλημμένην, ἐξ δὲ μυριάσι στίχων. There would be no point in this if the copies of the archetype were not to be uniform, at least in lineation.[b] It is significant, too, that Diogenes Laertius (vii. 33) refers to ' about l. 200,' κατὰ τοὺς διακοσίους, of Zeno's *Republic*, to ' about l. 600,' κατὰ τοὺς ἑξακοσίους στίχους, of Chrysippus, *On the Ancient Natural Philosophers* (187), and to ' about l. 1000 of the 3rd book of his *Justice*,' ἐν τῷ τρίτῳ Περὶ Δικαίου κατὰ τοὺς χιλίους στίχους (188). These references, vague as they are,[c] could only be of value if the *format* were fixed. And the survival of marginal ' hundred-marks,' *e.g.* in the Bankes Homer (cent. ii) and the Ambrosian Pentateuch (cent. v) would seem to imply an original fixed *format* as a standard of reference.

The importance, to emendation, of the establishment—if such it be—of these two line-units, 11-12 and 17-18, is clear. That of the column-unit is of less importance, but still, I think, of considerable value. And I think I may claim, at the risk of being told I am arguing in a circle, that the comparative ease with which most of the following solutions have come is corroborative evidence of the existence of the letter-units which led to them. I begin with[d]—

[a] Now that A. C. Clark has exploded the ' doctrine of the normal line,' *Descent*, p. 43.

[b] *Cf.* also the scribe's notes at the end of Philodemus περὶ Ῥητορικῆς and Epicurus περὶ Φύσεως, where the average line-lengths are respectively 20 and 14 letters.

[c] The texts probably indicated only ll. 100, 200, 300, etc.

[d] Not all emendations involving these units are mentioned below; see critical notes.

INTRODUCTION

(a) *Emendations involving the 17-18 letter line* :

I 2 * : Pre-Arch. may have omitted

$$\langle καὶ \ πρὸς \ οὓς \ ἀντιδικεῖ \rangle \quad (19)$$

over καὶ τούτοις συλλυπεῖσθαι   (22).

IV 11* : Arch. had lost ἀναστὰς ἐξιέναι from its margin
when *m* was copied, and

$$ἀναστὰς \ ἐξιέναι \ ζητῶν \quad (19)$$

(which came under ἀναμιμνῃσκόμενος   (17)
in Pre-Arch.) when the rest were copied.

VII 3 * : Pre-Arch. had

$$ἐπιβάλλειν \ εἴπας· \ Σὺ \ μὴ \quad (19)$$

over ἐπιλάθῃ ὁ μέλλεις   (16)

and the first ἐπι was corrected by a marginal adscript ὑπο,
which was copied as an adscript also by Arch. ; hence our
mss vary between ὑποβ. and ἐπιβ.

X 4 * : Here emendation is very uncertain; Pre-Arch. may
have had

$$καὶ \ ὅσα \ μικροῦ \ τις$$
$$πριάμενος \ λογίζεται \quad (18)$$
$$\langle αὐτῷ \ ἀποδοκιμάσαι \rangle \quad (17)$$
$$τοῖς \ ἀλλότρια \ δαπανῶσι \rangle \quad (20)$$
$$πάντα \ φάσκων \ \langle ὤνια \rangle \ εἶναι \quad (20).$$

XIV 5 * : Here emendation is very uncertain ; but one
thing is clear, the sentence must exemplify stupidity. I
suggest that two ll. of Pre-Arch. were omitted from Arch.
by πβλ ; Pre-Arch. then had

$$ἐπὶ \ θάκου \ ἀνίστασθαι \quad (18)$$
$$\langle καὶ \ ἐπανιὼν \ νύσταξαι \quad (18)$$
$$καὶ \ τὴν \ θύραν \ ἀλλογνοήσας \rangle \quad (22, \ ΑΛΛ$$
$$\qquad \text{written close as often)}$$
$$ὑπὸ \ κυνὸς \ τῆς \ τοῦ \ γει- \quad (17)$$
$$τονος \ δηχθῆναι.$$

THEOPHRASTUS

XVI 10 : Perhaps Pre-Arch. had

$$\pi\acute{\iota}\nu\alpha\kappa\alpha \ \kappa\alpha\grave{\iota} \ \epsilon\grave{\iota}\sigma\epsilon\lambda\theta\grave{\omega}\nu \ \epsilon\check{\iota}\sigma\omega \quad (21)$$
$$\langle\delta\iota\alpha\tau\epsilon\lambda\acute{\epsilon}\sigma\alpha\iota \ \acute{\epsilon}\pi\iota\theta\acute{\upsilon}\omega\nu \ \kappa\alpha\grave{\iota}\rangle \quad (20)$$

XVIII 6* : $\tau o\hat{\upsilon} \ \kappa\nu\alpha\phi\acute{\epsilon}\omega s$ is suspect. It ought to be dative, and the $\kappa\nu\alpha\phi\epsilon\acute{\upsilon}s$, if expressed, should have come in the previous clause. Pre-Arch. had

$$o\hat{\upsilon} \ \grave{\alpha}\nu \ \mathring{\eta} \ \mathring{\alpha}\xi\iota os \ \acute{\epsilon}\gamma\gamma\upsilon\eta\tau\acute{\eta}s, \ \kappa\alpha\grave{\iota} \quad (22)$$
$$\overline{\acute{o}\tau\alpha\nu \ \mathring{\eta}\kappa\eta \ \tau\iota s \ \alpha\grave{\iota}\tau\eta\sigma\acute{o}\mu\epsilon\nu os} \quad (22)$$

and Arch. changed $o\hat{\upsilon} \ \grave{\alpha}\nu$ to $\acute{o}\tau\alpha\nu$ by $\pi\beta\lambda$. With $\acute{o}s$ for $\acute{\omega}s$ above (Salm.) this is now good Greek (*see note*).

XX 9* : The remarks only have point if they are made when he is another's guest. Pre-Arch. may have had

$$\text{-}\delta\iota o\nu \ \mathring{\alpha}\nu\theta\rho\omega\pi o\nu \ \lambda\alpha\beta\epsilon\hat{\iota}\nu. \quad (18)$$
$$\langle\acute{\epsilon}\sigma\tau\iota\acute{\omega}\mu\epsilon\nu os \ \delta\grave{\epsilon} \ \epsilon\grave{\iota}\pi\overline{\epsilon\hat{\iota}\nu}\rangle \quad (18)$$

XXI 9* : Pre-Arch. probably had

$$\alpha\grave{\upsilon}\tau\hat{\omega} \ \mu\nu\hat{\eta}\mu\alpha \ \pi o\iota\hat{\eta}\sigma\alpha\iota \quad (17)$$
$$\kappa\alpha\grave{\iota} \ \sigma\tau\eta\lambda\acute{\iota}\delta\iota o\nu \ \underline{\grave{\alpha}\nu\alpha\sigma\tau\acute{\eta}\sigma\alpha s} \quad (21)$$

whence Arch. wrote $\sigma\tau\eta\lambda\acute{\iota}\delta\iota o\nu \ \pi o\iota\acute{\eta}\sigma\alpha s$ by $\pi\beta\lambda$.

XXI 11 : Pre-Arch. probably had

$$\delta\iota o\iota\kappa\acute{\eta}\sigma\alpha\sigma\theta\alpha\iota \ \pi\alpha\rho\grave{\alpha} \ \tau\hat{\omega}\nu \quad (19)$$
$$\pi\rho\upsilon\tau\alpha\nu\acute{\epsilon}\omega\nu$$

with $\sigma\grave{\upsilon}\nu$ in margin, whence it was wrongly attached by Arch. to $\delta\iota o\iota\kappa\acute{\eta}\sigma\alpha\sigma\theta\alpha\iota$.

XXIII 6* : It is as if we should say 'I gave A, B, C and D £50 apiece, E and F £25 apiece, and G, H, I, J and K £10 apiece,—in all £300' (*see note*). Pre-Arch. probably had

$$\mathring{\epsilon}\nu\alpha \ \alpha\grave{\upsilon}\tau\hat{\omega}\nu, \ \kappa\alpha\grave{\iota} \ \pi o\sigma\hat{\omega}\nu \quad (16)$$
$$\alpha\grave{\upsilon}\tau\grave{\alpha}s \ \kappa\alpha\theta' \ \acute{\epsilon}\xi\alpha\kappa o\sigma\acute{\iota}\alpha s \quad (17)$$
$$\langle\kappa\alpha\grave{\iota} \ \kappa\alpha\tau\grave{\alpha} \ \tau\rho\iota\alpha\kappa o\sigma\acute{\iota}\alpha s\rangle \quad (17)$$
$$\underline{\kappa\alpha\grave{\iota} \ \kappa\alpha\tau\grave{\alpha} \ \mu\nu\hat{\alpha}\nu \ \kappa\alpha\grave{\iota} \ \pi\rho o\text{-}} \quad (17)$$
$$\sigma\tau\iota\theta\epsilon\grave{\iota}s$$

INTRODUCTION

XXIV 2 * : Pre-Arch. seems to have had

$$\overline{\tau\hat\omega}$$
σπεύδοντι ἀπὸ δείπνου (19)
⟨ἐντυγχάνειν αὐτῷ⟩ (16)
ἐντεύξεσθαι φάσκειν (18)
$\overline{\dot{\epsilon}\nu\ \tau\hat\omega}$ περιπατεῖν· καὶ (18).

XXVII 15 * : Arch. seems to have telescoped Meister's reading

$$\omega\sigma\iota\nu\epsilon\gamma\overline{\gamma\upsilon\sigma\gamma\upsilon\nu\alpha\iota\kappa\epsilon\sigma}\ (17)$$

into ωσινεγγυναικεσ, which was corrected in such a way that v could not read it and wrote ὦσι . . . γυναικ . .

XXX 13 * : Pre-Arch. seems to have had

πρὸς τρόπου πωλεῖν· (16)
ἐπιβαλὼν ἀποδόσθαι (17)

and Arch. changed πωλεῖν to $\overline{\pi\omega\lambda\epsilon\hat{\iota}\sigma\theta\alpha\iota}$ by πβλ.

(b) *Emendations involving the* 11-12 *letter line* :

II 8 : If the words in question occupied a line of Arch. the last letters may have been written small, and this would account for the variants προσήγγελκα, προσήγγελκας, and προσήγγελκά σε.

XX 5 * : If, as seems likely, the mss other than V lost a part (*cd*) or the whole (*m*) of this § by πβλ of καί, it probably filled a certain number of lines in Arch. ; and yet 27 letters is rather too much for 2 lines and too little for 3 ; emendations of πανουργιῶν should therefore lengthen it. I suggest that Arch. had

om. *m* | om. *cd* | καὶ ὑποκορίζε- (12)
σθαι ποππύζων (12)
{ καὶ πανουργη- (11)
μάτιον (or -ματίδιον) τοῦ (9 *or* 11)
πάππου καλῶν. (11)
καὶ ἐσθίων δὲ (11).

XX 7 * : Here *CD* read με ἔτικτες and V ἔτικτές με, and *CD* omit εἶπ.—καί and read ὡς ποίᾳ ἡμέρᾳ for V's τίς ἡμέρα

23

(*see note*).   Moreover, *CD* omit the § καὶ ὑπέρ κτλ before
the § καὶ ὅτι κτλ.   I suggest that Arch. had

omit *c d* $\begin{cases} εἰπέ \langle μοι, ὦ\rangle \ μάμ- & (11) \\ μη, \ ὅτ' \ ὤδινες & (10) \end{cases}$

καί με ἔτικτες (12)

ποία τις ἡμέρα ; (12)

καὶ ὑπὲρ αὐτῆς (12).

XX 8 * :   Arch. probably had

ὡς ἡδύ ἐστι καὶ (12)

⟨ἀλγεινόν, καὶ⟩ (11)

ἀμφότερα δὲ (10).

(c) *Emendations involving both units* :

VI 3 * :   Arch. seems to have had

ὀρχεῖσθαι νή- (11)

φων τὸν κόρ- (9)

δακα καὶ προσω- (12)

πεῖον ἔχων ἐν (11)

κωμικῷ χορῷ (12)

with περιάγειν ἐν τῷ θεάτρῳ in the margin, this having been
dropped by the first hand by πβλ from Pre-Arch., which had

ἔχων ἐν κωμικῷ χορῷ (18).

περιάγειν ἐν τῷ θεάτρῳ (21).

The marginal adscript was apparently illegible when Arch.
was copied by all but *m*.   ἀνασεσυρμένος (above) and ὀρχεῖσθαι
were dropped by *m* and added in marg., whence a later
ancestor of M put them in in the wrong place.

VIII 2 * :   I suggest that Pre-Arch. had

καὶ πῶς ἔχεις ; καὶ ἔχεις τι (21)

περὶ τοῦδε εἰπεῖν καινόν ; (21)

and that Arch. telescoped the first line into καὶ ἔχεις τι,
adding καὶ πῶς ἔχεις in marg. ;   the marginal ἔχεις was afterwards corrected by an overwritten λέγεις which was wrongly
taken as a correction of the ἔχεις which remained in the text;

in re-inserting καὶ πῶς ἔχεις the ancestor of *CDE* dropped πῶς (by πβλ with the line above?).   Thus Arch. would have

λέγεις καὶ ἔχεις τι (10)
καὶ πῶς ἔχεις περὶ τοῦδε εἰ- (11)
πεῖν καινόν ;

which *ab* made into καὶ λέγεις τί καὶ πῶς ἔχεις κτλ, and the others into λέγεις τί καὶ ἔχεις κτλ.

XXI 14 (V 8) * : I suggest, in this extremely difficult passage, that Pre-Arch. had

ξένοις δὲ
συνεργεῖν ἐπιστάλματα (20)
καὶ ἅλας εἰς Βυζάντιον (19)
καὶ Λακωνικὰς κύνας (17)
εἰς Κύζικον πέμπειν καὶ (20)
μέλι Ὑμήττιον εἰς Ῥόδον, (20)

which Arch. copied thus

ξένοις δὲ
καὶ ἅλας συνεργεῖν ἐπι- (12)
εἰς Βυζάντιον στάλματα καὶ (11)
Λακωνικὰς κύ- (11)
πέμπειν νας εἰς Κύζικον (13)
καὶ μέλι Ὑμήτ- (11)
τιον εἰς Ῥόδον (12).

m, copying first (*see below*), could read συνεργεῖν but not the whole of καὶ ἅλας εἰς Βυζάντιον, which he therefore omitted ; the others could no longer read συνεργεῖν, but accepted the legible part of the adscript, viz. εἰς Βυζάντιον, as a correction of it. Hence M reads ξένοις δὲ συνεργεῖν Λακωνικὰς κύνας κτλ, ἐπιστάλματα being dropped as unnecessary by the epitomator ; and the others read ξένοις δὲ εἰς Βυζάντιον ἐπιστάλματα καὶ Λακωνικὰς κύνας κτλ.   The Papyrus (see p. 11 *n.*) copied a text which had lost ἐπιστάλματα as well as καὶ ἅλας εἰς Βυζάντιον but included πέμπειν, which standing doubtless in the margin of Arch. (having been omitted by the first hand because it comes in the *middle* of a list of accusatives) appears in M before, in *C* after, εἰς Κύζικον, and was (1) copied into the margin of *cd*, where *D* neglected it, (2) neglected by *abe*, etc.

THEOPHRASTUS

XXI 16 (V 10) * : I suggest that Pre-Arch. had

$$
\begin{array}{ll}
\text{αὐτὸς ἐν τοῖς ἀποδεί-} & (17) \\
\text{ξεσιν ὕστερον ἐπεισι-} & (18) \\
\text{έναι ἤδη συγκαθημένων} & (19) \\
\text{ἵν' εἴπη τῶν θεωμένων} & (18) \\
\text{πρὸς τὸν ἕτερον ὅτι τού-} & (19) \\
\text{του ἐστὶν ἡ παλαίστρα.} & (18).
\end{array}
$$

Arch. lost -έναι ἤδη συγκαθημένων by πβλ and read

$$
\begin{array}{lll}
& \text{αὐ-} & \\
& \text{τὸς ἐν τοῖς ἀπο-} & (12) \\
& \text{δείξεσιν ὕστε-} \quad \text{ἐπι} & (12) \\
& \text{ρον ἔπεισιν εἴ-} & (12) \\
& \text{πη τῶν θεωμέ-} & (11) \\
& \text{νων πρὸς τὸν} & (10) \\
& \text{ἕτερον ὅτι τού-} & (12) \\
& \text{του ἐστὶν ἡ} & (9) \\
& \text{παλαίστρα.} &
\end{array}
$$

P[a] and the ancestor of Pre-Arch. had already lost ὁ ἕτερος before πρὸς τὸν ἕτερον ; P's insertion of τις and omission of πρὸς τὸν ἕτερον are apparently an emendation of Philodemus or his authority. The ἐπι which apparently stood in the margin of Arch. as a correction of ἀπο(δείξεσιν) was taken by the ancestor of ABe as a correction of the now unintelligible εἴπη ; CDe kept εἴπη and changed it to εἰπεῖν, taking ἐπι rightly as a correction of ἀπο(δείξεσιν).

I now recur to the *Stemma*. The question arises, if all mss but the Papyri come from the divided 11-12 letter exemplar (Arch.), why have M and CD lost so much in the latter half of the book (β) ? Much of M's loss is of course due to the epitomator, but some, in all probability, to M's unepitomized ancestor *m*.

After *v* was made, β[b] became divided at many points. Some pieces were lost for good. The large piece containing XVI-XXVIII (β₁) was apparently missing when *abe* (see below) was made. One of the smaller pieces, however, that

---

[a] The Papyrus. [b] Or *q* (see p. 12 note *b*).

containing XXX 5-16 (β_3) was inserted in ά [a] (after Char.
XI) before any of the ancestors of ABCDEM were copied.
The ancestor of M (*m*) and that of CD (*cd*, see below) come
from α *plus* the recovered, but not everywhere legible or
unmutilated, β_1.

That *m* was made before any of the others (except
of course *v*) is indicated by some if not all of the
following readings of M :

III 1 οὐ καιρίων ἤ, 5 τὰ (bef. ’Απατούρια), IV 11 ζητῶν,
VI 6 κέραμον, 3 περιάγειν ἐν θεάτρῳ, IX 3 που κεκλημένος, 7
τοὺς (bef. χρήσαντας), X 13 ὀλάς, XIII 5 τὴν ὁδὸν καταλιπών,
XXI 15 (V 7) Sch. Ταραντινικόν. In β, *m*'s unique readings—
XVI 10 ἡμερῶν, XVII 1 τις, XVIII 2 ἐπιπέμπειν, 4 omit
τὴν θύραν, XX 2 συλλαλῇ, 4 βηματίσῃ—are not shared by
V, and it is possible that most of them originated with the
epitomator ; but βηματίσῃ, at any rate, must have stood as
an old variant in β's text or margin and been rejected by
v.[b] It should also be noted that in XVI M has two passages,
8 κἂν γλαῦκες—ταράττεσθαι, and 10 τετράσι—ἡμερῶν which
are lost in wider gaps by CD.

All this seems to indicate (1) that β_1 was recovered
torn and worm-eaten, (2) that it had suffered rather
less mutilation when *m* was made. It is thus probable that *m* was made from α($+ \beta_3$) $+ \beta_1$ before any
ancestor of ABCDE copied it.

I now pass on to CD. That these two families had
a common ancestor derived from α($+ \beta_3$) $+ \beta_1$ seems
to be proved by the gaps. In β they always coincide
in these as compared with V or M, and there is
nothing to belie it in their readings. In α, neither
has any considerable gap as compared with the other

[a] Or *p* (see p. 12 note *b*).
[b] For old (?) variants in the mss of the other works of T.
cf. a note in Parisiensis (P) of the *Hist. Plant.* Wimmer
(1842) p. xviii.

mss, but their shared errors, *e.g.* διεγείρειν XIII 5, βουλεύεσθαι 9, and the order Proem-Index instead of Index-Proem, are sufficient to indicate a common ancestry despite a few differences which may be ascribed to old variants in *a*:

I 1 *C* τὸ (so M), II 5 *c* μικρόν, IV 11 *C* λαμβάνων (M δεχόμενος), XXI 14 (V 8) *c* πέμπειν (so P, Ambr. P, and M).

The losses of this ancestor (which I call *cd*) in β, as compared with *v*, seem to be due to the following causes :—

(a) *parablepsia* (?), *e.g.* XVI 4 ἱερῶον εὐθύς, XX 9 καὶ τοὺς φίλους—ἐμπλῆσαι, XXI 6 καὶ κολοιῷ—πηδήσεται, XXIV 4 τὰς διαίτας—σχολάζειν, XXVI 5 καὶ ὡς θαυμάζω—διδόντος ; (b) some of these, since it is hard to see how πβλ should create gaps of 6-8 ll. in a column of 12-13 ll., may well be due to *designed shortening*, not necessarily from a desire to abridge, but because the partial mutilation of a § or §§ had put the passage beyond the scribe's powers of emendation ; (c) *mutilation* of β, *e.g.* XXI 9 Μελιταίου, XX 9 ὥστε εἶναι—σκευάζων, XXVII 4 καὶ ἐπ᾽ οὐράν—δικάζεσθαι (3 cols. of 11, 11, 12 ll.) ; (d) the *designed omission of incomprehensible passages*, *e.g.* XVI 2 ἐπιχρωνῆν, XXV 3 πεζῇ ἐκβοηθοῦντός τε, XXVII 11 καὶ ἔνδεκα λιταῖς—συναύξοντας. Gaps of a column and over would perhaps generally make absolute separation, but the preservation, for the most part, of the right sequence of §§ makes it necessary to suppose, despite the help doubtless got from the indices, that some of these large gaps were not actually missing from the recovered $β_1$, but wholly or partly illegible ; a medieval scribe would probably merely omit such passages. I may add here that somewhere in the *C*-tradition was an exemplar of about 21 letters to the line ; see gaps or transpositions of some *C* mss at IV 7, V 5, VII 3, X 8, XVII 8.

I now take A and B and the class *E*. The relations of the *E*-class have yet to be worked out.[a] Mean-

[a] For the Ambrosian mss see Bassi, *Riv. di Filol.* xxvi. 493.

while it may be said that it is highly probable that A and B had a common ancestor (*ab*), and that they share an ancestor (*abe*) with some of the *E*-class appears from Ambr. P's τούτοις τοῖς in VI 4, ἐκβαλλούσης (AB ἐκβαλούσης) and τοσαύτας in X 6 and 7.

Indications of an A→*e* tradition appear in ἐμπεσὼν λόγος II 2, ἔσχες and the position of ἔχεις 3, διαψιθυρίζειν 11, τὸ δεῖπνον III 2. For a B→*e* tradition *cf.* νεοττία (accent) II 6 (so Ambr. C), ἀνασυρόμενος XI 2. Suggestions of a *cd*→*e* tradition occur in II 4 ἄκοντος, XIII 4 διεγείρειν, XXI 16 (V 10) εἰπεῖν; and of a *c*→*e* tradition in IV 9 ἐπακοῦσαι, VII 9 κακωλῦσαι. Some of the above identities may of course be due to contamination.

It is at any rate evident that *E* is not really a family, but a class composed of all I–XV mss [a] other than A and B. An entirely independent *E*-tradition seems indicated by :—

Proem title προθεωρία (Ambr. E), II 6 ἀπίδια, 8 προσήγγελκά σε, VII 3 ἀφορμάς, X 8 ἐᾶσαι, XIV 6 τι (Ambr. E and I, with M). Ambr. P's ὁπόσας in X 3 points to *abe*'s having had in the margin an *o* which its ancestor, in common with A and B, wrongly prefixed to συσσιτῶν, but, unlike them, also copied into the margin, whence an intermediate exemplar prefixed it to πόσας.

To sum up, in the present state of our knowledge it may be said that the value of AB has been exaggerated at the expense of *CD* and M. The Epitome, particularly, has generally been underestimated—probably because it *is* an epitome, though surely where an epitome gives a longer or clearly better reading than the unabridged mss it is the

[a] A few have less; strictly, of course, A and B belong to this class.

more deserving of credit. Some of the mss of the
E-class appear to deserve closer attention than they
have hitherto received. V has long, and rightly,
been accorded first place ; but even here a warning
is needed—V is not *v*. Whether, as Navarre thinks,
our mss and papyri have a common ancestor in a
recension of Andronicus, is at present an open question. If traces of the 18-letter line are found in the
textual tradition of the other Peripatetic books it
will make it probable.[a] Meanwhile it may be said
that the displacements are in his favour, though if he
were right we should expect the *Characters* to share
codices not with various works of the rhetoricians
but with the rest of the writings precious to the
Peripatetics. However, this may be an accident of
their later history.

The following *Stemma* seems to me to account best
for the facts. *If the reader prefers the doctrine of a
double position for* XXX §§ 5-16[b] *to that of its trans-
ference, it will not greatly affect my main contentions.*
For even if the 12-13 line column be rejected—and
that does not necessarily follow—the two line-units
will stand, and it is on them that the emendations
made on pp. 21-26 are founded.

[a] For the early history of T.'s books see, besides Strab.
609, the note at the end of the Frag. of his (?) *Metaphysics*,
ap. Fabric. iii. 444.

[b] See above, p. 12, and note *a*.

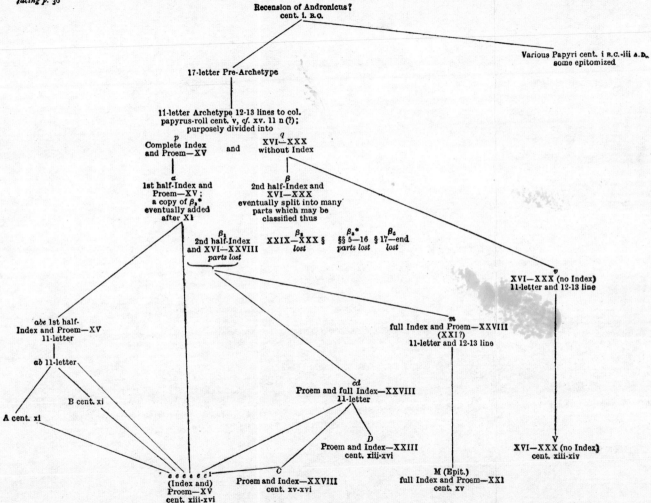

Recension of Andronicus?
cent. i. B.C.

Various Papyri cent. i B.C.-iii A.D.
some epitomized

17-letter Pre-Archetype

11-letter Archetype 12-13 lines to col.
papyrus-roll cent. v, *cf.* xv. 11 n (?);
purposely divided into

p
Complete Index
and Proem—XV   and

q
XVI—XXX
without Index

α
1st half-Index and
Proem—XV;
a copy of β_2*
eventually added
after XI

β
2nd half-Index and
XVI—XXX
eventually split into many
parts which may be
classified thus

β_1
2nd half-Index
and XVI—XXVIII
parts lost

β_2
XXIX—XXX §
lost

β_3*
§§ 5—16
parts lost

β_4
§ 17—end
lost

v
XVI—XXX (no Index)
11-letter and 12-13 line

abe 1st half-
Index and Proem—XV
11-letter

ab 11-letter

m
full Index and Proem—XXVIII
(XXI?)
11-letter and 12-13 line

B cent. xi

A cent. xi

cd
Proem and full Index—XXVIII
11-letter

D
Proem and Index—XXIII
cent. xiii-xvi

V
XVI—XXX (no Index)
cent. xiii-xiv

e e e e e e [1]
(Index and)
Proem—XV
cent. xiii-xvi

C
Proem and Index—XXVIII
cent. xv-xvi

M (Epit.)
full Index and Proem—XXI
cent. xv

[1] There has probably been some contamination in *E*.

BIBLIOGRAPHY

Editiones Principes : The *Characters* were not all recovered till the year 1786. *Characters* I-XV were first published by W. Pirckheymer at Nuremberg in 1527, XVI-XXIII by G. B. Camozzi at Venice in 1552, XXIV-XXVIII by Casaubon, in his 2nd edition, at Leyden in 1599, XXIX-XXX by J. C. Amaduzzi at Parma in 1786.

Books useful to the student :—

Theophrasts Charaktere herausgegeben erklärt und übersetzt von der PHILOLOGISCHEN GESELLSCHAFT ZU LEIPZIG 1897 (with an introduction by O. IMMISCH marking an epoch in the history of the text).

Theophrasti Characteres recensuit H. DIELS, Oxonii 1909 (text and textual introduction only).

The Characters of Theophrastus, an English Translation from a Revised Text, with Introduction and Notes, by R. C. JEBB, re-edited by J. E. SANDYS, London, 1909.

Teofrasto I Caratteri a cura di G. PASQUALI (Biblioteca di Classici Greci), Firenze, 1919 (text and translation).

Théophraste Caractères Texte et Traduction par O. NAVARRE (Budé), Paris, 1920.

Théophraste Caractères Commentaire, by the same (in the same series), Paris, 1924.

Theophrasti Characteres edidit O. IMMISCH, Lipsiae (Teubner), 1923 (text with brief textual introduction and *apparatus criticus*).

For the text by far the best guide is Immisch. For the commentary I should recommend the Leipzig Society *plus* Navarre. For introductory matter other than textual, *e.g.* comparison with Aristotle, and Theophrastus' English imitators, see Jebb-Sandys. In dealing with the text it should be remembered that the discovery of the Papyri has altered the situation in favour of Immisch and against Diels. A full bibliography could be compiled by combining Jebb-Sandys and Immisch. At the time of writing Dr. Pasquali's expected *editio maior* has not come out.

ALPHABETICAL INDEX OF THE CHARACTERS

COMPARATIVE INDEX OF TITLES

ΘΕΟΦΡΑΣΤΟΥ ΧΑΡΑΚΤΗΡΩΝ
ΠΙΝΑΞ

ΘΕΟΦΡΑΣΤΟΥ
ΧΑΡΑΚΤΗΡΕΣ

ΠΡΟΘΕΩΡΙΑ[1]

Ἤδη μὲν καὶ πρότερον ἐπιστήσας τὴν διάνοιαν
ἐθαύμασα, ἴσως δὲ οὐδὲ παύσομαι θαυμάζων,
τί ἄρα[2] δήποτε τῆς Ἑλλάδος ὑπὸ τὸν αὐτὸν
ἀέρα κειμένης καὶ πάντων τῶν Ἑλλήνων ὁμοίως
παιδευομένων, συμβέβηκεν ἡμῖν οὐ τὴν αὐτὴν
2 ἔχειν τάξιν τῶν τρόπων. ἐγὼ οὖν,[3] ὦ Πολύκλεις,
συνθεωρήσας ἐκ πολλοῦ χρόνου τὴν ἀνθρωπίνην
φύσιν, καὶ βεβιωκὼς ἔτη ἐνενήκοντα ἐννέα,[4] ἔτι
δὲ ὡμιληκὼς πολλαῖς τε καὶ παντοδαπαῖς φύσεσι
καὶ παρατεθεάμενος ἐξ ἀκριβείας πολλῆς, τούς
τε ἀγαθοὺς τῶν ἀνθρώπων καὶ τοὺς φαύλους
ὑπέλαβον δεῖν συγγράψαι ἃ ἕκαστοι[5] αὐτῶν

TITLE OF BOOK: mss Θεοφράστου χαρακτῆρες (ἰδιωμάτων),
Diog. Laert. v. 47-8 ἠθικοὶ χαρ. α΄, χαρ. ἠθ.: for χαρ. cf.
Men. 72 K(ock)   [1] only in e; if anything it would
probably be called in Hellenistic times Προοίμιον, cf.
Aristotle's *Dialogues* ap. Cic. *Att.* iv. 16. 2   [2] Madv:
mss γὰρ   [3] mss γάρ (from below?)   [4] καὶ βεβ. to
ἐννέα (we should expect ἅτε for καί), or to πολλῆς (ἐξ is
strange and φύσεσι after φύσιν clumsy), is probably interpolated   [5] only M: others ἑκάτεροι

THEOPHRASTUS
THE CHARACTERS

LETTER DEDICATORY

I HAVE often marvelled, when I have given the matter my attention, and it may be I shall never cease to marvel, why it has come about that, albeit the whole of Greece lies in the same clime and all Greeks have a like upbringing,[a] we have not the same constitution of character. I therefore, Polycles, having observed human nature a long time (for I have lived ninety years and nine [b] and moreover had converse with all sorts of dispositions and compared them with great diligence), have thought it incumbent upon me to write in a book the manners of each several

[a] Speaking generally, as we might of Europeans compared with Africans; cf. Zeno's book On Greek Education.
[b] If the preface is the work of Theophrastus, this reference to his age must be corrupt or interpolated (cf. Zeno, Diog. L. vii. 28); perhaps all within the brackets is spurious; there was a Polycles, adviser of Eurydice, wife of Arrhidaeus, Introd. p. 5.

3 ἐπιτηδεύουσιν ἐν τῷ βίῳ. ἐκθήσω δέ σοι κατὰ
γένος ὅσα τε τυγχάνει γένη τρόπων τούτοις
προσκείμενα καὶ ὃν τρόπον τῇ οἰκονομίᾳ χρῶνται·
ὑπολαμβάνω γάρ, ὦ Πολύκλεις, τοὺς υἱεῖς ἡμῶν
βελτίους ἔσεσθαι καταλειφθέντων αὐτοῖς ὑπο-
μνημάτων τοιούτων, οἷς παραδείγμασι χρώμενοι
αἱρήσονται τοῖς εὐσχημονεστέροις¹ συνεῖναί τε
καὶ ὁμιλεῖν, ὅπως μὴ καταδεέστεροι ὦσιν αὐτῶν.
4 τρέψομαι δὲ ἤδη ἐπὶ τὸν λόγον· σὸν δὲ παρ-
ακολουθῆσαί τε εὐμαθῶς² καὶ εἰδῆσαι³ εἰ ὀρθῶς
λέγω.

Πρῶτον μὲν οὖν ποιήσομαι τὸν λόγον ἀπὸ
τῶν τὴν χείρον' αἵρεσιν⁴ ἐζηλωκότων, ἀφεὶς τὸ
προοιμιάζεσθαι καὶ πολλὰ ἔξω⁵ τοῦ πράγματος
5 λέγειν· καὶ ἄρξομαι πρῶτον ἀπὸ τῆς εἰρωνείας
καὶ ὁριοῦμαι αὐτήν, εἶθ' οὕτως τὸν εἴρωνα
διέξειμι, ποῖός τίς ἐστι καὶ εἰς τίνα τρόπον
κατήνεκται· καὶ τὰ ἄλλα δὴ τῶν παθημάτων,
ὥσπερ ὑπεθέμην, πειράσομαι κατὰ γένος φανερὰ
καθιστάναι.⁶

---

¹ only M : others -τάτοις   ² E, cf. Aesch. 1. 116 : mss
ὀρθῶς (introd. p. 17)   ³ Arist. Eth. N. viii. 3. 8 al.
⁴ Büch.- E, cf. i. 7 and Nicol. 1. 20 (cf. 13) K : mss τὴν
εἰρωνείαν   ⁵ E : mss περὶ   ⁶ mss also ἐπεθέμην and
καταστῆσαι and καθεστάναι

38

kind of men both good and bad.[a] And you shall
have set down sort by sort the behaviour proper
to them and the fashion of their life ; for I am
persuaded, Polycles, that our sons will prove the
better men if there be left them such memorials
as will, if they imitate them, make them choose the
friendship and converse of the better sort, in the
hope they may be as good as they. But now to my
tale ; and be it yours to follow with understanding
and see if I speak true.

First, then, I shall dispense with all preface and
with the saying of much that is beside the mark,
and treat of those that have pursued the worser
way of life,[b] beginning with Dissembling and the
definition of it, and without more ado recount the
nature of the Dissembler and the ways to which
he is come ; and thereafter I shall endeavour, as
I purposed to do, to make clear the other affections
each in its own place.

[a] Or 'of either kind of men.'

[b] This, particularly, implies the project of a second volume
containing *good* Characters, which may have existed in
antiquity (Introd. p. 7), and is no certain argument against
the genuineness of the Proem as a whole ; the use of μὲν
οὖν at the beginning of Char. i. shows that, if lost, a genuine
preface or prefatory sentence was once here, *cf*. Xen. *Mem.*,
Arist. *Mag. Mor.*, *Oec.*, *Rhet.*, Cic. *Att.* iv. 16. 2 ; for such
a preface, spurious (?) but not necessarily very late, *cf*. that
to [Arist.] *Rhet. Alex.*, known to Ath. (xi. 508 a), and *Mund.* ;
Aristippus (died 350) dedicated his history of Libya to
Dionysius (Diog. L. ii. 83), *cf*. Arcesilaus and Eumenes,
ibid. iv. 38 ; *cf*. also iv. 14, vii. 185, and the list of Chrysippus's
works ; it may be noted that τὲ occurs five times here and
only four or five times elsewhere ; but the style of the preface
might well be rather different ; in any case it is not typically
Byzantine.

ΕΙΡΩΝΕΙΑΣ Α΄

Ἡ μὲν οὖν εἰρωνεία δόξειεν ἂν εἶναι, ὡς ἐν τύπῳ περιλαβεῖν, προσποίησις ἐπὶ τὸ χεῖρον[1] πράξεων καὶ λόγων, ὁ δὲ εἴρων τοιοῦτός τις, [2] οἷος προσελθὼν τοῖς ἐχθροῖς ἐθέλειν λαλεῖν οὐ μισεῖν,[2] καὶ ἐπαινεῖν παρόντας οἷς ἐπέθετο λάθρα, ⟨καὶ πρὸς οὓς ἀντιδικεῖ⟩[3] καὶ τούτοις συλλυπεῖσθαι ἡττωμένοις ὡς δὴ πάσχουσι κακῶς.[4] καὶ συγγνώμην δὲ ἔχειν τοῖς αὐτὸν κακῶς λέγουσι, καὶ ἐπιγελᾶν⟩[5] τοῖς καθ᾽ ἑαυτοῦ λεγομένοις· [3] καὶ πρὸς τοὺς ἀδικουμένους καὶ ἀγανακτοῦντας πρᾴως διαλέγεσθαι· καὶ τοῖς ἐντυγχάνειν κατὰ [4] σπουδὴν βουλομένοις προστάξαι ἐπανελθεῖν· καὶ μηδὲν ὧν πράττει ὁμολογῆσαι ἀλλὰ φῆσαι ἔτι[6] βουλεύεσθαι· καὶ προσποιήσασθαι ἄρτι παραγεγονέναι, καὶ ὀψὲ γενέσθαι αὐτῶν,[7] καὶ μαλακισθῆναι· [5] καὶ πρὸς τοὺς δανειζομένους καὶ ἐρανίζοντας ⟨εἰπεῖν ὡς οὐ πλουτεῖ, καὶ πωλῶν⟩[8] ὡς οὐ πωλεῖ, καὶ μὴ πωλῶν φῆσαι πωλεῖν· καὶ ἀκούσας τι μὴ προσποιεῖσθαι,[9] καὶ ἰδὼν φῆσαι μὴ ἑωρακέναι, καὶ ὁμολογήσας μὴ μεμνῆσθαι· καὶ τὰ μὲν σκέψεσθαι[10] φάσκειν, τὰ δὲ οὐκ εἰδέναι, τὰ δὲ θαυμάζειν, τὰ δ᾽ ἤδη ποτὲ καὶ αὐτὸς οὕτω διαλογίσασθαι. [6] καὶ τὸ ὅλον δεινὸς τῷ τοιούτῳ τρόπῳ τοῦ λόγου

---

[1] ⟨καὶ ἐπὶ τὸ ἔλαττον⟩?   [2] for μισεῖν cf. Ar. Eccl. 502, Dem. 54. 26, and for οὐ rather than καὶ οὐ Men. Pk. 867; but Nav. λαθεῖν ὅτι μισεῖ is perhaps right, cf. M ἐνδείκνυσθαι οὐ μισεῖν   [3] E, introd. p. 21   [4] E, from M καὶ συνάχθεσθαι πάσχουσι κακῶς ἢ ἡττημένοις; other mss omit ὡς . . . κακῶς   [5] E   [6] only M   [7] E: mss αὐτόν   [8] Ribb.-E   [9] cf. Lys. 13. 75, Men. 179 K   [10] Cas., cf. Men. 460 K: mss σκέψασθαι, ἐσκέφθαι

CHARACTER I

I. DISSEMBLING

Now Dissembling would seem, to define it generally, to be an affectation of the worse [a] in word and deed; and the Dissembler will be disposed rather to go up to an enemy and talk with him than to show his hatred; he will praise to his face one he has girded at behind his back; he will commiserate even his adversary's ill-fortune in losing his case to him. More, he will forgive his vilifiers, and will laugh in approval of what is said against him; [b] to such as are put upon and resent it he will speak blandly; [c] any that are in haste to see him are bidden go back home. He never admits he is doing a thing, but avows he's still thinking of doing it; and makes pretences, as that he's but now come upon the scene, or joined the company late, or was ill abed. If you are borrowing of your friends and put him under contribution, he will tell you he is but a poor man; when he would sell you anything, no, it is not for sale; when he would not, why then it is. He pretends he has not heard when he hears, and says he has not seen when he sees; and when he has admitted you right he avers he has no remembrance of it. He'll look into this, doesn't know that, is surprised at the other; this again is just the conclusion he once came to himself. He is for ever

[a] And the less?　　　　　[b] Reading uncertain.
[c] Cf. Xen. An. i. 5. 14 (Nav.).

χρῆσθαι· Οὐ πιστεύω· Οὐχ ὑπολαμβάνω· Ἐκ-
πλήττομαι· Λέγεις αὐτὸν ἑαυτοῦ ἕτερον γεγονέναι[1]·
Οὐ μὴν οὐ ταῦτα πρὸς ἐμὲ διεξήει·[2] Παράδοξόν
μοι τὸ πρᾶγμα· "Ἄλλῳ τινὶ λέγε· Ὁπότερον[3] δὲ
σοὶ ἀπιστήσω ἢ ἐκείνου καταγνῶ ἀπορούμαι·
Ἀλλ' ὅρα μὴ σὺ θᾶττον πιστεύῃς.[4]

ΚΟΛΑΚΕΙΑΣ Β′

Τὴν δὲ κολακείαν ὑπολάβοι ἄν τις ὁμιλίαν
αἰσχρὰν εἶναι συμφέρουσαν δὲ τῷ κολακεύοντι,
2 τὸν δὲ κόλακα τοιοῦτόν τινα, ὥστε ἅμα πορευό-
μενον εἰπεῖν· Ἐνθυμῇ ὡς ἀποβλέπουσι πρὸς σὲ
οἱ ἄνθρωποι; τοῦτο δὲ οὐθενὶ τῶν ἐν τῇ πόλει
γίγνεται πλὴν σοί· ἢ[5] Ηὐδοκίμεις χθὲς ἐν τῇ
στοᾷ· πλειόνων γὰρ ἢ τριάκοντα ἀνθρώπων
καθημένων καὶ ἐμπεσόντος λόγου τίς εἴη βέλτιστος,
ἀπ' αὐτοῦ ἀρξαμένους πάντας ἐπὶ τὸ ὄνομα αὐτοῦ
3 κατενεχθῆναι. καὶ ἅμα[6] τοιαῦτα λέγων ἀπὸ τοῦ
ἱματίου ἀφελεῖν κροκύδα, καὶ ἐάν τι πρὸς τὸ
τρίχωμα[7] ὑπὸ πνεύματος προσενεχθῇ ἄχυρον,
καρφολογῆσαι, καὶ ἐπιγελάσας δὲ εἰπεῖν· Ὁρᾷς;
ὅτι δυοῖν σοι ἡμερῶν οὐκ ἐντετύχηκα, πολιῶν
ἔσχηκας τὸν πώγωνα μεστόν, καίπερ εἴ τις καὶ
ἄλλος πρὸς τὰ ἔτη ἔχεις[8] μέλαιναν τὴν τρίχα.

[1] E: mss καὶ λέγει αὐτὸν ἕτ. γεγ.   [2] Ambr. E: other
mss καὶ μὴν οὐ κτλ.   [3] Cob: mss. ὅπως   [4] LATE ADDI-
TION: (7) Τοιαύτας φωνὰς καὶ πλοκὰς καὶ παλιλλογίας εὑρεῖν
ἔστι τοῦ εἴρωνος (mss ἐστιν οὐ χεῖρον ὂν and corr.)· ταῦτα δὴ
τῶν ἠθῶν μὴ ἁπλᾶ ἀλλ' ἐπίβουλα φυλάττεσθαι μᾶλλον δεῖ ἢ
τοὺς ἔχεις.   [5] E: mss πλὴν σοί, πλὴν ἢ σοί, ἤ σοι (i.e. ἢ
marg. arch.)   [6] Needh: mss ἄλλα   [7] mss add τῆς κεφαλῆς
[8] mss also ἔχεις πρὸς τὰ ἔτη (i.e. ἔχεις marg. arch.)

saying such things as ' I don't believe it '; ' I don't understand '; ' You amaze me '; ' If so, he must have changed '; ' Well, that's not what I was told '; ' I never expected this '; ' Don't tell *me* '; ' Whether to disbelieve *you* or make a liar of *him* is more than I can tell '; ' Don't you be too credulous.' [a]

II. FLATTERY

Flattery might be understood to be a sort of converse that is dishonourable, but at the same time profitable, to him that flatters ; and the Flatterer will say as he walks beside you ' Are you aware how people are looking at you ? [b] No man in Athens gets such attention '; or this, ' You were the man of the hour yesterday in the Porch ; why, although there was more than thirty present,[c] when the talk turned to who was the finest man there, the name that came to every lip both first and last was yours.' And while he says such things as these, he picks a speck from your coat [d] ; or if so be a morsel of chaff be blown into your beard, plucks it out and then says with a smile ' D'ye see ? because you and I be not met a whole day, your beard's full of grey hairs—though I own your hair is singularly dark of

---

[a] LATE ADDITION : Such be the speeches, tricks, and retractions to which dissemblers resort. These disingenuous and designing characters are to be shunned like serpents.
[b] *Cf.* Men. 402 K 5. [c] Or ' in Athens.' [d] *Cf.* Ar. 657 K.

4 καὶ λέγοντος δὲ αὐτοῦ τι τοὺς ἄλλους σιωπᾶν
κελεῦσαι· καὶ ἐπαινέσαι δὲ ἀκούοντας[1]· καὶ ἐπι-
σημήνασθαι δέ, ἐπὰν παύσηται,[2] Ὀρθῶς· καὶ
σκώψαντι ψυχρῶς ἐπιγελάσαι τό τε ἱμάτιον ὦσαι
εἰς τὸ στόμα ὡς δὴ οὐ δυνάμενος κατασχεῖν τὸν
5 γέλωτα. καὶ τοὺς ἀπαντῶντας μικρὸν ἐπιστῆναι
6 κελεῦσαι[3] ἕως ἂν αὐτὸς παρέλθῃ. καὶ τοῖς
παιδίοις μῆλα καὶ ἀπίδια[4] πριάμενος εἰσενέγκας
δοῦναι ὁρῶντος αὐτοῦ, καὶ φιλήσας δὲ εἰπεῖν·
7 Χρηστοῦ πατρὸς νεόττια. καὶ συνωνούμενος ἐπὶ
<πισυγγίου> κρηπῖδας[5] τὸν πόδα φῆσαι εὐρυ-
8 θμότερον εἶναι[6] τοῦ ὑποδήματος. καὶ πορευο-
μένου πρός τινα τῶν φίλων προδραμὼν εἰπεῖν
ὅτι Πρὸς σὲ ἔρχεται, καὶ ἀναστρέψας ὅτι Προσ-
9 ήγγελκά σε.[7] ἀμέλει δὲ καὶ τὰ ἐκ τῆς γυναικείας
10 ἀγορᾶς διακονῆσαι δυνατὸς ἀπνευστί.[8] καὶ τῶν
ἑστιωμένων πρῶτος ἐπαινέσαι τὸν οἶνον καὶ
παρακειμένῳ[9] εἰπεῖν· Ὡς μαλακῶς ἐσθίεις, καὶ
ἄρας τι τῶν ἀπὸ τῆς τραπέζης φῆσαι· Τουτὶ
ἄρα ὡς χρηστόν ἐστι· καὶ ἐρωτῆσαι μὴ ῥιγοῖ,
καὶ εἰ ἐπιβάλλεσθαι βούλεται, καὶ εἴ τι μὴ περι-
στείλῃ αὐτόν· καὶ[10] ταῦτα λέγων πρὸς τὸ οὖς
προσκύπτων[11] ψιθυρίζειν· καὶ εἰς ἐκεῖνον ἀποβλέπω

---

[1] mss ἀκούοντος, ἄκοντος, ἀκούοντα   [2] Foss: mss. εἰ
παύσεται, εἰ παύσηται with η corr. to ε, εἰ παύεται   [3] some
mss omit μικρόν   [4] most mss ἀπίους, but cf. Geop.
x. 74. 1 ὀπώρα . . οἷον δωράκινα μῆλα, ἀπίδια, δαμασκηνά
[5] E: mss ἐπικρηπῖδας, ἐπὶ κρηπῖδας (-ίδας)   [6] mss also φῆσαι
εἶναι (εἶναι φῆσαι) εὐρυθμ. (i.e. εἶναι marg. arch.)   [7] or
omit σὲ, cf. Plat. Prot. 314 D fin: mss. also προσήγγελκας,
-κα (introd. p. 23)   [8] some mss omit τῆς   [9] Gronov.-
E: mss παρακειμένων, παραμένων   [10] Pet.-E: mss ἔτι
περιστ., and καὶ μὴν, καὶ μὴ (μή from marg. arch., whence it
was intended to be added after τι)   [11] Valck: mss -πίπτων

your age.' He will desire silence when his friend
speaks, or praise the company for listening to him ;
when he comes to a stop, he will cry in approbation
' Quite right ' ; and if he make a stale jest will
laugh, and stuff the corner of his cloak in his mouth
as if he could not hold his merriment. Moreover,
any man that comes their way is bidden stand
awhile till the great one be gone past. He will buy
apples and pears and bring them in for the children,
and giving them before their father will kiss them
and cry ' Chicks of a good strain.' [a] When he buys
shoes with him at the cordwainer's, he will tell him
that the foot is shapelier than the shoe. And if he
go visiting a friend of his he will run ahead and tell
him he is coming, and then face round and say ' I
have announced you.' He is the man, you may be
sure,[b] to go errands to the women's market [c] there
and back without stopping for breath ; and of all
the guests will be first to praise the wine ; and will
say in his patron's ear ' You are eating nothing ' ;
or picking up some of the food upon the table
exclaim ' How good this is, isn't it ? ' and will ask
him whether he is not cold ? and will he not have
his coat on ? and shall he not draw his skirts a little
closer about him ? and saying this, bend forward to
whisper in his ear ; and will speak to another with

[a] *Cf*. Ar. *Av*. 767 ; probably a metaphor from fighting-
cocks.   [b] *Cf*. xiii. n. 1.
[c] Here were sold household requirements of all sorts (*not*
specially feminine—a mistaken interpretation of Poll. x. 18).

11 τοῖς ἄλλοις λαλεῖν. καὶ τοῦ παιδὸς ἐν τῷ θεάτρῳ
ἀφελόμενος τὰ προσκεφάλαια αὐτὸς ὑποστρῶσαι.
12 καὶ τὴν οἰκίαν φῆσαι εὖ ἠρχιτεκτονῆσθαι, καὶ
τὸν ἀγρὸν εὖ πεφυτεῦσθαι, καὶ τὴν εἰκόνα ὁμοίαν
εἶναι.[1]

ΑΔΟΛΕΣΧΙΑΣ Γ′

Ἡ δὲ ἀδολεσχία ἐστὶ μὲν διήγησις λόγων οὐ
2 καιρίων ἢ μακρῶν καὶ ἀπροβουλεύτων,[2] ὁ δὲ
ἀδολέσχης τοιοῦτός τις, οἷος ὢν[3] μὴ γιγνώσκει
τῷ[4] παρακαθεζόμενος πλησίον, πρῶτον μὲν τῆς
3 αὑτοῦ γυναικὸς εἰπεῖν ἐγκώμιον, εἶτα ὃ τῆς
νυκτὸς εἶδεν ἐνύπνιον τοῦτο διηγήσασθαι, εἶθ᾽
ὧν εἶχεν ἐπὶ τῷ δείπνῳ τὰ καθ᾽ ἕκαστα διεξελθεῖν·
εἶτα δὴ προχωροῦντος τοῦ πράγματος[5] λέγειν ὡς
πολλῷ[6] πονηρότεροί εἰσιν οἱ νῦν ἄνθρωποι τῶν
ἀρχαίων, καὶ ὡς ἄξιοι γεγόνασιν οἱ πυροὶ ἐν τῇ
ἀγορᾷ, καὶ ὡς πολλοὶ ἐπιδημοῦσι ξένοι, καὶ τὴν
4 θάλατταν ἐκ Διονυσίων πλόϊμον εἶναι, καὶ εἰ
ποιήσειεν ὁ Ζεὺς ὕδωρ πλεῖον,[7] τὰ ἐν τῇ γῇ
βελτίω ἔσεσθαι, καὶ ὃ ἀγρὸν[8] εἰς νέωτα γεωργήσει,
καὶ ὡς χαλεπόν ἐστι τὸ ζῆν, καὶ ὡς Δάμιππος
μυστηρίοις μεγίστην ⟨τὴν⟩[9] δᾷδα ἔστησεν, καὶ
πόσοι εἰσὶ κίονες τοῦ Ὠιδείου, καὶ Χθὲς ἤμεσα,
5 καὶ Τίς ἐστιν ἡμέρα τήμερον; καὶ ὡς Βοηδρομιῶνος μέν ἐστι τὰ μυστήρια, Πυανοψιῶνος[10] δὲ

---

[1] LATE ADDITION: (13) καὶ τὸ κεφάλαιον τὸν κόλακά ἐστι
θεάσασθαι πᾶν λέγοντα καὶ πράττοντα ᾧ χαριεῖσθαι ὑπολαμβάνει
(mss πάντα and ᾧ, ἃ, οἷς)   [2] οὐ κ..ρίων ἢ only in M
[3] mss also ὃν   [4] E: mss τούτῳ   [5] cf. Luc. D. Mer.
323   [6] mss also πολὺ   [7] some mss omit   [8] E (ὃ is
the crop): mss ὅτι ἀγρόν, ὃ (ὁ) ἀγρός, ὁ ἀγρὸς εἰ   [9] E
[10] mss Πυανεψ.

his eye on his friend. He will take the cushions from the lackey at the theatre and place them for him himself. He will remark how tasteful is the style of his patron's house ; how excellent the planting of his farm ; how like him the portrait he has had made.[a]

III. GARRULITY

Garrulity is the delivering of talk that is irrelevant, or long and unconsidered ; and the Garrulous man is one that will sit down close beside somebody he does not know,[b] and begin talk with a eulogy of his own wife, and then relate a dream he had the night before, and after that tell dish by dish what he had for supper. As he warms to his work he will remark that we are by no means the men we were, and the price of wheat has gone down, and there's a great many strangers in town, and that the ships will be able to put to sea after the Dionysia.[c] Next he will surmise that the crops would be all the better for some more rain, and tell him what he is going to grow on his farm next year, adding that it is difficult to make both ends meet, and Damippus' torch was the largest set up at the Mysteries,[d] and how many pillars there are in the Hall of Music, and ' I vomited yesterday,' and ' What day is it to-day ? ' and that the Mysteries are in September, and the

---

[a] LATE ADDITION : In fine the flatterer may be observed to say and do anything that he supposes will give pleasure.

[b] Perhaps in the ' Painted Porch,' cf. ii. 2, and Alciphr. iii. 17. 2 (iii. 52).

[c] Celebrated in March-April.

[d] Stale news ; this is clearly winter, and the Eleusinian Mysteries were in Sept.-Oct.

τὰ Ἀπατούρια,[1] Ποσιδεῶνος δὲ τὰ κατ᾽ ἀγροὺς
Διονύσια[2]· κἂν ὑπομένῃ τις αὐτὸν μὴ ἀφίστασθαι.[3]

ΑΓΡΟΙΚΙΑΣ Δ´

Ἡ δὲ ἀγροικία δόξειεν ἂν εἶναι ἀμαθία ἀσχήμων,
ὁ δὲ ἄγροικος τοιοῦτός τις, οἷος κυκεῶνα πιὼν
εἰς ἐκκλησίαν πορεύεσθαι, καὶ τὸ μύρον φάσκειν
οὐδὲν τοῦ θύμου ἥδιον ὄζειν, καὶ μείζω τοῦ ποδὸς
τὰ ὑποδήματα φορεῖν, καὶ μεγάλῃ τῇ φωνῇ λαλεῖν.
2 καὶ τοῖς μὲν φίλοις καὶ οἰκείοις ἀπιστεῖν, πρὸς
δὲ τοὺς αὐτοῦ οἰκέτας ἀνακοινοῦσθαι περὶ τῶν
3 μεγίστων· καὶ τοῖς παρ᾽ αὐτῷ ἐργαζομένοις
μισθωτοῖς ἐν ἀγρῷ πάντα τὰ ἀπὸ τῆς ἐκκλησίας
4 διηγεῖσθαι· καὶ ἀναβεβλημένος ἄνω τοῦ γόνατος
καθιζάνειν, ὥστε τὰ γυμνὰ αὐτοῦ ὑποφαίνεσθαι[4]·
5 καὶ ἐπ᾽ ἄλλῳ μὲν μηδενὶ ⟨μήτε⟩[5] θαυμάζειν μήτε
ἐκπλήττεσθαι ἐν ταῖς ὁδοῖς, ὅταν δὲ ἴδῃ βοῦν ἢ
6 ὄνον ἢ τράγον ἑστηκὼς θεωρεῖν. καὶ προαιρῶν
δέ τι ἐκ τοῦ ταμιείου δεινὸς φαγεῖν, καὶ ζωρότερον
7 πιεῖν· καὶ τὴν σιτοποιὸν πειρῶν λαθεῖν,[6] κᾆτ᾽
ἀλέσαι μετ᾽ αὐτῆς τοῖς ἔνδον πᾶσι καὶ αὐτῷ τὰ
8 ἐπιτήδεια. καὶ ἀριστῶν δὲ ἅμα καὶ[7] τοῖς ὑπο-
9 ζυγίοις ἐμβαλεῖν τὴν ὀλύραν· καὶ κόψαντος τὴν

---

[1] only M has τὰ   [2] M κατ᾽ ἀγρ. τὰ Δ., perhaps rightly ;
others omit τὰ   [3] all mss have this sentence after σήμερον
—sic—(introd. p. 17)   LATE ADDITION : (6) παρασείσαντα
δὴ δεῖ τοὺς τοιούτους τῶν ἀνθρώπων καὶ διαράμενον ἀπαλλάττεσθαι, ὅστις ἀπύρευτος βούλεται εἶναι · ἔργον γὰρ συναρκεῖσθαι
τοῖς μήτε σχολὴν μήτε σπουδὴν διαγινώσκουσιν, after which M
has ὁ γὰρ χρόνος οὐδὲ τοῖς καιριωτέροις ἐξαρκεῖ   [4] mss
also φαίνεσθαι : from ὥστε on may be a gloss   [5] Ast
[6] cf. Ar. Pax 1138, Lys. 1. 12   [7] some mss omit

Apaturia in October, and the country-Dionysia in December. And if you let him go on he will never stop.[a]

IV. BOORISHNESS

Boorishness would seem to be an unbecoming ignorance, and the Boor to be such as will take a purge before he goes to the Assembly,[b] declare that thyme smells every bit as sweet as perfume, wear shoes too large for his feet, and talk at the top of his voice. He distrusts his friends and kinsfolk, but confides matters of great import to his servants, and tells all that went on at the Assembly to the hired labourers who work on his farm. He will sit down with his cloak above his knee, and thus expose too much of himself.[c] Most things this man sees in the streets strike him not at all, but let him espy an ox or an ass or a billy-goat, and he will stand and contemplate him. He is apt also to take from the larder as he eats, and to drink his wine over-strong ; to make secret love to the bake-wench, and then help her grind the day's corn for the whole household and himself with it ; to fodder the beasts[d] while he munches his breakfast ; to answer a knock at

[a] LATE ADDITION : Such men as this anyone that would stay unburnt by the fire should flee by all and every means he can ; for it is hard to bear with one who cannot distinguish leisure from occupation. There is not time enough even for that which is relevant.

[b] This, in those days, would make him an unpleasant neighbour ; the next words refer to a different occasion.

[c] Cf. Philetaer. ii. 236 K.

[d] Lit. ' give the beasts their rice-wheat ' (Lat. far).

49

10 θύραν[1] ὑπακοῦσαι[2] αὐτός· καὶ ἐστιῶν[3] τὸν κύνα
προσκαλεσάμενος καὶ ἐπιλαβόμενος τοῦ ῥύγχους
εἰπεῖν· Οὗτος φυλάττει τὸ χωρίον καὶ τὴν οἰκίαν.
11 καὶ τὸ ἀργύριον δὲ παρά του λαμβάνων[4] ἀποδοκιμάζειν, λίαν λέγων μολυβρὸν[5] εἶναι, καὶ
ἕτερον ἀνταλλάττεσθαι.[6] κεῖ τὸ[7] ἄροτρον ἔχρησεν
ἢ κόφινον ἢ δρέπανον ἢ θύλακον, τοῦτο[8] τῆς
νυκτὸς κατὰ ἀγρυπνίαν ἀναμιμνησκόμενος <ἀναστὰς
12 ἐξιέναι> ζητῶν.[9] καὶ εἰς ἄστυ καταβαίνων ἐρωτῆσαι
τὸν ἀπαντῶντα πόσου ἦσαν αἱ διφθέραι καὶ τὸ
τάριχος, καὶ εἰ τήμερον[10] νουμηνίαν ἄγει, καὶ
<ἂν φῇ>,[11] εἰπεῖν εὐθὺς ὅτι βούλεται καταβὰς
ἀποκείρασθαι[12] καὶ τῆς αὐτῆς ὁδοῦ παριὼν[13] κομί-
13 σασθαι παρ' Ἀρχίου τοῦ ταρίχους.[14] καὶ ἐν
14 βαλανείῳ δὲ ᾆσαι. καὶ εἰς τὰ ὑποδήματα δὲ
ἥλους ἐγκροῦσαι.[15]

ΑΡΕΣΚΕΙΑΣ Ε΄

Ἡ δὲ ἀρέσκειά ἐστι μέν, ὡς ὅρῳ περιλαβεῖν,
ἔντευξις οὐκ ἐπὶ τῷ βελτίστῳ ἡδονῆς παρα-
2 σκευαστική, ὁ δὲ ἄρεσκος ἀμέλει τοιοῦτός τις,

[1] M. Schmidt: mss τὴν θύραν καὶ κόψαντος τὴν θύραν,
or omit κόψ. τ. θ. (introd. p. 18)   [2] Cas: mss
ἐπ.   [3] E, from M ἐσθίοντα: other mss omit   [4] mss
also λαβών, but M δεχόμενος   [5] Diels: mss λίαν μὲν
λυπηρὸν (λυπηρόν)   [6] Cob: mss ἅμα ἀλλάττ.   [7] E, cf.
Alciphr. 2. 16. 1 (3. 19): mss καὶ τὸ, καὶ εἰ τὸ, καὶ ὁ
[8] mss ταῦτα   [9] E, see introd. p. 21   [10] mss σήμ. ὁ
ἀγὼν (incorp. gloss; for nom. cf. Sch. M κόρδαξ 6. 3); for
ἄγει cf. Archil. 113 Bgk, where read Φησίν', ἕως φᾷ· νῦν ἄγει
Θαργηλία (subject once the king, cf. ὕει and ὕει Ζεύς)   [11] E
[12] mss also ὑποκ.   [13] cf. Ar. Pax 1155   [14] Sylb. partit.
gen.: mss τοὺς   [15] all mss have these two sentences after
ἀποκείρ. (introd. p. 18)

the door himself. When he gives a feast he calls
the dog, takes him by the snout, and says ' This
is the guardian of my house and farm.' When he
receives money [a] he tests it and finds it wanting ;
it looks, says he, too much like lead ; and changes
it for other. And if he has lent his plough, or a
basket, or a sickle, or a sack, he will remember it
as he lies awake one night and rise and go out to
seek it. On his way to the town he will ask any
that meets him the price of hides or red-herring,
and if 'tis new moon [b] to-day ; and should answer
come ' Yes,' declares he will go and be shorn out
of hand and get some herrings at Archias' shop on
the way to the barber's.[c] He is given also to singing
at the baths ; and loves to drive hobnails into the
soles of his shoes.

V. SELF-SEEKING AFFABILITY

Self-seeking Affability, to give it a definition, is
a sort of behaviour which provides pleasure, but
not with the best intentions ; [d] and it goes without
saying [e] that the Smoothboot or Self-seeking Affable

[a] Not necessarily ' *his* (due) money ' ; the article is often
used with this word when we should not expect it, *e.g.*
Diog. L. ii. 81 : so τὸ χρυσίον xxiii. 7.
[b] Observed as a holiday and a great day for marketing.
[c] Regardless of the noses of the barber's other customers.
[d] We have no single word for this unless it be Impression-
ism (and Impressionist) as it is sometimes transferred, in a
bon mot, from the realm of art : this man's behaviour comes
from a desire to produce a good impression *at all costs* ;
neither Complaisance nor Affability has this connotation ;
Healey's Smoothboot is unfortunately obsolete.
[e] *Cf.* xiii. n. *a.*

οἷος πόρρωθεν προσαγορεύσας καὶ ἄνδρα κράτιστον
εἰπὼν καὶ θαυμάσας ἱκανῶς ἀμφοτέραις ταῖς
χερσὶ λαβόμενος[1] μὴ ἀφιέναι, ἀλλὰ[2] μικρὸν ἐπι-
προπέμψας[3] καὶ ἐρωτήσας πότε αὐτὸν ὄψεται,
³ἐπαινῶν ἀπαλλάττεσθαι.[4] καὶ παρακληθεὶς δὲ
πρὸς δίαιταν μὴ μόνον ᾧ πάρεστι βούλεσθαι
ἀρέσκειν ἀλλὰ καὶ τῷ ἀντιδίκῳ, ἵνα κοινός τις
εἶναι δοκῇ.[5] καὶ τοῖς ξένοις[6] δὲ εἰπεῖν ὡς δικαιό-
τερα λέγουσι τῶν πολιτῶν. καὶ κεκλημένος δ'
⁴ἐπὶ δεῖπνον κελεῦσαι καλέσαι τὰ παιδία τὸν
⁵ἑστιῶντα, καὶ εἰσιόντα[7] φῆσαι σύκου[8] ὁμοιότερα
εἶναι τῷ πατρί, καὶ προσαγαγόμενος[9] φιλῆσαι καὶ
παρ' αὐτὸν καθίστασθαι,[10] καὶ τοῖς μὲν συμπαίζειν
αὐτὸς λέγων· Ἀσκός, πέλεκυς, τὰ δὲ ἐπὶ τῆς
γαστρὸς ἐᾶν καθεύδειν ἅμα[11] θλιβόμενος.[12]

ΑΠΟΝΟΙΑΣ Ϛ'

Ἡ δὲ ἀπόνοιά ἐστιν ὑπομονὴ αἰσχρῶν ἔργων τε
καὶ λόγων,[13] ὁ δὲ ἀπονενοημένος τοιοῦτός τις,

---

[1] only in P(ap. Herc. 1457)   [2] E : mss καὶ   [3] [ἐ]πι
in P only   [4] mss also ἔτι ἐπαινῶν ἀπ.   [5] τις
P : mss εἶς or omit   [6] Cor : mss and P accus.   [7] P εἰσελθόν-
τα, but cf. Ephipp. 6 K, Men. Pk. 193 (taken as singular ?)
[8] Nav. suggests σύκου ⟨σύκῳ⟩, cf. Herodas vi. 60   [9] mss
also and P προσαγόμ.   [10] so P or καθίσασθαι, cf. Lys.
18. 10 : mss also καθίσαι, -ίσασθαι   [11] ἀναθλιβόμενος? cf.
A.P. xii. 208 : P omits ἅμα   [12] all mss and P place
here the passage καὶ πλειστάκις κτλ. which most modern
editors transfer to xxi   [13] Gale : mss δικαιολόγων

is one that will hail you a great way off and call you
excellent fellow, and when he is done with admiring
you, seize you with both hands and not let go till
he have accompanied you some little way and asked
you when he can see you, and then go his way with
a compliment. When he is called to help settle a
dispute, his desire is to please the opposite party as
well as the friend he stands for, so that he may be
thought impartial. He will tell strangers, too, that
they are right and his fellow-countrymen wrong.
Bidden to a feast, he has his host call the children,
and they are no sooner come in than he declares
them to be as like as figs to their father, and drawing
them to him sets them beside him with a kiss, and
plays with some of them, himself crying 'Wineskin,
hatchet,' [a] and suffers others to sleep on his lap in
spite of the discomfort.

VI. WILFUL DISREPUTABLENESS

Wilful Disreputableness is a tolerance of the dishonourable in word and deed ; and your Scallywag

[a] These words were proverbial of lightness and heaviness,
originally in water, as in modern Greek a child learning to
swim floats like an ἀσκὶ or sinks like a τσηκούρι; this man,
then, lifts a child saying ἀσκός and drops it saying πέλεκυς
—or the like ; ' to try to sink an inflated skin ' was a proverb
for attempting the impossible, *Par. Gr.* ii. p. 311 ; inflated
skins were used for crossing rivers, etc., Xen. *An.* iii. 5,
Plut. *Thes.* xxiv. ; according to Hesychius there was a weight
called πέλεκυς=6 (or 12) minae (S. Koujeas, *Herm.* xli.
480, where see fig. Matz-Duhn. *Ant. Denk. in Rom,* ii. 2331) ;
cf. Aristotle and Diogenes' proffered figs, μετεωρίσας ὡς τὰ
παιδία, Diog. Laert. v. 18.

2 οἷος ὀμόσαι ταχύ, ⟨ἐκὼν⟩[1] κακῶς ἀκοῦσαι, λοι-
δορηθῆναι δυναμένοις,[2] τῷ ἤθει ἀγοραῖός τις καὶ
3 ἀνασεσυρμένος καὶ παντοποιός· ἀμέλει δυνατὸς
καὶ ὀρχεῖσθαι νήφων τὸν κόρδακα,[3] καὶ προσω-
πεῖον ἔχων ἐν κωμικῷ χορῷ περιάγειν ἐν τῷ
4 θεάτρῳ.[4] καὶ ἐν θαύμασι δὲ τοὺς χαλκοῦς ἐκλέγειν καθ᾽ ἕκαστον περιὼν[5] καὶ μάχεσθαι τούτοις
τοῖς τὸ σύμβολον φέρουσι[6] καὶ προῖκα θεωρεῖν
5 ἀξιοῦσι. δεινὸς δὲ καὶ πανδοκεῦσαι καὶ πορνο-
βοσκῆσαι καὶ τελωνῆσαι, καὶ μηδεμίαν αἰσχρὰν
ἐργασίαν ἀποδοκιμάσαι, ἀλλὰ κηρύττειν, μα-
6 γειρεύειν, κυβεύειν· τὴν μητέρα μὴ τρέφειν,
ἀπάγεσθαι κλοπῆς, τὸν κέραμον[7] πλείω χρόνον
7 οἰκεῖν ἢ τὴν αὑτοῦ οἰκίαν. καὶ τούτων[8] ἂν εἶναι
δόξειε τῶν περιϊσταμένων τοὺς ὄχλους καὶ προσ-
καλούντων, μεγάλῃ τῇ φωνῇ καὶ παρερρωγυίᾳ
λοιδορουμένων καὶ διαλεγομένων πρὸς αὐτούς· καὶ
οἱ μὲν μεταξὺ[9] προσίασιν, οἱ δὲ ἀπίασιν πρὶν
ἀκοῦσαι αὐτοῦ, ἀλλὰ τοῖς μὲν τὴν ἀρχήν, τοῖς
δὲ συλλαβήν, τοῖς δὲ μέρος τοῦ πράγματος λέγει,
οὐκ ἄλλως θεωρεῖσθαι ἀξιῶν τὴν ἀπόνοιαν αὐτοῦ
8 ἢ ὅταν ᾖ πανήγυρις. ἱκανὸς δὲ καὶ δίκας τὰς
μὲν φεύγειν, τὰς δὲ διώκειν, τὰς δὲ ἐξόμνυσθαι,
ταῖς δὲ παρεῖναι ἔχων ἐχῖνον[10] ἐν τῷ προκολπίῳ

---

[1] Herw., cf. Men. 614 K   [2] Foss, i.e. τοῖς δυν.;
partc. in the nom. (mss) cannot be right: or omit λοιδ. δυν.
as gloss?   [3] Sch. κόρδαξ εἶδος ὀρχήσεως αἰσχρᾶς καὶ
ἀπρεποῦς   [4] περιάγειν ἐν θεατρω (sic) only in M. introd.
p. 24   [5] Needh. i.e. περιὼν: mss παριὼν   [6] some mss
omit τούτοις   [7] only M: others have the gloss δεσμωτήριον
[8] Needh: mss τοῦτο δ᾽, τοῦτ᾽ ἂν   [9] E: mss μεταξὺ οἱ μὲν
[10] Sch. ἐχῖνός ἐστι σκεῦος χαλκοῦν τῆς δικαστικῆς τραπέζης, ἐν ᾧ
τὰ γράμματα ἤγουν τὰς ψήφους ἀπετίθεσαν

CHARACTER VI

or Wilfully Disreputable man [a] is quick to pledge his name, tolerant of slander, abusive of the great,[b] of a ne'er-do-weel, decency-be-damned, devil-may-care disposition. He is the man, I warrant you,[c] to dance the cordax sober, and when he wears a mask in a comic chorus to twist it hind-part before in the face of the house.[d] At a show he will go round collecting the pence from every man severally, and wrangle with such as bring the ticket and claim to look on for nothing. He will keep inns and brothels, he will farm the taxes; crier, cook, dicing-house man,[e] there's no trade so low but he'll follow it. He will turn his mother out of doors,[f] be apprehended for larceny,[g] spend longer time in the lock-up than in his own house. He would seem to be of those who gather crowds and abuse them and argue with them in a loud cracked voice, while some will come after he is begun and others go before he ends, this getting but the prologue, that the summing-up, the other a morsel of the theme itself, and no occasion reckoned so pat to his purpose as a fair.[h] In the courts of law he is alike fitted to play plaintiff or defendant; he may refuse his testimony on oath, or come to give it with a

---

[a] Perverse? cf. E. A. Poe, *The Black Cat.* Abandoned?

[b] Or, without emendation, 'able to be abused' (gloss; δύναμαι with pass. inf. is very rare in classical Greek).

[c] Cf. xiii. n. *a.*

[d] Cf. περιάγ. τὴν κεφαλήν, τὸν τράχηλον, κτλ: or 'do the scene-shifting in his mask'? cf. περίακτοι.

[e] The context belies the usual meaning 'dice-player.'

[f] Such people were classed by law as evil-livers and lost the right to speak in the Assembly, cf. Aesch. 1. 28, Diog. L. i. 55.   [g] Cf. Andoc. *Myst.* 1. 74.

[h] This sentence is perhaps an interpolation.

9 καὶ ὁρμαθοὺς γραμματειδίων ἐν ταῖς χερσίν. οὐκ
ἀποδοκιμάζειν δὲ ἀλλ' οὐδὲ πολλῶν ἀγοραίων
στρατηγεῖν[1] καὶ εὐθὺς τούτοις δανείζειν καὶ τῆς
δραχμῆς τόκον τρία ἡμιωβόλια τῆς ἡμέρας πράτ-
τεσθαι, καὶ ἐφοδεύειν τὰ μαγειρεῖα, τὰ ἰχθυο-
πώλια, τὰ ταριχοπώλια, καὶ τοὺς τόκους ⟨τοὺς⟩[2]
ἀπὸ τοῦ ἐμπολήματος εἰς τὴν γνάθον ἐκλέγειν.[3]

ΛΑΛΙΑΣ Ζ΄

Ἡ δὲ λαλιά, εἴ τις αὐτὴν ὁρίζεσθαι βούλοιτο,
εἶναι ἂν δόξειεν ἀκρασία τοῦ λόγου, ὁ δὲ λάλος
2 τοιοῦτός τις, οἷος τῷ ἐντυγχάνοντι εἰπεῖν, ἂν
ὁτιοῦν πρὸς αὐτὸν φθέγξηται, ὅτι οὐθὲν λέγει,
καὶ ὅτι αὐτὸς πάντα οἶδεν, καὶ ὅτι ἂν ἀκούῃ
3 αὐτοῦ μαθήσεται· καὶ μεταξὺ δὲ ἀποκρινομένῳ
ὑποβαλεῖν[4] εἴπας· Σὺ μὴ[5] ἐπιλάθῃ ὃ μέλλεις
λέγειν, καὶ Εὖ γε ὅτι με ὑπέμνησας, καὶ Τὸ
λαλεῖν ὡς χρήσιμόν που, καὶ Ὃ παρέλιπον, καὶ
Ταχύ γε συνῆκας τὸ πρᾶγμα, καὶ Πάλαι σε
παρετήρουν εἰ ἐπὶ τὸ αὐτὸ ἐμοὶ κατενεχθήσῃ·
καὶ ἑτέρας ἀρχὰς[6] τοιαύτας πορίσασθαι, ὥστε
4 μηδ' ἀναπνεῦσαι τὸν ἐντυγχάνοντα· καὶ ὅταν γε
τοὺς καθ' ἕνα ἀποκναίσῃ,[7] δεινὸς καὶ ἐπὶ τοὺς

---

[1] ἀποδοκιμάζειν Meier: mss -ων: ἀλλ' οὐδὲ E, cf. xxviii. 5
and Ar. Nub. 1395, Dem. 19. 37: mss οὐδ' ἅμα: Diels'
ἀλλαντοπωλεῖν does not suit the sequel   [2] Nav.
[3] LATE ADDITION: (10) ἐργώδεις δέ εἰσιν οἱ τὸ στόμα εὔλυτον
ἔχοντες πρὸς λοιδορίαν καὶ φθεγγόμενοι μεγάλῃ τῇ φωνῇ, ὡς
συνηχεῖν αὐτοῖς τὴν ἀγορὰν καὶ τὰ ἐργαστήρια   [4] mss
ὑποβάλλει(ν), ἐπιβ. (introd. p. 21): or ὑπολαβεῖν (old
corr. ?)   [5] mss also Εἶπας σύ; μὴ   [6] mss also ἀφορμὰς
[7] old variant ἀπογυμνώσῃ (early corruption of the spelling
ἀπογναίσῃ?): Nav. ἀπογυμνάσῃ

56

sealed box in his coat and bundles of documents [a] in his hands. Nor loath is he, neither, to play captain to much riff-raff of the market, lending them money the moment they ask it, and exacting three ha'pence a day usury on every shilling. And he makes his rounds of the cookshops, the fishmongers', the salters', and collects his share of their takings in his cheek.[b]

VII. LOQUACITY

Loquacity, should you wish to define it, would seem to be an incontinence of speech; and the Loquacious man will say to any that meets him, if he but open his lips, 'You are wrong; I know all about it, and if you will listen to me you shall learn the truth.' And in the midst of the other's answer he whispers him [c] such words as these: 'Pray bethink you what you are about to say'; or 'I thank you for reminding me'; or 'There's nothing like a talk, is there?' or 'I forgot to say'; or 'You have not taken long to understand it'; or 'I had long expected you would come round to my way of thinking'; and provides himself other such openings, so that his friend can hardly get his breath. And when he has worn out [d] such as go singly, he

---

[a] *i.e.* papyrus-rolls strung together.
[b] The usual place for carrying *small* change, *cf.* Ar. *Eccl.* 818.
  LATE ADDITION: Troublesome indeed are those who always have their tongue ready to let slip for abuse, and talk with loud voices; who make the market and the workshops to ring with their words.
[c] Or 'interrupts him with.' [d] Or perhaps 'disarmed.'

ἀθρόους[1] συνεστηκότας πορευθῆναι καὶ φυγεῖν
5 ποιῆσαι μεταξὺ χρηματίζοντας. καὶ εἰς τὰ διδα-
σκαλεῖα δὲ καὶ εἰς τὰς παλαίστρας εἰσιὼν κωλύειν
τοὺς παῖδας προμανθάνειν, τοσαῦτα καὶ προσ-
6 λαλεῖν τοῖς παιδοτρίβαις καὶ διδασκάλοις. καὶ
τοὺς ἀπιέναι φάσκοντας δεινὸς προπέμψαι καὶ
7 ἀποκαταστῆσαι εἰς τὴν οἰκίαν.[2] καὶ πυθόμενος
τὰς ἐκκλησίας ἀπαγγέλλειν, προσδιηγήσασθαι δὲ
καὶ τήν ποτε[3] γενομένην τοῖν ῥητόροιν μάχην,[4]
καὶ οὓς ποτε λόγους αὐτὸς εἴπας εὐδοκίμησεν[5] ἐν
8 τῷ δήμῳ· καὶ κατὰ τῶν πληθῶν γε ἅμα διηγού-
μενος κατηγορίαν παρεμβαλεῖν, ὥστε τοὺς ἀκούοντας ἤτοι ἐπιλαθέσθαι ἢ νυστάξαι ἢ μεταξὺ κατα-
9 λιπόντας[6] ἀπαλλάττεσθαι. καὶ συνδικάζων δὲ κω-
λῦσαι κρῖναι, καὶ συνθεωρῶν θεάσασθαι, καὶ συν-
δειπνῶν φαγεῖν, λέγων ὅτι χαλεπὸν τῷ λαλῷ
ἐστι σιωπᾶν, καὶ ὡς ἐν ὑγρῷ ἐστιν ἡ γλῶττα,
καὶ ὅτι οὐκ ἂν σιωπήσειεν οὐδ᾽ εἰ τῶν χελιδόνων
δόξειεν εἶναι λαλίστερος. καὶ σκωπτόμενος ὑπομεῖναι καὶ ὑπὸ τῶν αὑτοῦ παιδίων, ὅταν αὐτὸς
ἤδη καθεύδειν βουλόμενος κελεύῃ, λεγόντων Τάτα,[7]
λαλεῖν τι ἡμῖν, ὅπως ἂν ἡμᾶς ὕπνος τις[8] λάβῃ.

[1] some mss insert καί, but Nav. compares Plat. *Lys.* init.,
Xen. *An.* vii. 4. 47   [2] mss also ἐκ τῆς οἰκίας (but *cf.*
ἐκκεκρουμένῳ xxx. 11)   [3] some mss τὴν ἐπ᾽ Ἀριστοφῶντος
τότε (ποτε), incorporating gloss   [4] Diels-Hottinger: mss
τοῦ ῥήτορος μ. and add, after incorporation of gloss, καὶ τὴν
Λακεδαιμονίοις (-ων) ὑπὸ (ἐπὶ) Λυσάνδρου, confusing the archon
of 330 with the member of the Four Hundred: a *real* battle
has no point here   [5] arch. recorded variant εἶπεν εὐδοκιμήσας

58

is prone to march upon those who stand together
in troops, and put them to flight in the midst of
their business. It is a habit of his to go into the
schools and wrestling-places and keep the children
from learning their tasks, he talks so much to their
teachers and trainers.[a] And if you say you must
go your ways, he loves to bear you company and
see you to your doorstep. And when he has news
of the meetings of Assembly he retails it, with the
addition of an account of the famous battle of the
orators,[b] and the speeches he too was used to make
there so greatly to his credit, all this interlarded
with tirades against democracy, till his listeners
forget what it is all about, or fall half-asleep, or get
up and leave him to his talk. On a jury this man
hinders your verdict, at the play your entertainment,
at the table your eating, with the plea that it is
hard for the talkative to hold his peace, or that the
tongue grows in a wet soil, or he could not cease
though he should outbabble the very swallows. And
he is content to be the butt of his own children, who
when it is late and he would fain be sleeping and
bids them do likewise, cry ' Talk to us, daddy, and
then we shall go to sleep.'

[a] For construction cf. Alciphr. ii. 32. 3 (iii. 34).
[b] Demosthenes and Aeschines in 330 B.C.

---

[6] Herw. ⟨λαλοῦντα⟩ καταλ.   [7] E (Ribb. τατᾶ, but cf.
Herod. i. 60 τάταλίζειν): mss αὐτὸν ἤ. κ. βουλόμενον (βουλόμενον
corr. to -να) κελ. λέγοντα ταῦτα: for omission of the second
καθεύδειν cf. Dem. 54. 23 fin.   [8] most mss omit τις, but
(like ὅπως ἄν ; and λαλεῖν) it may be baby-language.

59

THEOPHRASTUS

ΛΟΓΟΠΟΙΑΣ Η΄

Ἡ δὲ λογοποιία ἐστὶ σύνθεσις ψευδῶν λόγων
καὶ πράξεων ὧν βούλεται ὁ λογοποιῶν, ὁ δὲ
2 λογοποιὸς τοιοῦτός τις, οἷος ἀπαντήσας τῷ
φίλῳ εὐθὺς καταβαλὼν τὸ ἦθος[1] καὶ μειδιάσας
ἐρωτῆσαι· Πόθεν σὺ καὶ πῶς ἔχεις καὶ ἔχεις τι
περὶ τοῦδε εἰπεῖν καινόν;[2] καὶ ὡς ἐπιβάλλων[3]
ἐρωτᾶν· Μὴ λέγεταί τι καινότερον; καὶ μὴν
3 ἀγαθά γέ ἐστι τὰ λεγόμενα· καὶ οὐκ ἐάσας
ἀποκρίνασθαι εἰπεῖν· Τί λέγεις; οὐδὲν ἀκήκοας;
4 δοκῶ μοί σε εὐωχήσειν καινῶν λόγων· καὶ ἔστιν
αὐτῷ ἢ στρατιώτης ⟨τις⟩[4] ἢ παῖς Ἀστείου τοῦ
αὐλητοῦ ἢ Λύκων ὁ ἐργολάβος παραγεγονὼς ἐξ
5 αὐτῆς τῆς μάχης οὗ φησιν ἀκηκοέναι· αἱ μὲν οὖν
ἀναφοραὶ τῶν λόγων τοιαῦταί εἰσιν αὐτῷ[5] ὧν
6 οὐδεὶς ἂν ἔχοι ἐπιλαβέσθαι[6]· διηγεῖται δὲ τούτους
φάσκων λέγειν ὡς Πολυπέρχων καὶ ὁ βασιλεὺς
7 μάχην[7] νενίκηκε καὶ Κάσανδρος ἐζώγρηται· καὶ
ἂν εἴπῃ τις αὐτῷ· Σὺ δὲ ταῦτα πιστεύεις; γεγονέναι
φησὶ[8] τὸ πρᾶγμα· βοᾶσθαι γὰρ ἐν τῇ πόλει, καὶ
τὸν λόγον ἐπεντείνειν, καὶ πάντας συμφωνεῖν,
ταὐτὰ γὰρ λέγειν περὶ τῆς μάχης καὶ πολὺν τὸν
8 ζωμὸν γεγονέναι· εἶναι δ' ἑαυτῷ[9] καὶ σημεῖον τὰ
πρόσωπα τῶν ἐν τοῖς πράγμασιν, ὁρᾶν γὰρ
αὐτῶν[10] πάντων μεταβεβληκότα· λέγει δ' ὡς καὶ

[1] sc. τὸ ἐπὶ τοῦ προσώπου ; cf. [Arist.] *Physiog.* i. 805 b 2,
and Eur. *Cycl.* 167 καταβάλλειν τὰς ὀφρῦς, Ar. *Vesp.* 655 χαλᾶν
τὸ μέτωπον, *Ach.* 1069 ἀνασπᾶν τὰς ὀφρῦς, Amphis 3. 305 M.
ἐπαίρειν τὰς ὀφρῦς   [2] introd. p. 24   [3] mss -βαλών   [4] *E*
[5] most mss -τοῦ   [6] Cas: mss -λαθέσθαι   [7] mss also
μάχη   [8] cf. Men. *Ep.* 79: most mss omit γεγονέναι, all
have φήσε   [9] Diels: mss δὲ αὐτῷ   [10] αὐτὸς τῶν ?
mss also αὐτὸν

VIII. NEWSMAKING

Newsmaking is the putting together of fictitious sayings and doings at a man's own caprice ; and the Newsmaker is one that no sooner meets a friend than his face softens and he asks him with a smile ' Where do you come from ? How do you ? and Have you any news of this ? ' and throwing himself, so to speak, upon him ' Can there be any greater news ? [a] nay, and it is good news ' ; and without suffering him to answer, ' What ? ' cries he, ' have you heard nothing ? methinks I can give you a rare feast.' And it seems he has some soldier, or a servant of Asteius the flute-player's,[b] or maybe Lycon the contractor, come straight from the battle-field, who has told him all about it. Thus his authorities are such as no man could lay hands on. Yet he recounts, with them for sponsors, how that Polyperchon and the King have won a battle, and Casander is taken.[c] And if it be asked him ' Do you believe this ? ' he will reply that it is so indeed, 'tis common talk, and the report gains ground, and everyone says the same ; all agree about the battle, and the butchers' bill is very long [d] ; he can tell it from the faces of the Government, they are all so changed. Moreover, he has been told in secret that they are keeping in

---

[a] *Cf.* Dem. *Phil.* i. 43. 10.
[b] Flute-playing was usual at sacrifices on the field of battle as elsewhere (Nav.).
[c] Introd. p. 5, and Index.
[d] Lit. ' the broth has been plentiful.'

παρακήκοε παρὰ τούτοις κρυπτόμενόν τινα ἐν οἰκίᾳ
ἤδη πέμπτην ἡμέραν ἥκοντα ἐκ Μακεδονίας ὃς
9 πάντα ταῦτα εἶδε[1]· καὶ ταῦθ᾽ ἅπαντα[2] διεξιὼν
πῶς οἴεσθε πιθανῶς σχετλιάζων λέγει[3]· Δυστυχὴς
Κάσανδρος· ὢ ταλαίπωρος· ἐνθυμῇ τὸ τῆς τύχης;
10 ἀλλ᾽ οὖν ἰσχυρός ⟨γε⟩ γενόμενος[4]—· καὶ Δεῖ δ᾽
αὐτὸν σὲ μόνον εἰδέναι· πᾶσι δὲ τοῖς ἐν τῇ πόλει
προσδεδράμηκε λέγων.[5]

ΑΝΑΙΣΧΥΝΤΙΑΣ Θ´

Ἡ δὲ ἀναισχυντία ἐστὶ μέν, ὡς ὅρῳ λαβεῖν,
καταφρόνησις δόξης αἰσχροῦ ἕνεκα κέρδους, ὁ δὲ
2 ἀναίσχυντος τοιοῦτος, οἷος πρῶτον μὲν ὃν ἀπο-
στερεῖ πρὸς τοῦτον ἀπελθὼν δανείζεσθαι· εἶτα
θύσας τοῖς θεοῖς αὐτὸς μὲν δειπνεῖν παρ᾽ ἑτέρῳ,
3 τὰ δὲ κρέα ἀποτιθέναι ἁλσὶ πάσας. καί ποι
κεκλημένος,[6] προσκαλεσάμενος τὸν ἀκόλουθον
δοῦναι ἀπὸ τῆς τραπέζης ἄρας κρέας καὶ ἄρτον,
καὶ εἰπεῖν ἀκουόντων πάντων· Εὐωχοῦ, Τίβειε.[7]

---

[1] mss also οἶδε   [2] mss πάντα, ταῦτα π., ταῦθ᾽ ἅμα
[3] E: M σχετλιάζων ἐπάγειν, others σχετλιάζει(ν) λέγων
[4] E   [5] LATE ADDITION: (11) τῶν τοιούτων ἀνθρώπων
τεθαύμακα τί ποτε βούλονται λογοποιοῦντες· οὐ γὰρ μόνον
ψεύδονται ἀλλὰ καὶ ἀλυσιτελῆ πλάττουσι (mss -λῶς ἀπ-
αλλάττ.).   (12) πολλάκις γὰρ αὐτῶν οἱ μὲν ἐν τοῖς βαλανείοις
περιστάσεις ποιούμενοι τὰ ἱμάτια ἀποβεβλήκασιν, οἱ δ᾽ ἐν
τῇ στοᾷ πεζομαχίᾳ καὶ ναυμαχίᾳ νικῶντες ἐρήμους δίκας ὠφλή-
κασιν.   (13) εἰσὶ δ᾽ οἳ καὶ πόλεις τῷ (mss πλεῖστοι) λόγῳ
κατὰ κράτος αἱροῦντες παρεδειπνήθησαν.   (14) πάνυ δὴ ταλαί-
πωρον αὐτῶν ἐστι τὸ ἐπιτήδευμα· ποία γὰρ (mss insert οὐ)
στοά, ποῖον δὲ ἐργαστήριον, ποῖον δὲ μέρος τῆς ἀγορᾶς οὗ οὐ
(mss οὐ or omit) διημερεύουσιν ἀπαυδᾶν ποιοῦντες τοὺς ἀκούοντας ;
(15) οὕτως καὶ καταπονοῦσι ταῖς ψευδολογίαις.   [6] only in
M (που κεκλ.)   [7] mss also τίμιε, τιμώσατε, Sch. only in M
Τίβιε δουλικὸν ὄνομα ὡς καὶ Δρόμων καὶ Γέτας καὶ τὰ τοιαῦτα

close hiding one that came four days ago out of Macedonia who has seen it all.[a] While this long tale is telling, you cannot think how true to life are his cries of woe : ' Poor Casander ! unhappy man ! do you see how luck turns ? Well, he was a strong man once, and now——! ' and he ends with saying, ' But mind you, this must go no further,' albeit he has been running up to all the town to tell them of it.[b]

IX. UNCONSCIONABLENESS

Unconscionableness, to define it, is a neglect of reputation for the sake of filthy lucre ; and he is unconscionable who, in the first place, goes off and borrows of a creditor he has already refused to pay.[c] Next, when he sacrifices, he dines abroad, and lays by the meat of the victim in salt.[d] When he is a man's guest, he calls his lackey and takes and gives him bread and meat from the table, and says in the hearing of the whole company ' Fall you to and

---

[a] Or, ' knows everything.'

[b] LATE ADDITION : It is a marvel to me what object such men can have in making their news. They not merely tell lies, but forge tales that bring them no profit. For often-times have they lost their cloaks gathering crowds at the baths, or been cast in their suits-at-law by default a-winning battles by land or sea in the Porch, or it may be have missed their dinner taking cities by assault of word. Their manner of life is hard indeed ; for what porch is there, or workshop, or part of the market-place which they do not haunt day in day out, to the utter undoing of their hearers, so do they weary them with their lying tales ?

[c] Cf. ἀδικεῖ=he has wronged ; Nav. compares Xen. An. vii. 6. 9, Isocr. 18. 53 ; for ἀπελθών cf. Diog. L. vi. 46.

[d] Instead of feasting his friends on it ; cf. Men. 518. 3 K.

4 καὶ ὀψωνῶν δὲ ὑπομιμνήσκειν τὸν κρεωπώλην εἴ
τι χρήσιμος αὐτῷ γέγονε, καὶ ἑστηκὼς πρὸς τῷ
σταθμῷ μαλίστα μὲν κρέας, εἰ δὲ μή, ὀστοῦν εἰς
τὸν ζυγὸν¹ ἐμβαλεῖν, καὶ ἐὰν μὲν λάθῃ,² εἰ δὲ μή,
ἁρπάσας ἀπὸ τῆς τραπέζης χολίκιον ἅμα γελῶν
5 ἀπαλλάττεσθαι. καὶ ξένοις δὲ αὐτοῦ θέαν ἀγοράσας
μὴ δοὺς τὸ μέρος θεωρεῖν, ἄγειν δὲ καὶ τοὺς
6 υἱεῖς εἰς τὴν ὑστεραίαν καὶ τὸν παιδαγωγόν. καὶ
ὅσα ἐωνημένος ἄξιά τις φέρει, μεταδοῦναι κελεῦσαι
7 καὶ αὐτῷ. καὶ ἐπὶ τὴν ἀλλοτρίαν οἰκίαν ἐλθὼν
δανείζεσθαι κριθάς, ποτὲ δὲ ἄχυρον,³ καὶ ταῦτα
τοὺς χρήσαντας⁴ ἀναγκάσαι ἀποφέρειν πρὸς αὐτούς.⁵
8 δεινὸς δὲ καὶ πρὸς τὰ χαλκεῖα τὰ ἐν τῷ βαλανείῳ
προσελθὼν καὶ βάψας ἀρύταιναν ⟨βίᾳ⟩⁶ βοῶντος
τοῦ βαλανέως αὐτὸς αὑτοῦ καταχέασθαι, καὶ
εἰπεῖν ὅτι Λέλουμαι, ἀπιών, κἀκείνου⁷ οὐδεμία
σοι χάρις.

ΜΙΚΡΟΛΟΓΙΑΣ Ι′

Ἔστι δὲ ἡ μικρολογία φειδωλία τοῦ διαφόρου
ὑπὲρ τὸν καιρόν, ὁ δὲ μικρολόγος τοιοῦτός τις,
2 οἷος ἐν τῷ μηνὶ ἡμιωβόλιον ἀπαιτεῖν ἐλθὼν⁸ ἐπὶ
3 τὴν οἰκίαν. καὶ συσσιτῶν⁹ ἀριθμεῖν τε πόσας¹⁰

¹ masc. in this sense: mss also ζωμὸν, but with ἐμβαλεῖν
this could only be taken as *into* not *for* his broth   ² old
var. ?: most mss λάβῃ, but *cf.* the reverse ἐπιλαθέσθαι viii. 4:
mss add εὖ ἔχει   ³ mss also ἄχυρα; for omission of the
μὲν-clause *cf.* Plat. *Theaet.* 101 D, Andoc. 1. 105   ⁴ M
τοὺς χρῶντας :' others χρησ.   ⁵ E : mss αὐτὸν   ⁶ E
⁷ Λέλουμαι Herw., κἀκείνου E : mss λέλουται ἀπ. κακεῖ; *cf.*
Ar. *Pax* 1103   ⁸ most mss omit   ⁹ introd. p. 29
¹⁰ varied order in mss, τε (τὰς or omit) κύλικας πόσας (ὁπόσας
Ambr. P, introd. p. 29), πόσας κύλ., shows that κύλικας was
in marg. arch. (gloss, *cf.* xiii. 4)

welcome, Tibeius.' Buying meat he will remind
the butcher of any good turn he has done him,
and as he stands by the balance, throw into the
scale a piece of meat or, failing that, a bone ;[a]
which doing if he be not seen, well and good ; else,
he will snatch a bit of tripe from the counter and
away laughing. He takes places for foreign friends
of his to see the play, and then sees it himself without paying his scot, and even takes his children the
next day and their tutor to boot.[b] One that carries
home something he has bought a bargain is bidden
share it with him ; and he will go to a neighbour's
to borrow to-day barley, to-morrow bran, and make
the lender fetch it when he pays it back. He loves
also to go up to the cauldrons at the baths, and
dipping the ladle despite the cries of the bathing-
man, do his own drenching, and exclaim as he runs
off, ' I've had my bath, and no thanks to you for
that ! '

X. PENURIOUSNESS

Penuriousness is an excessive economy of expenditure ; and the Penurious man is he that will come
to a man's house ere the month run out for a farthings-
worth of usury ; and at the club mess will reckon

[a] *i.e.* after the weighing, and before the meat is lifted
from the scale-pan.
[b] Apparently he takes a ' block,' say, of twelve seats,
and makes it do for thirteen the first day, and for even more
the second.

ἕκαστος πέπωκε, καὶ ἀπάρχεσθαι ἐλάχιστον τῇ
⁴ Ἀρτέμιδι τῶν συνδειπνούντων. καὶ ὅσα μικροῦ
τις πριάμενος λογίζεται ⟨αὐτῷ, ἀποδοκιμάσαι
τοῖς ἀλλότρια δαπανῶσι⟩¹ πάντα φάσκων ⟨ὤνια⟩²
⁵ εἶναι. καὶ οἰκέτου χύτραν ἔνην³ ἢ λοπάδα κατ-
⁶ άξαντος εἰσπρᾶξαι ἀπὸ τῶν ἐπιτηδείων. καὶ τῆς
γυναικὸς ἐκβαλούσης⁴ τρίχαλκον οἷος μεταφέρειν
τὰ σκεύη καὶ τὰς κλίνας καὶ τὰς κιβωτοὺς καὶ
⁷ διφᾶν τὰ καλύμματα. καὶ ἐάν τι πωλῇ, τοσούτου
⁸ ἀποδόσθαι ὥστε μὴ λυσιτελεῖν τῷ πριαμένῳ. καὶ
οὐκ ἂν ἐᾶσαι οὔτε συκοτραγῆσαι ἐκ τοῦ αὐτοῦ
κήπου,⁵ οὔτε διὰ τοῦ αὐτοῦ ἀγροῦ πορευθῆναι,
οὔτε⁶ ἐλαίαν ἢ φοίνικα τῶν χαμαὶ πεπτωκότων⁷
⁹ ἀνελέσθαι. καὶ τοὺς ὅρους δ᾽ ἐπισκοπεῖσθαι ὁση-
¹⁰ μέραι εἰ διαμένουσιν οἱ αὐτοί. δεινὸς δὲ καὶ
¹¹ ὑπερημερίαν πρᾶξαι καὶ τόκον τόκου· καὶ ἑστιῶν
¹² δημότας μικρὰ τὰ κρέα κόψας παραθεῖναι· καὶ
¹³ ὀψωνῶν μηδὲν πριάμενος εἰσελθεῖν· καὶ ἀπ-
αγορεῦσαι τῇ γυναικὶ μήτε ἅλας χρηννύειν⁸ μήτε
ἐλλύχνιον μήτε κύμινον μήτε ὀρίγανον μήτε ὀλὰς⁹
μήτε στέμματα μήτε θυληλήματα, ἀλλὰ λέγειν ὅτι
¹⁴ τὰ μικρὰ ταῦτα πολλά ἐστι τοῦ ἐνιαυτοῦ. καὶ
τὸ ὅλον δὲ τῶν μικρολόγων καὶ τὰς ἀργυροθήκας

---

¹ E, e.g. (introd. p. 21)   ² Unger   ³ E, cf. περυ-
σινόν Ar. Ran. 986 : mss (AB and Ambr. P) εἶναι or omi
⁴ old var. ἀποβ. but cf. Ar. Thesm. 481   ⁵ mss also σκοποῦ
⁶ perhaps ⟨εἰ μὴ ἐφ᾽ ᾧ⟩ μηδέ E ; cf. M μηδ᾽ ἐᾶν διὰ τοῦ αὐτοῦ
ἀγροῦ πορεύεσθαι ἐφ᾽ ᾧ μὴ συκοτραγήσῃ τις   ⁷ mss also
κειμένων, whence Cob. χαμαιπετῶν (χ. unaccented in some
mss)   ⁸ Foss : mss χρωνν.   ⁹ only M, others οὐλὰς

how many cups each has drunk, and of all the company offer the leanest firstlings to Artemis.[a] When one that has struck him a bargain comes to the reckoning with him, he rejects what he has bought him, saying that you can afford anything with other people's money.[b] And if a servant of his break a year-old pot or dish he will subtract the price of it from his food. Should his wife drop a half-farthing, he is one that will shift pots, pans, cupboards, and beds, and rummage the curtains [c]; and should he have aught for sale, sell it for so great a price that the buyer will make nothing by it. No man may take a fig from his garden, nor pass through his land, nor pick up a wind-fallen olive or date [d]; and his landmarks are visited every day in the year to make sure they remain as they were. This man is given to distraining for a debt and exacting usury upon usury ; to setting small slices of meat before his fellow-parishioners ; to returning empty-handed when he goes a-marketing ; and will forbid his wife to lend a neighbour salt, or a lampwick, or aniseed, or marjoram, or barley-groats, or garlands, or incense, 'for these little things,' says he ' come to so much in the year.' [e] In fine [f] you may see the money-

---

[a] The club must have been an association under the patronage of Artemis, Ἀρτεμισταί, probably for hunting purposes, cf. C.I.A. iv. 2. 1334 B (Holland).

[b] i.e. as principal he rejects a bargain struck in his behalf by a subordinate : but the reading is uncertain.

[c] Or, 'search between the floor-boards' (of the women's apartment, often upstairs), Studniczka.

[d] Or perhaps ' pass through his land except on condition that he will not pick up '; dates are the more in point because dates do not ripen well in Greece ; cf. Xen. An. ii. 3. 15, Paus. ix. 19. 8.   [e] Cf. Antiph. 135 K.

[f] The remainder is perhaps an addition by another hand.

ἔστιν ἰδεῖν εὐρωτίωσας καὶ τὰς κλεῖς ἰωμένας,
καὶ αὐτοὺς δὲ φοροῦντας ἐλάττω τῶν μηρῶν[1] τὰ
ἱμάτια, καὶ ἐκ ληκυθίων μικρῶν πάνυ ἀλειφο-
μένους, καὶ ἐν χρῷ κειρομένους, καὶ τὸ μέσον τῆς
ἡμέρας ὑπολυομένους,[2] καὶ πρὸς τοὺς γναφεῖς δια-
τεινομένους ὅπως τὸ ἱμάτιον αὐτοῖς ἕξει πολλὴν
⟨τὴν⟩ γῆν, ἵνα μὴ ῥυπαίνηται ταχύ.

ΒΔΕΛΥΡΙΑΣ ΙΑ΄

Οὐ χαλεπὸν δέ ἐστι τὴν βδελυρίαν διορίσασθαι·
2 ἔστι γὰρ παιδιὰ ἐπιφανὴς καὶ ἐπονείδιστος, ὁ δὲ
βδελυρὸς τοιοῦτος, οἷος ἀπαντήσας[3] γυναιξὶν
3 ἐλευθέραις ἀνασυράμενος δεῖξαι τὸ αἰδοῖον· καὶ
ἐν θεάτρῳ κροτεῖν ὅταν οἱ ἄλλοι παύωνται, καὶ
συρίττειν οὓς ἡδέως θεωροῦσιν οἱ λοιποί· καὶ
ὅταν σιωπήσῃ τὸ θέατρον ἀνακύψας ἐρυγεῖν, ἵνα
4 τοὺς καθημένους ποιήσῃ μεταστραφῆναι. καὶ πλη-
θούσης τῆς ἀγορᾶς προσελθὼν πρὸς τὰ κάρυα ἢ
τὰ μῆλα[4] ἢ τὰ ⟨ἄλλα⟩ ἀκρόδρυα[5] ἑστηκὼς
τραγηματίζεσθαι ἅμα τῷ πωλοῦντι προσλαλῶν.
καὶ καλέσαι δὲ τῶν παρόντων[6] ὀνομαστί τινα ᾧ
μὴ συνήθης ἐστί. καὶ σπεύδοντας δέ ποι[7] ὁρῶν
6 περιμεῖναι κελεῦσαι.[8] καὶ ἡττωμένῳ δὲ μεγάλην
δίκην ἀπιόντι ἀπὸ τοῦ δικαστηρίου προσελθεῖν
7 καὶ συνησθῆναι. καὶ ὀψωνεῖν ἑαυτῷ[9] καὶ αὐλη-

---

[1] mss also μικρῶν and μετρῶν (μετρίων?)   [2] mss also
ὑποδουμένους (Ambr. P ὑποδύμενος)   [3] some mss ὑπ. (from
marg. arch., whence M ὑποδεικνύειν below)   [4] mss also
μύρτα   [5] as ἀκρ. either includes all fruit or means nuts as

68

chests of the penurious covered in mould and their keys in rust, themselves wearing coats short of their thighs. You may see them anoint themselves from tiny oil-flasks, go close-shorn, put off their shoes at midday, and charge the fuller to give their coat plenty of earth so that it may stay the longer clean.

XI. BUFFOONERY

It is not hard to define Buffoonery; it is a naked and objectionable sportiveness; and the Buffoon is one that will lift his shirt in the presence of free-born women; and at the theatre will applaud when others cease, hiss actors whom the rest of the audience approves, and raise his head and hiccup when the house is silent, so that he may make the spectators look round. You will find him standing at the time of full-market where they sell nuts or apples or other fruits, and eating of them while he talks to the seller. He will call by name one of the company with whom he is not well acquainted; and should he see any man in a hurry, is sure to bid him wait. One that has lost a great suit he will accost on his way from court and give him his congratulations. He will do his own marketing and hire flute-

---

opposed to soft fruit, ὀπώρα, we must either read τὰ ἄλλα ἀκρ. or suppose τὰ κάρυα to be a gloss   [6] mss also παριόντων   [7] Cas: mss που   [8] some mss omit π. κ. (introd. p. 18)   [9] Cas: mss ἑαυτὸν or αὐτὸν

τρίδας μισθοῦσθαι, καὶ δεικνύειν δὲ τοῖς ἀπαντῶσι
8 τὰ ὠψωνημένα καὶ παρακαλεῖν Ἐπὶ ταῦτα,[1] καὶ
διηγεῖσθαι προσστὰς[2] πρὸς κουρεῖον ἢ μυροπώλιον
9 ὅτι μεθύσκεσθαι μέλλει.[3] καὶ ἐξ ὀρνιθοσκόπου τῆς
10 μητρὸς εἰσελθούσης[4] βλασφημῆσαι· καὶ εὐχομένων
καὶ σπενδόντων ἐκβαλεῖν[5] τὸ ποτήριον καὶ γελάσαι
11 ὥσπερ ἀστεῖόν τι[6] πεποιηκώς· καὶ αὐλούμενος δὲ
κροτεῖν ταῖς χερσὶ μόνος τῶν ἄλλων, καὶ συν-
τερετίζειν καὶ ἐπιτιμᾶν τῇ αὐλητρίδι ὅτι οὕτω
12 ταχὺ παύσαιτο[7]· καὶ ἀποπτύσαι δὲ βουλόμενος,
ὑπὲρ τῆς τραπέζης προσπτύσαι τῷ οἰνοχόῳ.

ΑΚΑΙΡΙΑΣ ΙΒ΄

Ἡ μὲν οὖν ἀκαιρία ἐστὶν ἀπότευξις ⟨καιροῦ⟩[8]
λυποῦσα τοὺς ἐντυγχάνοντας, ὁ δὲ ἄκαιρος τοιοῦτός τις, οἷος ἀσχολουμένῳ προσελθὼν ἀνα-
κοινοῦσθαι· καὶ πρὸς τὴν αὑτοῦ ἐρωμένην κω-
μάζειν πυρέττουσαν· καὶ δίκην ὠφληκότα ἐγγύης
5 προσελθὼν κελεῦσαι αὐτὸν ἀναδέξασθαι· καὶ μαρ-
τυρήσων παρεῖναι τοῦ πράγματος ἤδη κεκριμένου·
6 καὶ κεκλημένος εἰς γάμους τοῦ γυναικείου γένους
7 κατηγορεῖν· καὶ ἐκ μακρᾶς ὁδοῦ ἥκοντας[9] ἄρτι
8 παρακαλεῖν εἰς περίπατον. δεινὸς δὲ καὶ προσ-

---

[1] the use of ταῦτα rather than αὐτά suggests his actual words,
cf. ταύτην xxiii. fin.: Nav. δαῖτα, cf. Xen. Cyr. iv. 2. 37, Plat.
Phaedr. 247 B   [2] Fraenkel-Groeneboom: mss προστὰς
[3] here follows, in all mss but V, xxx. § 5 καὶ οἰνοπωλῶν—§ 16
λάβωσι; most editors transfer hither from xix. the following
passage; for early misplacements see introd. pp. 17 ff.   [4] mss
εἰς (V εἰς ἐξ) ὀρν. and ἐξελθ.   [5] Cas: mss ἐμβ.   [6] Bernard,
cf. Lys. 24. 18: mss ὡς τεράστιόν τι   [7] Eberhard: V τί
οὐ ταχὺ παύσαιτο, others μὴ ταχὺ παυσαμένη (emendation of
mutilated text)   [8] Schn: mss ἐπίτευξις (M ἐντ.)   [9] mss
also ·τα

players himself ; he will show his friends the good things he has bought, and invite them then and there to ' come and eat this with me ' ; and will stand beside the shop of the barber or the perfumer, and tell the world that he is about to get drunk. He will use words of ill-omen when his mother returns from [a] the diviner's ; and while the company is at their prayers and libations, will drop the cup and laugh as if he had done something clever. When he is listening to the fluteplayer he will be the only man present to beat time, and will whistle the air, and chide the girl for stopping so soon. And when he would spit something out, he spits it across the table at the butler.

XII. TACTLESSNESS

Now Tactlessness is a pain-giving failure to hit upon the right moment ; and your Tactless man he that will accost a busy friend and ask his advice, or serenade his sweetheart when she is sick of a fever. He will go up to one that has gone bail and lost it, and pray him be his surety ; and will come to bear witness [b] after the verdict is given. Should you bid him to a wedding, he will inveigh against womankind. Should you be but now returned from a long journey, he will invite you to a walk. He is given to bringing you one that

[a] *Or* is gone out to.
[b] Really to guarantee the correctness of his evidence when read by the clerk ; it would have been taken at the preliminary proceedings (Nav.).

9 ἄγειν ὠνητὴν πλείω διδόντα ἤδη πεπρακότι· καὶ
ἀκηκοότας καὶ μεμαθηκότας ἀνίστασθαι ἐξ
10 ἀρχῆς διδάξων.[1] καὶ προθύμως[2] δὲ ἐπιμεληθῆναι
ἃ μὴ βούλεταί τις γενέσθαι αἰσχύνεται δὲ ἀπ-
11 ειπάσθαι. καὶ θύοντας καὶ ἀναλίσκοντας[3] ἥκειν
12 τόκον ἀπαιτήσων. καὶ μαστιγουμένου οἰκέτου
παρεστὼς διηγεῖσθαι ὅτι καὶ αὑτοῦ ποτε παῖς
13 οὕτως πληγὰς λαβὼν ἀπήγξατο. καὶ παρὼν
διαίτῃ συγκρούειν ἀμφοτέρων βουλομένων δια-
14 λύεσθαι. καὶ ὀρχησόμενος[4] ἅψασθαι ἑτέρου μηδέπω μεθύοντος.

ΠΕΡΙΕΡΓΙΑΣ ΙΓ΄

Ἀμέλει ἡ περιεργία δόξει εἶναι προσποίησίς
τις λόγων καὶ πράξεων μετ᾽ εὐνοίας, ὁ δὲ περί-
2 εργος τοιοῦτός τις, οἷος ἐπαγγέλλεσθαι ἀναστὰς
3 ἃ μὴ δυνήσεται· καὶ ὁμολογουμένου τοῦ πράγματος δικαίου εἶναι ἑνί τινι ἐνστὰς[5] ἐλεγχθῆναι.
4 καὶ πλείω[6] δὲ ἐπαναγκάσαι τὸν παῖδα κεράσαι
5 ἢ ὅσα δύνανται οἱ παρόντες ἐκπιεῖν. καὶ διείρ-
γειν τοὺς μαχομένους καὶ οὓς οὐ γινώσκει. καὶ
6 ἀτραποῦ ἡγήσασθαι τὴν ὁδὸν καταλιπών,[7] εἶτα
7 μὴ δύνασθαι εὑρεῖν ᾗ πορεύηται.[8] καὶ τὸν

---

[1] Cor: mss -σκων   [2] Blaydes: mss -μος   [3] introd.
p. 14   [4] Cas: mss -άμενος   [5] E: mss ἐνστὰς, ἔν τινι
στὰς   [6] sc. ποτήρια, cf. x. 3   [7] all mss but M omit τὴν
ὁ. κ. (καταλιπεῖν c after πορεύεται), introd. p. 18   [8] -ηται
only M: other mss -εται: mss οὗ (corr. to ᾗ in marg. arch.,
whence the variant ἧς for οὓς above)

---

[a] A comparison of the uses of ἀμέλει by Plato, Xenophon, and the Comic poets shows that it introduces or

72

will pay more when your bargain is struck; and to rising from his seat to tell a tale all afresh to such as have heard it before and know it well. He is forward to undertake for you what you would not have done but cannot well decline. If you are sacrificing and put to great expense, that is the day he chooses to come and demand his usury. At the flogging of your servant he will stand by and tell how a boy of his hanged himself after just such a flogging as this; at an arbitration he will set the parties by the ears when both wish to be reconciled; and when he would dance, lay hold of another who is not yet drunk.

XIII. OFFICIOUSNESS

Officiousness, of course,[a] will seem to be a well-meaning over-assumption of responsibility in word or deed; and the Officious man one that is like to stand up[b] and promise to contribute what is beyond his means; and to object to some one particular of a matter on all hands admitted just, and be refuted. He will make his butler mingle more wine than the company can drink up; will part any that fight together even though he know them not; will leave the high-road to show you a footpath and then

reinforces a reply or virtual reply, with some such meaning as 'Never fear,' 'Oh that's all right,' cf. Modern Greek ἔννοια σοῦ; in Luc. and [Arist.] it varies between 'for instance' and 'at any rate' (cf. γοῦν); in T. the suppressed question is 'What is Officiousness, etc.?' At the beginning of a Char. it suggests 'I can easily answer that,' cf. xi. *init*. 'It is not hard to define Buffoonery'; and later in a piece it repeats the same idea; the notion that it means 'and moreover,' except perhaps in late writers, is a mistake. [b] Probably in the Assembly, cf. xxii. 5.

στρατηγὸν προσελθὼν ἐρωτῆσαι πότε μέλλει
παρατάττεσθαι, καὶ τί μετὰ τὴν αὔριον παραγ-
8 γελεῖ.¹ καὶ προσελθὼν τῷ πατρὶ εἰπεῖν ὅτι ἡ
μήτηρ ἤδη καθεύδει ἐν τῷ δωματίῳ. καὶ
9 ἀπαγορεύοντος τοῦ ἰατροῦ ὅπως μὴ δώσει οἶνον
τῷ μαλακιζομένῳ,² φήσας βούλεσθαι διαπειρᾶν
δοῦναι ⟨καὶ⟩³ ἀνατροπίσαι⁴ τὸν κακῶς ἔχοντα.⁴
10 καὶ γυναικὸς δὲ τελευτησάσης ἐπιγράψαι ἐπὶ
τὸ μνῆμα τοῦ τε ἀνδρὸς αὐτῆς καὶ τοῦ πατρὸς
καὶ τῆς μητρὸς καὶ αὐτῆς τῆς γυναικὸς τοὔνομα καὶ
ποδαπή ἐστι, καὶ προσεπιγράψαι ὅτι Οὗτοι πάντες
1 χρηστοὶ ἦσαν. καὶ ὀμνύναι μέλλων εἰπεῖν πρὸς
τοὺς περιεστηκότας ὅτι Καὶ πρότερον πολλάκις
ὀμώμοκα.

ΑΝΑΙΣΘΗΣΙΑΣ ΙΔ΄

Ἔστι δὲ καὶ ἡ ἀναισθησία, ὡς ὅρῳ εἰπεῖν,
βραδύτης ψυχῆς ἐν λόγοις καὶ πράξεσιν, ὁ δὲ
2 ἀναίσθητος τοιοῦτός τις, οἷος λογισάμενος ταῖς
ψήφοις καὶ κεφάλαιον ποιήσας ἐρωτᾶν τὸν παρα-
3 καθήμενον Τί γίνεται; καὶ δίκην φεύγων καὶ
ταύτην εἰσίεναι μέλλων ἐπιλαθόμενος εἰς ἀγρὸν
4 πορεύεσθαι, καὶ θεωρῶν ἐν τῷ θεάτρῳ μόνος
5 καταλείπεσθαι καθεύδων. καὶ πολλὰ φαγὼν τῆς
νυκτὸς⁵ ἐπὶ θάκου ἀνίστασθαι⁶ ⟨καὶ ἐπανιὼν
νυστάξαι καὶ τὴν θύραν ἀλλογνοήσας⟩⁷ ὑπὸ

---

¹ most mss παραγγέλλει   ² mss also καλλωπιζομένῳ
³ E, cf. τροπίζω: mss βουλ(εύ)εσθαι διάπειραν λαμβάνειν (cf.
Diog. L. vii. 36) εὐτρεπίσαι   ⁴ these three words are
perh. a gloss   ⁵ mss add καί   ⁶ introd. p. 21:
mss also ἐπὶ (ἀπὸ) θώκου; all mss ἀνιστάμενος (hence the
interpolated καί): for ἀνιστ. ἐπί cf. Dem. lix. 34 (πρός); cf.
also Ar. Lys. 1215   ⁷ E e.g. (introd. p. 21)

lose his way. He is the man that goes up to the general and asks when he means to give battle, or what his orders [a] will be for the day after to-morrow ; and to his father and says that his mother is by this time asleep in their chamber. When a sick person is forbid wine by the physician, he says that he'll make an experiment, and giving it him puts the poor fellow on his beam-ends. He will inscribe on a woman's tombstone the names of her husband and both her parents as well as her own name and birth-place, adding ' All these were worthy people.' And when he goes to take his oath he remarks to the bystanders ' This is by no means the first oath I have taken.' [b]

XIV. STUPIDITY

Stupidity, to define it, is a slowness of mind in word and deed ; and the Stupid man he, that after he has cast up an account, will ask one that sits by what it comes to ; when a summons has been taken against him, forgets about it and goes out to his farm on the very day he is to appear ; when he goes to the play is left at the end fast asleep in an empty house. When after a hearty supper he has to get up in the night, he returns only half awake, and missing the right door is bitten by his neighbour's

[a] Or the watchword, cf. Xen. i. 8. 15 f. (Nav.).
[b] Cf. Men. Pk. 569 K.

THEOPHRASTUS

6 κυνὸς τῆς τοῦ γείτονος δηχθῆναι. καὶ λαβών τι¹
καὶ ἀποθεὶς αὐτὸς τοῦτο ζητεῖν καὶ μὴ δύνασθαι
7 εὑρεῖν. καὶ ἀπαγγέλλοντός τινος αὐτῷ ὅτι τετε-
λεύτηκέ τις αὐτοῦ τῶν φίλων, ἵνα παραγένηται,
σκυθρωπάσας καὶ δακρύσας εἰπεῖν 'Αγαθῇ τύχῃ.
8 δεινὸς δὲ καὶ ἀπολαμβάνων ἀργύριον ὀφειλόμενον
9 μάρτυρας παραλαβεῖν· καὶ χειμῶνος ὄντος μάχε-
10 σθαι τῷ παιδὶ ὅτι σικύους οὐκ ἠγόρασεν· καὶ τὰ
παιδία² παλαίειν ἀναγκάζων καὶ τροχάζειν εἰς κό-
11 πους ἐμβάλλειν.³ καὶ ἐν ἀγρῷ αὐτοῖς φακῆν ἕψων
δὶς ἅλας εἰς τὴν χύτραν ἐμβαλὼν ἄβρωτον ποιῆσαι·
12 καὶ ὕοντος τοῦ Διὸς εἰπεῖν Ἡδύ γε τῶν ἄστρων
ὄζει, ὅτε δὴ οἱ ἄλλοι λέγουσι τῆς γῆς⁴· καὶ λέγοντός
13 τινος Πόσους οἴει κατὰ τὰς ἱερὰς πύλας ἐξενηνέχ-
θαι⁵ νεκρούς; πρὸς τοῦτον εἰπεῖν Ὅσοι ἐμοὶ καὶ σοὶ
γένοιντο.

ΑΥΘΑΔΕΙΑΣ ΙΕ΄

Ἡ δὲ αὐθάδειά ἐστιν ἀπήνεια ὁμιλίας ἐν λόγοις,⁶
2 ὁ δὲ αὐθάδης τοιοῦτός τις, οἷος ἐρωτηθεὶς Ὁ
δεῖνα ποῦ ἐστιν; εἰπεῖν Πράγματά μοι μὴ
3 πάρεχε· καὶ προσαγορευθεὶς μὴ ἀντιπροσειπεῖν·
4 καὶ πωλῶν τι μὴ λέγειν τοῖς ὠνουμένοις πόσου
5 ἂν ἀποδοῖτο, ἀλλ' ἐρωτᾶν τί εὑρίσκει· καὶ τοῖς
τιμῶσι καὶ πέμπουσιν εἰς τὰς ἑορτὰς εἰπεῖν ὅτι
6 οὐκ ἂν γένοιτο διδόμενα.⁷ καὶ οὐκ ἔχειν⁸ συγ-

¹ only in M and Ambr. E and I   ² mss add ἑαυτοῦ
(gloss, cf. xix. 5, xx. 5)   ³ mss also κόπον ἐμβαλεῖν
⁴ ὄζει Cor., ὅτε Jebb, τῆς γῆς Schw: mss νομίζει (corr. of
νόξει?) ὅτι and πίσσης (πήσσης): mss δὴ καὶ οἱ, δὴ καὶ, δὴ
οἱ   ⁵ mss also ἐξενεχθῆναι   ⁶ ⟨καὶ πράξεσιν⟩ Herw.
⁷ ⟨προῖκα τὰ⟩ διδ. Nav.   ⁸ mss ἔχων
76

dog.[a] If he receive a gift and put it away with his
own hands, he cannot find it when he seeks it. If he
be told of a friend's death so that he may come to
the house,[b] his face falls, tears come to his eyes,
and he says ' Good luck to him ! ' He is given to
calling witnesses to the repayment of money he
has lent ; to quarrelling with his man for not buying
cucumbers in the winter ; to making his children
wrestle and run till they are tired out. When he
boils his men's lentil-broth at the farm, he puts
salt in the pot twice over and makes it uneatable.
When it rains he remarks ' What a sweet smell from
the sky ! ' whereas others say ' from the ground.'
And when you ask him ' How many funerals do
you think have passed the Sacred Gate ? ' he replies
' I only wish you and I had so many.'

XV. SURLINESS

Surliness is a harshness of behaviour in words ;
and the Surly man, when you ask him ' Where is so-
and-so ? ' is like to reply ' Don't bother me ' ; and is
often mum when you wish him good-day. If he be
selling to you, he will ask what you will give,[c] instead
of naming his price. Any that give him [d] compli-
mentary gifts at feast-tide are told that they don't
do that for nothing ; and there is no pardon for

---

[a] Emendation doubtful.
[b] For the ceremonial πρόθεσις or laying-out.
[c] *Lit.* what it is worth (to you).   [d] *Not necessarily* send.

γνώμην οὔτε τῷ ἀπώσαντι αὐτὸν ἀκουσίως οὔτε τῷ
7 ἄρσαντι¹ οὔτε τῷ ἔμβαντι. καὶ φίλῳ δὲ ἔρανον
κελεύσαντι εἰσενεγκεῖν εἰπὼν ὅτι οὐκ ἂν δοίη,
ὕστερον ἥκειν φέρων καὶ λέγειν ὅτι ἀπόλλυσι
8 καὶ τοῦτο τὸ ἀργύριον. καὶ προσπταίσας ἐν τῇ
9 ὁδῷ δεινὸς καταράσασθαι τῷ λίθῳ. καὶ ἀνα-
10 μεῖναι οὐκ ἂν ὑπομεῖναι² πολὺν χρόνον οὐθένα·
καὶ οὔτε ᾆσαι οὔτε ῥῆσιν εἰπεῖν οὔτε ὀρχήσασθαι
11 ἂν ἐθελήσαι.³ δεινὸς δὲ καὶ τοῖς θεοῖς μὴ
ἐπεύχεσθαι.⁴

ΔΕΙΣΙΔΑΙΜΟΝΙΑΣ Ιϛ´⁵

Ἀμέλει ἡ δεισιδαιμονία δόξειεν ἂν εἶναι δειλία
2 τις⁶ πρὸς τὸ δαιμόνιον, ὁ δὲ δεισιδαίμων τοιοῦτός
τις, οἷος ἐπ᾽ Ἐννεακρούνου⁷ ἀπονιψάμενος τὰς
χεῖρας καὶ περιρρανάμενος, ἀπὸ ἱεροῦ δάφνης⁸ εἰς
τὸ στόμα λαβών, οὕτω τὴν ἡμέραν περιπατεῖν.
καὶ τὴν ὁδὸν ἐὰν ὑπερδράμῃ⁹ γαλῆ, μὴ πρότερον

---

¹ Groeneboom, cf. Sen. Ben. vi. 9. 1 (ἰπώσαντι sugg. E): mss
ὤσαντι   ² E : mss ὑπομεῖναι   ³ E : mss ἠθέλησε(ν),
θελῆσαι   ⁴ some mss add τέλος τῶν τοῦ Θεοφράστου
Χαρακτήρων· ἀλλ᾽ ἔστιν, ὦ Θεόφραστε, χαλεπὸν καθαροὺς
τῶν τοιούτων ἰδεῖν ἐν τῷ βίῳ καὶ τῆς ἐν τούτοις κακίας ὅλως
ἀφεστηκότας. εἰ μὴ γὰρ τὰ πάντα δοκοίη τις εἶναι κακός, τοῖς γοῦν
πλείοσι τοῦ χοροῦ τῶν ἀρίστων ἐξέωσται. ἡ τοίνυν σοὶ πειθομένους
ἡμᾶς τὰς ἀπάντων ὄψεις φυλάττεσθαι δεῖ, ἢ κοινωνοῦντας καὶ λόγων
καὶ πράξεων, τὴν ἑκάστου γνώμην (mss also μνήμην) μιμεῖσθαι.
ἀλλ᾽ οὕτω μὲν κακίας ἐσμὸς καὶ ἀρετῆς ἀλλοτρίωσις ἕπεται, ἐκείνως
(mss -νους) δὲ ἡ μισανθρωπία καὶ τὸ τοῦ Τίμωνος ἔγκλημα. ταύτῃ
78

such as unwittingly thrust him aside, bespatter him,[a] or tread on his toe. When a friend asks him the help of a subscription, it is certain he will first say he won't give it, and thereafter bring it saying ' Here's more good money gone ! ' He is prone, also, to curse the stone he stumbles over in the road. He will not abide to be kept long waiting ; he always refuses to sing, recite, or dance.[b] He is apt, also, not to pray to the Gods.[c]

XVI. SUPERSTITIOUSNESS

Superstitiousness, I need hardly say, would seem to be a sort of cowardice with respect to the divine[d] ; and your Superstitious man such as will not sally forth for the day till he have washed his hands and sprinkled himself at the Nine Springs,[e] and put a bit of bay-leaf from a temple in his mouth. And if a cat cross his path he will not proceed on his way

---

[a] *Or perhaps* squeeze him (in a crowd).   [b] After supper.
[c] *i.e.* refuse to pray : *or, regarding* μή *as a Christian interpolation,* he is apt to curse even the Gods (*cf.* § 1).
[d] *Or* spiritual.   [e] *Or* at three springs.

τοι καὶ χαλεπὸν ἐλέσθαι τὸ κρεῖττον καὶ δεινὸς ἑκατέρωθεν ὄλισθος
[5] Title in V: ἀπὸ τῶν τοῦ Θεοφράστου χαρακτήρων ιε΄. χαρακτήρ δεισιδαιμονίας   [6] only M   [7] E, cf. Isocr. Antid. 287 ; or ἐπὶ γ΄ κρουνῶν, cf. xxviii. 4 and Men. Phasm. 55 ; for ἐπί rather than ἀπό see § 12 : V ἐπιχρωνὴν (others omit), corruption of ἐπ' θ' κρηνῶν, from ἐπ' θ' κρούνου, or of ἐπὶ γ' κρουνῶν ; for confusion of η and ω cf. ἀλφίτην below   [8] comma E (so Nav.); δάφνης partit. gen. : V -νην   [9] Pauw: mss περιδ., παραδ.

πορευθῆναι ἕως διεξέλθῃ τις ἢ λίθους τρεῖς ὑπὲρ
4 τῆς ὁδοῦ διαβάλῃ.[1] καὶ ἐὰν ἴδῃ ὄφιν ἐν τῇ οἰκίᾳ,
ἐὰν ‹μὲν› παρείαν, Σαβάζιον[2] καλεῖν, ἐὰν δὲ ἱερόν,
5 ἐνταῦθα ἡρῶον εὐθὺς[3] ἰδρύσασθαι. καὶ τῶν λιπα-
ρῶν λίθων τῶν ἐν ταῖς τριόδοις παριὼν ἐκ τῆς
ληκύθου ἔλαιον καταχεῖν καὶ ἐπὶ γόνατα πεσὼν
6 καὶ προσκυνήσας ἀπαλλάττεσθαι. καὶ ἐὰν μῦς
θύλακον ἀλφίτων[4] διαφάγῃ, πρὸς τὸν ἐξηγητὴν ἐλθὼν
ἐρωτᾶν τί χρὴ ποιεῖν, καὶ ἐὰν ἀποκρίνηται αὐτῷ
ἐκδοῦναι τῷ σκυτοδέψῃ ἐπιρράψαι, μὴ προσέχειν
7 τούτοις ἀλλ' ἀποτροπαίοις[5] ἐκλύσασθαι. καὶ
πυκνὰ δὲ τὴν οἰκίαν καθᾶραι[6] δεινὸς Ἑκάτης
8 φάσκων ἐπαγωγὴν γεγονέναι· κἂν γλαῦκες βαδί-
ζοντος αὐτοῦ ‹ἀνακράγωσι›,[7] ταράττεσθαι καὶ
9 εἴπας Ἀθηνᾶ κρείττων παρελθεῖν οὕτω. καὶ οὔτε
ἐπιβῆναι μνήματι οὔτ' ἐπὶ νεκρὸν οὔτ' ἐπὶ λεχὼ
ἐλθεῖν ἐθελῆσαι, ἀλλὰ τὸ μὴ μιαίνεσθαι συμφέρον
10 αὐτῷ φῆσαι εἶναι. καὶ ταῖς τετράσι δὲ καὶ ταῖς
ἑβδομάσι[8] τῶν ἡμερῶν[9] προστάξας οἶνον ἕψειν τοῖς
ἔνδον, ἐξελθὼν ἀγοράσαι μυρσίνας, λιβανωτόν,
πίνακα,[10] καὶ εἰσελθὼν εἴσω ‹διατελέσαι ἐπιθύων

---

[1] Sylb: mss -λάβῃ   [2] V Σαβάδιον, but cf. xxvii. 8;
others omit ἐὰν παρ.—ἐὰν δὲ   [3] Düb: V ἱερῶον (from
above) εὐθ.; others omit (introd. p. 28)   [4] V ἀλφίτην,
cf. p. 79 n. 7   [5] Wytt: mss -πεὶς   [6] V καθᾶραι, others
καθαριεῖν   [7] Foss, cf. Men. 534. 1 K; or ‹κα(κ)-
καβίζωσι› βαδ. αὐτ. (Cob. κακκ. παριόντος), Ar. Lys. 760
[8] Im. -μαις: M ζ'   [9] E: M ἡμερῶν (without τῶν), others
omit   [10] λιβανωτὸν Foss: V -ωτῶν, others omit ἐθελῆσαι-
ἡμέραν: for πίνακες or πινάκια (which might be read here)
with myrtle and taenia cf. Boetticher, Baumcultus fig. 2;
it is a serious objection to Foss's πόπανα (cf. Men. 129 K,
Sch. Ar. Plut. 1126) that these would be made at home,
cf. Ar. Ran. 507

till someone else be gone by, or he have cast three stones across the street. Should he espy a snake in his house, if it be one of the red sort he will call upon Sabazius, if of the sacred, build a shrine then and there. When he passes one of the smooth stones set up at crossroads he anoints it with oil from his flask, and will not go his ways till he have knelt down and worshipped it.[a] If a mouse gnaw a bag of his meal, he will off to the wizard's[b] and ask what he must do, and if the answer be ' send it to the cobbler's to be patched,' he neglects the advice and frees himself of the ill by rites of aversion. He is for ever purifying his house on the plea that Hecate has been drawn thither.[c] Should owls hoot when he is abroad, he is much put about, and will not on his way till he have cried ' Athena forfend ! ' Set foot on a tomb he will not, nor come nigh a dead body nor a woman in childbed ; he must keep himself unpolluted. On the fourth[d] and seventh[e] days of every month he has wine mulled for his household, and goes out to buy myrtle-boughs, frankincense, and a holy picture,[f] and then returning spends the livelong day doing sacrifice to the

---

[a] Cf. Diog. L. vi. 37.   [b] Or the (official) diviner's.
[c] Cf. Hesych. ὠπωτῆρες, Diog. L. vi. 74.
[d] Cf. Ath. xiv. 659 d=Men. 292 K, 320 K.
[e] Or twenty-fourth (sc. φθίνοντος, which Im. inserts, needlessly, cf. Dem. xlii. 1) ; the 4th was Hermes' day, the 7th Apollo's, cf. Sch. Ar. Plut. 1126, but Apollo does not seem in point (see below), so Im. compares Hes. Op. 797.
[f] Or holy pictures (of the Hermaphrodites ? hung on the myrtle-boughs).

81

καὶ¹ στεφανῶν τοὺς Ἑρμαφροδίτους ὅλην τὴν
11 ἡμέραν. καὶ ὅταν ἐνύπνιον ἴδῃ, πορεύεσθαι πρὸς
τοὺς ὀνειροκρίτας, πρὸς τοὺς μάντεις, πρὸς τοὺς
ὀρνιθοσκόπους, ἐρωτήσων τίνι θεῶν ἢ θεαινῶν²
12 προσεύχεσθαι δεῖ.³ καὶ τελεσθησόμενος πρὸς τοὺς
Ὀρφεοτελεστὰς κατὰ μῆνα πορεύεσθαι μετὰ τῆς
γυναικός, ἐὰν δὲ μὴ σχολάζῃ ἡ γυνή, μετὰ τῆς
13 τίτθης καὶ τῶν παιδίων. καὶ τῶν περιρραινομένων
14 ἐπὶ θαλάττης ἐπιμελῶς⁴ δόξειεν ἂν εἶναι. κἄν ποτε
ἐπίδῃ σκορόδῳ ἐστεμμένην <τινὰ τῶν Ἑκατῶν>⁵
τῶν ἐπὶ ταῖς τριόδοις, ἀπελθὼν⁶ κατὰ κεφαλῆς
λούσασθαι καὶ ἱερείας καλέσας σκίλλῃ ἢ σκύλακι
κελεῦσαι αὑτὸν περικαθᾶραι. μαινόμενόν τε ἰδὼν
ἢ ἐπίληπτον φρίξας εἰς κόλπον πτύσαι.

ΜΕΜΨΙΜΟΙΡΙΑΣ ΙΖ´

Ἔστι δὲ ἡ μεμψιμοιρία ἐπιτίμησίς τις⁷ παρὰ
τὸ προσῆκον τῶν δεδομένων, ὁ δὲ μεμψίμοιρος
2 τοιόσδε τις, οἷος ἀποστείλαντος μερίδα τοῦ φίλου
εἰπεῖν πρὸς τὸν φέροντα Ἐφθόνησάς μοι τοῦ ζωμοῦ
3 καὶ τοῦ οἰναρίου οὐκ ἐπὶ δεῖπνον καλέσας. καὶ
ὑπὸ τῆς ἑταίρας καταφιλούμενος εἰπεῖν Θαυμάζω
4 εἰ σὺ καὶ ἀπὸ τῆς ψυχῆς οὕτω με φιλεῖς. καὶ τῷ

---

¹ Diels-*E* (introd. p. 22)   ² mss θεᾷ corr. *E, cf.* Antiph.
81 K   ³ V εὐχ. δεῖ   ⁴ *cf.* Men. *Pk.* 32, 325.
10 K, Heracl. Pont. ap. Diog. L. ii. 135   ⁵ *E*: V
ἐστεμμένων (for ω for η *cf.* ἐπιχρωνὴν above, § 2 n. 7, and
ἐπισκῆψαι xxix. 3)   ⁶ V ἀπελθόντων corrected from ἐπελθόν-
των: others, omitting κἄν—τῶν, καὶ ἐπὶ τοῖς τρ. ἀπελθὼν
⁷ only in M

Hermaphrodites and putting garlands about them.[a]
He never has a dream but he flies to a diviner, or
a soothsayer, or an interpreter of visions, to ask
what God or Goddess he should appease; and when
he is about to be initiated into the holy orders
of Orpheus, he visits the priests every month and
his wife with him, or if she have not the time,
the nurse and children. He would seem to be one
of those who are for ever going[b] to the seaside to
besprinkle themselves; and if ever he see one of
the figures of Hecate at the crossroads wreathed
with garlic,[c] he is off home to wash his head and
summon priestesses whom he bids purify him with
the carrying around him of a squill or a puppy-dog.
If he catch sight of a madman or an epilept, he
shudders and spits in his bosom.[d]

XVII. QUERULOUSNESS

Grumbling or Querulousness is an undue com-
plaining of one's lot; and the Grumbler will say to
him that brings him a portion from his friend's
table[e] 'You begrudged me your soup and your
swipes, or you would have asked me to dine with
you.'[f] When his mistress is kissing him, 'I wonder,'
says he, 'whether you kiss me thus warmly from

[a] Text uncertain, but cf. Men. Georg. 8 and 326 K.
[b] Instead of on occasions like the Great Mysteries? but
the trait is perhaps interpolated, cf. vi. 7.
[c] Reading uncertain.   [d] To avert the ill.
[e] When you sacrificed an animal you either bid your
friends to eat of it with you or sent them portions of the
meat only, cf. Men. Sam. 191.
[f] He confuses the servant with the master.

Διὶ ἀγανακτεῖν οὐ διότι οὐχ ὕει,[1] ἀλλὰ διότι
5 ὕστερον. καὶ εὑρών τι[2] ἐν τῇ ὁδῷ βαλλάντιον
6 εἰπεῖν 'Αλλ' οὐ θησαυρὸν εὕρηκα οὐδέποτε. καὶ
πριάμενος ἀνδράποδον ἄξιον καὶ πολλὰ δεηθεὶς τοῦ
πωλοῦντος Θαυμάζω, εἰπεῖν, ὅτι ὑγιὲς οὕτω ἄξιον
7 ἐώνημαι· καὶ πρὸς τὸν εὐαγγελιζόμενον ὅτι Ὑιός
σοι γέγονεν εἰπεῖν ὅτι "Αν προσθῇς καὶ τῆς οὐσίας
8 τὸ ἥμισυ ἀπέστης,[3] ἀληθῆ ἐρεῖς. καὶ δίκην
νικήσας[4] λαβὼν πάσας τὰς ψήφους ἐγκαλεῖν τῷ
γράψαντι τὸν λόγον ὡς πολλὰ παραλελοιπότι τῶν
9 δικαίων. καὶ ἐράνου εἰσενεχθέντος παρὰ τῶν
φίλων καὶ φήσαντός τινος Ἱλαρὸς ἴσθι, Καὶ πῶς;
εἰπεῖν, ὅτε[5] δεῖ τἀργύριον ἀποδοῦναι ἑκάστῳ καὶ
χωρὶς τούτων χάριν ὀφείλειν ὡς εὐεργετημένον;

ΑΠΙΣΤΙΑΣ ΙΗ'

"Εστιν ἀμέλει ἡ ἀπιστία ὑπόληψις τις ἀδικίας
2 κατὰ πάντων, ὁ δὲ ἄπιστος τοιοῦτός τις, οἷος
ἀποστείλας τὸν παῖδα ὀψωνήσοντα ἕτερον παῖδα
3 ἐπιπέμπειν[6] τὸν πευσόμενον πόσου ἐπρίατο. καὶ
φέρειν[7] αὐτὸς τὸ ἀργύριον καὶ κατὰ στάδιον
4 καθίζων ἀριθμεῖν πόσον ἐστί. καὶ τὴν γυναῖκα
τὴν αὑτοῦ ἐρωτᾶν κατακείμενος[8] εἰ κέκλεικε τὴν
κιβωτόν, καὶ εἰ σεσήμανται τὸ κυλικούχιον,[9] καὶ εἰ
5 ὁ μοχλὸς εἰς τὴν αὐλείαν[10] ἐμβέβληται· καὶ ἂν

---

[1] M ἀγ. ὅτι οὐχ ὕει, omitting ἀλλὰ δ. ὕ.: others οὐ διότι
ὕει κτλ.   [2] V omits: others τι καὶ, καὶ, τι (or βαλλάντιοσι
below), i.e. τι in marg. arch.   [3] Im: V ἀπέστη, others
ἄπεστιν   [4] Cas: mss νίκην ν.: mss add καί, but cf. xxii. 9
[5] Cas: mss ὅτι; cf. Ar. Nub. 716   [6] only M:
others πέμπ.   [7] Cor: mss. -ων   [8] M νυκτὸς
συγκαθεύδων   [9] mss κυλιούχιον, κοιλιούχιον   [10] M τῇ
αὐλαία, cf. Men. 564 K: others εἰς τὴν θύραν τὴν αὐλ.

your heart.' He is displeased with Zeus not because he sends no rain, but because he has been so long about sending it. When he finds a purse in the street, it is ' Ah! but I never found a treasure.' When he has bought a servant cheap with much importuning the seller, ' I wonder,' cries he, ' if my bargain's too cheap to be good.' When they bring him the good news that he has a son born to him,[a] then it is ' If you add that I have lost half my fortune, you'll speak the truth.' Should this man win a suit-at-law by a unanimous verdict, he is sure to find fault with his speech-writer[b] for omitting so many of the pleas. And if a subscription have been made him among his friends, and one of them say to him ' You may cheer up now,' ' What ? ' he will say, ' when I must repay each man his share and be beholden to him to boot ? '

XVIII. DISTRUSTFULNESS

It goes without saying that Distrustfulness is a presumption of dishonesty against all mankind ; and the Distrustful man is he that will send one servant off to market and then another to learn what price he paid; and will carry his own money[c] and sit down every furlong to count it over. When he is abed he will ask his wife if the coffer be locked and the cupboard sealed and the house-door bolted, and

---

[a] Cf. Men. Ep. 316.
[b] Litigants read speeches written for them by their counsel.
[c] Instead of intrusting it to his lackey.

ἐκείνη φῇ, μηδὲν ἧττον αὐτὸς ἀναστὰς ἐκ τῶν
στρωμάτων γυμνὸς καὶ ἀνυπόδητος[1] τὸν λύχνον
ἅψας ταῦτα πάντα περιδραμὼν ἐπισκέψασθαι, καὶ
οὕτω μόλις ὕπνου τυγχάνειν. καὶ τοὺς ὀφείλοντας
αὐτῷ ἀργύριον μετὰ μαρτύρων ἀπαιτεῖν τοὺς
6 τόκους, ὅπως μὴ δύναιντο[2] ἔξαρνοι γενέσθαι. καὶ
τὸ ἱμάτιον δὲ ἐκδοῦναι δεινός, οὐχ ὃς βέλτιστα
ἐργάσεται,[3] ἀλλ' οὗ ἂν[4] ᾖ ἄξιος ἐγγυητής. καὶ
7 ὅταν ἥκῃ τις αἰτησόμενος ἐκπώματα, μάλιστα μὲν
μὴ δοῦναι, ἂν δ' ἄρα τις οἰκεῖος ᾖ καὶ ἀναγκαῖος,
μόνον οὐ πυρώσας[5] καὶ στήσας καὶ σχεδὸν ἐγγυητὴν
8 λαβὼν χρῆσαι. καὶ τὸν παῖδα δὲ ἀκολουθοῦντα
κελεύειν αὐτοῦ ὄπισθεν μὴ βαδίζειν ἀλλ' ἔμπροσθεν,
9 ἵνα φυλάττηται αὐτῷ μὴ ἐν τῇ ὁδῷ ἀποδρᾷ. καὶ
τοῖς εἰληφόσι τι παρ' αὐτοῦ καὶ λέγουσι Πόσου,
κατάθου,[6] οὐ γὰρ σχολάζω πω πέμπειν, ⟨εἰπεῖν⟩[7]
Μηδὲν πραγματεύου· ἐγὼ γὰρ ⟨ἕως⟩[8] ἂν σὺ
σχολάσῃς, συνακολουθήσω.

ΔΥΣΧΕΡΕΙΑΣ ΙΘ′

Ἔστι δὲ ἡ δυσχέρεια ἀθεραπευσία σώματος
λύπης παρασκευαστική, ὁ δὲ δυσχερὴς τοιοῦτός
2 τις, οἷος λέπραν ἔχων καὶ ἀλφὸν καὶ τοὺς ὄνυχας
μεγάλους περιπατεῖν, καὶ φῆσαι ταῦτα εἶναι αὐτῷ
συγγενικὰ[9] ἀρρωστήματα· ἔχειν γὰρ αὐτὰ[10] καὶ τὸν·

[1] so M: others γ. ἐκ τ. στρ. καὶ ἀνυπ. (i.e. ἐκ τῶν στρ. in
marg. arch.)   [2] Jebb δύνωνται   [3] Salm: cf. ix. 6,
Ar. Pax 371, Lys. 614, Lysias 23. 2, Men. Ep. 218: mss
ὡς β. ἐργάσεται (V ἐργάσηται): for ἐργ. cf. Plat. Meno 91 D
[4] E: mss ὅταν (introd. p. 22)   [5] Foss ὄνομ' ἐντυπώσας
[6] or Πόσου κατάθου   [7] Cas.   [8] Madv. (see opp.)
[9] mss also -γενῇ   [10] Meier: mss -τὸν

for all she may say Yes, he will himself [a] rise naked
and bare-foot from the blankets and light the candle
and run round the house to see, and even so will
hardly go to sleep. Those that owe him money find
him demand the usury before witnesses, so that they
shall never by any means deny that he has asked
it. His cloak is put out to wash not where it will
be fulled best, but where the fuller gives him good
security. And when a neighbour comes a-borrowing
drinking-cups he will refuse him if he can ; should
he perchance be a great friend or a kinsman, he will
lend them, yet almost weigh them and assay them,[b]
if not take security for them, before he does so.
When his servant attends him he is bidden go before
and not behind, so that he may make sure he do
not take himself off by the way.[c] And to any man
that has bought of him and says ' Reckon it up and
set it down [d] ; I cannot send for the money just
yet,' he replies, ' Never mind ; I will go with you
till you can.' [e]

XIX. NASTINESS

Nastiness is a neglect of the person which is
painful to others ; and your Nasty fellow such as
will walk the town with the scall and the scab upon
him and with bad nails,[f] and boast that these ail-

---

[a] *i.e.* instead of sending a slave.

[b] *Or perhaps* scratch his name on them; contrast Arcesilaus, Diog. L. iv. 38.   [c] φυλάττηται passive.

[d] *Sc.* εἰς βιβλίον, *cf.* Dem. 1401. 19 ; *or perhaps* put down
how much (I owe you).

[e] *Or, keeping text,* if it is convenient to you, I will accom-
pany you home.   [f] *Lit.* great nails, *i.e.* from gout.

πατέρα καὶ τὸν πάππον, καὶ οὐκ εἶναι ῥᾴδιον
3 αὐτῶν[1] εἰς τὸ γένος ὑποβάλλεσθαι. ἀμέλει δὲ
δεινὸς καὶ ἕλκη ἔχειν ἐν τοῖς ἀντικνημίοις καὶ
προσπταίσματα ἐν τοῖς δακτύλοις, καὶ ταῦτα[2] μὴ
θεραπεῦσαι ἀλλ᾽ ἐᾶσαι θηριωθῆναι· καὶ τὰς μα-
σχάλας δὲ θηριώδεις καὶ δασείας ἔχειν ἄχρι ἐπὶ
πολὺ τῶν πλευρῶν, καὶ τοὺς ὀδόντας μέλανας καὶ
4 ἐσθιομένους.[3] καὶ τὰ τοιαῦτα· ἐσθίων ἀπομύτ-
τεσθαι· θύων ἅμ᾽ ἀδαξᾶσθαι[4]· προσλαλῶν ἀπορρί-
πτειν ἀπὸ τοῦ στόματος· ἅμα πιὼν προσερυγγάνειν·
5 ἀναπόνιπτος ἐν τοῖς ἐμβάσι[5] μετὰ τῆς γυναικὸς[6]
6 κοιμᾶσθαι· ἐλαίῳ σαπρῷ ἐν βαλανείῳ χριόμενος
7 φθύζεσθαι[7]· καὶ χιτωνίσκον παχὺν καὶ ἱμάτιον
σφόδρα λεπτὸν[8] καὶ κηλίδων μεστὸν ἀναβαλόμενος[9]
εἰς ἀγορὰν ἐξελθεῖν.[10]

ΑΗΔΙΑΣ Κ΄

Ἔστι δὲ ἡ ἀηδία, ὡς ὅρῳ περιλαβεῖν,[11] ἔντευξις
λύπης ποιητικὴ ἄνευ βλάβης, ὁ δὲ ἀηδὴς τοιοῦτός
τις, οἷος ἐγείρειν ἄρτι καθεύδοντα εἰσελθών, ἵνα
3 αὐτῷ συλλαλῇ[12]. καὶ ἀνάγεσθαι ἤδη[13] μέλλοντας
4 κωλύειν· καὶ προσελθόντων δεῖσθαι ἐπισχεῖν ἕως ἂν

[1] Meist: V -τὸν   [2] V omits   [3] mss incorp. gloss ὥστε
δυσέντευκτος εἶναι καὶ ἀηδής   [4] Diels: V θύων ἅμα δ᾽
ἄρξασθαι, others θύειν ἀρξάμενος and then προσλαλεῖν καὶ ἀπ.
[5] ἀναπόν. Badh: ἐν τ. ἐμβ. E, cf. xxi. 8 n. and ἐμβασικοίτας
Ath. 469 a and Petron. 24: V ἀναπίπτοντος ἐν τ. στρώμασι,
others omit ἀναπ. . . κοιμᾶσθαι   [6] mss insert αὐτοῦ, i.e.
αὑτοῦ, a gloss, cf. xiv. 10   [7] E, cf. ἐπιφθύζω: V χρώμενος
σφύζεσθαι, others χρίεσθαι, χρᾶσθαι, χρῆσθαι only   [8] <ἅμα
φορεῖν>? [9] Jebb: mss ἀναβαλλ.   [10] the remainder is
rightly transferred by most editors to Char. xi.   [11] V
λαβεῖν   [12] so M: others λαλῇ   [13] Schn: mss δὴ

ments are hereditary ; his father and his grandfather had them before him and 'tis no easy matter to be foisted into *his* family. He is like also, I warrant you, to have gatherings on his shins and sores on his toes, and seek no remedy, but rather let them grow rank. He will keep himself as shaggy as a beast, with hair well-nigh all over his body, and his teeth all black and rotten.[a] These also are marks of the man :—to blow his nose at table ;[b] to bite his nails[c] when he is sacrificing with you ; to spit from his mouth when he is talking with you ; when he has drunken with you, to hiccup in your face. He will go to bed with his wife with hands un-washed[d] and his shoes on; spit on himself at the baths when his oil is rancid[e] ; and go forth to the market-place clad in a thick shirt and a very thin coat, and this covered with stains.[f]

XX. ILL-BREEDING

Ill - breeding, if we may define it, is a sort of behaviour which gives pain without harm ; and the Ill-bred man is one that will awake you to talk with him when you are but now fallen asleep ; hinder you when you are this moment about to set forth on a journey ; and when you come to speak to him, beg

[a] *Cf.* Alciphr. ii. 25 (iii. 28).
[b] They used no handkerchiefs.   [c] *Or* scratch himself.
[d] It was usual to wash the hands after supper, *cf.* Ar. *Eccl.* 419; they used no spoons or forks.
[e] And therefore thickened, so as to require supplementing.
[f] *Or perhaps* wear a thick shirt with a very thin coat, and go forth into the market-place in a coat covered with stains.

βηματίσῃ¹· καὶ τὸ παιδίον τῆς τίτθης ἀφελόμενος,
μασώμενος σιτίζειν αὐτός, καὶ ὑποκορίζεσθαι
ποππύζων καὶ πανουργημάτιον² τοῦ πάππου
ικαλῶν. καὶ ἐσθίων³ δὲ ἅμα διηγεῖσθαι ὡς ἐλλέ-
βορον πιὼν ἄνω καὶ κάτω καθαρθείη, καὶ ζωμοῦ
τοῦ παρακειμένου ἐν τοῖς ὑποχωρήμασιν αὐτῷ
7 μελαντέρα ⟨εἴη⟩ ἡ χολή. καὶ ἐρωτῆσαι δὲ δεινὸς
ἐναντίον τῶν οἰκετῶν⁴ Εἰπέ ⟨μοι, ὦ⟩ μάμμη,⁵ ὅτ'
8 ὦδινες καί με ἔτικτες, ποία τις ⟨ἡ⟩ ἡμέρα;⁶ καὶ
ὑπὲρ αὐτῆς δὲ λέγειν ὡς ἡδύ ἐστι καὶ ⟨ἀλγεινόν,
καὶ⟩⁷ ἀμφότερα δὲ οὐκ ἔχοντα οὐ ῥᾴδιον ἄνθρωπον
9 λαβεῖν· καὶ ⟨ἑστιώμενος δὲ εἰπεῖν⟩⁸ ὅτι ψυχρόν
ἐστι παρ' αὐτῷ ⟨τὸ⟩ λακκαῖον,⁹ καὶ ὡς κῆπος
λάχανα πολλὰ ἔχων καὶ ἁπαλὰ¹⁰ καὶ μάγειρος εὖ
τὸ ὄψον σκευάζων· καὶ ὅτι ἡ οἰκία αὐτοῦ παν-
δοκεῖόν ἐστι, μεστὴ γὰρ ἀεί¹¹· καὶ τοὺς φίλους
αὐτοῦ εἶναι τὸν τετρημένον πίθον, εὖ ποτίζων γὰρ¹²
10 αὐτοὺς οὐ δύνασθαι ἐμπλῆσαι. καὶ ξενίζων δὲ
δεῖξαι τὸν παράσιτον αὐτοῦ ποῖός τίς ἐστι τῷ
συνδειπνοῦντι· καὶ παρακαλῶν δὲ ἐπὶ τοῦ ποτηρίου
εἰπεῖν ὅτι τὸ τέρψον τοὺς παρόντας παρεσκεύασται,
καὶ ὅτι αὐτήν, ἐὰν κελεύσωσιν, ὁ παῖς μέτεισι

¹ i.e. dum cacet: so M: others περιπατήσῃ correction of
gloss ἀποπατήσῃ, cf. δεσμωτήριον for κέραμον vi. 6   ² Cob.-E:
V πανουργιῶν, others omit καὶ παν. . . . καλῶν (introd. p. 23)
³ ἐστιῶν ? cf. xxiv. 9   ⁴ Courier, cf. xxx. 9: mss οἰκείων
⁵ E (introd. p. 23): V εἶπου (corr. to εἶπερ) μάμμη, others
omit εἰπ. . . . καί   ⁶ Foss-E: V ὅτ' ὦδ. κ. ἔτικτές με τίς
ἡμέρα, which would mean 'what day of the month,' cf. iii. 3
and Alciphr. 3. 4 init. (3. 7); other mss ὡς ποίᾳ ἡμέρᾳ με ἔτικτες
(introd. p. 24)   ⁷ Im.-E   ⁸ E (introd. p. 22)
⁹ E: mss incorp. gloss ὕδωρ after ψυχρόν   ¹⁰ V adds
incorp. gloss on λακκαῖον, ὥστε εἶναι ψυχρόν, others omit
ὥστε. . . . σκευάζων   ¹¹ Foss: mss ἐστι   ¹² Pas: mss
ποιῶν γάρ: cf. xiv. 12 for the corruption

you to wait till he have been round the corner. He will take the child from the nurse and feed it from his own mouth, and make sounds of kissing while he calls it by such pretty names as ' Daddy's bit of wickedness.' [a] When he is eating with you he will relate how he once took hellebore and was purged at both ends, and the bile from his bowels ' was as black as this soup.' He is prone to ask before the servants such questions as this : ' Tell me, Mammy, how went the day with you when you were brought to bed of me ? ' and will reply for her that there's both pleasure and pain to it, and that no man living can easily have the one without the other.[b] When he is out to dinner he will remark that he has *cold* water in his cistern at home, and *there*'s a garden with plenty of *excellent* vegetables and a cook that knows his *business* ; *his* house is a perfect inn, it is always so full of guests ; and his friends are like the leaky cask [c]—drench them as he will he cannot fill them. When he entertains strangers, he displays the qualities of his parasite or goodfellow ; and when he would make his guests merrier over the wine, tells them that the company's diversion is provided for ; they have but to say the word and his man shall go

---

[a] The rest of the Character shows that this is intended more literally than some editors would think.

[b] ἔχοντα neuter plural ; *lit.* can get things which have, etc.

[c] Of the Danaïds.

91

παρὰ τοῦ πορνοβόσκου ἤδη, "Ὅπως πάντες ὑπ'
αὐτῆς αὐλώμεθα καὶ εὐφραινώμεθα.

ΜΙΚΡΟΦΙΛΟΤΙΜΙΑΣ ΚΑ'

Ἡ δὲ μικροφιλοτιμία δόξει εἶναι ὄρεξις τιμῆς
ἀνελεύθερος,[1] ὁ δὲ μικροφιλότιμος τοιοῦτός τις,
2 οἷος σπουδάσαι ἐπὶ δεῖπνον κληθεὶς παρ' αὐτὸν τὸν
3 καλέσαντα κατακείμενος δειπνῆσαι· καὶ τὸν υἱὸν
4 ἀποκεῖραι ἀπαγαγὼν[2] εἰς Δελφούς. καὶ ἐπιμεληθῆναι δὲ ὅπως αὐτῷ ὁ ἀκόλουθος Αἰθίοψ ἔσται·
5 καὶ ἀποδιδοὺς μνᾶν ἀργυρίου καινὸν ποιῆσαι
6 ἀποδοῦναι. καὶ κολοιῷ δὲ ἔνδον τρεφομένῳ δεινὸς
κλιμάκιον πρίασθαι, καὶ ἀσπίδιον χαλκοῦν ποιῆσαι
ὃ ἔχων ἐπὶ τοῦ κλιμακίου ὁ κολοιὸς πηδήσεται·
7 καὶ βοῦν θύσας τὸ προμετωπίδιον ἀπαντικρὺ τῆς
εἰσόδου προσπατταλεῦσαι[3] στέμμασι μεγάλοις περι-
δήσας, ὅπως οἱ εἰσιόντες ἴδωσιν[4] ὅτι βοῦν ἔθυσε.
8 καὶ πομπεύσας δὲ μετὰ τῶν ἱππέων τὰ μὲν ἄλλα
πάντα ἀποδοῦναι[5] τῷ παιδὶ ἀπενεγκεῖν οἴκαδε,
ἀναβαλόμενος[6] δὲ θοἰμάτιον ἐν τοῖς μύωψι[7] κατὰ
9 τὴν ἀγορὰν περιπατεῖν. καὶ κυναρίου δὲ Μελιταίου
τελευτήσαντος αὐτῷ, μνῆμα ποιῆσαι καὶ στηλίδιον
10 ἀναστήσας[8] ἐπιγράψαι Κλάδος Μελιταῖος· καὶ

---

[1] mss also -ρου   [2] V ἀγαγών, but cf. ix. 2 ἀπελθών:
Foss ἀπάγειν : Schneid. ἀναγαγών perh. rightly, cf. Diog. L.
iii. 25 εἰς Ὀλύμπια ἀνιόντος   [3] V -λῶσαι   [4] εἰδῶσιν ?
[5] V δοῦναι   [6] mss ἀναβαλλ.   [7] cf. Ar. Lys. 1140,
Eccl. 47, 303, Men. Sam. 166   [8] introd. p. 22 : mss
ποιήσας : Im. στηλίδιον, ποιήσας ἐπιγράψαι

forthwith to fetch the girl from the brothel, ' so that we may all have the pleasure of listening to her music.' [a]

XXI. PETTY PRIDE

Petty Pride will seem to be a vulgar appetite for distinction ; and the Pettily-proud man of a kind that when he is invited out to dine must needs find place to dine next the host ; and that will take his son off to Delphi to cut his first hair. Nothing will please him but his lackey shall be a blackamoor. When he pays a pound of silver he has them pay it in new coin. He is apt, this man, if he keep a pet jackdaw, to buy a little ladder and make a little bronze shield for that jackdaw to wear while he hops up and down upon the ladder.[b] Should he sacrifice an ox, the scalp or frontlet is nailed up, heavily garlanded, over against the entrance of his house,[c] so that all that come in may see [d] it is an ox he has sacrificed.[e] When he goes in procession with the other knights, his man may take all the rest of his gear away home for him, but he puts on the cloak and makes his round of the market-place in his spurs. Should his Melitean lap-dog die, he will make him a tomb and set up on it a stone to say ' Branch, of Melitè.[f] ' Should he have cause to dedicate a bronze

---

[a] The ill-breeding prob. does not lie in speaking of the brothel, but the host should either have provided a flute-player or said nothing about it.

[b] Like a soldier on a scaling-ladder at the taking of a city.

[c] On the opposite side of the peristyle ?

[d] *Or perhaps more likely* know.

[e] That he was sacrificing *some* animal would be clear from the smell. [f] *See Index,* Melitè.

ἀναθεὶς δάκτυλον[1] χαλκοῦν ἐν τῷ Ἀσκληπιείῳ,
τοῦτον ἐκτρίβειν, στεφανοῦν,[2] ἀλείφειν, ὁσημέραι.
11 ἀμέλει δὲ καὶ διοικήσασθαι παρὰ τῶν συμπρυ-
τανέων[3] ὅπως ἀπαγγείλῃ τῷ δήμῳ τὰ ἱερά, καὶ
παρεσκευασμένος λαμπρὸν ἱμάτιον καὶ ἐστεφα-
νωμένος παρελθὼν εἰπεῖν Ὦ ἄνδρες Ἀθηναῖοι,
ἐθύομεν οἱ πρυτάνεις[3] τῇ Μητρὶ τῶν θεῶν τὰ
Γαλάξια,[4] καὶ καλὰ τὰ ἱερά,[5] καὶ ὑμεῖς δέχεσθε[6]
τὰ ἀγαθά· καὶ ταῦτα ἀπαγγείλας ἀπιὼν διηγήσασθαι οἴκαδε τῇ αὑτοῦ γυναικὶ ὡς καθ' ὑπερβολὴν
εὐημερεῖ.[7]

12 Καὶ πλειστάκις δὲ ἀποκείρασθαι, καὶ τοὺς
ὀδόντας λευκοὺς ἔχειν.[8] καὶ τὰ ἱμάτια δὲ χρηστὰ
13 μεταβάλλεσθαι, καὶ χρίσματι ἀλείφεσθαι. καὶ τῆς
μὲν ἀγορᾶς πρὸς τὰς τραπέζας προσφοιτᾶν,[9] τῶν
δὲ γυμνασίων ἐν τούτοις διατρίβειν οὗ ἂν οἱ[10] ἔφηβοι γυμνάζωνται, τοῦ δὲ θεάτρου καθῆσθαι, ὅταν
14 ᾖ θέα,[11] πλησίον τῶν στρατηγῶν. καὶ ἀγοράζειν
αὐτὸς μὲν[12] μηδέν, ξένοις δὲ συνεργεῖν ἐπιστάλματα, ⟨καὶ ἅλας⟩ εἰς Βυζάντιον καὶ Λακωνικὰς
κύνας εἰς Κύζικον πέμπειν[13] καὶ μέλι Ὑμήττιον εἰς
Ῥόδον· καὶ ταῦτα ποιῶν τοῖς ἐν τῇ πόλει δι-
15 ηγεῖσθαι. ἀμέλει δὲ καὶ πίθηκον θρέψαι δεινός, καὶ

---

[1] Naber: mss -ιον   [2] mss -οῦντα   [3] Herw: mss συνδιοικ.
and πρυτ. (introd. p. 22), after which they incorporate gloss
τὰ ἱερά   [4] Wil: V τὰ γὰρ ἄξια, others ἄξια   [5] V τὰ
ἱερὰ καλά, others omit τὰ ἱερά (i.e. τὰ ἱερὰ in marg.
arch.)   [6] V δέχ.: others ἐδέχ.   [7] for tense cf. νικᾷ
and for meaning Ath. 584 d: most mss -εῖν   [8] all mss
and P(ap. Hercul. 1457) have this and the following §§ after
θλιβόμενος Char. V, see opp.   [9] P προσέρχεσθαι   [10] οἱ
in P only   [11] mss also ἡ θέα   [12] mss and P αὐτόν μὲν,
mss also μὲν αὐτὸν   [13] introd. p. 25

finger or toe in the temple of Asclepius,[a] he is sure
to polish it, wreathe it, and anoint it, every day.
This man, it is plain, will contrive it with his fellow-
magistrates that it be he that shall proclaim the
sacrifice to the people ; and providing himself a clean
coat and setting a wreath on his head, will stand
forth and say ' The Magistrates have performed the
rites of the Milk-Feast, Athenians, in honour of the
Mother of the Gods ; the sacrifice is propitious, and
do you accept the blessing.'[b] This done he will
away home and tell his wife what a great success he
has had.

He is shorn, this man,[c] many times in the month ;
keeps his teeth white ; gets a new cloak when the
old one is still good ; uses unguent for oil. In the
market-place he haunts the banks ; of the wrestling-
schools he chooses those to dally in where the youths
practise ;[d] and when there is a show at the theatre
he will sit next to the generals. He does no buying
for himself, but aids foreigners in exporting goods
abroad, and sends salt to Byzantium, Spartan hounds
to Cyzicus, Hymettian honey to Rhodes ; and when
he does so, lets the world know it. It goes without
saying that he is apt to keep a pet monkey ; and

[a] As a votive offering in return for the cure of that member :
or, *keeping the text*, ring.
[b] Text uncertain ; the point would seem to lie either in
the (unusual ?) specification of the feast or in the unimport-
ance of this particular feast ; *cf.* [Dem.] *Proem* 54.
[c] The following passage, which the mss, including P, give
at the end of Char. V., is generally thought to belong here ;
but it may have belonged once to a separate Char., *cf.* the
previous § with § 16.
[d] *i.e.* the public ones, not the private ones for boys (Nav.).

τίτυρον[1] κτήσασθαι, καὶ Σικελικὰς περιστεράς,
καὶ δορκαδείους ἀστραγάλους,[2] καὶ Θουριακὰς[3]
τῶν στρογγύλων ληκύθους, καὶ βακτηρίας τῶν
σκολιῶν ἐκ Λακεδαίμονος, καὶ αὐλαίαν Πέρσας ἐν-
υφασμένην,[4] καὶ παλαιστρίδιον[5] κόνιν ἔχον καὶ
16 σφαιριστήριον· καὶ τοῦτο περιὼν χρηννύναι[6] τοῖς
φιλοσόφοις,[7] τοῖς σοφισταῖς, τοῖς ὁπλομάχοις,
τοῖς ἁρμονικοῖς ἐνεπιδείκνυσθαι.[8] καὶ αὐτὸς ἐν
τοῖς ἐπιδείξεσιν ὕστερον ἐπεισιέναι ἤδη συγκαθημένων, ἵν᾿ εἴπῃ τῶν θεωμένων ⟨ὁ ἕτερος⟩[9] πρὸς
τὸν ἕτερον ὅτι Τούτου ἐστὶν ἡ παλαίστρα.

ΑΝΕΛΕΥΘΕΡΙΑΣ ΚΒ΄

Ἡ δὲ ἀνελευθερία ἐστὶ πάρεσίς τις[10] φιλοτιμίας
δαπάνην ἐχούσης,[11] ὁ δὲ ἀνελεύθερος τοιοῦτός τις,
2 οἷος νικήσας τραγῳδοὺς ταινίαν ἀναθεῖναι τῷ
Διονύσῳ ξυλίνην,[12] ἐπιγράψας μόνον[13] αὐτοῦ τὸ
3 ὄνομα· καὶ ἐπιδόσεων γινομένων ἐκ τοῦ δήμου,[14]
4 ἀναστὰς σιωπᾶν ἢ ἐκ τοῦ μέσου ἀπελθεῖν· καὶ ἐκ-
διδοὺς αὑτοῦ θυγατέρα τοῦ μὲν ἱερείου πλὴν τῶν

[1] Sch. Δωριεῖς τὸν σάτυρον· καὶ ἔστι δὲ ὁ μικρὰν ἔχων οὐρὰν
πίθηκος and in one ms 3 obscure words, for the first 2 of
which Knox suggests 'Ρίνθωνος ἡ χρῆσις   [2] cf. Callim.
239 (85 Mair)   [3] Sch. (cf. Ambr. O) οἱ Θούριοι ἔθνος
Ταραντινικὸν ἐν ᾧ λήκυθοι εἰργάζοντο διαφέρουσαι τῶν ἄλλων
[4] Cob. and P: mss ἔχουσαν Πέρσας ἐνυφασμένους (cf. Diog. L.
vi. 102)   [5] so P: mss αὐλίδιον παλαιστριαῖον (παλαιστρικόν),
incorp. gloss   [6] P χρωννύναι   [7] P omits, perh. intentionally; Philodemus was a philosopher himself   [8] Cob.
and P: mss ἐπιδ.   [9] introd. p. 26   [10] E:
mss περιουσία τις ἀπὸ (ἀπὸ incorp. correction to ἀπουσία)
[11] Diels: mss -σα   [12] V ξυλίνην ἀναθ. τῷ Δ. (i.e. ξ. in
marg. of arch.)   [13] Hanow: V μὲν, others omit; Madv.
μέλανι   [14] Meier ἐν τῷ δήμῳ, cf. Dem. 21. 161
96

the ape he keeps is of the satyr kind ; his doves are
Sicilian ; his knuckle-bones [a] antelope ; his oil-flasks
the round flasks from Thurii ; his walking-sticks the
crooked sticks from Sparta ; he has a tapestry curtain
with Persians upon it ; and a little wrestling-place
of his own with a sanded floor and a ball-court.
The last he goes around lending to philosophers,
sophists, masters-at-arms, teachers of music, for their
displays ; [b] which he himself attends, coming in late
so that the company may say one to another, ' That
is the owner of the wrestling-place.'

XXII. PARSIMONY

Parsimony is a neglect of honour when it involves
expense ; and your Parsimonious man one that if
he win the prize for staging a tragedy will con-
secrate to Dionysus a diadem of wood [c] with his
own name and no other inscribed upon it ; [d] and
when a public contribution is asked in the Assembly,
rise without speaking or depart from the house.
At his daughter's wedding he will sell all the
meat of the sacrificial victim except the priest's

[a] For the game of that name *cf.* Ath. v. 194 a, *Pap. Soc.
Ital.* 331 (257 B.C.).
[b] *Cf.* Diog. L. vi. 104.
[c] *i.e.* a plaque in imitation of a headband (Nav.).
[d] He does not even give the poet's, let alone the tribe's.

ἱερέων[1] τὰ κρέα ἀποδόσθαι, τοὺς δὲ διακονοῦντας
ἐν τοῖς γάμοις οἰκοσίτους μισθώσασθαι· καὶ τρι-
ηραρχῶν τὰ τοῦ κυβερνήτου στρώματα αὑτῷ ἐπὶ
τοῦ καταστρώματος ὑποστορέννυσθαι, τὰ δὲ αὑτοῦ
6 ἀποτιθέναι. καὶ τὰ παιδία δὲ δεινὸς μὴ πέμψαι
εἰς διδασκάλου ὅταν ᾖ Μουσεῖα, ἀλλὰ φῆσαι κακῶς
7 ἔχειν, ἵνα μὴ συμβάλωνται. καὶ ἐξ ἀγορᾶς δὲ
ὀψωνήσας τὰ κρέα αὐτὸς φέρειν καὶ[2] τὰ λάχανα ἐν
8 τῷ προκολπίῳ· καὶ ἔνδον μένειν ὅταν ἐκδῷ θοἰμά-
9 τιον ἐκπλῦναι· καὶ φίλου ἔρανον συλλέγοντος καὶ
διηγγελμένου[3] αὐτῷ, προσιόντα προϊδόμενος ἀπο-
κάμψας ἐκ τῆς ὁδοῦ τὴν κύκλῳ οἴκαδε πορευθῆναι.
10 καὶ τῇ γυναικὶ δὲ τῇ ἑαυτοῦ ⟨πλέον ταλάντου⟩[4]
προῖκα εἰσενεγκαμένῃ μὴ πρίασθαι θεράπαιναν,
ἀλλὰ μισθοῦσθαι εἰς τὰς ἐξόδους ἐκ τῆς γυναικείας
11 παιδίον τὸ συνακολουθῆσον· καὶ τὰ ὑποδήματα
παλιμπήξει κεκαττυμένα φορεῖν, καὶ λέγειν ὅτι
12 κέρατος οὐδὲν διαφέρει· καὶ ἀναστὰς τὴν οἰκίαν
13 καλλῦναι καὶ τὰς κλίνας ἐκκορῆσαι.[5] καὶ καθεζό-
μενος παραστρέψαι τὸν τρίβωνα ὃν αὐτὸν φορεῖ.[6]

ΑΛΑΖΟΝΕΙΑΣ ΚΓ΄

Ἀμέλει δὲ ἡ ἀλαζονεία δόξει εἶναι προσδοκία
τις[7] ἀγαθῶν οὐκ ὄντων, ὁ δὲ ἀλάζων τοιοῦτός τις,
οἷος ἐν τῷ διαζεύγματι ἑστηκὼς διηγεῖσθαι[8] ξένοις

---

[1] Holl. γερῶν   [2] V omits   [3] Holl.: V διειλεγ., others
omit καὶ δ. . . . προσιόντα   [4] E   [5] mss also ἐκκρύσαι
[6] Münsterberg: mss αὐτὸς φ.   [7] mss also τινῶν   [8] mss
διηγεῖτο

portion, and covenant with the serving-men he hires
for the feast that they shall eat at home.[a] As
trierarch or furnisher of a galley to the state, he
makes his bed on the deck with the helmsman's
blankets,[b] and puts his own by. This man will never
send his children to school when it is the Feast of
the Muses, but pretend that they are sick, so that
they shall not contribute. He will come home from
market carrying his own buyings of meat and pot-
herbs in the fold of his gown ;[c] he will stay at
home when his coat is gone to the fuller's ; when a
friend of his is laying another's acquaintance under
contribution and he has wind of it, he no sooner sees
him coming his way than he turns into an alley and
fetches a compass home. The wife that brought him
more than three hundred pound is not suffered to
have a serving-maid of her own,[d] but he hires a
little girl from the women's market to attend her
upon her outings. The shoes he wears are all clouts,
and he avows they are as strong as any horn. He
rises betimes and cleans the house and brushes out
the dining-couches.[e] When he sits down he will turn
aside his frieze-coat when he has nothing under it.[f]

XXIII. PRETENTIOUSNESS

Pretentiousness, of course, will seem to be a laying
claim to advantages a man does not possess ; and
the Pretentious or Snobbish man will stand at the

---

[a] *Cf*. Men. 286 K, 450 K.
[b] The steersman on duty at night would not want them till
morning.   [c] *Cf*. Diog. L. vi. 36, 104.   [d] *Cf*. Men. *Sam*. 170.
[e] These naturally would be covered with crumbs.
[f] *Or perhaps* the frieze-coat which is all he wears ; *cf*.
Diog. L. vi. 13, vii. 22.

ὡς πολλὰ χρήματα αὐτῷ[1] ἐστιν ἐν τῇ θαλάττῃ·
2 καὶ περὶ τῆς ἐργασίας τῆς δανειστικῆς διεξιέναι
ἡλίκη, καὶ αὐτὸς ὅσα εἴληφε καὶ ἀπολώλεκε· καὶ
ἅμα ταῦτα πλεθρίζων πέμπειν τὸ παιδάριον εἰς τὴν
3 τράπεζαν δραχμῆς αὐτῷ κειμένης. καὶ συνοδοι-
πόρου δὲ ἀπολαῦσαι ἐν τῇ ὁδῷ δεινὸς λέγων ὡς
μετὰ Εὐάνδρου ἐστρατεύσατο, καὶ ὡς αὐτῷ εἶχε,[2]
καὶ ὅσα λιθοκόλλητα ποτήρια ἐκόμισε· καὶ περὶ
τῶν τεχνιτῶν τῶν ἐν τῇ Ἀσίᾳ, ὅτι βελτίους εἰσὶ
τῶν ἐν τῇ Εὐρώπῃ, ἀμφισβητῆσαι· καὶ ταῦτα
ψοφῆσαι[3] οὐδαμοῦ ἐκ τῆς πόλεως ἀποδεδημηκώς.
4 καὶ γράμματα δὲ εἰπεῖν ὡς πάρεστι παρ' Ἀντι-
πάτρου τριττὰ[4] δὴ λέγοντα παραγίνεσθαι αὐτὸν εἰς
Μακεδονίαν· καὶ διδομένης αὐτῷ ἐξαγωγῆς ξύλων
ἀτελοῦς[5] ὅτι ἀπείρηται, ὅπως μηδ' ὑφ' ἑνὸς
συκοφαντηθῇ· Περαιτέρω φιλοσοφεῖν προσῆκε
5 Μακεδόσι. καὶ ἐν τῇ σιτοδείᾳ[6] δὲ ὡς πλείω[7] ἢ
πέντε τάλαντα αὐτῷ γένοιτο[8] τὰ ἀναλώματα
διδόντι τοῖς ἀπόροις τῶν πολιτῶν, ἀνανεύειν γὰρ
οὐ δύνασθαι. καὶ ἀγνώτων[9] δὲ παρακαθημένων
κελεῦσαι θεῖναι τὰς ψήφους ἕνα αὐτῶν, καὶ ποσῶν
αὐτὰς καθ' ἑξακοσίας ⟨καὶ κατὰ τριακοσίας⟩[10] καὶ
κατὰ μνᾶν, καὶ προστιθεὶς πιθανὰ[11] ἑκάστοις

---

[1] Lycius: mss -τοῖς   [2] cf. Men. *Perinth.* 7   [3] Hottin-
ger: mss ψηφῆσαι   [4] mss also τρίτον   [5] some mss
add εἰπεῖν; cf. Andoc. 2. 11   [6] Cas: mss σποδιᾷ, σποδία
[7] V πλείους   [8] cf. xiv. 2 τί γίνεται; mss also γένοιτο αὐτῷ
[9] mss also ἀγνώστων   [10] E, introd. p. 22   [11] V -νῶς

Mole and tell strangers of the great sums he has
ventured at sea, and descant upon the greatness of
the usury-trade and his own profits and losses in it ;
and while he thus outruns the truth, will send off
his page to the bank, though he have there but a
shilling to his name. He loves to make sport of a
fellow-traveller by the way by telling him that he
served under Evander,[a] and how he stood with him,
and how many jewelled cups he brought home ; and
will have it that the artificers of Asia are better
craftsmen than these of Europe ;—all this talk though
he have never been out of the country. Moreover,
he may well say that he has no less than three letters
from Antipater [b] requesting his attendance upon him
in Macedonia,[c] and albeit he is offered free exporta-
tion of timber he has refused to go ; *he* will not lay
himself open to calumny ; the Macedonians ought
to have known better than expect it. He is like to
say, also, that in the time of the famine [d] he spent
more than twelve hundred pound in relieving the
distress,—he cannot say no ; and when strangers are
sitting next him he will ask one of them to cast the
account, and reckoning it in sums of ten, twenty-
five, and fifty, assign plausible names to each sum

[a] Apparently an intentionally thin disguise of the name
of Alexander, against whom T. had written the pamphlet
Callisthenes in 327.
[b] Regent of Macedonia after the death of Alexander,
323–319 ; *cf.* Xenocrates' refusal of Ant.'s offered gift, Diog.
L. iv. 8 ; *cf. ibid.* vi. 66.
[c] *Or* that a letter has come from Antipater bidding him
lead a commission of three to attend him in Macedonia.
[d] Prob. that of 329 B.C., *cf.* Dem. 34. 37 f.

τούτων ὀνόματα, ποιῆσαι καὶ δέκα τάλαντα·[1] καὶ
τοῦτο φήσας εἰσενηνοχέναι[2] εἰς ἐράνους αὐτῶν,
καὶ τὰς τριηραρχίας εἰπεῖν ὅτι οὐ τίθησιν οὐδὲ τὰς
λειτουργίας ὅσας λελειτούργηκε. καὶ προσελθὼν
δ᾽ εἰς τοὺς ἵππους, τοὺς ἀγαθοὺς τοῖς πωλοῦσι
8 προσποιήσασθαι ὠνητιᾶν· καὶ ἐπὶ τὰς κλισίας[3]
ἐλθὼν ἱματισμὸν ζητῆσαι εἰς δύο τάλαντα, καὶ τῷ
παιδὶ μάχεσθαι ὅτι τὸ χρυσίον οὐκ ἔχων αὐτῷ
9 ἀκολουθεῖ· καὶ ἐν μισθῷ τὴν οἰκίαν[4] οἰκῶν φῆσαι
ταύτην εἶναι τὴν πατρῴαν πρὸς τὸν μὴ εἰδότα,
καὶ διότι μέλλει πωλεῖν αὐτὴν διὰ τὸ ἐλάττω εἶναι
αὐτῷ πρὸς τὰς ξενοδοχίας.

ΥΠΕΡΗΦΑΝΙΑΣ ΚΔ΄

Ἔστι δὲ ἡ ὑπερηφανία καταφρόνησίς τις πλὴν
αὐτοῦ τῶν ἄλλων, ὁ δὲ ὑπερήφανος τοιόσδε τις,
οἷος τῷ σπεύδοντι ἀπὸ δείπνου ⟨ἐντυγχάνειν
3 αὐτῷ⟩[5] ἐντεύξεσθαι φάσκειν ἐν τῷ περιπατεῖν· καὶ
4 εὖ ποιήσας μεμνῆσθαι φάσκειν· καὶ βαδίζων ἐν
ταῖς ὁδοῖς[6] τὰς διαίτας κρίνειν ἐν τοῖς ἐπιτρέψασιν[7]·
5 καὶ χειροτονούμενος ἐξόμνυσθαι τὰς ἀρχάς, οὐ
6 φάσκων σχολάζειν· καὶ προσελθεῖν πρότερος οὐδενὶ
7 θελῆσαι.[8] καὶ τοὺς πωλοῦντάς τι ἢ μισθουμένους[9]

[1] ποιῆσαι καὶ V ; *i.e.* the five talents of § 5 have now grown
to ten ; mss also δέκα καὶ ποιῆσαι (*i.e.* καὶ in marg. arch.);
ποιῆσαι corresponds to γίγνεσθαι xiv. 2   [2] V εἰσενηνέχθαι,
which Foss keeps, reading αὐτῷ   [3] E: mss κλίνας   [4] Im.
(*cf.* ἔμμισθος and Xen. *Sym.* 4. 4): mss also μισθωτῇ οἰκίᾳ
[5] Ast-E (introd. p. 23)   [6] Schw : mss βιάζειν for βαδίζων,
some ἐν τ. ὁ. καὶ β. (*i.e.* ἐν τ. ὁ. marg.)   [7] ἐν is strange :
τοῖς ἐν⟨ὶ⟩ (*sc.* λόγῳ) ἐπιτρέψασιν, *i.e.* a form of arbitration where
the referee's decision was given in a single word (Yes or No?)?
cf. Men. *Ep.* 198 καταμενῶ | αὔριον ὅτῳ βούλεσθ᾽ ἐπιτρέπειν ἐνὶ
λόγῳ | ἕτοιμος   [8] mss -σας   [9] Stroth : mss μεμισθωμ.

given, and make it as much as three thousand pound.[a]
This he declares is what he contributed to these poor
men's subscription-lists, adding that he takes no
account whatever of the trierarchies and other state-
services he has performed. This man will go to the
horse-market and pretend to the dealers that he wishes
to buy thoroughbreds; and at the stalls [b] he asks
after clothing worth five hundred pound, and scolds
his lackey for coming out without gold.[c] And though
he live in a hired house, he tells any that knows no
better that he had this of his father, and is about to
put it up for sale because it is too small for the
entertaining of his friends.

XXIV. ARROGANCE

Arrogance is the despising of all the world but
yourself; and the Arrogant man of the kind that
will tell any that hastes to speak to him after supper,
that he will see him while he takes the air; [d] and
any that he has benefited, that he is bearing it in
mind. If he be made sole arbiter he will give judgement as he walks in the streets.[e] When he is to be
elected to office he excuses himself on oath, because,
please you, he has not the time. He will go speak
to no man before the other speak to him. It is his
way also to bid one who would sell to him or hire

[a] *Lit.* reckoning by 600 drachmas (=6 minas = a *tenth* of
a talent), and 3 minas (a *twentieth*), and 1 mina (a *sixtieth*),
make it ten talents: the ref. is not to the method of adding
up the total (why should he have an abacus with him?), but
to the (imaginary) list of his contributions; he does not
trouble to invent any but round numbers (see p. 22).
[b] Another part of the market-place.
[c] *Lit.* the gold; but the article is idiomatic, see p. 51 n. *a.*
[d] *i.e.* he won't put off his evening walk for him.
[e] See critical note 7.

8 δεινὸς κελεῦσαι ἥκειν πρὸς αὐτὸν ἅμ᾽ ἡμέρᾳ· καὶ
ἐν ταῖς ὁδοῖς πορευόμενος μὴ λαλεῖν τοῖς ἐντυγ-
χάνουσι,[1] κάτω κεκυφώς, ὅταν δὲ αὐτῷ δόξῃ, ἄνω
9 πάλιν· καὶ ἑστιῶν τοὺς φίλους αὐτὸς μὴ συνδειπνεῖν,
ἀλλὰ τῶν ὑφ᾽ αὑτόν τινι συντάξαι αὐτῶν ἐπι-
10 μελεῖσθαι. καὶ προαποστέλλειν δέ, ἐπὰν πορεύηται,
11 τὸν ἐροῦντα ὅτι προσέρχεται· καὶ οὔτε ἐπ᾽ ἀλειφό-
μενον αὐτὸν οὔτε λουόμενον οὔτε ἐσθίοντα ἐᾶσαι
12 ἂν εἰσελθεῖν. ἀμέλει δὲ καὶ λογιζόμενος πρός
τινα τῷ παιδὶ συντάξαι τὰς ψήφους διωθεῖν καὶ
13 κεφάλαιον ποιήσαντι γράψαι αὐτῷ εἰς λόγον· καὶ
ἐπιστέλλων μὴ γράφειν ὅτι Χαρίζοιο ἄν μοι, ἀλλ᾽
ὅτι Βούλομαι γενέσθαι, καὶ ᾿Απέσταλκα πρὸς σὲ
ληψόμενος, καὶ ῞Οπως ἄλλως μὴ ἔσται, καὶ Τὴν
ταχίστην.

ΔΕΙΛΙΑΣ ΚΕ΄

᾿Αμέλει δὲ ἡ δειλία δόξειεν ἂν εἶναι ὕπειξίς τις
2 ψυχῆς ἐν φόβῳ,[2] ὁ δὲ δειλὸς τοιοῦτός τις, οἷος
πλέων τὰς ἄκρας φάσκειν ἡμιολίας εἶναι· καὶ
κλυδωνίου[3] γενομένου ἐρωτᾶν εἴ τις μὴ μεμύηται
τῶν πλεόντων· καὶ τοῦ κυβερνήτου ἀνακύπτοντος
⟨εἰσομένου⟩ εἰ μεσοπορεῖ, πυνθάνεσθαι[4] τί αὐτῷ
δοκεῖ τὰ τοῦ θεοῦ· καὶ πρὸς τὸν παρακαθήμενον
λέγειν ὅτι φοβεῖται ἀπὸ ἐνυπνίου τινός· καὶ ἐκδὺς
διδόναι τῷ παιδὶ τὸν χιτωνίσκον· καὶ δεῖσθαι πρὸς
8 τὴν γῆν προσάγειν αὐτόν. καὶ στρατευόμενος δὲ

---

[1] ⟨ἀλλὰ παριέναι⟩?   [2] E: mss ἔμφοβος   [3] V κλύδωνος
[4] E; for εἰσ. cf. Men. Ep. 245: mss ἀνακόπτοντος (ἀνακύπτων
μὲν) πυνθαν. (αἰσθάν.) εἰ μεσ. καὶ

---

[a] i.e. without asking if you agree with his arithmetic.

him his labour to come to him at break of day.
When he is walking in the street, he never talks to
those that meet him, but goes by with his eyes on
the ground till it please him to raise them. When
he invites his friends, he does not dine with them
himself, but commands one of his underlings to see
to their entertainment. When he travels, he sends
a footboy before him to say that he is coming. No
man is admitted to his presence when he is anointing
himself, or at his bath, or taking food. No need to
say that when this man comes to a reckoning with
you he commands his page to do the counting and
adding and set the sum down to your account.[a] In
his letters you do not find ' You would oblige me,'
but ' My desire is this,' or ' I have sent to you for
that,' or ' Be sure that you do the other,' and
' Without the least delay.'

XXV. COWARDICE

Cowardice, of course, would seem to be a giving-
way of the soul in fear ; and your Coward he that
if he be at sea will have it that the jutting rocks are
pirate sloops, and when the sea rises asks if there's
not somebody aboard that's initiated.[b] If the helmsman look up to know if he is keeping mid-channel,[c]
he asks him what he thinks of the weather ;[d] or
tells one that sits next to him that a dream he has
had makes him uneasy : or takes off his shirt and
gives it to his man ;[e] or begs them put him ashore.

[b] Cf. Ar. Pac. 276.
[c] Or is halfway of his course (in either case he would go
by the relative position of mountain-tops, etc.).
[d] Cf. Eur. Cycl. 212 (Nav.).
[e] For ease in swimming ; the cloak, having no arm-holes,
could be thrown off with less delay.

πεζῇ[1] ἐκβοηθοῦντός τε[2] ⟨τοὺς συσσίτους⟩[3] προσ-
καλεῖν πάντας πρὸς αὑτὸν κελεύων στάντας[4]
πρῶτον περιιδεῖν, καὶ λέγειν ὡς ἔργον διαγνῶναί
4 ἐστι πότεροί[5] εἰσιν οἱ πολέμιοι· καὶ ἀκούων
κραυγῆς καὶ ὁρῶν πίπτοντας, εἴπας[6] πρὸς τοὺς
παρεστηκότας ὅτι τὴν σπάθην λαβεῖν ὑπὸ τῆς
σπουδῆς ἐπελάθετο, τρέχειν ἐπὶ τὴν σκηνήν,
⟨καὶ⟩ τὸν παῖδα ἐκπέμψας κελεύων[7] προσκο-
πεῖσθαι ποῦ εἰσιν οἱ πολέμιοι, ἀποκρύψαι αὐτὴν
ὑπὸ τὸ προσκεφάλαιον, εἶτα διατρίβειν πολὺν
5 χρόνον ὡς ζητῶν· καὶ ἐκ τῆς σκηνῆς[8] ὁρῶν
τραυματίαν τινὰ προσφερόμενον τῶν φίλων προσ-
δραμὼν καὶ θαρρεῖν κελεύσας ὑπολαβὼν φέρειν,
καὶ τοῦτον θεραπεύειν καὶ περισπογγίζειν, καὶ
παρακαθήμενος ἀπὸ τοῦ ἕλκους τὰς μυίας σοβεῖν,
καὶ πᾶν μᾶλλον ἢ μάχεσθαι τοῖς πολεμίοις. καὶ
τοῦ σαλπιστοῦ δὲ τὸ πολεμικὸν σημήναντος καθήμενος ἐν τῇ σκηνῇ ⟨εἰπεῖν⟩ "Ἄπαγ᾽ ἐς κόρακας·
οὐκ ἐάσει τὸν ἄνθρωπον ὕπνου λαβεῖν[9] πυκνὰ
6 σημαίνων. καὶ αἵματος δὲ ἀνάπλεως ἀπὸ τοῦ
ἀλλοτρίου τραύματος ἐντυγχάνειν τοῖς ἐκ τῆς
μάχης ἐπανιοῦσι καὶ διηγεῖσθαι ὡς Κινδυνεύσας
ἕνα σέσωκα τῶν φίλων[10]· καὶ εἰσάγειν πρὸς τὸν
κατακείμενον σκεψομένους τοὺς δημότας, τοὺς

---

[1] V πεζοῦ corr. to πεζῇ, others omit πεζ. . . . τε   [2] sc.
τοῦ στρατοῦ or τοῦ στρατηγοῦ (or ἐκβοηθούντων? cf. Xen. Cyr.
iii. 3. 54 ἰόντων εἰς μάχην, and συναγόντων below, xxx. 18)
[3] E, cf. Dem. 54. 4   [4] V κελ. πρ. αὐτ. στ., others πάντας
πρ. αὐτ. καὶ στ. (i.e. κελεύων, afterwards mutilated, in marg.
arch.)   [5] mss also -ρον   [6] Ilberg: mss εἰπεῖν, εἶπου (?)
[7] V καὶ κελεύσας, others κελεύειν   [8] E: mss ἐν τῇ σκηνῇ
[9] cf. Long. 4. 36 fin. ὕπνον εἵλοντο   [10] or, with V, ὡς
κινδυνεύσας "Ένα κτλ.
106

When he is serving on land and the troops are going into action, he will call his messmates and bid them all first stop and look about them ; it is so difficult to tell which is the enemy ; and then when he hears cries and sees men falling, he remarks to the men next to him that in his haste he forgot to take up his sword, and runs to the tent, and sending his man out with orders to reconnoitre, hides it under his pillow and then spends a long time pretending to seek for it. And seeing from the tent that they are bringing that way a wounded man that is a friend of his, he runs out, and bidding him be of good cheer, takes him on his back and carries him in ; [a] and so will tend the man, and sponge his wound clean,[b] and sit beside him and keep the flies from it, do anything, in short, sooner than fight the enemy. And indeed when the trumpet sounds the charge he never stirs from the tent, but cries ' Ill take ye ! he'll not suffer the man to get a wink of sleep with his continual bugling ! ' And then, covered with blood from another's wound, he will meet returning troops and tell them how he has saved one friend's life at the risk of his own [c] ; and bring in his fellow-parishioners, his fellow-tribesmen, to see the wounded

[a] *Or perh.* on his arm ; Nav. compares Plat. *Sym.* 212 D where, however, it is ἄγειν not φέρειν.

[b] *Cf.* περικαθαίρειν.

[c] *Or* tell each of them, as if he had risked his life, how he has saved one of his friends.

φυλέτας,[1] καὶ τούτων ἅμ᾽ ἑκάστῳ διηγεῖσθαι, ὡς αὐτὸς αὐτὸν ταῖς ἑαυτοῦ χερσὶν ἐπὶ σκηνὴν ἐκόμισεν.

ΟΛΙΓΑΡΧΙΑΣ ΚϚ΄

Δόξειεν δ᾽ ἂν εἶναι ἡ ὀλιγαρχία φιλαρχία τις ἰσχύος καὶ κέρδους[2] γλιχομένη, ὁ δὲ ὀλιγαρχικὸς[3]
2 τοιοῦτος, οἷος τοῦ δήμου βουλευομένου τίνας τῷ ἄρχοντι προσαιρήσονται τοὺς συνεπιμελησομένους τῆς πομπῆς,[4] παρελθὼν ἀποφήνασθαι ὡς δεῖ αὐτοκράτορας τούτους εἶναι, κἂν ἄλλοι[5] προβάλλωνται δέκα, λέγειν Ἱκανὸς εἷς ἐστι, τοῦτον δὲ ὅτι δεῖ ἄνδρα εἶναι· καὶ τῶν Ὁμήρου ἐπῶν τοῦτο ἓν μόνον κατέχειν ὅτι

Οὐκ ἀγαθὸν πολυκοιρανίη, εἷς κοίρανος ἔστω,

3 τῶν δὲ ἄλλων μηδὲν ἐπίστασθαι. ἀμέλει δὲ δεινὸς τοῖς τοιούτοις τῶν λόγων χρήσασθαι, ὅτι Δεῖ αὐτοὺς ἡμᾶς συνελθόντας περὶ τούτου[6] βουλεύσασθαι, καὶ Ἐκ τοῦ ὄχλου καὶ τῆς ἀγορᾶς ἀπαλλαγῆναι, καὶ Παύσασθαι ἀρχαῖς πλησιάζοντας καὶ ὑπὸ τούτων[7] ὑβριζομένους ἢ τιμωμένους ὅτε[8]
4 ἢ τούτους δεῖ ἢ ἡμᾶς οἰκεῖν τὴν πόλιν. καὶ τὸ μέσον δὲ τῆς ἡμέρας ἐξιὼν[9] τὸ ἱμάτιον ⟨μεμελημένως⟩[10] ἀναβεβλημένος καὶ μέσην κουρὰν κεκαρμένος καὶ ἀκριβῶς ἀπωνυχισμένος σοβεῖν τοὺς

---

[1] mss also τοὺς φ. τὸν δῆμον   [2] mss and P (*Oxyrh.* iv. 699) ἰσχυροῦ (-ρῶς) κέρδ.   [3] Cas: mss (and P?) -αρχος
[4] so V: other mss omit 2 ll. of arch. προσαιρ. τ. συν- and (from marg.) τῆς   [5] mss ἄλλοι   [6] so prob. V (Im.): others -των   [7] V adds αὐτούς: Nav. οὕτως   [8] *E*: mss ὅτι, cf. xvii. 9   [9] V adds καί, others omit καὶ τὸ ἱμ. ἀναβεβ.
[10] *E* (one line of arch. lost by πβλ), cf. Plat. *Prot.* 344 в

man, telling each and all that he carried him to the tent with his own hands.

XXVI. OLIGARCHY

It would seem that the Oligarchical or Anti-Democratic Spirit is a love of rule, covetous of power and gain; and the Anti-Democrat or Tory of the Old School [a] is he that steps forth when the Assembly is considering whom to join with the Archon for the directing of the pageant,[b] and gives his opinion that these should have full powers; and if the other speakers propose ten, he will say 'One is enough,' adding 'But he must be a man indeed.'[c] The one and only line of Homer's he knows is this :

'Tis ill that many rule; give one man sway.

It is only to be expected that he should be given to using such phrases as these :—' We should meet and consider this by ourselves '; ' We should rid ourselves of the mob and the market-place '; ' We should give up dallying with office and suffering ourselves to be insulted or exalted by such persons,[d] when either we or these fellows must govern the city.' And he will not go abroad till midday, and then it is with his cloak thrown on with studied elegance, and his hair and beard neither too short nor too long, and his finger-nails carefully pared, to

[a] Cf. Andoc. 4. 16.
[b] The procession at the Greater Dionysia.
[c] Cf. Men. Sam. 137, Pk. 260.
[d] The reference is to the initial and final scrutinies of magistrates before the Assembly.

τοιούτους λόγους ⟨λέγων⟩ τὴν τοῦ Ὠιδείου[1].
5 Διὰ τοὺς συκοφάντας οὐκ οἰκητόν ἐστιν ἐν τῇ
πόλει, καὶ ὡς Ἐν τοῖς δικαστηρίοις δεινὰ πά-
σχομεν ὑπὸ τῶν δικαζόντων,[2] καὶ ὡς Θαυμάζω
τῶν πρὸς τὰ κοινὰ προσιόντων τί βούλονται, καὶ
ὡς ἀχάριστόν ἐστι ⟨τὸ⟩[3] τοῦ νέμοντος καὶ διδόντος,
καὶ ὡς αἰσχύνεται ἐν τῇ ἐκκλησίᾳ ὅταν παρα-
6 κάθηταί τις αὐτῷ λεπτὸς καὶ αὐχμῶν· καὶ εἰπεῖν
Πότε παυσόμεθα ὑπὸ τῶν λειτουργιῶν καὶ τῶν τρι-
ηραρχιῶν ἀπολλύμενοι; καὶ ὡς μισητὸν τὸ τῶν
δημαγωγῶν γένος, τὸν Θησέα πρῶτον φήσας τῶν
κακῶν τῇ πόλει γεγονέναι αἴτιον,[4] καὶ δίκαια
παθεῖν,[5] πρῶτον γὰρ αὐτὸν ἀπολέσθαι ὑπ᾽ αὐτῶν.
7 καὶ τοιαῦτα ἕτερα πρὸς τοὺς ξένους καὶ τῶν
πολιτῶν τοὺς ὁμοτρόπους καὶ ταὐτὰ προαιρουμένους.

ΟΨΙΜΑΘΙΑΣ ΚΖ΄

Ἡ δὲ ὀψιμαθία φιλοπονία δόξειεν ἂν εἶναι
2 ὑπὲρ τὴν ἡλικίαν, ὁ δὲ ὀψιμαθὴς τοιοῦτός τις, οἷος
ῥήσεις μανθάνειν ἑξήκοντα ἔτη γεγονώς, καὶ
3 ταύτας λέγων παρὰ πότον ἐπιλανθάνεσθαι· καὶ
παρὰ τοῦ υἱοῦ μανθάνειν τὸ Ἐπὶ δόρυ καὶ Ἐπ᾽
4 ἀσπίδα καὶ Ἐπ᾽ οὐράν· καὶ εἰς ἡρῷα συμβάλλε-
5 σθαι τοῖς μειρακίοις λαμπάδα τρέχειν. ἀμέλει δὲ

---

[1] cf. βαδίζων ὁδόν Xen. *Mem.* ii. 1. 22, and Alciphr. 4. 7.
1 (1. 34) τὴν εἰς (*sic lege*) Ἀκαδήμειαν σοβεῖς (an imitation?)
[2] Schn: mss δικαζομένων : Meier δεκαζομένων   [3] Bersanetti,
cf. τὸ τῆς τύχης viii. 10 and Kühn.-Bl. ii. 1. 269   [4] V
adds incorp. gloss τοῦτον γὰρ ἐκ δώδεκα πόλεων εἰς μίαν
καταγαγόντα λυθείσας βασιλείας; cf. ὑπ᾽ αὐτῶν below, sc. τῶν
δημαγωγῶν: other mss omit αἴτιον . . . ὑπ᾽ αὐτῶν   [5] mss
αὐτὸν παθεῖν

strut it in the Street of the Music-House, saying,
'There's no dwelling in Athens for the informers';
or 'The juries are the curse of the law-courts'; or
'I marvel why men take up public affairs'; or
'How thankless the task of him that has to pay!'
or how ashamed he is when some lean and ill-kempt
fellow sits next to him in the Assembly. And he
will say 'When shall we cease to be victims of these
state-services and trierarchies?' or 'O this detest-
able tribe of demagogues!' and add 'Theseus was
the beginning of the misfortunes of our country;
and he got his deserts; he was their first victim
himself.' [a] And other such remarks does he make
to strangers or to such of his fellow-citizens as are
of his disposition and politics.[b]

XXVII. OPSIMATHY OR LATE-LEARNING

Opsimathy would seem to be an activity too great
for your years; and the Opsimath or Late-Learner
one that being past threescore years of age will
learn verses to recite,[c] and will forget what comes
next when he delivers them over the wine. He will
make his son teach him 'Right turn,' 'Left turn,'
and 'Right-about-face.' On the feasts of the
Heroes [d] he will compete in the torch-race for boys.

---

[a] *Cf.* Plut. *Thes.* 35.
[b] Perhaps an addition by another hand.
[c] At dinner-parties.
[d] *Or* to the shrines of the Heroes (Hephaestus and Prometheus?); but if so it must be emphatic, and in this context
one would expect the emphasis to lie on μειρακίοις; εἰς
rather than ἐν is due to the idea of entering *for* the race, *to
be* on a certain day; *cf.* the Orators *passim*.

κἂν που[1] κληθῇ εἰς 'Ηράκλεια,[2] ῥίψας τὸ ἱμάτιον
6 τὸν βοῦν αἴρεσθαι[3] ἵνα τραχηλίσῃ[4]· καὶ προσανα-
7 τρίβεσθαι εἰσιὼν εἰς τὰς παλαίστρας· καὶ ἐν τοῖς
θαύμασι τρία ἢ τέτταρα πληρώματα ὑπομένειν τὰ
8 ᾄσματα ἐκμανθάνων· καὶ τελούμενος τῷ Σαβαζίῳ
9 σπεῦσαι ὅπως καλλιστεύσῃ παρὰ τῷ ἱερεῖ· καὶ
ἐρῶν ἑταίρας[5] καὶ κριοὺς προσβάλλων ταῖς θύραις
10 πληγὰς εἰληφὼς ὑπ' ἀντεραστοῦ δικάζεσθαι· καὶ
εἰς ἀγρὸν ἐφ' ἵππου ἀλλοτρίου κατοχούμενος ἅμα
μελετᾶν ἱππάζεσθαι καὶ πεσὼν τὴν κεφαλὴν
11 καταγῆναι· καὶ ἐν δεκαδισταῖς[7] συνάγειν τοὺς
12 ⟨μὴ⟩[8] μετ' αὐτοῦ συναύξοντας· καὶ μακρὸν ἀν-
13 δριάντα παίζειν πρὸς τὸν ἑαυτοῦ ἀκόλουθον· καὶ
διατοξεύεσθαι καὶ διακοντίζεσθαι τῷ τῶν παιδίων
παιδαγωγῷ, καὶ ἅμα μανθάνειν παρ' αὐτοῦ
⟨παραινεῖν⟩,[9] ὡς ἂν καὶ ἐκείνου μὴ ἐπισταμένου.
14 καὶ παλαίων δ' ἐν τῷ βαλανείῳ πυκνὰ ἑδρο-
15 στροφεῖν,[10] ὅπως πεπαιδεῦσθαι δοκῇ· καὶ ὅταν ὦσιν
ἐγγὺς γυναῖκες[11] μελετᾶν ὀρχεῖσθαι αὐτὸς αὑτῷ
τερετίζων.[12]

[1] ποι? [2] E: mss -κλειον (εἰς=at or on, cf. Lys.
21. 3) [3] Meier: V αἱρεῖσθαι, others omit καὶ ἐπ'
οὐράν . . . δικάζεσθαι [4] ἵνα τρ. perh. a gloss; Theophr.'s
readers would surely not need this explanation [5] Schn:
V ἱερᾶς corr. fr. -ρὰς [6] E, cf. Plat. Gorg. 469 D:
mss κατεαγέναι [7] Wilhelm: V ἕνδεκα λιταῖς, others omit
καὶ . . . συναύξοντας [8] E [9] Hanow [10] E, cf.
ἑδροστρόφος: mss (τὴν) ἕδραν στρέφειν [11] Meister, cf. Ar.
Eccl. 880: V ὦσι . . . γυναικ. . . . (introd. p. 23) [12] LATE
ADDITION (only in V, where it follows Char. XXVIII):
(16) οὕτως ὁ τῆς διδασκαλίας ἐρεθισμὸς μανικοὺς καὶ ἐξεστηκότας
ἀνθρώπους τοῖς ἤθεσι ποιεῖ

CHARACTER XXVII

If he be bidden to any man's on a feast of Heracles, he is of course the man to throw off his coat and raise the ox to bend back its neck [a] ; when he goes to the wrestling-schools [b] he'll take a throw with the youngsters. At the jugglers' shows he will stay out three or four performances learning the songs by heart. When they are initiating him with the holy orders of Sabazius he takes pains to acquit himself best in the eyes of the priest. [c] If, when he is wenching and tries to break in the door, he be beaten by a rival, he takes it into court. He borrows a mount to ride into the country, and practising horsemanship by the way is thrown and breaks his head. At a tenth-day club's meetings he assembles men who have not the like objects with himself. [d] He will play long-statue [e] with his lackey ; he will shoot or throw the javelin with his children's tutor, and invite him the while to learn of him, as if he did not know his own business. When he is wrestling at the baths, he keeps wriggling his buttocks so that he may be thought to have had a good education. And when women are near, he will practise a dance, whistling his own tune. [f]

[a] For the knife. [b] A common diversion.
[c] Meaning uncertain.
[d] συνάγειν and συναύξειν are technical club-words, the latter meaning to further club-interests, cf. Lycon's will ap. Diog. L. v. 70.
[e] Prob. a children's gymnastic feat involving standing on another player's shoulders.
[f] LATE ADDITION : Thus can the prick of education make a man's manners those of one beside his wits.

ΚΑΚΟΛΟΓΙΑΣ ΚΗ'

Ἔστι δὲ ἡ κακολογία ἀγωγὴ[1] τῆς ψυχῆς εἰς τὸ χεῖρον ἐν λόγοις, ὁ δὲ κακόλογος τοιόσδε τις, 2 οἷος ἐρωτηθεὶς Ὁ δεῖνα τίς ἐστιν; ⟨εἰπεῖν⟩ "Ακουε δή,[2] καθάπερ οἱ γενεαλογοῦντες· Πρῶτον ἀπὸ τοῦ γένους αὐτοῦ ἄρξομαι· τούτου ὁ μὲν πατὴρ ἐξ ἀρχῆς Σωσίας ἐκαλεῖτο, ἐγένετο δὲ ἐν τοῖς στρατιώταις Σωσίστρατος, ἐπειδὴ δὲ εἰς τοὺς δημότας ἐνεγράφη, ⟨Σωσίδημος⟩[3]· ἡ μέντοι μήτηρ εὐγενὴς Θρᾷττά ἐστι, καλεῖται γοῦν ἡσυχῇ Κρινοκοράκα· τὰς δὲ τοιαύτας φασὶν ἐν τῇ πατρίδι εὐγενεῖς εἶναι[5]· αὐτὸς δὲ οὗτος ὡς ἐκ τοιούτων 3 γεγονὼς κακὸς καὶ μαστιγίας. καὶ ⟨περὶ γυναι-κῶν ἀ⟩κακῶν[6] δὲ πρός τινα εἰπεῖν Ἐγὼ δήπου τὰ τοιαῦτα οἶδα ὑπὲρ ὧν σὺ πλανᾷ[7] πρὸς ἐμὲ καὶ τούτους[8] διεξιών· αὗται αἱ γυναῖκες ἐκ τῆς ὁδοῦ τοὺς παριόντας συναρπάζουσι· καὶ Οἰκία τις αὐτὴ τὰ σκέλη ἠρκυῖα, ⟨καὶ⟩ Οὐ γὰρ οἷον[9] λῆρός ἐστι τὸ λεγόμενον, ἀλλ' ὥσπερ αἱ κύνες ἐν ταῖς ὁδοῖς

[1] Cas: mss ἀγών   [2] E, usual before a list, story, formal announcement, or emphatic statement, cf. Plat. Phaedr. 230 E, Sym. 214 B, Tim. Sch. 20 D, Plat. Com. Φάων 173. 5 K (cf. 174. 11) ἄκουε δή· ἄρξομαι κτλ, Eupol. Κόλ. 151 K, Men. Sam. 93 and frag. p. 468 l. 25 Allinson, Callim. Iamb. 201, Cleanthes 3 Powell, Luc. Gall. 12; οὐκοῦν δή quoted by Nav. from Plat. Soph. 256 D, 257 A is clearly unsuitable: V οὐκοῦνδε with mark of corruption; others omit, changing ἄρξομαι to ἄρξασθαι and omitting τούτου   [3] Meier   [4] E, cf. Diog. Laert. vi. 58, Theocr. 13. 27, Men. Her. 20: mss ἡ ψυχή, but the 'ornate alias' is hardly Greek (could it be an incorp. gloss translating κρ.?)   [5] introd. p. 14   [6] Im.-E   [7] Foss: V πλανᾶς, others omit καὶ . . . ἐμέ   [8] Ussing: mss -τοις   [9] Nav. compares Polyb. i. 20. 12

XXVIII. BACKBITING

Backbiting is a bent of the mind towards the worse in all a man says ; and your Backbiter one that, when you ask him ' Who is so-and-so ? ' is like to reply in the manner of a genealogist, ' Listen ; I will begin with his parentage ; this man's father was first called Sosias,[a] then among the troops [b] he became Sosistratus, and lastly when he was enrolled as a demesman or man of a parish,[c] Sosidemus ; but as for his mother, she's a high-born Thracian [d] ; at least she's called when nobody's listening [e] Krinokoraka,[f] and they say that women of that sort [g] are high-born in *her* country ; the man himself, as you might expect, coming of such a stock, is a knave and a villain.' And he will say to you about quite respectable women, ' I know only too well what trollops they are whose cause you are so mistaken as to champion to these gentlemen and me ; these women seize passers-by out of the street ' ;[h] or ' This house is simply a brothel ' ; or ' The saying is all too true, *They couple like dogs in the streets* ' ;

---

[a] Common as a slave-name, though also borne by freemen.

[b] Prob. mercenaries (Nav.).

[c] It was possible at this time, by questionable means, for a foreigner or even a slave to become an Athenian citizen (Nav.).　　　　　[d] Cf. Men. 469 K, Diog. L. ii. 31, vi. 1.

[e] Meaning doubtful ; perhaps Kr. is Thracian for ' courtesan.'

[f] The point perhaps lies in the outlandishness of the name ; attempts to derive it, *e.g.* from κρίνον and κόραξ, Lily-Crow, Black-and-White (ref. to the practice of tattooing ? Knox) should be given up ; the κρίνον, at any rate, was not proverbial for whiteness, as the lily is with us.

[g] *i.e.* prostitutes.　　　　　[h] Cf. Lys. 3. 46.

συνέχονται[1]· καὶ Τὸ ὅλον ἀνδρόλαλοί[2] τινες· καὶ
4 Αὐταὶ τὴν θύραν τὴν αὔλειον ὑπακούουσι. ἀμέλει
δὲ καὶ κακῶς λεγόντων ἑτέρων συνεπιλαμβάνεσθαι
καὶ αὐτὸς λέγων[3] Ἐγὼ δὲ τοῦτον τὸν ἄνθρωπον
πλέον πάντων μεμίσηκα· καὶ γὰρ εἰδεχθής τις ἀπὸ
τοῦ προσώπου ἐστίν· ἡ δὲ πονηρία, οὐδὲν ὅμοιον[4]·
σημεῖον δέ· τῇ γὰρ αὐτοῦ γυναικὶ ⟨γ′⟩[5] τάλαντα
εἰσενεγκαμένῃ προῖκα, ἐξ οὗ[6] παιδίον αὐτῷ γέγονε, γ′ χαλκοῦς εἰς ὄψον δίδωσι καὶ τῷ ψυχρῷ
λούεσθαι ἀναγκάζει τῇ τοῦ Ποσειδῶνος ἡμέρα.[8]
καὶ συγκαθήμενος δεινὸς περὶ τοῦ ἀναστάντος
εἰπεῖν ⟨κακά⟩,[9] καὶ ἀρχήν γε εἰληφὼς[10] μὴ ἀπο-
σχέσθαι μηδὲ τοὺς οἰκείους αὐτοῦ λοιδορῆσαι,
ἀλλὰ[11] πλεῖστα περὶ τῶν φίλων καὶ οἰκείων κακὰ
εἰπεῖν καὶ περὶ τῶν τετελευτηκότων, ⟨τὴν⟩ κακο-
λογίαν[12] ἀποκαλῶν παρρησίαν καὶ δημοκρατίαν καὶ
ἐλευθερίαν, καὶ τῶν ἐν τῷ βίῳ ἥδιστα τοῦτο ποιῶν.[13]

ΦΙΛΟΠΟΝΗΡΙΑΣ[14] ΚΘ′

Ἔστι δὲ ἡ φιλοπονηρία ὁμοπαθεία[15] κακίας, ὁ
2 δὲ φιλοπόνηρός ἐστι τοιόσδε τις, οἷος ἐντυγχάνειν
τοῖς ἡττημένοις καὶ δημοσίους ἀγῶνας ὠφληκόσι,[16]

---

[1] κύνες ὡς ἐν ὁδοῖς συνέχονται?   [2] Foss -λάβοι   [3] V
omits καὶ αὐτὸς and reads εἴπον (i.e. εἴπας), others καὶ
αὐτὸν λέγοντα   [4] V ὁμοία corr. from ὁμοῖα   [5] or
⟨ι⟩, cf. Men. 402. 11 K? Antiph. 224 K is not parallel
[6] οὗ Im: V ἦς   [7] γέγονε V marg., cf. Mach. ap. Ath. xiii.
581 d: text γεννᾷ, others omit τάλαντα ... γεννᾷ   [8] cf.
C.I.A. iii. 77. 16: or τοῦ Ποσειδεῶνος ὀσημέραι (E)?
[9] Cas.-E   [10] Schn: V -φότος, others omit καὶ ...
λοιδοοῆσαι; cf. Men. Pk. 45   [11] καὶ V, others καὶ ἄλλα

or 'Truth to tell, they are talkers with men'; or They answer the house-door themselves.' [a] I need not add that this fellow is apt, when others are maligning any man, to put *his* oar in and say, ' But I, I hate him above all men; what's more, he's ugly to look at, and his evil character—there's nothing to match it; and I'll tell you why: the wife that brought him two thousand pound, ever since she bore him a child has had but two farthings a day for her meat-money, and has been made to wash in cold water on Poseidon's day.' [b] He is prone to malign one of the company who is gone out; and, give him but the opportunity, he will not forbear to revile his own kin, nay he will often speak ill of his friends and kinsfolk, and of the dead, calling slander ' plain-speaking ' or ' the democratic spirit' [c] or ' in-dependence,' and preferring this among all the pleasures of life.

XXIX. FRIENDSHIP WITH RASCALS

Friendship with Rascals is a sympathy with vice; and the Friend of Rascals he that will seek the company of unsuccessful litigants or persons found guilty

---

[a] *Cf.* Ar. *Pax* 980, *Thesm.* 790, 797, Men. 546 K.
[b] 8th Dec.-Jan. (the washing would be ritual): *or* every day of December?
[c] *Cf.* Andoc. 4. 17.

---

12 *E*: mss κακῶς λέγειν   13 for the LATE ADDITION in V see Char. XXVII   14 V (the only ms for this Char.) φιλοπονίας here, and similar forms below   15 *E*, *cf.* Arist. 1495 b 14: mss ἐπιθυμία   16 V ὠφελήκ.

καὶ ὑπολαμβάνειν ἐὰν τούτοις χρῆται ἐμπειρό
3 τερος γενήσεσθαι καὶ φοβερώτερος· καὶ ἐπὶ τοῖς
χρηστοῖς εἰπεῖν Ὡς γίνεται καὶ Ὡς φασιν¹ ⟨καὶ⟩
ὡς οὐδείς ἐστι χρηστός, καὶ ὁμοίους πάντας εἶναι
4 καὶ ἐπισκῶψαι² δὲ Ὡς χρηστός ἐστι. καὶ τὸ
πονηρὸν δὲ εἰπεῖν ἐλεύθερον ἐὰν βούληταί τις εἰς
πεῖραν ἐλθεῖν³· καὶ τὰ μὲν ἄλλα ὁμολογεῖν ἀληθῆ
ὑπὲρ αὐτοῦ λέγεσθαι ὑπὸ τῶν ἀνθρώπων, ἔνια δὲ
ἀγνοεῖσθαι· εἶναι⁴ γὰρ αὐτὸν εὐφυῆ καὶ φιλέταιρον
καὶ ἐπιδέξιον· καὶ διατείνεσθαι δὲ ὑπὲρ αὐτοῦ
5 ὡς οὐκ ἐντετύχηκεν ἀνθρώπῳ ἱκανωτέρῳ. καὶ
εὔνους δὲ εἶναι αὐτῷ⁵ ἐν ἐκκλησίᾳ λόγον διδόντι
ἢ ἐπὶ δικαστηρίου⁷ κρινομένῳ. καὶ πρὸς ⟨τοὺς
παρα⟩καθημένους⁸ δὲ εἰπεῖν δεινὸς ὡς οὐ δεῖ τὸ
ἄνδρα ἀλλὰ τὸ πρᾶγμα κρίνεσθαι⁹· καὶ φῆσαι
αὐτὸν κύνα εἶναι τοῦ δήμου, φυλάττειν¹⁰ γὰρ αὐτὸ
τοὺς ἀδικοῦντας· καὶ εἰπεῖν ὡς Οὐχ ἕξομεν τοὺς
ὑπὲρ τῶν κοινῶν συνεπαχθισθησομένους,¹¹ ἂν τοὺς
τοιούτους προώμεθα. δεινὸς δὲ καὶ προστατῆσαι
6 φαύλων· καὶ συνεδρεῦσαι ἐν δικαστηρίοις ἐπὶ
πονηροῖς πράγμασι· καὶ κρίσιν κρίνων ἐκδέχεσθαι
τὰ ὑπὸ τῶν ἀντιδίκων λεγόμενα ἐπὶ τὸ χεῖρον.¹²

¹ E: V ὡς γίνεται ‖ (sic) καὶ φησὶν   ² Nast: V
-σκῆψαι, but cf. ἐπιχρωνῆν xvi. 2   ³ Naber: V εἰ
π . . . . . : Im. πλέον σκοπεῖν   ⁴ Schn: V ἀγνοεῖν φῆσα
⁵ Meier: V τῷ   ⁶ Diels: V λέγοντι (without λόγον
⁷ Meier: V -ίῳ   ⁸ Foss: V προσκαθήμενος   ⁹ cf. Diog.
L. v. 17 (ἄνθρωπον)   ¹⁰ cf. Alciphr. 2. 16 fin. (3. 19
¹¹ E: V συναχθεσθησ.   ¹² LATE ADDITION: καὶ τὸ ὅλον
φιλοπον⟨ηρ⟩ία ἀδελφή ἐστι τῆς πονηρίας. καὶ ἀληθές ἐστι τὸ τῆς
παροιμίας, τὸ ὅμοιον πρὸς τὸ ὅμοιον πορεύεσθαι

of crime, and suppose that their acquaintance will make him a man of the world and somebody to be afraid of.[a] Over the grave [b] of an honest man he will remark, 'As honesty goes,' or 'So they say,' and add 'No man is honest,' or 'We're all alike'; and when he says 'What an honest fellow,' it is a gibe. He declares of a scoundrel that he is a man of independent character if one shall only try him; and albeit he admits that all they say of him is mostly true, 'there are some things,' says he, 'they do not know; he is a man of parts, a good companion, and able too'; nay, will have it he has never met a more competent being. He is sure, moreover, to take his part when he has to pass scrutiny before the Assembly [c] or stand his trial at law; indeed at such a time he is like to remark to his neighbours, 'We should judge the act and not the person,' and to say that the man is the people's watchdog; for he keeps off evil-doers; and declare 'We shall have nobody to share our burdens for the public good if we throw over such men as this.' He is prone also to stand patron to worthless foreigners; [d] to form juntas on a jury in the support of bad causes; and when he is hearing a case,[e] to take the words of the parties in their worst sense.[f]

[a] For the disgrace attaching to 'evil communications' cf. Diog. L. vi. 6.

[b] For this use of ἐπί cf. Thuc. ii. 34. 8, Dem. 18. 285.

[c] As a magistrate, envoy, or the like.

[d] Resident foreigners were required to have a citizen as guarantor or legal representative.

[e] Certain kinds of cases went before a single judge as with us.

[f] Or accept the evil insinuations of the parties to the suit.

LATE ADDITION :—In fine, Friendship with Rascals is sister to rascality, and true is the saying 'like to like.'

ΑΙΣΧΡΟΚΕΡΔΕΙΑΣ Λ΄

Ἡ δὲ αἰσχροκέρδειά ἐστιν ἐπιθυμία[1] κέρδους
αἰσχροῦ,[2] ἔστι δὲ τοιοῦτος ὁ αἰσχροκερδής, οἶος
ἐστιῶν[3] ἄρτους ἱκανοὺς μὴ παραθεῖναι· καὶ δανεί-
4 σασθαι παρὰ ξένου παρ᾽ αὑτῷ καταλύοντος· καὶ
διανέμων μερίδας φῆσαι δίκαιον εἶναι διμοίρῳ τῷ
5 διανέμοντι δίδοσθαι, καὶ εὐθὺς αὑτῷ νεῖμαι· καὶ
οἰνοπωλῶν κεκραμένον τὸν οἶνον τῷ φίλῳ ἀπο-
6 δόσθαι· καὶ ἐπὶ θέαν τηνικαῦτα[4] πορεύεσθαι ἄγων
τοὺς υἱούς, ἡνίκα προῖκα ἀφιᾶσιν ἐπὶ θέατρον οἱ
7 θεατρῶναι.[5] καὶ ἀποδημῶν δημοσίᾳ τὸ μὲν ἐκ
τῆς πόλεως ἐφόδιον οἴκοι καταλιπεῖν, παρὰ δὲ
τῶν συμπρεσβευτῶν δανείζεσθαι[6]· καὶ τῷ ἀκο-
λούθῳ μεῖζον φορτίον ἐπιθεῖναι[7] ἢ δύναται φέρειν
καὶ ἐλάχιστα ἐπιτήδεια τῶν ἄλλων παρέχειν[8]· καὶ
ἀπὸ τῶν[9] ξενίων δὲ τὸ μέρος τὸ αὑτοῦ ἀπαιτήσας
8 ἀποδόσθαι· καὶ ἀλειφόμενος ἐν τῷ βαλανείῳ[10]
εἰπὼν Σαπρόν γε τὸ ἔλαιον ἐπρίω ὦ παιδάριον,[11]

---

[1] Cob: V (the only ms for §§ 1-4, 14-15, 17-end, introd. p. 12)
περιουσία   [2] Nav. sugg. ⟨καὶ τούτου μικροῦ⟩, cf. Arist. Eth.
N. iv. 3. 1122 a 2 (τούτου written τοῦ and then whole line
of arch. lost by πβλ?)   [3] Cor: V ἐσθίων   [4] V
τηνικαῦτα from text of arch., others ἡνίκ᾽ ἂν δέη from marg.
(old var.), τηνικαῦτα being lost before they were copied
[5] V ἐπὶ θεάτρων, others οἱ θεατρῶναι (i.e. ἐπὶ θέατρον in
marg. arch., whence V's ancestor corrected, incompletely,
οἱ θεατρῶναι): Holl. ἐπιθέατρον, cf. Bull. Corr. Hell. xviii.
120

XXX. MEANNESS

Meanness is the desire of base gain ; [a] and the
Mean man's way is, when he entertains his friends
to a feast, not to set enough bread before them ; to
borrow of a stranger that is staying in his house ; to
say as he carves the meat [b] that the carver deserves
a double portion, and help himself without more
ado ; and when he is selling his wine, to sell it
watered to his friend. He chooses those days to
take his sons to the play when the lessees of the
theatre throw it open for nothing. [c] When he goes
into foreign parts on the public service, he leaves at
home the travel-money given him by the State, and
borrows, as occasion demands, of his fellow-ambas-
sadors ; loads his lackey with a greater burden than
he can well carry, and of all his fellows feeds his
man the worst ; and even demands his share of the
presents they receive, in order to sell them. When
he is anointing himself at the baths he cries 'The
oil you bought, boy, is rancid,' and uses another's.

[a] Perhaps ' in small things ' has fallen out; ' Meanness'
is not quite low enough, but it is not avarice.
[b] At a club dinner or the like, where expenses are shared.
[c] Or perhaps throw open the upper rows for nothing.

164, cent. iii. B.C.   [6] V -βευόντων δανείσασθαι   [7] so V:
others ἐπιθ. μ. φ. (i.e. ἐπιθ. marg. arch.)   [8] some mss
prefer the old variant τῶν ἱκανῶν and some omit παρέχειν
(i.e. ἄλλων παρέχειν marg. arch.)   [9] some mss omit καὶ
ἀπὸ τῶν (lost by πβλ from under τῶν ἱκανῶν)   [10] mss
add καὶ   [11] Reiske: V only παιδ'ρ, others ἐπρίω (from
marg. ?) τῷ παιδαρίῳ (from τῷ ἀλλοτρίῳ below)

E   121

τῷ ἀλλοτρίῳ ἀλείφεσθαι. καὶ τῶν εὑρισκομένων
χαλκῶν ὑπὸ τῶν οἰκετῶν ἐν ταῖς ὁδοῖς[1] δεινὸς
ἀπαιτῆσαι τὸ μέρος, κοινὸν εἶναί φήσας τὸν
10 Ἑρμῆν· καὶ θοἰμάτιον[2] ἐκδοῦναι πλῦναι καὶ
χρησάμενος παρὰ γνωρίμου ἐφελκύσαι[3] πλείους
11 ἡμέρας ἕως ἂν ἀπαιτηθῇ. καὶ τὰ τοιαῦτα·[4]
Φειδωνίῳ[5] μέτρῳ τὸν πύνδακα εἰσκεκρουμένῳ
μετρεῖν αὐτὸς τοῖς ἔνδον σφόδρα δὲ ἀποψῶν τὰ
12 ἐπιτήδεια[7]· ὑποπρίασθαι φίλου[8]· δοκοῦντος πρὸς
13 τρόπου πωλεῖν· ἐπιβαλὼν ἀποδόσθαι. ἀμέλει[9]
δὲ καὶ χρέος[10] ἀποδιδοὺς τριάκοντα μνῶν ἔλαττον
14 τετραδράχμῳ[11] ἀποδοῦναι. καὶ τῶν υἱῶν δὲ μὴ
πορευομένων εἰς τὸ διδασκαλεῖον τὸν μῆνα ὅλον
διὰ τὴν ἀρρωστίαν,[12] ἀφαιρεῖν τοῦ μισθοῦ κατὰ
λόγον, καὶ τὸν Ἀνθεστηριῶνα μῆνα μὴ πέμπειν
αὐτοὺς εἰς τὰ μαθήματα διὰ τὸ θέας εἶναι πολλάς,
15 ἵνα μὴ τὸν μισθὸν ἐκτίνῃ· καὶ παρὰ παιδὸς κομιζό-
μενος ἀποφοράν, τοῦ χαλκοῦ τὴν ἐπικαταλλαγὴν
προσαπαιτεῖν, καὶ λογισμὸν δὲ λαμβάνων παρὰ
16 τοῦ χειρίζοντος ⟨τοῦ ἀργυρίου⟩.[13] καὶ φράτορας
ἑστιῶν αἰτεῖν[14] τοῖς ἑαυτοῦ παισὶν ἐκ τοῦ κοινοῦ
ὄψον, τὰ δὲ καταλειπόμενα ἀπὸ τῆς τραπέζης
ἡμίσεα τῶν ῥαφανίδων[15] ἀπογράφεσθαι, ἵνα οἱ δια-
κονοῦντες παῖδες μὴ λάβωσι. συναποδημῶν δὲ

---

[1] V ὑπὸ τ. οἰκείων ἐν τ. ὁ., others ἐν τ. ὁ. ὑπὸ τ. οἰκετῶν
(i.e. two 11–13 letter lines inverted)   [2] Mein: V ἱμ.
[3] cf. Herodas 2. 9, Long. 3. 5, Plut. Luc. 33   [4] old variant (?) τὰ δὲ δὴ τ.   [5] cf. Arist. Const. Ath. 10 (Φειδωνείων):
mss also φειδομένῳ   [6] E (κ for ιc): most mss ἐκκ.: Ambr.
Ο ἐγκ.   [7] V σφ. δὲ ὑποσπῶν τὰ ἐ., others τὰ ἐ. σφ. ἀποσπῶν
(i.e. σφ. δὲ ἀπ. in marg. arch.)   [8] E: mss ὑποθέω, but
cf. ὑποθέω and ὑποψωνίζω   [9] V omits ἐπιλ. . . .
ἀμέλει, others omit δοκ. . . . πωλ.: V πωλεῖσθαι (see
122

e is apt also, when his servants find ha'pence in the
treets, to cry 'Shares in thy luck!'[a] and claim
is part: and to put out his coat to wash and
orrowing a friend's, keep it for days till it be asked
ack.[b] These things likewise will he do: measure
ut his household's corn with his own hand, using a
heidonian measure[c] with a knocked-in bottom and
triking it off very even; buy a thing over a
iend's head;[d] offer to sell a guessed quantity; sell
bove the market. This fellow, I warrant you, will
ay a debt of fifty pound half-a-crown short; if his
ons go not to school the full month because of the
ickness, will reduce their school-money accordingly;
vill keep them from their lessons all the month of
'ebruary because there are so many festivals, so
hat he may save the fee. Receiving hire-money
rom a servant, he demands the discount on the
opper; and coming to a reckoning with his steward,
equires the premium on the silver.[e] When his
ellow-clansmen dine under his roof he will beg meat
rom the common table for his servants, and yet
iote down the half-radishes left over from the dinner
o prevent the hired serving-men carrying them off.

[a] *Lit.* Hermes (God of gain) is common (to both).
[b] *Cf.* Diog. L. vi. 62.   [c] *i.e.* obsolete (and smaller).
[d] By offering more for it.
[e] The servant works at a trade and pays his owner for the
right to do so; the steward or manager is entrusted with
money from his owner's chest.

(introd. p. 23): ἐπιβαλὼν Ussing: mss ἐπιλαβὼν   [10] V καὶ
χρέη δὲ   [11] sugg. Holl: mss τέτταρσι (τέτρασι) δραχμαῖς
(δραγμαῖς corr. to δραγμῶν B), τετραδράχμῳ in marg. arch.?
cf. Diog. L. ii. 34   [12] some epidemic; or read τιν'?
[13] E, *sc.* τὴν ἐπικαταλλαγήν   [14] V omits καὶ and ἐστ. αἰτ.
[15] V ῥαφ. ἡμίσεα: ἡμιρραφανίδια?

17 μετὰ γνωρίμων χρήσασθαι τοῖς ἐκείνων παισί, τὸ
δὲ ἑαυτοῦ ἔξω μισθῶσαι καὶ μὴ ἀναφέρειν εἰς τ
κοινὸν τὸν μισθόν. ἀμέλει δὲ καὶ συναγόντων παρ
18 ἑαυτῷ ὑποθεῖναι τῶν παρ᾽ ἑαυτοῦ δεδομένω
ξύλων καὶ φακῶν καὶ ὄξους καὶ ἁλῶν καὶ ἐλαίο
τοῦ εἰς τὸν λύχνον· καὶ γαμοῦντός τινος τῶ
19 φίλων καὶ ἐκδιδομένου θυγατέρα πρὸ χρόνου τινὸ
ἀποδημῆσαι, ἵνα ⟨μὴ⟩[1] προπέμψῃ προσφορὰ
καὶ παρὰ τῶν γνωρίμων τοιαῦτα κίχρασθαι
20 μήτ᾽ ἂν ἀπαιτῆσαι μήτ᾽ ἂν ἀποδιδόντων ταχέω
ἄν τις κομίσαιτο.

[1] Siebenkees

• Cf. Men. Ep. 195 ; Pk. 55.

f he travels abroad with men he knows, he will
make use of their servants and let out his own
without placing the hire-money to the common
account. Should his club meet at his house,[a] need-
ess to say he will put down to the common account
he fuel, lentils, vinegar, salt, and lamp-oil which he
provides.[b] When a friend or a friend's daughter is
o be married, he is like to go into foreign parts
some time before the wedding to avoid the giving
of a present. And all his borrowings from his
acquaintance are such as you would never ask back
nor readily accept the return of were it offered you.

[b] Such things would usually be left out of the reckoning;
for the genitive *cf.* Plat. *Gorg.* ταύτης τῆς εὐεργεσίας δύο
δραχμὰς ἐπράξατο, Xen. *Cyr.* iii. 1. 37 ἀπάγου τοὺς παῖδας
μηδὲν αὐτῶν καταθείς.

INDEX [1]

[1] The dates are those of the *floruit*, *i.e.* about the fortieth year.

THEOPHRASTUS

INDEX

E 2

INDEX

131

GREEK INDEX [1]

[1] containing the principal *cruces*.

132

HERODES, CERCIDAS

AND

THE GREEK CHOLIAMBIC POETS

(EXCEPT CALLIMACHUS AND BABRIUS)

EDITED AND TRANSLATED

BY

A. D. KNOX

LATE FELLOW OF KING'S COLLEGE, CAMBRIDGE

CAMBRIDGE, MASSACHUSETTS
HARVARD UNIVERSITY PRESS
LONDON
WILLIAM HEINEMANN LTD
MCMLXI

PREFACE

My aim has been to group together various writers whose works, from a similarity of metre, are connected with the study of Herodes. With the general literature on Herodes I have recently kept fairly well abreast; and if for other writers there are errors of acknowledgement and oversights I can only plead the schoolboy's argument of *tu quoque*: that every continental writer on Herodes (with the exception of R. Herzog) produces conclusions, readings and illustrations which may be found in the Cambridge edition to which presumably he has not access.[1]

My list of acknowledgements is very large. As to institutions, I owe very much to King's College, which enabled me to work many years unencumbered with duties of teaching: to the Cambridge Press, which has been exceedingly generous in other ways and in the matter of copyright: to the Bodleian Library and British Museum: and to the *Classical Review*, *Philologus* and *Phil. Wochenschrift*, which have enabled me to compress introductions and contro-

---

[1] On the other hand I have not neglected to view all the papyri which I publish. There is one anecdotum below: but I do not publish a photograph, since after having three separate exposures taken I have failed completely to secure a picture which distinguishes between ink and brown discolorations.

versial matter. To individuals my debt is great : far greatest to Mr. Milne of the British Museum, whose extraordinary skill in palaeography has recreated one writer and provided many valuable new readings in others. A similar debt I owe to Mr. Bell, on points of papyrology to Mr. Lamacraft of the British Museum, and on one matter to Prof. W. Schubart. I have had the benefit of discussion on several vital points with Mr. E. Lobel ; and I have to thank for courteous or useful communications Prof. P. Grooneboom, Dr. Hunt, Mr. J. U. Powell, Prof. Crönert of Baden, Prof. Collomp of Strassburg, Sir Frederic Kenyon, and Prof. R. Herzog, and of Cambridge scholars, Mr. E. Harrison, Prof. Pearson, Mr. Rackham, Dr. Nairn, and Prof. Adcock. My main debts to Kenyon and Mr. J. T. Sheppard are of the past : but in this way I owe an even larger debt to the dead, first to Dr. Walter Headlam (Cambridge edition of Herodas, 1922), and secondly to the researches of Dr. Gerhard of Heidelberg. At the last moment I have been fortunate enough to secure the expert assistance of Professor Bilabel of Heidelberg, whose careful work has far outweighed in value the little I could do in a brief stay.

Throughout the authors dealt with present problems of a controversial character, where it is impossible to sit on a fence ; and I have tried to express my views in full elsewhere, and in this book to take a bold and consistent line. For this reason much that has been written helps but little. As most of the writers included are poets or versewriters (too many, I fear, of the second category) and as, after all, the most important raw material of poetry or verse is metre, I have occupied some of

iv

PREFACE

the available space in the discussion of the iambic metre, the various types of which are not yet recognized. For general information on matters of life or philosophical ideas the reader should consult (according to the author) Headlam's notes on Herodes or Gerhard's edition of Phoenix of Colophon. On various archaeological details a small edition of Hero(n)d(a)s by R. Herzog may be consulted : always with the proviso that the author has not yet sufficiently reconsidered many of the errors of Crusius. For all this the text is good and up-to-date. There is an attractive edition of Herodes (Mimes 1-6) by P. Grooneboom.

Other recent work, Italian, French and English, is wholly different. Just as on the great arterial roads of England the traveller by night receives warning of pitfalls by an intricate system of red lamps, so these may serve for warning to the student or editor. But it is unhappily only too possible to see the warning signal and yet to end in the ditch. I have used the translation to give frankly my own idea of the character of the author. Where little metrical skill or individuality is shown I have used prose : where the metre is striking or impressive I have used metre ; and in order to restrain metrical discussion within a reasonable limit have given, in general, the metre of the original. The attempt to reproduce the metrical mastery of Hipponax is, of course, a failure ; and it is impossible to represent the tripping quality of Phoenix' work in a metre so unfamiliar to English ears as the lame iambus (ending with three long syllables). The advantage rests with Cercidas, whose very accurate metre is at the same time of a kind which is or could be used

nowadays, and deserves a metrist of the class of
W. S. Gilbert for translator.[1]

A. D. KNOX.

COURNSWOOD,
    HUGHENDEN,
        BUCKS.

---

[1] Perhaps I may be permitted the luxury of meeting some critics in advance. My translation of Herodes is unlike Spenser from whom I have borrowed many words. But for each mistake I will produce one from Herodes and another from his copyist. The structure of the sentence is often modern : but so is that of Herodes. Again, it is almost unintelligible. But it was two or three years before the Greek scholars of Europe made any headway in the interpretation of Herodes. The spelling adopted is a matter of necessity if we are to suggest the existence of pure Attic words (like δήπουθεν) in an Ionic dress (δήκουθεν): and inconsistency of spelling is necessary in translating an author, who, alone of all Greeks who dealt with every-day speakers, allowed the use of any or every form or scansion of words (*e.g.* κεῖνος, ἐκεῖνος, ὑγίη, ὑγιείη, κτλ.) even from the lips of the vulgar.

Again, I may be accused of giving too many or too few conjectural " supplements " in my text. My principle has been to complete standard phrases and insert necessary particles and formations of words. Further, the text of Herodes, at least, has not so much been read by palaeographers as guessed by scholars ; and where subsequent investigation by palaeographers has found many confirmatory traces, I give the whole guess. To give less would be sheer pedantry.

CONTENTS

CONTENTS

viii

CONTENTS

LIST OF ABBREVIATIONS

Bgk. = Bergk
Schnw. = Schneidewin
Cr. = Crusius
Wilam. = Wilamowitz
Kal. = Kalinka
P. = The Papyrus
R. = Rutherford
Mn. = Milne
K. = Kenyon
Hdl. = Headlam
Buech. = Buecheler
Bl. = Blass
M. = Meister

F.D. = quis (?)
C.E. = Cambridge Edition
  of Herodes
Herw. = Herwerden
J. = H. Jackson
Hg. = R. Herzog
H. = Hunt
A. = von Arnim
G. = Gerhard
Bi. = Bilabel
K.-Bi.: see page 229
Byz. = Byzantine version
Arm. = Armenian ver-
  sion
Müll. = Müller (Carolus)

GENERAL INTRODUCTION

OF the authors whose remains are collected below, and apart from the writers of one or two isolated fragments, Herodes possesses for us still the greatest interest. Yet this interest is in the main due partly to a misconception and partly to a mere chance. It is chance that has presented to us a papyrus which in length and preservation is unmatched except by those of Hyperides, Aristotle (*Resp. Ath.*) and Bacchylides. It was chance that gave the papyrus to the modern world before the lesser and incomplete papyri of Menander. And it is a malign chance that has given us Herodes when we might have had so much more of Hipponax or Callimachus' Iambi, or the whole of Cercidas' meliambi. This introduction is forced to view and measure other writers from the standpoint of Herodes : but this is merely because we live " not as we wish but as chance drags us," not because there should now be any misapprehension as to the merits of Herodes' work.

By common consent one of the greatest of Greek poets was Hipponax,[1] who was the founder of chol-

[1] His remains were collected by Welcker in a volume easily accessible. Others were added from a British Museum ms. of Tzetzes by Musgrave, by Herwerden and from an Etymologicum by Reitzenstein. The best collection is in

iambi[1]: for though this title was often given to
Ananius of whom we know nothing, yet
HIPPONAX the absurdity of Ananius' metre and the
and
ANANIUS poverty of his fragments prevent us from
considering his claim in any serious sense.
Hipponax wrote in a simple adaptation of the Ionic
plain iambus of his date, merely substituting a
final spondee for the final iambus of Archilochus.
The metre has always been misunderstood and
confounded with the iambus of Attic tragedy with
which it has nothing in common.

The metre was invented to suit the exceptional
bitterness of the man. Of his life we are fairly well
Life of informed. He was (Suid. *s.v.*) πατρὸς
HIPPONAX Πύθεω (whence Metriche's parentage in
Hrd. Mime I.). His mother was Protis.
A native of Ephesus [2] he was expelled by its tyrants
and went to Clazomenae.[3] His enmity with the
Bergk's *Poetae Lyrici Graeci*: and the best abbreviated
edition in Hoffmann's *Griechische Dialecte*, iii. p. 135 (including Reitzenstein's addenda). A long but not very able
discussion of the fragments is given by ten Brink in early
numbers of *Philologus*.

[1] Greek verse is measured by length of syllables, not by
stress (like English). The mark ∪ is for a short, − for a
long syllable. Breaks (*i.e.*, end of sense groups) are
marked |. The iambic metre of Hipponax' date was
≍−∪−≍ | −∪ | −∪−∪−, or ≍−∪−≍ | −∪ | −≍− | ∪−.
One or both of the first breaks are sufficient. Hipponax'
metre is ≍−∪−≍ | −∪ | −∪−−−, the two breaks being
again alternative. There is some evidence for ≍−∪−≍ |
−∪−≍ | −−−. The first two syllables are ≍−, but there
is slight evidence that he may also have permitted himself
∪∪∪ or −∪. Such substitutions are alleged in other
places, but the evidence proves worthless. See *Journal of
Cambridge Philological Society*, 1927, for a full discussion.

[2] Callim. *Iamb. passim*, Strabo, p. 642, Clem. Al. i. 308.

[3] So Sulpicia, *v.* 6.

sculptors Bupalus and Athenis is derived from the
insulting statues of him which they made. He must
have lived about 550 B.C. (Pliny, *N.H.* xxxvi. 5).
He is said by the author of the *Ibis* and a commentator on Horace (*Epod.* 6. 14) to have committed
suicide : but their accounts do not tally. In person
he was small, thin and ugly (Ael. *V.H.* x. 6), but
strong (Ath. 552 c).

Such details are in themselves unimportant Even
the scanty fragments show that the quarrel with
Bupalus was due not to the studied distortions of the
latter's art, but to the natural attractions of his
mistress, for whom Hipponax conceived an infatua-
tion. But they are evidence if not of the popularity,
at least of the great fame alike of his works and of
his very unpleasant character. This fame is further
attested by four epitaphs. That of Philippus (*A.P.*
vii. 405) scarcely deserves quotation : Alcaeus (of
Mitylene), *ib.* vii. 536, gives us little : Theocritus' (in
choliambics) is given below. Leonidas (*ib.* vii. 408)
adds one detail :—

> Ἀτρέμα τὸν τύμβον παραμείβετε, μὴ τὸν ἐν ὕπνῳ
> πικρὸν ἐγείρητε σφῆκ' ἀναπαυόμενον·
> ἄρτι γὰρ Ἱππώνακτος ὁ καὶ τοκέωνε[1] βαΰξας
> ἄρτι κεκοίμηται θυμὸς ἐν ἡσυχίῃ.
> ἀλλὰ προμηθήσασθε· τὰ γὰρ πεπυρωμένα κείνου
> ῥήματα πημαίνειν οἶδε καὶ εἰν Ἀίδῃ.

" Quietly pass by the tomb lest ye rouse the bitter
wasp that rests there. For but lately has rest been
found and quiet for the soul of Hipponax that barked
even at his parents. But beware : even in Hades
can his fiery words injure." [2]

---

[1] So W. Headlam for τοκεωνεια.
[2] The allusion (?) in [Archil.] 80 (D.) is too doubtful and
fragmentary.

GENERAL INTRODUCTION

The subject of so much curiosity and admiration, who inspired two of the world's greatest poets, Callimachus and Catullus, has left us a mere hundred verses or so. We owe them to the collection of a son of one who copied his style (Lysanias, son of Aeschrion). This book we have not: we only have some few verses quoted by Athenaeus, sometimes misquoted, often misattributed, and usually corrupt. Even some grammarians, like those on whose work Hesychius' dictionary rests, had very poor texts; though the Etymology has preserved us one or two fine and vigorous lines. Later Tzetzes, out of mere passion for the obscure, has preserved in his commentaries several quotations, haphazard, inaccurate and corrupt: we can still thank him for his habit of quoting complete lines and sense which has preserved for us of the poet far more than we otherwise might have had.

Fate of HIPPONAX' works

Beyond the shadowy name of Ananius we know nothing—perhaps there is nothing to be known of Hipponax' immediate successors. It may be held for certain that for the period when Athens ruled supreme over Greek literary taste the metre and manner was disused. The development of Greek literature was entirely in a different direction. There is indeed one remark in Aristophanes which shows that even at Athens these two writers had some readers: but it is perhaps even more remarkable that the poet makes an error in attribution.

Disuse of the metre

Simultaneously with the fall of Athens as a power, the old styles, subjects, metres and dialects were revived; but with the curious and wholly typical

Greek rule that these four ingredients must never
The
Revival be used in the exact and original manner.
It is true that until the third century A.D.
a certain weak reminiscence of the
Ephesian sixth-century dialect still flavours the
writings of those who employ this metre; and the
gradual relapse from this dialect is perhaps the
surest test of date. The metre of Hipponax was
wholly misunderstood and some writers substituted
the rhythms of Attic tragedy, preserving only the
final spondaic foot. Even Callimachus, who is the
nearest to Hipponax, does not fully represent him:
and Catullus, the Latin poet who copies Archilochus
faithfully, wholly deserts the Ephesian model. As
far as subjects go, it is impossible to draw any lines.
The metre was used for short poems on all subjects
by Phoenix, for dramatic idylls by Herodes, for
mythology or the like by Apollonius Rhodius and
Pseudo-Callisthenes, for fables by Babrius,[1] for
literary controversy by Callimachus,[1] for the introduction to a moralist anthology by [pseudo-]
Cerkidas, and in isolated epigrams by Theocritus
and Aeschrion. Of some of these a few words may
be said.

Aeschrion is said on doubtful authority to have
been a younger contemporary of Alexander. His
The writers
of the
revival,
AESCHRION son Lysanias may be the same as the
author of a book on the writers of choliambics, and this Lysanias a pupil of
Eratosthenes: the son then can hardly
have been born before 260 B.C. In this case it

---

[1] Not included here. I hope to help to revise Callimachus'
Iambi from the papyrus, a task which has not been attempted
since Hunt.

is a little difficult to accept the statement which Suidas gives on the authority of "Nicander" but is generally supposed to rest only on that of Ptolemaeus Chennus. But there appears to be no good grounds for refusing to place his floruit in the first years of the third century B.C. Some of his writings called *Ephemerides* concerned Alexander and may have been written in hexameters (Tz. *Chil.* viii. 404): others, whether on this or other subjects, were in choliambics and marked by extreme frigidity.

Perhaps a somewhat younger contemporary was Phoenix of Colophon. We are told by Pausanias

PHOENIX

i. 9. 7, that when Lysimachus destroyed Colophon its dirge was sung by Phoenix. It may be hoped that his dirge did not resemble the plea for Thebes which Pseudo-Callisthenes puts in the mouth of Ismenias the flute-player. He may have written as early as 280 B.C. He made no effort to copy the metre of Hipponax; his metre depends normally on the Athenian stage writers. But his short poems possess a certain tinkling elegance and follow closely the Alexandrine method of clothing in new garb hackneyed themes. The short moralistic excerpt quoted in the Anthology of [Cercidas] is considered by Gerhard [1] to display cynicizing tendencies: but it contains nothing which might not have been prompted by a normal indignation against war profiteers. We cannot conjecture what may have prompted Aeschrion (of Samos or Mitylene) to use this metre: but if Phoenix followed his compatriots

[1] In his magnificent collection *Phoinix von Kolophon* (Teubner, 1909), which must be consulted for references to the literature on these writers.

to the enlarged city of Ephesus his model was near
at hand ; and this accident may well have been the
reason which brought the metre into wide promin-
ence.   More probable is his intimate connexion with
Attica, which is now suggested by a coincidence in
his fourth poem.   It is, like his other poems, a brief
piece of about thirty verses, apparently an elegy on
Lynceus.   With Professor Crönert we could identify
Lynceus with Lynceus of Samos, a contemporary of
Menander, mentor of the young Poseidippus (Meineke, *Com. Gr.* i. p. 458) and writer of Attic comedy,
and further, identify Poseidippus of frag. 3 with the
comic writer and make Phoenix somewhat junior to
Menander.   We may, I think, go further and identify
with certainty the Strassburg papyrus from which
this poem is taken as containing some later sheets of
the " Cercidean " anthology.

Callimachus (who lived at Alexandria, 260–240),
Theocritus (more or less his contemporary)
and Apollonius Rhodius, who long outlived his instructor Callimachus, need no
introduction.   Theocritus and Apollonius
perhaps wrote hardly anything in this metre.   The
same may be true of Asclepiades of Samos who
ranks in time with the two first-named.   Of Diphilus,[1]
Parmeno and Hermeias of Curion we *know* nothing
whatever.   Others, like Alcaeus of Messene,[2] have
left nothing in this metre.   We may pass on to two
writers for us far more important and more dis-
putable.

The age of Cercidas[3] of Megalopolis, once a matter

Other names

---

[1] Gerhard, *op. cit.* pp. 211 *sqq.*
[2] *Ib.* p. 226.
[3] *Ib.* p. 206.

GENERAL INTRODUCTION

of dispute, is now fairly well known. The attack on CERCIDAS a disciple of Sphaerus, and the apparent censure of Stoicism as having degenerated since Zeno, would encourage us to place Cercidas in the second half of the third century B.C., when we know a famous Sphaerus to have been one of the diadochi of Zeno. In antiquity Cercidas, who had great weight in the councils of his country, was famed even above other learned poets for his literary enthusiasms. He hoped after his death to meet Pythagoras, Hecataeus, Olympus and Homer: the first two books of Homer were to be buried with him. Above all he appears passionately devoted to the Catalogue (Book II.): and the children of his city were compelled to learn it by heart. He boasts of his early devotion to the Muses: and it is no very wild guess that the anthology of which we have an introduction in choliambics comes from his selection. This theme I have developed in a separate book.[1] Whether he is actually the author of the sorry verses which formed the introduction thereto is another question. There is little doubt that Gregory of Nazianzus attributes them to him: but equally there is little doubt that the clumsy and almost random inanities are wholly unworthy of the skilled and competent metrist of the meliambs. If they are by him they are merely some juvenile epistolary doggerel preserved by Parnos to whom they are addressed: if not, they are an anonymous introduction to his collection. Wholly different from these are the meliambi. For the most part these are

[1] *First Greek Anthologist*, Cambridge, 1923. It may now be dated, on palaeographical grounds, as little later than 250 B.C. See below on the Strassburg fragment of Phoenix: also for the metres of Phoenix and [Cercidas].

metrically a clever and vigorous combination of the iambic and hexameter metres, each managed in the strictest and most graceful fashion. Whatever view be taken of their contents, in the narrower sense of the word style they are masterpieces. To our taste they suffer merely from their Alexandrinism : that is from the adaptation to one purpose of a form [1] designed for another use : the bombastic verbiage proper in a comedian or the writer of a mock cookery-book appears ill to become the gravity of a quite serious philosophy of life : and the excellent technique seems to detract from the seriousness of the writer.

Last—except for the verses in pseudo-Callisthenes [2] and some isolated epigrams—Herodes or Herodas.

HERODES : his date
The position of Herodes is an enigma to moderns. His immediate audience was the literary world of Alexandria and Attica in the middle of the third century B.C. Even this may be said with hesitation. There are several words and ideas which appear to belong to a later literature and life. The mention of an artistic idea—the Boy and the Goose [3]—associated with Boethus, an artist of the second century A.D., with these may be urged in support of a theory which, while allowing that his mimes were written *about* the third century B.C., would hold that they were written

---

[1] So too the use of Doric dialect (of a conventional kind) for Ionic metres.

[2] See below.

[3] In this matter Dr. Grooneboom says that the Boy and Goose cannot be derived from Boethus' famous statue because Herodes is earlier. But it would be fairer to say that this is *pro tanto* an argument for a later date for Herodes.

about a time long since past, and suffer, like Shakespeare's plays, from anachronisms. If, as appears to be the case, Professor Herzog has rightly identified the temple of Aesculapius at Cos with one which was replaced about 200 B.C., even so it would be just possible to suppose that the IVth mime rested on literary guide-books. The one solid argument against such a theory is that at no other time would such a method of writing have been tolerated or considered : that there are certain considerations which connect the VIIIth mime (Herodes' Introduction) with a similar poem by Callimachus in the same metre; and that such a connexion is incredible in a considerably later writer. Again, on the artistic side in Mime IV. there appear to be allusions to artistic feuds that at a later period may have been buried, and *v.* 25 suggests a date before 270 B.C.

It is useless to discuss further a theory which is rarely if ever heard now; except as a protest against too ready assumption that Herodes' date is, within limits, *certain.*[1]

Of his art many misconceptions are current. The recovery of parts of Mime VIII. should surely dispel these. Herodes puts on realism or doffs it with

---

[1] The only certain date is the superior date. It must have been possible to use the phrase 'demesne of the θεοὶ ἀδελφοί.' Prof. Herzog has adduced reasons for believing that the phrase may have been used of the first Ptolemy (Soter) and his consort. In the other direction we get no result. Queen Anne's Mansions tower to-day over St. James' Park; and Queen Anne (like St. James) is dead. If we could be certain that Stobaeus took over the citations of Herodes in his anthology from the old Cercidean anthology, we could be quite certain of a date before 240 B.C.

his subject. Mime I. is no more, or less, realistic
than the Middle or New Comedy : Mime II.
His art is sheer parody—which is very different.
Mimes III., IV., V. and VI. have a sort of realism
due to their being borrowed from the mime of
Sophron.[1] Mime VII. is a scene out of Middle
Comedy. Mime VIII. is a purely personal—even
sentimental fantasy. The treatment is, as literary
drama, magnificent : and may even be compared
favourably with that of Lucian, whose methods in
his dialogues are exactly parallel. Where Herodes
suffers is in his Alexandrine mannerisms.
His style He must at all costs be bookish and removed wholly from common life and common idiom.
Apart from his subjects (dubious, perhaps, but artist-
ically well-chosen) and his skilful miniature-work,
his whole idea is obscurantist. Lucian, it is true,
makes his hussies speak in pure Attic : but that was
intelligible and familiar to his literary audience.
Herodes' whole process is one of distortion. The
vocabulary is taken from the Attic drama. The
structure of the sentence is Attic. Over this is laid
a thick coating of Ionic forms taken perhaps largely
from corrupt mss of Hipponax. His metre is the
more or less loose metre of Attic tragedy, not of
old Ionic : with variations and licences introduced
arbitrarily. Even so Herodes' metrical talent is
too small for his task. He is compelled to mix
Attic and Ionic forms to suit his metre. A passion
for alliteration has the same distressing result. Even
with all these loosenesses his metrical ability is

[1] At the same time it must be noticed that in IV. we have
serious art criticism, not the sillinesses of the poor woman who
is supposed to be speaking.

at fault: and he is compelled constantly to distort sentences in such a manner that all illusion of real conversation is lost—still more all illusion of the plain simple tongue of vulgar folk. Where we might expect plain speech, we find a mass of literary allusions with difficulty woven into an unmetrical metre by the medium of an unreal, unstable and imaginary dialect. When Sappho wrote she turned the speech of those about her into poetry of beauty: when Herodes wrote he took the stuff of literature and converted it into a thing of ugliness.[1]

---

[1] The question of criticism of Herodes may be put very briefly. (*a*) The huge notes of Walter Headlam clearly reveal the numerous literary sources which Herodes employs. (*b*) But the negative argument which Headlam never expressed is far stronger. All Greek writers who took their language from the spoken language of one city used an exact and unvarying dialect. When Herodes, as in IV. 72 *sqq.*, uses the variant forms κεῖνος and ἐκείνου in one sentence spoken by one uneducated person he is using an imaginary and unreal language. And this instance is only one of a thousand. In real language, for example, 'doubtful quantities' do not occur. Where then a word-architect is so utterly careless in the choice of his main materials—where he romances about his words—it is idle to pay any attention to his facts. Archaeology has its uses in discovering the *latest* date at which he can have written: it has still failed to discover ἡ τύραννος of Ephesus and solve many other problems. But it will never convince anyone who has studied the regularities of the Attic comedians or many early poets that we have anything but a centoist *littérateur* writing for effect and with no eye on accuracy of speech, facts or details. Just as we know that Herodes' Ephesian boots came out of an Athenian bootmaker's, so at any moment his coins, statues, feasts, chronology or topography may be Attic or Ionic rather than Coan, or again Attic or Coan rather than Ionic. If anyone seriously believes Herodes to be a painter from life they must first make his speech realistic: expel all doubtful syllables, standardize

xxii

GENERAL INTRODUCTION

When Menander writes we can see an Athenian speaking plain and natural Attic. When Herodes

Detailed errors

writes we see an alleged Coan speaking in an Ionic dialect with many Attic phrases, and his sayings twisted into a clumsy metre. When Herodes tries to hint at a vulgarism he fails grotesquely. His proverbs are often misapplied : and from misunderstanding of the proverb-dictionary (such as had been collected by Aristotle, Theophrast and doubtless others) he either inserts words belonging to the dictionary, as ὁμοίως ᾽τὸν σίδηρον τρώγουσιν,᾽ and (μὴ) πρός τε (? καὶ πρός γε) ᾽κυσός᾽ φησὶ ᾽χὠ τάπης,᾽ or omits words quite essential to the phrase as belonging to the explanation—*e.g.* in κατὰ μυὸς ὄλεθρον he appears to divide **κατὰ μυός·** ὄλεθρον.[1] Quite impossible, in vulgar mouths, are such contortions as ἀλλὰ μὴ βροντέων αὐτὸς σὺ τρέψῃς μέζον ἐς φυγὴν ἡμέας, φέρειν ὅσας ἂν . . . σθένῃ and the like.

Such points are important when we consider the question of Herodes' home, and the period of his

his use of elisions, of ν ἐφελκυστικόν, insist that he should always write ἑῶν (or ἐῶν)—not just as suits his metre, rule out (as Meister did) all Attic forms, cut out all constructions that savour too much of Attic, and rewrite the Coan mimes in a Dorian dialect. When this task is completed they can prove that Herodes' borrowings from previous authors (unread by Coan schoolboys and bawds) are really pure coincidences. Then we shall consider their claims seriously. There is no evidence whatever of influence of the Κοινή, and the one Alexandrinism πάλι is probably a corruption.

[1] This, I think, is the solution of these strange difficulties : in my text and translation I have made the minimum corrections which give any sort of sense.

writing.   As to the first we may have his own word for

it that he was Athenian; for the only clue in Mime VIII. is where he says ' as we do at the Dionysia'; and the rite described is one which *in all literature* is associated with the Athenian villages alone.[1] He may have visited Cos (Mimes I.-IV.): perhaps he was familiar with Ephesus (V.-VII.). In either case there were literary reasons for placing his scenes at the homes of Philetas or Hipponax. It is not impossible that he may have lived at Ephesus, since in the Coan mime IV. he is careful to call the nomad Apelles an Ephesian. But his actual home is a matter of no moment whatever; though one would like to think that Mime II. was taken from a dull day's duty in the Attic courts, literary evidence is conclusive that it is mere parody of orators wholly or partially accessible to us. What is important to notice is that among the writers of the third century who used this metre, hardly any are pure Alexandrines. There is a far closer connexion with Attica. Phoenix is the friend of writers of Attic comedy.[2] Aeschrion defends a lady of Athenian ill-fame against an Athenian attack. Moschine, an Athenian lady (*Philologus*, lxxxi. p. 247), used this metre. Even the use of the metre for the *short* poem may be due less to Alexandrine canons than to the practice of Hipponax. Only the use of an old form for new ideas remains typically Alexandrine. Cercidas is a Megapolitan and follower (presumably) of Ananius. So we are left only with Callimachus, whose protests seem to be directed against the Atticism of Hipponax' followers.

[1] The Ptolemies introduced Attic rites into Alexandria: but climatic data preclude an Alexandrian scene.

[2] If the view given on p. xvii is right.

The popularity of this metre in the first three centuries A.D.[1]—extending even to the discovery of Herodes whom his contemporaries failed to notice—is perhaps partly due to its use by Roman poets. We have (besides Babrius) a few epigrams in quite vulgar style. Again, the choliambic metre, still more the second half of the verse, was commonly used in proverbs : and collectors tended to twist well-known quotations into this form. On the other hand these were again likely to degenerate into pure iambics ; and it is quite unsafe to take any of these as belonging even probably to early writers.

Late writers

Hipponax perished save as a quarry for the lexicographer and the pedant-poet. Herodes and Phoenix were barely known and little read. The paltry verses of pseudo-Cercidas were known only from their position at the head of a school-thumbed Anthology. Callimachus' Iambi are the least quoted, and now probably the least read of his works. Babrius' fables alone attained a wide public. But those who think of Greek writers as exclusively ' classics,' and ' classics ' as necessarily ' high-brow,' and vaguely picture a cultured antiquity which read the private speeches of Demosthenes without fear of impositions, or the *Electra* of Sophocles except at the risk of the birch, should study carefully the doggerel which is the basis of at least one-third of the pseudo-Callisthenic life of Alexander. For these are surely the worst verses, in every respect except that of metre, that

The Life of Alexander

---

[1] From 230 B.C. to about A.D. 100 there is a total eclipse of the metre. The revival is due to the popularity of the metre in Latin.

were ever written : bereft of humour, pathos, sense, truth, style and elegance. Despite considerable efforts I have been unable in my translation to avoid flattering them. Yet the work which was based on them, the life of Alexander, was edited and re-edited again and again by the Greeks : there was even a rendering into Byzantine politic verse. There was a popular Latin version. The Armenian read a literal translation of the doggerel. Persian and Syrian, Arabian and Ethiopian knew the book in their own tongue.[1] Early manuscripts of the more popular recensions, unread and uncollated, litter the libraries of Europe. Possessing no other quality except that they were easy to read, they had a circulation comparable with that of a modern novel. It is not inconceivable that these rhetorical ineptitudes and childish fables between the third and twelfth centuries A.D. reached a public as large as that which was attained by any other book except those of the New Testament.

[1] For references see Kroll, Introd. p. x.

HIPPONAX AND ANANIUS

INTRODUCTION

ONE difficulty in the study of Hipponax is the question of authenticity. Early editions usually contained a number of 'Hipponactean' verses of various length and rhythms having little but this in common that the final foot was a spondee (– –) or a trochee. But the various metrists who quote these do not profess that they come from the works of Hipponax, and Bergk (*P.L.G.*⁴) though giving the majority of them with asterisks rejected one as ' obviously a mere invention ¹' (p. 491) χαῖρ᾽ ὦ σὺ Λεσβικὰ Σαπφώ, and E. Diehl in his *Anthologia Lyrica* rightly follows Bücheler in omitting many more. For the sake of completeness I give the fragments in the order and with the numeration of Bgk.⁴, but without reference:

(1 inc.) *89 Ἑρμῆ μάκαρ, κάτυπνον οἶδας ἐγρήσσειν (so ten Brink): " Blest Hermes to awake sleepers knowing."

90 εἴ μοι γένοιτο παρθένος καλή τε καὶ τέρεινα. This verse is actually called τοῦ Ἱππώνακτος (Hephaest. 30 *al.*): but there can be little doubt that this is a slip for Ἱππωνάκτειον.

*91 ὁ Κιθαιρὼν Λυδίοισιν ἐν χοροῖσι Βακχῶν (so Gaisford-Bgk.).

---

¹ But ten Brink may be right in attributing it to Diphilus' play in which Hipponax was a character.

2

*92 καὶ κνίσῃ τινὰ θυμιήσας.

*93 ο θεοι τα λοινα τανταλοιο δοντες (Plotius 280):
it is not worth attempting to find an acceptable
reading for this or for

*94 πιcηνπαcαντεc (Plotius 293). Neither give as
they stand the metre which Plotius professes to
illustrate. Bk. rightly rejects them.

To these may be added without hesitation the
example of the ordinary choliambus given by Plotius
and Juba (ap. Rufin de Metr. Com. p. 386):

*13 ἀκούσατ' Ἱππώνακτος οὐ γὰρ ἀλλ' ἥκω. For we
know that this is the first verse of Callimachus' iambi.
Callimachus perhaps imitates Phoenix fr. 1. 15:
but οὐ γὰρ ἀλλά though an Atticism is common in the
later choliambists. Clearly it could not have been
used by Hipponax. See Callim. fr. 92 Schneider.
It is never attributed to Hipponax.

With this Bergk gives (2 Inc.) ὦ Κλαζομένιοι,
Βούπαλος κατεινε or καθηινε, e.g. τε κἄθηνις (Ργk.):
'Ye Clazomenians, Bupalus (and Athenis'). It
is quite possible that this verse is by Hipponax:
but the reading is wholly uncertain and it may well
be that Putsch the editor of Plotius was right in
supposing it to be a mere variant of Hippon. fr.
11. (Bgk.⁴) ὡς οἱ μὲν ἀγεῖ Βουπάλῳ κατηρῶντο. It is
quite possible that the two verses quoted by Rufinus
both come (as Bergk thought) from the same poet,
but that this poet is Callimachus.

Callimachus in his iambi professedly follows
Hipponax, saying that all those who wish to write
'lame' iambi must beg light from Ephesus. And
this would justify us if there were no evidence to the
contrary in supposing that in simple details the model
is the same as the copy. Now Callimachus rigorously

avoids the spondee (– –) in the fifth foot, and besides
this we have the direct testimony of Tzetzes and
others. If, therefore, it is true that Hipponax too
did so, Hephaestion the metrist when he was seeking
for an example of the spondee in the fifth foot would
have gone elsewhere ; and we need not allow our
judgement to be influenced by the anonymous citation (Bgk. 48* : Hephaest. 31. *Inc.* 3) εἰς ἀκρὸν ἕλκων
ὥσπερ ἀλλᾶντα ψύχων (l. ψήχων: ' as one that strokes
a sausage, drew tipward ')—the more so as ὥσπερ is
doubtful in early Ionic. The writer may be Herodes
since it is easy to take the words *in malam partem*.
No such disability attaches to the other example
quoted of the long fifth foot in Plotius (273) (Bgk. 44 :
Inc. 4) αναβιος (l. ἀνὰ δρίος : Simmias *fr.* 20, 15
(so Powell), *Lyr. Adesp.* 7, p. 185 in Powell's *Collectanea Alexandrina*) πλάνητι προσπταίων κώλῳ,
'stumbling about the dell with leg errant'; and
the example might be a mere mistake since the
syllable πταῖ- might be short. Quite possibly it is
from another writer : indeed it would be very
attractive to place it after *v.* 67 of Herodes' Mime
VIII. In fact it will be found on examination that
no satisfactory instance of a certain spondee in the
fifth foot occurs except in proper names : for a fuller
discussion see elsewhere. There is yet another
violation of Porson's law, this time as applied to
the beginning of a trochaic tetrameter in *fr.* 78*
(Hephaest. 34 : *Inc.* 5), Μητροτίμῳ [1] δηὖτέ με χρὴ τῷ
σκότῳ δικάζεσθαι, ' with Metrotimus runagate must

---

[1] The flaw could be removed by reading Μητρότιμε ; and
it would be strange were the runaway to possess such an
honourable name.

4

INTRODUCTION

I to law once more,' and it may be noticed that
this is again from the metrist Hephaestion (p. 34):
though ὁ σκότος (*tenebrio* Meineke) is, it is true,
found in an authentic fragment of Hipponax (51
Bgk.⁴). It is probably actually from Hipponax, but
may need alteration. With some misgivings I have
included certain anonymous citations (*e.g.* 61 Bgk.),
since this is attributed to ' one of the old iambists '
by grammarians : and it is certain that many grammarians had easy access to copies of Hipponax'
works and cared little for other writers in this metre.
But for them we should have little or no accurate
knowledge of what the poet did write.

It might be supposed that three citations in the
anthologist Stobaeus might help us. For what he has
preserved for us is, as far as text goes, fairly good.
But by some singular and unfortunate accident all
the passages which he attributes to Hipponax are
from other authors. As to two of these no serious
doubt exists. One is in a plain iambic metre of a
type at this time certainly non-existent. It runs
(Stobaeus lxxii. 5 : 72 Bgk., who agrees with Meineke
in attributing it to Hippothoon) :

> Γάμος κράτιστός ἐστιν ἀνδρὶ σώφρονι
> τρόπον γυναικὸς χρηστὸν ἔνδον λαμβάνειν·
> αὕτη γὰρ ἡ προὶξ οἰκίαν σώζει μόνη.
> ὅστις δὲ †τρυφῶς† τὴν γυναῖκ' ἄγει λαβών
> συνεργὸν οὗτος ἀντὶ δεσποίνης ἔχει,
> εὔνουν, βεβαίαν εἰς ἅπαντα τὸν βίον.

In *v.* 2 Haupt suggested ἔδνον. In *v.* 4 if τρυφῶσαν [1]
be read we must, of course, assume with Meineke a

---

[1] Better ἀτρύφερον perhaps. The first four verses all
contain rhythms impossible in any early Ionic writer.

hiatus, perhaps even allot the last two verses to
another author, and the sense is :

> Best marriage is it for a prudent man
> To take as dower a noble character :
> This bridal gift alone can save the house.
> But whoso takes to wife a spendthrift girl
>
> .   .   .   .   .   .
>
> He finds a helpmeet, not a mistress stern :
> A kind and true companion to the end."

Nor has another of Stobaeus' attributions found
any defenders : *Flor.* xxix. 42 (Bgk. 28 : *Inc.* 6) runs :
χρόνος δὲ φευγέτω σε μηδὲ εἷς[1] ἀργός. Apostolius
the collector of proverbs gives it as Δημώνακτος.
Style and subject are most akin to [Cercidas] : see
below. The sense is ' Let not one moment pass thee
by idle.' A third again seems equally unsound, and
has, like the foregoing, been generally rejected :

> Δύ᾽ ἡμέραι γυναικός εἰσιν ἥδισται[2]
> ὅταν γαμῇ τις κάκφέρῃ τεθνηκυῖαν (Bgk. 29 : *Inc.* 7),

' Two days in life of woman are sweetest, when she
is wed, and when she is buried.' These verses in a
Berlin anthology (P. 9773) recently discovered
(*Berliner Klassiker Texte* v. 2. 130) are attributed (the
lemma is very fragmentary) to . . . λυ . . . . s. Unhappily this does not quite remove all doubt. Professor Schubart has very kindly sent me a sketch of
the traces, pointing out that α is as likely as λ. σ as
against ν does not seem wholly certain. In the
jumbling of citations common to all Anthologies it is
possible that these verses were out of order and

---

[1] μηδὲ εἷς is Sicilian Doric, borrowed in Attic Comedy.
Hipponax would have divided μὴ δείς.

[2] Compare *Com. Fr. Adesp.* p. 1224.

INTRODUCTION

attributed to τῆς αὐτῆς or τοῦ αὐτοῦ 'by the same.'
At all events we are justified in leaving it out of
account in any generalization we may hope to make.
But there is one fragment which, though possessing
far higher claims than much which Bergk included,
may be relegated (*Inc.* 9, Meineke, *Anon.* 3) perhaps
to a very late date. It is the history of Hipponax'
discovery of the choliamb which I give from schol.
Heph. p. 214 (C.: for other references see Leutsch
and Schneidewin on Apostolius, viii. 59): . . . ἢ ἀπὸ
γραός τινος Ἰάμβης καλουμένης ἣ πλυνούσῃ συντυχὼν
ὁ Ἱππῶναξ καὶ ἁψάμενος τῆς σκάφης ἐφ᾽ ἧς ἔπλυνεν
ἡ γραῦς τὰ ἔρια ἤκουσε λεγούσης

> ῎Ανθρωπ᾽ ἄπελθε· τὴν σκάφην ἀνατρέπεις

(read -τρέψεις, Tricha p. 9 Herm.). 'Another derivation of the word iambus is from an old woman named
Iambé who was washing clothes when Hipponax came
along. He touched the wash-tub in which she was
washing her woollen clothes, and was met with :

> Hence sir ! you'll overbalance my wash-tub.'

To conclude the list of false fragments Suidas attributes to Hipponax the verse rightly assigned by
Meineke to Aristocles (Choerobosc. in *E.M.* 376. 21
says Aristotle).
(*Inc.* 10) εὐνοῦχος ὢν καὶ δοῦλος ἦρχεν Ἑρμίας.
The iota is short (Choerob.) and the fragment need
not delay us.
But perhaps even greater difficulties attach to those
citations, whose genuineness are undoubted, but
which are given by the Byzantine grammarian
Tzetzes. We cannot do better than to examine his
citations from other authors and select, at hap-

HIPPONAX AND ANANIUS

hazard, a few citations on Lycophron's *Cassandra*. In his citation (*v.* 87) of *Il.* Z 356 εἵνεκ' ἐμεῖο κυνὸς κακομηχάνου the last word really belongs to *v.* 344 (κυν. κακ.), two quotations having been boiled down into one.

On *v.* 39 he quotes ἀνήκεστον λάβεν ἄλγος as ἀν. ἄλγος ἔλαχεν which sheds a curious light on some of the metrical irregularities in his citations of Hipp.

Often his citations are mere rephrasings. On *v.* 175, Pindar's verse (*Pyth.* iv. 436), ὃς πάχει μάκει τε πεντηκόντορον ναῦν κρατεῖ appears as ὅσον π. ναῦς μάκει τε πάχει τε. Just above the same poem *v.* 175 is quoted with two words transposed.

On *v.* 209 Euripides' verse (*Bacch.* 920) is given as καὶ πρόσθε μὲν ἡγεῖσθαι δοκεῖ : Eur. wrote καὶ ταῦρος ἡμῖν πρόσθεν ἡγεῖσθαι δοκεῖς.

On 219-222 Aratus' verses, *vv.* 257-8 and 261-4, are run together and 261 is filled out from . . . ἑπτὰ δὲ κεῖναι to ἑπτὰ δή τοι ταίγε (from 257).

In the very next citation from the first verses of the *Lithica*, ὄϊζυος ἀτρεκὲς ἄλκαρ is cited as ὁ. ἄλκαρ αἰνῆς.

These verses are selected out of the few citations on Lycophron, 1-225. They are probably due to errors of memory or bad writing clumsily corrected. Another source of error was a habit of glossing, on the part of Tzetzes, as probably as of his copyists. Thus in citing (*l.c.*) Pind. *P.* iv. 149 over ἀταρβάκτοιο he wrote ἀφόβου, which duly appears in two codd. as ἀτὰρ ἀφόβου βάκτοιο. On *v.* 176 he cites a fragment of Hesiod, in which the reading we know from other sources to be τέκεν Αἰακὸν. Unfortunately he wrote (how inanely) υἱὸν over Αἰακὸν. So one ms has τέτοκεν υἱὸν, another τέκεν Αἰακὸν Αἰακὸν, and two

8

INTRODUCTION

leave out Αἰακὸν altogether. But the most striking verse in the narrow limits to which I have confined myself is Ap. Rhod. i. 755 τὸν δὲ μεταδρομάδην ἐπὶ Μυρτίλος ἤλασεν ἵππους, which appears (on v. 157) as τῷ δ' ἐπὶ Μυρτίλος (-ῳ) ἐκ στήθους γράφων ἤλασεν ἵππους. As we have a true text we can see that three words are parenthetical. But it is pertinent to ask, when we have no other text, how much of our Hipponax, as editors present it, is really a compound of glosses and parentheses. At any rate when a reading is on two or three accounts unsatisfactory, it is in the highest degree absurd to be satisfied with tinkering at two or three points. We can never be remotely certain of the cause of error. It is clear that in few, if any, of the cases above cited could the original have been restored with the smallest degree of certainty.

There is one hope, although I fear a slight one. It might be that in all these cases Tz., who had presumably no text of Hipp., always copied direct from the source: that is, from older scholia on Lycophron. Up to a point that is true. But these scholia were no doubt cramped and corrupt. Tzetzes had read them, but by no means always did he copy them where they belonged.[1] He was far too cunning and spread his citations over a wide area. Only too often it may be feared he quoted ἐκ στήθους, from memory. Only too often the junctures are invented and words are repeated to fill the gaps in his mnemonic exercises. As he had little metrical ear of his own he often transfers the order of words and gives merely

---

[1] All quotations including the word πάλμυς are presumably from one source: yet examine and see how they are scattered.

a rough notion of what the author conveyed. With
these facts in view we clearly cannot, if we are
honest, profess where there is a small difficulty to
recover the true text. Such corrections as seem to
me absolutely necessary for the sense I give in the
text, but for the most part we must never suppose
that we possess more than an outside chance of
recovering the truth.

For our other resources are slight. Aristophanes,
we are told, and certainly Callimachus and Herodes,
imitated him. But with writers of such genius we
cannot hope to disentangle whole phrases. There
is a profusion of words in Hesychius' dictionary:
but unfortunately the ms of Hipp. from which some
previous Alexandrine scholars took the words was
hopelessly corrupt: and the errors have grown in
transit. Test this where we have a sound text:
what can be made of διοπληητα : ἰσχυροπλήκτην ?

Our finest sources, the Etymologica, taking from
far older scholars, are liable to the corruption of
centuries. Erotian does not quote by verse or preserve the order of the original but subordinates
everything to medical interest. Despite the poor
character, in parts at least, of our mss of Athenaeus,
we might hope much from him. Yet here we are
faced by a strange but significant fact. Two citations
are admittedly second-hand, one from a critic of
Timaeus and one from a work on the (chol)iambo-
graphers: a third which gives two (really three)
passages is clearly from the same source since it
compares a use (of πέλλα) in Hipp. and Phoenix:
another is quoted with a parallel from Ananius (*fr.*
18 : see however p. 85) : a fifth is more probably
from Attic comedy : and we may take leave to

doubt the directness of a sixth[1] which is usually
connected with the second. That so voluminous a
reader should derive at second hand seems to show
that mss of Hipponax at his time were non-existent
or unprocurable. Plutarch appears to have had no
general knowledge of his works. Of other sources
Stobaeus the anthologist gives, as stated, extracts
none of which can conceivably be by Hipp.: and we
are left perhaps with a dozen verses.

To decide questions of dialect and metre on such
evidence is clearly difficult, but fortunately we have
better authority. Callimachus openly professes that
in his iambic he copies the *metre* of Hipponax:
Hephaestion, far our best metrical authority, allows
him great regularity: and even Tzetzes, who disputes
Hephaestion's rulings, can find no evidence against
them worth the name. The solitary dissentient voice
is that of a certain Heliodorus whose total incapacity
may be judged by such of his criticisms on other
authors as Priscian quotes.

It is impossible here to enter into an elaborate
inquiry. Elsewhere I shall show (*a*) that the early
iambus is the most strict of all metres, (*b*) that of
choliambic writers Hipponax alone observes all its
laws in a majority of his verses, (*c*) that of the minority
of verses a large minority are wholly unmetrical on
any standard, and, therefore (*d*) that having cast out
these verses we should not hesitate to remove also
the small minority of cases in which Hipponax appears
to use licences or metrical contrivances not found in

---

[1] There are three single citations, not included in this
collection. One comes to Athenaeus *via* Pamphilus (Bgk.
135), another *via* Hermippus (Bgk. 136), and the third (97)
from Theophrast (p. 87).

11

other Ionic poets. It is far easier to hold the hypothesis that Hipponax was wholly indifferent to metre
than to hold that he foresaw and forestalled contrivances and metres used by Attic poets : especially
as during a third of the long time between Hipponax
and Tzetzes these licences and contrivances were precisely those which were most likely to creep in. Only
after about A.D. 300 is there a probability of corruptions which offend any metrical canon of the iambus.

As we find on close examination [1] that Hipponax
obeys subtle rhythmic tests ; that, except on the direct
statement of metrists whose conclusions in eight cases
out of ten are mistaken, his rhythm is regularity itself;
that he is wholly consistent in his usage of dialectal
forms ; and above all that Callimachus in his carefully
restricted iambi openly claims to copy the example
of Ephesus, we may at least be pardoned if we prefer
the testimony of the poet-scholar of the third century
B.C. to the ignorant σχολαστικοί of the twelfth or
twentieth century A.D. For, as we have said, in reading a text of Hipponax over the second class of citations we are in a curious position : there is no evidence
that Tzetzes was successful in disentangling the text
of Hipponax from the comments of the scholiast. In
fr. 68. 6 one might even suppose a predecessor took
the comment for text: in *fr*. 61 Tzetzes is probably the culprit: while to complete the chain we
may quote the text of Hipponax as elicited from
Tzetzes by John Potter (*fr*. 59).

> δὸς χλαῖναν σφύκτουριν Ἱππώνακτι
> καὶ κυπασσίσκον καὶ σαμβάλικα κάσκέρικα
> καὶ χρυσοῦ μοι στατῆρας ἐξήκοντα
> τοῦ νερτέρου τοίχου.

[1] See my notes *Journal Camb. Ph. S.* 1927 p. xii.

INTRODUCTION

This was precisely the way in which some ancient scholars like the unreliable 'Heliodorus metricus' picked out the text for their metrical criticisms of Hipponax' versification. The sane critic will place as little trust in the discrimination of the pedants of Constantinople as in that of the future Archbishop who was probably a finer Greek scholar. For Tzetzes' metrical criticism, when we may suspect him of writing at first hand, is exceedingly poor. On Lycophron 167 he says that ἴσην is right whether short or long: in the later case it has merely πάθος τὸ λεγόμενον χωλίαμβον ! Yet it is, in the main, on the evidence of Tzetzes and on his ability to form an edition of fragments out of obscure and cramped scholia that Hipponax' work is commonly judged.

In closing a long and dull preface some apology for its length and dullness is necessary. But it is manifest that it is wholly impossible to judge of the aims or methods of the later writers who revived this metre unless we have a vague notion of its original character.

[*P.S.*—Much of what has been written above has been rendered superfluous by the discovery of a papyrus fragment printed on pp. 62–63. The thesis of the previous pages that Hipponax was neither an anticipator of metrical licenses used first in the Attic Tragic or Comic Drama, nor an incompetent versifier, is now established beyond the necessity of argument. As all readers of early Greek poetry, for instance of Sappho and Alcaeus, know, " the only correct procedure is to approach the quotations by way of the book texts." Unfortunately this course has not been open to me. Above all we see that there is no similarity between the metres of Hipponax and Herodes.]

HIPPONAX

EARLY CITATIONS

BOOK I

Genuine Fragments from Early Citations

1^{33}_{12} τίς ὀμφαλητόμος σε τὸν διοπλῆγα
ἔψησε κἀπέλουσεν ἀσκαρίζοντα.

(*Et. Vat.* ed. Reitz., *Ind. Lect. Rost.* 1890–91, p. 7. *E.M.*
154. 27 ἀσκαρίζειν· σημαίνει τὸ κινεῖσθαι Ἱππῶναξ (*v.* 2).
Hesych. ὀμφαλητόμος· μαῖα. διοπλῆτα· ἰσχυροπλήκτην cft.
Reitz.)

2_{14} δοκέων †εκτ†ῖνον τῇ βα[κ]τηρίῃ κόψαι . . .

3_{14} ἡμίεκτον αἰτεῖ τοῦ φάλεω κολαψ†αιε†

(Choerobosc. *Exeg. in Hephaest.* xlviii. 6 (τὰ ἄφωνα)
εὑρέθη ποιοῦντα σπανίως κοινὴν ἐν αὐτοῖς τὸ π̄τ̄ καὶ τὸ κ̄τ̄, οἷον
. . παρὰ Ἱππώνακτι ἐν τῷ πρώτῳ ἰάμβων (2) καὶ πάλιν παρὰ
τῷ αὐτῷ (3).)

1 The upper number 33 is that of the last edition of
Bergk's *Poetae Lyrici Graeci*; the lower, of Diehl's *Anth.
Lyrica.*   *v.* 1. -λιτομος cod.
2 *l.* τ' (δ') ἐκε. I doubt whether either illustration is really
sound. If Hippon. wrote βακτηρίη (-ᾳ ms), so must Herodes
have done (viii. 60) : and our choice lies between the two
traditions as to Hipponax' text. 3 ἡμίεκτον may scan ἡμῡεκτον.
If φάλεω (-εω)=φαλῆς (-ῆτος) as Θαλῆς (-ῆτος, -εω), we might
correct to κολάψασα, 'exsucta mentula,' or place a note of
interrogation after αἰτεῖ and read κολάψαι με. One cod. of
Choerob. has ἐν τῷ τρόπῳ ἴαμβον : corr. Hoffmann.

14

HIPPONAX

EARLY CITATIONS

BOOK I

Genuine Fragments from Early Citations

1 What navel snipstress[1] wiped you, dolt blasted,
And, as you hoofed around yourself, washed you.

('Hoofing around' means 'struggling.' *Hipp. Etymol.*
Navel-snipstress': midwife, *Hesych.* 'Blasted,' strength-
smiter.)

2 Thinking 'twas him I smote with my cudgel.

3 She asks eight obols for her tongue's service.[2]

(Mute consonants seldom allow the preceding syllable to
be of doubtful quantity in the case of pt and kt; *e.g.* . . .
Hipponax has băktēriai in his first book of Iambi (2). So
too the same writer has Hemiekton̆͞(3). *Choeroboscus.*)

---

[1] Midwife. Such allusions were the height of bad
manners. So presumably Theophrast's ἀηδής asks (xx. 7)
εἶπ' ὦ μάμμη ὅτ' ὤδινες καὶ ἔτικτές με τίς ἡ μαῖα (for ἡμέρα);
Hesych's second explanation is corrupt. The real meaning
is ἐμβρόντητος, 'dunderhead.'
[2] Videor mihi fata Aretes videre quae 'nunc in quadriviis
et angiportis glubit magnanimi Remi nepotes.'

4^{38}_{16} ἐκ πελλίδος πίνοντες· οὐ γὰρ ἦν αὐτῇ
κύλιξ· ὁ παῖς γὰρ ἐμπεσὼν κατήραξεν.

5^{39}_{17} ἐκ δὲ τῆς πέλλης
ἔπινον ἄλλοτ' αὐτός, ἄλλοτ' Ἀρήτη
προὔπινεν.

(Ath. xi. 495 c **πέλλα**· ἀγγεῖον σκυφοειδές, πυθμένα ἔχον πλατύτερον εἰς ὃ ἤμελγον τὸ γάλα. . . τοῦτο δὲ Ἱππ. λέγει πελλίδα (4), δῆλον, οἶμαι, ποιῶν ὅτι ποτήριον μὲν οὐκ ἦν, δι' ἀπορίαν δὲ κύλικος ἐχρῶντο τῇ πελλίδι. καὶ πάλιν (5). Φοῖνιξ δὲ . . Κλείταρχος πελλητῆρα μὲν καλεῖν Θεσσάλους καὶ Αἰολεῖς τὸν ἀμολγέα πέλλαν δὲ τὸ ποτήριον. Φιλητᾶς δὲ ἐν Ἀτάκτοις τὴν κύλικα Βοιωτούς.)

6^{40}_{18} σπονδῇ τε καὶ σπλάγχνοισιν ἀγρίης χοίρου

(Ath. ix. 375 c **χοῖρον** δὲ οἱ Ἴωνες καλοῦσι τὴν θήλειαν ὡς Ἱππ. ἐν ⟨α'⟩ (6).)

7^{41}_{19} βακκάρει δὲ τὰς ῥῖνας
ἤλειφον.

(Ath. xv. 690 a παρὰ πολλοῖς δὲ τῶν κωμῳδοποιῶν ὀνομάζεταί τι μύρον **βάκκαρις**· οὗ μνημονεύει καὶ Ἱππῶναξ διὰ τούτων (7). ἔσθ' οἵη περ κρόκος.)

8^{12}_{20} τί τῷ τάλαντι Βουπάλῳ συνοίκησας;

(Herodian ii. 301 (Choerobosc. i. 280. 31) ὅτι δὲ καὶ τοῦ τάλας τάλαντος ἦν ἡ γενική, δηλοῖ ὁ Ἱππ. εἰπὼν (8).)

4. 1 *v.l.* αὐτοῖς. So Eust. 1561. 37.
5. 2 Perhaps Ἀρήτῃ προὔπινον should be read, or ἔπινεν . . . Ἀρήτῃ (Schnw.). I have adopted the former for purposes of translation.
6 ἀγρίας codd. (em. by Bgk.: ⟨α'⟩ ins. id.).
7 ἔσθ' οἵη περ κρόκος] cod. E ἔστι δ'. Both are corrupt. The words probably belong to Ath., not Hipp.
8 συνῴκησας plerique codd.

16

4 Drank from a paillet : she had no tumbler:
Her slave had fallen on it and smashed it.

5   Now myself
I drank out of the pail, now Aréte
Had from me what I left.

(' Pail ' means a vessel shaped like a drinking-cup with
a rather broad bottom into which they used to milk. . .
Hipponax calls this paillet (4); and what he says shows
clearly that they had no cup, but in the absence of a tumbler
used the pail. And again (5). But *Phoenix* . . *Cleit-
archus* says that the Thessalians and Aeolians spoke of the
milking utensil as a ' paillier ' but of the cup as ' pail.'
Philetas in his *Stray Notes* says that the Boeotians gave the
name ' pail ' to the tumbler. *Athenaeus*.)

6 With drink offerings and a she-boar's entrails

(' Boar ' was used of the female by the Ionians. *Hipponax*
Book I. (6). *Athenaeus*.)

7   With bakkaris nostrils
Anointing

(Many of the comedians use the word ' bakkaris ' of a
kind of ointment : *Hipponax* too mentions it in these words
(7). It is rather like saffron. *Athenaeus*.)

8 Why with rogue Bupalus didst cohabit?

('τάλας' too (like μέλας) has the genitive ταλαντος as is
clear from *Hipponax* (8). *Herodian*.)

17

9^{63}_{21} ἐγὼ δὲ δεξιῷ παρ' Ἀρήτην
κνεφαῖος ἐλθὼν ῥωδιῷ κατηυλίσθην.

(Herodian ii. 924. 14 λέγεται δὲ (ἐρωδιός) ἔσθ' ὅτε καὶ
τρισυλλάβως ὥσπερ καὶ τὸ παρ' Ἱππώνακτι (9): id. i. 116. 25,
ii, 171. 7, 511. 28, E.M. 380. 40)

10^{10}_{22} κύψασα γάρ μοι πρὸς τὸ λύχνον Ἀρήτη

(Et. Vat. Reitzenstein, Ind. Lect. Rostoch. 1891–2, p. 14
λύχνος : λέγεται ἀρσενικῶς καὶ οὐδετέρως ὁ λύχνος καὶ τὸ λύχνον
Ἱππ. (10).)

$10B_{103}$ λίθινον ἀνδρίαντα

(Antiatt. Bekk. An. i. 82. 13 ἀνδριάντα τὸν λίθινον ἔφη
ππ. Βούπαλον τὸν ἀγαλματοποιόν.)

11^{22A}_{30} μάκαρς ὅτις . . . θηρεύει †πρήσας†.

12^{22B}_{31} καίτ<ο>ιγ' εὔωνον αὐτὸν εἰ θέλεις δώσω.

13_{32} †ἐκέλευε† βάλλειν καὶ λεύειν Ἱππώνακτα.

(Choerobosc. Exeg. in Hephaest. ὁμοίως καὶ τὴν εῦ εὑρίσκομεν ποιοῦσαν κοινήν, οἷον ἐν τῷ πρώτῳ Ἰάμβῳ (-ων Kal.)
Ἱππώνακτος, ἔνθα φησί (11), τὴν ρεῦ ἐν τετάρτῳ (?) ποδὶ
συνέστειλε· καὶ πάλιν ὁ αὐτὸς ἐν δευτέρῳ ποδὶ τὴν εῦ (12)· εἶτα
πάλιν ὁ αὐτὸς (13) τὴν λευ ἐν τετάρτῳ ποδί· λεύειν δέ φησιν
ἀντὶ τοῦ λιθοβολεῖν.)

9. 1 παρὰ ῥητήρ cod.: em. Schneidewin.
10 Probably the beginning of a tetrameter.
11 The Attic μακάριος ὅστις of two mss is clearly false.
Choeroboscus or his source may be deceived : or e.g. θύρετρα
of amatory quarries. μακηρ' ὅ τις one cod.
12 'him': since Hipponax appears to use μιν of things.
13 Scan ἐκέλεῦε, εῦωνον, λεύειν, θηρεύει.

18

9 So I with heron favouring[1] at nightfall
  Came to Aréte's dwelling and lodged there.

('ἐρῳδιός' is sometimes trisyllabic (ῥῳδιός) as *Hipponax'*
saying shows (9). *Herodian.*)

10 Facing the lamp stooped to me Aréte

(λύχνος and λύχνον are both used (masculine and neuter):
Hipponax (10). *Etymologicum Vaticanum.*)

10 B Statue of stone

(Statue of stone was the title given by *Hipponax* to Bupalus
the sculptor. An *antiatticist* in *Bekker's Anecdota.*)

11 Happy is he who hunteth (such quarries).

12 Yet, if you will, I'll give you him dirt-cheap.

13 He bade them pelt and stonecast Hipponax.

(In the same way we find εῦ, as in the first book of the
Iambi of *Hipponax*, where he says (11), he shortens ρεῦ
in the fourth foot; again he has εῦ in the second foot (12);
again (13) λευ in the fourth foot. 'Stonecast' is for
'stone.' *Choeroboscus.*)

[1] 'On my right': a favourable omen.

HIPPONAX

14²³   μ‹υ›δῶντα δὴ καὶ σαπρόν

(Erotian p. 115 σαπρόν: σεσηπότα ὡς Ἱππ. ἐν ᾱ Ἰάμβων
φησί (14).)

BOOK II

15²⁶₃₃   ἀκήρατον δὲ τὴν ἀπαρτίην ‹ἴσ›χει

(Pollux x. 18 τοὔνομα δὲ ἡ **ἀπαρτία** ἐστὶ μὲν Ἰωνικὸν
ὠνομασμένων οὕτω παρ' αὐτοῖς τῶν κούφων σκευῶν ἅ ἐστι παρ-
αρτήσασθαι· . . . εἰ μέντοι καὶ ἐν βιβλίῳ τινὶ τὴν ἀπ. εὑρεῖν
ἐθέλοις . . . εὑρήσεις ἔν τε τῷ δευτέρῳ τῶν Ἱππώνακτος ἰάμβων
(15) καὶ παρὰ Θεοφράστῳ . . .)

UNCERTAIN BOOKS

16³⁴₃₈   συκ‹έ›ην μέλαιναν ἀμπέλου κασιγνήτην

(Ath. iii. 78 b Φερένικος δὲ . . ἀπὸ Συκῆς τῆς Ὀξύλου
θυγατρὸς προσαγορευθῆναι· Ὄξυλον γὰρ . . . γεννῆσαι . . .
Ἄμπελον, Συκῆν . . . ὅθεν καὶ τὸν Ἱππ. φάναι (16).)

17³⁶₃₉   οὐκ ἀτταγᾶς τε καὶ λαγοὺς καταβρύκων,
           οὐ τηγανίτας σησάμοισι φαρμάσσων,
           οὐδ' ἀττανίτας κηρίοισιν ἐμβάπτων

(Ath. xiv. 645 c Πάμφιλος δὲ τὸν **ἀττανίτην** καλούμενον
ἐπίχυτόν φησι καλεῖσθαι. τοῦ δὲ ἀττανίτου Ἱππῶναξ ἐν τούτοις
μνημονεύει (17). ix. 388 b μνημονεύει αὐτῶν (ἀτταγῶν) Ἱππ.
οὕτως (17. 1). Hesych. ὀμπν[ε]ίῃ **δαιτί·** ἀντὶ τοῦ πολλῇ.)

14 μαδῶντα corr. by Stephanus.
15 ἀπαρτίαν codd.: -ίην Bgk.   ἔχει codd.
16 συκῆν codd.: corr. Schnw.   Perhaps Aeschriontic.
17. 1 Ath. 645 c ουκατταστε: ? ἀτταγέας.   In both places
λαγώς is given: corr. by Meineke.   καταβρύκων 645 c,
διατρώγων 388 b.   2 τηγανιας mss: corr. by Casaubon.
3 οὐκ Meineke, prob. rightly.

20

FRAGMENTS 14–17

14 Clammy and rotten

('Rotten': rotted. *Hipp.* Book I (14). *Erotian.*)

BOOK II

15 Untarnished his appendages keeping

(The word 'appendages' is Ionic, the name applying to light articles which may be hung on the belt; . . . if you wish for documentary evidence you may go to the second book of *Hipponax*' Iambi (15) and to *Theophrast* . . . *Pollux.*)

UNCERTAIN BOOKS

16 (?) The fig-tree black, which is the vine's sister

(*Pherenicus* . . says that the word συκῆ came from Suké, the daughter of Oxylus; he . . . . begat . . . . Ampelos and Suké . .; hence *Hipponax*, he says, said (16). *Athenaeus.*)

17 Not partridges and hares galore scrunching,
   Nor flavouring with sesamé pancakes,
   Nor yet with honey drenching fried fritters[1]

(*Pamphilus* speaks of the 'fritter' as a sort of cake. It is mentioned by *Hipponax* in the following verses (17). Of partridges *Hipp.* speaks as follows (17. 1). *Athenaeus. Here may belong* 'rich feasting': for 'much.' *Hesych.*)

[1] See on *fr.* 75.

HIPPONAX

$18^{3\ 7}_{4\ 0}$ ὁ δ᾽ ἐξολισθὼν ἱκέτευε τὴν κράμβην
τὴν ἑπτάφυλλον ᾗ θύεσκε Πανδώρη
Ταργηλίοισιν ἔγχυτον πρὸ φαρμάκου.

(Ath. ix. 370 a μήποτε δὲ ὁ Νίκανδρος μάντιν κέκληκε τὴν κράμβην ἱερὰν οὖσαν, ἐπεὶ καὶ παρ᾽ Ἱππώνακτι ἐν τοῖς ἰάμβοις ἐστί τι λεγόμενον τοιοῦτον (18). καὶ Ἀνάνιος δέ φησιν . . .)

$19^{4\ 6}_{4\ 3}$ καὶ τοὺς σολοίκους, ἢν λάβωσι, περνᾶσι
Φρύγας μὲν ἐς Μίλητον ἀλφιτεύσοντας,

(Herodian, de Barbarismo et Soloecismo, Valck. Ammon. p. 193 Σολοίκους δὲ ἔλεγον οἱ παλαιοὶ τοὺς βαρβάρους. ὁ γὰρ Ἀνακρέων φησί . . καὶ Ἱππῶναξ (19). v.l. in Eust. 368. 1.)

$20^{4\ 7}_{4\ 4}$ οἴκει δ᾽ ὄπισθεν τῆς πόλ⟨η⟩ος ἐν Σμύρνῃ
μεταξὺ Τρηχέ[ι]ης τε καὶ Λέπρης ἀκτῆς.

(Strabo p. 633 καὶ τόπος δέ τις τῆς Ἐφέσου Σμύρνα ἐκαλεῖτο, ὡς δηλοῖ Ἱππ. (20). ἐκαλεῖτο γὰρ Λέπρη μὲν ἀκτὴ ὁ πρηὼν ὁ ὑπερκείμενος τῆς νῦν πόλεως, ἔχων μέρος τοῦ τείχους αὐτῆς· τὰ γοῦν ὄπισθεν τοῦ πρηῶνος κτήματα ἔτι νυνὶ λέγεται ἐν τῇ Ὀπισθολεπρίᾳ· Τραχεῖα δ᾽ ἐκαλεῖτο ἡ περὶ τὸν Κορησσὸν παρώρειος.)

$21^{5\ 0}_{4\ 6}$ ἔπειτα μάλθῃ τὴν τρόπιν παραχρίσας

(Harpocrat. p. 123 μάλθη· ὁ μεμαλαγμένος κηρός· Ἱππ. (21).)

18. 1 ? ἐξόπισθεν Callim. *Iamb.* 413 s.v.l. ? ἱκέτευσε since Hrd. seems to shorten ἱκετεύω. But cf. καπηλεύει fr. 70. The forms θύεσκε and perhaps ἱκέτευε are not from the vernacular, the dialect being made appropriate to the myth. 3 vv.ll. Θαργ-, Ταργ-: Ταργ- Schnw.

19. 1 ἵν᾽ ἐθέλουσι Eust. 2 vv.ll. ἀλφιτεύοντας, -σαντας.

20. 1 ᾤκει codd.: corr. Schnw. and ten Brink. πόλιος cod.: corr. Bgk. πρηών also Anton. Lib. xi.

21 v.l. τρόπην.

22

18 So slipping off,[1] adjuréd the cabbage,
   The cabbage seven-leaved, which Pandora
   At the Thargelia gave as cake-off'ring
   Ere she was victim.

(We may suggest that *Nicander* (*fr.* 85) speaks of the
'cabbage' as 'prophetic' because it is holy since we find
in the Iambi of Hipponax something of this sort (18).
And Ananius too says . . . *Athenaeus.*)

19 And the soloeci sell, if they take them,
   The Phrygians to Miletus for mill-work,

(The ancients gave the name soloeci to barbarians.
Anacreon says . . And *Hipponax* (19). *Herodian* (explain-
ing the origin of the term solecism. The work is not considered authentic).)

20 Behind the city lived he in Smyrna
   Halfway between Cape Rough and the Crumbles.

(A part of Ephesus used to be called 'Smyrna' as is clear
from *Hipponax* (20); for the Crumbles was the name given
to the cape situate above the present city containing a
part of its wall; the property behind the cape is still
spoken of as 'in the Back Crumbles': 'Rough' was the
name given to the mountain side round Koressos. *Strabo*
(who further tells how Smyrna was founded thence).)

21 Anon the keel along with grease smearing

('Grease': melted wax, *Hipponax* (21). *Harpocration.*)

[1] *v.* 1 Presumably off a height. Bergk connects with
the accident to the slave (*fr.* 4 above). On the story see
Schweighäuser. Conceivably the verses are Callimachean.

23

22$^{52}_{48}$ καί μιν καλύπτει⟨ς⟩; μῶν χαραδριὸν πέρνης;

(Schol. Plat. 352 Bekker on *Gorg.* 494 B (χαραδριοῦ βίον λέγεις of the incontinent man) χαραδριὸς ὄρνις τις ὃς ἅμα τῷ ἐσθίειν ἐκκρίνει. εἰς ὃν ἀποβλέψαντες, ὡς λόγος, οἱ ἰκτεριῶντες ῥᾷον ἀπαλλάττονται· ὅθεν καὶ ἐγκρύπτουσιν αὐτὸν οἱ πιπράσκοντες ἵνα μὴ προῖκα ὠφεληθῶσιν οἱ κάμνοντες, (22) ὥς φησιν Ἱππ.)

23$^{53}_{49}$ ἀλλ' αὐτίκ' ἀλλήλοισιν ἐμβιβάξαντες

(*E.M.* 334. 1 ἐμβιβάξαντες: παρ' Ἱππ. (23) ἀντὶ τοῦ ἐμβοήσαντες.)

24$^{54}_{50}$ κριγὴ δὲ νεκρῶν ἄγγελός τε καὶ κῆρυξ

(*E.M.* 539. 1 (on κρίκε) καὶ ῥηματικὸν ὄνομα κριγή· ὡς παρὰ Ἱππώνακτι (24).)

25$^{55Λ}_{51}$ ὤμιξεν αἷμα καὶ χολὴν ἐτίλησεν.

(*E.M.* 624. 4 ὀμιχεῖν· . · ἐστὶ δὲ καὶ . . . ὀμίχω· ὁ μέλλων ὀμίξω ὡς παρ' Ἱππ., οἷον (25).)

26$^{56}_{52}$ σίφωνι λεπτῷ τοὐπίθ⟨η⟩μα τετρήνας

(Pollux vi. 19 καὶ σίφωνα μέν, ὅτῳ ἐγεύοντο, Ἱππ. εἴρηκεν (26).)

27$^{57}_{53}$ στάζουσιν †ὥσπερ ἐς τροπήϊον† σάκ⟨κ⟩ος.

(Pollux x. 75 καὶ ὁ τρύγοιπος καὶ ὁ σάκκος ἐπὶ τοῦ τρυγοίπου εἰρημένος, καὶ ὁ ὑλιστήρ. Ἱππ. δέ φησιν (27).)

22 Corr. Bgk. μήν for μιν is read in Suid. *s.v.* and Ar. *Av.* 266 schol. πέρας schol. Ar. (Ven.), -νᾶς cett., ὡς schol. Ar.

23 Also Zonaras, p. 706 Tittmann.

24 Also Zonaras, p. 1258 T., *An. Ox.* i. 268. 12, *Et. Gud.* 347. 27, Choerobosc. ii. 590, 657.

25 Also Zonaras, p. 1451 T., *An. Ox.* iv. 191. 6 (ὤμηξεν), 416. 7 (these have ἐτίλλησεν), schol. Hom. E 531.

26 ἐπίθημα for ἐπίθεμα Welcker.

27 ὥσπερ ἐκ τροπηῖου Bgk., since (Meineke) the wine goes from the vat into the sieve. Better ὥσπερ ῥεῖ τραπηῖου since ὥσπερ requires a main verb. σάκος corrected to σάκκος by Salmasius. τραπη- should probably be read (Hemsterhuys).

24

22 And veilest[1] it ? Sellest thou a bustard ?

(The ' bustard ' is a bird which evacuates while it eats.
People suffering from jaundice are eased by the sight of it;
so those who sell it wrap it up to prevent patients from being
relieved free of cost (22), as *Hipp.* says. *Commentator on
Plato, Gorgias*, 494 в, ' life of a bustard.')

23 Anon they shrieked aloud to each other,

(' Shriek to ' : in Hipponax (23)=' yell to.' *Etymologicum Magnum.*)

24 And screech, the ghost-announcer, ghost-herald

(There is also a noun ' screech,' *e.g.* in *Hipponax* (24). *id.*)

25 Bile in his urin, blood in 's stool brought up.

(Urine . . .; also . . . urin; *Hipponax* (25). (ὀμιχεῖν or
-ίχειν : fut. ὀμίξω.) *id.*)

26 With a thin tube he bored through the stopper.

(' Tube ' used for tasting mentioned in *Hipp.* (26). *Pollux.*)

27 They dribble like a winepress-sieve flowing.

(And ' strainer ' : and ' sieve ' in the same sense : and
'filter.' *Hipponax* says (27). *id.*)

---

[1] Perhaps καλύπτει could be kept as a middle (καλύπτῃ ;)
f ων is a part of the body.

HIPPONAX

28 ⁵⁸/₅₄ κἄλειφα Ῥόδι[ν]ον ἡδὺ καὶ λέκος πυροῦ

(Pollux, x. 87 ἐν δὲ τοῖς Δημιοπράτοις **λέκος** εὑρίσκομεν, εἰπόντος Ἱππ. (28).)

29 ⁵⁹/₅₅ πρὸς τὴν μαρίλην τὰς φ‹ο›ῖδας †θερμαίνωντ οὐ παύεται.

(Erotian p. 134 **φῷδες**· ἐστὶ μὲν ἡ λέξις Δωρική, καλοῦσι δὲ φῷδας τὰ ἐκ τοῦ πυρὸς γινόμενα μάλιστα δὲ ὅταν ἐκ ψύχους ἐν τῷ πυρὶ καθίσωσι στρογγύλα ἐπιφλογίσματα . . .· ὁτὲ δὲ καὶ ἐξανθήματα φοινικᾶ οἷον φῷδες περὶ τὸν θώρακά που γινόμενα. καὶ Ἱππ. δέ φησι (29). Tzetzes on Ar. *Plut.* 535 τὰ ἐκ ψύχους ἐκκαύματα ὡς καὶ Ἱππ. φησί (v. 1).

30 ⁶⁶/₅₈ κύμινδις ἐν λαύρῃ ἔκρωζεν.

(*Et. Flor.* p. 231 Miller *Mélanges* **Οὐδὸν ἐς λαύρην** (Hom. χ 128). τὴν δημοσίαν ὁδὸν . . .· τινὲς μὲν ὁδὸν ἀπέδοσαν, τινὲς δὲ τὸν κοπρῶνα, ὡς Ἱππ. (30). στολὴ (στόμα Mill.) δὲ λαύρης τὴν ἔξοδον τὴν εἰς αὐτήν (χ 137). *Cf.* Hesych. **ἐρκανήεντα πυλῶνα** (Dindorf for ἐρχ-)· τὸν πεπυκνωμένον καὶ συνεχόμενον.)

31 ⁶⁷/₅₉ ἐν ταμ[ε]ίῳ τε καὶ χαμευνίῳ γυμνόν

(*Mélanges* p. 402 Mill. **χαμεύνιον**· κραββάτιον καθάπερ καὶ παρ' Ἱππώνακτι (31). p. 307 Ἱππ. ἐν μιῷ τε κτλ. Hesych. **τάμ[ε]ιον**· θάλαμος.)

28 Ῥόδιον I conjecture as Ar. *Av.* 944, where Blaydes' crit. n. is most misleading. See Pape-Benseler *s.v.* Ῥόδος. The converse error in Poll. vi. 104. ἡδὺ with ῥόδινον appears otiose. Scan as Ροδυγον.

29 See note on opposite page.

31 The initial trochee may be supported from Herodes and is more likely than an initial dactyl, for which there is no good pre-Attic evidence. Corr. Hoffm. *Et. Vat.* has lost several sheets at the end, so that the entry χαμεύνιον is missing.

26

28 And Rhodian unguent sweet and a wheat-crock

(In the *Demioprata* (*Goods Sold by Public Auction*) we find ' crock,' used by *Hipp.* (28). *id.*)

29 Cease warming at the embers your chilblains.[1]

(' Chilblains ' : the word is Doric and applied to the round inflammations that result from the fire, especially when people sit right in the fire after being out in the cold. . . Sometimes it is applied to crimson eruptions in the region of the chest. *Hipponax* says (29). *Erotian*. Inflammations from cold as *Hipp.* says. *Tzetzes*' note on *Aristophanes*' *Plutus.*)

30   A raven was croaking
  In rear.

(' Passage to the " rear " *Homer* ' : the public way . . . Some explain the word as back-street, others as the privy : *cf. Hipp.* (30).[2] Mouth of the ' rear ' means the exit to it. *Etymologicum Florentinum*. *Cf.* ' Fenced gateway ' : narrow-set or straitened. *Hesychius.*)

31 Lay in a room on pallet-bed naked.

(' Pallet-bed ' : a small bed as in *Hipp.* (31). *Didymus Areius* on *Difficult Words in Plato*. So *Et. Flor.*)

---

[1] A most puzzling quotation. Erotian has τοὺς παῖδας for τὰς φωΐδας (Tzetzes); but Hoffmann, who rightly changes to φοΐδας, is also right in regarding this as a mere error. The verse . . . ας | θερμαίνων appears unmetrical. Perhaps it is an injunction, ' up and be doing ': θερμαίνων | π. τ. μ. τ. φ. οὐ παύσεαι; So I translate. μαρίλην is also cited as -ίλλαν or -ίλλην, here and in 39.

[2] *Et. Flor.* has ἔκρωζεν κ. ἐς λ. *Et. Vat.* Reitz. *Lect. Rost.*, 1891-2, p. 14, gives the true reading, ἐν λαύρῃ.

32 $^{6\ 5}_{6\ 0}$ καὶ νῦν ἀρειᾷ σύκινόν με ποιῆσαι.

(*Et. Flor.* p. 41 Mill. ἀρειῶ· τὸ ἀπειλῶ ὡς παρ' Ἱππ. (32)· τουτεστὶν ἀπειλεῖ. *E.M.* 139. 36 one cod. ἀρειᾷς . . . ἀπειλεῖς, sed ἀρειᾷ *Et. Vat.*)

33 $^{4\ 5}_{6\ 1}$ καὶ Μύσων ὃν ὡπόλλων
ἀνεῖπεν ἀνδρῶν σωφρονέστατον πάντων.

(Diog. L. i. 107.)

34 $^{6\ 8A}_{2}$ Σινδικὸν διάσφαγμα

(Schol. Ap. Rhod. iv. 321 καὶ Ἱππῶναξ δὲ μνημονεύει (τῶν Σίνδων) πρὸς τὸ (34). Hesych. **Σινδικὸν διάσφαγμα**· τὸ τῆς γυναικός.)

35 $^{6\ 8B}$ σηπίης ὑπόσφαγμα

(Ath. vii. 324 a Ἱππ. δ' ἐν τοῖς ἰάμβοις εἰπόντος (35) οἱ ἐξηγησάμενοι ἀπέδωκαν τὸ τῆς σηπίας μέλαν. ἐστὶ δὲ τὸ ὑπόσφαγμα ὡς Ἐρασίστρατός φησιν ἐν Ὀψαρτυτίκῳ ὑπότριμμα. Eust. *Il.* 1286. 6.)

36 $^{6\ 9}$ πασπαληφάγον γρόμφιν

(Phot. *Lex.* ii. 67. 12 Naber **πασπάλη**· τὸ τυχόν, οἱ δὲ κέγχρον· οἱ δὲ τὰ κέγχρινα ἄλευρα. Ἱππ. (36). *Cf.* Eust. 1752. 121.)

37 $^{7\ 0A}$ βολβίτου κασιγνήτην

(*E.M.* 204. 28 **βόλιτον**· βόλβιτον δὲ Ἴωνες οἵ τε ἄλλοι καὶ Ἱππ. οἷον (37). Bekk. *An.* 186. 10 **βόλβιτον** : Ἱππ.)

33 Probably Callimachean (ten Brink).
34 In the schol. Meineke reads πρώτῳ for πρὸς τὸ rightly: for a weak caesura would be incredible. All the same Cr. is very likely right in connecting with *fr.* 43, since Tz. appears to have quoted or meant to quote both verses.
36 πασπάλιν φαγών codd.: corr. Porson.

32 And menaces to render me senseless.

(To ' menace ' : threaten, as in *Hipp.* (32): *i.e.* threatens. *id.*)

33   Whom Apollo
    Declared the wisest man of all, Myson.

(*Diogenes Laertius.* (Probably from *Callimachus.*))

34   Sindian fissure[1]

(*Hipponax* mentions the Sindi in his first book (?) (34). *Commentator* on *Apollonius Rhodius.*)

35   Squid-pudding

(*Hipp.* in his iambi says (35). The interpreters explain it of the ink of the fish. It is really a pudding made of its blood as *Erasistratus* says in his *Cookery.* *Athenaeus.*)

36   Middlings-fed porker

(' Middlings ' : scraps. Others say millet, others millet-flour. *Hipp.* (36). *Photius.* *Hipp.* uses porker either of any sow or of an old one. *Eustathius* on *Homer's Odyssey.*)

37   Cow-dung's sister

(Bolitos was called bolbitos in general by the Ionians: and so *Hipp.* (37). *Etymologicum Magnum.*)

───────
[1] *i.e.* γυναικεῖον αἰδοῖον Hesych.

HIPPONAX

38⁷⁰ᴮ   ὥσ‹τε . . .› 'Εφεσίη δέλφαξ

(Ath. ix. 375 a καὶ Ἱππ. δὲ ἔφη (38).)

39⁷¹   πολλὴν μαρίλην ἀνθράκων

(Erotian p. 96 μᾶλλον δὲ ἡ θερμοσποδιὰ **μαρίλη** λέγεται ὡς
. . . καὶ Ἱππ. φησι (39).)

40⁸⁸   ‹τὸν δὲ› ληὸν ἀθρήσας

(Anon. *An. Ox.* i. 265. 6 τὸ λαὸς τῇ μεταγενεστέρᾳ 'Ιάδι
τραπέν· (40) Ἱππ.)

41⁷⁷₄₁   κρε‹ῖ›ας ἐκ μολοβρίτ‹εω›
         συός

(Eust. *Od.* 1817. 20 'Αριστοφάνης γοῦν ὁ γραμματικὸς . . .
ἐπάγει ὡς καὶ Ἱππ. τὸν ἴδιον υἱὸν μολοβρίτην που λέγει ἐν τῷ (41).
Ael. *N.H.* vii. 47 ἀκούσαις δ' ἂν καὶ τοῦ Ἱππ. καὶ αὐτὸν τὸν ὗν
μολοβρίτην που λέγοντος.)

42¹²⁷ μεσσηγυδορποχέστα

(Eust. *Od.* 1837. 42 κατὰ δὲ Ἱππ. καὶ ὁ μεσσηγυδορποχέστης
ἤγουν ὃς μεσοῦντος δείπνου πολλάκις ἀποπατεῖ ὡς πάλιν ἐμ-
πίμπλασθαι. Sueton. περὶ βλασφ. is no doubt the source:
Miller's text, p. 425 *Mél.*, gives the same explanation but
does not name *Hipp.*)

42ᴀ¹⁰⁰ ἄδηκε βουλή.

(Eust. *Od.* 1721. 61 χρήσεως Ἱππώνακτος ἦν Ἡρακλείδης
προφέρει, εἰπόντος (42ᴀ) ἤγουν ἤρεσκε τὸ βούλευμα. Compare
and perhaps add Hesych. Πανθρ‹ό›ῳ δήμῳ · παρρησίαν ἄγοντι
κτλ., 'Αελλῆσι | θυμοῖς· ἀνυποστόλοις μετὰ παρρησίας. Τίεσκε
μύθους· ἐτίμα λόγους.)

38 *e.g.* ‹δή τις›. Unless the word was pronounced 'Εφεγσίη.
'Εφεσηΐη ten Brink. Others suggest ἐπιστίη.
40 ‹δὲ› Bgk. invito metro.
41 μολοβρίτέω for -ου Schneidewin.

30

38   Like Ĕphēsĭān piglet

(*Hipponax* says (38).   *Athenaeus.*)

39 Embers of charcoal many

(Better to say that ' embers ' mean hot ashes as *Hipp.*
. . . says.   *Erotian.*)

40   Seeing the foulk

(Folk : the vowel is changed in later Ionic.   (40) *Hipp.*
Grammarian in *Cramer's Anecdota Oxoniensia.*)

41   Flesh from a beggar
     Pig

(*Hipponax* calls his own son [1] ' beggar pig,' in the following
(41).   *Aristophanes the grammarian* in *Eustathius* on
Homer's Odyssey (ρ 219).   You will find *Hipp.* calling even
the pig ' beggar.'   *Aelian.*)

42 In-mid-feast-voiding

(According to *Hipp.* we have also (42), that is one who
in the midst of dinner retires often in order to make room
for more.   *Eustathius* on *Homer* using *Suetonius'* work on
Opprobrious Names.)

42A (This) counsel pleased.

(A use of Hipponax adduced by Heracleides.   *Hipp.* says
(42A), *i.e.* The proposal met with favour.   *Eustathius* on
Homer's Odyssey.   Cf. 'Licentious-tongued people': speaking with license, etc.   *Hesych.* ' Flighty of spirit ': fearless
in license of speech, *id.* ' His rede did honour ' : honoured
his words, *id.*)

---

[1] There seems to have been some confusion in the text
of a previous grammarian between ὗς pig and υἱός son.
Aelian's version is clearly right.   It was fashionable to
explain μολοβρός, a Homeric word of doubtful meaning, as
food-seeker.   The Greeks turned their pigs loose early to
find food.   Hrd. Mime viii. init.

31

HIPPONAX

42B[109] βεβρενθ‹ονευ›μένον ‹δέ›

(Hesych. (42B)· παρ' Ἱππώνακτι ὀργιζόμενον.)

LATER CITATIONS, AND CITATIONS FROM CORRUPT TEXTS

BOOK I

43$\frac{3}{2}$ Κοραξικὸν μὲν ἠμφιεσμένη λῶπος

(Tzetz. *Chil.* x. 377 περὶ τῶν Μιλησίων μὲν ἔφαν πολλοὶ ἐρίων, περὶ ἐρίων Κοραξῶν ἐν πρώτῳ δὲ ἰάμβῳ Ἱππῶναξ οὕτως εἴρηκε μέτρῳ χωλῶν ἰάμβων (43). τοὺς Κοραξοὺς δὲ καὶ Σινδοὺς ἔθνη τυγχάνειν νόει. Hesych. **Κοραξοί**· Σκυθῶν γένος καὶ τὸ γυναικεῖον αἰδοῖον.)

44$\frac{1}{4}$ ἔβωσε Μαίης παῖδα Κυλλήνης πάλμυν.

(Schol. Lyc. 219 Μαίας καὶ Διὸς Ἑρμῆς, ὡς . . . ὁ Ἱππ. ἐν τῷ κατὰ Βουπάλου πρώτῳ ἰάμβῳ (44). Tzetz. *ad loc.*)

With this is generally connected :—

45$\frac{1}{4}$ Ἑρμῆ κυνάγχα Μηονιστὶ Κανδαῦλα
   φωρῶν ἑταῖρε δεῦρό [τί] μοι σκαπαρδεῦσαι.

(Tzetz. *An. Ox.* iii. 351. 7 τὸ δὲ Κανδαύλης Λυδικῶς τὸν σκυλλοπνίκτην λέγει, ὥσπερ Ἱππῶναξ δείκνυσι γράφων ἰάμβῳ πρώτῳ (45). So Tzetz. *on Iliad* p. 843 B.)

42B βεβρενθυόμενον Hesych. This is the only form which I can find which admits of easy scansion and appears to be sufficiently attested by such corrupt glosses as γρονθονεύεται and πραθενεύεσθαι. We might perhaps attribute to Hipponax forms in Hesychius like ἀναγαγγανεύουσι, (κατ)ιμονεύει, λαγγονεύει.

44 *vv.ll.* Κυκλήσιον, Κυκλίης, κυκλίης : βασιλέα πάλμυν almost all codd. ἐβόησε codd.: corr. Schneidewin.

45.2 [τί] bracketed by Bgk. σκαπαρδεῦσαι is explained by συμμαχῆσαι superscribed. **σκαπερδεῦσαι**· λοιδορῆσαι Hesych., who also explains κυνάγχα by κλέπτα. These and other glosses **σκαρπαδεῦσαι**· κρῖναι and **καπαρδεῦσαι**· μαντεύσασθαι are cited by Bgk.

32

42B With choler puffed

((42B): angry in Hipponax. *Hesychius.*)

LATER CITATIONS, AND CITATIONS
FROM CORRUPT TEXTS

BOOK I

43 Attired in a Koraxian mantle

(Many writers have mentioned Milesian wool, but *Hipp.* mentions Koraxian wool in his first book of iambi as follows in choliambic metre (43). You must know that the Koraxi and Sindi[1] are tribes. *Tzetzes.* Koraxians: A race of Scythians, etc. *Hesychius.*)

44 On Maia's son, Cyllene's tsar, called he.

(Hermes was son of Maia and Zeus, as . . . *Hipp.* says in the book of Iambi written against Bupalus (44). *Tzetzes* and *Commentator* on *Lycophron.*)

45 Dog-throttling Hermes, thief-mate, whom Maeons Kandaules call, come give me a shove up.[2]

(Kandaules in the Lydian tongue means puppy-throttler, as Hipponax shows in his first book of iambi (45). *Tzetz.* in *Cramer's Anecdota Oxoniensia* and on *Homer's Iliad.*) *Hesychius* translates dog-throttling as 'thief,' and gives several erroneous translations of 'to my aid come.'

---

[1] Hence **Cr.** is probably right in connecting this with *fr.* 34.

[2] *Cf.* λακκοσκάπερδος Hesych.

HIPPONAX

46$\frac{2}{5}$ Κίκων δ' ὁ †πανδαληκτος†, ἄμμορος καύης,
       τοιόνδε ⟨μο⟩ι κατ⟨εῖπε, κρῆτ'⟩ ἔχων
       ⟨δαῦλον⟩
       δάφν⟨η⟩σ⟨ιν⟩, οὐδὲν δ' αἴσιον προθεσπίζων

(Tzetz. on *Iliad* p. 76. 811 (δάφνη) ἦν οἱ ἱερεῖς τοῦ ἡλίου ἤτοι
μάντεις καὶ μάγοι, οἷος ἦν καὶ ὁ Χρύσης, στεφανούμενοι ἐπορεύοντο·
καθὼς δηλοῖ καὶ Ἱππ. ἐν τῷ κατὰ Βούπαλον ἰάμβῳ (46. 1) τοιόνδε
τι δάφνας κατέχων. id. on Lycophron *Alex.* 424. 5 καύηξ δὲ ὁ
λάρος κατὰ Αἰνιᾶνας, ὥς φησι καὶ Ἱππ. (46. 1). Hesych. (added
by ten Brink) **Κίκων**· ὁ Κίκων Ἀμυθάονος ἦν οὐδὲν αἴσιον προ-
θεσπίζων.

47$\frac{4}{6}$ πόλιν καθαίρειν καὶ κράδῃσι †βάλλεσθαι†

48$\frac{5}{7}$ βάλλοντες ἐν λειμῶνι καὶ ῥαπίζοντες
       κράδῃσι καὶ σκίλλησιν ὧσ⟨τε⟩ φάρμακον.

49$\frac{6}{8}$ δεῖ δ' αὐτὸν ἐς φάρμακον †ἐκποιήσασθαι†,
50$\frac{7}{9}$ †κἀφῆ παρέξειν† ἰσχάδας τε καὶ μᾶζαν
       καὶ τυρὸν οἷον ἐσθίουσι φάρμακοι·

51$\frac{8}{10}$ παλαὶ γὰρ αὐτοὺς προσ†δέχονται† χάσκοντες
       κράδας ἔχο⟨ντες⟩ . . . .
       . . . . . . ἔχο⟩ντας ὡς ἔχουσι φάρμακοι[ς]

46 The Hesychian gloss, whose language shows that it is
not a gloss but a quotation, was rightly incorporated by
ten Brink. 1 πανδάλητος, πανδαύληκτος, al. Κίκων is glossed
ὄνομα μάντεως and καύης λάρος. 2 Supplevi *e.g.*: τοιόνδε
τι δάφνης κατέχων Tzetzes. Hereabouts come the words
παῖς ὠμυθέωνος.

47 κρ. is glossed by συκαῖς. ?φαρμάσσειν for βάλλεσθαι, as Tz.
48. 2 ὥσπερ codd.

49-51A are probably misquoted in details. It cannot be
certain that they were not consecutive. In 49 ἐκπ. must
mean 'select': if corrupt it has replaced a passive. In 50. 1
I suspect the truth is πιέξειν (or -εῖν Hrd. viii. 47). On this
verse there is a note (ἀφή καὶ ἄρμα καὶ τὰ λοιπὰ οἱ Ἴωνες ψιλοῦ-
σιν) whence κάφῆ must be read. προσδοκεῦσι is probable for
προσδεχ.—a slip of memory. The ms. used by Herodes had

46 Kikon the hideous, cormorant[1] luckless,
  Amythaon's son, his head with bay-leaves crowned,
  With naught auspicious in his forecast

((Laurel) which the priests of the sun (*i.e.* prophets and
wise-men, like Chryses) wore as a crown when they walked
abroad, as is shown by Hipponax in his book of iambi
against Bupalus (46. 1, 2). *Tzetzes* on *Homer's Iliad.*
' Kikon ' was the son of Amythaon (46. 3). *Hesychius.*)

47 Must cleanse the city, and with twigs †pelted†

48 Pelting him in the meadow and beating
  With twigs and squills like unto a scapegoat.

49 He must be chosen[2] from you as scapegoat

50 And in his grip take barley-cakes, dried figs
  And cheese, such cheese as scapegoats may feed
  on.

51 For long have they awaited them gaping
  With twigs in hand ; . . . .
  . . . . . as trembling as scapegoats.[2]

[1] Priests are always represented as greedy. I translate
πανδήλητος : *cf.* πανλώβητος.
[2] If this fragment be not read consecutively it is possible
to explain φάρμακον as in *fr.* 18 and Tzetzes' comment as
equalling καθαρμόν (not -μα) : and (with scansion ἐκπὄγῆσ.) to
translate 'put him forth for a purification.' Again, if 51 be
not consecutive on 50, we could read :

  πάλαι γὰρ αὐτοῦ προσδέχονται χάσκοντες
  κράδας, ἔχοντες ὡς ἔχουσι φάρμακοι.

'They await there the twigs agape in such (pitiable) state
as scapegoats are in.'

χασκεῦντες : *cf.* Hrd. iv. 42. In 51. 2 the people who hold
the twigs are those who wait : hence -τες for -τας (Meineke).
But as ὡς ἔχουσι could only mean 'at once' in reference to
the subject of the sentence we need another ἔχοντας (*e.g.*
δέους) to refer to the state of mind of the victims.

HIPPONAX

52_{11}^{9} λιμῷ γένηται ξηρός, ἐν δὲ τῷ θυμῷ
[ὁ] φάρμακος ἀχθεὶς ἑπτάκις ῥαπισθείη.

(Tzetz. *Chil.* v. 726 ὁ φαρμακὸς τὸ κάθαρμα τοιοῦτον ἦν τὸ
πάλαι. ἂν συμφορὰ κατέλαβε πόλιν θεομηνίᾳ, εἴτ' οὖν λιμὸς, εἴτε
λοιμός, εἴτε καὶ βλάβος ἄλλο, τῶν (? τὸν) πάντων ἀμορφότερον
ἦγον ὡς πρὸς θυσίαν, εἰς καθαρμὸν καὶ φαρμακὸν πόλεως τῆς
νοσούσης· εἰς τόπον δὲ τὸν πρόσφορον στήσαντες τὴν θυσίαν τυρόν
τε δόντες τῇ χερὶ καὶ μᾶζαν καὶ ἰσχάδας, ἑπτάκις γὰρ ῥαπίσαντες
ἐκεῖνον εἰς τὸ πέος σκίλλαις συκαῖς ἀγρίαις τε καὶ ἄλλοις τῶν
ἀγρίων τέλος πυρὶ κατέκαιον ἐν ξύλοις τοῖς ἀγρίοις. . . ὁ δὲ
Ἱππῶναξ ἄριστα σύμπαν τὸ ἔθος λέγει (47), καὶ ἀλλαχοῦ
δέ πού φησιν πρώτῳ ἰάμβῳ γράφων (48), καὶ πάλιν ἄλλοις
τόποις δὲ ταῦτά φησὶ κατ' ἔπος (49-51), καὶ ἀλλαχοῦ δὲ
πού φησιν ἐν τῷ αὐτῷ ἰάμβῳ (52).)

53_{15}^{14} τούτοισι θηπ⟨έ⟩ων τοὺς Ἐρυθραίων παῖδας
τοὺς φησὶ† μητροκοίτας Βούπαλος σὺν
Ἀρήτῃ
[κνίζων καὶ] †φέλιζων† τὸν δυσώνυμον
⟨χό⟩ρτον

(Tzetz. on *Posthomerica*, 687 **θῆπον**· ἐθαύμαζον· τὸ θέμα
θήπω καὶ Ἱππ. (53). **ἐλλίζων**· τίλλων. *Cf. id.* **ψελιστήν**
λί⟨χ⟩νον (for λιγ- Mus.) and **χναύων**· περικνίζων, περιτίλλων ;
χναύει· λαμβάνει, κνίζει.)

52. 1 θυμός· τὸ ἄρρεν αἰδοῖον Sch. A rightly. Hesych.
confuses with θῦμος, thyme. 2 [ὁ] del. Blomfield.
53. 1 θήπων codd.: corr. Bgk. (Hesych. θηπητής· ἀπατεών).
2 *l.* τούς (ten Brink). 3 ἄρτον codd. κνίζων (in best
cod.) might be an explanation of a participle meaning eat,
gnaw: possibly δρυψελίζων (Bgk.). A simpler correction
would be καὶ κυψελίζων or ἐκυψέλιξε, in which case Hesych.
would be using a corrupt text. We should then further
read κυψελιστήν in gloss above. But there are many other
possibilities, *e.g.* κεῖται (ten Brink) with ψελίζων an otherwise
unknown verb.

52 That he be parched with famine and, led out
   A scapegoat, seven times on 's piece beaten.

(The scapegoat (expiatory offering) in old times was as
follows. Did misfortune, by the wrath of heaven, overtake
a city, whether famine or plague or other mischief, they led
out as to sacrifice the ugliest of all the citizens to be an
expiation and scapegoat of the diseased city. And having
set the sacrifice at such a spot as seemed fit they placed in his
hand cheese and barley-cake and dried figs. For after
beating him seven times on the penis with squills and (rods
of) wild fig and other wild trees they finally burnt him on a
fire of timber of such trees. . .[1] Hipponax describes the
custom best (47). Elsewhere he writes in the first book of
iambi (48), and again elsewhere in these words (49-51) and
elsewhere in the same book (52). *Tzetzes.*)

53 Th' incestuous Erythrean folk fooling
   With these things Bupalus with Aréte
   From day to day scuffled [2] his damned fodder.

θῆπον 'they marvelled [3]': pres. θήπω: so Hipp. (53).
Tzetzes. 'scuffle': tear. *Hesych. Cf. id.* 'scraping':
'scratching round, tearing round'; 'scrapes, gets, scratches.'

[1] Tzetzes first cites Lycophron 'as well as he can recall
him' and then these passages, which is merely a hypo-
critical cloak for the fact that he has borrowed them from
commentators on Lycophron.

[2] Like a hen, I take it.

[3] θηπ⟨έ⟩ω must, however, be taken transitively.

HIPPONAX

$54\frac{1\ 5}{3}$ †τε αρεδεύειε† τὴν ἐπὶ Σμύρνης

†ἴθι† διὰ Λυδῶν παρ[ὰ] τὸν †'Ατтάλεω†

τύμβον

καὶ σῆμα Γύγεω καὶ †μεγαστρυ† στήλην

καὶ μνῆμα †τωτος μυττάλυτα παλμυδος†,

πρὸς ἤλιον δύνοντα γαστέρα <σ>τρέψας.   5

(Tzetz. in *An. Ox.* iii. 310. 17 στίχοι 'Ιππ. τρισυλλάβους
ἔχοντες τοὺς παραλήγοντας πόδας . . καὶ †πᾶσαν† (54). Schol.
Nicander *Ther.* 633 Γύγου δὲ σῆμα τοῦ ἐκεῖ βασιλεύσαντος, ὡς
φησιν 'Ιππ. ἐν τῷ πρώτῳ τῶν [Λυδίας] ἰάμβων. **μυττάλυτα·**
μεγάλου Hesych.)

$55\frac{6\ 9}{2\ 3}$ [καὶ] τὴν ῥῖνα καὶ τὴν μύξαν ἐξαράξασα

(Tzetz. in *An. Ox.* iii. 308. 20 τὸ μέτρον τὸ Δωρικὸν παρέλειψα
λήθῃ· δέχεται δὲ πλεῖον τῶν ἄλλων ἰάμβ. μ. κατὰ τὴν β΄ χώραν ἢ
καὶ δ΄ ἢ ϛ΄ σπονδεῖον, σπανιάκις δὲ καὶ δάκτυλον ὡς ἰσόχρονον τῷ
σπονδείῳ· Δωρικὸν 'Ιππ. (55).)

54 In the text of Tzetzes read πάλιν (Meineke) for
πᾶσαν. In schol. Nicand. Λυδίας (idem) is a gloss on ἐκεῖ.
2 scans ἴθι δγὰ Λ.: but read ἰθύ. 4 μυτταλιδι Tz.: Hesych.'s
gloss was connected by Bgk. and M. Schmidt. For
suggestions on text see notes. No weight of textual evidence
will induce me to believe that the list contained foreign
dynasts, paramours and bastards. I fancy there is an
allusion to the conquest of Lydia. Perhaps begin ὁδὸν
τεωρεύεσκε . . . ἰθύ. **τεωρεύς·** . . . κακοῦργος, λῃστής (Hesych.).
55 ? μύσπαν : and give μυσπίη (Hesych.) to Hippon.

---

[1] Unfortunately we are helpless here. There seems no
reason to suppose the corruptions are slight. Attales (Nicol.
Dam. *fr.* 63) is mentioned as a bastard, Σεσώστριος Bgk.'s
suggestion in *v.* 3 intrudes a foreigner, and any unknown
name or person is improbable. Perhaps μεγαστρυ is partly

38

54 Along the road to Smyrna he ravag'd
　　Through Lydia straight by Alyattes' burrow,
　　By Gyges' grave, and Ardys' tomb mighty
　　And Sadyattes' monument, great tzar,
　　His belly turning, as he went, westward.[1]

(Verses of Hipp. with trisyllabic penultimate feet . . .
Again (54). *Tzetzes* [He mis-scans Ἀττᾰλέῶ as Ἀττᾰλέῶ!].
The tomb of Gyges who was king there, as Hipp. says in
the first book of his [Lydian] iambi. *Commentator* on
Nicander's Theriaca. μυττάλυτα: 'great.' *Hesychius*.)

55 [And] her nose, and the discharge therefrom
　　　knocking

(By a slip of memory I passed over the Dorian metre,
which more than other iambs contains spondees in the second,
fourth or sixth place, or rarely a dactyl as its metrical
equivalent. A Dorian verse of Hipponax (55). *Tzetzes*.)
[Tz.'s next citation suggests that he scanned μυξᾶν: but
I fancy he read τὴν μύξᾶν κᾰτᾰ τῆς ῥινὸς when we need only
read ἐκ for κατὰ to get good sense and metre.][2]

composed of an old gloss μεγίστου on †μυτταλυτα† (*infra*)
like Hesych.'s μεγάλου. The remainder may be καὶ ⟨παρ'⟩
Ἀρδυος στήλην. In *v.* 2 Ἀλυάττεω Schnw. is the nearest.
　　　　　　　　　　　　τοσαδυαττ
In *v.* 4 τωτοσμυττάλυτα might stand for τωλυαττεω. πάλμυδος
is known (Choerob. i. 232) to be an error, and anyhow it
must have ῠ. I suggest *e.g.* καὶ τὸ Σαδυάττεω μνῆμα Λυδίων
πάλμυνος or πάλμυν. Ἀτυος (Cr.) is nearer, but A. was never
a ruler (Hdt. i. 34): so παλμ. would have to go into another
verse. On the main point, that we have a list of Lydian
kings, I fancy the version is not misleading.
　[2] Before this may have come ἀποσκαμνυθίζειν: ἀπομυκτηρί-
ζειν Hesych.: *cf.* σκινθαρίζειν 'to strike the nose with the
middle finger,' id.

HIPPONAX

56 $\frac{17}{24}$ B δὸς χλαῖναν Ἱππώνακτι· κάρτα γὰρ ῥιγῶ
καὶ βαμβα‹λ›ύζω.

(Plutarch *Mor.* 1058 E ὁ δὲ ἐκ τῆς Στοᾶς βοῶν μέγα καὶ
κεκραγώς ' ἐγὼ μόνος εἰμὶ βασιλεύς, ἐγὼ μόνος εἰμὶ πλούσιος,' ὁρᾶται
πολλάκις ἐπ' ἀλλοτρίαις θύραις λέγων (56). The first verse is
quoted with variations of the moral 1068 B and 523 E. See
below. It is possible that the order is *fr.* 57 and *fr.* 56.
1 + ἐπεύχομαι—ῥιγῶ + καὶ β. So I translate. Then follows 59
perhaps with only two words missing.

57 $\frac{16}{24}$ $\frac{21}{A}$ ἐρ‹έ›ω, φίλ' Ἑρμῆ, Μαιαδεῦ Κυλλήν‹ε›ιε
[ἐπεύχομαί τοι· κάρτα γὰρ κακῶς ῥιγῶ].

(Tzetz. Lycophron 855 ἢ χρεία σοὶ καὶ ἑτέρας μαρτυρίας;
ἄκουσον (57)· καὶ μετά τινά φησιν (59). Priscian *de metr. Com.*
p. 251 L. ' Hipponactem etiam ostendit Heliodorus iambos
et choliambos confuse protulisse (57) ἐπεύχομαί τοι· κάρτα
γὰρ κακῶς ῥιγῶ. p. 247 L. (21 B Bgk.) Heliodorus metricus
ait: 'Ιππ. πολλὰ παρέβη τῶν νενομισμένων ἐν τοῖς ἰάμβοις. . .
Hipp. in primo ἐρέω [γὰρ οὕτω Κυλλήνιε Μαιάδος Ἑρμῆ]. Iste
enim versus cum sit choliambus, in quarto loco et quinto
habuit dactylos, cum in utroque debuerit a brevi incipiens
pes poni. In eodem (58). Iste iambus habet in secundo
loco spondeum et in quarto (*an error for* tertio) dactylum.)

58 $\frac{21}{28}$ B ἡ δ' ὀσφυῆγα καὶ ὀδυνοσπάδ' αἱρεῖται
γέροντα ‹νωδὸν . . . . . . κἀτερόφθαλμον›

(Plut. *Mor.* 1057 F καὶ κατ' Αἰσχύλου (an error of memory)
ἐξ 'ὀσφυαλγοῦς κὠδυνοσπάδος λυγροῦ γέροντος,' . . . *Lex. de*
Spir. p. 234 Valck. ὀσφυήξ· . . . ὡς τὸ ὀσφυῆγος γέροντος.
Priscian (*l.c.*) gives [τοὺς ἄνδρας τούτους] ὀδύνη παλλιρειτ (or π)αε.)

56. 2 βαμβακύζω: corr. Schnw.
57. 1 ὦ φίλ' Tz. ερμη or εραις Prisc.[1] ἐρέω Prisc.[2] Μαιάδος
Tz. ex gloss. quod integrum in Prisc.[2] habemus. In Prisc.[2]
ἐπεύχομαι is perhaps an explanation of ἐρέω. The words
from γὰρ to Ἑρμῆ are clearly a parallel citation, *e.g.*
'Αντίμαχος γὰρ οὕτω φησί κτλ. ' Iste enim versus,' etc.—not
unnaturally in a citation from Epic. κυλλήνειε Welcker.
58. 2 *e.g.* ὧδε. νωδὸν etc. Plut. *Mor.* 1058 A. The
Lexicon is no doubt quoting from a better ms. of Plutarch
than we possess.

56 I'll say dear son of Maia, Cyllene's
and Lord, give Hipponax a great coat : chilly
57 I am—I beg you I am right chilly
And my teeth chatter.

(But the Stoic philosopher, shouting aloud and crying
'I alone am king, I alone am rich,' is often seen at other
men's doors saying (56). *Plutarch* on the *Ultrapoetical
Absurdities of the Stoics* : also *On Common Conceptions*
and *On the Love of Riches*. Inaccurately quoted by *Heliodorus* the metrist as ' Verily I beseech thee : for full chilly
Am I,' and perhaps by *Tzetzes*, ' Give to Hipponax a great
coat, shirtlet,' etc. : see below, 59.)

57 See above and *fr.* 56.[1]

(If you need further evidence listen to this (57). Later he
says (59). *Tzetzes*. *Heliodorus* shows that Hipponax wrote
a mixture of choliambics and iambics (57). *Priscian*. *Heliodorus* the metrist says ' Hipponax broke many of the iambic
traditions. He says in the first book "For I will say thus :
son of Maia, Cyllenian Hermes." This verse, although
a choliambus, has dactyls in the fourth and fifth place,
although there should be in either place a foot beginning
with a short. In the same book (58). This iambus has
in the second place a spondee, and in the fourth (*he means*
" third ") a dactyl.' *Priscian*.)

58 ⟨She⟩ a hip-shot old man, pain-racked, chooses,[2]
⟨Toothless, one-eyed⟩

(And to be changed from what Aeschylus (? Hipponax)
calls a ' hip-pained sorry old man ' to a beautiful god-like
fair shaped youth. *Plutarch* on *The Stoics say*, etc. ' Hip-
shot': *e.g.* hip-shot old man. *Breathing Dictionary*.)

[1] It is clear that Heliodorus drew the verses from a copy
of Hipponax' works interlarded with glosses and marginal
comments. Perhaps these were the first verses.

[2] Priscian gives

Indeed all these men in a pain racked chooses.

Plutarch in the next sentence to that quoted, speaking of
Odysseus in Homer, introduces some details, I suggest from
Hipponax. The reference would be to Arete and Bupalus.

HIPPONAX

59₂₄⁸ δὸς χλαῖναν Ἱππώνακτι καὶ κυπασσίσκον
καὶ σαμβαλίσκα κἀσκερίσκα καὶ χρυσοῦ
στατῆρας ἑξήκοντα τούτερου τοίχου.

(Tzetz. Lycophron 855 οὗτος ἀσκέρας τὰ ὑποδήματα οὐ καλῶς
λέγει (59). ἀσκέραι¹ δὲ κυρίως τὰ ἐν τοῖς ποσὶ πιλία ἤτοι ὀρτάρια¹
λέγονται καὶ χλαῖναν¹ τὸ σφικτούριον¹ καὶ κυπασσίσκον¹ τὸ
ἐπιλωρικόν.¹ οὗτος δὲ ὁ Λυκόφρων, καίπερ ἀπ' Αἰσχύλου κλέπτων
λέξεις τινάς, ἐξ Ἱππ. δὲ πλέον, ἢ ἐπιλήσμων ὤν, ἢ μὴ νοῶν
ταύτας, ἄλλην ἄλλως ἐκτίθει . . . ἀλλ' ἄκουε πῶς φησιν Ἱππ.
(60). ἔγνως ὅτι διὰ τὸ εἰπεῖν δασείας τὰς ἀσκέρας τὰ ὀρτάριά
φησιν; ἤ . . (57). καὶ μετά τινά φησιν (59).)

60₂₅¹⁹ ἐμοὶ γὰρ †οὐκ ἔδωκας οὔτε χλαῖναν†
δασεῖαν, ἐν χειμῶνι φάρμακον ῥίγευς,
οὔτ' ἀσκέρῃσι τοὺς πόδας δασείῃσιν
ἔκρυψας ὥς <μοι μὴ> χίμετλα γί[γ]νηται.

(Tzetz. vide sup.)

61₂₀²⁹ ἐμοὶ δὲ Πλοῦτος, ἔστι γὰρ λίην τυφλός,
ἐς τὠικί' ἐλθὼν οὐδάμ' εἶπεν· Ἱππῶναξ,
δίδωμί <σ>οι μν<έ>ας ἀργύρ[ί]ου τριήκοντα.

(Tzetz. on Ar. Plut. 90 τυφλὸν δὲ τὸν Πλοῦτόν φησιν ἐξ
Ἱππώνακτος τοῦτο σφετερισάμενος· φησὶ γὰρ οὕτως Ἱππ. (61)
καὶ πόλλ' ἔτ' ἄλλα· δείλαιος γὰρ τὰς φρένας.

59 In almost all codd. the text is covered with glosses.
Besides the three explanations above, over τούτερου is
ἰωνικῶς (sc. for Attic θἀτ.) and μέρους over τοίχου. One
codd. has τοῦ νερτέρου τοίχου (? an error for ἐνδοτέρου). μοι after
χρυσοῦ codd. plur.
60. 1 One cod. has τὰν χλαῖναν. e.g. οὔτε κω Scaliger.
3 δασείῃσι: one cod. φησί. 4 ῥίγνυται one cod.: γίγν. corr.
Hoffmann. μή μοι codd.
61. 3 τοι codd.: σοι Bgk. ἀργυρίου codd.: corr. id.
καὶ πόλλ' κτλ. has falsely been given to Hipponax: cf.
καὶ πολλαχοῦ δυστηνὰ τοιαυτὶ λέγει Aeschrion (fr. 1 q.v.).
Those who insist on giving them to Hipponax should read
δείλαγος γὰρ and find a substitute for τὰς φρένας.

42

59 Give to Hipponax a great-coat, shirtlet,
   Sandals and carpet-slippers; and sixty
   Staters of gold by th' inner wall hidden.[1]

(Lycophron wrongly uses the word ' slippers ' for boots
(59). 'Slippers' properly mean the felt-shoes, that is
ortaria, worn on the feet, great-coat the *sphictorium*, and
shirtlet the *epiloricum*. This Lycophron, though stealing
some words from Aeschylus, while preferring Hippon., either
from forgetfulness or ignorance of their sense uses them
anyhow. . . . Listen to what *Hipp*. says (60). You realize
that by calling them ' shaggy ' he means *ortaria*. But *cf.*
(57). Later he says (59). *Tzetzes on Lycophron*.)

60 To me thou gavest never (yet) great-coat
   Shaggy, a cure for ague in winter,
   Nor hid'st in carpet-slippers right shaggy
   My feet, to hinder my chillblains growing.

(See above 59 *Tzetzes*.)

61 But never came there Plutus, the blind one,
   Unto my house, nor spake thus: ' Hipponax
   Minas of silver give I thee thirty.'
   [Etcetera : for his intelligence is paltry].[2]

(He calls Plutus blind, borrowing the epithet from
Hipponax, who says as follows (61). *Tzetzes on Aristophanes'
Plutus*.)

[1] τουτέρου τοίχου is of course the inner wall by which the
host sits (Hom. I 219), and the gold is to be there since
the task of the thief who digs under the walls (τοιχωρύχος)
would thereby be rendered more difficult. Refer perhaps to
this passage the word τοιχοδιφήτωρ=τοιχωρύχος cited by
Hesych. ὁρτάρια and σφικτ. are both late mediaeval words.
I note πόδορτα and σφικτ. in Achmes the oneiromancer.

[2] Tzetzes, who presumably borrowed this citation from
an earlier commentator, perhaps on Lycophron (1102 ?),
included the last words (which are really the grammarian's
criticism of L.) in his note. Or they may be Tz.'s own
criticism on Aristophanes' peculations from Hipponax.

LATE CITATIONS

From Uncertain Books

62$^{30A}_{34}$ ὦ Ζεῦ πάτερ ⟨Ζεῦ⟩ θεῶν Ὀλυμπίων πάλμυ

(Tzetz. on Lyc. 690 ἡ δὲ λέξις ὁ πάλμυς ἐστὶν Ἰώνων καὶ χρῆται ταύτῃ Ἱππ. λέγων (62, 63).)

63$^{30B}_{35}$ τί μ᾽ οὐκ ἔδωκας χρυσόν, ἀργύρου [πάλμυ];

(Vid. supra.)

64$^{31}_{36}$ †ἀπό σ᾽ ὀλέσειεν Ἄρτεμις, σὲ δ[ὲ κ]᾽ ὠπόλ-
λων†,

⟨σὲ δ᾽⟩. . . .

(Tzetz. An. Ox. iii. 310. 17 στίχοι Ἱππ. τρισυλλάβους ἔχοντες τοὺς παραλήγοντας πόδας (64). Contrast (Bgk.) Hephaestion p. 30 (33 Gaisf.) τὸ δὲ χωλὸν οὐ δέχεται τοὺς παραλ. τρισ. πόδ. id. Exeg. in Il. 797 B.)

65$^{32}_{37}$ παρ᾽ ᾧ σὺ λευκόπεπλον ἡμέρην μείνας
πρὸς μὲν κυνήσει⟨ς⟩ τὸν Φλυησίων᾽
Ἑρμῆν.

(Tzetz. Il. p. 83. 25 H. ἐπὶ μῦθον ἔτελλεν· ὑπερβατόν· ἐστι δὲ καὶ τοῦτο Ἰωνικὸν ὥς φησι καὶ Ἱππ. (64). καὶ ἀλλαχοῦ (65). Hesych. **Φλυήσιος·** Ἑρμῆς καὶ μήν τις.

62 ⟨Ζεῦ⟩ rectissime Meineke ex Archil. 88 (Bgk.). v.l. Ὀλ. θεῶν.
63 πάλμυ] v.l. πάλμυν : see opposite.
64 δὲ κῶπ. : corrected by Meineke.
65. 2 κυνήσειν cod.: corr. Welcker. Φλυησίων᾽ Bgk. olim rectissime. Hesych. φλυησί†ο†s is (?) corrupt, for months may end in -ων or -εών (so perhaps -εών᾽ here). Nor do they say ὁ Δηλίων Ἀπόλλων but ὁ Δήλιος.

44

LATE CITATIONS

FROM UNCERTAIN BOOKS

62 Zeus, tsar of Gods Olympian, father

(The word ' tsar ' is Ionic and used by *Hipponax* when he says (62, 63). *Tzetzes* on *Lycophron*.)

63 Why, tsar of silver, me no gold gav'st thou ?[1]

(See above.)

*64 May Artemis destroy thee, [and] Apollo,

(Verses of *Hipp.* (64) with the penultimate foot trisyllabic. *Tzetzes* in *Cramer's Anecdota Oxoniensia*. Contrast *Hephaestion* : the choliambic does not allow trisyllables in the penultimate foot.)

65 Whereat awaiting day of white raiment
    Phlyesiary Hermes thou 'lt worship.

(' Gave a harsh order ' : transposition (for made good his word) ; this is Ionic as *Hipponax* too says (64). And elsewhere (65). *Tzetzes.* ' Phlyesian ' : Hermes : also a month. *Hesych.*[2])

---

[1] 62 and 63 I have given separately. But more probably they came together and πάλμυν is mere dittography, ' Why gavest not gold nor mountains of silver,' *e.g.* χρ. ⟨ἢ⟩ (so Lobeck) ἄργυρον πολλόν ;

[2] Hesychius' note ' Phlyesian ' : Hermes, also a month— shows that Phlyesiary is the right reading.

66$^{4\ 2}_{4\ 1}$ ἐπ' ἁρμάτων τε καὶ Θρ‹ε›ϊκίων πώλων
    λευκῶν ὀ‹ρ›ούσ‹ας› ἐγγὺς Ἰλίου πύργων
    ἀπηναρίσθη Ῥῆσος Αἰν[ε]ίων πάλμυς.

(Tzetz. on *Posthomer.* 186 ὁ δὲ Ῥῆσος Αἰνειῶν Θράκης ἦν
βασιλεύς, υἱὸς Στρύμονος ἢ Ἠιονέος καὶ Τερψιχόρης . . . καὶ Ἱππ.
(66). On *Il.* 78. 1 H. καὶ ἀντὶ τῶν δασέων ψιλὰ ἐξεφώνουν ὡς
ἔχει ἡ ἀρχαία Ἰωνική, ἐπιβρύκων ἀντὶ τοῦ ἐπιβρύχων, καὶ τὸ
(66. 1), καὶ μεταρμόσας. Hesych. **Νεαίρησιν ἵπποις·** τοὺς ἀπὸ
Νεαίρης.

67$^{4\ 3}_{4\ 2}$ κακοῖσι δώσω τὴν πολύστονον ψυχήν,
    ἢν μὴ ἀποπέμψῃς ὡς τάχιστά μοι κριθέων
    μέδιμνον ὡς ἂν ἄλφιτον ποιήσωμαι,
    κυκεῶνα πίνων, φάρμακον πονηρ[ί]οῖσ‹ι›.

(Tzetz. *An. Ox.* iii. 308 δέχονται καὶ τρισυλλάβους πόδας εἰς (?)
ς´, πλὴν τοὺς ἀπὸ βραχείας ἀρχομένους, τὸν χορεῖον φημὶ καὶ τὸν
ἀνάπαιστον ὡς ὁ Ἱππ. (69) καὶ πάλιν (so Meineke) (68).
Hesych.)

68$^{4\ 2}_{4\ 5}$ Μιμνῆ, †κατωμμηχανετ· μηκέτι γράψῃς
    ὄφιν τριήρευς ἐν πολυζύγῳ τοίχῳ
    ἀπ' ἐμβόλου φεύγοντα πρὸς κυβερνήτην·
    αὕτη γὰρ ἔστ‹α›ι συμφορά τε καὶ κληδὼν
    †νικύρτα καὶ σαβωνι† τῷ κυβερνήτῃ   5
    ἢν αὐτὸν ‹ὁ› ὄφις †τὠντικνήμιον δάκῃ†.

(Tzetz. on Lycophron 425 **"Αποθεν** τὸ π̄ο̄ μικρὸν γράφε

66. 1 Θρηϊκίων : correxit Fick. 2 ὀείους κάτεγγυς codd. 3
παλάμας one cod.: βασιλεύς cett. Text Schneidewin. Perhaps
there was an incorrect variant ἰθύς, and καὶ ἐγγύς was written
in the margin. If so ὀ is all that is left of the participle
except that one cod. has an explanation ἰὼν in the margin.
67. 3 Scan πὄγήσωμαι or *l.* πονήσ. 4 πονηρίοις cod. : corr.
Fick. ? πᾶσι for πίνων with ἀλφίτων in 3.
68. 1 κακῶν μοχλητά ten Brink. If a vocative, κατωμόδαρτε
is near the traces, but perhaps it is a verb; *e.g.* κακοῦ μὴ
ἴχαινε or κατ' ὦν μὴ χαῖνε (Hes. **καταχηνη**) which might have
degenerated into ἔχανε. γράφῃς one cod. v.l. 4 ἔστι : v.l.
αὕτη. 5 vv.ll. σινωνι, δαβωνι, σαμαυνι. 6 vv.ll. τ' ἀνακείμενον
των τικνήμων, τῶν τι κνημένον. See Addenda.

46

FRAGMENTS 66–68

66 On cariot and Thracīan horses
 All white he sallied and near [1] Troy's castles
 There was he slain tsar Aeneian Rhesus.

(Rhesus was king of the Aeneians in Thrace, son of
Strymon or Eioneus and Terpsichore (66). *Tzetzes* on *Posthomerica*.[2] They used smooth consonants instead of aspirated
like old Ionic *souting* instead of *shouting*, and (66. 1), and
resaping. *id*. ' Neaerean Horses ': from Neaera. *Hesych*

67 To woe my weeping soul I 'll surrender
 Unless at once you send me a bushel
 Of barley, wherewithal I may find me,
 By drinking groats, of all my ills respite.

(Trisyllables are allowed in the sixth foot except those
beginning with a short vowel, *i.e.* ∪∪∪ and ∪∪ – : *e.g.*
Hipp. (67), and again (68). *Tzetz.* in *Cramer's Anecdota
Oxoniensia*.)[3]

68 Yearn not for mischief, Mimnes.[4] Cease painting
 A snake upon the trireme's benched bulwarks
 Which runs from prow abaft to the helmsman.
 For this brings evil fame and fate evil,
 Thou slave of slaves and yid, to the helmsman,
 If right upon his shin [the] snake bite him.

(ἄποθεν: write *sic* with omicron. Scribes ignorant of

---

[1] Read either 'straight for ' or ' sallied: hard by.'
[2] Tzetzes purloined this note from a long note by an
earlier editor of Lycophron on the use of πάλμυς ' tsar.'
[3] The criticism (that κριθεῶν is trisyllabic) is erroneous,
as erroneous as the criticism of the next citation ἄπōθεν.
Nor can anyone have written ὄφις in 68. 6, as the snake
has already been mentioned. In view of this, -τὠντῐκνήμιον
and δάκῃ, the verse may be an early gloss. If the steerer
exposes to the snake the *back* of his leg or calf the sense of
ἀντικν. in Hipp.'s time—' shin ' or the forepart—is somewhat
unsuitable. δάκη has been altered to δάκνῃ. Σάμορνα,
"God help us," is said to have been another name for
Ephesus from its Semitic inhabitants: Schmidt on Hesych.
s.v. Σαμονία.   [4] ? Mimnes thou well-bespankéd.

47

οὗτοι (the ms.?) δὲ ἀγνοήσαντες τὸ μέτρον μέγα τοῦτο γράφουσι. σὺ δὲ τοῦτο γίγνωσκε ὅτι τὸ δασὺ ἐκτείνειν δύναται ὅτε βούλεται ὁ στιχιστὴς ἴσως τοῖς διπλοῖς ὡς ... Τρῶες δ' ἐρρίγησαν ὅπως ἴδον αἰόλον ὄφιν (Hom. M 208). εἰ δὲ μείουρον τοῦτον νομίζεις ἄκουσον καὶ τῶν κατὰ Μιμνῇ τοῦ ζωγράφου χωλῶν ἰάμβων Ἱππωνακτείων στίχων (68). ἰδοὺ τοῦ ὄφις τὸ ο μακρόν ἐστιν ἐκταθὲν ὑπὸ τοῦ φ δασέος ὄντος. νικύρτας· δουλέκδουλος. Ath. vi. 267 c (cit. ten Brink) σίνδρωνα δὲ τὸν δουλέκδουλον.)

69 $^{7\,4}_{6\,7}$ οὔ μοι δικαίως μοιχὸς †ἀλῶναι δοκεῖ†
†Κριτίης ὁ Χῖος ἐν τῷ κατωτικῳ δούλῳ†

(Tzetz. vid. supra 68. Hesych. δοῦλος· ἡ οἰκία ἢ τὴν ἐπὶ τὸ αὐτὸ συνέλευσιν τῶν γυναικῶν.)

70 $^{5\,1}_{4\,7}$ ὁ δ' αὐτίκ' ἐλθὼν σὺν τριοῖσι μάρτυ<ρ>σιν
ὅκου τὸν ἔρπιν ὁ σκότος καπηλεύει
ἄνθρωπον εὗρε τὴν στέγην ὀφέλλοντα—
οὐ γὰρ παρῆν ὄφελμα—πυθμένι στοιβῆς.

(Tzetz. on Lycophron 579 ἔρπιν· χάλις καὶ ἔρπις ὁ οἶνος. χάλις μὲν παρὰ τὸ χαλᾶν τὴν ἵνα ἤγουν τὴν δύναμιν ἔρπις δὲ κτλ. ὅθεν καὶ οἱ Αἰγύπτιοι τὸν οἶνον ἔρπιν καλοῦσι. Ἱππωνάκτειοι δέ εἰσιν αἱ λέξεις. φησὶ γάρ (72). ἀλλαχοῦ δὲ πάλιν (70. 1-3). On 1165 ὀφελτρεύσωσι· σαρώσωσι· σάρον γὰρ καὶ ὄφελτρον καὶ ὄφελμα καὶ ὄφελμος ἡ σκοῦπα λέγεται. καὶ τοῦτο Ἱππ. φησίν (70). On Ar. Plut. 435 (v. 2). The second verse is quoted in an older scholium on Lyc. ll.cc. Hesych. Πέρδικος καπηλεῖον· χωλὸς καπηλὸς ὁ Π. ἦν. ἔνθεν ἔνιοι τὴν παροιμίαν φασὶ διαδοθῆναι.)

69. 2 mss give either κατωξ or κτωξ (i.e. κτωικῳ). See Bast's *Commentatio Palaeographica*, Tab. vii. 7, 8. Bgk.'s remark, ' Sunt enim iambi (sc. recti)' is inane, since Tz. quotes for trisyllables (exc. ⏑⏑⏑ and ⏑⏑–) in the final place of choliambi. On 2 see nn.

70. 1 ? αὐτις. μάρτυρσιν Buttmann. 2 ὅπου only schol. Ar. Plut. v.l. σκοπὸς. 3 εὑρών and ὁρῶν vv.ll.

---

[1] See crit. n. Bgk.'s suggestion κασωρ- is excellent. Hesychius' inane note rightly referred here by Ahrens should have provided food for thought for scholars who believe in

metrical rules write omega. But you, gentle reader, must
realize that an aspirate may at the will of the author count
two letters and lengthen the previous vowel, *e.g.* ὄφις in
Homer, *Il.* (M 208). If you think this verse ' docked '
cf. further *Hipp.'s* choliambi attacking Mimnes the painter
(68). Here you have ὄφις before φ aspirate. *Tzetzes* on
Lycophron. νικύρτας: slave of slave birth. *Hesychius.*)

69 †Unjust the Chian court that condemned you
   Tamquam adulter in lupanari [1]†

(*Tzetzes*: see on 68. *Slave*: House or a collection of
women in the same place. *Hesychius.*)

70 With three to witness he returned straightway
   To where the runaway his swipes peddles
   And found a man who, having no besom,
   Was besoming the house with a broom-stick.

(' Swipes ': booze and swipes are names for wine. The
former is derived from brawn and loose, *i.e.* loosening the
strength: the latter (etc.). Hence the Egyptians call wine
swipes. The words are used by *Hipp.*, who says (70).
Again elsewhere (70. 1-3). *Tzetzes* on *Lycophron*, 579).
On 1165 commenting on the unfamiliar verb " besom " *Tz.*
gives various forms for ' sweep,' ' sweeping,' and quotes all
four verses. He quotes *v.* 2 again on Aristophanes' *Plutus.*
They were also given by a previous critic of Lycophron.
' The hostel of Perdix ': Perdix was a lame innkeeper after
whom some say this proverb became traditional.[2] *Hesych.*)

the word μαλις and the like. As δοκεῖ is not a trisyllable
with a long vowel it follows that we must end the second
verse ἐν κασωρῖτέῳ: one may therefore write (*e.g.*) with
Ahrens οὔ μοι δικαίως ὥστε μοιχὸς ἁλῶναι δοκέει Κριτίης ὁ
Χῖος ἐν κ., but it is perhaps permissible to suspect that the
whole is a satirical attack on Bupalus: οὔ μοι δικαίως ἐν
κρίτῃσι Χίοισι δοκέεις ἁλῶναι μοιχὸς ἐν κασωρίτεω. This I
translate. There is a further doubt that really we may have
κατωτάτῳ, a favourite word of Tz. in explanation, *e.g.* on
Lyc. 121 ἐν τῷ τοῦ κρυπτοῦ καὶ κατωτάτου τόπου σήραγγι.
   [2] I suggest that there was an older Perdix who gave rise
to this tag if it is choliambic. The famous innkeeper (*Av.*
1292) of this name was, however, an Athenian   See Addenda.

HIPPONAX

71 $^{64}_{56}$ ⟨’Αθηνα⟨ίη⟩⟩
⟨ὶ⟩λ⟨ά⟩σκο⟨μαί σ⟩ε καὶ με δεσπότε⟨ω⟩
βεβροῦ
λαχόντα λίσσομαί σε μὴ ῥαπίζεσθαι.

(Tzetz. *An. Ox.* iii. 310. 17 στίχοι Ἱππώνακτος τρισυλλάβους
ἔχοντες τοὺς παραλήγοντας πόδας. . . πᾶσα (*l.* πάλιν Meineke)
(71). Hesych. **βεβρός·** ψυχρός, τετυφωμένος. **βέβροξ·** ἀγαθός,
χρηστός, καλός· and see below.)

DOUBTFUL FRAGMENTS

72 $^{73}_{66}$ †ολιγὰ φρον⟨έ⟩ουσιν οἱ χάλιν πεπωκότες.†

(Tzetz. on Hes. *Op.* 336 ὁ γὰρ οἶνος τὰς φρένας ἐξιστᾷ· ἐνίοτε
καὶ θυμὸν ἐπάγει ὡς καὶ Ἱππ. (72). Sch. Ar. *Plut.* 437, on
Lycophron 579 (see *fr.* 70), Miller, *Mél.* 307). Verses
possibly to be ascribed to Ananius.)

73*$^{55}_{26}$ ᴮ Ἑρμῆς δὲ Σιμώνακτος ἀκολουθήσας

(Miller, *Mél.* 19 ἀκολουθήσας (73).   ἐκτάσει τοῦ ᾶ· οὕτως
Ἡρωδιανός.)

71. 1 Ἀθηναίη ita Bgk.?   The word Ἀθηνᾶ is a gloss on
the corrupt μάλις : but it is quite probable that Ἀθ. preceded.
                    χαιρε
Μαλισκονισκε ms. A : κονισκελαιρε cett.   χαῖρε Bgk. rightly
explained as a gloss.   **μαλίς·** Ἀθηνᾶ Hesych.   For my
reading *cf.* Ἀληθι· χαῖρε Hesych.   2 δεσποτεα βεβροῦ : corr.
Schneidewin.   The last word is glossed μα[. . .]οῦ: ? μαλακοῦ
Hoffmann.
72 Very doubtful.   Perhaps οἱ . . . πεπώκασιν.   *v.l.* πεπτ-.
50

71   O Athéne,
I cry thee hail and beg that I gentle
Master may win, and feel not his cudgel.

(Verses of *Hipponax* with trisyllables in the penultimate
feet. . . Again (71). *Tzetzes* in *Cramer's Anecdota Oxoniensia*.)

DOUBTFUL FRAGMENTS

72 †Full little wit have men who sup on booze.†

(For wine removes wits: occasionally too it induces
passion as *Hipp.* says (72). *Tzetzes* on *Aristophanes' Plutus,
Lycophron*. Also the *Etymologicum*, but without naming
the author.)

73 †Hermes who followed, son of Simonax [1]†

(ἀκολουθήσας. So *Herodian* explains the scansion.)

[1] I am inclined to think the citation spurious and post-
Attic. See on Herodas ii. 47. I read ἁ or ὡκ.

---

73 If Herodian is to be trusted, and his authority is great,
it is perhaps more likely that ᾱκ is some peculiarity of
Ephesian dialect, than that it is an innovation of a later
writer. Lehrs reads Ἑρμῆς δ' ἐς Ἱππώνακτος. But even
Herodian may have been deceived by a false text, and ἀκολ.
is far more fitted to a gloss than to any early Ionic writer.
Even Hrd. eschews it. The real word may have taken the
genitive.

HIPPONAX

74*⁶¹₆₄   ἀνὴρ ὅδ' ἑσπέρης καθεύδοντα
ἀπ' ⟨ὦ⟩ν ἔδ⟨υ⟩σε †χλούνην.†

(Schol. Hom. I 539 χλούνην: οἱ μὲν ἀφριστήν· χλουδεῖν γὰρ
τὸ ἀφρίζειν τινες Δωριέων ἔλεγον· ἄλλοι δὲ κακοῦργον· καὶ γὰρ
τῶν ἀρχαίων ἰαμβοποιῶν τινα φάναι (74). Ξενοφῶντα δὲ γένος τι
Ἰνδῶν φάναι τὸν χλούνην εἶναι.)

(See also Introduction and after *fr.* 86.)

75³⁵₃₀ₐ See Phoenix *fr.* 8.

76*   ἐκ πελλίδος ⟨δὲ⟩ τάργανον κα[ι]τηγυίης
χωλοῖσι δακτύλοισι τήτέρη σπένδει
τρέμων οἷόν περ ἐν βορηΐῳ νωδός.

(Ath. 495 c Πέλλα· . . . εἰς ὃ ἤμελγον τὸ γάλα. . . Ἱππ.
λέγει πελλίδα (4, 5), Φοῖνιξ δὲ ὁ Κολοφώνιος ἐν τοῖς Ἰάμβοις
ἐπὶ φιάλης τίθησι λέγων οὕτως (Phoenix *fr.* 4). καὶ ἐν ἄλλῳ δὲ
μέρει φησίν (76). Hesych. τάργανον· ὄξος, Λυδοί.)

74 Dindorf may be right in placing χλούνην at the end of
v. 2, or Meineke in placing it at the beginning. More
probably Bgk. is right in placing χλούνης at the beginning
of *v.* 1. 2 οὖν codd.: corr. Schnw. ἔδησε codd.: corr.
Hermann.
76. 1 ⟨δὲ⟩ Schnw. καὶ τηγ. Ath.: corr. Porson.

---

¹ I translate Bergk's conjecture : see crit. n.
² Xenoph(anes) and (S)indi : so Hermann and Bergk.
³ 76 appears to me certainly Hipponactean. (*a*) There

52

74 †This rogue[1] here as I was at eve sleeping
   Stripped me.†

('Rogue' (of a boar): some explain as 'foaming' · for
certain Dorians spoke of foaming as 'roguing.' Others as
'villain': for, they say, one of the old (chol)iambic writers
said (74). Xenophanes says that rogue was the name of a
man of Sindi.)[2]

75 (See Phoenix *fr.* 8.)

76 And tarragon out of a smashed paillet
   With limping fingers of one hand dribbles,
   A-tremble like the toothless in north wind.[3]

('Pail': . . . into which they used to milk. . . *Hipp.*
speaks of it as 'paillet' (4, 5). Phoenix of Colophon in his
iambi uses it of a cup, as follows (Phoenix, *fr.* 4). And
in another portion of his works he says (76). *Athenaeus.*
'Tarragon': vinegar, a Lydian use. *Hesych.*)

re no difficulties of metre in the ascription. Every other
verse in our *frr.* of Phoenix is metrically impossible for
Hipp. So in *fr.* 1 v. 1, 3 ?, 6, 8 (*bis*), 9, 12, 14 (τοῖσι), 15,
17 (see *J. Camb. Phil.* 1927). (*b*) The tone is that of a virulent
lampoonist, not of a plaintive cynic. (*c*) The misery of the
sketch is accentuated if we transfer this paragraph to the
'pail' illustrations. (*d*) Hipp. certainly *used* not only
ἑλλίς but also the word τάργανον as the gloss shows. Phoen.
is not very fond of direct imitations, despite λέκος πυρῶν *frr.*
1, 2. If I am right in supposing Plut. had Hipp. in mind
when writing on the ultra-poetical absurdities of the Stoics
ᾠδός may also be Hipponactean. As against these argu-
ments we may set χωλοῖσι (deb. κυλλ.) and οἶονπερ (deb.
τονπ.). (*f*) They are far too good and concentrated for
Phoenix. Contrast his *fr.* 3. (*g*) What 'other portion'?

TRIMETER OR TETRAMETER

77⁷ ⁶₆ ₉ †λαιμώσσει δέ σ‹ε›υ† τὸ χεῖλος ὥσ‹τ›
ἐρῳδιοῦ.

(Schol. Nicand. *Ther.* 470 μαιμώσσων: ἀντὶ τοῦ ζητῶν κα
ὁρμῶν. γράφεται δὲ καὶ λαιμώσσων ἀντὶ τοῦ πεινῶν ὡς Ἱππ. (77)
Hesych. λαιμᾷ· εἰς βρῶσιν ὥρμηται.)

TETRAMETERS

78⁸ ³₇ ₀ λάβετέ μ‹ε›υ ταἰμάτι‹α›, κόψω Βουπάλο·
τὸν ὀφθαλμόν·
ἀμφιδέξιος γάρ εἰμι, κοὐκ ἁμαρτάνω κόπτων

(Suid. Βούπαλος· ὄνομα. Ἀριστοφάνης· εἰ νὴ Δί[α] ‹ἤδη› [τις
τὰς γνάθους τούτων ‹τις ἢ› δὶς ἢ τρὶς ἔκοψεν ὥσπερ Βουπάλου
φωνὴν ἂν οὐκ ἂν εἶχον. παρὰ τῷ Ἱππ. (78. 1). *id.* κόπτω· εἰ ν·
Δία . . . αὐτῶν . . . καὶ αὖθις (78. 1). Erotian p. 43 ἀμφιδέξιος . .
ὁ δὲ Ἱπποκράτης . . ἐπὶ τοῦ εὐχρήστου κατὰ ἀμφότερα τὰ μέρη .
ὁμοίως δὲ καὶ ὁ Ἱππῶναξ φησίν (v. 2). Galen, *Gloss. Hippocr*
430, *Aphorism.* xviii. 1. 148 also quote v. 2 but withou·
κόπτων.)

79⁷ ⁹₁ ₃ καὶ δικάζεσθαι Βίαντος τοῦ Πριηνέ‹ο›·
κρέσσων

(Strabo xiv. 636, Diog. L. i. 84, Suid. *s.vv.* Βίαντο·
Πριηνέως (one cod. -έος) δίκη and δικάζεσθαι.)

77 The words can easily be arranged, with slight altera-
tions, for a tetrameter. But see n. *v.l.* λαιμῷ. σου codd·
Some om. δέ σου.
78. 1 ? τῆτε for λάβετε. μου corr. by Schnw. θαἰμάτια Bgk
for θοἰμάτιον· ται. (trisyll.) Hi.-Cr. *v.l.* Βουπάλῳ. 2 Th·
fragments were connected by Bgk. καὶ οὐχ, κοὐχ mss.: corr
ten Brink. Suidas was copying a lost schol. on Arist·
Lys. 360.
79 ἃ καὶ κτλ. Diog. L.: Meineke cj. πρώτῳ. ἃ καὶ om
Suid. δικάσασθαι Strabo. Πριηνέως codd. omn. κρέσσο·
Strabo: κρείσσων Suid.: κρεῖσσον Diog. L.

FRAGMENTS 77–79

TRIMETER OR TETRAMETER

77 But thy lip raveneth as a heron's.[1]

('Raving': seeking and hastening. Some write 'raven-ing,' meaning hungry: *cf. Hipp.* (77). *Commentator* on *Nicander's Theriaca.*)

TETRAMETERS

78 Here take my clothes, so in the eye I 'll Bupalus
      pummel;
  For I am ambidexterous and pummelling miss
      not.[2]

('Bupalus': a name. Aristophanes 'In faith if some one twice or thrice the jaws of these had pummelled, as it was done to Bupalus, no voice would they have left them.' In *Hipp.* (78. 1). *Suidas.* 'Pummel.' 'In faith,' etc. And again (78. 1). *id.* 'Ambidexterous': . . . Hippocrates . . uses of those whose limbs are equally efficient on both sides of the body . . . So in *Hipp.* (78. 2). *Erotian.* Also twice cited by *Galen.*)

79 Than Bias of Priene far a better judge (finding)

(*Strabo, Diogenes Laertius, Suidas* on 'Bias of Priene' and 'judge.')

[1] With the Greeks almost all diving birds and sea birds are types of gluttony. With us only the cormorant enjoys that position. Probably read τὸ σεῦ δὲ χεῖλος ὥστε ῥωδιοῦ αἱμᾶ.
[2] It is by no means certain that these verses are consecutive.

HIPPONAX

80 $^{80}_{74}$ μηδὲ μοιμύλ[α]λειν Λεβεδίην ἰσχάδ' ἐι
Καμανδωλοῦ

(Sext. Emp. *adv. Math.* i. 275 Λεβεδίων γοῦν διαφερομένω
πρὸς τοὺς ἀστυγείτονας περὶ Καμανδωλοῦ ὁ γραμματικὸς τὸ 'Ιππωνά
κτειον παραθέμενος ἐνίκα (80). Hesych. μοιμύλλειν· θηλάζει
ἐσθίειν.)

81 $^{82}_{75}$ Κυπρίων ‹λ›έκος φαγοῦσι κἀμαθουσίω
†πυρῶν†

(Strabo viii. 340 συγκαταλέγειν τὸ μέρος τῷ ὅλῳ φασὶ τὸ
"Ομηρον. . . χρῶνται δὲ καὶ οἱ νεώτεροι· 'Ιππ. μὲν (81). Κύπρι
γὰρ καὶ οἱ 'Αμαθούσιοι. Eust. *Il.* 305. 23.)

82 $^{62}_{71}$ οἱ δέ μευ ὀδόντες
‹οἳ κοτ'› ἐν τοῖσι γναθοῖσι πάντες ‹ἐκ›
κεκινέαται.

(Cram. *An. Ox.* i. 287. 28 μεμετρέαται· . . . 'Ιωνικόν· . .
καὶ παρ' 'Ιππώνακτι (82). *Et. Mag.* 499. 41. Miller, *Mé*
181. 8 (omitting γναθοῖσι.)

83 $^{84}_{76}$ †ἐξ†. . . . | τίλλοι τις αὐτοῦ τὴν τράμιν τ
ὑποργά‹ζο›ι.

(Erotian p. 124 τράμιν· τὸν ὄρρον ὄνπερ καὶ ὑποταύρια
καλοῦμεν ὡς καὶ 'Ιππ. φησίν (83). μέμνηται καὶ 'Αρχίλοχος
Λυσίμαχος δὲ τὸν σφιγκτῆρα.)

80. 1 μοι μύ λαλεῖν codd.: corr. Meineke. Καμανδωδο
most codd. Λεβεδίην trisyll. ?
81 βέκος codd. φαγοῦσι om. Eust. πυρῶν Eust.: πυρ
Strabo: ? πυρέων Hrd.; *cf.* ii. 80.
82 Metre restored by Ahrens. 2 ‹ἐκ› ten Brink. οἳ κοτ'
have inserted *metri gratia*.
83 τράμιν ὑποργάσαι cod.: ‹τ'› Meineke. Clearly th
difference of tense is indefensible. For the alteration comp
crit. nn. on 79. I have placed the fragment here followin
Bgk. who suggested ἐκ ‹τρίχας›, but translate ἐξ — — | κτ
Certainly the more probable cause of corruption is the los
of a word after ἐξ. Meineke's ἐξάκις is wholly pointless
Erotian does not quote by verses, so that a trimeter is mor
probable.

80 Nor mumble figs Lebedian, from far Kamandolus

(When the Lebedians disputed with their neighbours over
Kamandolus, the scholar won the case by citing *Hipponax'*
verse (80). *Sextus Empiricus.* 'To mumble': chew, eat.
Hesychius.)

81 Of Amathusian loaves a crock and Cyprian eating[1]

(They say that Homer mentions together both the whole
and the part. . . So do later writers: *Hipp.* (81). For the
Amathusians are Cyprians. *Eustathius on Homer's Iliad.*)

82   But my grinders
   [That once] were in my jaws have now been all of
      them knock'd out.[2]

('Number'd': . . . Ionic. . . In Hipponax (82). *Etymologicum Magnum.*)

83   His anus
   Let some one pluck withal and knead gently.

('Anus': the rump or hypotaurium: *e.g.* Hipp. (83).
Archilochus too mentions it. Lysimachus says it is the
sphincter muscle. *Erotian.*)

---

[1] I do not believe in the form βέκος in Hdt. ii. 2, in view
of the ms. discrepancies and Aristophanes' βεκκεσέληνος.
Why βέκος Κυπρίων, not Κύπριον, and Ἀμαθουσίων not -ιον?
And why should a Greek in Lydian territory use a Phrygian
word of a Cyprian produce? λέκος removes these difficulties.

[2] Or simply 'have fallen out.' Teeth are thus said
κινεῖσθαι in the medical writers: Aretaeus, p. 17 Kuehn.

HIPPONAX

84 $^{24\ inc.}$ [ά] π‹έλ›λα γὰρ τρυγὸς γλυκείης ἦν ἔτικτεν
ἀνθηδών.

(*Et. Gud.* 57. 33 ἀνθηδών· ἡ μέλισσα παρὰ τὸ τὰ ἄνθη
ἔ[ν]δειν (so *Et. Gen.*) ἐν αὐτῇ ('Ιππ. ἐν πρώτῃ Wilam.) (84).)

[85 $^{81}_{57}$ στέφανον εἶχον κοκκυμήλων . . . καὶ
μίνθης]

(Ath. ii. 49 e ἐπεὶ δὲ πλεῖστον ἐν τῇ τῶν Δαμασκηνῶν ἐστι χώρᾳ
τὸ **κοκκύμηλον** καλούμενον . . . ἰδίως καλεῖται τὸ ἀκρόδρυον
Δαμασκηνόν. . . κοκκύμηλα μὲν οὖν ἐστι ταῦτα· ὧν ἄλλος
τε μέμνηται καὶ 'Ιππ. (85).)

86 ^{120} καὶ Διὸς κούρ‹α›ς Κυβή‹β›η‹ν› καὶ
Θρ‹ε›ϊκίην Βενδῖν

(Hesych. Κυβήβη· ἡ μήτηρ τῶν θεῶν . . . παρ' ὃ καὶ 'Ιππ.
φησι (86)· ἄλλοι δὲ Ἄρτεμιν.)

(*Inc.* 8) διὰ †δέρην† ἔκοψε μέσσην καδ δὲ λῶπος
ἐσχίσθη.

86 Cod. κοῦρος, -ηκη, -ικη : corr. Schmidt.
Inc. 8 I include here for convenience. It is attributed to
Anacreon by writers on Homer, P 542. It is difficult to
believe that Anacreon wrote scazons, but it is far more
probable that we should read ἔσχισεν than attribute to
Hipponax or Aeschrion. δέρην is impossible for Hipp. or
Anacreon, hence read δὲ ῥῖν(α).

58

84 A pail there was of honey sweet born of the
flower-eater.[1]

('Flower-eater': the bee because it sucks from the
flowers. (Hipp.) Book I. (84). *Etymologicum Gudianum.*)

85 A garland wore of damson flower, and mint [full
sweet smelling] [2]

(Since the 'damson' . . . grows in profusion in the
Damascene district . . . the fruit is specially named
'damascene.' Hipp. among others mentions it (85).
Athenaeus.)

86 Daughters of Zeus Cybebe hight and Thracian
Bendis

('Cybebe': the mother of the Gods. . . Whence Hipp.
has (86). Others identify her with Artemis. *Hesychius.*)

(Inc. 8) Clave through the middle of his (nose) and
rent was his mantle.[3]

[1] The fragment has been allotted to Aeschrion on the
ground of the pedantic word. But I find the diction no
more tasteless than that (*e.g.*) of *fr.* 15. πέλλα : so Bgk.

[2] In English damson is of course derived from damascene.
The Greek words differ. I have given the verse in the only
form in which it approaches metre : it is still irregular and
probably the attribution is mistaken. In Ionic tetrameters
separate words cannot form the first two feet,, and εἰχōν
is improbable. See however *Journal Camb. Phil. Soc.*, 1927,
p. 46. Perhaps read στέφεα μὲν . . . . . -λα καὶ μίνθην.

[3] *Inc.* 8 is really a plain tetrameter 'and rent his mantle
wide.'

H

87* (Anan. 4)   καί σε πολλὸν ἀνθρώπων

ἐγὼ φιλέω μάλιστα ναὶ μὰ τὴν κράμβην.

(Ath. 370 b μήποτε δὲ ὁ Νίκανδρος . . . (see on 18): καὶ
Ἀνάνιος δέ φησι (87*).)

(*Inc.* 9)   καὶ σαῦλα βαίνεις ἵππος ὣς κορωνίτης

(*E.M.* 270. 45 διασαυλούμενος· παρὰ τὸν σαῦλον, τὸν
τρυφερὸν καὶ ἁβρόν. Σιμωνίδης ἐν Ἰάμβοις (*Inc.* 9).)

(*Inc.* 10)   ὥσπερ ἔγχελυς κατὰ γλοιοῦ

(Ath. vii. 299 c Σιμωνίδης δ' ἐν Ἰάμβοις (*Inc.* 10).)

HEXAMETERS

89$^{85}_{27}$ Μοῦσά μοι Εὐρυμεδοντιάδε⟨ω⟩ τὴν π⟨α⟩ντο-
χάρυβδιν

τὴν ἐγγαστριμάχαιραν, ὅσ' ἐσθίει οὐ κατὰ
κόσμον,

ἔννεφ' ὅπως ψηφῖδι κακ⟨ῆ⟩ κακὸν οἶτον ὄληται

βουλῇ δημοσίῃ παρὰ θῖν' ἁλὸς ἀτρυγέτοιο.

(Ath. xv. 698 b Πολέμων δ' ἐν τῷ δωδεκάτῳ τῶν πρὸς Τίμαιον
περὶ τῶν τὰς παρῳδίας γεγραφότων ἱστορῶν τάδε γράφει . . .·
εὑρετὴν μὲν οὖν τοῦ γένους Ἱππώνακτα φατέον τὸν ἰαμβοποιόν.
λέγει γὰρ οὗτος ἐν τοῖς ἐξαμέτροις (89). Hesych. ἐγγαστριμάχαι-
ραν· τὴν ἐν τῇ γαστρὶ κατατέμνουσαν.)

87* Metre forbids us to accept the attribution to Ananius.
I suspect a dislocation in Ath.'s text or a misunderstanding
of Lysanias. As the rhythm of the first verse is unparalleled
in early Ionic writers, it may belong to Herodes.

Inc. 10 ὥσπερ γὰρ A.

89. 1 εὐρυμεδοντιαδεα: corr. Wilam.   ποντοχ.: corr. Bgk. ?
2 ὃς: corr. Kal. 3 κακῃ (om. tres codd.): corr. quis ? ἔννεπ'
inepte recentiores.

---

[1] If by Hipp. this must be satirical—' I swear on nothing.'
But the metre is late and the author more probably Phoenix
or Herodes. Ananius avoided all choliambi but those which
ended with four long syllables.

87*   Beyond all men
   I love thee most I swear by this cabbage.[1]

(Perhaps Nicander (. . . see on 18): and Ananius says
87). *Athenaeus.*)

Inc. 9) And treadest proudly like a horse arch-
            necked

("Proudifying": from proud = luxuriant, dainty. Simon-
des in his Iambi (*Inc.* 9). *Etymologicum Magnum.*)

Inc. 10)   Like eel on oil-scrapings [2]

(Simonides in his Iambi (*Inc.* 10). *Athenaeus.*)

HEXAMETERS

89 Eurymedontiades his wife with knife in her belly,[3]
   Gulf of all food, sing Muse, and of all her dis-
            orderly eating :
   Sing that by public vote at the side of th' un-
            harvested ocean
   Pebbled with stones she may die, an evil death to
            the evil.

(Polemon in his twelfth book of Criticisms of Timaeus
dealing with parodists writes as follows : Boeotus and
Euboeus . . surpassed their predecessors. But the actual
inventor of this class of poetry we must admit to have been
Hipp. the writer of (chol)iambics. In his hexameters he
says (89). *Athenaeus.*)

[2] *Inc.* 8, 9 and 10 are included here for convenience.
Their true authorship is uncertain and their resemblance to
Choliambi perhaps fortuitous. ὥσπερ (10) is probably unsound for the old Ionic. Aeschrion and Simonides are
confused (6).
[3] *v.* 1 That is she bolts her food without slicing it:
Hesychius' explanation appears to be very much abbreviated
and is as hard as the original.

HIPPONAX

90^{86}_{78} τί με σκιράφοισ' ἀτιτάλλεις;

(Eust. *Od.* 1397. 26 . . . 'Αθηναίοις οἳ καὶ ἐν ἱεροῖς ἀθροιζό
μενοι ἐκύβευον καὶ μάλιστα ἐν τῷ τῆς Σκιράδος 'Αθηνᾶς τῷ ἐπ
Σκίρῳ. ἀφ' οὗ καὶ τὰ ἄλλα κυβευτήρια σκιράφεια ὠνομάζετο. ἐ
ὧν καὶ πάντα τὰ πανουργήματα διὰ τὴν ἐν σκιραφείοις ῥᾳδιουργία
σκίραφοι ἐκαλοῦντο· Ἱππ. (90).)

91^{87}_{77} πῶς παρὰ Κυψοῦν ἦλθε

(*Gramm. Hort. Adonid.* p. 268^a οἱ δὲ Ἴωνες . . . Σαπφοῦ
καὶ Λητοῦν . . . ὁμοίως καὶ παρὰ 'Ιππώνακτι (91).)

91 Κυψοῦν is unlikely in an Homeric imitation: read with
Bergk (?) κῶς παρ Καλυψοῦν ἦλθε.

PAPYRUS FRAGMENT

92   ηὔδα δὲ λυδίζουσα β(ασγ)[ικορλαζε·
     πυγιστὶ τὸν πυγεῶνα παρ[,
     καί μοι τὸν ὄρχιν, τῇ σφαλ[ε
     κ]ράδῃ συνηλοίησεν ὡσ‹τε› [φαρμάκῳ,
     ἐ](ν τ)οῖς διοζίοισιν ἐμπε(δ)[ωθέντι.   5
     καὶ δὴ δυοῖσιν ἐν πόνοισ[ιν   •
     ἥ τε κράδη με τουτέρωθ[εν
     ἄνωθεν ἐμπίπτουσα· κ[ὼ
     π(αρα)ψιδάζων βολβίτῳ [
     ὦζεν δὲ λαύρη· κάνθαρο[ι δὲ   10
     ἦλθον κατ' ὀσμὴν πλεῦν[ες   •
     τῶν οἱ μὲν ἐμπίπτοντε[ς
     κατέβαλον· οἱ δὲ τοὺς ὀδό[ντας ὤξυνον·
     οἱ δ' ἐμπέσοντες τἀθυ(ρ)ά[†γ†ματ' ἔγραινον
     τοῦ Πυγέλησι [•   15

(For all notes see p. 65.)

90 Why cozenest me with thy dicings ? [1]

(. . . the Athenians who even used to assemble in temples
to play dice and most of all in that of Athene Sciras in the
quarter Sciron. Hence all other dicing-places were called
σκιραφεῖα. Hence too rogueries in general were called
σκίραφοι 'dicings' on account of the cheating that went on
in the dicing-places. Hipp. (90). *Eustathius* on Homer's
Odyssey.)

91 How unto Kypso came he

(The Ionians . . . formed the accusative of Sappho and
Leto in -oun. . . . So in Hipponax <you get Kypsoun>
(91). A Grammarian in the *Horn of Amalthea and Gardens
of Adonis, Aldine ed.* p. 268 verso.)

[1] ' In the quarter Sciron.' So clearly Eust. took it :
the derivation of Sciras is disputed.

PAPYRUS FRAGMENT

92 Then spoke she foreign wise : [Venez plus vite ;
   Hereafter I will pluck your foul anus ;
   Then with a bough [where tripped I lay kicking],
   Battered my . . . . s as though I were scapegoat,
   Emprisoned fast in place where twain planks split.
   Yes, truly was I [caught] in two evils ;   6
   On one side fell the rod above on me,
   [To my sore pain : below upon th' other]
   Befouled my . . . . dripped with fresh cow-dung.
   Then stank the midden ; [numberless] beetles 10
   Came at the stench [like flies in midsummer].
   Whereof some shoved away as they fell on
   [Perforce their neighbour] ; some their teeth
      whetted ;
   Some, that had fallen, first devoured th' ordure.
   More than Pygelean woes did I suffer.   15

COMPARISON OF NUMBERS OF FRAGMENTS OF HIPPONAX IN BERGK, *P.L.G.* AND THIS EDITION

Bgk.	Knox	Bgk.	Knox	Bgk.	Knox
1	44 and 45	32	65	64	71
2	46	33	1	65	32
3	43	34	16	66	30
4	47	35	75	67	31
5	48	36	17	68A	34
6	49	37	18	68B	35
7	50	38	4	69	36
8	51	39	5	70A	37
9	52	40	6	70B	38
10	10	41	7	71	39
11	2 Inc. (Introd.)	42	66	72	See p. 5
12	8	43	67	73	72
13	2 Inc.	44	Inc. 4	74	69
14	53	45	33	75	Herodas v. 74
15	54	46	19	76	77
16	57	47	20	78	Inc. 5 Introd.
17	56	48	Inc. 3	79	79
18	59	49	68	80	80
19	60	50	21	81	85
20	61	51	70	82	81
21	See 57	52	22	83	78
22A	11	53	23	84	83
22B	12	54	24	85	89
23	14	55A	25	86	90
24 (inc.)	84	55B	73	87	91
25	om.	56	26	88	40
26	15	57	27	89 and 91-99	om.
27	om.	58	28	90	See p. 2
28	Inc. 6	59	29	100	42A
29	Inc. 7	60	55	109	42B
30A	62	61	74	120	86
30B	63	62	82	127	42
31	64	63	9		

NOTE.—So profuse is Hesychius in glosses from Hipponax that I venture to suggest that some of the following anonymous citations may belong to him. Some I have included as illustrations in what *might* be their approximate contexts. In addition most of the Hesychian glosses referred in German texts to Herodes are more probably due to his original.

Words in ἰβυ-, various Lydian glosses, ἄρναν and other

FRAGMENTS AND NEW DISCOVERIES

Clazomenian glosses, Schmidt *s.v.* αὐριβάτας (Lyd. adv.), λουταρίξημα, μασίγδουπον | βασιλέα, Νεαίρῃσιν | ἵπποις, ὁδώδυσται, ὀμπνίῃ δαιτί, †ὀπωφᾶται†, Πέρδικος καπηλεῖον, τοιχοδιφήτωρ, τίεσκε μύθους, Τοξίου βουνός and *e.g.* τομεύουσι, χατεύουσα, φραδεύουσι.

To complete list of addenda to Bergk's edition, I give the following fragment (Diehl addenda): Inscr. Ostrak. Berolin. 12605 ὧρος· ἐνιαυτός . . . . 'Ιππώνακτος·

πονηρὸς [   ]οι πάντας

'Ασωποδώρου παῖδα κ[   ]

apparently with the sense ' wicked for all his years beyond the son of Asopodorus.'

Of certain fragments given by Bergk we may guess at metre in *fr.* 133 κύων λιμῷ | σαρκῶν, a dog gnawing In hunger, and *frr.* 110, 111 ἡ βορβορῶπις κἀνασυρτόλις πόρνη, which I do not translate.

Fragment 92 was found at Oxyrrhyncus.   Ed. pr. *Rivista di Fil. Class.* 1928, pp. 500 *sqq.* by G. Co[ppola].

1 ξι corr. from ξι P.   6 καιδη ex καινη.   8 πῖπτ ex πειπτ P. Iotas subscr. om P exc. βολβίτῳ (9).   Accents, etc., at 2 πυγεῶνα, 3 καί, 4 ηλοίη, 7 ἤ and τοὐτέρ, 8 ἐμπίπτουσα·κ, 9 ἄξων, 10 λαύρη, 11 κατ' and πλεῦν, 13 ον· οιδε, 14 οιδ', 15 πυγέλησι, and perhaps 10 ὦξεν.   Supplements *v.* 1 Vogliano and Lobel, *v.* 4 Coppola (corr. E. Lobel from ὥσπ[ερ], *v.* 5 (init.) Co., *v.* 10 Lobel, 11, 12, and 13 (ὁδόντας) Co., *v.* 4 . .]ποις Co., *vv.* 3, 5, 8, 13, 14 (ἔγρ. vel ἔχναυον) supplevi.

I translate *v.* 2 -ις ἐλάκτιζον, *v.* 6 ἠγρεύμην, *v.* 7 ἤλγυνεν, *v.* 9 κατῃσχύνθη, *v.* 10 τώριθμῷ, *v.* 11 ἢ θέρεος μυῖαι (following Co.), *v.* 12 ἐκ βίης ἄλλους.   Only a few letters of the three next verses remain.   In *vv.* 2 and 9 the sense is highly controversial.   I translate παρτιλῶ σ' αὖθις and φαλῆς καινῷ (vereor ne σπέρμα legendum sit).   τὰ διόξια sunt sedes (planks) τῆς λαύρης in quibus Hipponactem aut fraude (*Decameron*, ii. 5) aut casu captum et pronum jacentem Arete spe frustrata tamquam cinaedum (Petron. ch. 138) et impotentem (Burton, *Arabian Nights*, x. 250) contumelia punit.   Nescio an cantharorum dapes et titillationes providerit mulier.   βολβ. de stercore bovino tantum dici potest.   In λαύρη ('midden') excrementa omnis generis coacervantur.   Pro ἀθυράγματα vid. Hesych. θυραγμ- (extra ordinem): ἀφοδεύματα.

ANANIUS

1[1] Ἄπολλον ὅς <κ>ου Δῆλον ἢ Πυθῶν' ἔχεις,
ἢ Νάξον ἢ Μίλητον ἢ θεί<η>ν Κλάρον,
ἵκ<ε>υ κα<τ>' ἱ[ε]ρά· †ἢ† Σκύθας ἀ<π>ιξέαι.

(Ar. *Ran.* 659 Dionys. (1. 1). Xanth. ἤλγησεν· οὐκ ἤκουσας ; Di. οὐκ ἔγωγ' ἐπεὶ ἴαμβον Ἱππώνακτος ἀνεμιμνήσκομεν. Schol. ἴαμβον Ἱππ.· ὡς ἀλγήσας καὶ συγκεχυμένος οὐκ οἶδε τί λέγει· ἐπεὶ οὐκ Ἱππ. ἀλλ' Ἀνανίου. ἐπιφέρει δὲ ὁ Ἀνανίας αὐτῷ (1. 2, 3).)

2[2] χρυσὸν λέγει Πύθερμος ὡς οὐδὲν τἆλλα.

(Heraclid. Pont. (Ath. xiv. 625 c) οὗτός ἐστι Πύθερμος οὗ μνημονεύει Ἀνάνιος ἢ Ἱππῶναξ ἐν τοῖς ἰάμβοις †ἐν ἄλλῳ† οὕτως (2).)

1 που, θείαν, ἵκου, καθ', ἱερά, ἀφιξ-: corr. Meineke. 3 for ἢ read καὶ, the usual error, 'and then you may return home,' or better τί . . . ;
2 ? χρυσοῦ. On the score of metre Ananius must be the author. Note that Athenaeus quotes at second hand.

---

[1] The subject seems to be clear. It is an appeal to Apollo who had a tendency to wander to the north. Himerius (*Or.* xiv. 10) tells us (from Alcaeus) how on his birth A. was sent on his swan-car to Delphi by Zeus to give law to the Greeks. He immediately turned his team to the Hyper-

ANANIUS

1 Apollo, now at Delos, Pytho town,
Naxos, Miletus, or Claros divine,
First to our rites: why Scythiaward must hie?[1]

(*Dionysus* (1. 1). *Xanthias*. It hurt. Didn't you hear?
Dionysus. Not it indeed: a verse of Hipponax I hunted
for. *Aristophanes*, *Frogs*, 659. 'Hipponax': this is said
in his pain and confusion inaccurately, since the verse is
not by Hipp. but by Ananius. The next verses are (2, 3).
Commentator on this passage.)

2 Aught else but gold is naught, saith Pythermus.

(This is the Pythermus whom Ananius or Hipponax
mentions in his iambi †. . .†[2] as follows (2). *Heraclides
Ponticus* quoted by *Athenaeus*.)

boreans. He spent a year there before bidding his swans
return (ἐξ Ὑπερβορέων ἐφίπτασθαι). See Wernsdorf *ad loc.*,
J. U. Powell on Simias *fr.* 1 (*Collectanea Alexandrina*,
p. 111). Clearly the address is not that made on this
occasion but merely alludes to Apollo's migratory habits.

[2] († . . . †) perhaps ἐν ἀδήλῳ βιβλίῳ, ' I cannot say in which
book.

ANANIUS

3^3 εἴ τις καθείρξαι χρυσὸν ἐν δόμοις †πολὺν†
καὶ σῦκα βαιὰ καὶ δύ' ἢ τρεῖς ἀνθρώπους
γνοίη ‹κ›όσον τὰ σῦκα τοῦ χρυσοῦ κρέσσω.

(Ath. iii. 78 d ὅτι δὲ πάντων τῶν καλουμένων ξυλίνων καρπῶν
ὠφελιμώτερά ἐστι τοῖς ἀνθρώποις τὰ σῦκα . . . (f) καὶ Ἀνάνιο
δ' ὁ ἰαμβοποιὸς ἔφη (3). Stob. iv. 33 Ἱππώνακτος (3).)

4^4 = Hippon. 87.

5^5 ἔαρι μὲν χρόμιος ἄριστος, ἀνθί‹η›ς δ' ἐ‹ν›
χειμῶνι,
τῶν καλῶν δ' ὄψων ἄριστον καρὶς ἐκ συκέης
φύλλου,
ἡδὺ δ' ἐσθίειν χιμαίρης φθινοπωρισμῷ
κρε‹ῖ›ας,
δέλφακος δ' ὅταν τραπ‹έ›ωσι καὶ πατέωσιν
ἐσθίειν·
καὶ κυνῶν αὕτη τό‹τ›' ὤρη καὶ λαγῶν
κἀλωπέκων.
ὄϊος αὖτ' ὄ[ε]ταν θέρος τ' ᾖ κἠχέται βαβρά-
ζωσιν.
εἶτα δ' ἐστὶν ἐκ θαλάσσης θύννος οὐ †κακὸν†
βρῶμα,
ἀλλὰ πᾶσιν ἰχθύεσσιν ἐμπρεπὴς ἐν μυ‹σσ›ωτῷ.

3. 1 -ξει codd.　　　πολλὸν edd.　But it is doubtful if
Ananius *ever* used the verse-ending ◡ – – – and the right
reading might be *e.g.* ἅλις. δόμοις is not Ionic: δόμοισ' is.
3 γνώῃ σχάσοντας Stob.: γνοίη χ' ὅσῳ Ath. Both writers
(see on Hipp. 75) draw ultimately, I fancy, from Lysanias
on the Choliambists. This book probably contained a parallel
quotation from Hipp.
5. 1 -ίας: corr. Schn.　2 (Cas.) ἐν . . . φύλλοις. ὄψων
absent in some codd. 3 χιμέρης: corr. Heringa. 5 αὖ τῆμος

68

3 Should any in a room enclose much gold
  And a few figs and two or three mortals,
  He'd learn that figs than gold are far better.

(That figs are more useful than all so-called orchard fruits
.. Ananius the iambist says (3). *Athenaeus.* Also
quoted by *Stobaeus* the anthologist in his *Comparison of
Wealth and Poverty*.)

4 See Hippon. 87.

5 For best in spring the salmon[1] is, in winter the
        mack'rel[1];
  And best of dainties is the prawn that peeps from
        green fig-leaves,
  And sweet in autumn 'tis to eat the flesh of a
        young kid,
  And sweet to eat the flesh of pigs the autumn
        grapes treading.
  This is the time to eat of whelps, of hares and
        of foxes.[2]   5
  But mutton eat when summer comes and grass-
        hoppers chatter.
  And then the tunny from the sea no paltry food
        renders,
  But set in cheese-cake shineth out among other
        fishes.

[1] 'Salmon,' really umber: see Isaac Walton, *Compleat
Angler* ch. vi. I avoid the familiar English "grayling,"
since the date does not fit. *Our* mackerel is most pleasur-
ably caught in August (in a light wind, sails reefed) off the
Devon coast and eaten within an hour or two, but it keeps
ill in summer.   [2] See Casaubon.

Meineke is prob. right : τόθ' codd.   6 οἶος: expl. Casaubon.
ιυτοεταν: corr. Heringa.   7 ? for κακὸν—*e.g.* δειλὸν.   8 ἐμ-
πρεπεῖς *v.l.*   μυττ.: corr. Bgk. ?

69

ANANIUS

βοῦς δὲ πιανθείς, δοκέω μέν, καὶ μεσέων
    νυκτῶν ἡδὺς
κἠμέρης.   10

(Ath. vii. p. 282 b ἀνθίας· κάλλιχθυς. τούτου μέμνηται
Ἐπίχαρμος ἐν "Ηβας Γάμῳ (fr. 58 Kb.) καὶ σκιφίας χρόμις θ
ὃς ἐν τῷ ἦρι καττὸν Ἀνάνιον ἰχθύων πάντων ἄριστος ἀνθίας δὲ
χείματι. λέγει δὲ Ἀν. οὕτως (5).)

70

FRAGMENT 5

A fattened ox, I ween, is sweet o' day and at
    midnight.[1]

('Anthias': beauty-fish. Mentioned by *Epicharmus* in
his *Marriage of Hebe*: 'The sword-fish and the chromis
which in spring Ananius says Is best of fish, as winter brings
the beauty-fish the best.' Ananius' words are (5). *Athenaeus.*)

[1] One would have expected the sense 'when day and
night are equal.'

HERODES
MIMES AND FRAGMENTS

INTRODUCTION

THE papyrus of Herodes is in the British Museum (135).[1] The editio princeps by Kenyon dates from 1891. Rutherford's edition, based on Kenyon's proofs, was published soon after. Rutherford contributed something : but his very loose handling of the text drew violent criticisms from Nicholson (Librarian of the Bodleian, Oxford) in the *Academy*, September 26-October 31. Since then few English scholars have ventured to publish without an examination of the papyrus. Many other English critics, notably Walter Headlam and E. L. Hicks (subsequently Bishop of Lincoln), published in the same journal. In 1922 Bücheler published an edition based on a wide knowledge of classical literature, especially the more obscene Roman writers : Crusius' *Untersuchungen* appeared the same year. Crusius had spent great care on certain writers of whom Babrius was one : but his editions display a grave lack of judgement in preferring the text to the corrections, in sustaining the most obviously false readings, and in regarding Herodes as tending rather to the vulgar style than, as is the fact, to excessive artifice. His treatment of the text was honest and exceptionally careful, but he was quite devoid of palaeographical

---

[1] Milne, *Catalogue* 96, p. 66.

INTRODUCTION

skill. Blass was the only sound reader, always with the exception of Kenyon, who had to sustain the facts of palaeography like Athanasius against a world of heretical misreadings : and performed the task with extreme courtesy and an admirable firmness which in only one case [1] relaxed. The only flaw in Kenyon's work was that neither he nor anyone else had then any distinct idea of the proper treatment of papyri : in consequence the mounting was in places very faulty, and only lately several errors have been removed. In 1892 an edition by Herwerden appeared in *Mnemosyne* ; and in 1893 R. Meister published an edition, the interest of which lay in the view that Herodes wrote in perfectly good Ionic ; a view which can only be disproved by the number of cases (*e.g.* αἰκ-) where the true Ionic (ἀεικ-) does not suit the metre. For the following years only Crusius and Headlam continued the intensive study of Herodes : Headlam with an obstinate refusal to publish a full edition when problems remained of which an accurate solution might be found ; and Crusius with a stream of editions (last 1914) which displayed a satisfaction in a quite illiterate text and conjectural supplements. Meanwhile, however, R. Herzog made some excavations in Cos, which appear to complicate the problems of Mime IV., and some valuable notes on archaeological points. In 1904 (Dr.) J. A. Nairn, headmaster of Merchant Taylor's School, published an edition embodying most previous research : the main flaw being that the editor continually accepted theories based on quite inconsistent premises. In 1922 appeared an edition of Mimes I.-VI. by Professor

---

[1] Nairn's reading i. 82 is wholly impossible.

P. Grooneboom[1] : which displays the sound taste of a widely read scholar and clear, lucid and consistent judgement. The editor wisely follows Blass and Kenyon for text, but was unable himself to contribute anything. At about the same time Headlam's complete notes were published by the Cambridge University Press with an illustrative text and what was practically an editio princeps of Mime VIII., with the loose fragments pieced together. The main value of this edition (and, in a lesser degree, of Grooneboom's) should be to destroy the idea that Herodes was a writer who shows any relation to the ordinary speech, or that his connexions, aims, and methods are other than literary.

The following is a list of some recent work on Herodes :—

[2] Herodas: *The Mimes and Fragments*. With notes by Walter Headlam, Litt.D., Cambridge, 1922.

Les Mimiambes d'Hérodas I-VI par P. Grooneboom, Groningue, 1922.

[2] *Eroda I Mimiambi*. Testo Critico e Commento per cura di Nicola Terzaghi. Torino, 1925.

[2] Otto Crusius: *Die Mimiamben des Herondas.* . . . Zweite Auflage . . . von Rudolf Herzog. Leipzig, 1926.

[3] Articles (excluding reviews):

R. Herzog, *Philologus*, lxxix. pp. 370 *sqq.*, lxxxii. pp. 28 *sqq.*

[1] This edition should be consulted for work between 1906 and 1922.
[2] With translations.
[3] Mr. H. I. Bell's Bibliography of work on Papyri has been very helpful. Dr. P. Grooneboom has also sent me kind notes on recent literature.

INTRODUCTION

A. D. Knox, *C.R.* xxxix. pp. 13 *sqq.*, *Philologus*, lxxxi.
     241 *sqq.*, *Phil. Woch.*, 1926, 77 *sq.*, *C.R.* xlii. 163.
A. E. Housman, *C.R.* xxxvi. 109 *sqq.* (a certain ex-
     planation of ii. 65-7).
Kalinka (*Akad. der Wiss. in Wien Sitzb.*, 197 Bd. 6 Abh.).
Meerwaldt (*Mnemosyne*, liii. 393 *sqq.*).
Radermacher (*Der Lehrer des Herondas*: *Sonderabsdr. aus
     Wien. Zeitschr. für Volkskunde*, 30, 1925).
Vogliano (*Riv. di Fil.*, 1925, 395 *sqq.*).
W. M. Calder, *C.R.*, xxxviii. 113 *sqq.* (a useful note on
     Nannakos).
H. J. Rose, *C.Q.*, 1923, 32 *sqq.*
J. M. Edmonds, *C.Q.*, 1925, 129 *sqq.*
W. Vollgraff, *Mnemosyne*, 1927, p. 104.
W. R. Halliday, *C.R.* xxxvii. 115.

Of these writings it is only necessary for immediate
purposes to observe that Terzaghi (1925) makes no
effort to give a correct text, and that Edmonds'
notes are wholly deficient in objectivity and appear
to be wanting in appreciation of the author's meaning and style. Rudolf Herzog's[1] articles are of
course in a different category. Bound, in some sort,
to the cartwheels of earlier Teubner editions, he
has yet adopted and contributed a large number of
improvements. Unfortunately on many points he
retains theories of Crusius' which are obviously
inadmissible: and his valuable discoveries in Cos
have led him to take Herodes as a critic of actual
life in a way which would surprise no one more than
Herodes.

To return to the papyrus. It is of curious form,
with few verses to the column. It dates from perhaps about A.D. 100. It is written by an untrained

---

[1] Besides acknowledged points I owe to him the allocation
of parts in VII.

hand, and various errors suggest a more cursive
hand for its immediate archetype. It was checked
with indifferent care, the reviser writing the mark /
against the left of the dubious verse and calling
attention to false scansions by the usual method of
placing quantitative marks on the top. The actual
corrector missed many false verses even where his
attention was so called. Even so there are very
numerous corrections ; and apart from cases where,
as so often happens, the corrections (written above
or in the margin with occasional cancellation of the
false letters) are themselves inaccurately placed, all
corrections of every sort by whatever hand are for
the better.[1] The theory that corrections to normal
grammar were ever made is absurd, since it is patent
that no scholar ever touched this text or any ancestor ; otherwise we might have valuable marginal
notes. Long $\bar{\iota}$ is indifferently written ι or $\epsilon\iota$, and $\epsilon\iota$
is indifferently written $\epsilon\iota$ or ι or $\bar{\iota}$ or $\dot{\epsilon}\iota$. To save
space I have not noticed cases in my critical ap-
paratus. For $\chi\dot{\omega}$, etc. (P) I write $\langle\kappa\rangle\dot{\omega}$ without note in
crit. app. And so in other crases and elisions except
after prepositions : but see iv. 83, viii. 52. Similarly
I have standardized the contraction $\kappa\dot{\eta}$- for $\kappa\alpha\dot{\iota}$ $\dot{\epsilon}$-,
giving $\kappa\langle\dot{\eta}\rangle$- where P has $\kappa\dot{\alpha}$-. I have omitted to
note places where P gives punctuation (by gaps),
and numerous omissions of iota subscript. I give
the speakers' names, which are not given by P, and
note by the symbols [ ] in text, and $\langle$ $\rangle$ in translation where P fails to note change of speakers (by
paragraphus —). Further I have omitted to note

---

[1] Except at iii. 91, and vii. 104 where, in any case, the
erroneous correction is by the first hand. Occasionally, as
at iii. 53, the correction has miscarried.

INTRODUCTION

where **P** writes in full or contracts, except in cases of possible interest. It need only be pointed out that at vii. 96 either πρῆξις or πρήξεις is admissible.

The papyrus has suffered little from worms except at vii. *init.* Some damage due to incompetent handling before reaching the British Museum has been set right.

Of the Bude edition (1928 Laloy et Nairn) I have taken all the notice necessary for a student of Herodes: see the crit. nn. on ii. 15 and viii. 8. The reader should be warned that the Bude text (*e.g.* at i. 81, 82; viii. 47; ix. 8) is very inaccurate. I should have included among the list of signs omitted in my crit. app. cases (*e.g.* v. 6) where a hard verse is measured for metre by insertion of dots between feet. In iv. 70 I ought to have noted πημηῑνη.

I

ΠΡΟΚΥΚΛΙ[Σ] Η ΜΑΣΤ(ΡΟΠ)ΟΣ

ΜΗΤΡΙΧΗ

Θ[ρέϊσ](σ'), ἀράσσει τὴν θύρην τις· οὐκ ὄψει
μ[ή] τ[ις] παρ' ἡμέων ἐξ ἀγροικίης ἤκει;

ΘΡΕΙΣΣΑ

τ(ίς τ)[ὴν] θύρην;

ΓΥΛΛΙΣ

ἐγῶδε.

ΘΡΕΙΣΣΑ

              τίς σύ; δειμαίνεις
ἆσσον προσελθεῖν;

ΓΥΛΛΙΣ

ἢν ἰδού, πάρειμ' ἆσσον.

ΘΡΕΙΣΣΑ

τίς δ' εἶ σύ;

1. θύραν P, suppl. R.   2. μή τις Bl.   ἀποικίης P.
3. suppl. Bl.

80

I

THE BAWD OR MATCHMAKER

(Metriche, a respectable well-to-do lady, still young and attractive, is sitting at home with her slave Threissa in the room. A knock is heard. The season is winter. Time and (for us) place are not clearly marked. For the latter Cos is perhaps suggested. v. 56 has the clue.)

METRICHE [1]

Threissa, list, a rap at the door : go see an any of ours be here from the estate.

THREISSA

Who knocketh ?

GYLLIS

'Tis I.

THREISSA

Who art thou ?   Art afrayd to come nearer ?

GYLLIS

See there : I have come nearer.

THREISSA

Who art thou ?

[1] The speakers are allotted (mainly by punctuation) accurately except that in *v.* 8 δούλη ' wench,' is given to Gyllis.

HERODES

Γυλλίς, ἡ Φιλαινίδος μήτηρ.   5
ἄγγειλον ἔνδον Μητρίχῃ παρ(ε)ῦσάν με.

ΜΗΤΡΙΧΗ

κάλει. τίς ἐστιν;

ΓΥΛΛΙΣ

Γυλλίς, ἀμμί<η> Γυλλίς.

ΜΗΤΡΙΧΗ

στρέψον τι, δούλη. τίς σε μοῖρ' ἔπεισ' ἐλθεῖν,
Γυλλίς, πρὸς ἡμέας; τί σὺ θε[ὸς πρὸ]ς ἀνθρώπους;
ἤδη γὰρ εἰσι πέντε κου, δοκέω, (μῆνες)   10
ἐξ οὗ σε, Γυλλίς, οὐδ' ὄναρ, μὰ τὰς Μοίρας,
πρὸς τὴν θύρην ἐλθοῦσαν εἶδέ τις ταύτην.

ΓΥΛΛΙΣ

μάκρην ἀποικέω, τέκνον, ἐν δὲ ταῖς λαύραις
ὁ πηλὸς ἄχρις ἰγνύων προσέστηκεν·
ἐγὼ δὲ δραίνω μυῖ' ὅσον· τὸ γὰρ γῆρας   15
ἡμέας καθέλκει κἠ σκιὴ παρέστηκεν.

[ΜΗΤΡΙΧΗ]

. . .].ε καὶ μὴ τοῦ χρόνου καταψεύδεο·
οἴη τ' ἔτ' εἶ] γάρ, Γυλλί, <κ>ἠτέρους ἄγχειν.

5. γυλλλίs and φιλαινιου P, with correction in margin.

6. μητρίχηι P.   7. αμμια P : corr. R.   9. π^{ρος} P
(*i.e.* παρ' corr. to προς) K.   10. suppl. R.   10. suppl.
K.   12. ταυτην by correction from ταυτηs P (K.).
15. μυι, οσον P with μυσοσον in faint small letters in margin

GYLLIS

Gyllis, mother of Philaenis. Take news to Metriché within that I am here.

METRICHE (*hearing a woman's voice*)

Admit her. Who is it?

GYLLIS

Gyllis, nurse Gyllis.

METRICHE

To your wheel, wench. What fate, Gyllis, be-guyled you to come to us? Why camest angel-wise? 'Tis now, I ween, five months since any beheld you, even in fancy, come to this door, the Fates be witness.

GYLLIS

I live afar off, childe, and in the alleys the mud is knee-deep; and I can no more than a fly; for eld weigheth upon me, and the Shadow standeth by me.

⟨METRICHE [1]⟩

Frolick and belie not Father Time : for thous not past it yet, Gyllis.

[1] *vv.* 17-19 Changes of speakers may have been indicated in left margin.

(J. H. Wright).   16. ημε]ας P supplied by K. from Stob. *Fl.* cxvi. 18 where some codd. have *v.* 15 μνιοσων, μνοσων, κην for καὶ, and παραστηκει or παρεστηκη.   17. . . .] (δ)εκαιμη P.

(so Mn.): ? ἔρειδε, unless νέαζε be possible.   καταψευδου P.
18. suppl. by Tucker.

HERODES

⟨ΓΥΛΛΙΣ⟩

σίλ(λαιν)ε· ταῦτα τῆς νεωτέρης ὑμῖν
πρόσεστιν.

⟨ΜΗΤΡΙΧΗ⟩

ἀλλ' οὐ τοῦτο μή σε θερμήνῃ. 20

⟨ΓΥΛΛΙΣ⟩

ἀλλ', ὦ τέκνον, κόσον τιν' ἤδη χηραίνεις
χρόνον μόνη τρύχουσα τὴν μίαν κοίτην;
ἐξ οὗ γὰρ εἰς Αἴγυπτον ἐστάλη Μάνδρις
δέκ' εἰσὶ μῆνες, κοὐδὲ γράμμα σοι πέμπει,
ἀλλ' ἐκλέλησται καὶ πέπωκεν ἐκ καινῆς. 25
κεῖ δ' ἐστὶν οἶκος τῆς θεοῦ· τὰ γὰρ πάντα,
ὅσσ' ἔστι κου καὶ γίνετ', ἔστ' ἐν Αἰγύπτῳ·
πλοῦτος, παλαίστρη, δύναμις, εὐδί(η), (δ)όξα,
θέαι, φιλόσοφοι, χρυσίον, νεηνίσκοι,
θεῶν ἀδελφῶν τέμενος, ὁ βασιλεὺς χρηστός, 30
Μουσῆον, οἶνος, ἀγαθὰ πάν⟨τ⟩' ὅσσ' ἂν χρήζῃ[ς,
γυναῖκες, ὁκόσους οὐ μὰ τὴν Ἅιδεω Κούρην
(ἀστέ)ρας ἐνεγκεῖν οὐραν[ὸ]ς κεκαύχηται,
τὸ δ' εἶδος οἷαι πρὸς Πάρι[ν] κο⟨τ⟩' ὥρμησαν
θ(ε)αὶ κρι](θ)ῆναι καλλονήν—(λ)άθοιμ' αὐτάς 35
γρύξασα.] κο(ί)ην οὖν τάλαιν(α) σὺ ψυχήν
ἔχουσα] θάλπεις τὸν δίφρον; κατ' οὖν λήσεις
γηρᾶσα] καί σευ τὸ ὥριον τέφρη κάψει.
πάπτη]νον ἄλλη κἠμέρας μετάλλαξον
τ(ὸν)] νοῦν (δ)ύ' ἢ τρεῖς, ⟨κ⟩ιλαρὴ κατάστηθι 40
. . . . .(πρ)]ὸς ἄλλον· νηῦς μιῆς ἐπ' ἀγκύρης
οὐκ ἀσφ]αλὴς ὁρμ(ε)ῦ(σ)α· κεῖνος ἢν ἔλθῃ—

19. σιλ[(λ)α](ιν)ε P : suppl. by K.   νεωτερηισυμιν P.
                                                        λικος
23. μάνδρις P.   25. εκλελησται P, and καιν·ῆ·ς P : κυνης in

84

⟨GYLLIS⟩

Jest on : 'tis the way with you merrie wives.

⟨METRICHE⟩

Let not this irk thee.

⟨GYLLIS⟩

Well, childe, how long art thou a widow, in lone-
lihed wearying thy sole bedde ? Since Mandris fared
to Egypt 'tis ten months ne a jot sent thee. He
hath forgotten thee and quaffed anew. There is the
goddes house. No being nor creacioun but what is
in Egypt : wealth, grounds of disport, power, climate
fayr, fame, exhibiciouns, sages, gold, children, the
demesne of the Brethren Gods, right noble the king,
the Museum, wine, all boons man mote crave, women,
'a Hell-Maids name, more than sky vaunteth of stars,
and in countenance as what [goddesses] of yore came
unto Paris for deeming of their beautie, pray they
hear not my prating. [With] what intendiment then
warmest thy seat ? [Eld] will steal on thee and ash [1]
devour thy bloom. Spy elsewhither, and for two or
three days make change of your mind, and be chear-
full [once more] toward another. Ships ride [not]
safely on one anchor. An He come, ⟨thence⟩ shall

---

[1] As the ash on a torch creeps over the ember.

---

margin.　　26. κῖ P.　　28. πα'λαιστρη P.　　29. θέαι P.
　　　　　　　　　　　　　(θα)
31. marked as corrupt.　　αγα πανθ P.　　32. suppl. K.
33. so Hicks.　　34. (τηνδ)οψιν P with . . . . . δος superscr
explained by Hdl., Bl.　　35. so Buech.　　36. suppl. Hdl.
(e.g.)　　37. suppl. R.　　κατοῦνλησεις P.　　38. suppl. R.
　　　　　　　　　　　　　　　　　　　　·κ·
ωριμον P.　　39. suppl. Weil.　　χημ P.　　40. suppl. Bl.
χιλαρ.ηκαταστηθ.ι P.　　41. e.g. αὗτις.　　42. so Hicks.

HERODES

........] ..[..]ν[.] μηδὲ εἶς ἀναστήσῃ
ἡ]μεας φίλ(η) τὸ δεῖν(α) δ' ἄγριος χείμων
...............](λα), κοὐδὲ εἶς οἶδεν   45
τὸ μέλλο]ν ἡμέων· ἄστατος γὰρ ἀνθρώποις
......](θλη)[.]s. ἀλλὰ μήτις ἔστηκε
σύνεγγυ[s] ἡμῖν;

ΜΗΤΡΙΧΗ

οὐδὲ ε[ἶ]s.

ΓΥΛΛΙΣ

ἄκουσον δή

ἅ σοι χρ[εἴ]ζουσ' ὧδ' ἔβην ἀπαγγεῖλαι·
ὁ Ματαλ[ί]νης τῆς Παταικίου Γρύλλος,   50
ὁ πέντε νικέ[ω]ν ἆθλα, παῖς μὲν ἐν Πυθοῖ,
δὶς δ' ἐν Κορίνθῳ τοὺς ἴουλον ἀνθεῦντας,
ἄνδρας δὲ Πί(σῃ) (δ)ὶς καθεῖλε πυκτεύσας,
πλουτέων τὸ (καλόν), οὐδὲ κάρφος ἐκ τῆς γῆς
κινέων, ἄθικτ[ο]s [ἐς] (Κυ)θηρίην σφρη(γ)ίς,   55
ἰδών σε κ(α)θό(δ)ῳ (τῆς) Μίσης ἐκύμηνε
τὰ σπλάγχν', ἔρω[τι] καρδίην ἀνοιστρηθείς,
καί μευ οὔτε νυκτὸς οὔτ' ἐφ' ἡμέρην λείπει
τὸ δῶμα, [τέ]κνον, ἀλλά μευ κατακλαίει
καὶ ταταλ[ί]ζει καὶ ποθέων ἀποθνήσκει.   60
ἀλλ', ὦ τέκνον μοι Μητρίχη, μίαν ταύτην
ἁμαρτίην δὸς (τῇ) θεῷ· κατάρτησον
σαυτήν, τὸ [γ]ῆρας μὴ λάθῃ σε πρόσβλεψαν.

43. e.g. τέθνηκεν· (R.) οὔκουν.   44. φίλη· τὸ δεῖνα Bell,
Nairn. I conjecture and translate ·φιλεῖ τόδ' εἶν'· ὁ δὲ·
45. e.g. [(σε)ίει χαμαὶ τὰ φύλ]λα.   46.]νημεων P: τὸ μέλλον
                                   ανθρωποις
Buech., W.H., and others.   γαρημιων P (ανθρωπων first
written in superscr.).   47. e.g. ξοὴ (Cr.) γενέθλησ' with

none raise us again, deere. †So runs the world.†
The wild winter [shakes down the leav]es, and none
of us conneth [what will be]: for [life] is unstable
to the [generaciouns] of man. But say an any be
hard by.

METRICHE

None.[1]

GYLLIS

Hear then the newes whereof I wolde come here
messenger. Gryllos, son of Mataline, woman of
Pataikios, victor of five prizes, as boy at Pytho, twice
at Corinth over downy youth, while twice at Pisa in
boxing he overwent his rival men, of fair wealth,
moving no mote from ground, seal untouched to
Cytherea—he at the Descent of Misé set eyne on
thee, and his harte was stung with passion, and his
entrayles swollen: night and day long he quitteth
not my house, childe, but weepeth over me, calling
me fond names, and of yearning perdy dyeth. But
childe Metriche, prithee, this one errour grant to
the goddes: devote thyself to her,[2] lest eld espy

---

[1] 'None' is said by M., but the changes of speaker are
marked only by spaces.

[2] Understand ἐξ αὐτῆς: so Grooneboom. One might compare Michael Psellus (p. 244. 34 Sathas) ἐπειδὴ προσηλωμένην
εἶδον τῇ θεῷ καὶ οἶον ἐξηρτημένην (which normally takes genitive
or ἐκ . . .).

ἀνθρώπων.   εστηκεν P, a mark of error prefixed: ν
is cancelled before completion.   48. read and supplied by
Nicholson: ημων̣ P.   49. supp. Hardie.   50. Μᾱτᾰκ P.
γυλλος P, corrected in margin.   54. καλόν Hicks: καρπος
P.   55. suppl. Nicholson.   56. καθόδω and μίσης P.
57. suppl. Hicks, Hdl.   59. suppl. K.   60. τἀτᾰλιζει P.
61. μητριχηι P.   63. suppl. K.

καὶ δοιὰ πρήξεις· ἡδέω[ν] (τεύ)[ξ]ει (κα)[ί σοι
δοθήσεταί τι μέζον ἢ δοκεῖς· σκέψαι,   65
πείσθητί μευ· φιλέω σε, ναὶ μὰ τὰς Μοίρας.

ΜΗΤΡΙΧΗ

Γυλλί, τὰ λευκὰ τῶν τριχῶν ἀπαμβλύνει
τὸν νοῦν· μὰ τὴν γὰρ Μάνδριος κα[τ]άπλωσιν
καὶ τὴν φίλην Δήμητρα ταῦτ' ἐγὼ 'ξ ἄλλης
γυναικὸς οὐκ ἂν ἡδέως ἐπήκου(σ)α,   70
χωλὴν δ' ἀείδειν χώλ' ἂν ἐξεπαίδευσα
καὶ τῆς θύρης τὸν οὐδὸν ἐχθρὸν ἡγεῖσθαι.
σὺ δ' αὖτις ἔς με⟨υ⟩ μηδὲ ἕν⟨α⟩ φίλη τοῖον
φέρουσα χώρει μῦθον· (ὃν) (δ)ὲ γρῄαι(σ)⟨ι⟩
πρέπει γυναιξὶ ταῖς νέαις ἀπάγγελλε·   75
τὴν Πυθέω δὲ Μητρίχην ἔα θάλπειν
τὸν δίφρον· οὐ γὰρ ἐ⟨γ⟩γελᾷ τις εἰς Μάνδριν.
ἀλλ' οὐχὶ τούτων, φασί, τῶν λόγων Γυλλίς
δεῖται· Θρέϊσσα τὴν μελαινίδ' ἔκτ[ρ]ιψον
(κή)κτημόρους τρεῖς ἐγχέα(σα τ](οῦ ἀ)κρήτου   80
καὶ ὕδωρ ἐπιστάξασα δὸς πιεῖ[ν].

ΓΥΛΛΙΣ

κ(αλ)ῶ(ς).

ΜΗΤΡΙΧΗ

τῇ, Γυλλί, πῖθι.

64. δοια P: expl. Hdl.: suppl. Hdl., F.D. (καὶ σοι).
65. σκεψαι· P (? such marks after ι are often accidental; cf.
viii. 24 αμφι in Nairn's facs.).   65-66. a change of speakers
wrongly marked but cancelled.   67. β of απαμβλυνει ex
correctura. γυναι for Γυλλι Stob. *Fl.* cxvi. 24.   71. χωλον^α

thee ere thou wot. Twain ends shalt thou win :
thou shalt have joyaunce and gifts beyond thy fancy.
Think on't, be of my persuasioun. 'A Fates name
thy friend am I.

METRICHE

Gyllis, white hair blunteth wit : for, by Mandris
return and Demeter deare, had other woman spoken
so, I had not heard her out, but made her as lame as
her lays, and hate the threshold of my door. But
thou, deare, come thou never again to my house with
sike tale : tell girls what semeth old women ; but
let Metriché, childe of Pytheas, warm her seat ; for
none scoffeth at Mandris. But, 'tis said, 'tis not
words whereof Gyllis hath need : so Threissa, scour
out the chalice and pour in three noggins of neat
wine.

GYLLIS

That is well.[1]

⟨METRICHE⟩

There, Gyllis, drink.

[1] 'When !' see Appendix.

P.   73. corr. Buecheler ($\mu\epsilon$ P), and Cr. ($\epsilon\nu$ P).   76. π
                τον διφρον
εx δι P.   77. $\mu\eta\tau\rho\iota\chi\eta\nu$ P. $\mu\eta\tau\rho\iota$ cancelled. $\mu\acute{\alpha}\nu\delta\rho\iota\nu$ P.
                                    χι   α
ενγελαι P.   78. ουδε P.   φυσει P.   79. in margin
      ευ
κυλ γ(ε) ($\kappa\upsilon\lambda\acute{\iota}\kappa\omega\nu$ γένος εὐτελές Edmonds).   80. suppl. Hdl.,
Cr.   81. $\kappa\alpha\lambda\hat{\omega}\varsigma$ Alexis *fr.* 230. After ν there must
have been a large space. The change of speaker is marked
here only.

ΓΥΛΛΙΣ

δέξον· οὐ [ ] . . . . .(πον) [. .
πείσουσά σ' ἦλθον, ἀλλ' ἔ(κ)[ητι] (τ)ῶν ἱ(ρ)ῶν,
ὧν οὕνεκέν μοι—

ΜΗΤΡΙΧΗ

Γυλλί, ωνα[. . . . .
οσσοῦ γένοιτο.

ΓΥΛΛΙΣ

μᾶ, (τ)έκνον (π)[.] 85
ἡδύς γε, ναὶ Δήμητ[ρ]α, Μη[τρί](χ)[η]· τού[τ]ου
ἡδίον οἶνον Γυλλὶς οὐ πέ[π]ω(κέν) [κ](ω).
σὺ δ' εὐτύχει μοι, τέκνον, ἀσ[φα](λ)ίζ[ο]υ [δέ
σαυτήν· ἐμοὶ δὲ Μυρτάλη τε κ[αὶ] (Σί)μη
νέαι μένοιεν, ἔστ' ἂν ἐμπνέ[ῃ] Γυλλίς.   90

82. δείξον P corr. by Meister.   e.g. οὐ [σ]πεῖσαι
σπον[δήν (i.e. to give me a drink).   83. suppl. Cr.
84. distinxi. No Greek ever said ὤναό μοι 'you got from
me.' For the break compare vi. 15, iii. 58, 88, v. 73;
see pp. 177 sqq.: also Addenda, p. 354.   Perhaps ὠναγῆς

⟨GYLLIS⟩

Give it me: I came not here to persuade thee
[to spill liquor] but for holy rites'[1] sake, wherefore
my—

⟨METRICHE⟩

Gyllis, let yon mucky man [drub] his own.

⟨GYLLIS⟩

La! childe, [I am past that]. Good 'a Demeter's
name, Metriché: better wine than this Gyllis ne'er
drank. But fare thee well, childe, and hold thyself
in gard; but may my Myrtale and Simé remain
young while Gyllis hath breath in nostrils.

---

[1] The rites in *v.* 56.

ἴσχοι ὄσσ' οὗ γένοιτο (ii. 83). At 85 *e.g.* παρήβηκα.
μᾶ P.   86. suppl. Milne. 87. so Bl., al.: ηδέιον P.
88. suppl. Hdl. after Buech. 89. σαυτην by correction
from ταυτην P: suppl. Nicholson, Buech.

II

ΠΟΡΝΟΒΟΣΚΟΣ

ΒΑΤΤΑΡΟΣ

ἄνδρες δικασταί, τῆς γενῆς μ[ὲν] οὐκ ἐστέ
ἡμέων κριταὶ δήκουθεν οὐδὲ [τ]ῆς δόξης,
οὐδ' εἰ Θαλῆς μὲν οὗτος ἀξίην τ[ὴν] νηῦν
ἔχει ταλάντων πέντ', ἐγὼ δὲ μ[η]δ' ἄρτους,
. . . .] (ὑ)περέξει Βατταρόν [τι π]ημ[ήν]ας·   5
πολλο](ῦ γε) καὶ (δεῖ)· [τ]ωλυκὸν γὰρ [ἂν] κλαύσαι
. . . Κ](αρ)ίη (γ') ὄμαστος ᾗ ἀσ[τέω]ν χώρη.
. . . .]ος μέτοι(κός) ἐστι τῆς [πό]λιος κἠγώ,
καὶ ζ](ῶμεν) οὐχ ὡς βουλ(ό)[με<σ>]θ', ἀλλ' ὡς ἡμέας
ὁ και]ρὸς ἕλκει. προστάτην [ἔχ]ει Μέννην   10
ἐγὼ] δ' 'Αρισ[τοφ]ῶντα· πὺξ [νε]νίκηκεν
Μέν]νης, ('Αρισ)[τοφ]ῶν δὲ κ[ῆτι] νῦν ἄγχει·
κεἰ μ]ή ἐστ' ἀληθέα ταῦτα, το[ῦ ἡ](λ)ίου δύντος

---

1. ἐστε P : suppl. by K.   2. suppl. by K.   3. /ουδ
P, whence τ[ην] νηυν : explained by Bl.   4. εχει P who
started to write ειχ. μ[η]δαρτους P : suppl. by Cr.   5. *e.g.*
νομοῦ.   [τι π]ημ[ην]ας suppl. by Nicholson, Bl.   6 *sqq.*
first spaces missing with the two halves correctly mounted of
five letters narrowing to three.   6. πολλο]ῦ suppl. Mn.
γε και δι legi.   [τ]ωλυκον and [ἀν] C.E. *errata.*   7. so
Mn. : γ' ego : ἤν Bl.   fin. supplevi dubitanter : vid. n.
8. *e.g.* (κ)οῦτος Cr.   μέτοικος F.D. (rightly Mn.). Rest K.:
. . . λεω P.   9. suppl. Hdl., Cr. (init.).   ἡμεας P. Before

II

THE BROTHEL-KEEPER

(A court of law, nominally in Cos. Battaros, a villainous old rogue shoddily clad, addresses the jury. One of his protégées, whom he alleges to have been assaulted by the defendant Thales, is present.)

BATTAROS

Gentlemen of the jury ye wot ye are no judges of
our lineage nor renown: nor an Thales here hath a
ship worth five talents, and I lack loaves, shall he
[therefore] do Battaros a hurt and hold mastery of
law. Nay, far from it. Salt tears should he weep,
if Carian isle be a land of cities that are united
into one city.[1] For I am in this city as he—
an alien. We live not as we wolde but as needs
drive us. His patron is Aristophon, Mennes mine.
Mennes has won boxing bouts: Aristophon can still
hug. An this be not true, sirs, let him come out at

---

[1] Καρία or Καρίς = Κῶς, St. Byz. *s.vv.* For the end compare
Nairn's introduction, p. xix., Diod. Sic. xv. 76, *C.R.* xlii. 163.

αλλ a κ̄ deleted.   10. suppl. Stadtmueller.   [ε(χ)]ει P
(so Mn.) with νέμειν in margin, the ν being presumably a
slip.   11. suppl. Cr. and K. (νε).   12. suppl. Cr.
and Buech. (ητι).   13. suppl. Bl. (init.), K. fin.

ἐξε(λ)]θε(τω) ['χ]ων, ἄνδρες, [ἢν] (ἔ)χ(ει) χλαῖναν·
...]γνώσε‹τ›' οἵῳ προστάτ[ῃ τ]εθώρ(ηγ)μαι.   15
ἐρεῖ τ](ά)χ' (ὐ)[μῖ]ν '' ἐξ Ἄκης ἐλή[λου]θα
πυρ]οὺς ἄγ(ω)ν κήστησα (τὴν κακὴν λιμόν,''
ἐγὼ δ(ὲ) (πόρ)]νας ἐκ Τύρου· τί τῷ δήμῳ
........; δ]ωρεὴν γὰρ οὔθ' οὗτος πυροὺς
δίδωσ' ἀλλ]θειν οὔτ' ἐγὼ πάλιν κείνῃ.   20
εἰ δ' οὔνεκεν πλεῖ τὴν θάλασσαν ἢ χλαῖναν
ἔχει τριῶν μνέων Ἀττικῶν, ἐγὼ δ' οἰκέω
ἐν γῇ τρίβωνα καὶ ἀσκέρας σαπρὰς ἕλκων,
βίῃ τιν' ἄξει τῶν ἐμῶν ἔμ' οὐ πείσας,
καὶ ταῦτα νυκτός, οἴχε‹τ›' ἡμῖν ἡ ἀλεωρή   25
τῆς πόλιος, ἄνδρες, κ‹ἠ›φ' ὅτῳ σεμνύνεσθε,
τὴν αὐτονομίην ὑμέων Θαλῆς λύσει.
ὃν χρῆν ‹ἑ›αυτὸν ὅστις ἐστὶ κ‹ἠ›κ ποίου
πηλοῦ πεφύρητ' εἰδότ' ὡς ἐγὼ ζώειν
τῶν δημοτέων φρίσσοντα καὶ τὸν ἥκιστον.   30
νῦν δ' οἱ μὲν ἐόντες τῆς πόλιος καλυπτῆρες
καὶ τῇ γενῇ φυσῶντες οὐκ ἴσον τούτῳ
πρὸς τοὺς νόμους βλέπουσι κἠμὲ 'τὸν ξεῖνον
οὐδεὶς πολίτης ἠλόησεν οὐδ' ἦλθεν
πρὸς τὰς θύρας μευ νυκτὸς οὐδ' ἔχων δᾷδας   35
τὴν (ο)ἰκίην ὑφῆ[ψ]εν οὐδὲ τῶν πορνέων
β[ί]ῃ λαβὼν οἴχωκεν· ἀλλ' ὁ Φρὺξ οὗτος
ὁ νῦν Θαλῆς ἐών, πρόσθε δ', ἄνδρες, Ἀρτίμμης,
(ἄ)παντα ταῦτ' ἔπρηξε κοὐκ ἐπῃδέσθη
οὔτε νόμον οὔτε προστάτην οὔτ' ἄρχοντα.   40
καίτοι λαβών μοι γραμματεῦ τῆς αἰκείης
τὸν νόμον ἄνειπε, καὶ σὺ τὴν ὀπὴν βῦσον
τῆς κλεψύδρης, βέλτιστε, μέχρις οὗ εἴπῃ,

14. init. suppl. Cr.   ['χ]ων supplevi (or [ἐχ] Mn.).
fin. nescioquis.   15. Legi et εὖ supplevi (contra Hdl.)
94

sun wane in that cloke he weareth, and he shall know
what kind of patron is my habergeon. Perchance he
will tell you 'From Acre came I with cargo of wheat
and allayed the curst famine.' Aye but I have
brought giglots from Tyre. What is that to the folk?
Neither giveth he wheat free to grind, nor give I
her so. But an he claim, for that he sayle the sea
or be dight in a cloke worth three Attic minae,
while I live ashore trayling my ragged shoon—an
he claim therefore to take amaine of mine sans
mendes made, aye and by night, then gone is the
saufgard of the city, and your pride of self-rule by
Thales fordone. Nay he should know who he is and
of what clay mingled, and live as do I, in awe of the
least of his townsfolk: but in fact those who be
top-tiles of the city, and puffed of lineage far more
than he, these look to the laws, and no citizen ere
wronged me the straunger nor came of night to my
doors, nor with torches flamed my habitaunce, nor
took of my giglots amaine: but this Phrygian, now
Thales hight, but once Artimmes did this all sans
hede of law or governour or ruler. Now sir clerke,
take and read me the law of batterie, and thou, sir,
stop the hole of the water-clocke till he end his

---

p. 75 and crit. app., unde κεῦ Edmonds; ut suum profert
Nairn! Melius *e.g.* καί   16. init. Cr.   Fin.
Blass.   17. init. Cr. κήστηστα P with τ deleted.   (τ) vel
[τ]ην me iudice P.   18. suppl. Hdl.   19. suppl. Hicks.
Init. *e.g.* τοῦτ' ἐστί Hdl.   20. suppl. Hdl., Bl.   κ(ιν)ῆν P.
Can the accent be misplaced and point to ουτ εγω(γε) αλεῖν
κινην in the original? 24. ἐμ' P.   28. εχρην P, corr. Blass.
29. ζωιην P: ex compendio ζῶ' ortum (*cf. Philol.* 1925 Bd.
3-4).   36. (ο)ικιαν P.   38. After εων an α cancelled P.
43. I translate (ἀ)νείπῃ Herwerden.

†μὴ πρός τε κυσὸς φῇσι †‹κ›ὼ τάπης ἡμῖν,
τὸ τοῦ λόγου δὴ τοῦτο, ληῇς κύρσῃ.　　　　45

ΓΡΑΜΜΑΤΕΥΣ

ἐπὴν δ' ἐλεύθερός τις αἰκίσῃ δούλην
ἢ ἑκὼν ἐπίσπῃ, τῆς δίκης τὸ τίμημα
διπλοῦν τελείτω.

ΒΑΤΤΑΡΟΣ

　　　　　ταῦτ' ἔγραψε Χαιρώνδης,
ἄνδρες δικασταί, καὶ οὐχὶ Βάτταρος χρήζων
Θαλῆν μετελθεῖν. ἢν θύρην δέ τις κόψῃ,　　50
μ(ν)ῆν τινέτω, φ‹ήσ'›· ἢν δὲ πὺξ ἀλοιήσῃ
ἄλλ]ην πάλι μνῆν· ἢν δὲ τὰ οἰκί' ἐμπρήσῃ
ἢ ὅρους ὑπερβῇ, χιλίας τὸ τίμημα
ἔ(ν)ειμε, κἤν βλάψῃ τι, διπλόον τίνειν.
ᾤ[κ]ει πόλιν γάρ, ὦ Θαλῆς, σὺ δ' οὐκ οἶσθας　55
οὔ[τ]ε πόλιν οὔτε πῶς πόλις διοικεῖται,
ο[ἰ](κ)[εῖ]ς δὲ σήμερον μὲν ἐν Βρικινδήροις
ἐ(χ)θὲς δ' ἐν Ἀβδήροισιν, αὔριον δ' ἢν σοι
ν[α](ῦ)λον διδοῖ τις, ἐς Φασηλίδα πλώσῃ.
ἐ(γ)ὼ δ' ὅκως ἂν μὴ μακρηγορέων ὑμέας,　　60
ὦνδρες δικασταί, τῇ παροιμίῃ τρύχω,
πέπονθα πρὸς Θάλητος ὅσσα κἠμ πίσσῃ
μῦς· πὺξ ἐπλήγην, ἡ θύρη κατήρακται
τῆς οἰκίης μευ, τῆς τελέω τρίτην μισθόν,
τὰ ὑπέρθυρ' ὀπτά. δεῦρο, Μυρτάλη, καὶ σύ·　65
δεῖξον σεωυτὴν πᾶσι· μηδέν' αἰσχύνευ.
νόμιζε τούτους οὒ[ς] ὁρῇς δικάζοντας
πατέρας ἀδελφοὺς ἐμβλέπειν. ὁρῇτ', ἄνδρες,

44. Corrupt: see Hdl.: I suggest 'πρόετε' κυσὸς φῇσι.
ὁ λόγος huiusmodi fuerit. Venator post immodicam ficorum

96

reading, lest, as the saw goeth, arse cry 'shoot' and
sheets bag the spoyle.

CLERK

An a freeman assault a slave, or follow her of
malintent, let him pay double the assessment.

BATTAROS

So wrote Chaerondes, gentlemen of the jury, not
Battaros with intent to prosecute Thales. "An one
batter the dore, let him pay a mina ; an he pommel
with his fist, another mina ; an he burn the habitaunce, or trespass, a thousand minae is the price
set, and an he injure aught, restore double. For
Chaerondes was aedifying a city, Thales, but thou
knowest not city, nor how a city be aedified, but
livest to-day in Bricindéra, yesterday in Abdera, and
on the morn, an any give thee his fare, thou wilt
sayl to Phaselis. But I, leaste in long speche, gentlemen of the jury, I frett you with my saws, I have
been so entreated by Thales as mouse in pitch : I
was smot with fists, the dore of my house, wherefore
I pay a third as rent, is broken down, the lintell brent.
Come hither Myrtale : shew thyself to all : be
shamefast toward none : think, in this jury thou
seest, that thou beholdest fathers and brethren. See,

---

immaturorum cenam visus est audire consocios clamantes.

Cf. Philogelos 243   45 ληϊης P.   49. βατταωϛ^ρο P.
51 *sqq.* suppl. K.   φησιν P.   57. βρικινδήροιϛ P.
59. πλωση P.   61. I translate τῆ⟨ϛ⟩ παροιμίη⟨ϛ⟩ Blass.
62. καπισσηι^ημ P.   64. μισθον P corr. from μοῖραν.   67. οραιϛ^η P.

τὰ τίλματ' αὐτῆς καὶ κάτωθε κάνωθεν
ὡς λεῖα ταῦτ' ἔτιλλεν ὠναγὴς οὗτος,　　　　　70
ὅ‹τ›' εἷλκεν αὐτὴν κ‹ἠ›βιάζετ'—ὦ Γῆρας,
σοὶ θυέτω ἐπ[εὶ] τὸ αἷμ' ἂν ἐξεφύσησεν
ὥσπερ Φίλι[π]π(ο)ς ἐν Σάμῳ κοτ' ὁ Βρε‹ῦ›κος.
γελᾷς; κίν[αι]δ(ό)ς εἰμι καὶ οὐκ ἀπαρνεῦμαι
καὶ Βάτταρός μοι τοὔνομ' ἐστὶ ‹κ›ὠ πάππος 75
ἦν μοι Σισυ(μ)βρᾶς ‹κ›ὠ πατὴρ Σισυμβρίσκος,
κἠπορνοβόσ[κ]ευν πάντες, ἀλλ' ἔκητ' ἀλκῆς
θαρσέων λέ[ον]θ' [ἴλλ]οιμ' ἄν, εἰ Θαλῆς εἴη†ι†.
ἐρᾷς σὺ μὲν ἴσως Μυρτάλης· οὐδὲν δεινόν·
ἐγὼ δὲ πυρέων· ταῦτα δοὺς ἐκεῖν' ἔξεις.　　　80
ἢ νὴ Δί', εἴ σευ θ(ά)λπεταί τι τῶν ἔνδον
ἔμβυσον εἰς τὴν χεῖρα Βαττάρῳ τιμήν,
καὐτὸς τὰ σαυτοῦ θλῆ λαβὼν ὅκως χρήζεις.
ἒν δ' ἐστίν, ἄνδρες—ταῦτα μὲν γὰρ εἴρηται
πρὸς τοῦτον—ὑμεῖς δ' ὡς ἀμαρτύρων εὔντων 85
γνώμῃ δικαίῃ τὴν κρίσιν διαιτᾶτε.
ἢν δ' οἷον ἐς τὰ δοῦλα σώματα σπεύδῃ
κῆς βάσανον αἰτῇ, προσδίδωμι κ‹ἠ›μαυτόν·
λαβών, Θαλῆ, στρέβλου με· μοῦνον ἡ τιμή
ἐν τῷ μέσῳ ἔστω· ταῦτα τρυτάνῃ Μίνως 90
οὐκ ἂν δικάζων βέλτιον διήτησε.
τὸ λοιπόν, ἄνδρες, μὴ δοκεῖτε τὴν ψῆφον
τῷ πορνοβοσκῷ Βαττάρῳ φέρειν, ἀλλά
ἅπασι τοῖς οἰκεῦσι τὴν πόλιν ξείνοις.

69. κατωθεν P (ν deleted)　　70. λῖα P.　　ὠναγης P.
73. Φίλιππος can hardly be right but the correction above
ππ is unfortunately illegible.　ποτ (κ superscr.) and βρεγκος
(νθ)
P : corr. Hdl.　　76. βρίσκος P.　　78. λε(ων)[. .]οιμαν
P (teste Milne).　Perhaps in λέοντ' ἴλλοιμ' ἄν (cf. Hom. λ 573)
the second word was read as ‹ε›ίμ' οἶμ' ἄν and hence λέων

sirs, round about her smoothness, how smooth was
this pluckt by this mucky man when he raunched
and shent her.—Eld, let him render thankoffering to
thee : els had he spat forth his blood, as did once
Philip the Locust in Samos. Dost laugh ? I am a
Boye, I denay not—and my grandsire was Patchouli
hight, and my sire Patchouletto, and panders were
they all : but for prowes wolde I chivy a lion, were
I as Thales. You lust after Myrtale perchance ;
small matter that ; and I, after loaven : give one
and thou shalt get the other. Or els 'a god's name,
an thou be inly warmed, stuff the price into Boye
Battaros his hand, and take thine own and drub
thine own to thy desire. One thing, sirs—for this
has been said unto him—do ye sirs, since witnes is
there none, rule your sentence by aequitie. And,
an he will merely assay the bodys of slaves and call
unto torture, lo ! I offer mine own self freely : take
me Thales and torture me : only let the price be in
the midst : no better ruling could Minos himself
have made were he judge here with his balaunce.
For the rest, sirs, deme not that ye give vote
for Battaros the pandar but for all the straungers

---

arose. The false breathing (εἰλ-, ἴλλ-) is fairly common.
Ap. Rhod. ii. 27; Ruhnk. on Timaeus *Lex. Plat.* 80ᵇ. Fin.:
ιηι P, εἴην Kaibel; see Grooneboom's crit. n. which is very
sound.   79. συ superscribed. P here and 83 (fin.)
most falsely gives a change of speaker !   80. πυρεων
auctor non scriba.   82. ιωίτιμηνί P.   83. θλῇ P.
τασ, αυτου P (, deleted). Mark of corruption cancelled.
84. ενδετισ P, the last σ being deleted. ἔστ' ἐτ' Herw.,
which I translate.   ανδρας P.   87. οἶον (not οἴον)
Rutherford.

νῦν δείξε<τ>’ ἢ Κῶς κῶ Μέροψ κόσον δραίνει, 95
<κ>ὠ Θεσσαλὸς τίν’ εἶχε <κ>ἠρακλῆς δόξαν,
<κ>ὠσκληπιὸς κῶς ἦλθεν ἐνθάδ’ ἐκ Τρίκκης,
κἤτικτε Λητοῦν ὧδε τεῦ χάριν Φοίβη.
ταῦτα σκοπεῦντες πάντα τὴν δίκην ὀρθῇ
γνώμῃ κυβερνᾶτ’, ὡς ὁ Φρὺξ τὰ νῦν ὑμῖν 100
πληγεὶς ἀμείνων ἔσσετ’, εἴ τι μὴ ψεῦδος
ἐκ τῶν παλαιῶν ἡ παροιμίη βράζει.

95. δίξεθηκῶς P.   96. εἰχεν P.   97. κῶς P.
98. κήτικτε, λητοῦν and τεῦ.   Post φοιβη punctum P.

102. βαζει P : ? l. κράζει.

within your gates. Now shall ye prove Cos and Merops their puissaunce, and Thessalus and Hercules their glorie, and with what intencioun Aesculapius came hither from Tricca, and wherefore 'twas here that Phoebe bare Leto. Think on all these thynges and steer justice by aequity, sin now this Phrygian ye will find better for his beating, an out of ages past yon saw spit [1] sooth.

[1] Like the sea. Herodes is thinking of such phrases as ἐξήρυγες Callim. p. 32 Pfeiffer, ἐξερύγῃ (ita legendum) *fr*. 67 Schneider.

III

ΔΙΔΑΣΚΑΛΟΣ

ΜΗΤΡΟΤΙΜΗ

Οὔτω τί σοι δοίησαν αἱ φίλαι Μοῦσαι,
Λαμπρίσκε, τερπνὸν τῆς ζοῆς τ' ἐπαυρέσθαι—
τοῦτον κατ' ὤμου δεῖρον, ἄχρις ἡ ψυχή
αὐτοῦ ἐπὶ χειλέων μοῦνον ἡ κακὴ λειφθῇ.
ἔκ μευ ταλαίνης τὴν στέγην πεπόρθηκεν   5
χαλκίνδα παίζων· καὶ γὰρ οὐδ' ἀπαρκεῦσιν
αἱ ἀστραγάλαι, Λαμπρίσκε, συμφορῆς δ' ἤδη
ὁρμᾷ ἐπὶ μέζον. κοῦ μὲν ἡ θύρη κεῖται
τοῦ γραμματιστέω καὶ τριηκὰς ἡ πικρή
τὸν μισθὸν αἰτεῖ κἢν τὰ Ναννάκου κλαύσω,   10
οὐκ ἂν ταχέως λ<έ>ξειε· τήν γε μὴν παίστρην,
ὄκουπερ οἰκίζουσιν οἵ τε προύνεικοι
κοἱ δρηπέται, σάφ' οἶδε κἠτέρῳ δεῖξαι.
κἠ μὲν τάλαινα δέλτος, ἣν ἐγὼ κάμνω
κηροῦσ' ἑκάστου μηνός, ὀρφανὴ κεῖται   15
πρὸ τῆς χαμεύνης τοῦ ἐπὶ τοῖχον ἑρμῖνος,
κἢν μήκοτ' αὐτὴν οἷον Ἀίδην βλέψας
γράψῃ μὲν οὐδὲν καλόν, ἐκ δ' ὅλην ξύσῃ·

6. χαλκίνδα P.   7. αστραγάλαι P: αἱ δορκάδες R., M.
See Hippon. 31.   10. αιτι κην P.   11. ληξιε P: corr. by
102

III

THE SCHOOLMASTER

(Scene : A school, the master and boys present. There are statues of Muses round the walls. Enter Metrotime with her boy Kottalos. She addresses Lampriskos the master.)

METROTIME

An thou hope, Lampriskos, that the deare Muses mote give thee some pleasaunce and joyaunce of lyfe, so do thou beat this boye lefte ashoulder, till his last curst breath hang ons lips. Playing hazardry he hath spoiled the roof from his poor mother : for, Lampriskos, the knucklebones suffice not, but our affayres ever wax warre. Where lieth the dore of the writing-master, and the curst last day o' month ask his sold, weep I as much as Nannacus, this note he say forthright : but the gaming-place, where dwell the churles and runagates, he wotteth enow to direct his fellow. And the poor tablet which each month I werke to cere, lieth beraft before the wall-ward post of our pallet, an it so be he scowl not on it as 'twere Death, and write naught fair thereon, but

---

Bl., Hicks. 17. I take Ἀίδην as acc. after βλέψας : Callim.
Iamb. 297. 18. ξυλημι P.

αἱ δορκαλῖδες δὲ λιπαρώτεραι πολλόν
τῆς ληκύθου ἡμέων τῇ ἐπὶ παντὶ χρώμεσθα   21
ἐν τῇσι φύσῃς τοῖς τε δικτύοις κεῖνται.   20
ἐπίσταται δ' οὐδ' ἄλφα συλλαβὴν γνῶναι,
ἢν μή τις αὐτῷ ταὐτὰ πεντάκις βώσ⟨ῃ⟩.
τρι⟨τ⟩ημέρ⟨ῃ⟩ Μάρωνα γραμματίζοντος
τοῦ πατρὸς αὐτῷ, τὸν Μάρωνα ἐποίησεν   25
οὗτος Σίμωνα ὁ χρηστός· ὥστ' ἔγωγ' εἶπα
ἄνουν ἐμαυτήν, ἥτις οὐκ ὄνους βόσκειν
αὐτὸν διδάσκω, γραμμάτων δὲ παιδείην,
δοκεῦσ' ἀρωγὸν τῆς ἀωρίης ἕξειν.
ἐπεὰν δὲ δὴ καὶ ῥῆσιν οἷα παιδίσκον   30
ἢ 'γώ μιν εἰπεῖν ἢ ὁ πατὴρ ἀνώγωμεν,
γέρων ἀνὴρ ὠσίν τε κώμμασιν κάμνων,
ἐνταῦθ', ὅκως νιν ἐκ τετρημένης ἠθεῖ
'Ἄπολλον—Ἀγρεῦ'—, 'τοῦτο,' φημί, '⟨κ⟩ἡ
    μάμμη,
τάλης, ἐρεῖ σοι, κἠστὶ γραμμάτων χήρη,   35
κὠ προστυχὼν Φρύξ'· ἢν δὲ δή τι καὶ μ⟨έ⟩ζον
γρύξαι θέλωμεν, ἢ τριταῖος οὐκ οἶδεν
τῆς οἰκίης τὸν οὐδόν, ἀλλὰ τὴν μάμμην,
γρηῦν γυναῖκα κὠρφανὴν βίου, κείρει,
ἢ τοῦ τέγευς ὕπερθε τὰ σκέλεα τείνας   40
κάθη⟨τ⟩' ὅκως τις καλλίης κάτω κύπτων.
τί μευ δοκεῖς τὰ σπλάγχνα τῆς κακῆς πάσχειν,
ἐπεὰν ἴδωμι; κοὐ τόσος λόγος τοῦδε·
ἀλλ' ὁ κέραμος πᾶς ὥσπερ ἴτρια θλῆται,
κἠπὴν ὁ χειμὼν ἐγγὺς ᾖ, τρι' ἥμαιθα   45
κλαίουσ' ἑκάστου τοῦ πλατύσματος τίνω·
ἓν γὰρ στόμ' ἐστὶ τῆς συνοικίης πάσης,
τοῦ Μητροτίμης ἔργα Κοττάλου ταῦτα,

scrape it clene. But his dibs, glossier far than our
oil-flask, the which we use algates, lye in theyre bags
and nets. And he note conne the letter A, save one
schriech it to him five times. Two daies agone when
his father dictated ' Maron ' to him this fine fellow
made Simon o't : wherefore I dubbed myself fool
that taught him not to pasture asses but gave him
an educacioun in lettres, deming I sholde be holpen
when smit in yeres. And when or I or his father,
an old man ylfavoured of eyen and ears, bid him say
a speche, as one doth a child, then while he leaketh
the words—' Apollo '—' Hunter '—' why that,' quoth
I, ' even grandam could tell you albe she hath lost
her lettres, or any Phrygian serf in the stretes ' ;
and should we rate him more raucously, then for
three daies he knoweth not the threshold of our
habitaunce, but despoyleth his granddam, an old
dame beraft of sustenaunce, or else stretcheth his
legs astride the roof and sitteth pering alow like
some monkey. What thinkest my poor harte suffereth
when I see him ? Nay, and this is a small matter :
but all the tyling are disshivered like wafers, and
whensoever winter be nigh, sobbing I pay three
grotes for each tyle ; for all the tenement hath but
one voice, ' 'Tis the werke of Kottalos, childe of

19. δαιπαρωτεροι P.　21. τὴν P.　20, 21. transposed
by Pearson ; but see Addenda.　23. βωσαι P : corr. R.

24. τριθημεραι P : corr. Meister.　33. ἰθι P (first ι deleted).

34. αυρευ P.　Verse first punctuated by Tucker.　36. μιζον
P : corr. by M.　43. ιδωμι κουτόσος P.　44. ωσπερι
τια P : corr. by R.　45. . κημην P, with a dot, not a
mark of corruption.　ημεθα P.　46. . κλαιουσα εκαστου
P, perhaps the a is deleted.

κάληθίν', ὥστε μηδ' ὀδόντα κινῆσαι.
ὄρη δ' ὁκοίως τὴν ῥάκιν λελέπρηκε 50
πᾶσαν καθ' ὕλην, οἷα Δήλιος κυρτεύς
ἐν τῇ θαλάσσῃ τὠμβλὺ τῆς ζόης τρίβων.
τάς τ' ἑβδόμας δ' ἄμεινον εἰκάδας τ' οἶδε
τῶν ἀστροδιφέων, κοὐδ' ὕπνος νιν αἱρεῖται
νοεῖν‹τ›' ὁ‹π›ῆμος παιγνίην ἀγιν‹εῖ›τε. 55
ἀλλ' εἴ τί σοι, Λαμπρίσκε, καὶ βίου πρῆξιν
ἐσθλὴν τελοῖεν αἵδε κἀγαθῶν κύρσαις
μήλασσον αὐτῷ—

ΛΑΜΠΡΙΣΚΟΣ

                    Μητροτίμη, ‹μὴ› ἐπεύχεο·
ἕξει γὰρ οὐδὲν μεῖον. Εὐθίης κοῦ μοι, 59
κοῦ Κόκκαλος, κοῦ Φίλλος; οὐ ταχέως τοῦτον
ἀρεῖτ' ἐπ' ὤμου τῇ 'Ακέσεω σεληναίῃ
δείξοντες; αἰνέω τἄργα, Κότταλ', ἃ πρήσσεις·
οὔ σοι ἔτ' ἀπαρκεῖ τῇσι δορκάσιν παίζειν
ἀστράβδ, ὅκωσπερ οἵδε, πρὸς δὲ τὴν παίστρην
ἐν τοῖσι προ‹υ›νείκοισι χαλκίζεις φοιτέων; 65
ἐγώ σε θήσω κοσμιώτερον κούρης
κινεῦντα μηδὲ κάρφος, εἰ τό γ' ἥδιστον.
κοῦ μοι τὸ δριμὺ σκῦτος, ἡ βοὸς κέρκος,

---

49. καληθιν' ωστε P. Verse marked as corrupt.　50. ορη-
δεκοιως P.　53. εβδομασταμ P (correction miscarried).
Terzaghi reads δ' on other grounds.　55. οτημος P : corr.
Hdl.　αγινητε corr. R.　58. μὴ inserted by Jackson.
μητροιτ P.　59. που P.　61. ακέσεω P.　62. Κοτταλα-
πρήσσις P.　63. ταισι P : corrected by R.　πεμπειν P,
corrected to παιζειν.　64. ἀστράβδ P.　65. προνικοισι P :
corrected by K.　68. σκυλος P : corrected by Jackson.
106

Metrotime,' and sooth is it, so they may keep their
teeth whole.[1] And see how he hath peled all his
chine in the woodland, like some Delian lobster-
fisher,[2] dragging out his blunted life afloat. But the
seventh daies and twentieth he wotteth of better
than the stargazers, and not e'en sleep o'ertaketh
him as he reckoneth when ye kepe playday. But
Lampriskos, as thou hopest these dames [3] may render
thee fair avauntage in life, and mayest encounter
fortune, give him not less—

LAMPRISKOS

Metrotime, cease imprecaciouns : he shall lose
naught. Hither Euthies, hither Kokkalos, hither
Phillos ; lift him forthright ashoulder and shew him
to Aceses' full moon.[4] (*They do so.*) Kottalos, I
admire your haveour. Sufficeth it not to play dibs
quick-eyed [5] like these, but must hie to the gaming-
place and play with the churles at toss-penny ? I
will make thee moe modest than a maid ne'er moving
mote, an that be thy pleasaunce. Bring hither the
smarting lash, the bull's pizzle wherewith I flay the

---

[1] 'Otherwise I would have knocked them out.' See
Philologus, lxxxi. 246 n. 7. A similar interpretation was
simultaneously proposed by Radermacher.

[2] The absurdity of statement (chine for back), and of
metaphor (for the Delians were not idle lobster-fishers but
divers) is possibly designed.

[3] The Muses.

[4] *i.e.* my patience is exhausted, though I have waited as
long as A.—a proverbial dawdler.

[5] ἀστράβδα I take of the quick graceful glances (Dictt. *s.v.*
ἀστράπτω) of the youths engaged at the game.

ᾧ τοὺς πεδήτας κἀποτάκτους λωβεῦμαι;
δότω τις ἐς τὴν χεῖρα πρὶν χολῇ βῆξαι.　　70

ΚΟΤΤΑΛΟΣ

μή ⟨μ⟩᾽ ἱκετεύω, Λαμπρίσκε, πρός σε τῶν Μουσέων
καὶ τοῦ γενείου τῆς τε Κόττιδος ψυχῆς
μὴ τῷ με δριμεῖ, τῷ ᾽τέρῳ δὲ λώβησαι.

⟨ΛΑΜΠΡΙΣΚΟΣ⟩

ἀλλ᾽ εἶς πονηρός, Κότταλ᾽, ὥ⟨στ⟩ε καὶ περνάς
οὐδείς σ᾽ ἐπαινέσειεν, οὐδ᾽ ὅκου †χώρης†　　75
οἱ μῦς ὁμοίως τὸν σίδηρον τρώγουσιν.

ΚΟΤΤΑΛΟΣ

κόσας, κόσας, Λαμπρίσκε, λίσσομαι, μέλλεις
ἔς μ᾽ ἐ⟨μ⟩φορῆσαι;

⟨ΛΑΜΠΡΙΣΚΟΣ⟩

μὴ ᾽μέ, τήνδε δ᾽ εἰρώτα.

⟨ΚΟΤΤΑΛΟΣ⟩

ταταῖ, κόσας μοι δώσετ᾽;

⟨ΜΗΤΡΟΤΙΜΗ⟩

εἴ τί σοι ζώην,
φέρειν ὅσας ἂν ἡ κακὴ σθένῃ βύρσα.　　80

70. χολη P: corrected by Hicks, Tucker.　　71. μημημι-
κετεύω προσπρισκε P: over προς λαμ is written, προσ being
cancelled. The marks over ευ may be an error (washed
out) for ου which in 72 is written over των and γενειων.
              τ
-εὐω is short (Buech.).　72. κουτιδος P.　74. ἰς P.　　ωτεκαι
108

gyved and unruly : put it in mine hand ere I
choke with choler.

KOTTALOS

I adjure thee, Lampriskos, by the Muses, and thy
beard and the life of thy deare Kottalos, damnify
me not with the smarter but with the other.

⟨LAMPRISKOS⟩

But thou art bad, Kottalos. E'en selling none
would prayse thee, e'en where mice eat iron summer-
tyde[1] and winter-tyde alike. (*He beats him.*)

KOTTALOS

How many, how many blows, Lampriskos, wilt lay
on me ?

⟨LAMPRISKOS⟩

Ask not me, but her.

⟨KOTTALOS⟩

Ow ! how many will ye give ?

⟨METROTIME⟩

As thou wishest me life, as many as your wicked
hyde can bear.

[1] See crit. note.

πέρνας P. 75. ὄκως P. ?χῶρης or κῶρης should be read :
So I translate (= καὶ θέρους καὶ χειμῶνος). 78. εσμεν P.
ἔς μ' ἐνφ. Rth. 79. τᾱτᾱ P. ἰτίσοιζωην P. 80. φερ
P with mark of corruption. βυρσαι (ι deleted) P.

⟨ΚΟΤΤΑΛΟΣ⟩

παῦσαι· ἱκαναί, Λαμπρίσκε.

ΛΑΜΠΡΙΣΚΟΣ

                καὶ σὺ δὴ παῦσαι
κάκ' ἔργα πρήσσων.

⟨ΚΟΤΤΑΛΟΣ⟩

              οὐκέτ' οὐχί ⟨τι⟩ πρήξω,
ὄμνυμί σοι, Λαμπρίσκε, τὰς φίλας Μούσας.

ΛΑΜΠΡΙΣΚΟΣ

ὅσσην δὲ καὶ τὴν γλάσσαν οὗτος ἔσχηκας·   84
πρός σοι βάλεω τὸν μῦν τάχ', ἢν πλέω γρύξῃς.

ΚΟΤΤΑΛΟΣ

ἰδού, σιωπῶ· μή με, λίσσομαι, κτείνῃς.

ΛΑΜΠΡΙΣΚΟΣ

μέθεσθε, Κόκκαλ', αὐτόν.

ΜΗΤΡΟΤΙΜΗ

                οὐ⟨κ ἔ⟩δε⟨ι⟩ λῆξαι,
Λαμπρίσκε, δεῖρον δ'—

⟨ΛΑΜΠΡΙΣΚΟΣ⟩

                ἄχρις ἥλιος δύσῃ;

110

⟨KOTTALOS⟩

Stop ! Enow, Lampriskos.

LAMPRISKOS

Stop thou too thy villainy.

⟨KOTTALOS⟩

Ne'er again will I do aught, I swear to thee,
Lampriskos, by the deare Muses.

LAMPRISKOS

And what a tongue hast thou gotten, boye ! I
will set the gag on thee an thou prate moe.

KOTTALOS

See, I am silent : prithee slay me not.

LAMPRISKOS

Kokkalos, lose ye him.   (*They do so.*)

METROTIME

Thou shouldest not have ceast, Lampriskos, but
beat him—

⟨LAMPRISKOS⟩

Till sun welke ?

---

82. πρησων P.   ουκετουχιπαιξω P : οὐχί τι or τοι Ellis.
83. ομνυμιλοι P.   84. εσχηκε(ν) P.   87. ουδεκληξαι P.
Here as L. *has* stopped ἔδει (Buecheler?) is necessary (C.E.)
with λῆξαι or ἐκλῆξαι (Pearson).   88. δὺς ῇ Meister.
δειρονδαχρι P.

HERODES

⟨ ΜΗΤΡΟΤΙΜΗ ⟩

ἀλλ' ἐστὶν ὕδρης ποικιλώτερος πολλῷ,
καὶ δεῖ λαβεῖν νιν—

⟨ ΛΑΜΠΡΙΣΚΟΣ ⟩

κ⟨ἠ⟩πὶ βυβλίῳ—

⟨ ΚΟΤΤΑΛΟΣ ⟩

δήκου 90
τὸ μηδέν—

⟨ ΜΗΤΡΟΤΙΜΗ ⟩

ἄλλας εἴκοσίν γε, κἢν μέλλῃ
αὐτῆς ἄμεινον τῆς Κλεοῦς ἀναγνῶναι.

⟨ ΚΟΤΤΑΛΟΣ ⟩

ἰσσαῖ.

⟨ ΜΗΤΡΟΤΙΜΗ ⟩

λάθοις τὴν γλάσσαν

⟨ ΛΑΜΠΡΙΣΚΟΣ ⟩

ἐς μέλι πλύνας.

⟨ ΜΗΤΡΟΤΙΜΗ ⟩

ἐρέω ἐπιμηθέως τῷ γέροντι, Λαμπρίσκε,
ἐλθοῦσ' ἐς οἶκον ταῦτα, καὶ πέδας ἤξω 95
φέρουσ', ὅκως νιν σύμποδ' ὧδε πηδεῦντα
(αἱ) π(ότνι)αι βλέπ(ωσι)ν ἃς ἐμίσησεν.

91. μηδεν P.   92. κλεοῦς P.   93. ισσᾶι P.   ιλασσαν
P : corr. K.   97. αἱ π. legit Hdl.
112

⟨METROTIME⟩

Aye, far more knavish than hydra is he, and he
must get—

⟨LAMPRISKOS⟩

An he studie his book?

KOTTALOS

Naught whatsoever.

⟨METROTIME⟩

Aye, twenty moe blowes, e'en though he shall
read better than Clio herself.

⟨KOTTALOS⟩

Yah!

⟨METROTIME⟩

Mayst wake to find tongue cu—[1]

⟨LAMPRISKOS⟩

—ltured in honied eloquence.

⟨METROTIME⟩

I will hie home, Lampriskos, and tell the old man
of this so een he can grasp [2] it, and return with gyves
that the Ladies [3] whom he hated may see him daunce
here foot-tight.

[1] M. would have gone on to say ' cut out,' but this word
(which also meant ' castrated ') would have shocked the
prim pedagogue. He substitutes a phrase which implies
' skilled in poetry and oratory,' σοφός, educated. Many may
prefer van Leeuwen's conjecture μάθοις . . . . . . πλῦναι.

[2] ἐπιμηθέως is objective, not subjective. Herodes recalls
Thuc. i. 140 ἐνδέχεται γὰρ τὰς ξυμφορὰς τῶν πραγμάτων οὐχ
ἧσσον ἀμαθῶς χωρῆσαι ἢ τὰς διανοίας τοῦ ἀνθρώπου.

[3] The Muses.

IV

ΑСΚΛΗΠΙΩΙ ΑΝΑΤΙΘΕΙСΑΙ ΚΑΙ
ΘΥСΙΑΖΟΥСΑΙ

ΚΥΝΝΩ

Χαίροις, ἄναξ Παίηον, ὃς μεδεῖς Τρίκκης
καὶ Κῶν γλυκῆαν κἠπίδαυρον ᾤκηκας,
σὺν καὶ Κορωνὶς ἥ σ' ἔτικτε κὠπόλλων
χαίροιεν, ἧς τε χειρὶ δεξιῇ ψαύεις
Ὑγίεια κὠνπερ οἵδε τίμιοι βωμοί,   5
Πανάκη τε κἠπιώ τε κἰησὼ χαίροι,
<κ>οἳ Λεωμέδοντος οἰκίην τε καὶ τείχ<εα>
πέρσαντες, ἰητῆρες ἀγρίων νούσων,
Ποδαλείριός τε καὶ Μαχάων χαιρόντων
<κ>ὦσσοι θεοὶ σὴν ἑστίην κατοικεῦσιν   10
καὶ θεαί, πάτερ Παίηον· ἵλεω δεῦτε
τὠλέκτορος τοῦδ', ὄντιν' οἰκίης τοίχων
κήρυκα θύω, τἀπίδορπα δέξαισθε.
οὐ γάρ τι πολλὴν οὐδ' ἕτοιμον ἀντλεῦμεν,
ἐπεὶ τάχ' ἂν βοῦν ἢ νενημένην χοῖρον   15
πολλῆς φορίνης, κοὐκ ἀλέκτορ', ἴητρα
νούσων ἐποιεύμεσθα τὰς ἀπέψησας
ἐπ' ἠπίας σὺ χεῖρας, ὦ ἄναξ, τείνας.

1. α(ν)αξ, παι(η)ον, and (μ)εδις P.   3. χωπολλων P,
corr. to κωπ.   5. υγιιατεκ' marked as corrupt P:
114

IV

OFFERINGS AND SACRIFICES

(The Temple of Aesculapius at Cos. There are two poor women, Kynno and Kokkale, with their slave and a cock which they bring as an offering. They are early for the moment of entering the inner chamber and they look round at the statues and sculptures.)

KYNNO

Hail, King Paieon, that art sovran of Tricca and hast gotten braw Cos and Epidaurus as thine habitaunce, and Koronis withal that bare thee and Apollo I cry hail, and Hygieia whom thou touchest with thy right hand, and those whose honoured shrines are here, Panace and Epio and Ieso and Podalirius and Machaon that sack'd house and walls of Leomedon, physickers of fell sicknesses, and all gods or goddeses, father Paieon, that inhabit thine hearth : hither come graciously to accept as side-dish this cock, herald of the walls of my habitaunce whom I sacrifice. For small and scanty are our sources : els might no cock but some ox or sow crammed with mochell fat be our guerdon for physicking of those sicknesses which thou, O King, hast brushed away by laying on of

corr. Bl.   11. $\overset{\lambda}{\iota(\delta)\epsilon\omega}$ P.   12. τουαλ. P with ω superscr.
16. αλεκτορ' ἰητρία P.

115

ἐκ δεξιῆς τὸν πίνακα, Κο‹κκ›άλη, στῆσον
τῆς Ὑγιείης.

‹ΚΟΚΚΑΛΗ›

μᾶ καλῶν, φίλη Κυννοῖ,   20
ἀγαλμάτων· τίς ἦρα τὴν λίθον ταύτην
τέκτων ἐπο‹ί›ει καὶ τίς ἐστιν ὁ στήσας;

‹ΚΥΝΝΩ›

οἱ Πρηξιτέλεω παῖδες· οὐχ ὁρῇς κεῖνα
ἐν τῇ βάσει τὰ γράμματ’; Εὐθίης δ’ αὐτ‹ήν›
ἔστησεν ὁ Πρήξωνος.

‹ΚΟΚΚΑΛΗ›

ἵλεως εἴη   25
καὶ τοῖσδ’ ὁ Παιὼν καὶ Εὐθίῃ καλῶν ἔργων.
ὅρη, φίλη, τὴν παῖδα τὴν ἄνω κείνην
βλέπουσαν ἐς τὸ μῆλον· οὐκ ἐρεῖς αὐτήν,
ἢν μὴ λάβῃ τὸ μῆλον ἐκ τάχα ψύξει‹ν›;—
κεῖνον δέ, Κυννοῖ, τὸν γέροντ’—ἆ πρὸς Μοιρέων 30
τὴν χηναλώπεκ’ ὡς τὸ παιδίον πνίγει.
πρὸ τῶν ποδῶν γοῦν εἴ τι μὴ λίθος, τοὖργον,
ἐρεῖς, λαλήσει. μᾶ, χρόνῳ κοτ’ ὤνθρωποι
κῆς τοὺς λίθους ἕξουσι τὴν ζοὴν θεῖναι—
τὸν Βατάλης γὰρ τοῦτον, οὐχ ὁρῇς, Κυννοῖ,   35
ὅκως βέβ(η)[κ](ε)ν, ἀνδρ[ι]άντα τῆς Μύττεω;
εἰ μ(ή) [τι]ς (αὐ)τὴν εἶδε Βατάλην, βλέψας
ἐς τοῦτο τὸ εἰκόνισμα μὴ (ἑτέρ)ης δείσθω.

19. κοτταλη P: corr. R., Buech.   20. μᾶ P.   21. τον η
P.   24. αυτα P: corr. Richards.   26. ευθιης P:
116

gentle hands. Kokkale, set the picture by the right
hand of Hygieia.

⟨KOKKALE⟩

Lo! Kynno deare, what fayre statues: what
artificer, prithee, made this stone, and who was it
that did set it here?

⟨KYNNO⟩

The children of Praxiteles: seest not yon letters
on the base? And Euthies son of Prexon set it up.

⟨KOKKALE⟩

Gracious be Paion unto these and Euthies for their
fayre werkes. See deare, yon child looking up toward the apple: woldest not say that, an she get
not the apple, she will expire forthwith? Aye and
yon old man, Kynno! Lo, 'a Fates' name how the
babe doth throttle the goose. Were it not at close
quarters of stone, the werke, motest say, wolde
speke. La! time will be when man shall wot to
put life e'en into stones! This image of Batale,
daughter of Myttes, seest not, Kynno, its gait?
None that had seen not Batale but only glaunced
at this likenes wolde need the other.

---

corrected by Bl., R.   27. κειμένην P.   29. ψυξι
P: corrected by Buech.   30. ιτονγεροντάπρος P.

                                        χ
32. Marked as corrupt.   33. λαλήσειν R.   μακρονωι P.

                                      κ
34-5. There is a paragraphus in P.   36. οπως P.   suppl.
Bl.   ανδρ[ι]αντα suppl. K.   37. supplied by

                    e   σ
Hicks, R.   38. εικονισμα P.   ηδισθω P.

HERODES

ἔπευ, φίλη, μοι καὶ καλόν τί σοι δείξω
πρῆγμ' οἷον οὐχ ὥρηκας ἐξ ὅτ<ε>υ ζώεις.   40
Κύδιλλ', ἰοῦσα τὸν νεωκόρον βῶσον.
οὐ σοὶ λέγω, αὕτη, τῇ ὧ(δε) <κ>ῶδε χασκεύσῃ;
μᾶ, μή τιν' ὥρην ὧν λέγω πεποίηται
ἔστηκε δ' εἴς μ' ὀρεῦσα κα(ρ)κ[ί]νου μέζον.
ἰοῦσα, φημί, τὸν νεωκόρον βῶσον.   45
λαίμαστρον, οὔτ' †ὀργήτ σ[ε] κ(ρ)ηγύην οὔτε
βέβηλος αἰνεῖ, πανταχῆ δ' (ἴσω) κεῖσαι.
μαρτύρομαι, Κύδιλλα, τὸν θ[εὸν] τοῦτον
ὡς ἔκ με κάεις οὐ θέλουσαν οἰδῆσαι·
μαρτύρομαι, φήμ'· ἔσσετ' ἡμ(έρη) κείνη   50
ἐν ᾗ τὸ βρέγμα τοῦτο τὸ ἀσυρὲς κνήσῃ.

μὴ πάνθ' ἑτοίμως καρδιη<βολεῦ>, Κυννοῖ·
δούλη 'στί, δούλης δ' ὦτα νωθρίη θλίβει.

ἀλλ' ἡμέρη τε κἠπὶ μέζον ὠθεῖται·
αὕτη σύ, μεῖνον· ἡ θύρη γὰρ ὤϊκται   55
κἀνεῖ<τ>' ὁ παστός·

< ΚΟΚΚΑΛΗ >

                οὐχ ὁρῇς, φίλη Κυννοῖ;
οἷ' ἔργα! <ν>αὶ <μ>ὴν ταῦτ' ἐρεῖς Ἀθηναίην

---

40. οτου P: corrected by M.   41. κυδιλλ' P.   sqq. suppl.
K.   42. αυτη P.   χασκούσῃ Bl.   43. over ι of τιν
P has an accent deleted.   44. suppl. by K.   46.
λαίμαστρον P.   46. ? ἀργή.   fin. suppl. K.   47. αἰνῖ
118

KYNNO

Follow, deare, and I will shew you a fayre thynge
such as hast not seen in thy life. Kydilla, go and
cry lowd to the sacristan. Speke I not to thee that
starest hither and thither? La! no reke hath she
of what I say, but standeth goggling at me more
agape than a crab. Go, I repeat, and cry lowd to
the sacristan. Thou gluttonry, ne close ne common
clepes thee werthy, but algates art thou held naught.
Kydilla, I call this god to witnes that thou flamest
me albeit I wolde not rage : god be witnes, I repeat :
day shall tide when thou shalt scratch this fowl noddle
of thine.

KOKKALE

Lay not all things to heart readily, Kynno : she is
a slave, and slaves ears are choked with slombrihed.

KYNNO

But 'tis day, and the pres increaseth. So bide
thou : for the door is oped, and the sanctuary is
free of ingate.

⟨KOKKALE⟩

See'st not, Kynno deare? What werkes! In
sooth motest say 'twas Athena did chisell the fayre

γλύψαι τὰ καλά—χαιρέτω δὲ δέσποινα.
τὸν παῖδα δὴ ⟨τὸν⟩ γυμνὸν ἦν κνίσω τοῦτον
οὐχ ἕλκος ἕξει, Κύννα; πρὸς γάρ οἱ κεῖνται   60
αἱ σάρκες οἷα θερμὰ θερμὰ πηδεῦσαι
ἐν τῇ σανίσκῃ· τὠργυρεῦν δὲ πύραυστρον
οὐκ ἦν ἴδῃ Μύελλος ἢ Παταικίσκος
ὁ Λαμπρίωνος, ἐκβαλεῦσι τὰς κούρας
δοκεῦντες ὄντως ἀργυρεῦν πεποιῆσθαι;   65
ὁ βοῦς δὲ ⟨κὠ⟩ ἄγων αὐτὸν ἤ ⟨τ⟩' ὁμαρτεῦσα
⟨κ⟩ὠ γρυπὸς οὗτος κὠ ἀνάσιλλος ἄνθρωπος
οὐχὶ ζόην βλέπουσι ⟨κ⟩ἡμέρην πάντες;
εἰ μὴ ἐδόκ⟨ε⟩υν τι μέζον ἢ γυνὴ πρήσσειν,
ἀνηλάλαξ' ἄν, μή μ' ὁ βοῦς τι πημήνῃ·   70
οὕτωτς† ἐπιλοξοῖ, Κυννί, τῇ ἑτέρῃ κούρη.

ΚΥΝΝΩ

ἀληθιναί, φίλη, γὰρ αἱ Ἐφεσίου χεῖρες
ἐς πάντ' Ἀπελλέω γράμματ', οὐδ' ἐρεῖς " κεῖνος
ὤνθρωπος ἕν μὲν εἶδεν, ἕν δ' ἀπηρνήθη,"
ἀλλ' ὅ οἱ ἐπὶ νοῦν γένοιτο †καὶ† θεῶν ψαύειν   75
ἠπείγετ'· ὃς δ' ἐκεῖνον ἢ ἔργα τὰ ἐκείνου
μὴ παμφαλήσας ἐκ δίκης ὀρώρηκεν,
ποδὸς κρέμαιτ' ἐκεῖνος ἐν γναφέως οἴκῳ.

ΝΕΩΚΟΡΟΣ

κάλ' ὕμιν, ὦ γυναῖκες, ἐντελέως τὰ ἱρὰ
καὶ ἐς λῶον ἐμβλέποντα· μεζόνως οὕτις   80

59. τονπαιδαδη γυμνον P : corrected by K.   60. κύννα P.
61. θερμαπηδωσαι P. [θερμα]   62. δὲ πῦρᾰ(σ)τον P : corr. W. Voll- [ρ]
graff.   63. ιδημυλος P with mark of corruption. ἴδησ[ε]
120

thynges—Lady I cry mercie. This bare boye, an I
scratch him, wolde he not be wounded, Kynno?
For his flesh lieth on him in the picture as with right
warm pulsaciouns; and the silvern fire-box—an
Myellos or Pataikiskos see it, wolde not their eyne
fall out for belief 'twere in sooth silvern ywrought?
And the ox and his leader and her that followeth,
and this man of hooked nose, and this of heyre erect.
are not day and livelihed in their eyne? An I
demed not I sholde defame my sex, I sholde have
cryed out for feare the ox mote do me an hurt: so
askaunce looketh he with one eye.

KYNNO

Yea, deare, for true are the hands of Apelles of
Ephesus in all paintings ne motes say 'Yon man
looked on one thynge, and gave no thought to
another,' but all that was his of wit or inspiracioun,
he was fain to assay: and whoso examine not him
ors werkes with judicious **oeillades** may he hang by
the foot in fullers house.

SACRISTAN

Full fayre, dames, are your meat-offerings, and
fayrer their significaunce: none hath ere found moe

Μύλλος Hdl.   66. χο P.   67. χω P.   ουτοσουκκω
λλ
[αν]ασι(μ)ος P. ουκ is cancelled by line and dots superscribed.
u itself is formed out of a λ. Verse marked corrupt.
68. ζόην P.   σινημερην P: corr. Hicks.   69. -κουν P.
75. ωι P: explained by Hdl.   Read κἀκ: *i.e.* ὅ τι καὶ
οἱ θεοὶ ἐπὶ νοῦν αὐτῷ ποιήσειαν Hdt. i. 27.   76. Verse
τα
marked corrupt.   ηἐργαεκεινου P.   79. εντελεωσ-
σταῖρα P but the second σ is cancelled by a vertical stroke.
80. μεζονω° ουτις P.

ἠρέσατο τὸν Παιήον᾽, ἥπερ οὖν ὑμεῖς.
ἰὴ ἰὴ Παίηον, εὐμενὴς εἴης
καλοῖς ἐπ᾽ ἱροῖς ταῖσδε κεἴ τινες τῶνδε
ἔασ᾽ ὀπυιηταί τε καὶ γενῆς ἆσσον.
ἰὴ ἰὴ Παίηον· ὧδε ταῦτ᾽ εἴη.   85

ΚΥΝΝΩ

εἴη γάρ, ὦ μέγιστε, <κ>ὑγίη πολλῇ
ἔλθοιμεν αὖτις μέζον᾽ ἴρ᾽ ἀγινεῦσαι
σὺν ἀνδράσιν καὶ παισί.—Κοκκάλη καλῶς
τεμεῦσα μέμνεο τὸ σκελύδριον δοῦναι
τῷ νεωκόρῳ τοὔρνιθος, ἔς τε τὴν τρώγλην   90
τὸν πελανὸν ἔνθες τοῦ δράκοντος εὐφήμως
καὶ (ψ)αιστὰ δεῦσον· τἄλλα δ᾽ οἰκίης ἕδρῃ
δαισόμεθα—καὶ ἐπὶ μὴ λάθῃ φέρειν, αὔτη,
τῆς ὑγιῆς δ᾽, ὅ οἱ προσδός· ἦ γὰρ ἱροῖσιν
μέ(ζ)ων ἁμαρτ<εῖν> ἢ ὑγίη 'στὶ τῆς μοίρης.   95

83. καλοισεμπροις P, but μ is cancelled and so is a mark
of corruption at the beginning of the verse.   86. χυγιηι P,
corrected by R.   88. Change of speaker falsely marked

favour in Paieons eyne than ye.   Hail, hail Paieon;
mayst be propitious for fayre offerings to these and
any that be their spouses or near sybbe.   Hail, hail,
Paieon.   Amen.

KYNNO

Amen, most mighty, and may we return anon in
goodly health, bearing withal larger offerings, with
husbands and children.—Kokkale, take hede fayrly
to cutte the leg of the fowl and give it to the sacristan,
and silently set the cake in the snakes den, and dip
the wafer [1]: of the rest shall we make feast in the
seats of our habitaunce, and don't forget to give
him some too of the health-offering: for soothly in
sacrifices a health-offering is sorer loss than the
portion.

[1] The 'cake' is probably (Hg.) a piece of money and the
'den' a collecting-box. 'Him' two lines below is the
husband, implied from οἰκίης ἕδρῃ.

89. τεμοῦσα most edd.   90. τῲι P.   91. πὲλανον P.
94. δωι P, *i.e.* δ', ὅ οἱ (ωι for ωι).   95. αμαρτιης P: corr.
Hdl.

V

ΖΗΛΟΤΥΠΟΣ

ΒΙΤΙΝΝΑ

Λέγε μοι σύ, Γάστρων, ⟨εἶ⟩ δ' ὑπερκορὴς οὕτω,
ὥστ' οὐκέτ' ἀρκεῖ τἀμά σοι σκέλεα κινεῖν
ἀλλ' Ἀμφυταίῃ τῇ Μένωνος ἔγκεισαι;

ΓΑΣΤΡΩΝ

ἐγὼ 'Αμφυταίῃ; τὴν λέγεις ὀρώρηκα
γυναῖκα;

⟨ΒΙΤΙΝΝΑ⟩

προφάσεις πᾶσαν ἡμέρ⟨η⟩ν ἕλκεις. 5

ΓΑΣΤΡΩΝ

Βίτιννα, δοῦλός εἰμι· χρῶ ὅτι ⟨μοι⟩ βούλει
καὶ μὴ τό μευ αἶμα νύκτα κἠμέρην (πῖ)νε.

ΒΙΤΙΝΝΑ

ὅσην δὲ καὶ τὴν γλάσσαν, οὗτος, ἔσχηκας·
Κύδιλλα, κοῦ 'στι Πυρρίης; κάλει μ' αὐτόν.

1. η P : corr. Buech.   4. αμφυταιην P : corr. J.   μενων
crossed out and λεγεις superscr. P.   5. προφασῖς P.
ημεραν P.   6. βίτιννα P.   μοι inserted by R.
after βούλει; but cf. Hippon. fr. 45.   7. suppl. K.

        κ
9. πουμοι P (μο crossed out and στ superscr.)
124

V

A JEALOUS LADY

(*Scene: A lady's chamber in a house in Ephesus. Bitinna the lady harangues Gastron, her slave, also her unfaithful paramour. Kydilla, her confidential slave-girl, is also present.*)

BITINNA

Tell me Gastron, art so surfeited, that it sufficeth thee not to stir my legs, but must woo Amphytaea, Meno's woman[1]?

GASTRON

Amphytaea? I. Have I e'en seen her of whom thou speakest?

⟨BITINNA⟩

Excuse on excuse all day long!

GASTRON

Bitinna, thy slave am I: use me as thou wilt, ne sup my blood day and night.

BITINNA

And what a tongue hast gotten, slave! Kydilla, where is Pyrrhies? Call him to me.

[1] Probably wife.

HERODES

τί ἐστί;

ΒΙΤΙΝΝΑ

      τοῦτον δῆσον—ἀλλ' ἔθ' ἔστηκας;—   10
τὴν ἱμανήθρην τοῦ κάδου ταχέως λύσας.
ἢν μὴ καταικίσασα τῇ σ' ὅλῃ χώρῃ
παραδεῖγμα θῶ, μᾶ, μή με θῇς γυναῖκ' εἶναι.
ἦρ' οὐχὶ μᾶλλον Φρύξ; ἐγὼ αἰτίη τούτων
ἐγῶμι, Γάστρων, ἤ σε θεῖσ' ἐν ἀνθρώποις.   15
ἀλλ' εἰ τότ' ἐξήμαρτον, οὐ τὰ νῦν εὗσαν
μῶρ‹ο›ν Βίτινναν, ὡς δοκεῖς, ἔ‹τ›' εὑρήσεις.
φέρ', εἷς σύ, δῆσον, τὴν ἀπληγίδ' ἐκδύσας.

ΓΑΣΤΡΩΝ

μὴ μή, Βίτιννα, τῶν σε γουνάτων, δεῦμαι.

ΒΙΤΙΝΝΑ

ἔκδυθι, φημί. δεῖ σ' ὁτεύνεκ' εἶ δοῦλος   20
καὶ τρεῖς ὑπέρ σευ μν‹έ›ας ἔθηκα γινώσκειν.
ὡς μὴ καλῶς γένοιτο τἠμέρῃ κείνῃ,
ἥτις σ' ἐσήγαγ' ὧδε. Πυρρίη, κλαύσῃ·
ὁρῶ σε δήκου πάντα μᾶλλον ἢ δεῦντα.
σύ‹σ›φιγγε τοὺς ἀγκῶνας, ἔκπρισον δήσας.   25

ΓΑΣΤΡΩΝ

Βίτιννα, ἄφες μοι τὴν ἁμαρτίην ταύτην.
ἄνθρωπός εἰμι, ἥμαρτον· ἀλλ' ἐπὴν αὖτις
ἕλῃς τι δρῶντα τῶν σὺ μὴ θέλῃς, στίξον.

   11. τουτον P with second του crossed out.   14. ειρ P
changed to ηρ.   15. εγωιμι P.   17. μῶραν P: corr. Hdl.

18. φερῖς P : **expl. by Ellis.**   δῦσον P.   19. δουμαι was

PYRRHIES

What is it ?

⟨BITINNA⟩ [1]

Bind this fellow—what ? Standest still ?—loosing anon the rope of the bucket. An I mar thee not and set thee as an example to the countriesyde, la ! call me no woman. Am I not rather an Eunuch ? 'Tis I, Gastron, I that fault herein, that I set thee among men.[2] But, an I erred then, thou shalt find Bitinna a fool now no moe, for all thou thinkest. Come, thou, bind him unayded when thou hast stripped him of his smock.

GASTRON

Nay, nay, Bitinna—by thy knees, prithee.

BITINNA

Strip him, I repeat. Must wot that art a slave and that I payd for thee three minae. Ah ! ill betyde that day that brought thee hither. Shalt rue it, Pyrrhies—I see that dost aught els save bind him. Truss his arms ; bind till they be perdy severed.

GASTRON

Bitinna, forgive me this errour. Mortal am I, I have erred ; but an thou find me moe doing aught thou woldest not, then tattoo me.

[1] The second change of speaker is adequately indicated by a large space.
[2] Treated you as fellow man.

---

first written by P.   20. ὁτευνεκ P.   21. μνας P with
dot below μ.   γινωισκειν P.   25. συγϲφ P : corr.
                  η
Buech.   26. αμαρτιαν P.

ΒΙΤΙΝΝΑ

πρὸς Ἀμφυταίην ταῦτα, μὴ ’μὲ πληκτίζευ,
μεθ’ ἧς ἀλινδῇ καὶ ἐμὲ χρὴ π(ο)δόψηστρον   30

. . . . . .

⟨ ΠΥΡΡΙΗΣ ⟩

δέδεται καλῶς σοι.

ΒΙΤΙΝΝΑ

           μὴ λάθῃ λυθεὶς σκέψαι.
ἄγ’ αὐτὸν ἐς τὸ ζήτρειον πρὸς Ἕρμωνα
καὶ χιλίας μὲν ἐς τ⟨ὸ⟩ νῶτον ἐγκόψαι
αὐτῷ κέλευσον χιλίας δὲ τῇ γαστρί.

ΓΑΣΤΡΩΝ

ἀποκτενεῖς, Βίτιννα, μ’ οὐδ’ ἐλέγξασα   35
εἶτ’ ἔστ’ ἀληθέα πρῶτον εἴτε καὶ ψευδέα;

ΒΙΤΙΝΝΑ

ἃ δ’ αὐτὸς εἶπας ἄρτι τῇ ἰδί⟨η⟩ γλάσσῃ
‘Βίτινν’, ἄφες μοι τὴν ἁμαρτίην ταύτην’;

ΓΑΣΤΡΩΝ

τήν σευ χολὴν γὰρ ἤθελον κατασβ⟨έσ⟩σαι.

ΒΙΤΙΝΝΑ

ἕστηκας ἐμβλέπων σύ, κοὐκ ἄγεις αὐτόν   40
ὅκου λέγω σοι; ⟨θλ⟩ῆ, Κύδιλλα, τὸ ῥύγχος

---

30. δι καιεμ(ε)χρηπ(ο)δοψ P (read by Milne). There is no
doubt as to this reading. I translate a v. 30ᵃ ὑμέων γενέσθαι

BITINNA

Playne not to me, but to Amphytaea with whom thou lyest, and needs must I ⟨your⟩ foot towell ⟨be
· · ⟩.

⟨PYRRHIES⟩

Thou hast him well bound.

BITINNA

See he escape not loose. Take him to the abode of torment to Hermon, and bid him hammer thousand stripes into his back and thousand into's belly.

GASTRON

Wilt kill me, Bitinna, ne try first an it be sooth or false?

BITINNA

What of thine own tongues utteraunce ' Bitinna forgive me this errour ' ?

GASTRON

Aye, for I wolde quench your choler.

BITINNA

Standest agape, and leadest him not where I bid thee? Kydilla, dint this losells beak, and thou,

---

$\overset{\eta}{\text{. . . .}}$ 31. μέθλαθη P.   33. τον/νωτον P.   36. ψευδεα
P (doubtful mark over ε).   37. ιδιαι P: corr. by R.
39. κατασβωσαι P: corr. by Bl.   41. οδῇ P: corr. by Hdl.

129

τοῦ παντοέρκτεω τοῦδε, καὶ σύ μοι, Δρήχων,
ἤδη 'φαμάρτει ⟨τῇ σ' ἂν⟩ οὗτος ἡγῆται.
δώσεις τι, δούλη, τῷ κατηρήτῳ τούτῳ
ῥάκος καλύψαι τὴν ἀνώνυμον κέρκον,   45
ὡς μὴ δι' ἀγορῆς γυμνὸς ὢν θεωρῆται;
τὸ δεύτερόν σοι, Πυρρίη, πάλιν φωνέω,
ὅκως ἐρεῖς Ἕρμωνι χιλίας ὧδε,
καὶ χιλίας ὧδ' ἐμβαλεῖν· ἀκήκουκας;
ὡς, ἤν τι τούτων ὧν λέγω παραστείξῃς,   50
αὐτὸς σὺ καὶ τἀρχαῖα καὶ τόκους τίσεις.
βάδιζε καὶ μὴ παρὰ τὰ Μικκάλης αὐτόν
ἄγ', ἀλλὰ τὴν ἰθεῖαν. οὗ δ' ⟨ὑ⟩πεμνήσθην—
κάλει, κάλει δραμεῦσα, πρὶν μακρήν, δούλη,
αὐτο⟨ὺ⟩ς γενέσθαι.

ΚΥΔΙΛΛΑ

                    Πυρρίης, τάλ⟨η⟩ς, κωφέ, 55
καλεῖ σε. μᾶ, δόξει τις οὐχὶ σύνδουλον
αὐτὸν σπαρά⟨σσ⟩ειν ἀλλὰ σημάτων φῶρα·
ὁρῇς ὅκως νῦν τοῦτον ἐκ βίης ἕλκεις
ἐς τὰς ἀνάγκας, Πυρρίη; ⟨σ⟩έ, μᾶ, τούτοις
το⟨ῖ⟩ς δύο Κύδιλλ' ἐπόψε⟨τ⟩' ἡμερέων πέντε 60
παρ' Ἀντιδώρῳ τὰς Ἀχαϊκὰς κείνας,
ἃς πρῶν ἔθηκας, τοῖς σφυροῖσι τρίβοντα.

ΒΙΤΙΝΝΑ

οὗτος σύ, τοῦτον αὖτις ὧδ' ἔχων ἧκε
δεδεμένον οὕτως ὥσπερ ἐξάγεις αὐτόν,
Κόσιν τέ μοι κέλευσον ἐλθεῖν τὸν στίκτην 65
ἔχοντα ῥαφίδας καὶ μέλαν. μιῇ δεῖ σε

42. τουτο και P : το is crossed out and δε superscr.   43. αμ-
αρτισοιεαν P : corrected by Danielss.   49. -κᾶς P.   53. επεμν.

Drechon, follow now by the way thy fellow leadeth.
Slave, wilt give a rag to this curst fellow to hyde his
bestiall nakedness, that he be not seen bare through
the market? Once moe a second time I cry thee
Pyrrhies to tell Hermon that he lay on thousand
here and thousand there: hast heard? Soothly an
thou traverse aught of my orders thou shalt thine
own self pay debt and interest. Walk on and lead
him not by Mrs. Smallwaies[1] but on the Mall. But
I mind—run, slave-girl, and call them, call them ere
they be afar.

KYDILLA

Pyrrhies, deaf wretche, she calleth thee. La,
one mote deme 'twas no fellow-slave he mauleth,
but a grave-robber: look how dost drag him perforce
to the torments, Pyrrhies. La! 'tis thee that
Kydilla will live to see with this pair of eyne in
five daies time rubbing with thine ankles at Antidorus
abode those Achaean gyves that but yestereen didst
doff.

BITINNA

Ho there, come back bringing him bound even as
dost lead him out, and enjoyne Kosis the tattooer
to come with needles and ink. Thou must be spotted

[1] *i.e.* through the back slums.

P: corr. Hdl.   54. δραμοῦσα is usually read.   55. Mark
of change of speakers misplaced below 56: *i.e.* at μᾶ.

αυτος P: corr. J., Bl.   ταλας P.   56. ουχιδουλον P.
59. verse marked as corrupt.   πυρριηεμα P: corr. by Bl.

60. τους P: corr. Bl.   61. αχαϊκας P.   63. αυθις P.
66. φ of ραφιδας first written as δ.   δῖ P.

HERODES

ὁδῷ γενέσθαι ποικίλον. κατηρτήσθω
οὕτω †καταμνος† ὥσπερ ἡ Δάου τιμή.

ΚΥΔΙΛΛΑ

μή, τατί, ἀλλὰ νῦν μὲν αὐτόν,—οὕτω σοι
ζῴη Βατυλλὶς κἠπίδοις μιν ἐλθοῦσαν   70
ἐς ἀνδρὸς οἶκον καὶ τέκν' ἀγκάλαις ἄραις—
ἄφες, παραιτεῦμαί σε· τὴν μίαν ταύτην
ἁμαρτίην—

ΒΙΤΙΝΝΑ

   Κύδιλλα, μή με λυπεῖτε,
ἢ φεύξομ' ἐκ τῆς οἰκίης. ἀφέω τοῦτον
τ[ὸ]ν ἑπτάδουλον; καὶ τίς οὐκ ἀπαντῶσα   75
ἔς μευ δικαίως τὸ πρόσωπον ἐμπτύοι;
ο(ὐ), (τ)ὴν Τύραννον, ἀλλ' ἐπείπερ οὐκ οἶδεν,
ἄνθρωπος ὤν, ἑωυτόν, αὐτίκ' εἰδήσει
ἐ(ν) τῷ μετώπῳ τὸ ἐπίγραμμ' ἔχων τοῦτο.

ΚΥΔΙΛΛΑ

ἀλλ' ἔστιν εἰκὰς καὶ Γερήνι' ἐς πέμπτην—   80

68. see nn. 69. τατί P. ^{οι}σω P. 70. μεν P:
corr. R. 71. Non αγκα'λ. 73 μηλυπιτεμε P: corr.
by R. 77. επε(π)ειπερ P, who wrote επει first but oddly
turned the ι into π. 80. εστιν—the ι is a correction as if
the writer had started to write ε.

---

¹ Herodes may have misread an old proverb collection :
see introd. The proverb, which refers to a quiet death, is,
however, inapposite. The correct sense is given by Horace.
Sat. ii. 5. 91 *Davus sis comicus atque stes capite obstipo,
multum similis metuenti.* There is fair evidence for καταμν
in the sense 'capite obstipo,' perhaps by early confusion with

attone. Let him be taught to cringe as low as his
honour Davus.[1]

KYDILLA

Nay, mamma, but now—e'en as thou hopest
Batyllis may live and maiest one day see her come
to a mans house, and maiest lift her children in thine
arms—now let him be : this one errour—

BITINNA

Kydilla, vex me not, all of you : or will flee the
habitaunce. Am I to let be this slave of slaves ?
Who then that encountred me wolde not rightly spit
in my face ? Nay by the Queen,[2] but since, though
mortal he be, he knoweth not himself, soon shall he
know it with this inscripcioun[3] on his forehead.

KYDILLA

But 'tis the twentieth, and but four days to the
Gerenia.

the Doric κατᾰμύω. Either Herodes coined κατάμνος incor-
ectly or καταμύων should be read.
[2] οὐ τὴν Τύραννον. The title is unknown for any Greek
divinity : yet it is fairly clear that v. 80 suggests an Ionic
colony and that the immediately following mimes are likely
o be Ephesian. There the oath is ' by Artemis,' and it
may be presumed that we have Artemis here. The com-
monest error in Greek texts, as in proofs and books to-day,
is the writing of a somewhat similar word for another by
false association : cf. vi. 34-38. I fancy Herodes wrote
Κυναγόν, ' Huntress.'
[3] Inscripcioun: ĀNOC EIMI?

BITINNA

νῦν μέν σ᾽ ἀφήσω, καὶ ἔχε τὴν χάριν ταύτῃ,
ἢν οὐδὲν ἦ<σσ>ον ἢ Βατυλλίδα στέργω,
ἐν τῇσι χερσὶ τῇσ᾽ ἐμῇσι θρέψασα.
ἐπεὰν δὲ τοῖς καμοῦσιν ἐγχυτλώσωμεν
ἄξεις τότ᾽ ἀμελι<τῖτι>ν ὁρτὴν ἐξ ὁρτῆς.   85

82. ηττον P: corr. by Meister.   83. εμησι P.
85. αμ(ε)λιτ(η)ν εορτην εξ εορτης P: corr. by Hdl.

134

BITINNA

Now shall I let thee be, and be thankfull to this girl whom I love as Batyllis and in mine own hands did noursle. But whenas we have done libacioun to those that sleep, then shalt have unhonied [1] festivall on festivall.

---

[1] *i.e.* πικράν 'bitter.' Honey was not offered to the dead.

VI

ΦΙ(Λ)ΙΑΖ(Ο)ΥCΑΙ Η ΙΔΙΑΖΟΥCΑΙ

ΚΟΡΙΤΤΩ

Κάθησο, Μητροῖ· τῇ γυναικὶ θὲς δίφρον
ἀναστα(θ)ε(ῖσα)· πάντα δεῖ με προστά‹σσ›ειν
αὐτήν, σὺ δ' οὐδὲν ἄν, τάλαινα, ποιήσαις
αὐτὴ ἀπὸ σαυτῆς· μᾶ, λίθος τις, οὐ δούλη
ἐν τῇ οἰκίῃ ‹κ›εῖσ'· ἀλλὰ τἄλφιτ' ἢν μετρῇ   5
τὰ κρίμν' ἀμιθρεῖς, κἤ‹ν› τοσοῦτ' ἀποστάξῃ
τὴν ἡμέ[ρ]ην ὅλην σε τονθορύζουσαν
καὶ πρημονῶσαν οὐ φέρουσιν οἱ τοῖχοι.
νῦν αὐτὸν ἐκμάσσεις τε καὶ ποεῖς λαμπρόν,
ὅτ' ἐστὶ χρ[εί](η), ληστρί; θῦέ μοι ταύτῃ   10
ἐπεί σ' ἔγ(ευ)σ' ἂν τῶν ἐμῶν ἐγὼ χειρέων.

ΜΗΤΡΩ

φίλη Κοριττοῖ, ταῦτ' (ἐ)μ(ο)ὶ ζυγὸν τρίβεις.
κἠγὼ ἐπιβρύχουσ' ἡμέρην τε καὶ νύκτα
κύων ὑλακτέω ταῖ[ς] ἀνωνύμοις ταύταις.
ἀλλ' οὕνεκεν πρός σ' (ἦλ)[θ]ον—

---

1. κιδθεσ P (δ cancelled by vertical stroke and θ formed
out of ο (Buech.)).   2. legit K.   ταττειν P : corr.
by R.   3. some marks over δε of ουδεν.   5. εις P : corr.
Richards.   μετρεω P. (with η above)   6. κη P : corr. by Bl.

136

VI

A PRIVATE CHAT

(Scene: Ephesus? The house of Koritto, a lady. Her friend Metro bursts in unannounced. A slave-girl is present.)

KORITTO

Sit down, Metro—Arise and set a chayre for the lady! Must I bid thee myself do all thy devoyrs, and thou woldest do naught of thine own self? La! thou'rt a stone in the house, not a slave-girl: but an thou takest thy measure of wheat, each crumb thou tellest, and an ne'er so litell driblet escape, the walls burst with thy day-long playnts and lamentaciouns. So thou dost wipe it and render it clean now, thou thief, when need is? I counsell thee render oblacioun to this lady: els had I given thee taste of my handes.

METRO

Deare Koritto thou'rt galled by the same yoke as I. I too day and night long yap like a dog gnashing at these bestiall wenches. But for my errand—

7. suppl. by K.   10. suppl. by Bl.   11. χέιρεων is a customary hyper-Ionicism due doubtless to Herodes: χειρῶν editors.   13. ε of επιβ. is due to a correction by P. 14. suppl. by K.   non ὑλακτέω P.   15. suppl. by K.

137

KOPITTΩ

ἐκποδὼν ἡμῖν 15
φθείρεσθε, νώβυστρ᾽, ὦ(τ)[α] μοῦνον καὶ γλάσσαι
τὰ δ᾽ ἄλλ᾽ ἑορτή—

MHTPΩ

λίσσομα[ί σ](ε), μὴ ψεύσῃ,
φίλη Κοριττοῖ, τίς ‹κ›οτ᾽ ἦν ὅ σοι ῥάψας
τὸν κόκκινον βαυβῶνα;

KOPITTΩ

κοῦ δ᾽ ὀρώρηκας,
Μητροῖ, σὺ κεῖνον;

MHTPΩ

Νοσσὶς ε[ἶ]χεν ἡρίννης 20
τριτήμέρη νιν· μᾶ, καλόν τι δώρημα.

KOPITTΩ

Νοσσίς; κόθεν λαβοῦσα;

MHTPΩ

διαβαλεῖς ἤν σοι
εἴπω;

KOPITTΩ

μὰ τούτους τοὺς γλυκέας, φίλη Μητροῖ,
ἐκ τοῦ Κοριττοῦς στόματος οὐδεὶς μὴ ἀκούσῃ
ὅσ᾽ ἂν σὺ λέξῃς.

MHTPΩ

ἡ Βιτᾶ‹δ›ος Εὐβούλη 25
ἔδωκεν αὐτῇ καὶ εἶπε μηδέν᾽ αἰσθέσθαι.

⟨KORITTO⟩

Get ye gone, ye slightfull ones ; naught but ears
and tongues, and the rest of ye idlenes—

METRO

Prithee, lie not, Koritto deare ?   Who did stitch
thee the scarlet baubon ?

KORITTO

Where hast seen it, Metro ?

METRO

Nossis, Erinna's childe, had it two daies agone.
La ! a fayre gift.

KORITTO

Nossis !   Whence gat she it ?

METRO

Wilt bewray an I tell thee ?

KORITTO

By these sweet eyne, Metro deare, none shall hear
from Koritto's mouth aught thou saiest.

METRO

Eubule, wife of Bitas, gave it her and bade her
that none discover it.

---

16. suppl. by Hicks.   17. εορτηι P : corr. by Bl.
Suppl. by K.   19. κονκινον (κ above) P.   25. ἡβῖτᾶτος P :
corr. W. Schulze.

ΚΟΡΙΤΤΩ

γυναῖκες, αὕτη μ' ἡ γυνή ⟨κ⟩οτ' ἐκτρύψει.
ἐγὼ μὲν αὐτὴν λιπαρεῦσαν ἠδέσθην
κἤδωκα, Μητροῖ, πρόσθεν ἢ αὐτὴ χρήσασθαι.
ἡ δ' ὥ⟨σ⟩περ εὕρημ' ἁρπάσα⟨σα⟩ δωρεῖται   30
καὶ τ⟨ῇ⟩σι μὴ δεῖ. χαιρέτω, φίλη, πολλά,
ἐοῦσα τοίη, ⟨κ⟩ἠτέρην τιν' ἀνθ' ἡμέων
φίλην ἀθρείτω τἆλλα. Νοσσίδι χρῆσθαι
τῇ Μηδοκέω—μέζον μὲν ἢ δίκη γρύζω,
λάθοιμι δ' Ἀδρήστεια—χιλίων εὔντων   35
ἕν' οὐκ ἂν ὅστις σαπρός ἐστι προσδοίην.

ΜΗΤΡΩ

μὴ δή, Κοριττοῖ, τὴν χολὴν ἐπὶ ῥινός
ἔχ' εὐθύς, ἤν τι ῥῆμα μὴ καλὸν πεύθῃ.
γυναικός ἐστι κρηγύης φέρειν πάντα.
ἐγὼ δὲ τούτων αἰτίη λαλεῦσ' εἰμί   40
†πολλά† τήν μευ γλ⟨ά⟩σσαν ἐκτεμεῖν δεῖται.
ἐκεῖνο δ' οὗ σοι καὶ μάλιστ' ἐπεμνήσθην,
τίς ἔσ⟨τ⟩' ὁ ῥάψας αὐτόν; εἰ φιλεῖς μ' εἶπον.
τί μ' ἐ⟨μ⟩βλέπεις γελῶσα; νῦν ὀρώρηκας
Μητροῦν τὸ πρῶτον; ἢ τί τἀβρά σοι ταῦτα;   45
ἐνεύχομαι, Κοριττί, μή μ' ἐπιψεύσῃ,
ἀλλ' εἰπὲ τὸν ῥάψαντα.

ΚΟΡΙΤΤΩ

          μᾶ, τί μοι ἐνεύχῃ;
Κέρδων ἔραψε.

27. ποτ P : corr. R.   30. omissions suppl. by K.
31. ταῖσι P : corr. R.   33. χρησθ P (with *αι* superscr.).   34. ηγυ-
νηγρυξω P with ηδικηγρυξ(ω) superscr.   36. λεπρος and
140

KORITTO

Oh womankind, this woman shall one day fordo me. I granted her prayers, and gave it her, Metro, ere I used it myself : and she seized it like trove, and gives it to whom she ought not. To such an one, dere, bid I long farewell, and let her quest henceforward other friend in my room. To Nossis, wife of Medokes—I speke beyond due limit and may Adrasteia hearken not—though I had a thousand yet wolde I not lend one that were rotten.

METRO

Prithee, Koritto, let not ire sit anon on thy nostrils an thou hear word of no fayre import. Gentle woman sholde suffer all things. 'Tis I that fault herein for speking o'ermuch : I sholde cut out my tongue. But—to my main intendiment—who did stitch it ? Say, an thou love me. Why these mowes at me ? Hast neer seen Metro before ? What mene these bashings ? I adjure thee, Koritto, false me not, but say who stitched it.

KORITTO

La ! why adjure ? 'Twas Kerdon.

προσδωσω (ωσω erased) P.   _{οιην}   37. κόρη τυ Stob. *Fl.* lxxiv.
14.   _{καλ}   38. σοφον P : σοφὸν Stob.   41. ⟨ἤ⟩ πολλά K.
But the writer is here half asleep and quite probably has substituted πολλά (as λεπρός) for a word of the same sense : *e.g.* περισσά or ἄκαιρα (Greg. Naz. ii. 726, *v.* 984 ἰδοὺ προτείνω τὴν ἄκαιρον καὶ λάλον γλῶσσαν· ὁ θέλων νηλέως ἐκτεμνέτω). γλωσσαν P : corr. by M.   43. ἴπον P.   44. ενβ. P. 46. μαημοι P : corr. Bl., Hdl.

‹ ΜΗΤΡΩ ›

κοῖος, εἰπέ μοι, Κέρδων;
δύ' εἰσὶ γὰρ Κέρδωνες, εἷς μὲν ὁ γλαυκός
ὁ Μυρταλίνης τῆς Κυλαίθιδος γείτων·   50
ἀλλ' οὗτος οὐδ' ἂν πλῆκτρον ἐς λύρην ῥάψαι·
ὁ δ' ἕτερος ἐγγὺς τῆς συνοικίης οἰκέων
τῆς Ἑρμοδώρου τὴν πλατεῖαν ἐκβάντι,
ἦν μέν κοτ', ἦν τις, ἀλλὰ νῦν γεγήρακε·
τούτῳ [Κ](υλ)αιθὶς ἡ μακαρῖτις ἐχρῆτο—   55
μνησθεῖεν αὐτῆς οἵτινες προσήκουσιν.

ΚΟΡΙΤΤΩ

οὐδέτερος αὐτῶν ἐστιν ὧ‹ν› λέγεις, Μητροῖ,
ἀλλ' οὗτος οὐκ οἶδ' ἢ '‹κ› Χίου τις ἢ 'ρυθρεών
ἥκει, φαλακ(ρ)ός, μικκός—αὐτὸ ἐρεῖς εἶναι
Πρηξῖνον· οὐδ' ἂν σῦκον εἰκάσαι σύκῳ   60
ἔχοις ἂν (οὔ)[τ]ω· πλὴν ἐπὴν λαλῇ, γνώσῃ
Κέρδων ὀτεύνεκ' ἐστὶ καὶ οὐχὶ Πρηξῖνος.
κατ' οἰκίην δ' ἐργάζετ' ἐ‹μ›πολέων λάθρη,
τοὺς γὰρ τελώνας πᾶσα νῦν θύρη φρίσσει—
ἀλλ' ἔρ(γ)' ὁκ(οῖ)' (ἔ)στ' ἐργάτης; Ἀθηναίης   65
αὐτῆς ὁρ‹ῆ›ν τ(ὰς) χε[ῖ]ρας οὐχὶ Κέρδωνος
δόξεις· ἐ[γὼ] μὲν—δύο γὰρ ἦλθ' ἔχων, Μητροῖ—
ἰδοῦσ' ἅμ' ἰ(δμ)ῇ τώμματ' ἐξεκύμηνα·
τὰ βαλλί' οὕτως ἄνδρες οὐχὶ ποιεῦσι—
αὐταὶ γάρ ἐ(σ)μεν—ὀρθά· κοὐ μόνον τοῦτο,   70
ἀλλ' ἡ μαλακό(τ)ης ὕπνος, οἱ δ' ἱμαντίσκοι
ἔρι', οὐχ ἱμ(ά)[ντες]· εὐνοέστερον σκυτέα
γυναικ[ὶ] διφῶσ' ἄλλον οὐκ ἀνευρ[ή]σ[εις].

ΜΗΤΡΩ

κῶς οὖν ἀφῆκας τὸν ἕτερον;
142

⟨METRO⟩

Which Kerdon ? Tell me. There are two Kerdons,
one of grey eyne, neighbour of Myrtaline daughter
of Kylaithis: but yon note stitch plectre for
lyre. The other has habitaunce forby the tenement
of Hermodorus as one quitteth the Broad Way:
of mark once but now eld hath him. Him had
Kylaithis, who is now at peace. May her kin
memorize her.

KORITTO

'Tis neither of these, Metro. This one haileth
from Chios or Erythrae, I wot not which: bald and
short: a very Prexinos motest say: fig to fig notest
so compare: but whenas he prateth thou'lt ken him
to be Kerdon not Prexinos. At home he werketh
bartering by stealth, for every door now shuddereth at
the tax-gatherers. ' But what werkes is he werker ? '
Athenes own handes woldest deme to see, not
Kerdons. I—for he came with twain of them, Metro
—at first glaunce were mine eyne extent: e'en
straighter than the livelihed—none listeth—: nay
moe—as soft as sleep, and the thonglets no thongs
but wool: kinder cobbler to feminitee notest find,
quest how thou wilt.

METRO

How gattest not the other ?

---

52. οικ^εων P.   57. ως P: corr. Bl.   58. ηχιου P:
corr. W. Schulze.   60. αισσυκωι P.   61. suppl. by K.
63. κατοικειν P with mark of error at beginning: corr. R.
65. I give the letters as Milne reads them exc. (ε)στ for (α)στ.
Construction as τὰ μετεωρὰ φροντιστής (Plat.), μυρία πεμπαστάν
(Aesch.).   66. ορ(α)ν P.   67. suppl. Bl., Buech.
68. ἀμι(δμ)η P.   72. suppl. R.   73. suppl. Hdl.
(ησ.[.] superscr.).   74 etc. suppl. K.

< ΚΟΡΙΤΤΩ >

τ[ί] δ' οὐ, Μητροῖ,
ἔπρηξα; κοίην δ' οὐ προσήγαγον πειθοῦν   75
αὐτῷ; φιλεῦσα, τὸ φαλακρὸν κ[α]ταψῶσα,
γλυκὺν πιεῖν ἐγχεῦσα, ταταλίζ[ο]υσα,
τὸ σῶμα μοῦνον οὐχὶ δοῦσα χ[ρ]ήσασθαι.

ΜΗΤΡΩ

ἀλλ' εἴ σε καὶ τοῦτ' ἠξίωσ' ἔδει δοῦ[ν]αι.

ΚΟΡΙΤΤΩ

ἔδει γάρ· ἀλλ' ἄκαιρον οὐ πρέπον (γ') εἶναι·   80
ἤληθεν ἡ Βιτᾶ<δ>ος ἐν μέσῳ <Εὐβ>ούλη·
αὕτη γὰρ ἡμέων ἡμέρην τε καὶ νύκτα
τρίβουσα τὸν ὄνον σκωρίην πεποίηκεν,
ὅκως τὸν ωὑτῆς μὴ τετρωβόλο[υ] κόψῃ.

ΜΗΤΡΩ

κῶς δ' οὗτος εὗρε πρός σε τὴν ὁδὸν ταύτην,   85
φίλη Κοριττοῖ; μηδὲ τοῦτό με ψεύσ(ῃ).

ΚΟΡΙΤΤΩ

ἔπεμψεν αὐτὸν Ἀρτεμῖς ἡ Κανδᾶ<δ>(ο)[ς
τοῦ βυρσοδέψεω τὴν στέγην σημήνασα.

ΜΗΤΡΩ

αἰεὶ μὲν Ἀρτεμῖς τι καινὸν εὑρήσει,
πρόσω 'πιεῦσα τὴν προκυκλίη   90
ἀλλ' οὖν γ' ὅτ' οὐχὶ τοὺς δύ' εἶχες ἐ<κ>λῦσαι
ἔδει πυθέσθαι τὸν ἕτερον τίς ἡ ἐ<κ>δοῦσα.

⟨KORITTO⟩

All things tryed I: all persuasiouns trayned:
kissing, stroking his bald pate, flagons of mead, fond
names, albut surrendring mine own bodie.

METRO

But an he asked, e'en this sholdest have given.

KORITTO

Aye—but all things in tyde. Eubule wife of Bitas
was grinding before us. For day and night long
doth she weare our stone into scrapings, enaunter
she pay a grote to set her own.

METRO

And how found he his way hither to thee, deare
Koritto? Eke herein false me not.

KORITTO

Artemis, wife of Kandas the tanner, sent him
hither, shewing the house.

METRO

Artemis will aye find some new device drinking
deep down in bawdy bottles. But sin notest salve the
twain, algates sholdest have found who bid the other.

---

81. ηληθενγαρ P.　τατος corr. W. Schulze.　ενμεσ(ω)ι-
δουλη P : corr. Jevons.　86. ψευσ(η)[ι] P.　87. Καν-
δατος P (so Bl.): corr. W. Schulze.　90. P has ιηνθα(λπην),
but there is a quite different correction (unfortunately illegible) above. I imagine τῆς προκυκλίης στάμνης.　91, 92. εγ
for εκ P.

HERODES

ἐλιπάρεον ὁ δ' ὤμνυ' οὐκ ἂν εἰπεῖν μοι·
†ταύτη γὰρ ‹ἥλω› κἠγάπησέ ν‹ιν›, Μητροῖ.†

‹ΜΗΤΡΩ›

λέγεις ὁδόν μοι· νῦν πρὸς Ἀρτεμῖν εἶ‹μι›·   95
ὅκως ὁ Κ(έρδω)ν ὅστις ἐστὶν εἰδ[ή](σ)ω.
ὑγίαινέ μ(ο)[ι, Κοριτ]τί· λαιμᾶ τ[ις] ‹κ›ὤρη
ἡμῖ[ν] ἀφ[έρπειν] ἐστί.

ΚΟΡΙΤΤΩ

                      τὴν θύρην κλεῖσον,
αὖτ[η σ]ύ, (ν)[εο]σσοπῶλι, κἀξαμίθρησαι
αἱ ἀλ(ε)κτ[ορῖ]δες ε(ἰ) [σ]όαι εἰσί, τῶν τ' αἰρέων   100
αὐτῆσ[ι ... ο]ν· οὐ γὰρ ἀλλὰ πορθεῦ(σι)
ὠρν[ι]θ(ο)[κ]λέ[π]ται, κἢν τρέφῃ τις ἐν κόλπῳ.

94. This verse at top of the column with ἄ right mg.
of 93.   The article was only granted to a lady in return

146

KORITTO

I besought but he swore he nould say : †for he was charmed with her and she with him, Metro.†

METRO

Thy tale speedeth me : now hie I to Artemis to know what man Kerdon be.   Fare thee well, Koritto : one hungereth and I must move off.

KORITTO

Shut the door—ho you there, chick-girl—and tell an the hens be safe, and toss darnel to them.   For indeed the bird-thieves spoyle e'en an one rear abosom.

---

for services.   ιναι P : corr. by R.   96. suppl. Buech.
97. init. suppl. Buech.   fin. corr. (λαιμαι) and suppl. by
Grooneboom.   98. init. suppl. Cr.   99. init. suppl. R.,
med. Diels.   100. suppl. by Cr.   101. *e.g.* ῥῖψον Bl.
102. suppl. Hdl.

VII

C]ΚΥ(Τ)[Ε]ΥC

ΜΗΤΡΩ

Κέρδων, ἄγω (σ)οι τάσδε τὰς (γ)[υνάς, εἴ] τι
τῶν σῶν ἔχεις αὐτῆσιν ἄξιον δεῖ(ξ)αι
χειρέων νοῆρες ἔργον.

ΚΕΡΔΩΝ

          οὐ μάτην, Μητρ(οῖ),
ἐγὼ φ[ι]λέω σε. ταῖς γυναιξὶν οὐ θήσεις
τὴν μέζον' ἔξω σανίδα; Δριμύλῳ φωνέω·   5
πάλιν καθεύδεις; κόπτε, Πίστ(ε), τὸ ῥύγχος
αὐτοῦ, μέχρις τὸν ὕπνον ἐκχέῃ πάντα·
μᾶλλον δὲ τὴν ἄκανθα[ν], ὡς ἔχ[ω]ν κ‹λά›ῃ,
ἐκ τοῦ τραχήλου δῆσο[ν. εἶ]α δή, [κέρκω]ψ,
κίνει ταχέως τὰ γοῦνα· μέζον [ἴχη](νας)   10
τρίβειν ψοφεῦντα νου(θ)[ετημάτων] τῶνδε;

1. γυνάς Diels, εἴ τι Ellis.   3 fin. an erasure.   4. φ[ι]λω
P.   8. καληι P : correxi et supplevi.   9. εἶα δή suppl.
Diels, κέρκωψ Hdl.   10. supplevi dubitanter.   11. supplied by Hdl.   τουτωνδε P (του being cancelled by
dots). The gap here when the mounting is corrected is of
about one letter more than would appear from the facsimile;

VII

THE COBBLER

(Scene : A street in Ephesus (?) by a cobbler's shop. Metro arrives and introduces two customers to Kerdon. Slaves are at work inside. Metro appears to have made Kerdon's acquaintance since Mime VI— and to some effect.)

METRO

Kerdon, I bring thee these dames an hast slie handycraft to shew them.

KERDON

My loves labour for thee, Metro, is not lost. Set the larger plank outside for the dames. 'Tis Drimylos I speke to. Asleep again? Smite his snout, Pistos, till he shed all his sleep. Nay rather, that his penaunce may endure, hang the teasell from his neck. Ply thy knees apace, sir Kerkops; yearnst to chafe louder[1] chastisements than these? *Now*

---

[1] 'louder,' *i.e.* chains.

---

here of seven or eight letters. See Kenyon in the Cambridge Edition.

νῦν ἔκ μιν αὐτήν, λε[. . . . . ., λαμπ]ρύνεις
κ(α)[ὶ] ψ[ῆ]ς; (ἐ)γώ] σευ τὴ(ν) [. . . . .]ψήσω.
ἔ(ζεσ)[θε, Μ](η)τροῖ. Πίστ[ε τὴν . . . . . o]ιξας
πυργῖδα, μὴ τὴν ὧδ[ε, ...](ν),   15
τὰ χρήσιμ᾽ ἔργα, τοῦ τρ[ιωρόφου . . .]ος
ταχέως ἔνεγκ᾽ ἄνω(θ)[εν. . . . . . Μη]τροῖ,
οἳ᾽ ἔργ᾽ ἐπόψεσθ᾽. ἡσυχῆ [. . . . .]ον
τὴν <σ>αμβαλούχην οἰ(γ)[ε. . . . . . .] πρῶτον,
Μητροῖ, τελέων ἄρη[ρεν ἐκ μερ](έ)ων ἴχνος·   20
θηεῖσθε κύμε[ῖ]ς, ὦ γυ[ναῖκες· ἡ πτ]έρνη
ὀρῆθ᾽ ὅκως πέπηγε, <κ>[ὼς σά]φ᾽ ἠν[ίσκ]οις
ἐξηρτίωται πᾶσα, κ[οὐ τὰ] μὲν κ[αλῶ]ς
τὰ δ᾽ οὐχὶ καλῶς, ἀλλὰ πά[ν]τ᾽ ἴσαι χ[εῖρε]ς.
τὸ χρῶμα δ᾽, οὕτως ὑμ[ι]ν ἡ Πα[. .] δοίη   25
.[. . . . . π]ερ ἰχανᾶσθ᾽ ἐπαυρέσθαι,
(π)[. . . . . ἄλ]λο τῷδ᾽ ἴσον χρῶμα
κ[οῦ . . . . οὔτ]ω, κοῦ δὲ κηρὸς ἀνθήσει;
χ[ρυσοῦ στατῆρα](ς) τρεῖς ἔδωκε Κανδᾶ<δ>(ι)
Κ[έρδων . . . . . .] τοῦτο κἤτερον χρῶμα·   30
β[ραχεῖ λόγῳ δ᾽ ὄμνυ]μι πάν<τ>᾽ ὅσ᾽ †ἔστ᾽† ἱ[ρ]ά
κὤ[σσ᾽ ἐστὶν ὅσια] τὴν ἀλη[θείη]ν βάτ . . †ζειν
. . . .] οὐδ᾽ ὅσον ῥοπὴν ψεῦδος
. . . .] Κέρδωνι μὴ βίου ὄνησις
μ[ηδ᾽ . . . .]ων γίνοιτο—κα[ὶ] χάριν πρός με 35
. . . . οὐ γ](ὰ)ρ ἀλλὰ μεζόνων ἤδη
. . . .] κερδέων ὀριγνῶνται.

12. If λαμπ]ρύνεις (Blass ?) is right at most six letters
are missing. λειόπυγε may be better than λευκόπυγε Cr.
13. init. supplevi (judice H. Rackham certissime): ψ superscr.
ἐγώ Cr.   fin. *cf.* Diels. κοχώνην ἐκψήσω fills the space well.
14. init. suppl. by Hdl.   τὴν Cr., *e.g.* διπλῆν Hg.   15. τὴν
δ᾽ ἐκεῖσ᾽, ἆρον.   16. supplevi *e.g.* with δ᾽ οἶος. They are
so precious as to be kept at the top of the house and none
150

⟨smooth-rump⟩, dost clene and wipe it : I'll wipe thy
⟨posteriours⟩ for thee. Sit ye down, Metro. Pistos,
ope the ⟨double⟩ chest—not this ⟨here but yon, and
have out⟩ my noble werkes, bringing them ⟨thyself⟩
speedily the third floor adown. Happy Metro, what
werkes shalt behold ! Quietly, ⟨sir greedy-belly⟩,
ope the shoecase. ⟨This⟩ sole Metro is fixed of perfect ⟨parts⟩ : descern ye, too, ladies : see how fast
it is, and how truly finished with straps all about,
nor is it part-fair part-fowl, but equall handicraft
algate. And for tint,—so may Paphos queen grant ye
joyaunce of all things ⟨soever⟩ ye yearn for—, no tint
like this hath ⟨any yet chaunced on⟩. Where shall
⟨dye or⟩ wax bear sike flowers ? Three gold staters
did K⟨erdon⟩ pay to Kandas who sold him this and
another colour,—nay I swear by all things holy ⟨and
hallowed⟩ that I speke sooth and that no lye ⟨shall
escape the barrier of my teeth⟩ one moment : or
may Kerdon have no profit of life ⟨or trafficking⟩—
and bade me thank him : for, and true is it, ⟨the
skinners⟩ clutch after greater gains now. ⟨As with

---

but Pistos may touch them.   17. suppl. Bl., K. *e.g.* ὀλβίη
(Hdl.).   18. 9 or 10 letters missing, *e.g.* σύ, λαίμαστρον.
19. corr. by Bl.   Seven letters missing after οἶγε : *e.g.*
τοῦτο (Bl.) δὴ or σοι.   20. supplevi.   21. suppl.
by R.   22. ὅπως P (who started to write ορ).   supplevi
e.g.   23. suppl. Bl., Hdl.   24. supplied by Cr., Bl.
25. ? Πάφου,   26. *e.g.* μεδέουσ', with ὅσωνπ]ερ Hdl.
27. *e.g.* ⟨ε⟩τληχεν οὐδ⟨ε⟩ὶς   28. suppl. Cr. Hg. : *e.g.* φῦκος.
29. supplevi : ἁτ(ι) P : corr. W. Schulze.   30. suppl. Cr.
Then *e.g.* ὁ δ᾽ ἐδίδου.   31. εστινι[.] α P : ὄμνυμι
πάνθ᾽ ὅσ᾽ ἔστ᾽ ἱρά Bl.   32. init. suppl. Hdl.   βαδίζειν
P : suppl. and corrected by Bl.   A mark of doubt is
prefixed.   33. *e.g.* ἕρκος δ᾽ ὀδόντων.   34. *e.g.* ἀμείψεται ἤ.
35. supplevi *e.g.* ἐμπολέων.   36. suppl. Cr.   init. *e.g.*
ᾔτησεν.   37. *e.g.* οἱ ῥινοδέψαι.

............] τἄργα τῆς τέχνης ἡμ‹έ›ων
.... ὁ πίσ]υγγος δὲ δειλαίην οἰζύν
.....] . ναν[. .]έων νύκτα ‹κ›ἡμέρην θάλπω· 40
.....]s ἡμέων ἄχρις ἑσπέρης κάπτει
....](α)ι πρ[ὸς] ὄρθ[ρ]ον; οὐ δοκέω τόσ‹σ›ον
τὰ Μικ‹ί›ωνος (κ)ηρί' εὐπ[. . . .]
κοὔπω λέγω, τρεισκαίδε[κ' . . . . . . β](ό)σκω,
ὁτεύνεκ' ὦ γυναῖκες ἀργ[. . . . . . .]s,   45
οἵ, κἢν ὔη Ζ(ε)ύ(s), τοῦτο μοῦ[νον . . . . .]ν
'φέρ' εἰ φέρεις τι,' τἄλλα δ' ἀψ[. . . . ἐ](ά)ται
ὅκως νεοσσο[ὶ] τὰς κ‹ο›χώνας θά[λ]π[ο]ντες.
ἀλλ' οὐ λόγων γάρ, φασίν, ἡ ἀγο(ρ)ὴ δεῖται
χαλκῶν δέ—τ(ο)ῦτ' ἢν μ(ὴ) ὗμιν ἀ[νδ]άνῃ, Μητρ[οῖ,
τὸ ζεῦγος, ἕτερον ‹κἤ›τε[ρ]ον μάλ' ἐξοίσει, 51
ἔστ' ἂν (ν)ό(ῳ) πεισθῆτε [μὴ λ]έγει[ν] ψευδέα
Κέρδωνα. τάς μ(οι σ)α[μβα]λουχίδας πάσας
ἔνεγκε, Πίστε· (δεῖ '[γ]κ)αλίστ' (εὖ) νηθείσας
ὑμέας ἀπελθεῖν, ὦ γυναῖκες, εἰς [ο]ἶκον.   55
θήσεσθε δ' ὑμ[εῖς]· (γέ)νεα ταῦτα πα[ν]τοῖα·
Σικυώνι', 'Αμβρακίδια, Νοσσίδες, ‹Χ›ῖαι,
ψιττάκια, κανναβίσκα, Βαυκίδ[ες], βλαυττία,
'Ιωνίκ' ἀμφίσφαιρα, νυκτιπήδηκες,
ἀκροσφύρια, καρκίνια, σάμβαλ' 'Αργεῖα, 60
κοκκίδες, ἔφηβοι, διάβαθρ'· ὦν ἐρᾷ θ[υ]μός
ὑμέων ἑκάστης εἴπατ'· ὡς ἂν αἴσθοισθε
σκύτεα γυναῖκες καὶ κύνες τί βρώζουσιν.

38. τα εργα and ημων P.   e.g. ὅκως μελίσσης.   39. suppl. Bl.
e.g. φορεῖτ'. De mensura huius loci mire agit Edmondsius
C.Q. 1925, qui ea quae falsis rationibus adductus conjecerat,
tamquam spatiis congruentia iterat.   40. e.g. πάσχων, and
ἀνώγεων Postgate.   41. e.g. ἐπ‹ε›ὶ τίς.   42. e.g. ἢ πίεται: cett.

bees, so ye enjoy⟩ my handicraft, dames, but I, the
cobbler, ⟨suffering⟩ piteous woe, ⟨this⟩ ⟨chamber⟩
warm night and day long. ⟨Which of us⟩ eateth
till even? ⟨Or shall drink⟩ at dawn? Not
Mikion's ⟨combs⟩ I ween are so ⟨bounteous to all
els⟩. And—which is more—tho' thirteen slaves I
browse—they are all idleness itself, and e'en an rain
come know naught but 'Bring an bringest': but for
aught els sitt croakles, like chicks warming their
posteriours. But say they, 'Market needs not words
but brass.' So, an this pair beseme thee not Metro,
he will bring out another and yet another till ye
be persuaded o' mind that Kerdon telleth no lies.
Bring me, Pistos, the shoecases all: soothly, dames,
must ye have arms well laden ere ye go home. Ye
shall descern: here are all these kinds: Sicyonian,
little Ambracians, Nossians, Chians, parrots, hemps,
Baucises, slippers, Ionian buttoned, hop-o'-nights,
ankle-tops, crabs, Argive sandals, scarlets, lads,
stairs; say each what heart wish, that ye may
know why women and dogs devour leather.

---

suppl. K.   τοσον P: corr. K.   43. μικρωνος P: corr. Cr.
κηρία recte Cr.[1], Hg.   fin. e.g. εὖ ποιεῖν ἄλλους. 'Sic vos
non vobis mellificatis apes.'   Mikion misellus apibus suis ne
decimam quidem partem mellis (Geopon. xv. 5. 4) reliquerit.
44. ·κου P: suppl. Buech., Cr.   fin. e.g. εἰ Κᾶρας.
45. οτουνεκ with ε superscr. P.   e.g. ἀργίη πάντες Hdl.   46. οἳ
e.g. μοῦνον ᾄδουσι Hdl.   47. suppl. by Cr.: e.g. ἀψόφως
Hdl.   48. ὅπως P with κ superscr.: corr. and suppl. by
Jackson.   κηχωνας P.   51. χατε[ρ]ον P.   52. (ν)ο(ω) P:
·ead and corrected by Bl.   fin. supplied by Buech. (?).
53. σαμβαλουχίδας Buech.   μοι Bl.   56. θήσεσθε P? rest
                 ω
·s R.   57. σικυνια P and λειαι: corr. Hdl.   58. ψιντακαια
P: ψιττακια in E.M., Hsch.   βλαυττια P.   See Proc.
Camb. Phil. Soc. 1927.

ΜΗΤΡΩ

κόσου χρεῖζεις κεῖν' ὃ πρόσθεν ἤειρας
ἀπεμπολῆ⟨ν τὸ⟩ ζεῦγος; ἀλλὰ μὴ βροντέων   65
οὗτος σὺ τρέψον μέζον εἰς φυγὴν ἡμέας.

⟨ΚΕΡΔΩΝ⟩

αὕτη σὺ καὶ τίμησον εἰ θέλεις αὐτό
καὶ στῆσον ἧς κοτ' ἐστὶν ἄξιον τιμῆς.
(εἶ)τ', (ἐκ) τό(σ)ων γὰρ οὔ σε ῥηδίως κρ(ῖ)ναι
ζευγέων, γύναι, τὠληθές—

⟨ΜΗΤΡΩ⟩
                    ἢν θέλῃς, ἔργον   7(
ἐρεῖς τι—

⟨ΚΕΡΔΩΝ⟩

        ναὶ μὰ τήνδε τὴν τεφρὴν κόρσην,
ἐφ' ἧς ἀλώπηξ νο[σ]σίην (π)ε(πο)ί(η)τ(αι)—
τάχ' ἀλφιτηρὸν ἐρ(γ)α(λε)ῖα κινεῦσι.
Ἑρμῆ τε Κερδέων καὶ σὺ Κερδείη Πειθοῖ,
ὡς, ἤν τι μὴ νῦν ἦμιν ἐς βόλον κύρσῃ,   7(
οὐκ οἶδ' ὅκως ἄμεινον ἢ ⟨κ⟩ύ⟨θ⟩ρη πρήξει.

ΜΗΤΡΩ

τί τονθορύ⟨ζ⟩εις κοὐκ ἐλευθέρη γλάσσῃ
τὸν τῖμον ὅστις ἐστὶν ἐ⟨ξ⟩εδίφησας;

ΚΕΡΔΩΝ

γ(ύ)να(ι), μιῆς μ[νῆ](ς) ἐστιν ἄξιον τοῦτο
τὸ ζεῦγος· ἢ ἄνω "σ⟨τ⟩' ἢ κάτω βλέπειν· χαλκοῦ 8(

65. (marked as corrupt): ⟨ν τὸ⟩ inserted by K
69. (κ)ῇ(ει)ναι and (εκ) το(σ)ων legi: ('possible' Milne)
70. ζευγεων legit Milne: sed vide addenda.   72. αλωπη(

METRO

That pair thou tookest up just now—at what price
woldest barter ?   Ho, thou, roar not overlowd ne put
us to flight.

⟨KERDON⟩

Ho thou, prithee, price it thine self and weigh the
price thereof : next, for 'twas no random chance,
lady, that led thee, out of all these pairs, to the true
one—

⟨METRO⟩

Prithee talk some busines.

⟨KERDON⟩

Aye, busines indeed will I talk—I swear by this
grey pate whereon fox nests [1]—to bring quick bread
to toolpliers.   Ah gainster Hermes and gainstress
Suasioun in troth, an naught now rencounter our
casting, I know not how pot shall prosper.

METRO

Why mumblest ne freetonged descryest the pryce ?

KERDON

Lady this pair is worth a mina, scan sky, scan

[1] *i.e.* bald.

P. suppl. Hdl.   73. marked as corrupt : suppl. Diels.
74. Κερδέων Danielss. and others.   76. χυτρη P by
correction of some letters : κύθρη Buech., Meister.
77. τονθορυ̅ξ̅ει P : corr. by Buech.   78. εξεδιφ (imitating the
form of ξ used in the text copied) P : *cf.* on 77.   79. supplied by K.   80. ηνωση P : corr. by Hdl.

L   155

ῥίνημ' ὃ δήκοτ' ἐστὶ τῆς Ἀθηναίης
ὠνευμένης αὐτῆς ἂν οὐκ ἀποστάξαι.

ΜΗΤΡΩ

μάλ' εἰκότως σευ τὸ στεγύλλιον, Κέρδων,
πέπληθε δαψιλέων τε καὶ καλῶν ἔργων.
φύλασσε κἄ[ργ]ασ' αὐτά· τῇ γὰρ εἰκοστῇ   85
τοῦ Ταυρεῶνος ἡ 'κατῆ γάμον ποιεῖ
τῆς Ἀρτακηνῆς, κὐποδημάτων χρείη·
τάχ' οὖν, τάλης, (ἄξουσι) σὺν τύχῃ πρός σε,
μᾶλλον δὲ πάντως· ἀλλὰ θύλακον ῥάψαι
τὰς μνέας ὅκως σοι μὴ αἱ γαλαῖ διοίσουσι.   90

ΚΕΡΔΩΝ

ἤν τ' ἡ 'κάτ‹η› ἔλθῃ, μνῆς ἔλασσον οὐ‹κ› οἴσει,
ἤν τ' ἡ Ἀρτακηνή· πρὸς τάδ', εἰ θέλεις, σκέπτευ.

ΜΗΤΡΩ

οὔ σοι δίδωσιν ἡ ἀγαθὴ τύχη, Κ[έ]ρδων,
ψαῦσαι ποδίσκων ὧν πόθοι τε κήρωτες
ψαύουσιν, ἀλλ' εἶς κνῦσα καὶ κακὴ λώβη·   95
ὥστ' ἐκ μὲν ἡμέων †Λιολέος† ἔω πρήξεις,
τ(α)ύτῃ δὲ δώσεις κεῖνο τὸ ἕτερον ζεῦγος
κόσου; πάλιν πρήμηνον ἀξίην φωνήν
σεωυτοῦ.

85. φυλασσεκα[.]ασ P : two short letters missing.
87. [τ] ησα(ρ)[τα](κ)ηνῆσ P : supplied by K.   88. marked
as corrupt. Reading (Cr.) is doubtful.   91. ηκατελθη

earth¹ : no fyling of copper whatsoever might ooze therefrom were Athena customer.

METRO

Full metely, Kerdon, is thy hovel packed with plenty of fayre werkes : keep them and make them. On the twentieth of Taureon Hecate holds marriage of the Artacene, and need is of shoon. Mayhap, wretche, nay assuredly will they hye to thee. Stitch thee a purse enaunter the cats dispred thy minas.

KERDON

Come Hecate, come th' Artakene, a mina, no less, ere they take them : prithee recorde that.

METRO

Fayre Fortune, Kerdon, granteth thee not to touch dainty feet that loves and desires touch : thous a scald knave and an infamy. So from us thou'lt get no more than Aeoleus' dawn² : but at what price wilt give yon other pair to this lady ? blatter thilk time some utteraunce beseming thee.

---

¹ The ὑπερήφανος of Theophrast carefully cuts people in the street, looking above or beneath them : so here the sense is ' affect to despise ' (περιορᾶν, ὑπερορᾶν).

² Conceivably ⟨Α⟩ιολεὺς dreamt of great riches and woke to find himself robbed. The whole would mean ' less than nothing.'

---

and ουχοισι P.   92. ηντηι P.   96. marked as corrupt.
97. κ ex χ.   99. σεωτου in left margin with σεωυτου στατη.
at top of column.

157

ΚΕΡΔΩΝ

στατῆρας πέντε, ναὶ μὰ θεούς, φο[ι]τᾷ
ἡ ψάλτρι' ‹Εὐ›ετηρὶς ἡμέρην πᾶσαν   100
λαβεῖν ἀνώγουσ', ἀλλ' ἐγώ μιν [ἐ](χθ)[α]ίρω,
κἢν τέσσαράς μοι Δαρ‹ι›κοὺς ὑπόσχηται,
ὀτεύνεκέν μευ τὴν γυναῖκα (τ)ωθάζει
κακοῖσι δέννοις· εἰ δὲ [. . . . ἔχ]ει χρείη
φέρ',—εὐλαβοῦ‹μαι› τῶν τριῶν . . . . δοῦναι—
καὶ ταῦτα καὶ ταῦτ' ἢ ὑμῖν ἑπτὰ Δαρεικῶν   106
ἕκητι Μητροῦς τῆσδε· μηδὲν ἀντεί(πῃς)·
δύ]ναιτό μ' ἐλάσαι σ‹ὴ› ἂν [ἰὴ] τὸν πίσ[υγγον
ἐόντα λ‹ί›θινον ἐς θεοὺς ἀν(απ)τῆ(ν)αι·
ἔχεις γὰρ οὐχὶ γλάσσαν ἡδο‹ν›ῆς δ' ἠθ(μό)ν· 110
ἆ, θεῶν ἐκεῖνος οὐ μακρὴν ἀπ(ε)[στ' ὢν](ήρ)
ὀτέῳ σὺ χείλεα νύκτα κἠμέρην οἴγ[εις.
φέρ' ὧδε τὸν ποδίσκον· εἰς ἴ‹χ›νος θῶ (μιν).
πάξ· μήτε προσθῇς μήτ' ἀπ' οὖν ἕλῃ[ς] μηδέν·
τὰ καλὰ πάντα τῆς καλῆισιν ἁρμόζει·   115
αὐτὴν ἐρεῖς τὸ πέλμα τὴν 'Αθηναίην
τεμεῖν. δὸς αὕτη καὶ σὺ τὸν πόδ'· ἆ, ψωρῇ
ἄρηρεν ὁπλῇ βοῦς ὁ λακτίσας ὑμ‹έ›ας.
εἴ τις πρ[ὸ]ς ἴχνος ἠκόνησε τὴν σμιλήν,
οὐκ ἄν, μὰ τὴν Κέρδωνος ἑστίην, οὕτω   120
τοὔργον σαφέως ἔκειτ' ἂν ὡς σαφ‹έ›ως κεῖται.
αὕτη σύ, δώσεις ἑπτὰ Δαρικοὺς τοῦδε,
ἡ μέζον ἵππου πρὸς θύρην κιχλίζουσα;
γυναῖκες, ἢν ἔχητε κἠτέρων χρείην
ἢ σαμβαλίσκων ἢ ἃ κατ' οἰκίην ἕλκειν   125

100. corr. by Bl. R (ευ om. P).   101. suppl. by K.
102. δαρεικους P.   103. οτουνεκεν P: corr. by Meister.

104. δεννοις P.   *e.g.* τῶνδ'.   105. correxi et supplevi *e.g.*
The placing of a fragment is uncertain (Lamacraft) : perhaps
158

KERDON

Five staters, 'a gods name, doth the harpist Eueteris
bid me take, and haunteneth me daylong, but I hate
her, tho' she promise me four Darics, in that she
wyteth my wyfe with ill reprieves. But an ye nede
such, come—⟨I am ware of giving les than the three⟩
—let these and these be [1] yours for Darics seven, for
Metros sake : gainsay thou me naught. Thy voice
might drive me the stony cobbler to fly heavenward :
for no tongue hast thou but a sieve of joyaunce : in
sooth not far from heaven is he unto whom thou
opest thy lips day and night long. Here with thy
dainty foot : let me set shoe thereon. Ah ! no more,
no les : all things fayre fit the fayre : Athena herself,
motest say, cut the sole. Give me thy foot, eke thou :
the lout that trod on you had a clumsy hoof.[2] Had
one but whetted his knife on the sole, 'a Kerdons
hearth, the werke were not so true as true 'tis. Ho
thou, woldest give seven Darics for this, thou that
gigglest against the door moe lowd than horse ?
Dames, an ye have need of other sandals dainty or

---

[1] $\tilde{\eta}$: the subjunctive (as Soph. *Phil.* 300) is softened by
the sense ($\delta\hat{\omega}$) as in Soph. ($\delta\iota\delta\acute{\alpha}\xi\omega$).

[2] Appears to be a mere touch of picturesque flattery.

$\acute{o}\nu[\alpha\rho]$, perhaps $[\mu\epsilon]\hat{\iota}o\nu$. I translate the latter. He does not
want to 'split the set.' 106. $\kappa\alpha\iota\tau\alpha\upsilon\tau\alpha\kappa\alpha\iota\tau\alpha\upsilon\tau$ P :
corrected by K. η $\upsilon\mu\iota\nu$ P. 107. ita Hg.
108. $\delta\acute{\upsilon}\nu\alpha\iota\tau o$ Buech., marked as doubtful. $\epsilon\lambda\hat{\alpha}\sigma\alpha\iota$ P.
supplevi et correxi: η om. P (*cf.* v. 91): post $\alpha\nu$ unius
literae spat. 109. $\epsilon o\nu\tau\alpha\lambda\eta\theta\iota\nu o\nu$ P. corrected
by Hdl. 110. $\eta\delta\eta\nu\eta\sigma\delta\eta\theta(\mu\eta)\nu$ (or $(\iota)\nu$) P. The verse
is marked as doubtful. 111. supplied by Buecheler.
112. supplied by Bl. 113. legit id. 114. $\pi\alpha\xi$. $\mu\eta\tau\epsilon$ P.

115. $\tau\eta s$ P. 118. $o\pi\lambda\eta$ P : corr. Hdl. $\upsilon\mu\alpha s$ P : corr.
Meister. 121. $\sigma\alpha\phi\omega s$ P : corr. Meister.

HERODES

εἴθισθε, τήν μοι δουλ[ίδ'] ὧδε ⟨δεῖ⟩ πέμπειν.
σὺ δ' ἧκε, Μητροῖ, πρός με τῇ ἐνάτῃ πάντως
ὅκως λάβῃς καρκίνια· τὴν γὰρ οὖν βαίτην
θάλπους ἄνευ δεῖ ⟨καὶ⟩ φρονοῦντ' ⟨ἔ⟩νδον ῥάπτειν.

126. marked as doubtful.
crossed out P: corr. Bl.
φρονουντακαιραπτιν P.

πεμπετει the last ι being
crossed out P: corr. Bl.
129. correxi: ανευδεινδον-

160

housewear ye mote send me the handmaid.[1] But be
ware Metro that thou come to me on the ninth to
get thy 'crabs,' for jerkins inner seam must be
stitcht sans haste and warily withal.

[1] The suggestion seems to be that Metro's commission
needs inordinate care. The subject matter of Mime VI. is
perhaps suggested. ἔνδον objective 'on its inside.'

VIII

ENΥΠΝΙΟΝ

Ἄστηθι, δούλη Ψύλλα· μέχρι τέο κείσῃ
ῥέγχουσα; τὴν δὲ χοῖρον αὐόνη δρύπτει·
ἢ προσμένεις σὺ μέχρι σευ ἥλιος θάλψει
τὸν] κυσὸν ἐσδύς; κῶς δ᾽, ἄτρυτε, κοὐ κάμνεις
τὰ πλ]ευρὰ κνώσσουσ᾽; αἱ δὲ νύκτες ἐννέωροι.
ἄστη]θι, φημί, καὶ ἅψον, εἰ θέλεις, λύχνον,   6
καὶ τ]ὴν ἄναυλον χοῖρον ἐς νομὴν πέμψον.
τ](όν)θρυζε καὶ κνῶ, μέχρις <ο>ὖ παραστά[ς σοι
τὸ] βρέγμα τῷ σκίπωνι μαλθακὸν θῶμα[ι.
δει]λὴ Μεγαλλί, κ(α)[ὶ] σὺ Λάτμιον κνώσσεις;   10
οὐ] τάρ(γ)α σὲ τρύχ[ου]σιν· ἀλλὰ μὴν στέμμ[α
ἐπ᾽ ἰρὰ διζόμε(σ)[θ]α; βα(ιὸ)ς οὐχ ἡμῖν
ἐν τῇ οἰκίῃ <᾽σ>τι μα[λ]λὸς εἰρίων. δειλή,
ἄστηθι· σύ τέ μοι τ[οῦ](ναρ), εἰ θέλεις, Ἀννᾶ,
ἄκουσον, οὐ γὰρ ν(η)[πίας] φρένας βόσκεις.   15
τράγον τιν᾽ ἕλκειν [διὰ] φάραγγος ᾠήθ[ην
μακρῆς, ὁ δ᾽ εὐπώ[γω]ν τε κεύκέρως [ἦεν·

3. θαλψηι P (ηι deleted and ι superscr.).   4. τον] (κ)υσον.
The supplements in this and following vv. are due to Diels,
Palmer, Hdl.   6. αστη](θ)ι φημι P.   αστησον P but
with σησ cancelled and τ changed to ψ.   8. τον]θρυζε P.
ρισευ P : correxi Camb. Ed. 1922.   9. το]βρεγμα P.   θωμα[ι
P.   10. δι]λημεγαλλί P.   κ(α)[ι]συ P.   11. ου]ταερ(γ)α
P. 'The width of the damaged surface is so small that if

VIII

THE DREAM

A monologue (probably) on a winter's day at dawn in a country farm. Herodes, as master of the house, rises and wakes the servants. A sow grunts outside.)

Rise up, Psylla wench! How long wilt lye snoring
and the sow forswat? Tarriest till the sun steal into
thy parts and warm them? Art not thy ribs tired,
tireless one, of sleping these agelong nights? Rise
up, again I say, and light the lamp, prithee, and
escort her unmelodious pigship to pasture. Oh,
mutter and scratch thyself till I stand o'er thee and
make me thy noddle soft with my stave. Megallis,
wretche, snorest thou too like ympe of Latmos[1]? Not
with werkes art weary: for seeke we a wool fillet
for rytes, not a wisp of wool is in our habitaunce.
Wretche rise up: and thou Annas, prithee, list to
my dreme, for thou nourslest not sorry wits. Mesemed
    dragged through a long gorge[2] a gote, fayre of

---

[1] Like Endymion.

[2] 'led a goat'; the phrase implies 'to sacrifice.'

---

t (the letter after ρ) is a $\bar{\gamma}$ the horizontal stroke must have
been exceptionally short' K.   13. ευτηι P.   ετι P: corr.
Idl.   μα[λ]λοσ P.   14. P, suppl. by Bl.   αυυᾶ P. Verse
marked as doubtful.   15. suppl. by K.   16. ηθ[superscr.
above ισμ[P.   suppl. Cr.   17. med. suppl. by Cr.

HERODES

ἐπεὶ δὲ δή [μ](ιν) [. . . . . .](α) τῆς βήσσης,
ἔω φα[ούσης . . . οὐ] γὰρ ἐσσῶμαι,
σύ[ριγξι. . . . . .ν]τες αἰπόλοι πλέ[γδην   2
τῇ[ις . . . . .χλ]ωριῶντ' ἐποιεῦ[ντο.
κἠγὼ οὐκ ἐσύλευν [. . . .] (αἴξ)[. . . . .ἄλλης
καὶ ἄλλης δρυὸς [. . .] (γ)ε[
οἱ δ' ἀμφὶ κάρτα (ὁ)[ρῶν]τες [
τὸν αἶγ' ἐποί<ευ>ν [. . . .] π[2
κα[(ὶ)] [π]λησίον με[. . . . .](ιν)
κ[. . . . .](αν)μα, (μ)[εχρὶ] (τῶ)[ν
σχ[ιστ. .] κροκωτ[. . . .]φι
ω[. . . .] λεπτῆς ἄντυγος .αθ(υξ)[
σ[(τ)ικτῆ]ς δὲ νεβροῦ χλαν[ι]δίῳ κατέζω[στ]ο   3
κ[αθειμέν]ην κύπα[σσι]ν ἀμ[φ]ὶ τοῖ[ς] ὤμοις,
κό[ρυμβα δ'] ἀμφὶ κ(ρ)[η]τὶ (κ)[ίσσι(ν)]' ἔστεπτο·
κνήμη κο]θόρνου [. . . .]η κα[τ]αζώστρη
<ε>ἵλικτο· κ]ὼ μὲν το[σσάδ]ε α(ἱ)[θρίου] φρίκη[ς
. . . . ἀλ(ε)]ώρην εἶχ[. . .] .θι .[. . . . .]   3

18. e.g. εἰς τὸ τέρμα Hg.   19. η[. .] σφα[P: supplev
e.g. <ε>ἴρυσ', οὐ (i.e. I was late for the beginning
20. supplevi e.g. coll. Milton, Sams. Ag. 1596, 'Occasion
drew me early to this city And as the gates I entered wit
sunrise The morning trumpets . . .' Here the dreamer w
always going to the festival or he would not have bee
dragging the goat. After συριγ. e.g. τέρπν' αὐλοῦντες: the
πλέγδην: cf. Eratosthenes fr. 27 Powell περιπλέγδην κρεμόνεσ
(from the Erigone, which I conjecture to be related to the
verses).   21. marked as corrupt. init. suppl. Herzo
fin. Cr. cett. e.g. χερσὶ δεσμά, like the oscilla: cf. Eratost
fr. 26 μόσχους καὶ χλώρας κλήματος ἐκφυάδας. For th
whole scene, Greg. Naz. ii. 11ʙ γηπόνων χορὸν στησάμεν
καὶ ἀμησάμενος στάχυν ὡραῖον πλεκέτω στέφανον ἡμερίδος τε πε
κεφαλῆς ἐγειρέτω κισσῷ κτλ.   22. supplevi e.g. ἱρ' ὁ δ' (Hg
φυγών.   23. e.g. διήγγεν ἀμπέλους τρώγων: cf. Hesychi
δρύες οἰνοχίτωνες.   24. e.g. ἔκδικ' ἔρδοντα.   25. e.g. θῦμ

164

beard and horn.   And whenas at long last I ⟨dragged
him⟩ from the dell—with dawn for I failed not my
task, ⟨mid pleasaunt ditties on⟩ flutes goteherds were
twining grene ⟨bonds⟩.   No hurt did I but ⟨the gote
scaped⟩ and nibbled ⟨of the vine shoots now from
this⟩ tree now from that.

But those around, seeing how he ⟨did⟩ right
⟨wantonly⟩, made the gote ⟨an oblatioun⟩.   Now
against the altar and hard by me saw I ⟨a young
man clad⟩ in a very fayre cloke of gold to his feet.[1]
He was dight with a slit frock round ⟨his thighs⟩ so
as it mote reach down to their thin curve : and he
had about his shoulders a long gowne bound by a
stole of dappled fawn, and a crown of ivy tendrils
around his hed.   His nether shin was ⟨swathed⟩ with
the binding of a high boot.   Such a garb had he as fayre
protectioun from savage chill,[2] e'en as real.[3]   Mean-

---

[1] For the number of clothes see the excerpts from Athenaeus in the Cambridge edition.

[2] The supplement is certain enough from Hesych.
Ἀλεξαίθριον· θερμὸν σκέπασμα· Σοφοκλῆς Ἀμφιαράῳ. αἶθρος·
ψύχος τὸ ὀρθρινόν id.

[3] Init. e.g. : καλὴν : fin. e.g. εἴχ' ἀληθίνησ' ἴσα (v. 38).

πρὸς δὲ τῷ βώμῳ.   26. e.g. μευ δή τιν' εἶδον ἕλκοντα.   27. e.g.
καλὸν μάλ' (ε)ἶμα, and ποδῶν, χρυσοῦν (the punctuation is
certain from the space in P).   μᾶ (feminina ejulatio) is impossible.   χρυσοῦν and εἶμα are necessary : see Callixen. Ath.
197 e and Cambridge Ed. p. 384.   28. e.g. σχιστὸν κροκωτὸν
(Vogl.) ἠμφίεστο τοὺς μηρούς.   29. ὦν δόξε and καθίξεσθαι.
30. supplevi. fin. suppl. Hg.   Traces of last letter (in ad-
joining column) noted by Cr[5].   στικτῆς ex v.l. in v. 32
certum : improbat Edmondsius.   31. init. supplevi (vel Κορα-
ικ
ξικὴν) : καὶ is impossible.   32. supplevi.   εστεπτο P (from v.
30).   33. supplevi : e.g. ν⟨ε⟩ιάτη.   34. supplevi : longiora
ἔσφικτο (Hg.) etc.   35. supplevi.

οἱ δὲ αὖ τ]ὸ λῶπο[ς ἡλί]κον [πε]π(ο)ιῆσθαι
...... 'Οδ]υσσέος ο[ἰκὸς Αἰόλ[ου] δῶρον
..................] τὸ (δ)[έρμ]α λακτίζειν
.... βεβη](κ)έν[αι] λῶστον
ὥσπερ τελεῦμεν ἐν χοροῖς Δι‹ω›νύσου.   40
‹κ›οἱ μὲν μετώποις ἐ[ς] κόνιν κολυμβῶντες
ἔκοπτον ἀρνευτῆρ[ε](ς) ἐκ βίης οὖδας
οἱ δ' ὕπτι' ἐρριπτεῦντο· πάντα δ' ἦν 'Ανν[ᾶ
εἰς ἓν γέλως τε κἀνίη [......]έντα.
κ‹ἠ›γὼ δόκεον δὶς μ(οὖ)[νο]ς ἐκ τόσης λείης   45
ἐπ' οὖν ἀλέσθαι, κἠλά(λα)ξαν ὤνθρω[ποι
ὥς μ' εἶδ[ον ...]ως τὴν δο[ρὴ]ν πιεζεῦσαν
καί φ[.................]τ(α)[......
οἱ δ' ἐ[.................   .   .
γρυπ[.   50
ρυπ[.   .   .   .   .
τ[.   .   .   .
τ[.   .   .   .
      .   .   .   .   .
        55
      .   .   .   .

'τὰ δεῖνα πνεῦσαι λὰξ πατέ[ων
ἔρρ' ἐκ προσώπου μή σε καίπ[ερ ὢν πρέσβυς
οὔλῃ κατι(θὺ) τῇ βατηρίῃ κό[ψω.'   60

36. init. supplevit e.g. Lobel.   αυτω(ι) primum scrip-
serit.   λῶπος = δέρμα (Hg.).   med. supplevi.   ω̇λωπος (ο above)

P.   πεποιῆσθαι Mn. recte   37.]υσσεως ὁ P.   suppl.
Cr.: correxi et med. supplevi.   init. e.g. εἰς πλοῦν Hg.
38. supplevi e.g. προύθεντ'· ἔ]φη [δὲ δεῖν.   39. e.g. κήχειν
τὸν αὖτ]ε π[ροσβ.   40. Διον. P: corr. K.   42. ἀρ-
νευτῆρες ceu urinatores explicavi (C.E. trad.).   44. e.g.
166

time they ⟨set forth⟩ the hide in size such as mote
have been the gift of Aeolus for Ulysses ⟨voyaging,
while he bade that they⟩ sholde lepe on the skin[1]
⟨while he sholde win that⟩ was best at landing again
thereon, e'en as we observe in the dances of Dionysus.
And some plunging with their foreheds on to the
dust smit as dyvers the erthe amain : others were cast
aback ; and all thynges, Annas, both laughter and
payne were mingled in one. And mesemed I too
had share and alone of that sore havocke leped on
twice, and they acclaymed me as they saw me
burdened and ⟨o'erprest with the⟩ skin ⟨around my
shoulders after the order of victors⟩. But others
⟨did cast me out with mocking words . . .⟩. But an
⟨old⟩ man hooked of nose and fowl of . . . .

'to be prowd for thy tramplings. Out of sight, leaste
aged though I be I smit thee athwart with my rod.'

[1] I give a suggestion in accordance with δίς in 45. After
the first impact the leaper would bound up.

'ναμιχθέντα.   45. καγω P with mark of doubt.   μοῦνος
rectissime Hg.   δις may have been explained as δ' εἷς (so
Hg.?) in right hand margin.   47. supplevi.   e.g. αἰνῶς :
in fine δορήν suppl. Cr.   48. e.g. καὶ φλῶσαν ἀμφὶ ὤμοισιν
οἷα νικῶντα (Ar. Ran. init.).   49. e.g. οἱ δ' ἐξέβαλλον ἔπεσι
μιξιάμβοισι.   50 sqq. a description of the old man (ed.).
57. fin. e.g. κῶς δ' ἤρθης.   58. fin. e.g. δορήν μοῦνος.
59 sq. supplied by K. from Schol. Nicander, Ther. 397
'Ηρώδης . . . ἐν τῷ ἐπιγραφομένῳ Ὕπνῳ (l. ἐνυπνίῳ) φεύγωμεν
ἐ. π. μή σ' ἐκπερῶν π. ο. κ. β. καλύψῃ.

κἠγὼ μεταῦτις ' ὦ παρεόν[τες ' ἠμείφθην
' θανεῦμ' ὑ(π)ὲρ γῆς εἰ ὁ γέρων μ[
μαρτύρ[ο]μαι δὲ τὸν νεην[ίην
ὁ δ' εἶπεν [ἄ]μφω τὸν δορέα (ξ)[ύλῳ δῆσαι.
καὶ τοῦτ' ἰ[δ]ὼν ἔληξα. τοὔνδυ[τον   65
'Αν]νᾶ δ[ὸς] ὧδε. τ<οὖ>ναρ ὧδ' ἰ[δὼν
. . . . . .]ν αἶγα τῆς φ[άραγγος ἐξε]ῖλκον
ἔξω τι κ](α)λοῦ δῶρον ἐ(κ) (Δ)[ιων](ύ)σου·
ὡς δ' οἱ αἰ]πόλοι μιν ἐκ βίης [ἐδα](ι)τρεῦντο
[τ]ὰ ἔνθεα τελεῦντες καὶ κρεῶ[ν ἐδαί]νυντο   70
τὰ μέλεα πολλοὶ κάρτα τοὺς (ἐ)[μοὺς (μ)]όχθους
τιλεῦσιν ἐν Μούσῃσιν· ὧδ' ἔγω[γ]' (οἴ)[μαι.
τὸ μὴν ἄεθλον ὡς δόκ<εο>ν ἔχ[ει]ν μοῦνος,
πολλῶν τὸν ἄπνουν κώρυκον πατησάντων,
κἠ τῷ γέροντι ξύν' ἔπρηξ' ὀρινθέντι,   75
ἐπὶ] κλέος ναὶ Μοῦσαν ἤ μ' ἔπεα κ[λήσει
μ]έγ' ἐξ ἰάμβων, ἤ με δευτέρη γν[ώμη
ἐ]([μοῖ)ς μεθ' Ἱππώνακτα τὸν πάλαι [κεῖνον
(τ)ὰ κύλλ' ἀείδειν Ξουθίδαις ἐπι<θ>ύσει.

61. κηγω (η ex ω) P.   supplevi.   62. *e.g.* με κικλήσκει.
63. end ? αὐτόν.   64. suppl. Hg. (me judice proba-
biliter).   65. suppl. Cr. Then *e.g.* κού μοι;   66. supplevi.
τωναρ P : correxi. in fine *e.g.* κρίνω.   67. suppl. Cr.   init.
e.g. ὡς καλόν.   68. init. supplevi, fin. Cr.   69. init.
supplevi : fin. (Mn.) : non fuit ἐμετρεῦντο.   70. suppl.
Cr.   71. suppl. Cr.   72. supplevi dubitanter.
73. δοκουν P.   76. supplevi *e.g.*   77. init. suppl.
nescioquis : fin. γνώμη Cr.[1]   78. init. suppl. Hg. vel
τι[(μη)]s Mne. ἐμοί = οἱ 'Αθηναῖοι.   fin. Cr.   79. κυλλ' P.
επ†ουσι P : correxi.

And I answered back ' O folk, I will die for the country an the old man ⟨summon⟩ me : thereunto call I the young man to witnes.' And he bad the flogman to ⟨bind⟩ both in the stocks. Thereat ended my swevening. ⟨Where is my⟩ coat [1]? Hither with it, Annas. Thus saw I : thus expound I. ⟨E'en as fayre⟩ was the gote I dragged out of the gorge, e'en so shall I have some gift from Dionysus fayre : and as amain the goteheards cleved him and rendered their rites and ate the flesh thereof, e'en so shall a many poetards [2] clever rend my writings. So reckon I. But as mesemed alone to have the guerdon, while many trod in vain the breathles [3] skin, for all I shared [4] with the old man enraged, e'en so by Muses troth, either shall iambickes call me to great fame, or my second intendiment gode me after the order of Hipponax of yore to sing halting measures to my Xuthos-born kin.[5]

---

[1] He shivers with *fear*: *cf.* Callim. *fr. anon.* 80, and my note in C.E. So Ovid *Heroides* xv. 173 *ego frigida surgo* after a dream: *Amor.* iii. 5 *dixerat interpres : gelido mihi sanguis ab ore fugit.*

[2] The dream is interpreted by a series of puns to retain which I have taken liberties with the Greek, which runs : ' Many in a literary line (high-brows) shall tear up (criticize) my poems.

[3] ' breathles ': *i.e.* air-tight ; see Camb. Ed.

[4] ' fared alike ' Hg.

[5] my Ionian brethren ; *i.e.* to Athens.

ΑΠΟΝΗCΤΙΖΟΜΕΝΑΙ

Ἔ]ζεσθε πᾶσαι. κοῦ τὸ παιδίον; δέξ[ον
κ]αὶ π[ρ]ὸς Εὐέτειραν [κ]αὶ Γλύκην· (β)[......
χ]ιτ[ῶνα λ]αιδρή· τὴν ἑτοῖμον οὐ [.........
........]εις; μή σε [κν]ισμάτων [.......
........]ινα τ[αῦτ' ἀ]νηνύτω[ς ....
........]ν ἤ[δη κἀλλ]αχῆ πεπο[ίκιλσαι.
..................] φέρ' [ἐς] κό[ρον ....
(κ)ρ[..](ο)(λλ)[............]α δειλαίοις βλέ[ψαι.
φέρ' ὦ(δ)[ε] (κ)[αὶ τὴν κύλι](κ)α· καὶ τὰ νῦ[ν ....
αὕτη σύ, [..........]ζεται νό[ου 1
οὐ πρόσθ' ἀ[..........]νις η ξ[........
τίθεσθ' ἄμ[ιλλαν .... ἄ]εθλον ἐξοί[σ....
γλή[χωνα ...... τοῖς το]κεῦσί σ' ἤειρα

1. suppl. K.   fin. supplevi.   2. suppl. K.   Εὐέτ-
Cr. rightly.   fin. *e.g.* βρέχεις τόν μεν.   3. sup
plevi.   fin. *e.g.* σμήχεις.   4. *e.g.* ἀεὶ καθεύδεις
quamvis probante Edmondsio.   fin. *e.g.* μνήσω.   5. *e.g.*
ἤνπερ τὰ δεινά.   fin. *e.g.* κνώσσῃς.   6. *e.g.* ὅσσοισιν   med
ἤδη κ ego ἀλλαχῆ Cr.   fin. supplevi.   7. *e.g.* τὴν Εὐέτειρα
πρόσφερ'.   med. suppl. by Cr.   fin. *e.g.* ἐς κόρον δ' ὅσσοις
8. so Mne.   *e.g.* χρὴ πολλὰ καὶ δυστηνὰ ...   9. supplev

IX

BREAKING FAST

(Scene and plot unknown.)

Sit ye all down. Where is the baby? Bring him
hither—and Eueteira too and Glyke. Clumsy thing,
thous ⟨soaking my dress⟩. ⟨Soap⟩ the one that's
ready. ⟨Ever⟩ asleep? I fear lest I mind thee of
all those prickings wherewith hast oft been tattooed
e'er now, an thou continue these fearsome ⟨yawns⟩.
Hither with ⟨Eueteira⟩—⟨sholdest⟩ have had enow
of all these ⟨sorry⟩ hangdog grimaces. Hither too
with the ⟨cup⟩. Still ⟨asleep⟩? Ho there—has
⟨Nossis⟩ lost all those wits that once ⟨were hers⟩?
—and our visitaunt, are ye in pitched combat? Seekst
to carry off yon salad for prize? Yet sooth I raised
thee to be thy parents ⟨staff and . . . . .

(φέρ' ὧδε Cr. rightly).　　　fin. *e.g.* εὕδεις.　　　10. *e.g.* μᾶ μὴ

πλάζεται.　　　　　　　in fine nomen: φρ P (*i.e.* φρ[ενῶν]). ^(νο)
11. *e.g.* ἁμαρτοῦσ'· ἤ τε νῆνις ἡ ξείνη.　　　12. init. supplevi,
fin. Cr.[2]　　in med. *e.g.* μῶν . . . -οίσεις.　　　13. init. suppl.
Cr.　　med. *e.g.* ; καίτοι.　　fin. supplevi.　　14. *e.g.* σκίπωνα
γήρως.

X

*Ἡ χαλκέην μοι μυῖαν ἢ κύθρην παίζει
ἢ τῆσι μηλάνθ‹η›σιν ἄμματ' ἐξάπτων
τοῦ κεσκ‹ί›ου μοι τὸν γέροντα λωβῆται.

Stob. *Fl.* lxxviii. 6 (51 Hense) (περὶ νηπίων) Ἡρώδου
Μιμιάμβων.

1. *vv.ll.* χαλκαίην, μυίην.   2. *vv.ll.* ταῖσι, τμῆσι: corr.
by Meineke.   μηλάνθασιν, μηλολόνθης : corr. Gaisford.
3. κεσκέου codd.: corr. by Salmasius.

XI

Ὡς οἰκίην οὐκ ἔστιν εὐμαρέως εὑρεῖν
ἄνευ κακῶν ζώουσαν· ὃς δ' ἔχει μεῖον,
τοῦτό‹ν› τι μέζον τοῦ ἑτέρου δόκει πρήσσειν.

Stob. *Fl.* xcviii. 28 (27 Hense) Ἡρωδα Μιμιάμβων (sine
accentu duo codd.)

3. τούτου corr. by Schneidewin.   δοκεῖ corr. id.   μεῖζον
corr. Meister.

SMALLER FRAGMENTS

X

Or 'brassfly'[1] or 'pot'[1] playeth he, or tying
threads to cockchafers robbeth my distaff of flax.

Mimes of Herodes . . .   *Stobaeus* in his *Anthology*: book
On Infants.

[1] Forms of blind-man's-buff.

XI [2]

Sin 'tis no light task to find a habitaunce that
liveth sans ills : but whoso hath least thereof him
reckon to fare better than another.

Mimes of Herodas . . .   *id.*

[2] X and XI. Either or both of these might belong to
Mime IX.

XII

ΜΟΛΠΙΝΟC

Ἐπὴν τὸν ἑξηκοστὸν ἥλιον κάμψῃς
ὦ Γρύλλε, Γρύλλε, θνῆσκε καὶ τέφρη γίνευ·
ὡς τυφλὸς οὐπέ[ρ]κειν⟨α⟩ τοῦ βίου καμπτήρ·
ἤδη γὰρ αὐ⟨γ⟩ὴ τῆς ζοῆς ἀπήμβλυνται.

Stob. *Fl.* cxvi. 21 (56 Hense) Ἡρώδου ἐκ Μολπεινοῦ (corr.
by Meineke).

3. ὁ ὑπὲρ κεῖνο or ὑπερκεῖνο codd.: corrected by Porson
4. (Stob. *ibid.* 22 Ἡρώδου μιμάμβων) : the conjunction is due
to Salmasius. αὕτη codd.: αὐγή Salm. ζωῆς codd.
corrected by Porson. ἀπήμβλυτο codd.: corrected by
Salm.

XIII

CΥΝΕΡΓΑΖΟΜΕΝΑΙ

προσφὺς ὅκως τις χοιράδων ἀν⟨η⟩ρίτης

Ath. 86 b Ἡρώνδας δ᾽ ἐν Συνεργαζομέναις.

προσφῦσ᾽ Buecheler. ἀναρίτης codd.

SMALLER FRAGMENTS

XII

MOLPINOS

Gryllus, Gryllus, when hast entered lifes sixtieth
lap,[1] die and become ashes : for blind is the lap that
follows, seeing that lifes ray is dimmed.

From Herodes' *Molpinos* . . . *id.*

[1] The MSS of Stobaeus give a most unusual phrase for
'passed your sixtieth birthday'—'rounded your sixtieth
sun' as a runner entering the straight rounds the corner.
ἥλιον ' sun,' can hardly be correct. I have omitted it and
slightly changed the metaphor.

XIII

FACTORY GIRLS

Clinging like limpet to rocks

But Herondas in the *Factory Girls* says . . . . *Athenaeus*
(discussing the word limpet).)

HERODES (?)

From Cn. Mattius (see Cambridge Herodas, p. 419).

XIV

1 Nuper die quarto, ut recordor ; et certe
   aquarium urceum unicum domi fregit.

2 iam iam albicascit Phoebus, et recentatur
   commune lumen hominibus voluptatis.

3 quapropter edulcare convenit vitam
   curasque acerbas sensibus gubernare.

4 sinuque amicam refice frigidam caldo
   columbulatim labra conserens labris.

5 iam tonsiles tapetes ebrii fuco
   quos concha purpura imbuens venenavit.

6   ficorum
   in milibus tot non videbitis grossum.

7 sumas ab alio lacte diffluos grossos.

8 pressusque labris unus acinus arebat.

†9 dein coquenti vasa cuncta deiectat
   nequamve scitamenta pipulo poscit.†

APPENDICES

APPENDIX I

(i. 80-85)

The readings of P proposed and generally accepted here (in col. 6) are quite impossible : this is due in the main to mismounting. There are several strips but these may be considered as two strips since some join up. A the left hand strip is mounted touching B the right hand : really there is a gap throughout of one letter (τ in the top line (τοῦ ἀκρήτου) and η in the bottom line (where the δ of μη(δ)᾽ ἄρτους would have filled the slight gap shown). The following *placita* are all wrong.

Line 2. C. E. presents Cr.'s reading as πιει[ν αδρ](ω). The gap is of 5 letters, not 3½. Nor can the traces be fitted. Moreover, if the μελαινίς is a ποτήριον, ἀδρῷ (*sc.* ποτηρίῳ) is nonsense.

Line 3. δεῖξον · οὐ (παραλλάττειν) Nairn. This does not fit the traces. Further (*a*) there is a letter (ε) of which some traces are visible before (π). (*b*) Before this another letter must have gone. Blass' οὐ[κ] (ἐγὼ) (πάμ)π(α)ν fits the spaces. I doubt, however, if it or (οὐδὲ γὰρ) be right.

Line 4. If ἔ(κ)[ητι] (τ)ῶν is right, the gap here = τι in space.

Line 5. The traces after ωνα [　] are far too dubious for discussion.

177

But there is another error of mounting. At the bottom line the strip (or combined strips) B are $\frac{1}{3}$ of a letter too low. But the papyrus has stretched unequally and at the top verses the letters on B are a whole letter too low. At line 6 τεκνον (π) they would be about $\frac{3}{4}$ of a letter too low. The distinct traces after (π) (*i.e.* after (π)[.]) give therefore the tops of letters.

Only at line 2 can guessing at the exact word be profitable. Here Mne. read πιεί[ν] (κ). .(ως) and between (doubtfully) (νδ) or (νδρ). But here I think it is safe to leave the shadowy traces, merely noting that they are all diagonal, that there must have been a wide gap after [ν], and that there is a paragraphus, which can only refer to a change of speaker in or at the end of this verse.

Alexis (*fr.* 230) reads μὴ παντελῶς αὐτῷ διδοὺς ὑδαρῆ· κατανοεῖς; ἴσον ἴσῳ μικροῦ· καλῶς! ἡδύ γε τὸ πῶμα. We may I think safely read πιεῖν (space) καλῶς and give this word to Metriché in the sense of 'Thanks' or 'When!' See also Alexis 111, Men. 292. Milne considers this reading a legitimate interpretation of the traces. There would, with change of speaker, probably be a gap of the space of about one letter before κ.

It is not my purpose to argue in favour of any 'supplements.' It is rather to draw attention to a point which should have been noted before. As Crusius and Headlam certainly read a vast amount of Greek literature, it is quite safe to assume that there is in Greek literature no parallel whatever for ὤναο μού τινος, 'you got something at my hands.' As well might you say ἔλαβεν ἑαυτῷ μοι ἵππον, 'he got a horse from me.' The dative of advantage inherent in the middle form wholly precludes another dative of advantage (or disadvantage); and the common use is, of course, παρ' ἐμοῦ. The question is simply where to divide the speakers (for P gives no paragraphi and no clues). Anyone familiar with the style of Herodes will easily recognize, I hope, that ὧν οὔνεκέν μοι can hardly be other than an introduction to a request and that it is suitably followed by an interruption—precisely because the speaker falters: compare exactly vi. 15 (at the beginning of a conversation) :—

vi. 15 A. ἀλλ' οὔνεκεν πρός σ' ἦλθον—
            B. ἐκποδὼν ἡμῖν
        φθείρεσθε, νώβυστρ' . . . .
    A.   λίσσομαί σε.

Even if the speakers be not changed, the interruption remains.

But we have a similar phenomenon (without the speaker faltering, but at the *end* of a plea) in iii. 56 :—

A. ἀλλ' εἴ τί σοι, Λαμπρίσκε . . . ἀγαθῶν κύρσαις
    μή λασσον αὐτῷ—
B.   Μητροτίμη, μὴ ἐπεύχεο.

The final appeal is interrupted. Probably too iii. 88 A. δεῖρον δ'— B. ἄχρις . . . So in v. 73 τὴν μίαν ταύτην ἁμαρτίην— B. Κύδιλλα, μή με λυπεῖτε. A. . . .

In fact in almost all cases where there is an appeal we have the request broken off in mid verse. In all the wholly visible words you have here exactly the same thing almost as if it were traditional to the mime :—' I came for no petty ends, but for those sacred rites for whose sake . . .' 'Gyllis . . .' 'La! child . . .'

HERODES

Appendix II

vi. 94. It is amazing to see the egregious blunder of Buecheler in reading καὶ as ἴσθι (!!) still repeated by editors. Yet there is no palaeographer in Europe who has or could support such an attempt. In editing a text it is fatal to proceed without expert advice.

Appendix III
(on vii. 8. 9)

vii. 8. The spacing of the papyrus here which I gave in 1922 and for which I had secured Dr. Kenyon's assent in 1913 (C.E. p. 230 *inf.*) is sound; like Dr. Headlam's conclusions. The exact reading is μᾶλλον δὲ τὴν ἄκανθα[ν] ὡς εχ[   ]ν καληι ἐκ τοῦ τραχήλου δῆσον, the space left being of one large or two small letters. Now no satisfactory explanation of καληι has been given : it could only mean ' with a fair bond,' which is absurd. Wrongly I have suggested the reading δεῖρον and supposed a blow to be indicated. But this is inconsistent with τρίβειν which must be of something galling which is worn (v. 62). ' Do you wish to wear louder reminders than these ' indicates a heavier form of the same unpleasant gyves. Dr. Headlam might have noted that though ἄκανθα itself is not used elsewhere of any instrument of this sort, yet similar words are so used. On κήρυκες or sharp shell-shaped prongs Christian martyrs were made to lie (*Eccl. Smyrn. Ep.* Jacobsen, p. 590). The Latin is *murices*, a phrase also used to translate the Greek τρίβολοι, so called from the plant or ' burr.' As an instrument in the shop we have no evidence for ἄκανθα : but a spiked instrument hung down the back underneath the dress would certainly prevent the slave from going to sleep.[1]

What of ὡς εχ ν κάλῃ? ὡς εχει εν is not only meaningless but impossible. As I have shown (C.E. *l.c.*) ὡς ἔχεις is necessary. ὡς ἐχρῆν which I suggested *F.G.A.* 1923) lacks support. They did not say ' Do so as you ought to have done.' Moreover καληι is at fault. Far the easiest correction is to κλάῃ, and this with ἔχων gives excellent sense : *Eccl. Sm. Ep. l.c.* κήρυκας ὑποστρωννύμενοι . . . ἵνα . . . διὰ τῆς ἐπιμόνου κολάσεως . . . That at least they did say : Ar. *Nub.* 58 δεῦρ᾽ ἔλθ᾽ ἵνα κλάῃς, and the order is good, for ἔχων is stressed as *ibid.* 131 τί ταῦτ᾽ ἔχων στραγγεύομαι ;

APPENDIX IV

(vii. 31 and 40 *sqq.*)

vii. 31. Of this verse we have only β. . . . . ιι πάνθ᾽ ὅσ᾽ ἐστὶν ι[.]α, and yet it is very probable that the whole can be reconstructed. Building

[1] See also Wesseling on Hdt. i. 92.

on Blass' sure foundation we get ὄμνυμι πάνθ' ὅσ
ἔστ' ἱρά. Now very often the Greeks avoided
anything so bold as the use of πᾶς, οὐδείς, etc., with
out an apologetic phrase. In an Attic tragedian, i
we had πάντας ὡς ε[, we might with fair safety
conjecture ὡς εἰπεῖν (ἔπος): and it is attractive to
suppose that this line is whole and that we have
another and common phrase here :—

Aesch. *P.V.* 521 βραχεῖ δὲ μύθῳ πάντα συλλήβ
δην μάθε.

715 πάντα γὰρ Δαρεῖ' ἀκούσῃ μῦθον ἐν βραχεῖ λόγῳ
(so recc.).

Eur. *Or.* 446 πάντων πρὸς ἀστῶν ὡς θάνω· βραχὺ
λόγος.

Lucian iii. 362 ἀνδρὸς ὡς βραχεῖ λόγῳ περιλαβεῖ
. . οὐδεπώποτε . . . ἄπαντα . . .

The same phrase is used with πολλά: βραχεῖ δ
μύθῳ πολλὰ συλλαβὼν ἐρῶ Eur. *fr.* 362. 5; *cf*
704. 3. Contrast Mime iv. init.

vii. 40 *sqq.* The conditions have been changed by
recent work on the papyrus. Herzog ('rightly
Bell) has recalled the reading κηρί(α) in 43, giving
it the signification of 'wax-lights.' At first sigh
neither 'honey' nor 'honey-combs' gives sense
and the apparent verbal resemblance in Theocr. v
126 τὸ πότορθρον ἁ παῖς ἀνθ' ὕδατος τᾷ κάλπιδι κηρίᾳ
βάψαι (with 112 τὰ Μίκωνος) cannot possibly assist
Perhaps Kerdon likens himself to the 'little busy
bee' *Coll. Alex. Lyr.* Ad. 7, which works for others
Lucian, *A.P.* x. 41. There is a chance that †Μικρων
is plagued with κηρία (an unpleasant type of sore) and
that Kerdon complains that his sedentary habits have

182

given him an even more distressing disease ; and this
can easily be reconciled with Greek diction and the
traces in P leaving a wide choice of alternatives,
e.g. :—

$$ἐντεῦθεν ὑμεῖ](s) τἄργα τῆς τέχνης ἡμέων \quad 38$$
$$φορεῖθ', ὁ πίσ]υγγος δὲ δειλαίην οἰζύν·$$
$$γάγγρα]ιναν . .έων νύκτα κἠμέρην θάλπω \quad 40$$
$$ἢ σάρκα]s ἡμέων ἄχρις ἑσπέρης κάπτει·$$
$$. . . ί]αι πρὸς ὄρθρον ! οὐ δοκέω τόσσον$$
$$τὰ Μικίωνος κηρί' εὐπ[ορεῖν . . .$$

See Aesch. *fr.* 253, Eur. *fr.* 792 (φαγέδαινα quod
fort. leg.). There is then a wide choice of unpleasant details to fill up the gaps still left. Without
leisure to read Greek medical works again for this
one purpose, I suggest at random *v.* 40 ἀλγέων, *v.* 43
ὑπνίαι (Herzog), and *v.* 43 ψώρης. But I hope that
this restoration is not the true one.

Appendix V

viii. (The Dream)

Herodes, who is at no point in contact with life
except where it touches letters, gives us plenty of
clues for the identification of the scene. It is a feast
to Dionysus at midwinter where a game of leaping
on a bladder is played. At all points this tallies
with the country festivals of Dionysus in Attica ;
and no other festival of this sort is known in Greek

183

letters. Herodes appears to be defending himself against a criticism of Callimachus in his iambi that the modern writers of lame iambi did not use the metres of Hipponax. Herodes replies with a poem in which he uses the 'Ephesian' metre at least as accurately as Callimachus. Resolved feet are rare (only one except in the first foot): and there are no verses ending in four long syllables. Herodes professes to have attended the festival, won the prize and contested afterwards with an old man. The old man is Hipponax: and other punning prophecies are made. Callimachus appears to have known of Herodes' work; presumably because the first seven mimes were current earlier.

It may be remarked that Phoenix' verses also show changes of this type. His moralist poem follows the licence of Ananius: his other two poems avoid the four long syllables at the end of the verse: and to the (oriental) Ninos he gives frequent use of the resolved syllable, following Aeschylus in the *Persae*.

The idea that the speaker is a woman (Terzaghi Vogliami) has been mercilessly refuted in reviews by Herzog and by the present writer. In *vv.* 27 and 47 I have chosen illustrative supplements to show on how shadowy a foundation the idea rests. Many will prefer my earlier version of 47, especially as the skin at the county Dionysiaca was not fully blown up. In 45 δ' εἰς seems possible.

There is no reason to suppose that I was right (in C.E.) in making a story out of *vv.* 20 *sqq.* The whole thing is quite normal and τὸ λῶπος covers all need for details. Herodes merely dreamed he was going to a country Dionysia and chooses to paint the

APPENDIX V

dress and the leaping scene, rather than recount
familiar details like a scholiast. How far the
quarrel with the old man is a new incident, or part
of the normal ritual, is uncertain. At least, there is
nothing in it to conflict with theories of vegetation
festivals so familiar to us from the *Golden Bough*.

If this be so, we must explain on normal principles
for such dreams. The priest of Dionysus (*vv. 26 sqq.*)
both is (*v. 68*), and must be referred to, the god whose
priest he is. Artemidorus is quite definite on the
point at issue (ii. 30 οἷον δ' ἂν ὑπολάβῃ τις θεοῦ
ἱερεὺς εἶναι, τοιοῦτον αὐτῷ καὶ τὸ ἀγαθὸν ἀποβήσεται
ἢ ἀπὸ τοιούτων ἀνδρῶν ἢ γυναικῶν. Conversely *id.*
iii. 13).

Whatever men may say, Dionysus, the god of all
dramatic art, will place Herodes next to Hipponax
among all those who have used his metre. There
is no evidence that Muses were present : indeed
Herodes especially uses an odd and forced expression
ἔνθεος (*v. 70*) to introduce the Muses (*v. 71*).

CERCIDAS
MELIAMBS, FRAGMENTS, AND CERCIDEA

M

INTRODUCTION

THE papyrus of Cercidas is in the British Museum. For a description see the *editio princeps* (A. S. Hunt, *P. Oxy.* viii. 1082). Latest edition in *Coll. Alex.* (J. U. Powell), p. 203. See also Diehl, *Anthologia Lyrica*, iii. 305. For recent work on the papyrus see articles by the present writer in *C.R.* xxxviii-xxxix. There are still a large number of small isolated fragments : but there is no reason to believe that they were all once contiguous (Hunt). The general character of the metre was pointed out by P. Maas and von Arnim. For references to periodicals see Milne *Catalogue* 59, p. 45 (where read 1138 for 1158).

I

col. i]ε γὰρ ο[.]ξεν.s εἰδέμεν   1
          ]νετοι[. . .] αδ' ἐπ' εἰλαπι-
          ]αιρω(ν)[. . . .β]λεννο(το)ι(σ)υ-
          πηρί](δ)as αλ[. . . . .]υσω καὶ δο-
          ]υυν[. . . .]   5
                    ]ρ τον λαμβα[ν]
                    ]μι τοῦτο· (ν)[ ]
                              εκτε
                    ]συντελῖς τ[ ]
                    ]φέρει καὶ γ(α)[ ]
                    ]ως μὴ λεγο[ ]   10
                    ]ελθε· (δω).[ ]
          ](ν)εσυμ[. . .]ηνα· καιτ[ ]   12
          ](ο)μιζ[. . . .]υτευσηι[ ]
                    ]μ[. . . . .]αρ μοι το[ ]
          ]ατα .[. . .]. αλαιος [ ]   15
          ]ινο[. . . .]τεων· ὤ[ ]
                    (νμ)
          ]των α(ὐτῶ)ν ἁ λαβοῦ[σα]
                    ]Ζεὺς κοιραν[ ]
          (σ). .ορειν παρεστιν ε[ ]

Col. i. 1. The placing of ξεν is doubtful: nor can we be certain how many letters are missing at the beginning of the lines.   εἰδέμεν P.   3. λέννο(τ)οί(ο)υ P (marked as (part of) one word).   τ(ο)ι not τει (Lobel, Bell): (σ) me

190

I

Col. i

. . . but little in feasting   2
                    This man delighteth
Child of oily-ragged clothes . . .

. . . how
If Zeus be master   18
Never fair result we see?

---

iudice, (possible) Bell: βλεννοτ = βλεννο-νοτ-οισυπ-[. . . .
7. τοῦτο P.   8. as above P.   11. ελθε· P.   12. ηνα·
P.   16. so P.

CERCIDAS

col. ii κα[. . . . . .γ]ὰρ ὁ
σχ(ε)[. . . . . ἀλ]λὰ
<small>.˙τι(λλ)</small>
τα(η)[. . . .]εν
τ' ὀυ[. . . .](γ)ας
καιτ[. . . .]   5
μυε[. . . .]ν
πιδ[. . . .]   7
. . . .]α

fr. 9   ]η πολιο[? 7
]ινακολα[? 8
]λεων πυκιν[? 9
]χουσι γήρᾳ δ[? 10
ο]ὐκέτι πάνθ' ὠ[? 11
]σᾶπ.[? 12

marg. σπ]ανιοψιάδᾳ   12
]ros   13
]καὶ σπυροὶ οἱ πυροί   14

Col. ii. 1. κᾰ P (*e.g.* καλὸν).   3, 4. ita P.   3. superscr. ?
τι(ν).   10. (?)]χου σιγηροί H.   12. schol. suppl.
Wilamowitz.   Perhaps we have (*fr.* 26) the ends of some

192

Col. ii (?)

Fragment 7 (? = 25 *fr*. H. : see crit. n.).

So it appears to me that our 'pot friend' Ulpian, as my Cercidas of Megalopolis says, watches his fellow guests to see if they have overlooked a fish-bone or lumpy piece of gristle in their food before them (Athenaeus).

' Child of but frugal repasts '

---

verses (about 12-14) (δυσ)παλεστωι.[/(ι)λον ἔνθα/(κι)ς καθιζε[: also below this and just above κ.λ. *fr*. 25 αλ](λ)ους ακα[/]ω παλι. [/]εσσοσι ..]/. . . (κελευ). This fragment suggests a loose citation in Ath. viii. 347 e οὕτω μοι δοκεῖ καὶ ὁ λεβητοχάρων Οὐλπιανός, κατὰ τὸν ἐμὸν Μεγαλοπολίτην Κερκίδαν, (. . . . .) τηρεῖν (. .) τοὺς ἐσθίοντας εἰ παρεῖδον ἢ ῎ΑΚΑνθαν ἢ τῶν τραγανῶν ⟨τι⟩ [ἢ] χονδρῶδες τῶν παρατεθέντων, which agrees well enough with the margination just *above* it. In this case *fr*. 26 probably belongs elsewhere, since it is hard to bring this in line with the notes. (λ)ους ακα [. . .) would be 14 fin, (κελευ) [. . .] 17 fin., μέχρι 18 fin., γερπε[20 fin., καυτῶν 22 fin., and λάρον 23 fin. It is not possible to read σπ](ῡ)ριδια in *fr*. 32 nor to place it by the lowest note.

CERCIDAS

II

          ....]κ.λ.[
          ....] μέχρι
          ....](β)ριδιατριβᾶ[
          ....]´ γερπε[
          ....

col. ii.   ....εἰς [. .]κʹ αὐτῶν
fin.   .... ὀ]λβοθύλακον
col. iii. λαρόν | τε καὶ ἀκρασίωνα
           θῆκε πενητ(υλίδ)αν
           Ξένωνα, ποτάγαγε δ' ἁμίν | 5
           ἄργυρον ⟨τὸν   ⟩
              ⟨εἰς ἀνόνατα⟩ ῥέοντα; |
           κα[ὶ] τί τὸ κώλυον ἦς
           αἴ τι⟨ς⟩ σφ' ἔρο[ι]το,
           (ῥεῖα γάρ ἐστι θεῷ
           πᾶν ἐκτελέσ⟨σ⟩αι
           χρῆμ' | †ὅκκ' ἐπὶ νοῦν ἴῃ†),
           ἢ τ[ὸ]ν ῥυποκιβδοτόκωνα | 10
           καὶ τεθνακοχαλκίδαν |,
           ἢ τὸν παλινεκχυμενίταν
           τῶν κτεάνων ⟨ὄ⟩λεθρον |,
           τοῦτον κενῶσαι
           τᾶς συοπλουτοσύνας, |

ante 1. ? ἁ]βρίδια, γ' ἔρπε., (εριδια H.).   1. εἰσόκ':
cf. μέχρι supra.   2. ταγὸν (e.g.). Up to this point
I have not attempted to place the words in metrical
setting. Between γερπε and εισοκ' might be two—three
194

II

. . . . . .

Chose out that greedy
  Cormorant, of wealthy purse,
And child of licentiousness, Xeno,
  Turn him to poverty's child,
And gave unto us ⟨who deserve it⟩[1]   5
  Rivers of silver that now
Are wasted on profitless uses?
  What should there be to prevent
—Ask God the question,
  Since it is easy for him,
Whate'er he fancy,
  Sure execution to find—,   10
10 If one be the ruin of money,
  Pouring out whate'er he has,
Or usurer dross-stain-begrimed,
  Ready to perish for gold,
That God should drain him,
  Void of his swine-befouled wealth,

[1] The lacuna may have been ἄργυρον τὸν αὐτόθεν νῦν.

---

verses (or half-verses). (The numeration at the side is
that of J. U. Powell, *Coll. Alex.*; the vertical lines mark the
lines of the ed. pr.) On Ξένωνα is a note ἀκρατὴς [ὁ Ξένων
καὶ ἀπο]/γνωστός τις καὶ (π)ι(κ)ρός (supplevi post Hunt), and
on ii fin. ἀ(πό)λαυο(ν) (?).   3. ἀκρασίωνα P.   5. ξένωνα·
ποταγαγε δ' P.   7. εροιτο· P.   σ om. P: correxit H.
αι ex ει P. *sqq.* ἴδαν, ἴταν P.   8. τελεσαι P: corr.
A(rnim).   9. μ' ὅκ. P.   *e.g.* ἐπὶ νοῦν ὅκ' ἴῃ A.   13. for
τῶν perhaps read τὸν with M(aas).   πλεθρον but ολεθρον
in margin.   14. -σύνασδομενδ' P.

M 2   195

δόμεν δ' ἐπιταδεοτρώκτᾳ   15
κοινοκρατηροσκύφῳ |
τὰν ὀλλυμέναν δαπάννλλαν; |
μήπο<κ>' οὖν ὁ τᾶς Δίκας
ὀφθαλμὸς ἀπεσπαλάκωται, |
χὠ Φαέθων μονάδι   20
γλήνᾳ παραυγεῖ, |
(κ)αὶ Θέμις ἁ λιπαρὰ
καταχλύωται; |
πῶς ἔτι δαίμονες οὖν
τοὶ μήτ' ἀκουὰν
μήτ' ὄπα<ς> πεπαμένοι; |
καὶ μὰν τὸ τάλαντον ὁ σεμνὸς |
ἀστεροπαγερέτας   25
col. iv.   μέσσον τ' <ἀ>ν' Ὄλυμπον [. . . . .†]
     (ο)ρθον[†. . . . . . |
[κ](α)ὶ νένευκεν οὐδ(α)μῇ· |
καὶ τοῦθ' Ὅμηρος
εἶπεν ἐν Ἰλιάδι· |
ῥέπην, ὅταν αἴσιμον ἆμαρ,   30
ἀνδράσι κυδαλίμοις †ην†|
πῶς οὖν ἐμὶν οὐ ποτέρεψεν
ὀρθὸς ὢν ζυγοστάτας, |
τὰ δ' ἔσχατα Βρύγια Μυσῶν— |
ἄζομαι δέ θην λέγ<η>ν—   35

15. -τρωκται· (and so often) P.   **16.** φωι·   **17.** δα-
πανύλλαν P.   **18.** μηποτ P.   **19.** schol. ζῷον δ
τύπους μ(ὲν) ὀφθαλμ(ῶν) ἔχει, ὀφθαλμο(ὺ)s δ' ο(ὐ), (οὐ)δ(ὲ) βλ[έ]πει
(ita Mn.).   **20.** ·χω, φιεθων, μονάδι, P.   schol.
ἐν̀ ὀφθαλμῷ π(αρα)βλέπει.   **21.** αι· πως P.   schol.
                τοι
ἐπεσκότισ[τ]αι.   **22.** οντοιμη P, but ουνοιμη in margin.
23. οπαν P.   **25.** Delirant Powell, Wilamowitz, alii
196

15 And give to one frugally feeding,   15
  Dipping cup at common bowl,
The cash that is wasted on trifles ?
  Is the eye of Justice then
Beshrunk that a mole might outsee her ?
  Phaethon, too, doth he squint   20
With single pupil ?
  Themis the bright—doth a mist
Bedim her vision ?
  How can man hold them for gods
That neither hearken,
  Nor have any eyes to see ?
Yet say they the gath'rer of lightning
  Mighty monarch holds the scales   25
Aloft in the midst of Olympus,
  Nodding not a moment's space.
E'en so doth Homer [1]
  Set in his *Iliad* down :—
' By fate to the mighty of valour
  Sinks the balance of the day.'
Why then doth the balancer even
  Never unto me incline ?   30
But Brygians,[2] farthest of mortals,—
  Clearer words I dare not say—   35

---

[1] Θ 72.   [2] Apparently the Macedonians.

Homerici στεροπηγερέτα immemores.   26. τον P:
correxi. Between Ὄλυμπον and ὀρθον 5-11 letters missing :
I suggest *metri gratia* ἀνορθοῖ glossed ἀνὰ τὸ ὀρθον ἔχει.
27. suppl. H.   30-31. ρεπειδ P: -ειν A. †ην·† del. A. :
fuit verborum ρεπειδ correctio (*cf.* H. praef. 24-5) : ῥέπειν
G. Murray : terminationes huiusmodi tacite (⟨η⟩ν) mutavi.
32. εμεν is corrected into εμιν in P.   34. φρυγια
P, while εσχάτᾱ has an accent on ε cancelled : the truth is
given in the margin.   35. ἄζομαι P.

197

CERCIDAS

ὅσον [κατά]γει τὸ παρ' αὑτοῖς |
τῶ Διὸς πλα[στ]ίγγιον. |
ποίους ἐπ' ἀνάκτορας οὖν τις |
ἢ τίνας οὐρανίδας
κιὼν ἀνεύροι |
πῶς λάβῃ τὰν ἀξίαν,   40
ὅθ' ὁ Κρονίδας, ὁ φυτεύσας |
πάντας ἁμὲ καὶ τεκών, |
τῶν μὲν πατρωός,
τῶν δὲ πέφανε πατήρ; |
λῶον μεθέμεν περὶ τούτων
τοῖς μετεωροκόποις· | 45
τούτους γὰρ ἔ(ρ)γον
οὐ‹δὲ› ἐν ἔλπομ' ἔχην· |
ἁμὶν δὲ Παιάν
καὶ τἀγαθὰ Μετά[δως μελέτωτ, |
—θεὸς γὰρ αὕτα—
καὶ Νέμεσις κατὰ (γ)ᾶν;
μέσφ' οὖν ὁ δαίμων |
οὔρια φυσιάει
τιμ‹ῆ›τε ταύταν   50

col. v.   φῶ(τ)[ες]· ἐ(λα[
         κα]ταιξ
    ἀντε(π)[

36. supplevi.   37. suppl. H.   stop after πλα[. .]ιγγιον.
               οι
39. ευρη· P.   40. πῶσλ P.   41. ὁθ P.   42. ἁμε P.
43. πατρωος P. cited from Cercidas by Poll. iii. 27 as less
198

How far they pull down in their favour
  Zeus' scales of equity !
What lords them that lord it above us,
  Whom then of Uranos' sons
May any seeking
  Merit's retribution find,   40
When the offspring of Kronos, our parent
  Who begat us one and all,
Some men as father,
  Others as stepfather know ?
Fit talk for astrologers truly ;
  Let us refer it to them :   45
For them to settle
  It will be slightest of tasks ;
To us is Paean
  Good, and fair-dealing is good—
A very goddess—
  Nemesis too, upon earth :
What time the godhead
  Blows in our favour astern,
Hold *her* in honour,   50
  Mortals : though bravely they fare,
A sudden tempest
  Swooping down from other airt
Sinks to perdition

---

correct than ἐπιπάτωρ. **44.** ʹλωιον P. **45.** μετεωροκοποις·
is glossed in margin by αστρολογοις. **46.** ουθεν P ?
corr. Wilam. εχειν· ἀμιν P. **47.** ἀγαθὰ secl. Wilam.
μεταιδως P : corr. Wilam. ; schol. has ἐπεὶ δὼς ἀγαθή, whence
it appears that καὶ Μετάδως ἀγαθὰ must have been the reading. **48.** (γ)αν· P. **50.** suppl. H. **51.**]ταῖξ supplevi
et correxi : pessime H., cett. με]τάξαντες. **52.** αντ(· π)
vel (· γ) : non fuit (εσ). *Cf. e.g.* Theod. Presb. *de incarn.*
Dom. p. 245 ἔνθα καὶ ἑτέρας καταιγίδος ἀντιπνευσάσης·

```
        ]σητον ὄλ[βον
                ]τύχα(ς)·
ταῦτ' ε[. . . .]μιν                           55
νείοθεν ἐξεμέσαι;
```

53. suppl. H.   50-55. I translate ἐλαυνομένως ἄλλος κατᾶιξ
ἀντέπνευσε ποντιῶν φυσητὸν (-ατὸν) ὄλβον χὐπεραφανεῖς τύχας·
ταῦτ' ἔσθ' ὃς ὑμῖν . . .; The exact size of the various gaps

III

```
Δοιά τις ἅμιν ἔφα                            1
γνάθοισι φυσῆν |
τὸν κυανοπτέρυγον
παῖδ' 'Αφροδίτας, |
Δαμόνομ'· οὔτι (γ)[ὰ]ρ εἶ
λίαν ἀπευθής· |
καὶ βροτῶν [ὅτῳ] γὰρ ἂν
πραεῖα καί <πως>                             5
εὐμενε|δεξιτέρα
πνεύσῃ σιαγών, |
οὗτο(ς) (ἐν) ἀτρεμίᾳ
τὰν ναῦν ἔρωτος |
```

The new poem is marked by a coronis.   It bears no title.

1. schol. δοι[α   ]: δοιάτισἅμιν P.   3. Δαμονομ'· and
ἀπευθης· P.   4. βροτων [?]μεναν^{γαρ}πραειακαιευμενὲ[?]δεξιτεραν
200

Puffed-up wealth or fortunes proud :
And who can youward   55
  Vomit them back from the deep ?

---

is uncertain. The meaning of the end is hard to fit: the
nautical metaphor is clear from the schol., and the use of
ἐξεμέω in Hom. μ 237, 437. On 56 there is a marginal
note ἐκ βαθ(έω)[ν.   **54.** τύχας· P.   **55.** ταυτ' P.

III

Thou, O Damonomus, art
  Not ill instructed :
' Twain are the blasts ' we are told
  ' That Aphrodité's
Offspring doth breathe from his cheeks,
  The azure-wingéd.
Unto whomsoe'er of men
  With gentle mildness
Kindlily-out-of-the-right
  His jaw hath breathéd,
Tranquil the sea of love,
  Whereon that mortal

---

with ν cancelled: supplevi et correxi. There is no need
(apart from metre) to assume gaps at either point: possibly
⟨ὅτῳ⟩. [ὅτῳ] Hunt.

CERCIDAS

σώφρονι πηδαλίῳ
πειθοῦς κυβερνῇ· |
τοῖς δὲ τὰν ἀριστερὰν
λύσας ἐπόρσῃ |
λαίλαπας ἢ λαμυρὰς   10
πόθων ἀέλλας, |
κυματίας διόλου
τούτοις ὁ πορθμός· |
εὖ λέγων Εὐριπίδας·
†οῦ κάρρον οὖν ἐστὶν
δύ᾽ ὄντων |† ἐκλέγ‹η›ν
τὸν οὔριον ἇμιν ἀήταν |
καὶ μετὰ σωφροσύνας   15
οἴακι πειθοῦς |
χρώμενον εὐθυπλο‹ῆ›ν
ὅκ᾽ ᾖ κατὰ Κύπριν ὁ πορθμός·
μὴ[18

col. vi.   ]α[18 a

fr. 13
⎜......]στω βι[
⎜......].κυβερν[
⎜......]σω δόξα[
⎜......]ν μὲν ἀλλ[

fr. 53
⎜......]καν Ἰκάρω[
⎜.........]φ...πι[

⎜νομ[19
⎜δαπ[20
              ]καὶ τ[...(..)   21
.(..)...(τ).(ῥ)ηξεῖ.[
ἀ]στρα(π)[..] (σ)[...](π)λόος·
πᾶν γ[ὰρ] τὸ βι[(αι)οπόν]ηρον
(κ)αὶ προκοθ[η]λυμαν[ὲς]

-202

Ruddered by discipline calm
    His ship directeth.
But 'gainst whomsoe'er the boy,
    His left jaw loosing,
Rouseth the storms or the fierce
    Typhoons of passion,
These have their voyages fraught
    With waves unceasing.'
Nobly said, Euripides !
    Since twain the choice is,
Better far it is for us
    To choose out the wind in our favour,
So that with calmness of soul,
    Where leads the goddess,
Voyage we straight on our course
    And steer us by discipline's tiller.

Icarus . . . .

    Lightning besetting his course :   23
For all that is violent, wicked,
    Mad in pursuit of its mate,

---

7. ατρεμια P, and 8. πηδαλιωι and κυβερνη· P.   9. ορση
quae exempla sufficiant.   10. αελλᾶς P.   12. ευρι-
πιδας· P.   οὐκοῦν δύ' ὄντων κάρρον ἐστὶν ἐκλ. recte Maas.
14. ἀμιναηταν· και P.   16. ευθυπλοειν ὅκῆ P.   17. πορθμος.
P. schol. ἀφροδίσιος.   col. vi. fr. 13 huc certe referen-
dum : dubites de columnae lineis. conieceram νομ .. σω/δαπ ..
ν/καὶ τὸκ' ἀνίκα : sed refragantur vestigia πι/πλ.   Ἰκάρω
bene Powell.   21. e.g. τόκα πρὸς ταῦτα ῥηξεῖν.   ηξεῖ P.
22. στρᾶπ. P.   ? -όβλητος.   23. supplevi.   24. προ-
κοθηλ. A.

φέρει ταναβλαψιτέλειαν   25
(κ)αὶ μεταμελλοδύναν·
ἀ δ' ἐξ ἀγορᾶς 'Αφροδίτα,
καὶ τὸ μη[δε]νὸς μέλ⟨η⟩ν
ὁπ[α]νίκα λῆς, ὅκ(α) χρῄζῃς,
οὐ φόβος οὐ ταραχά·   30
τ(α)[ύ]ταν ὀβόλω κατακλίνας
Τ[υν]δαρέοιο δόκει
γαμβ(ρ).[

| τημεν· κο
| γα
| γα
| ρ(ε)

(Stob. *Fl.* lviii. 10 περὶ ἡσυχίας: Κερκίδα μελιάμβων : (ἡμιάμβων codd.: corr. Meineke) ⟨τ⟩ὸ τᾶς ρικνᾶς χελώνας †α†μναμονεῦ (em. Meineke)· οἶκος γὰρ ἄριστος κτλ. : *vid. inf.*)

25. λειαν· and δυναν· ἀ P.   28. suppl. H.   29. νίκαλῆσδ P.   30. ταραχα· P.   31. κατακλίνας· P. (There are faint traces of scholia against *vv.* 22, 23, 30, 31.)

32. γαμβρέστατ' ἦμεν potius quam γαμβρὸς το⟨κ⟩ ?   33. τει
                                                      η
     κο
μεν· νυ P. si huc pertineret fr. 7 (H.) legi non posset quod

Engendereth woe of repentance [1]   25
  And ruin [1] far-spread in the end :
But Venus that paces the market—
  In repletion of desire
Demanding no thought or attention:—
  Here is no fear and no care :   30
One obol will win you a mistress,
  Son-in-law fancy yourself
To Tyndarus (favoured 'mong suitors) :
  (Yet remains one more advice) :—
⟨Remember always
  What the wrinkled tortoise said :
' Both dearest and best, my good masters,
  Truly, of all things, is home.'⟩

---

[1] These Greek words ταναβλ. and μεταμελλ. appear easiest
as two words despite the strange nature of the compounds.
The latter would have to be connected with μεταμέλειν, which
may be compared with, but not excused by, e.g. Nicand.
Alex. 81 ξηρὰ δ' ἐπιλλύζων ὀλοῇ χελλύσσεται ἄτῃ.   μέλος
Ebeling, Lex. Hom. s.v.

proposui γαμβρες (nam ρ vix aut ne vix quidem possibile):
metri et spatiorum gratia potest e.g. γαμβρ(ὸ)[ς χαρι]έσ[τατά] τ'
ἦμεν· . . . [τὸ] τᾶς ῥ[ικνᾶς] γὰ[ρ δὴ χελώνας μναμόν]ευ(ε)· οἶκος γὰρ
[ἄριστος ἀλαθέως] καὶ φίλο͞ς, [˘]ρε̄[˘—]. Certe hic poema finem
habet: sub καιφιλος spatium: e.g. ὦνδρες ἔφα.

IV

col. vii.   ά]κις

δμαθεὶς βροτὸς οὔτι ἑκὼν |
ἔκλαξε κανθώς.

τὶν δ' ἀμάλακτον ἔσω |
στέρνων καὶ ἀνί-
κατον κέαρ ἔσκεν |

πιμελοσαρκοφάγων
πάσας μελεδώνας.   5

†τοι† τὶν διέφευγε†ν† καλῶν
οὐδέν ποκα· πάντα τ' ὑπὸ
σπ[λ]άγχνοις τεοῖς†ι† ἔσκ'

(ά)βρ(ὰ) Μουσ<ᾶ>ν κνώδαλα· |

Πιερίδων θ' ἀλ[ι]ευ-
τὰς ἔπλεο, θυμέ, καὶ ἰχν-   10
(ευτ)ὰς ἄρισ(τ)[ο]ς. |

νῦν δ' τὄκκα μὲν†τ ἐκφανέες
λευκαὶ κορυφ[ᾶ] (περι)αι- |
ωρεῦντ' ἐ(θ). . . (ν).

(ἀκαλέω) < > λάχνα,
κνα[κ]ὸν δὲ (γένη)-
ον, καί τι ματεύει |

1, 2. metre uncertain. Above at top of column a schol.
]μενον. The writer appears to address himself. In this poem
the metrical divisions do not appear to correspond, as they
do elsewhere, to sense divisions.   1. *e.g.* — ◡◡ μυριάκις.
                                             'ως'
2. ἐκλᾶιξε κανθους P.   3. τῐν P.   ἀμάραντον P: superscr.
(α)·πε·(ραντον): margin 'αμαλακτον·   4. εσκ'εν (ἦν εἰς)
Powell: dubito.   'πῐμελὸσαρκοφαγων πασᾶς . . . νᾱς' P.

IV

Many a time
Man loses the fight e'er his orbs
Full loath he closes.

Thou hadst a heart in thy breast
Unsoftened and un-
Tamed ever in fighting

'Gainst all the desires of fat flesh
Which gluttons may cherish.

Nothing on earth that was fair
Escaped you : but ever you kept
Within your bosom

All the Muses' cublets young.

Thou wert a fisher my soul
Of all the Pierian maids
And keenest tracker.

But now that there gleam on my head
White hairs but a few at the edge
Around encircling

Still with incipient down,
Still yellow my beard,
And still doth my summer

---

6. *e.g* τὶν διέφευγε(ν) (ex τοιδιεφ).: τιν Wilam. τοι delen-
dum. P καλον. 7. ουδένποκα· παντα τεοισιν (ν cancelled)
δυποσπ P. 8. Μουσῶν P. 9. ·πε(cancelled)ιεριδων P.
11. †. . .† *e.g.* ὅκα τ'. νῦν P. 12. -ωρευνται P. *e.g.*
ἇμιν. ἀκαλέφ(α) is false (?) Doricism for ἠκαλέφ(η). A
short syllable is missing: *e.g.* 'πὶ. λαχναι P. κνα[κ]ον
suppl. H. γέν(ε)ιον H.

CERCIDAS

‹χοῖον› κολακεύει‹ν›

‹τῶ› χρόνῳ τ' ἐπάξιον

εὐρὺν (ποτὶ) (τέ)ρματος οὐδ-
όν· | τᾶμος ἐσλᾶς

14. κάι P (non κάι). superscr. (above (κρ)αγυον) .(τ)[.].
ἀλικία Murray, which I translate.   **15** is devoid of metre
and sense. It runs χρ. τ. ἐ. κολακεύει. It seems necessary
to make the half iambus correspond to ἀβρὰ M. κ.
16. βιοτᾶς P.

IV (?)

(a) col. viii.	(b) *fr.* 59 + 11 + 39	(c) col. ix
μὲν	δ[όμον	]ον· μὴ νόμιζ[ε	
	[	]τω ῥευσε[ι	
	γ[	π]όκα· μία πέλ[λα	
	νο.[	]. μην[..].μι· τουτῶ[	]οτ[
	σὶκ 5	]οις· .[..]με(ι)[	]. ευτω
	ἄχαρι(ν)	πολ]λο(ὶ) [(δ)ἐ] κ(αὶ)[	]ονμ
	ναν, (ο)[	σοφ]ίας·	πολλᾶ[ν] δ[ὲ	
	μεθα.[		σό](φ)οις· ἁ δὲ (π)υ[	

17. τᾶμος εσλᾶς P with gloss τᾶμος ἔ[πειτα: suppl. H.

(a) 1. *e.g.* μὲν δόμον – ∪∪ ἐκ κρηπῖδος ... In margin
opposite *v.* 9 (κνώδαλα): ἀγρεύματα κ(αὶ) ἐνεργήματα ('objects
of chase,' *i.e.* activities), opp. 14: ἠ[(λικίαν) φ. ματεύ[ει]ν ἀν(τὶ
τοῦ) (τ)[ούτοις] ἤδ[ε](σ)θ[αι ἢ] μέλ(ειν)['Age,' he says,
'seeks': that is, delights in these things or has a care
for them. Opp. 16: (πρ)ο(ορ)ῶν(τι) [δη](λαδὴ) [εἰς] π(ο)[λὺν
τ](ὸ)ν and a much rubbed line: *e.g.* τοῦ γήρως χρόνον:
'looking forward to a long span of old age.' I give the be-

Seek for the thing that is fair
And able to flatter

Worthy of my riper years

Looking ahead to my life's
Broad threshold of eld at its close,
Then from foundation
Fair ⟨

IV (?)

Think not

One cup

Mind doth see
And mind doth hearken

⟨Poets have said⟩: can they then
Though standing ⟨. . .⟩ at their doors
Behold true wisdom

---

ginnings of col. viii. and ix. (*e.g.*) which it appears hopeless to combine as viii. init. and fin. Between I give *e.g.* the *frr.* 59 + 11 + 39 and the literary *fr.* 4 connecting παλῶ with Prometheus : for a correction of a previous error of mine my thanks are due to Hunt. There is of course no certainty that ix. follows on viii., nor that (*b*) and (*c*) should be connected. (*b*) 7. πολλᾱ P et cett.; vid. Hunt. 8. metri gratia σοφοῖς· ἃ δὲ πυνθανόμεσθα, κοὐκ ἀπάτυλλα φάτις. 9. suppl. H. (*c*) *ll.* 4, 5, 6 (οὕτως μέν), 14, 18. are scholl. The juncture of *fr.* 41 (and 9*) is certain; of 40 probable.

τὶς ἀλα[ἀ]πα ^{ˊτˋ} υλλα.[
περ.[10   ]καλον[
νοω[
ταν[   ]. .δρυ[
ηκὸρυ[φ   ]..[.]υ.[φῦναι . . . .
(τ)ας δα[πα]λῶ· πέφ(υ)κε . αλλ' ὀλ.
κτο[15   ][ ]ρ Προμαθεὺς
πάιλ.[   ](ισαρ)ο
εκτα[   ](τ)άχα ῥη-
στακ.[(λ)[.]
βεβ[
με.[20
ἀκτ(ι)[

(Stob. *Fl.* iv. 42, 43 M. (περὶ ἀφροσύνης | **:** νοῦς ὁρῇ | καὶ νοῦς ἀκούει . ⟨‒◡◡⟩ πῶς κεν ἴδοι|εν τὰν σοφίαν πέλας ἐστ|ακνίαν ⟨‒‒ | ‒◡◡‒◡◡‒ | ‒⟩ ἀνέρες ὧν τὸ κέαρ παλ⟨ῶ⟩ σέσακται καὶ δυσεκνίπτω τρυγός (παλος and -τῳ cod.): corr. Bentley.)

17. τάχαρῇ P.

V

col. x.   οὐ. [. . . . .]νης πυ[θι ‖   1
          ουτ[. . . .] ἀκάρδιον[2
          [. . .](φ)ρίκαν τ' ['Α]πό(λ)[λων ‖ συγ-]   3
          κροτησιγόμφιον ‖   4

The conjunction of the col. which I call (*e.g.*) ix. and x. is certain. I conjecture that no verse is missing and that *fr.* 37 (with coronis) may begin. The spot above, if ink, might be part of a gloss. Metre as poems 2, 3 but without equal correspondence of sense and cola.   1-2. *e.g.* οὐ μάταν ἦς Πύθιος

<. .   .   .   .   .   .>

Those <. . .> mortals whose heart
    With mud is filléd,
Stained with lees that wash not out.

(Cercidas quoted in Stobaeus' *Anthology* : *On Madness*.)

V

    Not in vain the Pythian [1]
Is so entitled :
     Unto each man cowardly blight
Apollo sendeth
    Or cold fear teeth-chattering,

[1] The Cynic regarded Apollo and the Muses (music) with
as great suspicion as any other patrons of pleasure.

βοατὸς οὕτως· ἀλλ' .... βλάβαν.   3-4. γόμφ P.   supplevi.
e.g. νέμει: gaps [   ] from two to eight letters.   τωι P.

κα]τὰ καιρὸν ἑκάστῳ,   5
(π)[άντα] θεῖ κὴ(λ)αύνεται
γὰρ (ἀ)[   ]τα
φευξιπόνων ἀν[ὰ γᾶν
φῦλα σκιόθρεπτ'
†ἀδον[ο]π[λ]άκτων βροτῶν   10
ἀκ[ήρ]ιος ἐγχεσίμωρος†·   9
καὶ μ[ά]λ' ἐπισταμένως   11
[ὕ]ψ[ι]τράγ[ῳδο]ς   13
(θεὰ) χ(λ)[ι]δᾶγας ὤπας(ας)   12
πί[ειρ]ατ†ἱ μὲν ὠλεσίκαρπο⟨ς⟩   14
[δὲ Φρ]ύγα φυσαλέ†ατν   15
(Λ)υδάν [τ' . . . . . .]ῇ·
νεῦρα δὲ καὶ κρα[δα . .
δι'] ὦτ' ἐλέλιγμα[. . . . .]ς
εὖπα(λ)[αμ

About four lines lost in col. x. and ten in col. xa. The
next ten lines begin ταυτα|γαρου|αθεσ|ναται.|τοσαεικ|ω φιλος
τασι|ησκαι(ν)οωκ.|πενιᾳ ποτιφ|τιμοτάτω δεπ|π[. .](α)μυρο[. There
the poem ends and the remainder of the column is lost.

5. suppl. H.   6. θεῖκὴλαύ P.   *e.g.* ἀΐοντα.   7. supplevi.
10. suppl. Wilam.   9. supplevi *e.g.* et transtuli.   φῦλαι

VI

. . . .

col. xi. αιο]λόπωλον[| |
       βουσόω | μύω[π | | 2
       ιππον χρέ[ων;| | 3

1. suppl. H.   2. σόω P: suppl. Wilam.   fin.
et 3 supplevi.   3. fin. supplevi.

Alike unto each in their season.
    See how smoothly all things glide,
For those that hearken,
    Races that live in the shade
Avoiding turmoil,
    Men by stroke of pleasure numbed—
The spear-spurning spiritless godhead :
    Aye, and with cunning intent
The lofty-tragic,
    Fertile dam of sterile stock,
Muse gendereth luxury-shattered
    Phrygian of puffing cheeks
And Lydian wanton :
    Strings and reverberant twang
Of dexterous fingers resounding

.   .   .   .   .

P (ι cancelled).   13, 12. ωπασ(ασθεα) χλ. [υ]ψ P.
suppl. et transtuli.   14. ν seclusi.   -καρπον
P : correxi. Accents on σκιοθ., -ίμωρος, -άκτων, χλιδᾱγας, πῑ.
15. φῡσἀλέαν P : read φυσαλέον. 16. χυδαν might just be read:
not αὐδάν.   17. ἦ·νεῦρα P.   e.g. κραδαλᾱ̆ . . . ἐλέλιγμα . . . . . .s
εὐπάλαμός τε λύρα. schol.] . . σκρα [ ] (αια)s.   18. ωτ'
ελέλ P.   19. suppl. Maas.

VI

.   .   .   .   .   .

What driver of team of four horses
    Brightly sparkling in the sun
Should use to spur them
    Goad that galleth oxen's flanks ?

| τοῦ]το γάρ ἐστ' ἀγάθω   4
τοῦτ' εὐθυδίκω [δελ]εαστᾶ,   5
Στωικὲ Καλλιμέδων·
. . . . . . π[.](σ)[.]στι πονηρὰ
καὶ [. . . . .]μένα·
Σφαίρω γὰρ [αἴ τι
. . . .](π)ροβάλῃς   10
ἢ καί τι [. . . . .
οὐ]χὶ τὸν εἰς ἀρετὰν
[καὶ . . . .]δες ἰχνεύεις
ἀλ[λὰ τὸν εἰς . . . . .]
φέροντ' ὀπώραν   15
[. . . . .]·
κο(ὐ) (το)ῦτ[ο]ν (α)ὐ[τὸν
[<, ἀλλ>   ]
[   ]

5. τᾶ and δων· P.   1-4. e.g. ποτ' αἰολόπωλον ◡--ὠμο-
πληξιβουσόῳ μύωπι χρῆσθαι ἀνδρὶ τέθριππον χρέων; πολλοῦ δεήσει.

VI (?)

col. xii.   ]ηθρα   1
(e.g. 20) σκωπτίλλ(ιο)[. .] αὖ, |
          (λ)η[. . . . . . .]ιδ[ίκ]ως,
          βλαβὰν (ἀκλ)η[[
(e.g. 25) . . . .]ετρ[. . .]μοφλυακῆν†   5

col. xii. (e.g.) probably from same poem and possibly
the next column. See appendix.   ληρολογ. K. F. W.
Schmidt: φόβος, ἀποστομοῖ H.   **1.** ηθρασκωπτίλλ.ο P.
214

‹Far be it from him.›
This is the action of one,
O Stoic Callimedon, seeking
To entice the good and just :
Nay, this is the pathway of villains
Trodden by the base and ill :
Whoso to Sphaerus
Giveth up aught that is dear,
Or aught confideth,
It is no guide unto calm
Or virtuous life he pursueth :
Nay, it is one who will lead
To madness' harvest

. . . .

π

7. π superscr.　　e.g. τᾷδ' ἀτρακτὸς ἐστι.　　8. e.g. κακοῖς
τετριμμένα : μενᾱ P.　　9. supplevi.　　10. e.g. τῶν ἰδίων.
11. e.g. πεισθῇς.　　12. supplevi.　　13. supplevi e.g.
ἀταραχῶδες (ita fere Mayer).　　14. supplevi : e.g μανίας.
16. e.g. κἀσεβῆ διδάσκαλον.　　17. supplevi.

VI (?)

Of idle jestings
Pettifogging lawyers they,
Disaster ‹bringing
With their sharp and prickly thorns›
To babbling of pitiful nonsense
‹Whetting well their pointed tongue› :

---

2. ἀν· P : but corrected to circumflex.　λη is more probably a
gloss. There is a stop after ωs.　5-6. ἀκεῖν τοπος (o is certain)
? : ? κοπος.　　αυτο P.　　There is not room for Φοῖβος.
see Appendix.

215

| τόπος ἢ φ[ό]βος αὐτὸ
συ(μ)[πα]|ρῶν [ἀ]ποστ(ο)μ[οῖ];
τᾶς δὴ το[ι]αύτας
σκεπτοσύνας κεν[ὰ] | μὴ
(e.g. 30) σπουδὰν ποιεῖσθ[αι
τῶ] | στρέφ‹η›ν ἄνω κάτω,   1(
†(ἀ)[λλ', αἴ] | (τ)[ι]ν' εὕρῃς διὰ (π)ασᾶν
(μ)[ου]|σικῶς ἁρμοσμένον, |
†.]οτανισοντον πόθον ἕλκ[ε],
(e.g. 35) (κ)αὶ | [(μ)ά]θ' εὖ τὸν ἵμερον,
τ[ί]s [τ'] ἐστὶ ποτ' ἄρσενας ἄρσ(η)[ν | 1(
τίs] τ' ἔ[ρ]ως Ζα(ν)ωνικός.

Κερκίδα
κυνός
με]λίαμβοι

Nor habit of discipline blunteth
    Nor fatigue its bitter edge.
Aspire not therefore
    Into the follies to probe
Of suchlike tenets,
    Turning on from page to page,
But an thou discover a fellow
    Formed in perfect harmony,
To companionship equal of passion
    Take him, finding what desire
Can be for a man of another,
    And what Zeno's love doth mean.

9-10. κενὰ is object of στρέφειν.   11. suppl. Wilam.
for εὕρῃς e.g. ἀθρῇς, ἴδῃς.   διὰ (π)ασαν lucide P: . (θεα)ν H.
hic quidem dormibundus.   12. suppl. H.   14-16. supplevi post H.   13. locus desperatus.   After ἕλκε εἰς πόθον
would be usual. I suggest ποτὰν ἴσον εἰς πόθον ἕλκε κτλ. (C.R.).

FRAGMENTS

(All fragments of papyrus of over thirty letters have received some adjuncts and been placed in their columns: except those to which I give the name of column xi. (e.g.) and col. viii. 9. The remainder, with one possible exception, appear, as long as they remain separate, of little interest. The following meliambic fragments must be added to those read, or cited, above.)

1. (2 Bgk. ii. P.)

οὐ μὰν ὁ πάρος ⟨γα⟩ Σινωπεύς,
τῆνος ὁ βακτροφόρ⟨ο⟩ς,
διπλ†οτ†είματος, αἰθεριβόσκας,
ἀλλ' ἀν' ⟨‿ – ‿ ⟩ ἔβα
χ⟨ῆ⟩λος ποτ' ὀδόντας ἐρείσας
καὶ τὸ πνεῦμα συνδακών·
⟨Ζανὸς γόνος⟩ ἦς γὰρ ἀλαθέως †Διογένης† 5
†Ζανὸς γόνος† οὐράνιός τε κύων.

(Diog. L. vi. 76 οἱ δὲ τὸ πνεῦμα συγκρατήσαντα, ὧν ἐστι καὶ Κερκίδας ὁ Μεγαλοπολίτης ἢ Κρῆς (? ἀντίκρυς) λέγων ἐν τοῖς Ἰάμβοις οὕτως (1).) So perhaps *fr.* 19 αταν|(ο)υ(μα) above which is a note which *might* be expanded into ἐκ τούτων ἀκριβ]ῶς γν(ῶ)[ναι . . . . ὁποί](αν δ)[ἢ τοῦ βίου τελευτὴν εἶχεν ὁ Διογέν]ης.

2. (5 Bgk., 15 P.) Θέσσαλος δὲ ἅμα τοῖς ἑαυτοῦ σοφισταῖς ἐφ' ὑψηλοῦ θρόνου καθήμενος ἐν κριομύξ⟨α⟩ις ἀνδράσιν, ὡς ὁ Κερκίδας φησίν, εὐδοκιμήσει. Galen (x. 406). C. may have written

ἐν κριομύξ⟨α⟩ις
ἀνδράσιν εὐδοκιμῶν.

FRAGMENTS

1. Others say that he committed suicide by holding his breath : among these is Cercidas of Megalopolis [or Crete ?], who says ⟨plainly ?⟩ as follows in his *Iambi* :—

Not so did the old Sinopean
　　Famed for the cudgel he bore,
The double-cloaked liver in ether ;
　　Nay but he rose to the sky
By clipping his lips with his grinders,
　　Thereby biting off his breath :
Zeus' son was he rightly entitled,
　　Rightly ' the heavenly dog.' [1]

(*Diogenes Laertius's Lives.*)

2. But Thessalus sitting among his sophists on a lofty seat will, as Cercidas says,

find favour
'mong sheepishly-drivelling [2] folk.

(*Galen.*)

---

[1] From the Dog (κύων) the Cynics took their name.
[2] -μυξης is the common form, *e.g.* Anon. c. Synes. 32 fin. The writer like Synes. may have read Cercidas.

---

1. 1. γεα codd. : corr. Bgk.　　2. φορας codd.　　3. ο seclusit A.　　4. *e.g.* ⟨Ὄλυμπον⟩.　　χεῖλος codd.
5-6. Διογένης seclusit et Ζ. γ. transtulit A.
2. 1. κριομύξοις codd.

　　　　　　　　　　　　　　　　　　219

CERCIDAS

3. (1 Bgk., 15 P.)

ἦν καλλιπύγων ζεῦγος ἐν Συρακούσαιs.

(Ath. xii. 554 d αὗται ὑπὸ τῶν πολιτῶν καλλίπυγοι ἐκαλοῦντο ὡς καὶ ὁ Μεγαλοπολίτης Κ. ἐν τοῖς ἰάμβοις ἱστορεῖ λέγων (3).)

4. (7 Bgk., 16 P.) Greg. Naz. ii. 213 is a mere paraphrase of portions of [Cercid.] προοιμίον.

5*. (10 P. : Cronert, *Rh. Mus.* lxii. 311.)

τῷ περι‹σσαν›-
θηροπέπλου μανίας
ὕβρεός τε περιστάσιμον
στοὰν ἔχοντι
Πυθαγόρου πελάτᾳ   5

(Ath. iv. 163 e πρὸς ὃν ἐπιστέλλων ὁ Στρατόνικοs ἐκέλευσε τὸν ἀπαίροντα τὸ ῥηθὲν ἀπαγγεῖλαι (5).)

6. (28 H.)

αρσε
ῥέθος βλε[π
β]λοσυρομ[ματ

7. See above (on col. ii.).

4. See my *First Greek Anthologist*, Cambridge, 1922.
5. 1-2. σσαν inserui (*cf.* Eur. *I.A.* 73).   5. πελαιτᾳ cod. The metrical agreement of this *fr.* with that of poem iv. is extraordinary : but it should be remembered that the metre is also that of Philoxenus and no doubt others. Chronological considerations preclude the authorship of Cercidas, unless we suppose that the characters Strat. and Demetrius Aspendius (πρὸς ὅν) are wrongly given by Athenaeus.
220

3. These girls were called ' fair-rumped ' by their fellow-citizens as ⟨pseudo-?⟩Cercidas of Megalopolis narrates in his *Iambi.* Here are his words :—

> There was a fair-rumped pair in Syracuse.
> <div align="right">(<i>Athenaeus</i>.)</div>

4. (*Fr.* 17 Bgk., 16 Powell from *Gregory of Nazianzus* : see over and n.)

5. Stratonicus sent a message to Demetrius of Aspendus and told the messenger dispatched to deliver his words to the

> Pythagorean expert
> Whose portico ever is thronged
> With pride and over-
> Gorgeously-raimented crowds.
> <div align="right">(<i>Athenaeus</i>.)</div>

(These verses—older than C.—are interesting as showing that his style and one at least of his metres had previously been applied to kindred topics.)

6. (See n.) It is not probable that he will brace himself up and

> with austere eyes

look gold in the face : nay rather would he be struck with awe thereof and yield and finally embrace it. (*Synesius*.)

7. (See col. ii.).

---

6. 3. Supp. H. ?ὁ βλοσυρομματίας. I subjoin this fragment which might belong to our second column in order to call attention to a possible adaptation of it in Synesius, *de Regno*, p. 54 Krabinger οὐκ εἰκός γε αὐτὸν διαράμενον βλοσυροῖς ὀφθαλμοῖς ἀντιβλέψαι χρυσίῳ· τοὐναντίον μὲν ⟨οὖν⟩ αἰδεσθῆναί τε καὶ ἐνδοῦναι καὶ τελευτῶντα περιπτύξασθαι.

APPENDIX

THE last column of the papyrus of Cercidas' *Meliambi*
provides several problems of difficulty : of some of
these I have attempted to provide a solution. But
the gravest difficulties lie in the first few lines.
Scanty as the remains are, they should be sufficient
to guide us as to the general sequence of thought
and metre ; and this they fail to do.

Here are the traces as I see them :

$$[\ ]\eta\theta\rho\alpha\sigma[\ ]\ \kappa\dot{\omega}\pi\tau\acute{\iota}\lambda\lambda.\ .\alpha\hat{\upsilon}\cdot(\lambda\eta)[$$
$$[.\ .\ .\ .\ .\ ]\iota\delta[.\ .\ ]\omega\varsigma\ \cdot\ \beta\lambda\alpha\beta\alpha\nu(\alpha\kappa\lambda)\eta$$
$$[.\ .\ .\ .\ .\ ]\epsilon\tau.[.\ .\ ]\mu o\phi\lambda(\upsilon)\alpha\kappa\epsilon\hat{\iota}(\nu)$$
$$\tau o\pi o\varsigma\ \eta\phi[.\ ]\ (\beta)o\sigma\alpha\upsilon\tau o\sigma\upsilon(\mu)[.\ .\ .\ .\ ]$$
$$\rho\omega\nu[.]\pi o\sigma\tau(o)\mu[.]\ \tau\alpha\varsigma\ \delta\eta\tau o[.]\ \kappa\tau\lambda.\qquad 5$$

1. $\alpha\hat{\upsilon}$ by correction from $\alpha\dot{\upsilon}.\lambda\eta$ or $\sigma\eta.\eta\theta\rho\alpha\varsigma$ may or may not
join $\kappa\dot{\omega}$.   2. parts of two letters below $\eta\theta\rho\alpha$ (ν.) visible.
3. no room for $o\iota$ after ϕ. $\upsilon(\mu)$ or $\upsilon(\delta)$ only.
4. $\tau\acute{o}\pi o\varsigma$ certain.

Hunt read *v.* 4. $\tau\acute{o}\pi(o)\varsigma\ \mathring{\eta}\ \phi\acute{o}\beta o\varsigma$. As to the second
o of $\tau\acute{o}\pi o\varsigma$ his doubts are to me unintelligible. The
fragment fits close up not as in the facsimile and o
is as certain as any letter in the papyrus (and that
is a high order of certainty). Further Hunt, dis-
regarding $\dot{\upsilon}\pi\grave{o}\ \sigma\tau\acute{o}\mu\ddot{\alpha}$ which we know now to be
metrically false, rightly read $\dot{\alpha}\pi o\sigma\tau o\mu o\hat{\iota}$.

It may safely be predicted of the metre of this

poem (especially if *frr.* 5 and 6 belong to it) that it
follows the common metre of Cercidas, that is

$$\text{A} \begin{cases} -\cup\cup-\cup\cup-{}^1 \\ \text{or} -\cup-\underset{\smile}{\smile}-\cup-{}^2 \end{cases} + \text{B} \begin{cases} \underset{\smile}{\smile}-\cup\cup-\cup\cup-\underset{\smile}{\smile}{}^1 \\ \text{or} \underset{\smile}{\smile}-\cup-\underset{\smile}{\smile}-{}^2 \end{cases}$$

Whether this is the *whole* law we do not know.

Now these verses flagrantly transgress this rule.
At $(\sigma)\nu\mu\ldots \, \dot{a}\pi o\sigma\tau o\mu oî$ we are in A² and at $\tau\hat{a}s \, \delta\grave{\eta}$
$\tau o\iota a\acute{v}\tau a s$ in B². Hence at $\tau\acute{o}\pi o s \, \mathring{\eta} \, \phi\acute{o}\beta o s \, a\mathring{v}\tau\acute{o}(s)$ we
are at the end of B¹. But immediately before this

$\tau \ldots \mu o\phi\lambda.$ or $\tau \ldots . \mu o\phi\lambda\breve{v}a\kappa\hat{\eta}\nu$ is also an end of B¹.
In view of the punctuation—for Cercidas always unites

metre and sense in cola—$\iota\delta \,\breve{.}\, \omega s \cdot \beta\lambda a\beta a\nu$ is clearly
the end of A¹ or A² and beginning of B¹ or B²
Line 1 is hopeless.

Of this phenomenon (the complete disappearance
of two As running) there can be three solutions :—

(*a*) One A is really B. This is secured in current
texts by three errors (or wholly improbable corrections) :—

(α) Reading $\tau\grave{o} \, \pi(\hat{\omega})s$: this is impossible.
(β) Followed by $\mathring{\eta} \, \Phi oî\beta o s$: this is impossible.
(γ) By the metre $-\cup\phi\lambda\breve{v}a\kappa\epsilon\hat{\iota}\nu \, \tau\grave{o} \, \pi\hat{\omega}s$: this is un-
    heard of.

(*b*) Extensive lacunae. But why should these
lacunae be so regular ?

(*c*) The only theory which seems conceivable is
that the *Meliambi* of Cercidas in the papyrus from
which this is copied ended the roll : that a square
piece was torn out : and that the writer simply
missed the letters which he did not see. It is a
simple calculation that a gap averaging ten syllables

would account for all difficulties after line 1. If the letters (λη) there are an adscript, there is a certain improbability, since, *ex hypothesi*, the parent papyrus had no adscripts here. They would have either to be text or an adscript (λε)[ίπει . . . .] due to the actual scribe.

Clearly we must consider on independent grounds of language whether the view (*a*) with its corrections of text is more or less probable than (*c*). We have to choose—since τὸ and even τὸ π[τ can well follow –φλυακεῖν—between (*c*) τ]όπος ἢ φόβος αὐτὸ (for H.'s αὐτὸς is meaningless) συμ[ ]ων ἀποστομοῖ, and (*a*) ἢ Φοῖβος αὐτὸς ὑμ´ [ὁ]ρῶν ἀπ., always remembering that the papyrus in no way favours this reading.

Now to (*a*) there are three further several objections.

(i) It appears that here as in *frr.* 5 and 6 only one person is addressed (*l.* 9 εὕρῃς). Probably H. was right in reading ποιεῖσθ[αι in 7.

(ii) Phoebus is never spoken of, as far as I know, as blunting anything or anybody.

(iii) ὁρῶν is wholly pointless.

To (*c*) I can only see one reason why it should fail here of general acceptance. That is that it falls in line with a commonplace figure in Greek poetry which has no exact counterpart in modern languages. I will take the words singly.

(i) -ος ἢ φόβος. Fear has several companions, *e.g.* Menand. *fr.* 418 λύπη (so often) φόβος φροντίς, Callim. *fr.* Anon. 176 αἰδὼς καὶ δέος ἀλλήλων, φόβοι καὶ πόνοι, Plat. *Legg.* 635 c, Plut. *M.* 128 c (so that you can go as far back as κ]όπος), Plat. *Symp.* 197 D, ἐν πόνῳ, ἐν φόβῳ, ἐν πόθῳ, ἐν λόγῳ.

APPENDIX

(ii) φόβος συμπαρών. In certain writers, especially Xenophon and Plutarch, συμπ. means little more than συνεῖναι (*Thes. s.v.*). Compare *Rep. Lac.* 2. 2 ὥστε πολλὴν μὲν αἰδῶ, πολλὴν δὲ πειθὼ ἐκεῖ συμπαρεῖναι, *Cyrop.* viii. 7. 7 φόβος μοι συμπαρομαρτῶν. But this is of an ever-haunting fear and probably the sense is nearer 'reverence.' For the Greek συνών we use some wholly different metaphor such as 'ingrained.' If κ]όπος be right we should think of some rather strained sense such as 'pain': Soph. *Phil.* 880 ἡνίκ᾽ ἂν κόπος μ᾽ ἀπαλλάξῃ ποτε. Ar. *Plut.* 321 has τῷ κόπῳ ξυνεῖναι.

(iii) Fear blunts. Pind. *Nem.* iii. 39 οὐδέ νιν φόβος ἀνδροδάμας ἔπαυσεν ἀκμὰν φρενῶν—just as in old age αἱ φρένες ἀπαμβλύνονται Hdt. iii. 134. Conversely courage sharpens: so expressly Christodor. *Ecphr.* 295 θάρσεϊ τολμήεντι τεθηγμένος.

(iv) What is blunted? Clearly anything that has an edge on which fear operates unfavourably. Edged tools are :—

(*a*) The person sharpened : Ar. *Nub.* 1107 εὖ μοι στομώσεις αὐτόν (Blaydes), Poll. ii. 100 Ἀριστοφάνης δὲ στ. εἴρηκε τὸ λάλον ἀπεργάσασθαι.

(*b*) γνάθος: *ibid.*

(*c*) ὀδόντες :｜ Ar. *Ran.* 815 ἡνίκ᾽ ἂν ὀξυλάλου †περὶ† ἴδῃ θήγοντος ὀδόντας.

(*d*) γλῶσσα : Soph. *Aj.* 584, Pindar, *Ol.* vi. 82 δόξαν ἔχω τιν᾽ ἐπὶ γλώσσᾳ ἀκονᾶς λιγυρᾶς, *Trag. Fr. Anon. Adesp.* 423 γλῶσσαν ἠκονημένος.

(*e*) λόγοι: Lucian, ii. 517, Aesch. *P.V.* 327.

(*f*) φρένες : Eur. *Hipp.* 689.

(*g*) ψυχήν : Xen. ; see Index *s.vv.* ἀκονᾶν, θήγειν.

Thus we see that speakers, instruments of speech,

or words spoken are most commonly sharpened whether by courage or anger. But we are seeking a neuter noun (αὐτό) and the choice lies between λῆμα Eur. *Or.* 1625, or, what seems more suitable, στόμα :—

Soph. *O.C.* 794 τὸ σὸν ... στόμα πολλὴν ἔχων στόμωσιν.
  Trach. 1176 μὴ 'πιμεῖναι τοὐμὸν ὀξῦναι στόμα.

(v) Can fear blunt the mouth or tongue ? Though this exact metaphor does not occur we have—

Soph. *Ant.* 180 ὅστις ... ἐκ φόβου του γλῶσσαν ἐγκλῄσας ἔχει, 505, *Ajax* 171 σιγῇ πτήξειαν ἄφωνοι: whence it may be questioned whether Sappho's texts (p. 16 Lobel) had not once ἀλλὰ κἂμ μὲν γλῶσσ‹α †τέθ›αγε† by error for τέθαπε : if such be possible in Aeolic.[1] So interlinked are the ideas of fear, silence, confidence and loquacity.[2]

A case has, I hope, been made out for a lacuna -μοφλυακῆν τὸ [στόμ'   κό]πος ἢ φόβος—the intervening words being *e.g.* εὖ τεθαγμένο— ; τίς ἢ ... For the rest we can hope for little. But βλάβαν (ἀκλ)η strikes no obvious note and it might be considered whether λη is not part of the same verse as -φλυακῆν (*e.g.* λήρημα δὲ τρισμοφλυακῆν—with κι](να)ιδ[ικ]ῶς above), and whether ἀκ does not belong to βλάβαν. Certainly ἀκ- sharp gives us a wide field of choice, with ἀκμά, ἀκονά (Pind. *ll.cc.*), ἀκι-, or even ἄκμων : *P.* i. 86 ἀψευδεῖ δὲ πρὸς ἄκμονι χάλκευε γλῶσσαν. But I prefer ἀκονα- in view of those two difficult sayings of Aeschylus :—

[1] Hesychius's gloss θάπαν shows that the *root* is not only found in Ionic.
[2] *E.M. s.v.* βοή· ... ἡ μὲν γὰρ δειλία θραύουσα τὸ πνεῦμα βραχίστην ἀπεργάζεται τὴν φωνήν. Ach. Tat. ii. 25.

APPENDIX

Ag. 1537 Δίκᾳ δ' ἐπ' ἄλλο πρᾶγμα θήγεται βλάβης
πρὸς ἄλλαις θηγάναισι Μοῖρα,

Eum. 861 αἱματηρὰς θηγάνας, σπλάγχνων βλάβας
νέων,

where, however you read or explain, it seems to me
that some subtle and lost connexion between βλάβη
and θηγάνη lies—as if, for instance, βλάβη could bear
the sense of a good or true sharpening surface. As
to the first lines of the column in Cercidas palaeographical difficulties are so grave that it seems idle to
make suggestions : on metrical grounds it would be

desirable to separate (σ)κωπτίλλ . . . and αὖ . . . But
κ(αὶ ὀ)πτίλλ⏑⏑ also gives sense and, if the theory of
a considerable gap is right, it is useless to attempt
precision.

CERCIDEA

THE following verses appear to be continuous and to have been attributed to Cercidas at least as early as the end of the fourth century A.D. The evidence is produced and considered in a work by the present writer (*The First Greek Anthologist*, Cambridge, 1922). They clearly formed the beginning of an Anthology. But it is difficult to believe they actually were by Cercidas, though the anthology may have been due to his efforts. The chief discrepancy lies not so much in style, as Mr. W. E. Barber thinks, but in metre. For style may easily be assumed but, once a metrist as skilful as the writer of the *Meliambi*, always a metrist. Not that the metre is irregular (see on Phoenix *fr.* 4). It is the norm of the moralist, admitting the spondee freely in the fifth foot, and rigidly limiting resolution. But the adaptation of sense to metre is careless and clumsy. As I find it impossible to represent such metrical shortcomings, I translate into prose.

Such an unfavourable verdict could not fairly be given on evidence of the text of the two English papyri [1] which is very unsound : but what remains of the Heidelberg [2] papyrus is excellent. On this

[1] Lond. 155 verso, Bodl. ms gr. class. f, 1 (p).
[2] No. 310.

magnificent [1] work was done by Dr. G. A. Gerhard of Heidelberg (*Phoinix von Kolophon*, Teubner, 1909): full illustrations being given of the moral ideas underlying these lines of doggerel verse. Dr. Gerhard's work is also of great bibliographical value for other choliambic writers: but it loses to some extent by a failure to recognize essential metrical differences, and by a theory that the metre was used especially by moralist writers (see on Phoenix). Recently I have visited Heidelberg and with the subsequent aid of Prof. F. Bilabel solved one or two doubtful points. Professor Bilabel has also very kindly examined many doubtful passages. Where he has confirmed my reading I use the symbol (K.-Bi.); where he has detected flaws and helped with sketches to the establishment of a new reading, I use the symbol (Bi.-K.). Where the suggestion is due entirely to him, it is so accredited.

Later leaves of our anthologist may be found at Strassbourg (*Wiss. Ges. Pap.* 304-7: see Phoenix, *fr.* 4).

[1] Dr. Gerhard, however, was not a skilled palaeographer. Among several errors one may especially mention his failure to allow for the form of τ used by the scribe. The text of the London papyrus is almost entirely due to Milne, assisted, or hindered, by the present writer.

CERCIDEA

........](οὐδ)εὶς οὐ[........ ἀνθ](ρ)ώποις
........](ι) κ(ατ)εἰδ(ε)[ν .... ἀ](ν)θρώπων
........]σα(ς) οὓς κα(τ)[εἶδεν] ἀνθρώπο(υ)ς
........](δ)ὲ (π)ρός (σ)ε χ[ρήσο]μαι πάσῃ
........](π)ο[ιή](μ)α(τ)' οὐ μάτ[. .] ἀκούοντα·   5
........] . (παρνεσωσπα)[.] ἀνθρώπων
........](καιδ)[. .]εν καλὴ κεῖ(ται)
.... κυλλ]όχειρες ὥ[σπ]ερ Ἁρπυῖαι
..... ἄναγ]νον κέρδος ἐκ λίθου παντός
.....έ]καστος ἔνθεν ἁρπάξῃ   10
.... κ]υβιστᾷ κἠπινήχεται πᾶς τις
.... ἑ]ταῖρον καὶ (κασί)γν[ητ]ον κ[αὶ] ὦρα
.... ἑ]αυτοῦ τὴν τρισο[ιζύρη]ν ψυχήν
.... οὐ](δὲν) [. . . ἠ] θάλασσα μὲ]ν πεζῇ
.... ἀν]θρώποι[σιν ἠ δὲ] (γ)ῆ πλωτή·   15
...... περ]ιφέρουσι τήνδ[ε τ]ὴν ῥῆσιν
κέρδαιν' ἑταῖρε καὶ θέρευς κ(αὶ) χειμῶνος
.... πάντοθε]ν κέρδ(αι)νε· μηδέν' αἰσχύνου
.... α]ἰδοῦ· τοῦτ' ὀνειδ(ι)εῖτα(ί σοι).

1. *e.g.* τοῖς νῦν μὲν and καταρᾶται.   2. *e.g.* ὃς κᾶν ὅσον and
ἦθος.   3. *e.g.* ἀποστυγήσας : fin. supplevi.   4. *e.g.* προθυμίῃ
(Πάρνε vix legi potest).   suppl. G(erhard).   5. supplevi.
e.g. χρηστῶν and μάτην.   6. *e.g.* ἐὰν διδάξω, Πάρνε σ' ὡς παρ'.
7. *e.g.* οἴχωκεν Αἰδὼς κοὐδ' ἐφ' ἕν.   8. suppl. Hdl.   *e.g.* αὐτοὶ
δὲ.   ὥσπερ Kenyon.   9. suppl. Cr.   *e.g.* ζητοῦσ' id.

230

CERCIDEA

There is no one who has glanced ⟨for a moment⟩ on the ⟨character⟩ of mankind at present, without ⟨cursing⟩ mankind, and ⟨hating⟩ mankind on whom he has glanced : but to you I shall display all ⟨zeal⟩, since you are no idle listener to poems of ⟨worthy⟩ writers, ⟨if, maybe, I might teach⟩ you, Parnos, that from mankind ⟨Shame has departed⟩ and in no respect is considered fair : while ⟨men themselves⟩ with ⟨crooked⟩ fingers like Harpies seek from every stone an unholy gain : and each ⟨hunting⟩ for a stretch to pillage, dives thither and swims to his prey, ⟨destroying⟩ comrade, brother or wife, but ⟨preserving⟩ his own thrice wretched life. ⟨To them⟩ nothing is ⟨sacred⟩ : ⟨by such⟩ of mankind the sea is trodden under foot and the land sailed over : all alike they carry on their lips this saying : ' win gain, my friend, summer and winter alike : from everywhere win gain : have no reverence or shame of any man : he will merely mock you for it.' ' Un-

10. *e.g.* διζήμενος δ'.   11. suppl. Cr.   *e.g.* ἐκεῖ *id.* or εὐθύς.
12. *e.g.* ὀλλύς.   13. *e.g.* σῴζων δ' cett. ex P Bodl.
14. *e.g.* οὐδὲν ἱρὸν (Mn.), and τοῖς δ'.   ηθαλλα(σ)α P Bodl. :
corr. *id.*   15. *e.g.* τοίοισιν Mn.   (σηδετν) P Bodl. : corr.
id.   16. *e.g.* πάντες δὲ.   τουτο το ρη P Bodl.   17. κην
κερους P Bodl. : see Sext. Emp. *adv. Dogm.* v. 122.
18. ἀπαντόθεν Sext. Emp. rightly. ? P habuerit ἀπανταχόθεν.
19. *e.g.* καὶ μηδένα. See Addenda.

231

. . . .](ν) τὴν χεῖρ᾽ ὅκου λαβεῖν δεῖ τι   20
ὅκου [δ]ὲ δοῦναι μηδ᾽ ὅλως φόρει χεῖρα
ἐροῦσι πολλοί· πολλὰ σαυτὸν ἀσπάζου
ἐπὴν ἔχῃς τι· πάντα σοι φίλων πλήρη·   23
πένητα δ᾽ ὄντα χἠ τεκοῦσα μισήσει·   25
πλουτοῦντα γάρ σε χοἰ θεοὶ φιλήσουσι,   24
ἐὰν ⟨δὲ⟩ μὴ ἔχῃς μηδέν, οὐδὲ κηδεσταί.   26
ἐγὼ μὲν οὖν, ἆιτα, καὶ καταρῶμαι   27
τοῖς νῦν βίοις καὶ πάντας ἀνθρώπους μισῶ
τοὺς ζῶντας οὕτω, καὶ ἔτι μᾶλλον μισήσω,
ἀνεστρόφαν γὰρ τὴν ζ⟨ό⟩ην ἡμῶν οὗτοι·   30
†τῇ γὰρ πάροιθεν ἦν δ᾽ [ἄ]χρ[ι [ν]ῦν (ἐστὶν σεμνή)†
δ]ικαιότης ᾧ(χωκεν) ἔ(νθ)ε[ν ο]ὐχ ἥξει·
ἀπιστίη ζῆ· π(ίστι)ς (ε). . . . .
ἴσχυκεν ἡ (ἀναίδε)ια (τ)οῦ [Δ]ιὸς μεῖζον·
ὅρκοι τεθ[νήκα]στιντ· οἱ θ(εο)ὶ δ᾽ (εἰά)κασ(ιν)·   35
ἡ δυσγένεια κριθ(ι)ᾷ κατ᾽ ἀνθρώπους
τῆς δ᾽ εὐγενεί[ας ἁ]λμυρὸν κ(ατ)έπτυσ(ται).
†γῆμαι δ᾽ ἂν οὐ[δεὶ](ς) ο[ὐ]δὲ τὴν (Ἥρ)⟨η⟩ν θέλοι†
πτωχὴν (ἐοῦσα)ν τ[. . . . . .](ε). . .(ο)ντο(ς),
μᾶλλον δ᾽ ἕλοι(τ)[ο τὴν (ἐ)[π](ὶ [σ](τέ)γους Λυδήν
ἔχων ὀπυίειν (ἔνδ)ο[ν ἢ]ν φέρῃ χαλκοῦς.   41
κα(ὶ) [
οἱ τἀ[
(ἐὰν) [   ]την
ο. . .[45
μο.[
αι.[
ε(χ).[
κα(ὶ).[
ὅτα[ν   50

fold your hand when you are to receive anything; but when you are to give have no hand at all,' is what many will say: 'embrace yourself heartily when you have anything: then the world is full of friends for you: but if you are poor even your mother will hate you. For if you are rich even the gods will love you: if you have nothing, not even your relatives will love you.' I then, my comrade, curse the lives men lead now, and hate all mankind who live thus, and shall hate them even more. For these have overturned our life; for justice, holy until now, has departed beyond recall. Faithlessness flourishes, faith ⟨has left the earth⟩: shamelessness has won greater strength than Zeus. The sanctity of oaths has perished, while the gods suffer it. Low birth runs riot among mankind and men spit salt on noble birth. And none now would wed even Hera herself, were she poor, and bereft of all that might profit him; rather would he choose to keep in his house as wife a Lydian harlot, if he[1] get brass with her.

[1] *Not* ' she bring,' which would be φέρηται.

---

20. *e.g.* διπλῆν φορεῖ: better perhaps ἀναπέτ(α)σο]ν. fin. ὅκου (τι) δει λ(αβει)ν P Lond. ὅκου λαβει[P Bodl. which has the middle portions of 22, 23, 26 in this order. I follow J. U. Powell. 21. suppl. Kenyon. 26. corr. id. δε om. P Lond. P Bodl. χεις μηδεν ο(ιη) absurdly. 27. αιτεια P : corr. J. U. Powell. 29. l. καὶ ἐπὶ. 30. ζωην P : corr. C. 31. supplevi. fin. (lectio vix dubia) Mn. : *e.g.* del. ην δ Mn. 32. suppl. Mn. 33. *e.g.* ἐκ τῆς γῆς ἔρρει. 34. suppl. Mn. l. μέξον. 35. suppl. Mn. (there are vague traces of (νηκα)). 37. suppl. Mn. κ(ατ) επτυσ(. .) P : text Sitzler, dubitante Mn. 38. suppl. Mn. -αν P. *e.g.* γ. θ. δ' ἂν. οὐδὲ τ. ᾿Η. οὐδείς. 39. εουσαν K.-Mn. *e.g.* τοῦ νιν ὠφελήσοντος. 40. suppl. Mn. (ἀπὸ). 41. supplevi: ἣν Cr. οπνειν P.

233

```
κ[                      οὐ](δ)ὲ μαίον[ται
(π)[λὴν                        ]ων
·[                      γα](σ)τρος
· ·[                     (υ)]σεν
χρ[                                              55
α.[.]ν[
```

```
                              ]σων
                              ]α
                           ο](ῦ)τοι
                                                60
                              ]φης
· · · ·[                      ]
ὁσ.[                          ]
· ·[                          ]
ὁν . . .(α)[                  ]               65
κε(ν) . . . .[               ]
```

P Heid ἔοικ' ἐνεῖναι· π[αντό](θ)εν γὰρ ἕλκουσιν
κοὐκ ἔστιν οὔ[τ]ε [σ]υγγενὴς οὔτε ξεῖνος
ὃ[ς ο]ὐχ[ὶ λα]ιμᾷ τ[οῦδ'] (ὅ)κως ἕξει μέζον·
χ[ω]ρὶς δέατος ὁ (θ)εσ[μὸς ο]ὐδὲ μέμνηται
θεοῦ Δικαίης ἀλλ(ὰ) [. . .](χλ)ενάζουσιν· 71
ὅκως δὲ χ(ρ)ὴ ζῆν [.].[. . .] (ἔγ)ωγε θαυ-
μ(ά)[ζω·
ἐν θηρίοισιν; ἀλλὰ δ.[.]. .(ζ)ωαί·
ἀπιστίη γε παντα[. . .].[. . . .].[. . . .]αι[
τὸ τῆς (ἀχ). . . .[. .]†πενια† τ' ἴσως πάντα[75
τὸ μειλιχῶδες κ(α)ὶ προσηνὲς δὴ τοῦτο.
ἐκεῖνο μ[ὲ]ν γὰρ ο[ἶδ]α, σὺν θεοῖς εἰπεῖν,
ὅπερ κ(ρά)[τιστ](όν) [ἐ]στιν, οὐ νενίκημ(α)[ι
[. . .].[. . . . . .] καὶ γαστ[ρὸ](ς) ἀλλ' ἀπ-
(α)ρ[κ]εῦμαι
· · · ·] (ἔχε)ις γὰρ πρῆ(ον, ἢ) τ(ί) κερδαί(ν)[εις

234
```
```

⟨51. How well could I have spared, for thee, young swain,
    Enow of such as for their bellies' sake
    Creep and intrude and climb into the fold;
    Of other care they little reckoning make
    Than . . .

            MILTON, *Lycidas*, 112 *sqq.*⟩

Such goad ⟨of avarice⟩ is in their souls: they drag
gain from every source: and there is neither kin nor
friend but ventures all in quest of gain. Divine Law
has no terrors, nor are they mindful of the goddess
of justice but mock at her. I wonder only how
one should live among these beasts: nay here life is
unlivable. All around faithlessness overcomes the
cause of spotless faith and all things, perchance,
riot on this comfortable and attractive doctrine.
Nay, but, by heaven's grace, I know that old rule
which is best: I am no slave of pleasures or of my
belly, but am content with little. What[1] civil-

---

[1] One is tempted to *conjecture* πρῆξιν or πλεῖον 'profit,' but neither can be read.

---

55. A mark of corruption. If the equation with P Heid. is sound five *vv.* have dropped out. The endings of *vv.* from P Heid. are *v.* 38 and *v.* 40 ἦν etc. 55. ? χρόνος δὲ φευγέτω σε μηδὲ εἷς ἀργός (p. 6). 57-61. ? om. P Lond., which marks corruption. 59, 61. So Bi. 66. *e.g.* κέντρον: or κε(ί)νοις? (Mn.) 67. . . . κ.ε(ν)[(optime quadrat εοικε εν vel εοικ ειν) P Lond.: εοικεν P Heid. suppl. G. 68. καὶ οὐκ P Heid.: vestigia P Lond. cum κουκ εστιν quadrant. suppl. G. 69. non fuit το[λμ]ᾷ π[άνθ' Bi.-K.: supplevi. 70. θεσμὸς supplevi probante Bi.: cett. Gerhard. 71. suppl. Hense: praecessit *e.g.* νιν. 72. supplevimus ego et Powell: *e.g.* τοῦσδε. 73. (K.-Bi.) *e.g.* δ(ύσβιοι). 74. *e.g.* πανταχοῦ πίστεως νικᾷ. 75. *e.g.* ἀχράντου Sitzler: nullum spatium ante πενία G.-Bi.: στρηνιᾷ reposui, coll. *v.* 36. fin. legi rectissime (iudice Bi.). 77, 78, 79. suppl. G. 79. init. *e.g.* λαιμαργίης. 80. πρηον Bi.: ad *v.* 73 refero: init. *e.g.* τί δῆτ'. cett. leg. K.-Bi.

ἰδώ](ν γ)έ πως κάνδ(υλ)ον (ὠ)ς οὕτως εἰ-
π(ώἰνἰ);
                                                81
εἰς] (γ)ὰρ στόμ' ὡς ἔοικ[εν] (ἴ)στ(α)[τ]αι
μο(ῦ)νον
χρό]νον τοσ[οῦ]τον [ὅσσον ἄν] τις ἔσθη [τι],
(ὅτα)ν δ' ἀμείψητα[ι αὐτ](ὸ) καὶ τ(ὸ)[ν ἤκι-
σ](τ)ον
εἰς ζῆν χ(ά)ρυβδ(ιν) [. . . . .]. οἴχεται πά[ν-
τ](α)·
                                                85
καὶ ταῦτα τεν[. . . .].[.]. .ε καὶ ἑτερ(ο)
[. . . . .]
ὑπὲρ δὲ τούτων [μ]ὴ πάτει λίνων [. . . . .
ἐγὼ μὲν οὖν, ὦ Π[άρ]νε, (τα)ῦτ' οὐχὶ ζ[ηλῶ
ἀλλ' ἐν χαλ[ινοῖς .].[.] ἐ(μ)αυτὸν ὡ(ς [. . . . . .
γαστρὸς κατ(ί)σ(χ)[ω. .].[. . .]βιά[ζ]ομαι τ[οῦ-
τον
                                                90
πρὸς εὐτέλε(ια)ν τ[ὸ]ν [βί](ον) κα(θ)ίστασ(θ)[αι
καὶ μὴν ὅτ[α]ν γε (θἠὸ).[. .] σ(π)έν(δ)ειν . [
κάμνω· με[γ]ίσ(τη δ') [. .].[. .]. [.].(μοι) χό(ν)-
[δρος
τέρπει δέ μ' οὕτως (ο)[ὐ](δ)[ἐ]ν ὡς τὸ κερ-
δ(αί)[νειν
ἐκ] τοῦ δικαίου το[. . . . .]. [τ]οῖς ἀν[θ]ρώ-
(π)[οις
                                                95
. .λαμ]βάνειν .[.].[. .].[. . .] ἐκ τρόπ[ων] α[ἰ-
σχρῶν
. . . .].[.](νενο)ν . .[. . . .]. ουθεν . .[.].[
. . . . . . χρ]όνῳ π[λ]ο(υ)τοῦντας ἐξ ἀ[. . . . . .
. . . .]. (τ). .(ν). . . (ὤ)σπ(ερ) ουδ(ο). .[
ἔστιν γάρ, ἔστιν, ὅ(ς τ)ά(δε σ)κοπεῖ (δ)αίμων
ὃ(ς ἐ)ν χρόνῳ τὸ θεῖον οὐ καταισχύνει,   101
νέ]μει δ' ἑκάστῳ τὴν καταίσιον μοῖραν.

ization is it, what boots it, to glimpse, so to say, a
bonne bouche? For what is set in the mouth remains
only for the moment of eating : after it has passed
through but a moment, all goes into a live [1] abyss.
Eat then cheerfully just so much as I do and no
more : beyond this walk not as a bird into the
net. These maxims, Parnos, I not only admire, but
keep myself obedient as ⟨a horse⟩ in belly-bands,
and force myself to order my life to simplicity. Aye
and when I must sacrifice to some pleasure I am
weary of it, since a pinch of salt is enough pleasure
for me, and nothing delights me so much as to win
from just dealing that ⟨which never⟩ comes to men
from base courses, ⟨as I now see many⟩ for a short
while enriching themselves by shamelessness,⟨though
their wealth vanishes⟩ as if ⟨it had never come⟩. For
there is indeed a divinity who looks on these things
and in time's course brings not to shame the godhead, but gives to each his due portion. So I,

---

[1] γαστήρ is derived (*E.M.*) to mean ἡ πάντα τὸν βίον λαμ-
βάνουσα μὴ πληρουμένη.

---

81. init. leg. Bi.-K.   supplevi. fin. leg. εἴπω.   82. supplevi: ἵσταται K.-Bi.   83. init. supplevi ex Greg. Naz.
(ii. 444).   ἐσθῃ .. vel ἐσθίη Bi.   supplevi.   84. supplevi.   85. suppl. G. init. K.-Bi.   med. *e.g.* δή τιν'.
86. *e.g.* τένδειν χρή σε καὶ ἑτέρῳ δοῦναι.   87. πατ. K.-Bi.
[ὄρνις.   88. suppl. G.   89. suppl. G.   *e.g.* νῦν]
ἐμαυτὸν ὡς (leg. K.-Bi.) [πῶλον.   90. *e.g.* καὶ ἐκβ. Hense.
τοῦτο G.: τοῦτον Hense.   91. suppl. G.   92. suppl. G.
θηδονὴ K.   σπένδειν K.-Bi.   93. supplevi *e.g.* ἐσθ' ἁλός γ'
ἐμοί: praecesserit (92) χρήζω.   94. suppl. Kroll, Powell, ed.
95. suppl. G.   *e.g.* τοῦθ' ὅπερ.   96. init. suppl. G.
e.g. οὔ, ἔξεστιν.   fin. supplevi. *Cf. e.g.* Plut. *Mor.* 570
πλουτοῦσιν ἀπὸ πραγμάτων αἰσχρῶν.   97 sqq. I translate
as *F.G.A.* p. x.   102, 103. suppl. G.   102. καταισιαν
P. After this *v.* follows Ἴαμβος Φοίνικος, another citation
(from Phoenix ?), then a comic *fr.*

CERCIDEA

> ἐγ]ὼ μὲν οὖν, ὦ Πά(ρ)νε, βουλοίμην εἶναι
> τἀρκεῦντ’ ἐμαυτῷ καὶ νομίζεσθαι χρηστός
> ἢ πολλὰ πρήσσειν, καί ποτ’ εἰπεῖν τοὺς
>   ἐχθρούς   105
> ‘ ἁλῶν δὲ φόρτος ἔνθεν ἦλθεν ἔνθ’ ἦλθεν.’

106. αλων ex αλλων.

Parnos, would wish to have just what sufficeth me, and to be considered worthy, rather than to busy myself and give my enemies scope for saying ' The salt cargo returns whence it came.'[1]

[1] A proverb of wasted labour—with a gibe at the Cynic's diet (*v.* 93).

FRAGMENTA
CHOLIAMBICA

EUPOLIS

Ἀνόσια πάσχω ταῦτα ναὶ μὰ τὰς νύμφας.
πολλοῦ μὲν οὖν δίκαια ναὶ μὰ τὰς κράμβας.

(Priscian *de metr. Com.* 415 K. Eupolis Βάπταις . . . hos
. . . posuit in fine habentes spondeos (1, 2).

PHOENIX

ΙΑΜΒΟϹ Α. ΝΙΝΟϹ

fr. 1 (1 Powell)

Ἀνὴρ Νίνος τις ἐγένετ᾽ ὡς ἐγὼ κλύω
Ἀσσύριος ὅστις εἶχε χρυσίου πόντον,
τὰ δ᾽ ἄλλα πολλῷ πλε<ῦ>να Κασπίης ψάμμου·
ὃς οὐκ ἴδ᾽ ἀστέρ᾽ οὐ [δίζ]ων ἐδίζητο,

1. ἐγὼ ᾽κούω Bgk.   3. τάλαντα πολλῷ Ε: καὶ τἄλλα πολλὸν
cod. A.   The above reading seems to explain the variants,
but it may be Ph. wrote τὰ δ᾽ ἀγαθά: *cf.* the proverb πόντος
ἀγαθῶν.   4. *e.g.* οὐχ ἅλων.

242

EUPOLIS

Unholy wrongs I bear by Nymphs swear I!
Nay rightfully by cabbages swear I.

(Eupolis in the *Baptae* wrote the following verses with
spondees at the end (1, 2). *Priscian* on *Comic Metres*.)

PHOENIX

POEM I. NINOS[1]

1

There was a man called Ninos, I am told,
Assyrian, who possessed a sea of gold
And all things else more than the Caspian sand :
Who ne'er the stars nor orb of heaven scanned

[1] The song is one of many variants of an alleged inscription
on the tomb of Sardanapallus in the Chaldaean tongue, of
which two translations, one in verse and one in prose, were
current in Greek. The poise of the fingers of the statue
was interpreted as dismissing everything else as worth no
more than a flick. I do not think that Phoenix wrote *books*
of Iambi. This was the first poem in his book.

FRAGMENTA CHOLIAMBICA

οὐ παρὰ μάγοισι πῦρ ἱερὸν ἀνέστησεν,
ὥσπερ νόμος, ῥάβδοισι τοῦ θεοῦ ψαύων.
οὐ μυθιήτης οὐ δικασπόλος κεῖνος·
οὐ λεωλογεῖν ἐμάνθαν' οὐκ ἀμιθρῆσαι.
ἀλλ' ἦν ἄριστος ἐσθίειν τε καὶ πίνειν
κηρᾶν, τὰ δ' ἄλλα πάντα κατὰ πετρῶν ὤθει
ὡς δ' ἀπέθαν' ὡνήρ, πᾶσι κατέλιπε ῥῆσιν
ὅκου Νίνος νῦν ἐστί †καὶ τὸ σῆμ' αϊδέ‹ς›†
"Ακουσον εἴτ' 'Ασσύριος εἴτε καὶ Μῆδος
εἷς ἢ Κοραξός, ἢ 'πὸ τῶν ἄνω λιμνῶν
‹Σ›ινδὸς κομήτης· οὐ γὰρ ἀλλὰ κηρύσσω· 1⟨
ἐγὼ Νίνος πάλαι ποτ' ἐγενόμην πνεῦμα,
νῦν δ' οὐκέτ' οὐδέν, ἀλλὰ γῆ πεποίημαι·
ἔχω δ' ὁκόσον ἔδαισα [χὠκόσσ' ἤεισα]
χὠκόσ[σ] ἠράσθην,
τὰ δ' ὄλβι' ἡμέων δήιοι συνελθόντες
φέρουσιν ὥσπερ ὠμὸν ἔριφον αἱ Βάκχαι· 2⟨
ἐγὼ δ' ἐς "Αιδην οὔτε χρυσὸν οὔθ' ἵππον
οὔτ' ἀργυρῆν ἄμαξαν ᾠχόμην ἕλκων·
σποδὸς δὲ πολλὴ χὠ μιτρηφόρος κεῖμαι.

(Ath. 530 e Φοῖνιξ δὲ ὁ Κολοφώνιος ποιητὴς περὶ Νίνου λέγω⟨
ἐν τῷ πρώτῳ τῶν 'Ιάμβων γράφει οὕτως (1).)

7. μυθιήτης codd. : corr. Schweighäuser.   12. is often
regarded as an insertion.   σῆμα (ϊ)δει cod. A.   15. corr.
by Schweig.   18. χὠκοσσ' ἐράσθην cod. : corr. Bgk.
Perhaps we should write two verses : so translation.   Hdl.
read ὁκόσσ' ἔπαισα (Kaibel), χὠκ. ἤεισα, χὠκόσσ' ἔδ‹ωκα γαστρί›,
κτλ. (v.l. ὁκόσσον ἔδ.).   For this I would compare exactly
Greg. Naz. Carm. (ii. 780 Colon) ἔπαιξεν, ἦσε, γαστρὸς ἔπλησεν
νόσον.

PHOENIX

Nor duly at his magi's side with rod
Stirred up the holy fire and touched his god.
No spokesman was, nor counsellor this man,
No marshal, no reviewer of his clan ;
Wine, food, and lust of all men he adored
The most : aught else but these went by the board :
And when he died he left, to all to say
(Where town and tomb alike are hid to-day) [1] :—
' Assyrian and Median, give ear
Unto my preaching ! hear Koraxian ! hear
Thou long-haired Sindian from the Upper Mere :
I Ninos once of yore was living breath :
And now am nought but common earth in death.
All that I ate ⟨or drank⟩ †and all my song†
And all my lechery to me belong.
But all my goods my foes have ravishéd
And sundered as a Maenad doth a kid.
And I to Hades neither gold did bring
Nor horse, nor car of silver panelling :
I that did wear the diadem on my brow
A far-flung scattering of ash [2] am now.'

(Phoenix the poet of Colophon speaking of Ninos in his
first Iambus says (1). *Athenaeus.*)

---

[1] See Addenda.
[2] πολλή whether " wide-spread " as I take it, or " a heap "
as Mr. J. U. Powell suggests to me, is probably right. To
my ear it suggests ὥσπερ οἱ πολλοί, which is the point of the
poem. I have introduced this in *v.* 16 (transl.). Ninos did
not have the grand burial of the old Assyrian princes, as to
which we are learning new details. For the earliest burials
with jewelled cars and asses see C. L. Woolley in the *Times*,
p. 11, Jan. 12, 1928.

FRAGMENTA CHOLIAMBICA

ΚΟΡΩΝΙϹΤΑΙ

fr. 2 (2 Powell)

Ἐσθλοί, κορώνη χεῖρα πρόσδοτε κριθέων,
τῇ παιδὶ τὠπόλλωνος, ἢ λέκος πυρῶν
ἢ ἄρτον, ἢ ἤμαιθον, ἢ ὅτι τις χρῄζει.
δότω, 'γαθοί, τις, τῶν ἕκαστος ἐν χερσίν
ἔχει, κορώνη. χάλα λήψεται χονδρόν·   5
φιλεῖ γὰρ αὕτη πάγχυ ταῦτα δαίνυσθαι·
ὁ νῦν ἅλας δοὺς αὖθι κηρίον δώσει.
ὦ παῖ, θύρην ἄγκλινε, Πλοῦτος †ἤκουσε†,
καὶ τῇ κορώνῃ παρθένος φέρ‹ο›ι σῦκα.
θεοί, γένοιτο πάντ' ἄμεμπτος ἡ κούρη   10
κἀφνειὸν ἄνδρα κὠ‹υ›νομαστὸν ἐξεύροι
καὶ τῷ γέροντι πατρὶ κοῦρον εἰς χεῖρας
καὶ μητρὶ κούρην εἰς τὰ γοῦνα καθείη,   13
‹   .   .   .   .   ›   13a
θάλος, τρ‹ό›φ[ε]ιν, γυναῖκα, τοῖς κασιγνήτοις.
ἐγὼ δ' ὅκο‹ι› πόδες φέρ‹ω›σιν, ὀφθαλμούς
†ἀμείβ†ομαι Μούσῃσι, πρὸς θύρῃσ' ᾄδων,   16
καὶ δοντὶ καὶ μὴ δοντί, πλεῦνα ‹τετ›τίγων.   17

ἀλλ', ὦγαθοί, 'πορέξαθ' ὧν μυχὸς πλουτεῖ·   18
δός, ὦ ‹ἄ›ναξ, δὸς καὶ σὺ πότνα μοι νύμφη·

1 (and 20). ‹s› χεῖρα?   4. τις after ἕκαστος codd.
Ath.   7. αὖθις codd.   8. e.g. l. ἥκει σοι.
9. φέρει codd.: corr. Bgk.   14. τρέφειν codd.
15. ὅκου, φέρουσι codd.: corr. Dind., Bgk.   16. -αισι,
-αις codd.: corr. Cr.   16. See on Herodas (C.E.), p. 395,
where add Opp. Cyn. iv. 199, ii. 222.   e.g. ἐρείδομαι:
Greg. Naz. Or. i. 477 Β οἱ μὲν πόδες ἐφέρον[το] ἡ δὲ ὄψις εἶχε
τὴν θάλατταν fixes the sense and punctuation.   17. τωνγεω
codd.   19. so Cr.

PHOENIX

THE CHOUGH-BEGGARS

2

Good sirs, give to Apollo's child the chough
A fist of barley, crock of loaves, enough
Of bread, a farthing.   Each give what he will
Of what he has in hand, kind sirs, to me
The chough.   Coarse salt will not distasteful be.   5
On all these things she loves full well to thrive.
Who now gives salt a honeycomb shall give.
Sir slave ! open the door.   Let wealth come in
What time the girl brings figs from store within.
Pray God the maiden lead a virtuous life   10
And to a famous man and rich be wife.
And set a son upon her father's knee,   12
A daughter on her mother's ; and may she
As child or girl or woman ⟨bring delight,
When forth she ventures⟩ [1] to her brothers' sight.
I, as I wander over dale and hill,
Keep my eyes fixed upon the Muses still ;   15
And, be ye churl or lavish, at your wicket
More blithely will I sing than any cricket.   17

. . . . . .

Kind sirs, set forth what cupboard has in store,   18
Kind master give, kind mistress give me more.

---

[1] Clearly a verse is missing.   The sense is secured by
Hom. ζ 154 sqq. τρισμάκαρες μὲν σοί γε πατὴρ καὶ πότνια μήτηρ,
τρισμάκαρες δὲ κασίγνητοι· μάλα πού σφισι θυμὸς αἰὲν εὐφροσύνησιν
ἰαίνεται εἵνεκα σεῖο λευσσόντων τοιόνδε θάλος χορὸν εἰσοιχνεῦσαν.
The line lost was something like κῆρ εὐφρανέουσαν ἡνίκ' ἐς
χορὸν φοιτῇ.   The Greeks (in literary tradition) were very fond
of their sisters.   We are not.

FRAGMENTA CHOLIAMBICA

νόμος κορώνῃ χεῖρα δοῦν᾽ ἐπαιτούσῃ.
†τοιαῦτ᾽ εἰδὼς† δός τι καὶ καταχρήσει.

(Ath. viii. 359 e οἶδα δὲ Φοίνικα τὸν Κολοφώνιον ἰαμβοποιὸν
μνημονεύοντά τινων ἀνδρῶν ὡς ἀγειρόντων τῇ κορώνῃ καὶ λέγοντα
(? -ων) ταῦτα (vv. 1-17). καὶ ἐπὶ τέλει δὲ τοῦ Ἰάμβου φησίν
(vv. 18-21).)

It is remarkable that these verses differ (metrically) *toto
caelo* from those of I and III : perhaps they are written
after Callimachus' criticisms in his *Iambi*. More probably
Phoenix varies metre with subject.

21. *e.g.* τοσαῦτ᾽ ἀείδω Bgk.

‹ΝΕΟΠΛΟΥΤΟΙ›

fr. 3 (6 Powell)

π(ολ)λοῖς γε θνητῶν τἀγ[ά]θ᾽, ὦ Ποσείδιππε,
οὐ [σύ]μφορ᾽ ἐστίν, ἀλλὰ δεῖ τοιαῦτ᾽ αὐτούς
τ](έμν)ειν, ὁκοῖα καὶ φρονε[ῖ]ν ἐπίστανται·
(νῦν) δ᾽ ο[ἴ] (μ)ὲν [ἡ]μῶν κ(ρή)[γυ]οι καθεστῶτες
(π)ολλὴν ἀ(φ)ειδέως ν(η)[σ](τίην) ἐρεύγοντα[ι   5
(οἱ) δ᾽ οὔτε σῦκα, φασίν, οὔτ᾽ ἐρίν᾽ εὔντες
(π)λουτοῦσι. τῷ πλούτῳ δὲ πρ(ὸς) τί δεῖ χρῆ[σθ]αι
τοῦτ᾽ αὐτὸ πάντων πρῶτον οὐκ ἐπίστανται,
ἀλ(λ)᾽ (ο)ἰ(κ)[ία]ς μὲν ἐκ λίθου σμαραγδίτου,
εἴ πω[ς] ἀνυστόν ἐστι τοῦτ᾽ αὐτοῖς πρήσσει(ν)   10
πά]το(ν) [τ᾽] ἔχουσας καὶ στοὰς τετραστύλους
πολλῶ]ν τ(α)λάντων ἀξίας κατακτῶ(ν)ται.
. . . . . .](δ)᾽ ἑαυτῶν τὴν ἀναγκαίην (ψυχ)ὴν
. . . .]η σκ[ωρίη το]ύτων πάντων·
. . . .].ρα [πλοῦ](τ)[ο]ν ἐκπορίζουσιν   15
. . . . λ](ό)γοις χρηστοῖ(σ)ι σωφρονισθεῖσα

1, 2. so Gerhard.   3. suppl. Bi.-K.; *cf.* Poseidippus
A.P. ix. 359.   4. νῦν etc. Cr.   κρήγυοι G.   5. νηστίην
Bücherer-Cr.   6. ερινα Papyrus.   7, 9, 10. so G.

PHOENIX

So give the chough a fistful as is fit.   20
So sing I.   Give.   You 'll ne'er repent of it.

(I recall that Phoenix the (chol)iambist of Colophon mentions certain men as collecting for the chough, and says
(saying ?) as follows (1-17).   At the end of the Iambus he
says (18-20).   *Athenaeus.*)

[THE PROFITEERS]

3

Unto full many mortals goods are not
Good, Poseidippos : such should be men's lot
As is their power to stomach.   Now, God wot,
Our nobles belch not save on sorry fare,
Those who nor garden figs nor wild figs are,   5
Are rich.   But how their riches they should spend
They know not.   An they gain their dearest end,
Houses they buy for millions houses bright
With colonnades and floor of malachite.
But for the food whereon their souls should feed,   10
They mix it with the scourings of their greed.
For base are gains when men seek wealth alone
And listen not to words of righteous tone,
To learn precisely what is right and fit.
O Poseidippus let us say of it :   15
Their houses costly are and fair of note

---

11. . .](στου)[.] Heidelb. legere visus sum : sed "besser]τον["
monet Bi.   12. so G.   13. see G. and read with him
ψυχῇ.   Beginning *e.g.* τροφήν.   14. το]ύτων G.   beginning (for sense) ἔφυρεν ἀργή.   15. *e.g.* κέρδη γὰρ αἰσχρά.
πλοῦτον dubium (Bi.).   16. *e.g.* οὐ μὴ.   λόγοις G.

249

FRAGMENTA CHOLIAMBICA

. . . . . .] (τ)ὰ χρηστὰ καὶ τὰ συμφέροντ' εἰδῇ.
[. . . . . .] τοιούτοις ἀνδράσιν, Ποσείδιππε,
. . σ]υ(μ)βέβηκεν (οἰκ)ίας μὲν κεκτῆσ(θ)α(ι)
κ](α)λὰς καταξίας τε χρημάτων πολλῶν,   2(
α]ὐτοὺς δ' ὑπάρχειν ἀξίους τ[ρι]ῶν χ(α)[λκῶ]ν;
κ]αὶ μάλα δικαίως, ἤν τις ἐνθυμῇτ' [ὀρ]θῶς
. . . .]ν γὰρ καὶ λίθων φροντίζουσιν.

(In Cercidas' Anthology with lemma Ἴαμβος Φοίνικος (η')
Follows at once (? τοῦ αὐτοῦ))

3*

. . . .(μ') [οἱ]κι. [. .] (ἀ)νιστᾶσιν

    .   .   .   .   .   .

17. *e.g.* ὀρθῶς.   18. *e.g.* τοῖς οὖν G.   19. οὐ συμβ. G
20, 21, 22, 23. So G.

---

[1] The anthology does not add materially to the reputation
of the poet. Athenaeus would appear to have selected hi
two best pieces. But it gives us their scope—say twenty t
fifty lines—and shows us that 1 and 2 may be nearly complete. Moreover, Poseidippus gives us a clue as to date
that is that this poem may be later than 275, if this (Gerhard

PHOENIX

But they themselves are worth not half a groat.[1]
And rightly, too, such verdict may we give,
‹For stones they are and› unto stones they live.[2]

(The first citation in *Cercidas*' anthology, ' One of *Phoenix*'
Iambi.' The citation which follows in the same metre—the
title has been lost—runs :)

3*

. . . set up hous. . .

is the Poseidippus who was then studying in Athens under
Zeno and Cleanthes. Another identification (see below) is
with the comic poet who lived later. But again, if my
reading in *v. 2* is rightly approved by Bilabel, the epi-
grammatist (of the same date as the comic poet) must also
be considered. Indeed the piece might be a commentary on
the epigram ποίην τις βιότοιο τάμοι τρίβον ;

[2] Such seems to be the most apposite ending but it is
somewhat hard to fit in. See Gerhard pp. 134, 140. Perhaps
λίθοι τ' ἔφυν (Pind. *P*. i. 42), written ἔφυσαν.

PHOENIX (?)

A Papyrus at Strassburg (*W.G.* 304-307)[1] contains on the recto an anthology of lyrics from tragedy. On the verso is what appears undoubtedly to be part of the Cercidas anthology. In general the metres are iambic and the subjects chosen for their ethical value. There are no names of authors given. The date of the hand, according to Bell, Lobel, and Bilabel, is the middle of the third century B.C. It can hardly be doubted that the author of the choliambi given below is Phoenix. The metre is identical with that used by Phoenix in the Heidelberg fragment; and the loose flowing repetitive style is typical of all we have of him. Another reason, observed by W. Crönert, is that the name Lynceus occurs in this, and Poseidippus in the Heidelberg fragment. Lynceus is known to have written letters to Poseidippus, possibly those of an elder to a pupil. If, as may be, it is Lynceus who is dead, the verses may have been written about 280 B.C.: for Lynceus is called a contemporary of Menander, Poseidippus being younger, or at least younger as a writer: see Suid. *s.vv.*, Ath. viii. 337 d. The anthology, then, is almost contemporary with the verses, if these names are those of the well known writers of Attic comedy.

[1] *Gött. Gel. Nachr.*, 1922, i. 31.

FRAGMENTA CHOLIAMBICA

This may be a convenient place to note two points : *firstly*, the metre of the fragment. There are two licenses employed by Greek writers as a variant of the rigid form $\smile - \smile - \smile | - \smile - \smile - - -$. One is to allow many resolutions. Phoenix adopts this in two pieces. The other is to allow the ending $- - - -$. This is adopted by Phoenix in two pieces ; also by the author of the anthology whom Gregory calls Cercidas. Callimachus eschews both licences, though occasionally admitting an undivided trochee : Herodes uses both. *Secondly*, we may now place the anthology collector, who contributed the preface, as writing about 250 B.C., and roundly assert that this metre was as far as we know and in all probability not used between 200 B.C. and the Christian era. Earlier columns of the Strassburg portion of the Anthology are not well re-assembled yet. Below this poem we have the verses (already edited by Crönert) :

> ἀγαπᾶτε τοῦτον πάντες ὃς ἔχει τἀγαθά[1]
> ἅπαντ᾽ ἐν αὐτῷ, χρηστός, εὐγενής, ἁπλοῦς,
> φιλοβασιλεύς, ἀνδρεῖος, ἐν[2] πίστει μέγας,
> σώφρων, φιλέλλην, πραΰς, εὐπροσήγορος,
> τὰ πανοῦργα μισῶν, τὴν ἀλήθειαν σέβων.

Next column contains three pseudo-Epicharmic verses, ἐπιστα . . . | τιμαν θεοι . . . | αὐτὸν κυβερ(ν)[—clearly of ruling the tongue. At the bottom is a fragment of Attic comedy of which I give the beginnings of the last nine verses :Ἄπολλον Ἀ(γρ εὖ ? ?) | οὕτως δ᾽ ἂν ἐμ | ἡμῖν ὑβριζ . . . | καὶ τρίποδες ἀλ. . | καὶ μὴν ἀδικεῖται ψ. . . . . . . | νῦν μοι διακόνουν . . παιδίον | ἀστεῖον οὐχ ὁμ. . . . ἐκ κει. | ἃ δ᾽ ἂν λάβω τοι δεῖ

---

[1] a horrid pun, αγαπα and αγα(θα) πα(ντ).
[2] for εμ.

διπλο᾿ ἀπο[δοῦναι | τὰ πάτρια γὰρ δὴ τῆς τέχνης |.   In
between are the interesting verses:

οὔτ(ω) τὰ πρόσθεν[
κοινῆς τραπ[έζης ἀξίωμ᾿ ἔχων ἴσον,
ἀκόλαστον ἔσ[χε γλῶσσαν αἰσχίστην νόσον.
κορυφῆς ὑπε[ρτέλλοντα δειμαίνων πέτρον[1]
τυχ. . .ετα[
ἢ πού τ[

These I quote, (a) since they give clearly the subject
of this section of the anthology—praise or blame of
the tongue: (b) since, as will be seen, the three
verses taken from the first ten lines of Euripides'
Orestes may be choliambic (ἴσον, νοῦσον, πέτρον).

We must consider briefly the subject matter. A
poet is dead. The speaker (Phoenix or, as in the
Ninos poem, another) wishes consolation for the
loss. He longs to see Lynceus, and will render him
famous by iambi at feast of bowls (and in the
country ? ?). For us there is an unfortunate am-
biguity. Does Apollo or some representative of
poetry mourn a dead writer, *e.g.* Menander, and
beseech Lynceus to replace him, with promises to
inspire him at the Dionysia in city (see *ap.* Dem.
531) and country? Or is the request for the robe
merely an aside to a slave, and is "that which was
my robe" Lynceus, and the iambi those of Phoenix
who speaks? On the whole, I believe this is so,
but have no confidence in either interpretation.

[1] *vv.* 2, 3, 4 suppl. E. Lobel.

<ANΩNYMOY EΠITYMBIOΣ>

fr. 4

```
• • • • • • • • • • .].. o.[o .] (ελπ)[. . . .] δεινοῖς
• • • • • • • • • • ] .. (μι)[..](π)ε[. . . .]ν λέσχη
.].. . .[. . . .].. (συ).[.](ν) δὲ (λ)αυψηρήν
.].. . .[. .].. (ι)δαι .[. .] (ἀσφαλ)ῆ ᾽π(οὐ)ρ(α)s
.].. . .[.].. . . . ην.(φ). [ἐν]αύεσθαι λύχνον·          5
.].. . . . . .(ε).(αλ)os, καὶ πα(νοι)κίη θάλλων
ἑτοῖμον †.. τον κ(τῆσι)ν ὦ(ν) ἐ(κ)εῖ† τήρει,
καὶ κάε χρείην καὶ π[έν](η)τος ἐμβλέψας.
. . .[. . .].. ε(s) τ. (θοιλπα) τῆς τύχης κρίνων
• • • • • •] τὸ μηδὲν καὶ κενῷ προσεμβ(α)[. . . .     10
• • • • • •](ω)δεστ.ν[ε](ξ)αγ.. πάρ σευ
• • • • • •]. .[. . . . . . . . .]. .[. . . . . .          12
              (duo versus desunt)
• • • • • • α](φν)εα .[. . .] (μηδ)[. . . . . . . .      15
• • • • • • .δ]εξιῆς ἤψ(ω) τ᾽ ἡμῶ[ν
• • • • • • .]τι τ(ῷ) θεῶν ξείνῳ
.](α)[. .].οι(το) (σοὶ) μὲν (X)εῖos (ἤ) (ἀ)πὸ τῆς
                                  Σμύρνης
```

3. *e.g.* σεαυτὸν ἴσθι τὴν τύχην . . .   4. *e.g.* δαίμον᾽
(init. ἐνταῦθα μίμνε).   5. *e.g.* ἔνθεν δέ σ᾽ ἐχρῆν ὀψ᾽.   6. *e.g.*
πρόφαινε καλός: l. -οικίη.   7. . . . τογ P: ? l. αὐτοῦ. Dein
suspicor ὡς ἔχει.   8. εβλ. P with μ superscr.: l. χρείῃ.
9. *e.g.* τὰ κοινά, τὰ δεινά cett.: init. *e.g.* σὺ δ᾽ ἥλιτες.
256

⟨EPITAPH (ON LYNCEUS?)⟩

4

Full often would I say in idle] talk,
" Beware of] dangers [if abroad you walk.
Know you are mortal] and swift Fate is not:
Abide at home where] safety is your lot.   **4**
There are the fires] from which your lamp to light,
Flourish both you and yours, and shining bright
Keep it a ready vessel there [1] with heed
And burn it, apt to serve the poorest's need.
Alas! you] scoffed at Fate's alarms, and found
Faring abroad] your [feet] on hollow ground.   **10**
No profit is there more of you for me

.   .   .   .
.   .   ' rich '   .   .   .   **15**
.   . ' my right hand clasped ' .   . **16**
.   . ' the host of gods '   .   **17**
Praise you in Smyrna, †Crete†, or Chios [2] bred   **18**

[1] In *v.* 7 I translate αὐτοῦ . . . ὡς ἔχει. P seems to have
ωνεκει. There may be an allusion here to Lynceus as a
poet: Callim. *Iamb.* 334 Ἔφεσον ὅθεν πῦρ οἱ τὰ μέτρα μέλ-
λοντες τὰ χωλὰ τίκτειν μὴ ἀμαθῶς ἐναύονται. *v.* 8 'Give a light
even to the poorest' encourages this interpretation.

[2] Clearly Homer who was born at Smyrna, Chios, Colophon, Salamis, Rhodes, Argos or Athens. The reading
'Crete' is an error, perhaps for ἢ 'Ακτῆς—'from Smyrna
or Attica.'

---

10. *e.g.* εἶναι and προσεμβαίνων.   16. ? ἡμέων.   18 *e.g.*
κλήζοιτο.

FRAGMENTA CHOLIAMBICA

(ἦ) (Κρὴs) ὅ,τ᾽ εἴη καὶ κεν(ὸν κεν)ῷ (β)ά(ξ)α(ι)·
ἐγὼ δ᾽ ὑπ᾽ ῞Αιδου (δή σε πε)[ί]θομαι γλῶσσαν   20
....[......](τα π)[ερὶ] πασ(ῶ)ν χελιδόνων·
ὃ δ᾽ (εὔκο)[.......](π)[....](φ)η(μ)[.](μυστα)ισι[.]
(σὺ)ν εὐλαβείη τ(ρι)[....]..[.....].[......
τί πόλλ᾽ ἀείδω; μ(ω)ρίη γὰρ ἡ λέσχη·
στεῖλόν μ(ε χ)λ(αί)νη· κῶς δ᾽ ἔχω ποθέω(ν) βλέψαι
Λυγκεῦ σε; ....σύ· νῦ(ν γ)ὰρ ᾧ κατέσταλμαι 26
κατερρύηκε καὶ εἰς τὸν ᾽Αίδη βαίνει.
ἐγὼ δ᾽ ἰάμβ(οι)s κἠπὶ Κρητήρων Θοί(ν)ῃ
θήσω σε τιμήεντα καὶ ἐν χώρῃ παντί.

19. Beginning very uncertain.   (ἄκρωs) would fit traces
better.   21. read περὶ χ. π.   25. στειλομ P.   26.
lectio incertissima: μή olim dedi: fort. ἄγρει.   νυγ ex
νῦν?   29. εγ P.

fr. 5 (3 Powell)

Νίνου κάδοι μάχαιρα καὶ κύλιξ αἰχμή,
κ⟨ύ⟩μ⟨β⟩η δὲ τόξα δήιοι δὲ κρητῆρες,
ἵπποι δ᾽ ἄκρητος κἀλαλὴ ῾ μύρον ⟨χ⟩εῖτ⟨ε⟩.᾽

(Ath. x. 421 d καὶ ὁ Κολοφώνιοs δὲ Φοῖνίξ φησιν (5).)

5. 2. κόμη corrected by Haupt.   3. κεῖται by Lachmann.

ANECDOTUM ARGENTINENSE

Some empty singer to an empty head [1] :
But you have ta'en below, I wot, a tongue   20
That has all twittering swallows far outsung.[2]   21
.   .   .   .   22
' with caution '   23
Why sing I long ; for idle talk is folly.   24
Robe me ! How suffer I, who long to see   25
You, Lynceus, once again ! Come ! robe thou me.
For that which was my robe has vanished quite [3]
And treads the path to Hades out of sight.
But I at country-side and Feast of Bowls [4]
Will win your verses honour from all souls.   30

[1] See *Paroem.* κενοὶ κενὰ βουλεύονται and πρὸς κενὴν (or -ὸν) ψάλλεις.
[2] *vv.* 20 and 21 echo Phoenix *fr.* 1 *v.* 21 and *fr.* 2 *v.* 17 .
[3] See Headlam's note on Herodes ii. 15.
[4] ' Feast of Bowls ' : conceivably two mixing-bowls, one for the living and one for the dead. Ionic has no dual. As Phoenix lived at Ephesus, the probable scene for Mime V. of Herodes, this appears as a *possible* name of the feast which Herodes paraphrased with the words ἐπεὰν δὲ τοῖς καμοῦσιν ἐγχυτλώσωμεν (84). But see above.

5

For casks were Ninus' sword and jugs his spear,
Cups were his arrows, bowls his enemy,
Ho ointment ! his alarm, liqueurs his cavalry.

(And Phoenix of Colophon says (5).   *Athenaeus.*)

FRAGMENTA CHOLIAMBICA

fr. 6 (4 Powell)

Θαλῆς γὰρ †ὅστις† ἀστέ[ρ]ων ὀνήιστος
καὶ τῶν τότ᾽, ὡς λέγουσι, πολλ⟨ὸ⟩ν ἀνθρώπων
ἐὼν ἄριστος, ἔλαβε πελλίδα χρυσῆν.

(Ath. xi. 495 d Φοῖνιξ δ᾽ ὁ Κολοφώνιος ἐν τοῖς Ἰάμβοις ἐπὶ
φιάλης τίθησι τὴν λέξιν λέγων οὕτως (6).   καὶ ἐν ἄλλῳ δὲ μέρει
φησίν (7).)

fr. 7 (5 Powell)

Hippon. *fr.* 76*.

fr. 8

ὁ μὲν γὰρ αὐτῶν ἡσυχῇ τε καὶ ῥύδην
θύνν†ον† τε καὶ μυττωτὸν ἡμέρας πάσας
δαινύμενος ὥσπερ Λαμψακηνὸς εὐνοῦχος
κατέφαγε δὴ τὸν [σ]κλῆρον, †ὥστε χρῆ†
σκάπτειν

6. 1. ὅστις : read *e.g.* ἀστοῖς.   ἀστέων (from false mss. of
Hdt.) : Casaubon's certain correction (quam nemo umquam
dubitavit literarum Graecarum vel minime peritus). Here are
the disjecta membra in Hdt. alone :—τῶν τότε + superlative
i. 23, viii. 8, ix. 72, *cf.* iii. 125 : ἀνθρώπων + sup. i. 24, 45, iv.
91, viii. 68 : τῶν ἀστῶν + sup. or δόκιμος i. 158, iii. 20, iv. 14,
161, v. 63, 97, 126, vi. 61, 101, vii. 118, viii. 46, ix. 93.   It is
true that the expression is intolerably diffuse, but so is all
that we have of Phoenix.   Compare Theogn. v. 23.   On
ἀστεύς see my *First Greek Anthologist*, p. 24.   2. -ῶν
A : corr. by Toup.   3. *v.l.* πελλιάδα.

PHOENIX (?)

6

For Thales, to his townsmen usefullest
Of townsmen, and, say they, by far the best
Of men then living took the paillet gold.

(Phoenix of Colophon in his *Iambi* uses the word (paillet)
of a cup as follows (6). Elsewhere[1] he says (7). *Athenaeus*.)

7

Hippon. *fr*. 76.

8

One day by day luxuriously dined
In ease on cheese-cake spiced and tunny brined,
Like eunuch Lampsacene : his portion done
He fain would dig 'mid mountain rocks and stone ;

[1] It is clearly impossible to suppose these words are right.
In what other part? For these are iambi like the others.
But we know of various books of Hipponax, and if we transfer
the text of Athenaeus (or of Lysanias behind it) we get a
natural sequence καὶ πάλιν (495 d) . . . καὶ ἐν ἄλλῳ δὲ μέρει
(495 e). The gravest stylistic argument is that Phoenix was
wholly incapable of such compression as the three verses
show.

---

8. 2. θύνναν A, θύννον C, θυννίδα Meineke.   4. σκληρὸν
cod. Ath.: corr. Dalecamp.   ὥστε χρὴ cod. Ath.: leg.
χρῇ: Soph. *Ant*. 887 (Jebb).   So ten Brink.

FRAGMENTA CHOLIAMBICA

πέτρας [τ'] ὀρείας σῦκα μέτρια τρώγων   5
καὶ κρίθινον κόλλικα δούλιον χόρτον.

(Ath. vii. 303 c θυννίς . . . 304 b Ἱππῶναξ δὲ ὡς Λυσανίας ἐν
τοῖς περὶ ⟨τῶν⟩ ἰαμβοποιῶν παρατίθεται, φησίν (8).)

The evidence for attributing this fragment to Hipponax
appears faulty. On the one hand Athenaeus' attribution is plain, the divisions and the breaks are good,
and the connexion with *fr.* 17 (so most edd.) attractive.
Against this we have (*a*) ῥύδην so typical of later choliambists (ἐμπτύοι Hrd., καταπτῦ (?) Cercid., κλύω Phoenix).
(*b*) The moral tone. (*c*) Three cases of resolution in the first
foot—for Athenaeus seems to have read θυννίδα in *v.* 2. Of
course his text may have been corrected from better codd.,

AESCHRION

fr. 1. μήνη τὸ καλὸν οὐρανοῦ νέον σίγμα
  2*. στενὸν καθ' Ἑλλήσποντον ἐμπόρων χώρην
     ναῦται θαλάσσης ἐστρέφοντο μύρμηκες.
  3*. ὁ δ' ἐξελὼν ἱμάντα φορτίου ζώνην
  4*. ἶρις δ' ἔλαμψε καλὸν οὐρανοῦ τόξον.
  5*. καὶ πίσσαν ἐφθὴν ἣν θύραι μυρίζονται

(Tzetz. *Rhet. Gr.* iii. 650 Walz ὡς τὴν σελήνην οὐρανοῦ
πάλιν Αἰσχρίων σίγμα· οὕτω γὰρ λέξεσιν αὐταῖς αὐτὸ Αἰσχρίων
λέγει (1)· τὸν λόγον ἐκτραχύνουσι, σκληρύνουσι δὲ πλέον ἢ μᾶλλον
εἰς ψυχρότητα σύρουσι γελαστέαν, ὡς καὶ ὁ γράψας τὰ ψυχρὰ
ταυτὶ τῶν ἰαμβείων (2) καὶ πολλαχοῦ δυστηνὰ τοιαυτὶ λέγει
(3-5).

AESCHRION

And peck at fodder whereon slaves are fed,
A modicum of figs and barley bread.

(Tunny . . . ; Hipponax, as Lysanias says in his work
on the (chol)iambic poets, remarks (8). *Athenaeus.*)

---

if these were extant. Again, *v.* 4 is wholly unsatisfactory
though the resolution is not objectionable. (*d*) The fact
that the citation is second-hand. If genuine we should have
to read *e.g. v.* 1 ῥύβδην (Bgk.), *v.* 2 μυσσωτὸν *id.*, *v.* 3 ὥστε,
v. 4 κατ' **ὧν** φαγὼν and ὥστε θὴς σκάπτει and in *v.* 2 keep
θυννόν C (θύνναν A). Even so μέτριᾶ τρώγων is wrong for
Hipponax, but right for Phoenix (2. 1, 6. 3).

AESCHRION

1. O Moon the heaven's pretty new sigma [1]
2*. Sea-ants the sailors swarmed, where their
     business
   The merchants have in Hellespont's narrows.
3*. So he unloosed a strap, a bale's girdle
4*. A rainbow shone, the heaven's fair iris. [2]
5*. And boiling pitch, a portal's anointment

(Or again as Aeschrion calls the moon the heaven's
pretty sigma. Here are his exact words (1). Thus style is
rendered ' rougher,' I should rather say ' harsher,' or better
still ' diverted to a ridiculous bathos,' as is the case with
the author of these iambi which are typical of bathos (2).
With him these unfortunate effects are common (3-5).
Tzetzes in *Rhetores Graeci.*)

[1] C, not Σ.   [2] Transposing the original.

FRAGMENTA CHOLIAMBICA

fr. 6

ἐγὼ Φιλαινὶς ἠπίβωτος ἀνθρώποις
ἐνταῦθα γήρᾳ τῷ μακρῷ κεκοίμημαι.
μή μ', ὦ μάταιε ναῦτα, τὴν ἄκρην κάμπτων
χλεύην τε ποιεῦ καὶ γέλωτα καὶ λάσθην·
οὐ γὰρ μὰ τὸν Ζῆν', οὐ μὰ τοὺς κάτω Κούρους,   5
οὐκ ἦν ἐς ἄνδρας μάχλος οὐδὲ δημώδης·
Πολυκράτης δὲ τὴν γενὴν Ἀθηναῖος
λόγων τ⟨ε⟩ παιπάλημα καὶ κακὴ γλῶσσα
ἔγραψεν ⟨ὅ⟩σσ' ἔγραψ'· ἐγὼ γὰρ οὐκ οἶδα.

(Ath. viii. 335 b Φιλαινίδος εἰς ἣν ἀναφέρεται τὸ περὶ
Ἀφροδισίων ἀκόλαστον σύγγραμμα ὅπερ φησὶ ποιῆσαι Αἰσχρίων
ὁ Σάμιος ἰαμβοποιὸς Πολυκράτη τὸν σοφιστὴν ἐπὶ διαβολῇ τῆς
ἰνθρώπου σωφρονεστάτης γενομένης. ἔχει δὲ οὕτως τὰ ἰαμβεῖα (6).
Α.P. vii. 345 ἀδέσποτον· οἱ δὲ Σιμωνίδου.)

fr. 7

καὶ θεῶν ⟨βρῶσιν⟩
ἄγρωστιν εὗρες ἣν Κρόνος κατέσπειρεν.

(Ath. vii. 296 e Αἰσχρίων δ' ὁ Σάμιος ἔν τινι τῶν ἰάμβων
Ὕδνης φησὶ τῆς Σκύλλου (*cf. Α.P.* ix. 296)(Hdt. viii. 8) τοῦ
Σκιωναίου κατακολυμβητοῦ θυγατρὸς τὸν θαλάσσιον Γλαῦκον
ἐρασθῆναι. ἰδίως δὲ καὶ περὶ τῆς βοτάνης λέγει ἣν φαγὼν
ἀθάνατος ἐγένετο (7).)

6. *vv. ll.* 4 λάσθηνν, 5 Ζεῦν, οὐδὲ, 6 ἠιν, 7 γυνὴν, 8 οἷα
and ἄσσα.   8. τι Ath., *Α.P.*
7. 1. so Haupt.

AESCHRION

6

Philaenis I, the whole wide world's byword,
Lie resting here after a long old age.
O idle sailor, rounding the headland,
Spare me your jeers, derisions and mockings,
For so I swear by Zeus, and by Hell's Youths [1]
Ne'er was I common woman, nor lustful.
Polycrates, Athenian native,
Evil of tongue and crafty word-monger,
Wrote of me what he wrote : for I know not.

(Philaenis, to whom is ascribed the obscene work on erotics,
said by Aeschrion of Samos, the writer of iambi, to have
been written by Polycrates the sophist to libel the woman,
who was, in fact, a model of chastity. *Athenaeus.* Also in
the *Palatine Anthology* with lemma "On Philaenis the
courtesan from Elephantiné who painted on a tablet the
famous γυναικείας μίξεις on account of which she is lampooned
by the Athenian wits." A scholiast (*A.P.*) repeats the
charge quoting Lucian (*Amor.* 28).

7

And agrostis
Did'st find, the Gods' repast, sown by Kronos.

(Aeschrion of Samos in one of his iambi says that the
sea deity Glaucus was enamoured of Hydna, daughter of
Scyllus [2] the Scionean diver. And he has an original statement about the food which he ate and became immortal
(7). *Athenaeus.*)

[1] The Dioscuri. For the ellipse of (Dios) compare
Herodes, i. 32.
[2] Scyllus or Scyllies was (Hdt. viii. 8) the famous diver
who deserted to the Greeks before the naval fighting round
Artemisium in connexion with the battle of Thermopylae.
He swam ten miles under sea ! Agrostis is a kind of grass.
Glaucus was originally a fisher of Anthedon.

FRAGMENTA CHOLIAMBICA

THEOCRITUS

ὁ μουσοποιὸς ἐνθάδ' Ἱππῶναξ κεῖται·
εἰ μὲν πονηρός, μὴ προσέρχευ τῷ τύμβῳ·
εἰ δ' ἐσσὶ κρήγυός τε καὶ παρὰ χρηστῶν,
θαρσέων καθίζευ, κἢν θέλῃς ἀπόβριξον.

(*A.P.* xiii. 3 and one cod. Theocr.)

2. *A.P.* ποτέρχευ: cod. Med. προσέρχου.   3. χρηστῶ
A.P.   4. καθίζου cod. Med.

DIPHILUS

στρωφᾷς δὲ πώλους ὡς ὁ Μαντινεὺς Σῆμος
ὃς πρῶτος ἅρματ' ἤλασεν παρ' Ἀλφειῷ.

(Scholl. Pind. *Ol.* x. 83 (*a*) παρατίθεται δὲ (Δίδυμος) καὶ τὸν
γράφοντα τὸν Θησηίδα μαρτυροῦντα τῷ Ἥρωι τὴν τοῦ ἅρματος
ἡνιοχευτικὴν ἀρετήν· τρέψας δὲ πώλους ὡς ὁ Μαντινεὺς Ἥρως.
(*b*) Ἀριστόδημος δέ φησι μὴ δύνασθαι συγχρονεῖν Ἁλιρρόθιον τὸν
κατὰ Κέκροπα Ἡρακλεῖ ἀλλὰ μηδὲ Ἀρκάδα εἶναι ἀλλ' Ἀθηναῖον.
Σῆμον δέ τινα νῦν νενικηκέναι ἅρματι ὥς φησι Δίφιλος ὁ τὴν
Θησηίδα ποιήσας ἔν τινι ἰάμβῳ οὕτω τρέψας δὲ κτλ. (*vv.* 1-2).

1. *v.l.* τρέψας, Ἥρως schol. (a).

VARIOUS FRAGMENTS

THEOCRITUS

Stranger, here lies the poet Hipponax :
If thou art wicked, to his tomb come not ;
If thou art goodly and thy sires gentle,
Be bold : sit here : and if thou wilt, slumber

(In the *Anthologia Palatina* and one ms. of *Theocr.*)

DIPHILUS[1]

And swervest colts like Mantinese Semus
Who won the car race first by Alpheus.

((a) Didymus cites the author of the *Theseis* as witness
to the driving skill of the Hero (*v.* 1). (b) Aristodemus says
that Halirrhothius being contemporary of Cecrops cannot
have been alive with Heracles, nor was he an Arcadian but
an Athenian. In fact the victor in the car race was a certain
Semus, as is stated by Diphilus the author of the *Theseis*
in a (chol)iambic verse as follows (*vv.* 1, 2). Two *Commentators* on an *Olympian Ode* of *Pindar*.)

[1] Of Diphilus nothing is known beyond the statements
above. In the second verse it is not clear whether πρῶτος
means 'was first to' or 'to victory.' The second schol.
suggests that this was part of a fugitive epigram. Quite
possibly a quotation from the *Theseis* is lost and these
iambi are by another hand. The Diphilus of schol. Ar.
Nub. 96 might be the same, but this is improbable.

FRAGMENTA CHOLIAMBICA

RHINTHON

(*fr.* 10 Kaibel)

Α. ὁ σὲ Διόνυσος αὐτὸς ἐξώλη θείη.
Β. Ἱππωνά[κ]τ‹ειον› τὸ μέτρον.
  Α. οὐδέν μοι μέλει.

(Hephaest. p. 9 Ῥίνθων μὲν γὰρ καὶ ἐν ἰάμβῳ ἐπισημασίας ἠξίωσε τὸ τοιοῦτον. ἐν γὰρ Ὀρέστῃ δράματί φησιν (v. 1), εἶθ' (v. 2). So Choerob. in Theodos. ii. 796 Hillgard πολλάκις εὑρίσκονται καὶ ἐν τοῖς μέτροις ἀποτελοῦντα κοινὴν τὸ κτ καὶ πτ, . . . ὡς παρὰ τῷ Ῥ. (v. 2).)

1. θείης ἴθ' cod.
2. Ἱππῶνάκτος codd.: correxi.
The apparent choliambic fragment in Clement of Alexandria, p. 14 Potter, attributed to Rhinthon, is really a trimeter : see Potter's citations. For another fragment of Rhinthon see my *First Greek Anthologist*, p. 22.

ASCLEPIADES OF SAMOS

fr. 1

ὃ καὶ κυνὸς καλοῦσι δυσμόρου σῆμα

(Schol. Eur. *Hec.* 1273 περὶ δὲ τοῦ κυνὸς σήματος καὶ Ἀσκληπιάδης φησὶν ὅτι κυνὸς καλοῦσι δυσμόρου σῆμα. Schol. Lyc. 315 σκύλαξ· . . . σκύλακα τὴν Ἑκάβην λέγει, ὅτι κύων ἐγένετο ὥς φησι μυθικῶς Εὐριπίδης (*l.c.*). . . . καὶ Ἀσκληπιάδης περὶ τοῦ τόπου οὗ ἀνηρέθη (1).)

1. ὃ καὶ om. schol. *Hec.*
268

VARIOUS FRAGMENTS

RHINTHON

A. May Dionysus be thy perdition.
B. A Hipponactean [1] verse !
    A. I do not mind.

(Rhinthon in an iambus calls attention to this practice. In his play *Orestes* he says (*v*. 1) and proceeds (*v*. 2). *Hephaestion.* *Kt* and *pt* often have the syllable before them either short or long : *e.g.* Rhinthon (*v*. 2). *Choeroboscus.*)

[1] Rhinthon is satirizing the scansion θεὶη (Hephaestion) and ἄκτ- (Choeroboscus). The latter depends on the false reading βἄκτηρίη in Hipponax (p. 14).

ASCLEPIADES OF SAMOS

1

The luckless ' bitch's tomb ' they now call it.

(About the ' bitch's tomb ' Asclepiades says that (1). *Commentator* on *Euripides' Hecuba.* ' Whelp ': . . . Lycophron gives this name to Hecuba since she was turned into a bitch according to Euripides' legend. Asclepiades says about the place where she was killed (1).)

FRAGMENTA CHOLIAMBICA

fr. 2

κούφῃ κεραί⟨ῃ⟩ κεύσταλεῖ παρήνεγκεν

(Plut. *Mor.* 476 A κἄν τις ἔξωθεν ἀρχὴ πάθους ὥσπερ διαδρομὴ γένηται σπιλάδος (ε. καὶ κ. κ. π.) ὥς φησιν ᾿Ασκλ.)

APOLLONIUS RHODIUS
CANOBUS
fr. 1

Κορινθιουργές ἐστι κιόνων σχῆμα.

(Steph. Byz. Κόρινθος· . . . ·καὶ σύνθετον Κορινθιουργής ὡς ᾿Αττικουργής. ᾿Απ. ὁ ῾Ρόδιος Κανώ†π†ῳ [δευτέρῳ] (1).)

fr. 2

†τρέψει δὲ νηὸν† ὁ γλυκύς σε χωρίτης
πλόος κομίζων δῶρα πλουσίου Νείλου.

(Steph. Byz. χώρα· . . . ᾿Απολλώνιος ἐν τῳ Κ. (2).)

1. δευτέρῳ del. Meineke.   In text ?? σῆμα.
2. 1. τέρψει δὲ νηῶν Pinedo, which I translate.   χωρίτης : em. Meineke.   2. Νείλου πλουσίου codd. : em. Gavel.

270

2

Rides out the storm with light and bare yard-arm

(And if from outside comes the beginning of any evil like the passage of a storm[1] he as Asclepiades says (2). *Plutarch* on *Tranquillity*.)

[1] σπιλάς 'storm': see *J.Th.S.* xiv. 56, xvi. 78. Add Plut. *Dio* 10 τοῦ χειμῶνος παραφερομένου.

APOLLONIUS OF RHODES

CANOBUS

1

A pillared group Corinthian-fashion

('Corinth': . . . there is a compound 'Corinthian-fashion' like 'Attic-fashion.' Apollonius of Rhodes in his [second] *Canobus*.[1] *Stephanus of Byzantium*.)

2

Thou shalt delight in the ships' sweet passage
That brings the countryfolk rich Nile's presents.

('Country' . . .: compound 'countryfolk.' Apollonius in his *Canobus*. *Id*.)

[1] Canobus was the steersman of Menelaus who was turned into a star. The Corinthian pillars marked his alleged grave. Out of Helen's tears for him grew, as Apollonius no doubt did not fail to mention, the plant ἑλένειον. *E.M. s.v.* Neither Apollonius nor Asclepiades seem to have written more than one choliambic poem.

271

FRAGMENTA CHOLIAMBICA

PARMENO

fr. 1 (1 Powell)

ἀνὴρ γὰρ ἕλκων οἶνον, ὡς ὕδωρ ἵππος,   1
Σκυθιστὶ φωνεῖ   2
          οὐδὲ κόππα γιγνώσκων   3
κεῖται δ' ἄναυδος ἐν πίθῳ κολυμβήσας   4
κάθυπνος ὡς μήκωνα φάρμακ‹ο›ν πίνων.   5

(Ath. v. 221 a (1) φησὶν ὁ Βυζάντιος Παρμένων.)

fr. 2 (2 Powell)

ἦλθον μακρὴν θάλασσαν, οὐκ ἄγων σῦκα
Κα[ι]ν‹αῖ›α φόρτον.

(Ath. iii. 75 f Παρμένων ὁ Βυζάντιος ἐν τοῖς ἰάμβοις τὰ ἀπὸ
Κανῶν τῆς Αἰολικῆς πόλεως ὡς διάφορα ἐπαινῶν φησίν (2).)

fr. 3 (3 Powell)

Αἰγύπτιε Ζεῦ Νεῖλε
(Ath. v. 203 c.   Schol. Pind. *P.* iv. 97.)

fr. 4 (8 Powell)

παῖδ' οὔτε γέν‹υσι› πυρρὸν οὔθ' ὑπηνήτην

(Schol. Theocr. vi. 3 πυρρός· ὁ ἀρτίχνους . . . Παρμενίσκος
(-ων Haupt) (4).)

1. 3. κόππα A : κάππα cett.   5. φαρμάκων AC : corr. Cas.
Meineke saw that the order was unsatisfactory.   For
sense lost *e.g.* πρῶτον· εἶτά που πλεῖον πιὼν σεσίγηκ'

2. 2. Καινεα A : corr. Palmerius.   φόρτου A : corr.
Cas.   Sense ἀλλὰ —◡— πόρνας?

4. γένειον sch. : corr. Bücheler.

272

VARIOUS FRAGMENTS

PARMENO

1

For one that drinketh wine, as horse water,
First speaks like Scythians: ⟨then when drunk
    deeper⟩
Silent he lies, and cannot say ' Koppa,' [1]
Since he has fallen to a tub's bottom,
As with some opiate, with sleep druggéd.

(Parmeno of Byzantium says (1).   *Athenaeus*.)

2

          ⟨Crossing⟩
Far seas I came hither, no figs bringing,
Produce of Canae, ⟨but some fair ladies⟩.

(Parmeno of Byzantium in his iambi praises figs from
Canae the Aeolian city as of superlative quality. *Athenaeus*.)

3

O Nile, Egyptian Zeus,

(*Athenaeus*. A *Commentator* on a *Pythian* ode of *Pindar*.)

4

A boy nor yellow-chinned nor yet downy

(' Yellow ': used of one whose beard is just beginning to
grow. . . . Parmeniscus (4). *Commentator* on *Theocritus*.)

[1] To the Greeks the northern tongues appeared to have
an undue preponderance of ugly guttural sounds (Hdl. on
Hrd. vi. 34). *ko* is both the 'first' letter of the Scythian
or as the hiccup of the drunkard's alphabet. The Greeks
said οὐδ' ἄλφα.

FRAGMENTA CHOLIAMBICA

HERMEIAS

(p. 237 Powell)

Ἀκούσατ', ὦ Στοίακες, ἔμποροι λήρου,
λόγων ὑποκρ⟨ι⟩τῆρες, οἳ μόνοι πάντα
τὰν τοῖς πίναξι, πρίν ⟨τι⟩ τῷ σοφῷ δοῦναι
αὐτοὶ καταρροφεῖτε, κᾷθ' ἁλίσκεσθε
ἐναντία πράσσοντες οἷς τραγῳδεῖτε.   5

(Ath. xiii. 563 d τούτων τῶν Ἀλέξιδος ἀπομνημονεύσας ὁ
Μυρτίλος κᾷτα ἀποβλέψας εἰς τοὺς τὰ τῆς Στοᾶς αἱρουμένους
τὰ Ἑρμείου τοῦ Κουριέως ἐκ τῶν ἰάμβων προειπών (vv. 1-5),
παιδοπῖπαι ὄντες καὶ τοῦτο μόνον ἐξηλωκότες τὸν ἀρχηγὸν ὑμῶν
τῆς σοφίας Ζήνωνα τὸν Φοίνικα, ὃς οὐδέποτε γυναικὶ ἐχρήσατο
παιδικοῖς δ' αἰεί, ὡς Ἀντίγονος ὁ Καρύστιος ἱστορεῖ ἐν τῷ περὶ
τοῦ βίου αὐτοῦ.)

1. στόιακες A : στοίακες (E).   2. ὑποκρητῆρες corr. Mus.
3. πρινὴ : corr. Porson. Read προεῖπεν in Ath. Perhaps
continue (for otherwise there is no construction), e.g.

ὡς παιδοπῖπαί τ' ἐστὲ καὶ μόνον τοῦτο
Ζήνωνα τὸν Φοίνικα ἐοίκατε ζηλοῦν
ὃς οὐδ' ὄναρ γυναικί, παιδικοῖς δ' αἰεί
ἐχρήσατ'.

CHARINUS

Ἔρροις πλανῆτι καὶ κακὴ πέτρη Λευκάς·
Χαρῖνον, αἰαῖ, τὴν ἰαμβικὴν Μοῦσαν
κατηθάλωσας ἐλπίδος κενοῖς μύθοις.
τοιαῦτ' Ἔρωτος Εὐπάτωρ ἐρασθείη.

(Ptolemaeus Chennus (Phot. Bibl. p. 153. 5) Χαρῖνος δὲ
ἰαμβογράφος ἠράσθη Ἔρωτος εὐνούχου τοῦ Εὐπάτορος οἰνοχόου, καὶ
πιστεύσας τῷ περὶ τῆς πέτρας λόγῳ κατέβαλεν ἑαυτόν. ἐπεὶ δὲ
καταβαλὼν τὸ σκέλος κατεάγη καὶ ὑπὸ ὀδύνης ἐτελεύτα ἀπέρριψε
τάδε τὰ ἰαμβεῖα (vv. 1-4).)

VARIOUS FRAGMENTS

HERMEIAS

Hear me, ye Stoics, merchants of twaddle,
Verbiage-fakers : you yourselves gulp down
All that is in the dishes, ere wise men
Can get a sup or bite : and your actions
Belie your fair pretences : [1] †you're caught out   5
In lust unnatural, herein Zeno
Your founder, and herein alone, aping :
For this Phoenician never knew woman.†

(After quoting these verses of Alexis, Myrtilus stared round
at those of the Stoic persuasion present and quoted the words
of Hermeias of Curium (*vv.* 1-8), as Antigonus the Carystian
states in his *Life*. *Athenaeus*.)

[1] Verses 5-8 are merely paraphrased in Athenaeus : see
crit. n. Of Hermeias of Curium (in Cyprus) nothing more
is known.

CHARINUS

Damn thee, Leucadian rock,[1] thou vile truant :
Alas the Muse iambic Charinus
Thou didst burn up with flattering tales empty.
Eupator's love for Love I pray end thus.

(Charinus a (chol)iambic poet fell in love with Love, a
eunuch who was cup-bearer to Eupator, and trusting in the tale
about the rock threw himself over the edge. In falling
he broke his leg and just as he was dying in agony threw
off these iambic verses (*vv.* 1-4). *Ptolemaeus Chennus* in
Photius's Catalogue.)

[1] Diving over the Leucadian precipice into the sea was
supposed to have the effect of winning the love of a
reluctant loved one. The whole of the narrative of Ptolemaeus is suspect : but these verses can hardly be later than
A.D. 100 or 200. πλανῆτις seems to mean ' deceitful.' See
[Ovid], *Heroid.* xv. 163 *sqq.*

FRAGMENTA CHOLIAMBICA

APOLLONIDES (NICAENUS)

Γλῆνιν παρηονῖτις ἀμπέχω χερμάς
πικρῇ κατασπασθέντα κύματος δίνῃ,
ὅτ' ἰχθυάζετ' ἐξ ἀκρῆς ἀπορρῶγος·
χῶσαν δέ μ' ὅσσος λαὸς ἦν συνεργγήτης,
Ποσεῖδον, οὓς σὺ σῷζε καὶ γαληναίην   5
αἰὲν διδοίης ὁρμιηβόλοις θῖνα.

(*A.P.* vii. 693 Ἀπολλωνίδου ἰαμβικόν.)

4. ὅσσος ἦν συνεργάτης λαός conj. Jacobs.

HERODIANUS

Ἡρῳδιανὸς Νι[κί]ου πα[τ]ρὸς [σ]τῆσεν
χαλκεῖον ἀνδριάντα πατρίδος ψήφῳ
γνώμης τ' ἔκ‹η›τι, μείλιχος γὰρ ἦν [π]ᾶ[σιν]
τερπνῶν τε μ[ί]μων οὓς ἔγραψεν ἀσ[τ]ε[ί]ως.

(Cougny, *A.P.* iii. p. 589, from a grave-stone at Ergissa (Eski-Zaghra).)

3. τε ἔκατι lapis.

PARDALAS

Ὁ Σαρδιηνὸς Παρδαλᾶς δὶς ἤκουσα·
μεμνήσομαί σου κἂν ἐμῇσι βύβλοισι.

(Cougny, *A.P.* iii. p. 30. One of a number of inscriptions on the left leg of the famous statue of Memnon in Egypt.)

2. Num σευ?

VARIOUS FRAGMENTS

APOLLONIDES (OF NICAEA?)

Here, sea-side cairn, do I embrace Glenis,
In woeful whirl of wave to death sucked down,
What time he sat on rugged cliff fishing.
His mates did pile me here, O Poseidon :
Them save thou : evermore give calm weather
To all who from this sea-board their lines cast.

(In the *Anthologia Palatina*.)

HERODIAN

Herodianus set this bronze statue
To Nicias his sire by his town's vote
Memorial to his character gentle
And to his pleasant mimes with wit written.

(On a grave-stone : see *Cougny's Appendix to A.P.*)

PARDALAS OF SARDIS

I, Pardalas of Sardis, twice heard thee
And in my books I promise thee mention.[1]

(*Appendix* to the *Palatine Anthology*.)

[1] Ancient tourists who listened for the sound of Memnon's
statue at dawn scrawled their semimetrical testimonies all
over the statue and base. Cougny i. 175, 184, 185 are
mainly in pure iambi and I omit them despite an occasional
choliambus, due to the incompetent author or authoress.
Pardalas seems to have had some knowledge of the metre
and appropriate dialect.

FRAGMENTA CHOLIAMBICA

ANON. I

Ὁ κλεινὸς ἶνις βασιλέως Ἀμάζασπος,
ὁ Μιθριδάτου βασιλέως κασίγνητος,
ᾧ γαῖα πατρὶς Κασπί⟨οι⟩s παρὰ κλήθρ⟨οι⟩s
Ἴβηρ Ἴβηρος ἐνθαδὶ τετάρχυται
πόλιν παρ' ἱρὴν ἣν ἔδειμε Νικάτωρ
ἐλαιόθηλον ἀμφὶ Μυγδόνος νᾶμα.
θάνεν δ' ὀπαδὸς Αὐσόνων †ἀγήτορι†
μολὼν ἄνακτι Παρθικὴν ἐφ' ὑσμίνην,
πρίν περ παλάξαι χεῖρα δηΐῳ λύθρῳ,
ἴφθιμον, αἰαῖ, χεῖρα δουρὶ †κανοζωρ†   1
καὶ φασγάνου κνώδοντι, πεζὸς ἱπ⟨πεύς τε⟩.
ὁ δ' αὐτὸς ἶσος παρθένοισιν αἰδοίαις . .

(Cougny, *A.P.* iii. p. 132. In Rome? Non inveni.)

3. -ιας -ρας corr. by Meineke.   7. ? ταγήτορσι an
ἄναξι (8).   10. καὶ τόξῳ M. Haupt.   11. supplie
by Scaliger.

ANON. II

. . . .]ιων ἴχνος, εἰ θέλεις γνῶναι
. . . .]ις τῇδε λαίνῃ στήλῃ.
. . . .] ἐν φθιτοῖς ἀνὴρ χρηστός,
. . . .] λέλοιπεν ἡλίου φέγγος,
. . . .]ων μηδέπω τελειώσας.
πάντ' . . . .]ι δέδοκτο, μοῦνος ἀνθρώπωι
καὶ πάντας] ἀρετῇ τοὺς ὁμήλικας προὖχεν
εἰς πᾶν δί]καιος, θεοσεβής, φιλάνθρωπος.
τίς οὐχ ἑ]ταίρων τὸν τεὸν μόρον κλαίει;

1-5. I translate the general sense given by Cagnat (s
7, 9, 10, 12, 13 (δεινὸν) and 14).   3. χρ. ἐν φθ. ἀν. lapis
6. δέχοιτο lapis : corr. Cagnat.
278

ANONYMOUS FRAGMENTS

ANON. I

The famous son of a king, Amazaspus,
And of king Mithridates own brother,
Who by the Caspian gates was born, here lies,
Iberian of Iberian, balméd,
By holy city [1] built by Nicator   5
On the Mygdonian stream 'neath grey olives.
Unto the Roman emperor [2] fighting
Against the Parthian he went ally,
(And fell his hand not yet in foes' blood steeped,
That hand alas ! both with the bow mighty   10
And with the sword-hilt) horse and foot leading.
Withal he was of modesty maiden . . .

[1] Nisibis.
[2] The emperor seems to have been Trajan.

ANON. II

⟨Halt passing⟩ if thou wouldest learn, stranger,
⟨Who buried lies⟩ beneath this stone pillar.
Once was he ⟨so and so⟩, a man righteous,
⟨But now hath gone and⟩ left the fair sunlight
And left unfinished ⟨his life's due course⟩.   5
Alone of men was he ⟨in all blameless⟩
⟨And all⟩ his fellows he in worth outdid.
⟨In all things⟩ just, humane, and god-fearing.
⟨Which of⟩ thy comrades at thy fate weeps not ?

279

FRAGMENTA CHOLIAMBICA

ἅπας] μὲν ὄχλος οἰκετῶν σε δακρύει,   1⟨
ἐν παν]τὶ δ' ἦσθα σεμνὸς ὡς δοκεῖν εἶναι
ἔτ' ὄν]τα παῖδα τοῖς νοήμασιν πρέσβυν.
. . . .]ον, ποθητὴ μῆτερ, εὔνασον θρῆνον,
πέ]νθους τιθηνόν, ὃς μάτην σε πημαίνει·
οὐδεὶς γὰρ ἐξήλυξε τὸν μίτον Μοιρῶν,   1⟨
οὐ θνητός, οὐκ ἀθάνατος· οὐδ' ὁ δεσμώτης
οὐδ' αὖ τύραννος βασιλικὴν λαχὼν τιμήν
θεσμοὺς ἀτρέπτους διαφυγεῖν ποτ' ᾠήθη.
Φαέθοντα Τιτὰν οὐκ ἔκλαυσ' ὅτ' ἐκ δίφρων
ἀπ' οὐρανοῦ κατέπεσεν εἰς πέδον γαίης;   2⟨
Ἑρμῆς δ' ὁ Μαίας οὐκ ἔκλαυσεν ὃν παῖδα
[Μυρτίλον †ἀπὸ δίφρων† κύμασιν φορούμενον]
οὐδ' αὖ Θέτις τὸν σ‹θ›εναρὸν ἔστενεν παῖδ⟨
ὅτ' ἐκ βελέμνων θνῆσκε τῶν Ἀπόλλωνος;
οὐδ' αὖ βροτῶν τε καὶ θεῶν ἄναξ πάντων 2⟨
Σαρπηδόν' οὐκ ἔκλαυσεν, οὐκ ἐκώκυσεν;
οὐδ' αὖ Μακηδὼν ὁ βασιλεὺς Ἀλέξανδρος
ὃν τίκτεν Ἄμμων θέμενος εἰς ὄφιν μορφήν . .

(Cougny, *A.P.* iii. p. 123.   In Alexandria.)

16. read οὐδὲ.   22. is corrupt.   23. στεναρόν lapis
25. πάντων ἄναξ lapis.   28. incomplete.

ANONYMOUS FRAGMENTS

⟨Aye all⟩ thy household servants are mourners; 10
And always wast thou dignified, seeming,
Though yet a boy, in intellect man-like.
O yearning [1] mother, thy lament cease thou:
It doth but nurse the grief that hurts idly.
For none have yet escaped from the Fates' thread,
Nor mortal nor immortal: nor pris'ner [2] 16
Nor tyrant borne to consequence kingly
Has ever thought to flee their laws fixéd.
Titan did mourn for Phaethon fallen
Out of his car from heaven to earth's plain. 20
And Hermes Maea's son his own son wept,
Myrtilus, thrown to waves ⟨that his name bear⟩. [3]
Thetis lamented for her son valiant
When by Apollo's darts he lay stricken.
Aye and the king of all gods and all men 25
Bewailéd and lamented Sarpedon.
Aye Alexander, Macedon's ruler,
Whom Ammon did beget disguised snakewise . . .

---

[1] ποθητή must mean weeping. Read ποθῆτι.
[2] *Cf.* Ps.-Call. pp. 290 *sqq.* for these and following verses.
They might actually be by the same writer.
[3] I suppose the author to have written something like
Μυρτίλον ἰαφθέντ' εἰς φερώνυμον κῦμα. φορηθέντα would suffice.

FRAGMENTA CHOLIAMBICA

DIOGENES LAERTIUS

1 (1 Meineke)

Τί δὴ γέρων ὢν καὶ φάλανθος, ὦ 'ρίστων,
τὸ βρέγμα δῶκας ἡλίῳ κατοπτῆσαι;
τ‹οι›γὰρ τὸ θερμὸν πλεῖον ἢ δέον ζητῶν
τὸν ψυχρὸν ὄντως εὗρες οὐ θέλων Ἅιδην.

(Diog. L. vii. 164 τοῦτον λόγος φαλακρὸν ὄντα ἐγκαυθῆναι
ὑπὸ τοῦ ἡλίου καὶ ὧδε τελευτῆσαι . . . (1).)

2 (2 Meineke)

Οὐκ ἄρα μῦθος ἦν ἐκεῖνος εἰκαῖος
 ὡς ἀτυχής τις ἐών·
τὸν πόδα κολυμβῶν περιέπειρέ ‹πως› ἥλῳ·
 καὶ γὰρ ὁ σεμνὸς ἀνήρ,
πρὶν Ἀλφεὸν ποτ' ἐκπερᾶν, Ἀλεξῖνος   5
 θνῆσκε νυ‹γ›εὶς καλάμῳ.

(Diog. L. ii. 109 ἔπειτα μέντοι νηχόμενον ἐν τῷ Ἀλφειῷ
νυχθῆναι καλάμῳ καὶ οὕτω τελευτῆσαι . . . (2).)

3 (3 Meineke)

Εἰ καὶ σέ, Ξενοφῶν, Κραναοῦ Κέκροπός τε πολῖται
 φεύγειν κατέγνων τοῦ φίλου χάριν Κύρου,
ἀλλὰ Κόρινθος ἔδεκτο φιλόξενος, ᾗ σὺ φιληδῶν
 οὕτως ἀρέσκῃ· κεῖθι καὶ μένειν ἔγνως.

(Diog. L. ii. 58 ὡς ἐτελεύτα (3). A.P. vii. 98 (3) ἐκ τῆς
βίβλου τῆς ἐπιγραφομένης Βίων Φιλοσόφων. vv. 3, 4 Suid.
s.v. φιληδῶν from A.P.)

1. 3. τὺ γὰρ corr. Meineke.
2. 3. τὸ cod.: em. Stephanus.   6. νυχθεὶς corr. Hermann.
3. 2. φευγέμεναι A.P.   4. ? ὅκως.

DIOGENES LAERTIUS

1

Why, O Ariston old and bald-headed,
Did'st to the sun to bake give thy noddle ?
Withal didst thou, excess of heat seeking,
Discover that cool death which thou shunnédst.

(It is said that Ariston, who was bald, was scorched by
the sun and so died. Here is an epigram of mine (1).
Diogenes Laertius, Lives of the Philosophers.)

2

That witty jest was no mere jest random
  How an unfortunate wight,
In swimming, on a nail his foot piercéd :
  So did that reverend man
Named Alexinus crossing Alphéus
  Pierced by a bulrush expire.

(Later while swimming in the Alpheus Alexinus was
pierced by a reed and so died. Here is my epitaph (2).
id. See Addenda.)

3

Xenophon, though by the townsmen of Cecrops
  and Cranaus dooméd
  To exile since thou followedst Cyrus,
Yet did Corinth receive thee hospitable : where
  both in comfort
  Thy life thou passed'st and wast there buried.

(On Xenophon's death *id.* Also in the *Palatine Anthology*
whence *Suidas* quotes the last two verses.)

FRAGMENTA CHOLIAMBICA

4 (om. Meineke)

Καὶ σὲ Πρωταγόρη σοφίης ἴδμεν βέλος ὀξύ
ἀλλ' οὐ τιτρώσκον⟨τ⟩', ⟨ὄντα⟩ δὲ γλυκὺ
⟨χ⟩ρ⟨ί⟩μα.

(*A.P.* vii. 132.   Not in our codd. of Diog. L.)

5 (om. Meineke)

Ἰλιγγίασε Βάκχον ἐκπιὼν χανδόν
Χρύσιππος, οὐδ' ἐφείσατο
οὐ τῆς Στοᾶς, οὐχ ἧς πάτρης, οὐ τῆς ψυχῆς,
ἀλλ' ἦλθε δῶμ' ἐς Ἀΐδεω.

(Diog. L. vii. 184 τοῦτον ἐν τῷ Ὠιδείῳ σχολάζοντά φησιν
Ἕρμιππος ἐπὶ θυσίαν ὑπὸ τῶν μαθητῶν κληθῆναι· ἔνθα προσ-
ενεγκάμενον γλυκὺν ἄκρατον καὶ ἰλιγγιάσαντα πεμπταῖον ἀπελθεῖν
ἐξ ἀνθρώπων ... (5).   *A.P.* vii. 706.)

4. 2. -ον, -ων corrected by Jacobs.   κρῆμα corrected
by Boissonade.
5. 3. οὐχ ἧς *A.P.*: οὐδ' ἧς some codd. D.L. (vitiosissime):
Jacobs οὐ τῆς perhaps rightly.   πάτρας *A.P.*

4

Thee too Protagoras do we know, sharp spear-
  point of wisdom,
  Not wounding us but sweet as an ointment.

(In the *Palatine Anthology* only.)

5

Chrysippus had a fit upon gulping
  A drink, and spared not anyone,
Nor Stoa, nor his land, nor his own self,
  But into Hades passed away.

(Hermippus says that Chrysippus was resting in the
Odeum when he was summoned by his pupils to a sacrifice:
there he took a liqueur and had a fit and five days later
departed this life . . . (5). *Diog. L.* Also in the *Palatine
Anthology*.)

ANON. AP. PSEUDO-CALLISTHENEM

Poems I and II and those later ones which concern
the death of Darius were edited by Kuhlmann, a
pupil of W. Kroll (Munster, 1912). Since then Kroll
has produced a text of the one best codex, or recension of the life of Alexander (Berlin, 1926). This
is codex A (Paris Graec. 1711). Some other codices
present quite different versions, B and C (codd. dett.):
and I have constantly referred to the Bodleian cod.
Barocc. 20, a ms. in the main of type C. Further
we have the excellent Armenian version (Arm.)
translated into Greek by Richard Raabe [1] (Leipzig,
1896), the Latin translation of Valerius (Val. : printed
by Müller-Didot : Arrian etc. 1865), and the
Byzantine version (Byz.) into politic verse (W.
Wagner,[2] Berlin, 1881), all of which preserve something of value. Of the recensions A (only preserved
in one bad codex) is by a stylist more or less faithful
to his original : B and C represent a version into the
vulgar language. In a way they are more helpful,
since wherever a literary metrical phrase peeps out
that is necessarily original.

Besides the verses in i. 42 preserved only in the Latin
of Julius Valerius, Kuhlmann recognized only three

[1] To whom most of the improvements in the text of i. 46
are due.
[2] *Trois Poèmes grecs du moyen âge.*

choliambic portions : and to these Kroll in his critical notes adds an oracle (which is quite separate) and an account of Darius' appearance when Alexander goes to the Persian camp as his own herald. But, as the verses in i. 46 show, there is far more. For we have no mere song of Ismenias the flute-player : the narrative between his verses and those of Alexander—and indeed, though obscuredly, the narrative before—is all choliambic. Further, in the fable of the mice and wasps, which I give below in verse for the first time,[1] the conclusion is

ὡς δ᾽ εἶπε[ν ὁ] βασιλεὺς πάντες αὐτὸν ηὐφήμουν

and the verses continue. It is clear that for large portions this life of Alexander rests on a choliambic basis : and we may hazard a guess that the whole is based on an anthology of Alexander's deeds in which the choliambic verses (as far as they extended) occupied pride of place. The only known poet who wrote of the fall of Thebes was Soterichus, who lived under Diocletian ; but he seems to have been an epic poet.[2] There are difficulties in placing our choliambist later (when the art of the iambus was beginning to be lost), or earlier (when Soterichus must have merely copied the theme of the fall of Thebes). But the first appears the less unlikely hypothesis. The coincidence of parts of the story with far earlier sources is by no means fatal to this. It is best merely to give what can be found of these verses and leave entirely the question as to when this curious narrative—compound of Egyptian and

[1] So with many other portions.
[2] For another epic poem on this subject introduced into a history see *P. Oxy.* 1798.

ANON. AP. PSEUDO-CALLISTHENEM

Aethiopian fable, anecdote, forged letters and choliambic verse, with some traces of sound historians as sources—finally took shape. The only certain test of a very late date does not apply to our author, who uses words like the nominative 'Aλέξανδρος in which the accent does not fall on the penultimate.[1]

---

[1] As the verses have to be picked from various sources I use the following signs :—

i. The reading of Codex A is given without mark.

ii. Insertions from codd. dett. are given in round brackets ( ).

iii. Insertions or corrections whether conjectural or from the versions are marked ⟨ ⟩. When they are from the versions the source is given in the crit. app.

iv. Where I indicate omissions (. . .), I give the general sense in italics on the English side. Often one or two isolated traces of metre are omitted. Where no traces of metre occur I give a résumé in English in italics and round brackets.

1

i. 42. 9 καὶ παραγίνεται εἰς Φρυγίαν καὶ εἰσελθὼν
εἰς αὐτὴν Ἴλιον τὴν πόλιν ἔθυσεν Ἕκτορι καὶ Ἀχιλλεῖ
καὶ τοῖς ἄλλοις ἥρωσιν. praecipue tamen Achillem
veneratur ac rogat uti sibi et ipse faveat et dona
quae ferret dignanter admittat; haec enim a sese
non ut ab externo ac superstitioso verum ut con-
sanguineo ac religioso dedicari;

> hinc primus exstat Aeacus Iovis proles,
> atque inde Peleus Phthiae regna possedit,
> quo tu subortus inclyta cluis proles.
> Pyrrhusque post id nobile adserit sanguem,
> quem subsecuta est Pie‹l›i fama non dispar ;   5
> Pie‹l›ique proles Eubius dehinc regnat.
> post Nessus ardens excipit domus nomen,
> Argusque post id, qui potens fuit Xanthi ;
> ex hoc Arete nobilis genus ducit.
> Areta natus Priami nomen accepit,   10
> Tryinus unde et Eurymachus post illum,
> ex quo Lycus fit dives et dehinc Castor.
> Castore natus est Dromon qui dat Phocum ;
> atque hinc suborta est Metrias, quae suscepit
> Neoptolemei nominis vicem dignam,   15
> cui substitutus Charopus.   hic Molossorum

5. Pieri *codd.*: *corr. Mai.*

1

i. 42. 9 [1] Alexander arrived in Phrygia and entered the city of Ilium itself and sacrificed to Hector and Achilles and the other heroes. Most of all he honoured Achilles and asked him to favour him and deign to accept the gifts he bore. These he dedicated not as a superstitious stranger, but as a relative and a religious man.

> Aeacus son of Jove your race founded,
> Next Peleus held the Phthian dominion,
> Whose world-famed progeny you are cálled.
> Next Pyrrhus vindicates thy blood nobly,
> And Pielus of equal fame follows.   5
> Thereafter Eubius, Pielus' son, reigns.
> Next glorious Nessus name of thy house bore;
> Thereafter Argus, master of Xanthus,
> From whom Arete noble her race drew.
> Priamus was the son of Arete,   10
> Tryinus and Eurymachus next came;
> Whence wealthy Lycus and anon Castor.
> Dromon was Castor's son and bore Phocus;
> Hence Metrias was born, and her son bore
> The name Neoptolemeian with full worth;   15
> Charopus, his successor, the kingdom

---

[1] All our Greek MSS. omit this poem.

regni potitus auctor extitit stirpis
nostrae <
      > eritque viscus inclytum matris.
e qua subortus vestro sanguini adnector,   20
quaesoque nomen adseras tuum nobis,
bellisque praestes gloriasque subtexus
velut feracis seminis <   > fructum,
quod cuncta late spatia terrae pervadat;
unaque metis nostra fac Phaethonteis   25
regna explicari mundus adserat cunctus.

II

(ii. 46. 11)

χεὶρ δὲ Μακεδονικὴ οὐκ ἔκαμε τὸν
    πολυσφαγῆ σίδηρον αἱματώσασα.   1

•   •   •   •

(46a. 3)

Ἰσμηνίας Θηβαῖος, τῆς αὐλομελῳδίας ἔμπειρος
ἄνθρωπος, ... τὴν χεῖρα προτείνας
     ἄρχεται λέγειν οὕτως·   2

(Βασιλεῦ μέγιστε, φεῖσαι ἡμῶν εὐτελῶν· μὴ τοιού-

Molossian gat, and of our race founder
Became . . .[1]
       will be his mother's famed offspring.
Whose son I, with your race thus connected, 20
Beg that your name by us be asserted,
Given to wars and crownéd with glories :
For fruit are we of a seed right fertile,
A seed to range over the whole wide earth.
Grant the whole world declare that our realm be 25
By Phaethontean goals alone bounded.[2]

(*Alexander wins over the cities on the Black Sea, and
nters Greece. The first resistance comes from Thebes.*)

[1] Here should follow the names of Alcetas and Neoptole-
nus (Kuhlmann).
[2] As we should say, ' the sun should never set on it.'

II

(*The Thebans close their gates but Alexander forces
n entrance.*)

The hand of Macedon tired not

    Dipping in gore its sword all blood-spattered. 1

.   .   .   .   .   .

A certain Ismenias of Thebes, a flute-player,
tretched forth his hand and with many tears)

    did thus begin speaking :—   2

Spare, Alexander of all kings greatest,[1] our sorry

[1] *v.* 1 was *e.g.* φεῖσαι μέγιστε βασιλέων Ἀλέξανδρε. Where
ve can see a basic verse I drop into verses in the translation.

τῳ κινδύνῳ τὴν πόλιν ἡμῶν εἰς τέλος ἀφανίσῃς)
Ἀλέξανδρε, νῦν πείρᾳ μαθόντες τὸ σὸν (ἰσόθεον)
κράτος σεβόμεθα[a]· ἐπίσχες τὰς ἀνικήτους χεῖρας
ἀπὸ Θηβαίων ⟨ἀγνοίᾳ μήπως ἀσεβεῖν δόξεις
τὰ συγγενῆ σου. Ἡράκλεος, Διόνυσος, οὗτοι
θεοὶ Θηβαῖοι⟩,[b] ἐπιδοξότατοι θεοὶ καὶ προγονικῆς
μίξεως ἀρχέγονον βλάστημα. Διός τε καὶ Σεμέλης
πυριλοχευτὸς Διόνυσος ἐν Θήβαις ⟨ἐτέχθη⟩[b]·
Ἡρακλῆς ⟨παρὰ⟩[b] Διός τε καὶ Ἀλκμήνης
⟨ἐσπάρη⟩[c]· οὗτοι[d] πᾶσιν ἀνθρώποις ⟨βοηθοὶ καὶ
εἰρηνικοὶ⟩[e] σωτηρίας φύλακες ἐφάνησαν

σοῦ δὲ τυγχάνουσ᾽[ιν] Ἀλέξανδρε **3**
προπάτορες ὄντες. **4**

τούτ⟨ους⟩[f] σε χρὴ μιμήσασθαι καὶ εὐεργετεῖν
ὥσπερ ἐκ θεῶν γενόμενος. μὴ ὑπερίδῃς τὰς
Διονύσου καὶ Ἡρακλέους τροφοὺς Θήβας ἀπολ-
λυμένας μηδὲ τὸ βοόκτιστον ἄστυ κατασκάψῃς·
ὄνειδος γὰρ ὕστερον Μακεδόσι γενήσεται.

ἀγνοεῖς Ἀλέξανδρε **5**
⟨   ⟩ Θηβαῖον [καὶ] οὐχὶ Πελλαῖον· **6**

⟨ὅλη⟩[g] σε Θηβαίων χώρα λιτανεύει

⟨θρηνοῦσα⟩, τοὺς σοὺς προπάτορας κομίζουσα **7**
θεούς, Λυαῖον **8**

εὐφροσύνης καὶ χορείης θιασώτ⟨ην⟩,[h] Ἡρακλέα

δίκαιον ἔργοις καὶ βοηθὸν ἀνθρώποις. **9**

---

[a] from σεβόμεθα we have only the versions as a check on
the readings of cod. A.   [b] Byz.   [c] Byz.: κατέσπειραν A.
[d] οὕτω A.   [e] Arm. (Byz.)   [f] Byz.: τούτῳ A.   6. e.g.

persons. Do not in such a disaster destroy our city completely.

> Taught by experience your divine puissance [1]
> We worship thee : keep off from us Thebans
> Your hands unconquered,

lest you appear in ignorance to wrong your kin. Heracles and Dionysus are the gods of Thebes, most glorious gods and ancestral offspring of earliest union between Zeus and Semele. Dionysus,[2] with fire for his midwife, was gotten in Thebes. In Thebes was born Heracles, offspring of Zeus and Alcmene. These appeared to all the world preservers, as helpers and peaceful guardians of safety. (3, 4) And they are your ancestors, Alexander. As you are born of gods, you should imitate these and do good. Do not allow the continuance of the destruction of Thebes which nursed Dionysus and Heracles, nor raze the ox-founded city. For hereafter it will be a reproach to the Macedonians. (5, 6) Do you not know, Alexander, that you are a Theban and not a citizen of Pella ? The whole land of Thebes calls on you wailing and entreats you through my mouth, (7, 8) Thebes that displays your ancestral gods, Lyaeus, god of delight and revel-leader of the dance, and Heracles

> Righteous of deed and all mankind's helper.   9

---

[1] *e.g.* ἰσόθεον τὸ σὸν κάρτος.
[2] Dionysius Zagreus, distinguished thus by later writers from D. the late-born.

ἔχων γένος   *a* πόλις A : ὅλη Byz. : *e.g.* ὅλη δὲ λιτανεύει σε
Θ. χ.   7. Byz. : διὰ τῆς ἐμῆς φωνῆς A.   Num νομίζουσα ?
8. Byz. : λῦσαι οὓς A.   *h* -ας A.

ἤδη καὶ μιμητὴς τῶν προγόνων ⟨φαινόμενος⟩,
καλῶν καὶ ἀγαθῶν ὄντων τὸ πλεῖον, εἰς εὐεργεσία**

    μετατρ⟨απεὶς ἐκ⟩ τῆς ὀργῆς,   10

[πρὸς]*b* τὸ προχειρότατον ⟨πρὸ⟩*c* τοῦ κολάζει
τὸ ἐλεεῖν ἔχε.

μὴ θῆς ἐρήμους   1**
τούς σε σπείραντας θεούς,

  τῶν σῶν γεν[ε]αρχῶν ⟨ἄστυ⟩ μὴ καθαιρήσῃς,
  ἰδίαν πατρίδα σου μὴ ἀγνοῶν κατασκάψῃς.
  ὁρᾷς τὰ τείχη ταῦτα; ⟨ταῦτα δέδμηνται⟩
  Ζῆθός ⟨θ'⟩ ὁ ποιμὴν καὶ ὁ λυρῳδὸς Ἀμφίων, 15
  οἱ Ζην[ων]ὸς υἱοί, ⟨τ⟩οὺς λάθρα ἔτε⟨κ⟩εν νύμφη
  ἡ Νύκτεως ⟨παῖς⟩ ἐν χοροῖς πλανηθεῖσα.
  [τὰ] θεμέλια ταῦτα καὶ τὸ πλούσιον δῶμα
  πύργωσε Κάδμος. ὧδε λαμβάνει νύμφη⟨ν⟩ 1*9*
  ⟨τὴν⟩ Ἁρμονίαν ἣν ἔτεκεν ἀφρογενὴς Κύπρις
  τῷ κλεψικοίτῃ Θρηκίῳ συνελθοῦσα.
  τὴν σὴν ἄρουραν μὴ ἀκρίτως ἐρημώσῃς,
  μη⟨δὲ⟩ καταφλέξῃς πάντα Θηβαίων τείχη.
  ⟨τῇ Λαβδακοῦ⟩ [ἔ]στι [α]δώμα⟨θ'⟩· ὧδε δυσ-
      δαίμων
  ⟨ὁ⟩ Λάϊο⟨ς⟩ ⟨γυναῖκα λαμβάνει⟩· τίκτει 25
  ⟨τὸν⟩ πατρο[ς]⟨φ⟩ό[γο]ντην ⟨Οἰδίπουν⟩ λυγρὰ
    μήτηρ.
  τοῦ⟨θ'⟩ Ἡρακλ⟨ῆ⟩ος τέμενος ἦν, τὸ μὲν πρῶτον
  Ἀμφιτρύωνος οἶκος· ⟨ᾧ⟩δ' ἐκοιμήθη
  τρεῖς νύκτας ὁ Ζεὺς εἰς μί⟨η⟩ν ἀριθμήσας.

---

a ἂν φαίνῃ Byz.   10. Byz.: -τρέπε τὰ A.   *b* del. Kroll.
e Müller, Arm.   12. καθ. πόλιν A.   13. σου π. A.
14. δεδομημένα A. A verse is lost ' with poems, lyre and
lute ': Byz., Arm.   15. Kroll.   λοίδορος A; *cf.* Arm.

Do you too imitate your ancestors, persons of
general excellence ;

Turn your anger to benevolence,   10
prefer pity to over-hasty punishment.

Desolate not   11
the gods that begat you,

The city of your ancestors raze not :   12
Nor thine own land in ignorance ruin.
Seest thou yon walls ? they are the walls builded
By shepherd Zethus, poet Amphion,   15
The sons of Zeus, whom at a feast erring
The child of Nycteus secretly brought forth.
And these foundations here, and the rich house
Were built by Cadmus, who to wife took once
Harmonia nymph, child of foam-born Cypris,   20
By union with ravishér Thracian.
Lay not thine own demesne thus unjudged waste
Nor burn down all the walls of us Thebans.
This is the house of Labdacus : here took
A wife the ill-starred Laius ; here bore   25
Oedipus patricide his poor mother.
Here shrine of Heracles : it was erstwhile
Amphitryon's house : here on a time Zeus slept
Three nights which he did turn to one only.

---

16. Müll., Arm.   ἔτεμεν A.   17. Arm.   χοροῖς Byz.,
Arm.: χρόνοις A.   18. Byz., Arm.: δόγμα A.   19. Kroll
ex Byz. προσεπύργωσε: πύργος καὶ A.   ὦδε Arm.   τὴν ν.
Ἀ. A: corr. Kroll.   21. κλεψοκύτει θρησκείῳ A : corr. Müll
22. ἀκρίτως μὴ A.   24. πλαγίου τε A.   ὅδε A.
25. πλαγίου τε A.   τίκτει: τί δὲ A, which gives one verse:
suppl. et corr. ex Byz., Arm.   26. -ψ- A.   27. Kroll.
-κλέος A.   28. Arm.: Ἀμφικτύονος A, Byz.   ὅδε A.
29. εἰς μίαν ἀθροίσας A: ἀριθμήσας Arm., Byz.

ὁρᾷς ἐκείνους τοὺς πεφλεγμένους οἴκους   30
ἀκμὴν ἔτ' ἐκ‹στάζ›οντας οὐρανοῦ μῆν‹ι›ν;
ἐκ‹εῖ› κεραυνῷ τὴν ποθουμένην βάλλει
Σεμέλην ποθ' ὁ Ζεύς· ‹ὧ›δε τοῦ πυρὸς μέσ‹σ›ον
τὸν Εἰραφιώτην ἀπεκύησε ‹Ληναῖον›.
‹ὧ›δ' Ἡρακλῆς μέμηνεν· ἔνθεν οἰστρηθεὶς   35
Μεγάραν ἀνεῖλεν τὴν γυναῖκα τοξεύσας.
ὁ βωμὸς οὗτός ἐστιν ὃν βλέπεις Ἥρας,
‹ᾗ τις› λόφου τέτμηκε βῶλον ἀρχαῖον,

ἔνθ' Ἡρακλῆς κιθῶνι σάρκα δαρδάπτων   40
κατηθαλώθη, χερσὶ τῆς Φιλοκτήτου
‹δοὺς τόξα βαφθένθ' αἵματι δρακοντείῳ›.
ταῦτ' ἐστὶ Φοίβου λόγια, Τειρεσίου δῶμα·
ὁ τρισγέρων ‹ἐν τοῖσδε› γίνεται μάντις
ὃν εἰς γυναῖκα μετετύπωσ‹ε› Τριτων‹ίς›.   45
Ἀθάμα‹ς› μανεὶς ἐνταῦθα παῖδα Λε‹ί›αρχον
τόξοις ἀνεῖλεν εἰς νε‹β›ρὸν τυπωθέντα·
ἐνθένδε ‹δ'› Ἰνὼ ‹φ›ήλατ' εἰς βυθοῦ κῦμα
σὺν τῷ Μελικέρτῃ τῷ νεογνῷ λυσσώδης.
ἐνθένδε πηρὸς Οἰδίπους ἀπηλάσθη   50
ταγ‹αῖ›ς Κρέοντος· οὗ τὸ βάκτρον Ἰσμήνην
‹ἔπεφνε Τυδεύς· ἧς ἐπώνυμος κρήνη›

31. Byz.: -ταξ- A.   -ην A : μῆνιν Arm., Byz.   32. ἐκεῖ
Arm.: ἐκ A.   κεραυνῷ Kroll: -νοῦ A.   33. ὅδε A.   μ. τ. π.
A.   34. ἡρα- A, Byz.   Ληναῖον Byz., Arm.: λινεύχην A.
35. ὅδε A.   38. ᾗ τις inserui: conf. HPHC et HITIC.
λ. τ. β. Byz. fere: ὑψηλὰ κέκμηκεν βῶμον ἀρχαῖον A.   A verse
is missing, e.g. βάθροισιν ὑψηλοῖσι χωρὶς ἱδρύσας; cf. Arm.
40. κιθῶνα A.   δαρδάπτειν A : corr. Maas.   41. καθηλώθη
A : corr. Maas.   42. supplevi e.g. ex Arm.   43. ταύταις τῇ A : corr. Müller.   44. ἐν οἷς Byz.   45. -α -α
A : corr. Müller.   47. Arm.: νεῦρον A.   48. ἐκεῖνο
A : δ' Müll. (Arm.).   49. λυσσότην A : corr. Müll.

Beholdest over there those burnt houses,   30
That even now do heaven's wrath ooze out ?
[1] There Semele belovéd did Zeus once
With levin smite ; and in the fire's own midst
Th' Eiraphiot Lenaean from thigh brought forth.
Here was to madness Heracles goaded   35
And Megara his wife slew with arrow.
This altar that thou see'st is of Hera,
Where the hill's ancient sod is by man cut
With lofty steps apart : Heracles here,
In anguish of the shirt his flesh burning,   40
Was burnt on pyre : unto Philoctetes
His arrows steeped in dragon's blood leaving.
See here is Phoebus' pulpit ; three ages
Teiresias living in this house outlived ;
Tritonis changed to woman his manhood.   45
Here Athamas went mad and Leiarchus
His child did shoot with bow a deer deeming.
Hence Ino leapt into the sea's depths down
With Melicertes her young child frenzied.
Hence Oedipus was driven, at Creon's   50
Behest, all lame : his staff, his Ismene,[2]
⟨Did Tydeus slay : from whom this spring gat
    name⟩

[1] *vv.* 14 *sqq.* may be older. Not once is 'O Alexander'
—useful padding in this metre—introduced. The sack is
only mentioned in 22 and 23. The diction is not so late,
the style high-faluting instead of prosaic, the catalogue
straightforward, and the metre excellent. But it is very
poor stuff. *A Midsummer-Night's Dream* provides an easy
model for translation.

[2] Schol. Eur. *Phoen.* 53 Ἰσμήνην ἣν ἀναιρεῖ Τυδεὺς ἐπὶ κρήνης
καὶ ἡ κρήνη ἀπ' αὐτῆς Ἰσμήνη ἐκλήθη.

---

l. τ. ν. τ. M.   50. ἀπελάσθην A : corr. Müller.   51. ταγες,
οὕτω A.   52. supplevi ex schol. Eur. *Phoen.*

οὗτός ⟨θ᾽⟩ ὁ ποταμὸς ἐκ μέσου Κιθαιρῶν⟨ο⟩ς
Ἰσμηνός ἐστι Βάκχιον φέρων ὕδωρ.
ἐλάτην ὁρᾷς κλάδοισιν ὑψόσ᾽ ἀρθεῖσαν;   55
ἐν τ⟨ῇ⟩δε Πενθεὺς[ιν] τοὺς χοροὺς κατοπτεύων
πρὸς τῆς τεκούσης δυστυχ⟨ῶ⟩ς διεσπάσθη.
πηγὴν ὁρᾷς βρύουσαν αἱμόχρουν ὕδωρ,
ἐξ ἧς βοὸς μύκημα δεινὸν ἠχεῖται;
τοῦτ᾽ ἐστὶν αἷμα τ⟨ῆς⟩ σεσυρμένης Δίρκης. 60
ὁρᾷς ἐκείνην ⟨ὑ⟩στάτην ἀκρώρειαν
τὴν ἐξέχουσαν τῆς ἀταρπιτοῦ ⟨τ⟩αύτης;
ἡ Σφὶγξ ἐπ᾽ αὐτῆς ἕζεθ᾽ ἡ τεραστ⟨ε⟩ία
πρόσταγμα προστάττουσα δημ⟨ό⟩ταις πᾶσιν
ἣν Οἰδίπους ἀνεῖλε πολλὰ μερμήρας.   65
αὕτη θεῶν πηγή 'στι καὶ ἱερὰ κρήνη,
ἐξ ἧς ἀναβλύζουσ⟨ιν⟩ ἀργυραῖ νύμφαι.
εἰς ⟨ταῦ⟩τα λιβάδι᾽ Ἄρτεμις κατελθοῦσα
φαίδρυν⟨ε⟩ χρῶτας· ὁ δὲ δύσαγνος Ἀκταίων
ἃ μὴ θέμις κατεῖδε λουτρὰ ⟨Λητ⟩ώας.   70
⟨μετ⟩αλλαγεὶς ⟨δ᾽ ἐς⟩ ἔλαφον ἀκλεῶς σῶμα
κυ⟨σ⟩ὶν ⟨ὠ⟩μοδ[ι]αίτοις διὰ τὸ λουτρὸν ἠγρεύθη.
⟨ὁρ⟩ᾷς ἵν᾽ Ἄρης ἐπολέμησε τὰς Θήβας,
ἔνθα Πολυνείκης ἦρξεν Ἀργείου λ⟨ηοῦ⟩,
στράπτων λοχαγὸς ⟨ἑπτὰ⟩ θ⟨ο⟩υρίων λόγχη⟨ς⟩; 74
ἐνταῦθα Κα[μ]πανεὺς παρὰ τὸ χεῖλος ἐφλέχθη.
τὰς μὲν πύλας καλοῦσι ⟨ταύ⟩τας Ἠλέκτρας.

53. οὗτω ἀπότομος A: ποταμ. Kroll.   εἰς μέσον and -νως
A: corr. Müll.   54. -εον φέρον corr. id.   55. εἰς ὕψος
ἀρ. κλ. A.   56. τιδε A.   57. τῇ -σῃ and -χοις A: corr.
Müll.   58. τὴν Ἀγήνορος A: πηγὴν ὁρᾷς Müll. (Arm., Byz.)
ἔμοχθον A: αἱματόεν Arm.: αἷμα χρυσοῦ κτλ. Byz.: ita Kroll.
60. τι A.   61. Müll.: ὑ om. A.   62. σατάρπη· τοῦ
A: corr. Müller, Arm.   αὑτῆς A: ταύτης Sitzler.
63. εἰσφῇξ A: corr. Müll., Arm.   64. -ώταις A.
300

And eke Ismenus from mid Cithaeron
In his stream bearing Bacchian water.
Dost see that fir with branches aloft borne ?   55
Thence Pentheus Dionysus' rites witnessed
Whom did his mother tear apart sadly.
Dost see the fount whose waters are bloody
And echo up a dreadful bull's bellow ?
This is the blood of Dirce, by bull dragg'd.   60
Dost see that ridge upon the horizon
That juts from out the path of man trodden ?
Upon it sat the Sphinx, that great marvel,
And bade the townsfolk all do her bidding,
Till she was slain by Oedipus crafty.   65
This is the Gods' Well and the spring sacred
From which do silver nymphs gush out water.
Unto these pools did Artemis climb down
To wash her body ; impious Actaeon
Saw the Letoan's bath that none may see.   70
His form uncouthly to a stag's changéd,
Slain by his ravening hounds he paid dearly.[1]
See'st thou, when Ares fought 'gainst Thebes' city,
Where Polynices led the host Argive,
Gleaming of seven spear hosts commander ?   75
There Capaneus was burnt at wall's coping,
Where are the gates men call the Electrae.

---

[1] διὰ τὸ λουτρὸν can hardly be correct. A phrase like δι'
ἀσέβειαν, ' for his impiety,' is needed. I translate λυτρόν.

---

65. μερμήνας A : corr. Müll., Arm.   66. π. θ. ἐστί A :
corr. Müll.   67. -σα A.   69. Byz. : -αι A.   70. Arm. :
διστ· A.   71. ins. Kroll : -αγῆς A.   72. κυριν A : corr.
Müll.   ὁμοδι- A : corr. Sitzler ex Arm.   73. ἐν πᾶσιν
A : παῖδες Arm.   74. λεῶς A (Byz.).   75. Byz. :
ἔνθα A.   -ην A.   77. Kroll.   δε υλοκορας A : corr. Müll.,
Kroll.

πύλαις δὲ ταύταις Προίτισιν ⟨τὸν⟩ ἄρρηκτ⟨ον⟩
Ἀμφιάραον χαί⟨ν⟩ουσα δέχ⟨νυται⟩ γαῖα.
Ὠγωγίαις πύλ⟨αι⟩σιν ἐν τρίταις κλήθρ⟨ῳ⟩ 80
⟨Ἱπ⟩πομέδοντα ⟨παῖς⟩ Μεγα[νευ]σθέν⟨ους⟩
κτείνει.
ἔπεσε ⟨δὲ⟩ Νηίσταισι παρὰ πύλαις ⟨ταύταις⟩
Παρθενοπαῖος· ὁ δ᾽ Ὁμολωίσιν γαί⟨ων⟩
πύλαισ⟨ι⟩ ⟨Τυδεὺς⟩ μυρί⟨οι⟩σιν ἐ⟨β⟩λήθη. 84
⟨φεύγει δ᾽ Ἄδραστος· ἑβδόμαι πύλαι δ᾽ αὗται⟩.

θάν⟨ο⟩ντα [ἐ]θάψ⟨αι⟩ τὸν λ⟨οχ⟩αγὸν Ἀργείων
[ἤ] διώ⟨ρι⟩σ᾽[α] ἁγνὰ ⟨πα⟩ῖς ἔτ᾽ εὖσα[ι] Καδ-
με⟨ί⟩α[ν],

αὗται Λυ⟨αί⟩ου τοῦ φιλευίου Θῆβαι   90
αὐ⟨λ⟩αὶ πέφυκαν ἃς ἐπ⟨έκτ⟩ισ᾽ Αἰσώπῳ,
⟨   ⟩ Βακχίους ⟨   ⟩ 91a
ἃς ⟨νῦν⟩ κελεύεις ἐκ βάθρων ἀναιρεῖσθαι.
ὁρᾷς σὺ σηκὸν Ἡρακλέους πυρὸ⟨ς μεστόν⟩;
τοῦ σοῦ γεν[ε]άρχου καὶ πατρὸς φιλ⟨ανθρώ⟩που
τεμένη σεαυτό⟨ν⟩ ἀγνοῶν θέλεις φλέξαι.   95
τί τοὺς γον⟨ῆ⟩ας τοὺς τεκόντας ὑβρίζεις,
Ἡρακλέους γένος ⟨τε⟩ καὶ κλυτοῦ Βάκχου;
   Ἰσμηνίας μὲν ἱκέτευσε τοσ⟨σ⟩αῦτα
πεσὼν παρὰ ποσὶ βασιλέως Ἀλεξάνδρου.

78. προσθεθείσαις ἡμῖν: corr. Müller, Kroll.   -τες A:
corr. Müll.   79. Arm.: χαιρ- A.   Kroll: δεχοίοιτε
A.   80. -εσιν A.   -ρε A.   81. παῖς Arm.: τὸν A.
ειτ᾽ A: ἀναιρεῖ Arm.   82. ἔπεσε Arm.: εἶπεν τὲ A.   δὲ
suppl. Sitzler.   Νηίσταισι Arm.: κεδίστεσιν A.   83. Arm.:
ὅτε ἦν μόλην A.   γαίης A: cf. θαρρῶν Arm.   84. Arm.
-εσιν A, ἐκλ. A, Arm.   85. supplevi e Byz., Arm.   86.
e.g. ἐνταῦθα πόλεως Ἀντιγόνη παρὰ γνώμην.   87. -ψε A.

At these the Proetid gates the unshatter'd   78
Amphiaraus was by earth swallow'd.
At third Ogygian gates with the gate-bar [1]   80
Hippomedon Megasthenes' son felled.
Fourth at the Neistean gates perish'd
Parthenopaeus ; at th' Homolóid
Slain Tydeus was, struck down by darts countless.
Adrastus fled : these are the gates seventh.   85
⟨Here notwithstanding the townsfolk's bidding,⟩
Antigone, unwedded maid Theban,
The leader of the Argive host buried,
⟨And with her love in living tomb perished⟩.
These Thebes upon Asopus are founded   90
Courts of Lyaeus that doth love ' Evoe,'
⟨That⟩ Bacchic ⟨revelry once supported⟩   91a
Which now to be uprooted thou biddest.
Dost see the shrine of Heracles song-famed ?
Homes of thine ancestor and sire, lover
Of all mankind, would'st burn ?   Thyself know'st
     not ?   95
Why dost insult thy parents, thy fathers,
Scion of Heracles and famed Bacchus ?
     Ismenias did supplicate thuswise
Falling at feet of King Alexander.

[1] I translate κλήθρῳ and what the Armenian version
suggests, παῖς Μεγασθένους for slayer of Hippomedon. But
I find no warrant for either guess.

-έντα and λαυ- A : corr. Müll.   88. λισετευσαι A. From
this verse to end of speech we have only A.   89. see
translation.   90. Λυεου τοῦ φιλέα υἱὸς ὡς οὐ A : corr. Kroll.
91. αὗται A.   ἐσωπω A : corr. Müll.   92. σὺ A :
corr. Kroll.   93. πυρούμενον A.   94. σ ευγενεαρχου A.
Φιλίππου absurde A.   95. σεαυτοῦ τεμ. A.   96. -εας A.
97. Ἡρ. γεν. A : corr. Müll.   98. -τος αὐτὸς μὲν ἱκετεύσας
Ἰσμ. ἔπεσεν π. π. Ἀ. β.

ὁ δὲ Μακεδὼν πρὸς αὐτὸν ὄμμα ⟨τρηχ⟩ύνας 100
καὶ τοὺς ὀδόντας τοῖς ὀδοῦσι συντρίζων
ὀργὴν ἀναπ⟨ν⟩έων τοῖον εἶπε τὸν μῦθον·
ὦ παγκάκιστ⟨ον⟩ ἐκλόχευμα Καδμείων,
ὦ παγκάκιστον ζῷον, ⟨ὦ⟩ θεοῖς μῖσος,
ὦ δήμι⟨ο⟩ν βλάστημα βαρβάρου ῥίζης, 105
ὦ τῆς ἐπ' Ἰσμήνῃ σ⟨ὺ⟩ λείψανον λύπης,
⟨. . . . .⟩,
σοφιστικούς μοι καὶ πεπλασμένους μύθους
εἰπὼν ὑπέλαβες ὅτι πλανᾷς Ἀλέξανδρον;
⟨ἢν⟩ γὰρ προ[σ]πᾶσαν τὴν πόλιν καθαιρήσω, 110
καὶ πυρὶ τεφρώσω ⟨   ⟩,
καὶ πάντας ὑμᾶς μετὰ πάτρας κατασκάψω,
⟨πῶς⟩ τῶν ⟨γενεαρχῶν ἐξέκοψα τὴν ῥίζαν⟩;
εἰ γὰρ σὺ πᾶσαν τὴν σπορὰν ⟨ἐ⟩γίνωσκε[ι]ς
[καὶ] πόθεν ⟨π⟩έφυ⟨κ⟩α, καὶ τίνες λοχεύσαντες,
οὐκ ἦν σε Θηβαῖοις⟨ι⟩ ταῦτα κηρύ⟨σσ⟩ειν; 116
ὅτι ἐστὶν ἡμῖν συγγενὴς Ἀλέξανδρος,
μὴ πρὸς πολίτην [α]πο⟨λέμιοι⟩ καταστῶμεν·
⟨θ⟩ῶμεν στρατηγ⟨ὸ⟩ν· σύμμαχοι γενηθῶμεν·
ἡμεῖς πολῖται, συγγενεῖς Ἀλεξάνδρου. 120
δόξ' ἐστὶν ἡμῖν τῆς γεραι[ο]τάτης ῥίζης,
⟨ἢ⟩ν οἱ Μακεδόνες ἐπιπλακῶσι Θηβαίοις.
ὅτ⟨ε⟩ δ' εἰς ἄμυναν οὐδὲν †ἀτονησατε†
καὶ τὸ θράσος ὑμῶν τῆς μάχης κατῃσχύνθη,
τότε ⟨δὴ⟩ μεταβολὴ καὶ δέησις ἀγνώμων, 125

100. Kroll?: ὃ. π. αὐ. A.   μηκύνας A.   102. Byz.:
-πτεων A.   103. Arm., Byz.: -τε A.   104. καὶ A:
(or ἄνθρωπε καὶ θ. Arm.: τῶν κακίστων Byz.).   105. -ων

The latter gave at him a glance savage, 100
And gnashing upper teeth upon lower
Spake out as follows his irate answer :
Most evilly begotten of Thebans !
Most evil beast ! Of heaven's hate object !
Of root barbarian a growth common ! 105
Last relic of the woe of Isméne !
⟨O dotard of blind mind and of blind eyes⟩ ! 107
With barrister-like cunning of false tales
Didst thou expect to cheat Alexander ? 110
Suppose that I destroy the whole city
And burn to ashes ⟨all the walls Theban⟩
And raze you all to earth with your township,
How do I then root out my forefathers ?
If thou hadst known of my descent truly
Whence I was born and who they were gat me, 115
Should'st not have told the Thebans as follows ?—
' Since Alexander is our own kinsman,
Let us not go to war 'gainst our fellow :
Let 's make him general, be his allies :
Kin are we, fellow-citizens are we. 120
To us the honour of the branch eldest
If Macedonians join with us Thebans.'
Now when you 've shown no spirit in combat,
And all your boast of battle disgraced lies,
Now you revert to prayers and pleas idle, 125

A.   106. -νησι A.   107. Arm. : see transl.
110. ἐν A : recte Arm. (Byz.).   111. om. A, Arm., Byz. :
e.g. πάντα Θηβαίων τείχη.   113. τὴν A, Byz. cett.   Byz. :
γονέων A.   114. σύ μου γ. τ. σ. π. A.   115. -σα A.
? κἀκ τίνων -ων.   116. -ττ- A.   118. παραταχθῶμεν Byz. :
                                                                    λ
πο for ἀπο.   119. δῶμεν -ίαν A.   122. ἐὰν A.   123.
Arm. : ὅτι A.   ηὐτονήσατε Raabe ex Arm. : l. -άντων τὸ
θάρσ.   125. Müller.

⟨οἵ, μὴ δυνάμενοι νο⟩ῦν ἔχοντ⟨ες αἱρεῖσθαι   126
δόξῃ⟩ ᾽δύνασθε πρὸς μάχην ᾽Αλεξάνδρ⟨ου⟩. 126a
ἀλλ᾽ οὐδὲ Θηβαίοι[ει]σιν οὐδέ σ⟨οι⟩ πρ⟨ῆξις⟩,
κάκιστα ⟨ἐφ᾽ ὑμᾶς⟩ τοῦ τέλους ⟨ἐπ⟩ελθόντος
Θήβας ⟨μὲν⟩ αὐτ⟨ὰ⟩ς ⟨αὐτόθεν⟩ καταφλέξω.
[καὶ] ᾽Ισμηνίαν ⟨δ⟩ὲ τὸν κράτιστον αὐλητήν   130
τ⟨ῶ⟩ν ἡμιφλέκτ⟨ω⟩ν δωμάτων ἐφεστῶτα
οὕτω [σε] κελεύω δίδυμ⟨ο⟩ν ὀργάνων ἦχος
βοιωτιά⟨ζει⟩ν ⟨τήν θ᾽⟩ ἅλωσιν αὐλῆσαι.
⟨οὕτω⟩[ς εἰπὼν ἐ]᾽κέλευσε τοῖς στράτοις κατα-
        σκάπτειν
ἑπτάπυλα τείχη καὶ πόλισμα Θηβαίων.   135
πάλιν ⟨Κιθ⟩αιρὼν ἐπεχόρευε Θηβαίοις·
᾽Ισμην[ι]ος αὐτὸς αἱμόφυρτος ⟨ἔρ⟩ρευσ⟨ε·
βέβλητο τείχη καὶ πόλισμα Θηβαίων.
καὶ πᾶσα γαῖα ταῖς σφαγαῖς κοπωθεῖσα,   139
κατα⟨ρ⟩ριφέντων δωμάτων πολυκ⟨λ⟩αύστων,
βαρὺ σ⟨τ⟩ένουσ⟨α τ᾽,⟩ ἀπ᾽ ἐ⟨δαφ⟩ῶν ἐμυκᾶτο.
᾽Ισμηνίας δὲ δίδυμον ὀργάνων ἦχος
ἦν ἁρμοσάμενος, τ⟨ῶ⟩ν ⟨ἐ⟩ρειπί⟨ω⟩ν ἑστώς
⟨ἧ⟩περ ἐκέλευσεν ὁ Μακεδὼν ᾽Αλέξανδρος.
ἐπεὶ δὲ τείχη πάντ᾽ ἔπιπτ⟨ε⟩ Καδμείων   145
καὶ μέλαθρα ⟨τὰ⟩ Λύκου καὶ τὸ ⟨Λα⟩βδάκου
        δῶμα,
εἰς εὐσέβειαν τῆς πάροιθε παιδείας
τὴν Πινδάρου ⟨᾽τήρησεν οἰ⟩κ⟨ί⟩αν ⟨μούνην⟩,

126, 126 a. iniuria desperat Kroll: ita Arm., nisi quod
σωφρονοῦντες et ἠβούλεσθε τὴν δόξαν vertit Raabe: μὴ δυνα-
μένη συνεχόντων ἀναιρῆσαι ὅτι οὐ δύνασθε πρ. μ. ᾽Αλεξάνδρῳ
A.   127. Arm.: σὺ A.   πρωτο A: συμφέρει
Arm.   128. Byz.: sive ὑμῖν κάκ.   αὐθέντος A: ἐλθ.
Byz.: ἐπιφανέντος Arm.   129. δὲ A: μὲν Byz., Arm.: ὸς
A.   Kroll e Byz. (ἐκ ῥιζῶν): Arm. ἐν ταύτῃ τῇ ὥρα.
306

Who, since before you could not choose rightly, 126
Imagined you could fight Alexander. 126a
But neither do the Thebans, nor dost thou
Avail : and now the evil end cometh,
When I will burn the town of Thebes wholesale.
And bid Ismenias, ' best flute-player,' 130
Standing upon the half-consumed houses,
The double harmony of pipes ⟨pouring⟩
Boeotian-wise [1] to play the town's sacking.
Thus did he bid his hosts to earth raze down
The seven-gated walls and fort Theban. 135
Once more Cithaeron raved and Ismenus
With stream of blood did rush on Thebes' city.
Fallen the walls and fort of the Thebans.
And all the earth was by the spade harassed,
As were cast down the houses much wept for, 140
And bellowed from its very foundations.
Ismenias stood there on the ruins,
The harmony of his twin pipes fitting,
Where he was bidden by Alexander.
But as fell all the walls of the Thebans, 145
And Lycus' halls and Labdacus' mansion,
In pious mem'ry of his young training
The house of Pindar did he spare only,

[1] The Boeotian νόμος here alluded to was symbolical of an unhappy ending.

130. σε A.   Arm., Byz. : κάκιστον A.   131. Arm. :
τὴν -ιν A.   132. Byz. : -ων A, Arm.   133. δύο τι ἀναλ.
A : recte Arm., Byz. : sive Βοιώτιον χεῖν.   134. Byz. :
αὐτὸν A.   136. Arm., Byz. : ἐκεῖ χαίρων A.   137. Byz. :
'Ισμηνίας Arm., -νιος A.   ῥεύσας A.   140. cf. Arm.
141. Arm. : γένους A.   ἀπελθών A.   142. τῆς μηνίας
A : corr. Müll.   143. τὸν ἡρίπιον corr. Müll.   144. ὅπερ A :
ὡς Arm.   145. -ον corr. Müll.   146. Λαβ. Arm.
148. codd. dett. i. 27 (Arm. ἐπῆρεν).   codd. dett. ibid.
μόνην : A κατανα τύμβον, Arm. πύργον : fort. οἰκίας πύργον

FRAGMENTA CHOLIAMBICA

ἐν‹θ᾽› ἦλθε παῖς ὢν καὶ μετέσχε ταῖς Μούσαις
πρὸς τὸν λυρ‹ω›δὸν τὸν γέροντα φοιτήσας. 150
πολλοὺς μὲν ἄνδρας περὶ πάτραν κατασφάξας
ὀλίγους κατέλιπε παντελῶς ἔτι ζῶντας,
καὶ τοὔνο‹μ›᾽ αὐτῶν τοῦ γένους ἀπήλειψεν.
Θήβας γὰρ εἶπε μή‹τιν᾽› ἔτι ‹κ›αλεῖν Θήβας
ἀλλ᾽ ἄπολιν αὐτῶν τὴν πόλιν γεν[ν]ηθῆναι, 155
ὡς ‹οὐ›νομ‹ῆ›ναι τὸν τοιοῦτον ἄνθρωπον.

(ii. 14. 5.)

ἔξω‹θεν› ἐπὶ λόφου (γὰρ) ἦν ὁ Δαρεῖος
(τάφρους) ὀρύσσων καὶ φάλαγγα[ς] συντάσσων
[ὡς] δέ‹ει› [τῶν] Μακεδόνων ‹οὐ μενοῦσαν›
    ὑσμίνην.
ὁ δὲ ‹τότ᾽› ἀθρήσας τὸ πολὺ θαῦμα Δαρείου 160
παρ᾽ ὀλίγον αὐτὸν προσεκύνησεν ὡς Μίθραν
θεὸν νομίζων οὐρανοῦ κατελθόντα
τοῖς βαρβάροις πέπλοισιν ἐγκοσμηθέντα.
ἦν γὰρ ‹καθάριον› τῶν τύπων τὸ προσχῆμα·
‹ἀνὴρ μεσῆλιξ›· ‹καὶ› λίθοι πολύ†τιμοι† 165

149. ἔνθ᾽: ἐν ᾧ A.   πάϊς ὢν Arm.: πεσὼν A.   150. -οδὸν
A.   153. Arm.: τοῦ νοῦ A.   154. μηκέτι λαλεῖν A:
recte Arm. καλεῖν.   156. ὡς ἔννομον εἶναι A: ἄνομον Arm.
Fuit ὃς ἂν ὀνομήνῃ vel εἴ τις . . . -ήναι.   157. Byz.: order
varies in A, B, C: γὰρ C.   158. Byz.: τάφους cod.
Barocc. 20: στράτους cett.   ὑποτάσσων A.   159.
ὡς δὲ ὁ A.   συνεισμηνιοδῳ (i.e. φόβῳ) A: recto propius
Byz.: καὶ φόβῳ συστελλόμενος πολλῷ τῶν M.   160. Arm.
161. θεὸν Μίθραν A: Μιθρ. om. cett.   Hic demum usque ad
σῶμα Δαρείου choliambos agnovit Kroll.   163. στολαῖς
308

Where as a boy he went to learn music—
His master the old lyrical poet.[1]   150
Many he slew around their own city,
And very few indeed he left living,
The very name of all their race rubbed out.
He bade that Thebes should be on no man's lips,
And that their city should be no city,   155
When anyone should speak of such fellows.

(Here the traces of choliambi cease for the time till ii. 13,
when Alexander is in Persia. But, as the last verse shows,
the story of the refounding of Thebes, and much else, was
in this metre once.)

(ii. 13-14. 5 *Alexander sees a vision of Ammon in
guise of Hermes with wand and cloak (and staff) and
Macedonian felt hat and is told to proceed in this disguise
as his own herald. He crosses the frozen Strangas and
tells the outposts of his errand. They take him to
Darius.*)

Apart upon a hill sat Darius   157
Deep ditches digging, and his hosts training
That feared the Macedonian combat.
When he saw Darius, that wonder,   160
He very nearly worshipped him ; Mithras
He thought to see from heaven descended,
Adornéd with barbarian raiment ;
For holy was the monarch's appearance.
He was of middle age. With stones precious   165

---

[1] Comment is perhaps superfluous.

---

cett.   164. Arm.: κατ᾽ αὐτόν A.   165. Byz.: A
and Arm. paraphrase: ad fin. ἐκ λίθων πολυτίμων dett.

διαδήματος [τὸ] κάρηνον ἔσκεπ‹ο›ν σφιγχθέν[τος]·
πέπλῳ δ' ἐχρῆτο ‹ὁπ›οῖον ἄλλον οὐκ εἶδ‹ε›ν·
Βαβυλωνί‹ω›ν (ὕφασμα) χρυσί‹ω›ν νῆμα
σειραὶ δὲ χρυσ[ει]αῖ καὶ πέδιλα [χρυσέων]
    φοινικ‹ᾶ›,   169
‹σκέποντα› δε‹ιρ›ὴν καὶ δυοῖν ποδοῖν κνῆμα[ι].

(χρύσεα δὲ λυχνίδια ἐπάνωθεν αὐτοῦ ἥπτοντο·
ἕτερα δὲ περὶ τοῖς πόσιν αὐτοῦ καὶ κύκλῳ περι-
έστραπτον λυχνία.)

λοχαγέται ‹δὲ› μυρίοι‹σι› κηρύκων   171
(σκήπτροισιν) ἑκατέρωθε[ν] μυρίων φωτῶν
κυκληδὸν ἐστέψαντο σῶμα Δαρείου.

        .   .   .   .   .   .

σοὶ μηνύω 'γών, (ὡς) παρὼν Ἀλέξανδρος,   174
βασιλεὺς βραδύνων εἰς μάχην ‹κατέρχεσθαι› 175
ἤδη πρόδηλός ἐστιν ἀσθενῆ ψυχήν
‹κεκτημένος καὶ δειλός›· ὥστε μὴ μέλλε,
‹πότε δὲ συνάπτεις τὸν πόλεμον›, (ἀνάγ-
    γειλον).   178

        .   .   .   .   .   .

οὐ μὴ [με] ταράξῃς ‹. . .›· ἀλλ' ἐπεὶ δεῖπνον
[τὸ] συνηθὲς [τοῖς] ἀγγέλοισ‹ι› δεῖ τελειοῦ-
    σθαι,   180
καὶ γὰρ αὐτὸς Ἀλέξανδρος (δεῖπνον ἐποίησε τοῖς
ἐμοῖς γραμματοφόροις, συνδείπνησόν μοι. καὶ)
χειρὸς (κρατήσας) δεξιᾶς ('Αλέξανδρον)   181

----

166. A δ. σ. τὸ κ. ἔσκεπεν : φορῶν cett.   167. A (ο)ῖον οὖν οὐκ
εἶδον ἅ.   168. A -ιον (bis) et εὔφασιν.   169. -κων A:
codd. dett. give the colours *vice versa*.   170. σκῆπτρον A.
171. ἀλλ' οἱ λ. A.   172. ἔθνεα ταῖς A : σκῆπτρα (and στίφη)
cett.   174. ἐγώ σοι μηνύω omnes : ὡς om. A.   175.

A diadem his head around girded.
A robe he wore,—the other had ne'er seen
Its like, of Babylonian gold lace :
Necklets of gold he wore and shoes crimson
Cov'ring his neck and calves of his two legs.   170

Golden lamps were alight above him, and larger
lamps shone at his feet and around him.

While generals with countless heraldic   171
Sceptres arrayed on this and on that side
Circled around the form of Dareius.

(*Alexander is brought to Darius and delivers his
message* :—)

I tell thee, as I were[1] Alexander,   174
A king who is sloth to enter the combat,   175
At once is shown to have a weak spirit
And cowardliness of heart.   Without halting
Announce to me when combat may open.   178

(*Darius, after commenting on A.'s boldness, says* :—)

Thou shalt not trouble me.   But, since dinner   179
Must be prepared as usual for heralds,   180

for so did Alexander himself give dinner to my envoys,
dine with me.   So

He took the right hand of Alexander   181

---

[1] ὥσπερ ὤν.

ὀφείλεις εἰδέναι βασιλεῦ Δαρεῖε ὅτι βρ. ε. μ. β. πρ. ἐ. τῷ ἀντιδίκῳ :
τῷ ἀντιδ. om. Byz. recte.   176. ἀσθενῆ ἔχων τὴν A.
177. κεκτημένος Byz. : καὶ ἄνανδρον Arm.: δειλ- and μαλθακ-
Byz.   178. init. Byz. (exc. δέ): codd. dett. ἀλλὰ ἀνάγ-
γειλόν μοι πότε βούλῃ σύναψαι . . .   180. τὸ σ. δ. τοῖς ἀγ. A :
sim. Byz.   181. τῆς δ. χ. A.

FRAGMENTA CHOLIAMBICA

[εἰσ]ήνεγκεν αὐτὸν ‹τῶν ἀνακτόρων εἴσω›
ὁ δ᾽[ε Ἀλέξανδρος] (ἀγαθὸν) ἔσχ᾽ ἐν καρδίᾳ τὸ
σημεῖον
ἤδη κρατήσ‹ειν› τῶν τυραννικῶν ‹ἑδρῶν›.
ὁ δὲ ‹οὖν› ἐ[ι]σελθὼν εἰς τὰ μέλαθρα Δαρείου
καὶ †ἐπὶ τὸ[ν] δεῖπνον εὐθέως ἐκηρύχθη.   186
πρῶτος δ᾽ ἄνω κλιντῆρος ἦν ὁ Δαρεῖο‹ς›,

δεύτερος δὲ ἀδελφὸς ἦν Ὀξυάθρης ‹ὁ› Δαρείου,

τρίτος δὲ ‹Δίοχος› σατράπης Ὀξυδράκ‹ων›,   188

εἶτα πάλιν ‹Ἀ›δου‹λ›ίτης[a] ὁ ἐπὶ Σούσης,[b] καὶ
Φραόρτης[c] ‹. . .›

μετ᾽ αὐτὸν ‹ἐκλίθη δὲ› Μιθριδάτης ἕκτος   189
καὶ Τιριδάτης τοξοτῶν ‹ὃς ἦν› πρῶτος,   190

ἔτι τε Κανδαύλης ὁ νυκτίχρωος †Μένωπος†,[d] εἶτ᾽
ἀνέκειτο Αἰθιόπων ἄναξ,

καὶ Πολυάρης ἔγγιστ‹ος› ἡγέμων   191
μέγας,[e] Ὀρνιράτης, Διόσιος, Καρδερωκέτης, Σουλ-
βάτης, Ἀλκίδης,

τοῖσ‹ι› δ᾽ ἀντίκρυς   192
ἀνέκειτο μο‹ῦ›νος αὐτὸς ἐπὶ μιᾶς κλίνης
ὁ πάντ᾽ ἄριστος ὁ Μακεδὼν ‹Ἀλέξανδρος›.   194

ch. 15   .   .   .   .   .   .

.   .   .   .   .

182. Byz. (except for ἔσω): ἔνδον τῶν βασιλείων A.   183.
better ‹ἐνὴν δὲ› (καλὸν).   184. -ήσης A.   τόπων Byz.: δε-
σποτῶν absurde Arm.: τὸν τύραννον νικῶν A.   185. οὖν inserui.
186. e.g. πρὸς (πρῶτος codd. dett.).   187. Arm., Byz.: -ου
312

And led him by it into his palace ;
The other treasured up the fair omen,
That he would take the tyrant's throne right soon.
So to Darius' halls did he enter   185
And even unto dinner was summoned.
Now first on couch aloft lay Darius,   187

second came Oxyathres brother of Darius,

Third Diochus the Oxydrak's satrap,   188

then next Adoulites warder of Susa, and Phraortes
‹   .›,

And Mithridates next to him lay sixth   189
And Tiridates chief of the archers,   190

and Menops' son the dusky Candaules, then the king
of the Ethiopians ‹. . .›,

And Polyares nearest great general,   191

Ornirates, Diosius, Carderocetes, Sulbates, Alcides.

                              over   192
Against them lay alone on one divan
Hero of Macedon Alexander.   194

(*The Persians marvelled at his small size, not knowing
that a drop of heavenly soul resides in a small vessel.
Now the cupbearers plied the cup freely.*)

---

a.   188. Byz.: δὲ ὦχος A.   Kroll : -ησαν A.
δουρίτης A : -λίτης Byz. : 'Ανδ- Arm.   b Arm.: ἐκ πισσ- A.
Here and elsewhere the forms differ in our three authorities
between whom I choose : all miss the description of Ph.
189. συνανεκλ. post ἕκτος A.   190. τόξων τῶν A.   d Per-
aps ὁ νυκτίχρωος παῖς Μέροπος ὁ Κανδαύλης.   191. ἔγ-
ιστα A.   e e.g. δεινός.   193. αὐ. μ. ἀν. A.   194.
Αλ. Byz.

μεσάσαντος δὲ τοῦ πότου ἐπινοεῖ τι ὁ Ἀλέξανδρος·

(ὅσους σκύφους ⟨γὰρ⟩ ἔλαβ') ἔσωθεν ἔκρυ⟨π-
τ⟩εν·   195

οἱ δὲ [πινεγχύται] βλέποντες ἐνεφάνιζον Δαρείῳ.
ὁ δὲ Δαρεῖος ἐκ τοῦ κλιντῆρος ἀναστὰς εἶπεν· ὦ
γενναῖε

πρὸς τί ταῦτ' ἐγκολπίζ[ῃ];   197

(νοήσας δὲ ὁ Ἀλέξανδρος ἀπὸ τοῦ σχήματος τῆς
ψυχῆς ⟨τὴν μωρίαν⟩[a] εἶπε· μέγιστε βασιλεῦ,

οὕτω ⟨γὰρ⟩ (ὁ ἐμὸς δεσπότης Ἀλέξανδρος   198
ὅταν δεῖπνον ποιῇ τοῖς ταξιάρχαις καὶ ὑπερ-
ασπισταῖς)

τὰ κύπελλ' ⟨ἐν οἷσιν ἂν πίωσι⟩ δωρεῖται   199
⟨αὐτοῖσιν⟩· (ὑπενόουν δὲ καί σε τοιοῦτον,   200
καὶ) ὡς παρὰ τῷ ἐμῷ βασιλεῖ ἐνεκολπισάμην . . .

. . . .
πρὸς ταῦτα [. . .]ὁρῶντες ⟨τῶν λόγων Ἀλεξ-
άνδρου⟩   201
(τὴν πιθανότητα) ⟨πάντες ἦσαν ἔκθαμβοι⟩·
πλαστὸς (γὰρ) ἀεὶ μῦθος ⟨ἢ⟩ν (ἔ)χῃ πίστιν
(εἰς ἔκστασιν) πεποίηκε τοὺς ἀκούοντας.
[. . .] σιγῆς γενομένης ⟨οὖν τις⟩ ἀνεπόλησ[εν
αὐτόν   205
ὄνομα[τι] (Πασάργης), [. . .] ἡγεμὼν γῆς Περ-
σίδος·

195. ἔκρυβε A.   [a] Arm.   199. ενσιπῆνοις A (i.e. ἐν ⟨οἶ⟩σι
πίνουσ⟨ι⟩).   200. Arm., Byz.   201. [οἱ Πέρσαι ἀφ] delen-
dum.   fin. Byz., Arm.   202. πιθανότητι (misplaced)
codd. dett.: τῇ π. Arm., Byz.   Byz. (ἄπ-).   203. ἐὰν codd
σχῇ A.   204. Better ἐξιστάναι πέφυκε.   205. [   ]: πολλῆ
314

And when the drinking was well started Alexander
devised a ruse.

As the cups came to him, in his bosom   195
He hid them : which was shown to Darius.   196

Darius leaping up from his couch said, ' Good sir,

Why put these in your bosom ?   197

Alexander, diagnosing from his appearance the folly
of his soul, said, ' O most mighty King,

My master even so, Alexander,[1]   198

if he gives a feast to his own spearmen and
colonels

Gives them the cups whereof they have drunken[2];
And I supposed you had the same custom,   200

and put them in my bosom as I would at my king's
table. (But if you have not this custom, take them
back.)

Wherefore they when they saw the persuasion   201
Of Alexander's words were astonished.
For ever lying tale if it wins faith
Drives to bewilderment all its hearers.
Silence ensuing, one, the embassy's   205
Chief leader, called Pasarges, remarked him.

---

[1] Om. Ἀλέξ. et lege ὅτ. δ. τ. τ. καὶ ὑ. ποιῇ.

[2] Professor Kroll adds to our difficulties by reading
ἐκείνοις for ἐνσιπήνοις. What A copied badly was ἐν οἶσι πίνουσι
and the original perhaps κύπελλ' ἐν οἶσιν ἂν πίωσι. See also
crit. n.

οὖν codd.: ἧς A.   206. A: ὀνόματι ἀσάργης: παράγης C.
[   ]: ὃς ἦν γενόμενος. Notandum Περσίδος. ἢ τῆς πρεσβείας.

ᾔδει γὰρ αὐτὸν κατὰ πρόσωπον, εἰς Πέλλην
ἡνίκα τὸ πρῶτον ἦλθε[ν ὑπὸ] Δαρεί‹ῳ› πεμφθεὶς
Μακεδονίας ‹γ›ῆς (τοὺς) φόρους ἀπαιτῆσαι.
(ἔστη δ' ἐπιστὰς ἀντίκρυς Ἀλεξάνδρου)·   210

καὶ πρὸς ἑαυτὸν ἔλεγεν,

οὐκ ἐστὶν οὗτος ὃν λέγουσ'[ιν] Ἀλέξανδρον; 211
ἔστιν ‹γε›· δεῖ με τοὺς τύπους ἐπιγνῶναι.   212

καὶ κατανοήσας ἐκ δευτέρου εἶπεν· αὐτός ἐστιν
ἀσφαλῶς·

          ἡ φωνὴ γὰρ αὐτὸν ἤλεγξε   213
‹εἰ καὶ πλανᾷ τύπος με›·   214

(πολλοὶ γὰρ ἄνθρωποι τῇ φωνῇ γινώσκονται κἂν
ἐν σκότει διάγωσιν). . . . παρανακλιθεὶς δὲ τῷ
Δαρείῳ εἶπε· [μέγιστε]

(βασιλεῦ ‹τε› καὶ δυνάστα ‹Περσικῆς› χώρας)
οὗτός ‹γ'› ὁ πρεσβεὺς αὐτὸς ἔστ'[ιν] Ἀλέξανδρος

(ὁ παλαὶ Φιλίππου ‹γενόμενος› ἀριστεύων) 217

•   •   •   •   •   •   •   •

ὁ δὲ Ἀλέξανδρος ὑπὸ τοῦ θεοῦ βοηθούμενος

ὤξυνε ([τὸν] πῶλον τὴν ὁδὸν διευθύνων)·   218
νὺξ γὰρ βαθεῖα (καὶ σκότος κατ' Ο‹ὔ›λυμπον)·
‹πλεῖστοι δ' ἐφ' ἵππων βάρβαροι διώκοντες› 220
‹ἴσχυσαν οὐδὲν καταλαβεῖν› ‹Ἀλέξανδρον›·
(ὁ μὲν γὰρ εἶχε τὴν ὁδευτικὴν) πεύκην

207-8. order ἡνίκα . . . ἦλθεν εἰς Πέλλην τῆς Μ. ὑπὸ
Δαρείου π.   209. Better ἀπαιτήσων.   210. so codd.
Barocc. 20 (ἐπιστὰς ἔστη).   212. ἀσφαλῶς ἐστι Α.   213. ἔστιν
γάρ?   214. ita fere Byz.: sim. codd. dett.   215. πάσης
316

For by his face he knew him, since erstwhile
He came to Pella town, for Darius
Demanding Macedonian tribute.
He took his stand facing Alexander   210

and said to himself

Is not this he they call Alexander?   211
'Tis he.   I ought to recognize full well.   212

And observing again he said: Certainly it is he;

His voice so betrays him,   213
Even if his shape trick me.   214

For many people even in the dark are recognized
by their voice. (*Pasarges then concluding certainly
that he was Alexander himself*) lay down beside Darius
and said,

The envoy, King and Lord of all Persia,   215
Is none but Philip's son Alexander
Who among Philip's sons (?) showed most manhood

(*Alexander seeing he is recognized escapes with the
cups and a torch which he snatches from a sentry.*)

And with God's aid   217
He spurred his colt and held on a straight course.
The night was deep, and dark was Olympus.
And many following him on horseback   220
Entirely failed to catch Alexander.
For he held out, unto himself shining,

B: Περσ. Byz.   217. γεγονὼς B (num τῶν γόνων !?)
Mox τοῦ θεοῦ βοηθοῦντος.   218. δι. τὴν ὁ. αὐτῷ B; cf. Byz.
219. ἦν γὰρ ν. β. A.   "Ολ. C, Byz.   220. Byz.: πλ.
δὲ τοῦτον β. δ. μεθ' ἵπ. κατ. οὐκ ἴσχ. sim. B.   222. C, Arm.
γῆν C: πεύκην A, Arm.

λάμπ⟨ων⟩ ἑαυτῷ, (φῶ⟨ς⟩ ἄπειρον ἔμπροσθεν)·
(ἦν δ' ὥσπερ ἀστὴρ ⟨τῶν ἐν⟩ οὐρανῷ φαιδρός
μόνος τ' ἰὼν εἰς οὐδὲν ἦγε[ιτο] τοὺς Πέρσας), 225
οἱ δ' εἰς φάραγγας ⟨ᾗ⟩ ἔτυχον ⟨διώλοντο⟩. 226
ὁ δὲ Δαρεῖος συνεφοράζετο ἐπὶ τοῦ κλιντῆρος
καθεζόμενος· ἐθεάσατο δὲ [τι]ᵃ ἐξαίφνης

                κρήγυόν τι σημεῖον·   227
⟨Ξέρξου⟩ γὰρ εἰκὼν τοῦ ὀρόφου διαστάντος
κατέπεσε⟨ν⟩ ἥνπερ ἠγάπ⟨ησε⟩ Δαρεῖος.   229

. . . .
. . . . .ᵇ

μηδὲν δυνάμενοι τῶν τόπων ἀπέστησαν, 230
ποταμὸς γὰρ οὗτος πᾶσίν ἐστιν ἄπλευστος. 231
καὶ οἱ μὲν Δαρείῳ ἔλεγον

             τὸ εὐτύχημ' Ἀλεξάνδρου. 232
ch. 16   .   .   .   .   .   .
   .   .   .   .   .   .

        ἕωθεν τὸν στράτον συναθροίσας 233
(ἐξ ὀνόματος καθώπλισ'), ἐν μέσ⟨οις⟩ ἑστώς
ὁποῖος ⟨ὁ⟩ Ζεὺς [. . . .] δαίμονας διακρίνων. 235
καὶ πάντας [τοὺς ἑ]αυτοῦ ⟨τοὺς στράτους⟩
    ἀριθμήσας   236
(εὗρεν τὸν ἀριθμὸν χιλιάδας ἑκατὸν εἴκοσι,ᶜ καὶ
στὰς ἐφ' ὑψηλοῦ τόπου τινὸς παραινεῖ αὐτούς
λέγων· ἄνδρες συστρατιῶται,

εἰ καὶ ⟨παρ' ἡμῖν⟩) ὁ ἀριθμὸς βραχὺς λίαν, 237

223. κατέλαμπεν A.   φῶτ' B, which places this after next
verse. 224. ἐξ codd. dett. 225. ἀνύων τὴν ὁδὸν μόνος C:
ἀνιών B. 226. ᾗ : or ἐν [τῷ] σκότει Byz.: A καὶ οἱ μὲν διώκοντες
εἰς ὃ μέρος ἔτυχον ἐδίωκον· ὁ μὲν γὰρ . . . οἱ δὲ εἰς τὰς φάραγγας

The guiding torch of infinite splendour,
And was as one of heaven's stars radiant,
Lone traveller outwitting the Persians,   225
Who perished in the dells, as chance led them.   226

Now Darius bemoaned his fate, seated on his divan;
where he

Saw suddenly a trustworthy omen.   227
The roof cracked and a picture of Xerxes,
By King Darius treasured much, fell down.   229

*(Alexander escapes over the river just before it thaws :
the Persians arrive too late and)*

Retreating from the riverside baffled,   230
(For this is an impassable river)
Of Alexander's luck told Darius.   232

(Alexander next day)

Full early did assemble his hosts all,   233
Armed them and called by name, in midst standing,
Like Zeus the heavenly deities counting.   235
And having counted up all his soldiers   236

found there were 120,000. He stood on a high hill,
and harangued them :

Fellow soldiers and friends !
Full small, as well I know, are our numbers,   237

κατεκρημνίζοντο.   *a* del. Kroll.   228. Arm. : εἰκὼν
γὰρ ἔξω A.   κατ. δι. A.   229. -πα A.   *b* There
are only isolated traces of verses in Alexander's escape
across the river, *e.g.* τὸν δ' Ἀλέξανδρον ἔρριψεν· ἐρρύσθη ⟨δὲ⟩
γῆς ἐπὶ στερρᾶς.   230. ἀπ. τῶν τ.· ὁ γὰρ π. οὗ. ἄ. ἐ. π. A.
233. συν. τ. σ.   234. ἐκέλευσεν ἐ. ὁ. καθοπλισθῆναι C, Arm.
μέσῳ A.   235. τοὺς οὐρανίους A, ἐν οὐράνῳ Arm.   *c e.g.*
δὶς ἑξήκοντα χιλιάδας εὗρεν.   237. A in false place : B
εἰ καὶ β. ὁ ἀ. ἀλλὰ φρ. μεγάλη παρ' ἡμῖν κτλ.

FRAGMENTA CHOLIAMBICA

ἀλλὰ φρόνησις μεγάλη [παρ᾽ ἡμῖν] καὶ θράσος κα
δύναμις

    ὑπὲρ ‹γε› Πέρσας τοὺς ἐναντίους ἡμῶν·   238
    ἡμῶν δὲ μηδεὶς ἀσθενέστερόν . . .   239

τι λογίσηται

    ‹. . . . .› θεωρῶν τὸ ‹μέγα› βαρβάρωι
      πλῆθος·   240
    εἷς γάρ τις ἐξ ἡμῶν ‹γε› χεῖρα γυμνώσας)
    †τῶ νῶ θεωρῶν† (χιλίους ἀναιρήσει.   242

μηδεὶς οὖν ὑμῶν δειλιάσῃ·

    πολλαὶ γὰρ εἰσὶ μυριάδες ‹. . . . .› μυιῶν   243
    λειμῶνας ‹. . . . .› θλίβουσαι·
    ὁπόταν δὲ ταύταις ἐμπέσωσιν ‹αἱ› σφῆκες   245
    σοβοῦσιν αὐτὰς ταῖς πτέρυξι) κλά‹ζ›οντες·
    οὕτω τὸ πλῆθος οὐδέν ἐστι πλὴν πλῆθος·
    σφηκῶν γὰρ ὄντων οὐδέν εἰσιν (αἱ μυῖαι).
    ὡς δ᾽ εἶπε[ν ὁ] βασιλεύς, πάντες αὐτὸν ηὐφήμουν.
    πολλὰς ‹δὲ› χέρσους καὶ †στόμους† διευθύνας   250
    ‹ἦγεν› τὸν ὄχλον ἐπὶ τὰ νῶτα τοῦ Στράγγου.
    Δαρεῖος ‹οὖν› ὡς ‹εἶδε› τόν ‹τ᾽› Ἀλέξανδρο‹ν›
    ὀλιγοστὸν ὄντα, (καὶ παγέντα) ‹. . . . . .›
    [ ] τὸν ποταμὸν εὑρὼν διεπέρασ᾽[εν], ἐπιστῆναι
    βουλόμενος . . . . . . .τοῖς στρατοῖς Ἀλεξάνδρου·   255
    . . . . κήρυκας εἰς ‹μέσον› πέμπει
    καλεῖν ‹ἀνώγων› (εἰς μάχην [τοὺς] ἀριστ‹ῆ›ας)

(ὁ δὲ στρατὸς Δαρείου

---

238. τοὺς B.   239. μηδ. οὖν ἡμ. B.   ἀσθενέστερον : -ος
φανείη Byz.: e.g. -ραν ψυχὴν ἔχοι.   240. Byz.: τὸ πλ. τῶν
β. B.   242. τῶν ἀντιμάχων codd. dett.; verss.: τῶν

but we have great resource and courage and personal
strength

Beyond our adversaries the Persians.   238
Let none of us display the least weakness
Seeing the vast barbarian numbers.   240
For one of us even with hand empty
Of idle fools like these will slay thousands.
For there are flies <. . .> in thousands
Thronging in days of summer the meadows;
But when the wasps attack them in battle   245
They rout them merely by their wings' whistle.
So numbers count as nothing but numbers.
When there are wasps mere flies count for nothing.
The king spoke and his soldiers all cheered him.
And after many lands and paths traversed   250
He led them to the borders of Strangas.
Darius when he saw the commander
Had few with him, and saw the stream frozen,
Crossed it in haste, desiring to surprise
By stealth the armies of Alexander,   255
Yet heralds sent to summon to combat
The chosen men of all the brave foemen.

Now Darius' host

ἀντιδίκων οὕτω τῷ νῷ θεωρῶν (οὕτω τι νωθρῶν Kroll).   Vestigiis
propius τῶν ὧδε μωρῶν, which I translate.   243. *e.g.* ἀεί.
244. ἡμέρᾳ θερινῇ Arm., *e.g.* -να θερινῆσ' ἡμέρῃσι: θλίβουσαι λει-
μῶνας B: αἱ σκοποῦσαι τὸν ἀέρα misere cod. A.   246. κλαγόντες
A.   247. πλὴν πλῆθος: πρὸς ἡμᾶς or σύνεσιν codd. dett.
248. codd. omnes?: παρόντων inepte Kroll.   250. οὖν
omnes.   ὁδοὺς καὶ ἄκρα Arm., στίβους Kroll.   251. εὗρεν A.
252. ὁ δὲ Δ. omnes.   ἰδών: ἐθεάσατο A.   στράτον -ρου A.
254. A ἐχλεύασεν ὡς μηδὲν (om. cett.) καὶ εὖ. ἐπιπήκτον τ. π.
255. *e.g.* ἄφνω: πρῶτος dett.   256. καὶ A: *e.g.* ὅμως
(Byz.) γε μήν.   ἐκπέμπει A.   257. καλεῖν τὴν μάχην A:
καλοῦντας κτλ. cett.   -εας codd. dett.

FRAGMENTA CHOLIAMBICA

⟨πᾶς ὅπλοις ἐθωρήχθη⟩.

ὁ δὲ ἅρματος Δαρεῖος ἦν ἐφ' ὑψηλοῦ

καὶ οἱ σατράπαι αὐτοῦ ἐπὶ δρεπανηφόρων ἁρμάτων
ἐκαθέζοντο). τῶν δὲ Μακεδόνων προῆγεν ὁ
Ἀλέξανδρος ἐγκαθίσας τὸν Βουκέφαλον ἵππον·
προσεγγίσαι δὲ τούτῳ οὐδεὶς ἠδύνατο. . . .

ὡς δ' ἑκατέρους ἔκληζε πολέμιος σάλπιγξ   260
πολὺς δέ τις θροῦς συνεκλονεῖτο καὶ κλαγγ⟨ή⟩
στράτων, προθυμίᾳ ⟨γὰρ⟩ ἦλθον εἰς δῆριν,
(οἱ μὲν λίθους ἔβαλλον, οἱ δὲ τόξ.   263
ἔπεμπον ὡς ὄμβρον ἀπ' οὐρανοῦ φερόμενον,
ἕτεροι δ') ⟨ἔκρυπτον⟩ βέλεσιν (ἡμέρας φέγγος),
ἄλλοι δ' ⟨ἄρ'⟩ ἐξοιστροῦντο ⟨ταῖς⟩ μαχαίραισιν·
[καὶ] ὤλοντο πολλοί, πολὺς ὀδυρμὸς ὠρώρει·
⟨ὡς⟩ οἱ μὲν ἐσφάζοντο (βέλεσι τρωθέντες),
ἡμισφαγεῖς δ' ἔκειντο . . . . (ἄλλοι·   268
γνοφερὸς δὲ ἦν ὁ ἀὴρ καὶ αἱματώδης).

πολλῶν δὲ Περσῶν ὀλεθρίως τελευτώντων,   269
ὁ Δαρεῖος ἔστρεψε τὰς ἡνίας τοῦ ἰδίου ἅρματος,[a]
καὶ πᾶν τὸ Περσῶν πλῆθος εἰς φυγὴν ὦρμα.   270
δρεπανηφόρων ⟨οὖν⟩ ἁρμάτων τροχαζόντων
(ἐθέριζ⟨ο⟩ν αὐτο⟨ὶ⟩ τοὺς πλείστους τῶν Περσῶν
ὄχλους ὡς [ἐπὶ]

258. ἐθωρακίσαντο πανοπλίαν codd. dett.: π. ὅ. ἐθωρακίσθη Byz.
259. ὁ δὲ Δ. ἦν ἐφ' ἅρματος ὑψηλοῦ A.   260. ἔκλαγξε codd.
dett.: οὖν -ους ἔκλιζε A (Kr.).   261. κλαγγείων A: i.e.
κλαγγὴ τῶν Kroll.   262. δὲ A.   263. e.g. οἱ δ' ἐτόξευον
πέμποντες — ὡς ἀπ' οὐρανῶν ὄμβρον.   264. βολίδας ἐσφεν-
δόνιζον ὥστε ἐπικαλύπτειν codd. dett.: ἐσκέπασαν A.   τὸν
ἀέρα A: ἡμέρας φέγγος codd. dett., Byz. (Arm.).   265. ἅ.
δὲ μ. ἐξ. A.   266. πολλοὶ μ. ὤ., πολὺς δὲ A.   267. καὶ

322

was all in arms ready.   258
Darius sat on chariot lofty

and his satraps were seated on scythed chariots.
The Macedonians were led by Alexander on his
horse Bucephalus that none could approach.

Now when the martial trumpet called both sides 260
And mighty din and shouting of armies
Clattered together, eagerly fighting,   262
Some hurled great stones, and others shot arrows,

like rain falling from heaven,

Others with missiles the daylight clouded,   264
Others with swords to frenzy were goaded.   265
Many did fall, and many cries rose up,
As some were slain of wounds from thrown missiles
Or lay half slain . . .

The air was thick and blood-tainted.

When many Persians were by doom taken,

Darius turned the reins of his car,

And the whole Persian host to flight urgéd.   270
Then on their chariots scythed, in haste wheel-
ing,[1]   271

the satraps mowed down the common herd of the
Persians like

---

[1] vv. 271-2 may be continuous, e.g. πεζοὶ 'θερίζονθ' ὥσπερ
ὑπ' ἀγροτῶν σῖτος, which is nearer the A version.

---

codd.   268. ἕτεροι δὲ ἠ. ἔ. A, Byz. : ἄλλοι δὲ ἠ. ἔ. codd.
dett.   ^a e.g. Δ. ἔφυγεν ἡνιοστροφῶν ἄρμα.   270. τὸ πλ.
τῶν Π. A.   271. δὲ πολλῶν A.   ^b So in general
codd. dett.: -εν -os codd. dett.: e.g. ἐθέριζον ὄχλους ὥσπερ
ἐν θέρους ὥρῃ.

FRAGMENTA CHOLIAMBICA

στάχυας ἀρούρης ἀγρόται ἐπικείροντες).   272

κάτωθε[ν] δ'[ι] ἐλύθη κῦμα καὶ ἥρπασε‹ν› πάντας
οἱ δὲ μὴ φθάσαντες διαπερᾶσαι τὸν ποταμόν

ὑπὸ τῶν Μακεδόνων (νηλεῶς) ἀνῃροῦντο.   274
ὁ δὲ Δαρεῖος φυγὰς γενηθεὶς καὶ εἰσελθὼν εἰς τὰ
βασίλεια[a]

(ῥίψας ἑαυτὸν εἰς [τὸ] ἔδαφος, ἀνοιμώξας,   275
σὺν δάκρυσι ἐθρήνει ἑαυτὸν ἀπολέσας πολὺ πλῆθος
ἀνδρῶν

κ̓αὶ τὴν Περσίδα ὅλην ἐρημώσας).   276

ch. 20 . . . .

(οἱ δὲ σατράπαι Δαρείου ἔγνωσαν τὸν Ἀλέξανδρον
ἐγγίζοντα ὅ τε Βῆσσος καὶ ὁ Ἀριοβαρζάνης· καὶ

παρατραπέντες [οὗτοι] τὰς φρενοβλαβεῖς γνώμας
ἐβουλεύσαντο Δαρεῖον ἀναιρῆσαι . . . .) οὕτως
ἐπήνεγκαν Δαρείῳ

ἐξιφωμένας [τὰς] χεῖρας.   278
ὁ δὲ τοὺς πονηροὺς ἰδὼν εἶπεν·

ὦ ἐμοῦ δεσπόται [οἱ] τὸ πρὶν [μου] δοῦλοι,
τί τοσοῦτον ἠδίκησα (βαρβάρῳ τόλμῃ[ματι])   280

---

272. ἀρούρης στάχυας ἀγρότητι κείροντες cod. Barocc.: first
ἐπὶ rightly omitted by Byz.: ὥσπερ σῖτος ὑπ' ἀρότρῳ, ne mur-
murante quidem Krollio, A: nostrates aratris haud ita utun-
tur: στ. ἀρούρας etiam Byz.   [a] e.g. φ. γ. δ' εἰς δόμους ὁ Δ.
276. e.g. ἑαυτὸν ἐθρήνησεν ἀπολέσας πλῆθος μέγιστον ἀνδρῶν γῆν
θ' ὅλην ἐρημώσας.   280. β. τολ. after ἀνέλητε codd. dett.
324

The husbandmen the plough-land corn reaping.

he Persian host attempt to flee across the Strangas
)

The ice gave way and the wave engulf'd them. 273

ose who failed to cross in time

Were by the men of Macedon butcher'd.

arius fled to his palace and

Casting him on the floor, with a loud groan, 275

d floods of tears wept for his loss of so numerous
host,

And desolation of his own country. 276

(*Darius after vain appeals* [1] *flees to Ecbatana and the*
spian gates. Alexander pursues.) Now the satraps
Darius Bessus and Ariobarzanes learnt that Alex-
der was approaching, and,

By evil stroke from God their hearts smitten, 277

ey plotted to kill Darius. . . They attacked Darius,

swords in their hands holding. 278

hen he saw the villains he said :

My masters, my slaves once ! 279
How have I wronged you that with cruel spirit 280

[1] Darius cites some pure iambic verses: and one letter in
s correspondence with Alexander which ensues, unlike the
st of the letters of which this history is full, shows traces of
re iambi. These, like others (i. 33, iii. 24. 3), have no
ace in this collection.

ἵνα με ἀνέλητε;

(μὴ πλε⟨ῖ⟩ον ὑμεῖς Μακεδόνων τι δράσητε·) 28
ἐάσατ᾽[ε με] οὕτως ἐπὶ τὰ μέλαθρα ῥιφ⟨θ⟩έντ
ἀναστενάζειν τὴν (ἀνώμαλον ⟨μοῖραν⟩).
ἐὰν γὰρ ἐλθὼν ὁ βασιλεὺς Ἀλέξανδρος
εὕρῃ σφαγέντα †βασιλέα† ληστρικῇ γνώμῃ, 28
ἐ⟨π⟩εκδικήσει ⟨μ'⟩· οὐ θέμις γὰρ ὀφθῆναι 28
βασιλέα[a] δολοφονηθέντα οἰκτίστω⟨ς⟩.[b]

οἱ δὲ ἀσεβεῖς μαθόντες τὴν εἴσοδον (Ἀλεξάνδρου
. . . προλείψαντες τὸν Δαρεῖον ἡμίπνουν ἀπο
φεύγουσιν . . . καὶ (εἰσελθὼν πρὸς αὐτὸν Ἀλέξ
ανδρος
⟨. . .⟩ εὗρεν αὐτὸν ⟨αἱμόφυρτον⟩ ἡμίπνουν), 28
καὶ (ἀνοιμώξας

⟨ἐλέου γέμοντα⟩ θρῆνον ἄξιον λύπης 28
δάκρυα ἐξέχεεν [καὶ]

τῇ χλάμυδι ⟨δ᾽⟩ ἐσκέπα⟨ζ⟩ε [τὸ] σῶμ
Δαρείου),
28
ἐπιθεὶς δ᾽ ἑαυτοῦ χεῖρας ἐπὶ τὸ Δαρείου 29
στῆθος τοίους ἔλεξε συμπαθεῖς μύθους·
ἀνάστα, φησί· τῆς τύχης, ὦ Δαρεῖε,
καὶ τῶν σεαυτοῦ δεσπότης πάλιν γίνου.
δέξαι σ[ο]ὺ τὸ διάδημα Περσικοῦ πλήθους,
ἔχε σοῦ τὸ μέγεθος τῆς τυραννικῆς δόξης. 29
ὄμνυμί (σοι) Δαρεῖε τοὺς θεοὺς πάντας
⟨ὡς ταῦτ᾽⟩ ἀληθῶς καὶ οὐ πεπλασμένως (φράζω)

281. δράσηται cod. Barocc. : -σετε codd. dett. ?? 283
ἀνώμαλόν μου (ἀνομαλῆ cod. Barocc.) τύχην: δυσέκβατον A
326

ou come to kill me ?

Excel not Macedon in your actions.	281
Suffer me thus upon the earth rolling	
To weep aloud at my fate's injustice.	
For if there come the king Alexander,	
And find a king by pirates slain lying,	285
He will avenge me : Right doth not suffer	286

hat a king should be seen slain by guile most
pitifully.

*(After a struggle they decamp leaving Darius half
dead. Alexander arrives and)*

found him half alive with blood spatter'd.   287

With a loud groan he uttered

A lamentable dirge and right piteous,   288

hed tears

And with his cloak Darius' form veiling,	289
Upon Darius' breast his hands laid he,	290
And words of sympathy spoke as follows :—	
Arise, quoth he ; Darius, of fortune	
And of your own be once again master.	
Receive the Persian diadem once more,	
The might of all your kingly fame keeping.	295
I swear to you, Darius, by heaven,	
I speak this truly with no feigned utt'rance,	

---

285. ἄνακτα Kroll.   286. ἐπ- : εὖ A: cett. ἐκδικ. τὸ αἷμά μου·
₁ ⟨βασιλεῖ⟩ β. Ausfeld; but sterner measures are needed.
ᵇ -των A.   287. Byz.: ἐκκεχυμένον . . . τὸ . . . αἷμα C.
288. θρ. ἄ. λ. C : ἐλ. γέμ. B later.   289. -ασε C.   290. τὰς
χεῖρας δὲ αὐτοῦ ἐπ. A.   296. σε A.   297. Kroll (ὡς Byz.,
ταῦτα Arm.) : ὅτι ἐγώ A.

FRAGMENTA CHOLIAMBICA

μόνος παρέ‹ξ›ω τὸ διάδημα τῶν σκήπτρων.
μετὰ σοῦ γὰρ αὐτὸς καὶ τροφῆς ἐκοινών‹ουν›
ἐπὶ ‹σ›αῖς τραπέζαις ‹σ›ὴν ἀν' ἑστίαν, χ‹ρεί›‹
ἡνίκα παρήμην ἀγγελ‹ῶν› 'Αλεξάνδρου.   3‹
ἀλλ' ἐξανάστα καὶ κράτυνε τῆς χώρας.
οὐ δεῖ βασιλέα δυστυχοῦντα λυπεῖσθαι·
ἰσότης γὰρ ἀνθρώποισ‹ι περὶ τέλους μοίρης›·
τίνες δέ σ' οἱ τρώσαντες, εἶπε, Δαρεῖε·   30
μήνυσον αὐτοὺς (ἵνα σε νῦν, ἄνα‹ξ, τί›σω.)
ταῦτα ‹οὖν› λέγοντος [   ] ἐστέναξ[εν] ὁ Δαρεῖο
καὶ ἐπισπασάμενος (τάς ‹τε› χεῖρας ἐκτείνας
στῆθος φιλήσας ‹τ'› εἶπε· τέκνον 'Αλέξανδρε
μη‹δέ›ποτ' ἐπαρθῇς (τῇ τυραννικῇ δόξῃ)·   31
(ὁπόταν) γὰρ ἔργον ἰσόθεον κατορθώ‹σῃς›,   31
καὶ χερσὶ ταῖς σαῖς οὐραν(οῦ θέλ)ῃς ψαύειν,
σκόπει τὸ μέλλον· ἡ τυχὴ γὰρ οὐκ οἶδεν
‹   › (βασιλέ' οὔτε μὴν πλῆθος),
ἀκρίτῳ δὲ ῥοίζῳ πάντ‹α› (πανταχ)ῶς (ῥέμβε
   [τα]ι).   31
ὁρᾷ‹s› τίς ἤμην καὶ τίς ἐγενόμην τλήμων·
ὁ τῆς τοσαύτης ἄρτι ‹κύριος γαίης›
νῦν οὐδ' ἐμαυτοῦ δεσπότης ἀποθνήσκω.
θάψον με ταῖς σαῖς εὐσεβεστάτ‹α›ις χερσίν·
κηδευσατώσαν Μακέδονες (με) καὶ Πέρσαι·   32‹

        .   .   .   .   .   .

μί‹η› γενέσθω συγγένεια Δαρείῳ.   32‹
τὴν δ' ἐμὲ τεκοῦσαν παρατίθημί σοι τλήμων,

298. -έχω Α.   299-300. Kroll: -νουν, ταῖς, τὴν Α.   300‹
χεῖραν Α (χειρὶ Arm.).   301. ἄγγελος Α.   304. ἡ π. τ. μύρι‹
Α: corr. Kroll ex Arm.   306. ἀναπαύσω Β: ἵνα με ἔκδικον‹
ἔχῃς Α.   307. 'Αλεξάνδρου.   308. καὶ codd. dett., Byz.‹
328

That you may have again the sole sceptre.
For I myself at meat with you sat once
At table by your hearth, when I came here   300
To bring you message from Alexander.
But now arise and be your land's master :
A king should suffer not nor be wept for.
For all are equal at their last hour's end.
Who are they who did wound you, Darius ?   305
Tell me their names, O King : I 'll avenge you.
As Alexander spake thus, Darius   307
Groaned, drew him nigh to him, his hands stretch'd
     forth,
And kissed his breast and quoth : Alexander,
Be not elated by your proud kingship :   310
When you have wrought a deed of god worthy
And fancy with your hands to touch heaven
Think of what is to be : for fate knows not
Or king or commoner : all things cruelly
In undistinguished eddy she whirls round.   315
See what I was, and what my fate now is ;
I, who was once of all this land owner,
Am master now not even of myself.
Me with your hands most pious here bury,
Let Macedonians tend me, and Persians : [1]   320

. . . . . .

Let all as kindred do my kin's functions.
Alack for me, I give you my mother !

[1] Probably the account in C, according to which the king
summons his harem is, for the choliambic writer, original.
But, as usual in this version, traces of metre are few.

---

310. Kroll.   311. -σεις A.   312. οὐρανοὺς A, οὐρανὸν
codd. dett. (φθάσαι).   314. e.g. ὅλως τιν' οὔτε : A βασιλέα
ἢ λῃστὴν οὔτε πλῆθος.   315. παντὶ κακῶς A : πανταχόθεν
cett.   317. Arm. (om. cett.) : κύρον γύης A.   319. -οις
A.   321. μία codd.

καὶ τὴν γυναῖκα ⟨δ'⟩ ὡς σύν⟨αι⟩μον οἴκτειρον·
καὶ τὴν θυγατέρα σοι δίδωμι Ῥωξάνην,
ἵν' εἴ τι κἂν φθιτοῖσι λείπεται γνώμη⟨ς⟩   325
⟨οἱ δύο γονῆες⟩ ἐπὶ τέκνοισ⟨ι⟩ κα(υ)χῶνται.
σ⟨οὶ⟩ μὲν Φίλιππ⟨ος⟩, Ῥωξάνη[s] δὲ Δαρεῖ⟨ος⟩.
τοσαῦτα λέξας ὁ βασιλεὺς ⟨ὁ⟩ Δαρεῖος
τὸ πνεῦμ' ἔλειψε⟨ν⟩ ἐν χερ⟨οῖ⟩ν Ἀλεξάνδρου.

323. Kroll.   σῦνεμὸν A : corr. Raabe ex Arm.   324. Ῥ.
δ. σοι A.   325. γνώμη A.   326. Kroll : σὺ δυὸ
γενεαῖς A.   κάχονται A : καύχ. cett.   327. σὺ, -πῳ,
-ης, -ίῳ codd. : corr. Kroll.   329. ἔ. τὸ π. and χερσὶν A.

Pity my wife here as a kinswoman !
My daughter give I also Roxanes,
That if sense liveth yet among dead men 325
Two parents in their offspring may glory,
Philip in you, and I in Roxanes.
After this utterance King Darius
In Alexander's hands the ghost gave up.[1]

[1] Further traces of metre are few : and it is very doubtful whether Book III. containing Alexander's expedition into Judea, his journey to Candace, and his death, owes anything to the versifier. See p. 357.

331

FRAGMENTA CHOLIAMBICA

ORACULUM

ap. Ps.-Call. i. 3. 4.

Ἐν δὲ τῷ Αἰγύπτῳ ἀφανοῦς γενομένου
τοῦ Νεκτανεβῶ ἠξίωσαν οἱ Αἰγύπτιοι τὸν προ-
πάτορα τῶν θεῶν Ἥφαιστον τί ἄρα ὁ τῆς Αἰγύπτου βασιλεὺς ἐγένετο. ὁ δὲ ἐπεμψεν αὐτοῖς
χρησμὸν πρὸς τὸν ἀόρατον τοῦ Σεραπείου[a] στῆναι[b]
ὃς χρησμοδοτεῖ αὐτοῖς οὕτως·

Αἴγυπτον ὁ φυγὼν κρατερὸς ἄλκιμος πρέσβυς
βασιλεὺς δυνάστης †ἥξει† μετὰ χρόνον νέος,
τὸ γηράλαιον ἀποβαλὼν τύπων εἶδος,
κόσμον κυκλεύσας ἐπὶ τὸ πεδίον Αἰγύπτου,
ἐχθρῶν ⟨ἁπάντων⟩ ὑποταγὴν διδοὺς ἡμῖν. 5

οὕτω δοθέντος . . .

---

[a] Σεραπείου: v.l. Σινωπείου.   [b] στῆσαι A.   iambos no-
tavit W. Kroll.   1. ἐκφυγὼν [cod.] L[eid].   κραταιὸς A :
-ερὸς L.   2. *e.g.* μ. χ. ν. θ' ἥξει.   3. γεράλαιον A, L.
τύπον εἶδον κόσμου A.   4. Αἰγ. π. A, L (Αἴγυπτον L).
5. ἐλθὼν διδοὺς L.

332

ORACLE

Ps.-Call. i. 3. 4

Now in Egypt after Nectanebos' disappearance
the Egyptians saw fit to ask Hephaestus the
grandsire of the gods what had happened to the
king of Egypt. And he sent to them an oracle to
go to the recess of the Serapium. And Serapis
delivered an oracle to them as follows :—

> The strong, brave sire that has fled Egypt
> Monarch and king will come again youthful,
> Having put off his features old semblance,
> Circling the world to Egypt's plain once more,
> Giving of all our enemies conquest. 5

After this oracle had been thus delivered, [failing
to discover its meaning they wrote the verses on the
base of Nectanebos' statue, as a memorial against
such time as the oracle should come to pass.]

UNCERTAIN FRAGMENTS

The search for anonymous choliambics has met with
but little success.   It is very easy for prose passages
to appear to belong to such a metre.   An excellent
instance of this kind appears in Polyb. i. 32 :

τοὺς ἀπολογισμοὺς παρὰ τί νῦν σφαλείησαν
καὶ πῶς δύναιντο τοὺς ἐναντίους νικᾶν;

as quoted by Suidas.   Under the heading ' Spuria '
I give a few instances of verses which, it appears to
me, are either fortuitous, or belong to another metre.
But there is another class, not yet noted by editors,
as to which, it seems, some room for doubt exists.
The collectors of Greek proverbs normally threw
these into the rhythm of the end of a verse, or indeed
a whole verse ; and where the choliambic rhythm
predominates it seems possible to claim a few of
these, not indeed from writers in choliambi, but as
conscious choliambi produced by the editor of proverbs.   This is why I have ventured to give the late
fifteenth-century choliambi of Arsenius, who after
the fall of Constantinople augmented Apostolius' (his
father's) collection of proverbs ; and drawn attention
to a place where a far earlier writer, Synesius, bishop
of Cyrene, deliberately casts a proverb into this
metre, or uses a metrical authority.   Thus Hesiod's
δῶρα θεοὺς πείθει degenerates into a verse-end δῶρα

καὶ θεοὺς πείθει and ἡ ἀπὸ Σκυθῶν ῥῆσις assumes an illogical accusative. Since distinction is not always possible I include a certain number of cases where there may actually be a quotation from a choliambic writer (other than a proverb-collector); but I do not suppose that there are more than four or five of these. The division into (a) Dicta and (b)[1] is unsatisfactory. It is further possible that of the four or five some like ἀεί με κτλ. and μύωπι κτλ. are from lost fables of Babrius. Where all is so hypothetical detailed discussion is unnecessary; and this warning must suffice.

[1] Proverbs proper.

FRAGMENTA INCERTA

(1-10, *vid*. pp. 2-7)

Inc. 11 (Bgk. 25)

ὁ τὸν κυσὸν τρωθείς
ἤδ‹ει›ς ‹ὅ›που μάλιστα τοῦ κράνους χρεί‹η›.
(Photius, ii. 33 Naber.)

Inc. 12 (Bgk. 26 A)

A. βαύ, βαύ.

B. καὶ κυνὸς φωνὴν ἵεις;

(Joan. Alex. *de ton.* p. 32. 23 βαὺ ... ὀξύνεται (12).)

Inc. 13

στροβεῖς σεαυτὸν κοχλίου βίον ζώ‹ω›ν.

(Plut. *Mor.* p. 525 Ε σὺ δὲ τοσαῦτα πράγματα συγχεῖς καὶ
ταράττεις καὶ (13).)

Inc. 14 (Bgk. 27)

ἐγὼ μὲν ὦ Λεύκιππ‹ε› δεξίῃ σίττῃ

(Schol. Ar. *Av.* 704 Δίδυμος δέ, ἐπεὶ ἡ σίττη καὶ εἴ τι
τοιοῦτον ὄρνεον δεξιὰ πρὸς ἔρωτας φαίνεται (14). Suid. ἀεὶ τοῖς
ἐρῶσιν.)

11. 2. ἤδη Αἰσώπου : corr. Dobree.　　χρεία corr. Bgk.
12. interpunxi.　　13. ζῶν : corr. Crusius.　　14. ὦ
Suid.: ὡς schol. Ar.　　Λευκίππη corr. Bentley.　　-η -η
corr. Meineke.

336

UNCERTAIN FRAGMENTS

(*For* 1-10 *see above*)

11

In the rump wounded
Thou knewest where a helmet was needed

(*Photius's Lexicon.*)

12

A. Bow ! Wow !

B. Do'st bark dog-like ?

(*John* of *Alexandria* on *Accents.*)

13

You lead a shell-fish life of inquietude.

(You confound all these matters [1] and in your worry (13).
Plutarch on *Avarice.*)

14

Leucippus, I with favouring parrot

(Didymus' explanation rests on the ground that parrots
and suchlike birds are favourable to lovers (14). *Commentator* on *Aristophanes' Birds* : also in *Suidas' Lexicon.*)

[1] The reading is uncertain and unsatisfactory.

FRAGMENTA CHOLIAMBICA

Inc. 15

†ἐπ' ἀνδ†ρὸς ἄνδρα Κερκίδας ἀπέκτεινεν.

(Arist. 673 a 13 τὸ περὶ τὴν κεφαλὴν ὡς ἀποκοπεῖσα φθέγγεται.
. . τοῦ γὰρ ἱερέως τοῦ Ὁπλοσμίου Διὸς ἀποθανόντος . . ἔφασάν
τινες ἀκοῦσαι τῆς κεφαλῆς ἀποκεκομμένης λεγούσης πολλάκις (15).
διὸ καὶ ζητήσαντες ᾧ ὄνομα ἦν ἐν τῷ τόπῳ Κερκίδας ἔκριναν.)

Inc. 16

ἐγὼ μέντοι ἡ τοσαύτη τρεῖς ἤδη
καθεῖλον ἱστοὺς ἐν βραχεῖ χρόνῳ τούτῳ.

(Strabo, p. 378 μνημονεύεταί τις ἑταίρα πρὸς τὴν ὀνειδίζουσαν
ὅτι οὐ φιλεργὸς εἴη οὐδ' ἐρίων ἅπτοιτο εἰπεῖν (16).)

Inc. 17

μὴ πάντοθεν κέρδαινε σαυτὸν αἰσχύνων.

(Greg. Naz. περὶ ἀρετῆς ii. 432. v. 387 καὶ ταῦτ' ἐπαινεῖ
τῶν σοφῶς εἰρημένων (17) . . .)

Inc. 18

τέττιγα ⟨μέντοι⟩ τοῦ πτεροῦ συνείληφας.

(Lucian, iii. 162 τὸ δὲ τοῦ Ἀρχιλόχου ἐκεῖνο ἤδη σοι λέγω
ὅτι (18). Apostol. xvi. 32.)

15. I doubt whether there be a verse at all, and whether
the head said more than Κερκίδας ἀπέκτεινεν. The first
two words are anyhow corrupt. The obvious correction
of ΕΠΑΝΔΡΟC is (Ε)ΗΜΙΑΡΟC, which I translate.
17. The verse is expressly attributed by Gregory to an
older writer. However, it may well have been an ordinary
iambus (αἰσχυνῶν). The next citation is from Eur. (*fr.* 20).
See my *F.G.A.* p. 4.

UNCERTAIN FRAGMENTS

15

Foul Cercidas his fellow-man murder'd.[1]

(The story of the head speaking when severed from the body. . . When the priest of Hoplosmian Zeus was mysteriously slain, some alleged that the head though cut off kept on repeating (15). So they hunted out one of this name there and accused them. *Aristotle.*)

16

I at my age three times
In this brief space have undone three pieces.[2]

(A certain courtesan is said to have remarked to a lady who rebuked her for idleness nor putting her fingers to the loom (16). *Strabo.*)

17

Gain not from every source thyself shaming.

(You must approve the following wise utterances ' (17) . . .' *Gregory, Bishop of Nazianzus.*)

18

You've taken by the wing a grasshopper.

(It is time for me to tell you of Archilochus'[3] dictum (18). *Lucian's Liar.* Also in *Greek Proverbs.*)

---

[1] Some have actually sought to connect this with Cercidas (the law-giver of Megalopolis or the cynic) or a relative !

[2] Should probably be classed among paroemiac dicta : it may not occur in any literary writer.

[3] Pfeiffer has recently shown that Archilochus wrote τέττιγος ἐδράξω πτεροῦ: so this fragment belongs to p. 347.

FRAGMENTA CHOLIAMBICA

Inc. 19

λευκήν

μᾶζαν φυρῶ σοι;

(Diogen. vi. 12 ἐπὶ τῶν μεγάλως ὑπισχνουμένων. Other references *Paroem. Gr.* i. 271.)

Inc. 20

ζῷον ἐν πυρὶ σκαῖρον

(Cram. *An. Ox.* ii. 371. 19.)

Inc. 21

⟨τέρψιν⟩ ἣν χαρίζονται νύκτες

(*Ibid.* 483. 3.)

19. *vv. ll.* φύρωσιν, μεγάλους, μεγάλα.   20, 21. indicavit Headlam.

UNCERTAIN FRAGMENTS

19

May I

A white cake mix you ?

((19) refers to those who make lofty promises. *Greek Proverbs.*)

20

An animal in fire leaping

(*Grammarian* in *Cramer's Anecdota Oxoniensia.*)

21

That pleasure which nights give

(*Ibid.*)

PAROEMICA

(a) Dicta

1. φιλεῖν ἀκαίρως ἶσον ἐστὶ τῷ μισεῖν.

(*Paroem. Gr.* ii. 778.)

2. εἰ τυρὸν εἶχον οὐκ ἂν ἐδεόμην ὄψου.

(Apostol. vi. 76 ἐπὶ τῶν ὀλίγοις ἀρκουμένων καὶ ἐγκρατῶν from Plut. *Mor.* 234 E εἰς πανδοκεῖον (Λάκων τις) καταλύσας καὶ δοὺς ὄψον τῷ πανδοκεῖ σκευάσαι, ὡς ἅτερος τυρὸν ᾔτει καὶ ἔλαιον, ' εἶτ᾽,' ἔφη (2).)

3.   ζημίαν αἰροῦ μᾶλλον
ἢ κέρδος αἰσχρόν· τὸ μὲν [γὰρ] ἅπαξ σε λυπήσει
τὸ δὲ διὰ παντός.

([Apostol.] viii. 34 b from Stob. *Fl.* v. 31 (i. 20 H.). Χίλωνος.)

4. ἡ βραχυλογία ἐγγύς ἐστι τοῦ σιγᾶν.

([Apostol.] viii. 41 c from Stob. *Flor.* xxxv. 9 Λυκοῦργος πρὸς τὸν εἰπόντα ' διὰ τί Λακεδαιμόνιοι τὴν βρ. ἀσκοῦσιν ;' εἶπεν ὅτι ἐγγὺς κτλ.)

1-5. It is possible that at some period before Plutarch (or Stobaeus) certain dicta may have been given in a metrical choliambic form.   **4.** *e.g.* τὸ γὰρ βραχυλόγον if the story is adopted from a metrical writer.

342

PROVERBS

(a) Sayings (cf. Inc. 16)

1. Untimely love 's than hatred no better.

(*Greek Proverbs.*)

2. If I had cheese what use to me were meat?

(*Greek Proverbs* from the story in *Plutarch*: A certain
Spartan put up at an inn and gave meat to the innkeeper
to cook: when the latter asked for cheese and oil, he rejoined
(2).)

3.   For loss is far better
  Than gain with shame: the one for one moment,
  The other aye will irk.

(*Greek Proverbs* from *Stobaeus' Anthology*, where it is
attributed to *Chilon*.)

4. For brevity to silence is next door.

(*Greek Proverbs* from *Stobaeus' Anthology*: Lycurgus
when asked why the Spartans practised brevity replied (4).)

FRAGMENTA CHOLIAMBICA

5.   ἐξ ἴσου δίδου πᾶσιν.

(Plut. *Mor.* 208 B (Agesilaus is the speaker) is thus given by Apostol. vii. 51, with the lemma ἐπὶ τῶν ὀρθῶς διανεμόντων καὶ δικαίως κρινόντων.)

6. ἀκραῖς ἐπὶ ῥηγμῖσιν Εὐξείνου πόντου

(Plut. *Mor.* 602 A διὸ καὶ Διογένης ὁ Κύων πρὸς τὸν εἰπόντα ' Σινωπεῖς σου φυγὴν ἐκ Πόντου κατέγνωσαν,' ' ἐγὼ δέ,' εἶπεν, ' ἐκείνων ἐν Πόντῳ μονήν ' (6).)

6. Diogenes was well-read but is not likely to have cited Hipponax or Ananius or a contemporary. It is usual to read πόρου.

(b)[a]

Ἀεί με τοῖ[ουτ]οι πολέμιοι διώκοιεν, Ἀκάνθιος τέττιξ, "Ἁλμη ⟨γὰρ⟩ οὐκ ἔνεστ᾽ αὐτῷ, Ἀκαρπότερος εἶ ⟨τῶν⟩ Ἀδωνίδος κήπων, Ἀκόλω [τὰ] χειλ⟨έ⟩ οὐ σύκῳ βῦσαι, Ἀπὸ ξύλου καλοῦ[b] ⟨γε⟩ κἂν ἀπάγξασθαι, Ἀρουραία μάντις, Βία πενήτων πλουσίων παράκλησις, Γῆς ⟨μὲν⟩ οὐκ ἔνεστ᾽ αὐτῷ,[c] Δηλίου κολυμβητοῦ, Δίκτυον φυσᾶς,[d] Δῶρα καὶ θεοὺς πείθει, Ἐγένετο καὶ Μάνδρωνι συκίνη ν⟨ῆ⟩ῦς, Εἴληφεν ἡ παγὶς τὸν μῦν, Ἐμπεδοκλέους ἔχθρα, Ἐν θέρει [τὴν] χλαῖναν[e] κατατρίβεις, Ἐξ ἑνὸς πηλοῦ, Ἔχεται δ᾽ ὥσ⟨τε⟩ πο⟨υ⟩λύπους πέτρ⟨η⟩ς, Ἡ τρὶς ἓξ ἢ τρεῖς οἶνας, Θρᾷκες ὅρκι᾽ οὐκ ἐπίστανται, Κάκιον ἢ Βαβῦς (?)

[a] References will readily be found in the Indexes of Leutsch and Schneidewin, *Paroemiographi Graeci*, Gottingae

344

PROVERBS

5.   Equal shares all round.

(*Greek Proverbs* : ' applies to fair and just apportionment.'
Plutarch is the source where it is part of a saying of *Agesilaus*.)

6. Upon the furthest shores of the Euxine

(Hence Diogenes the Cynic when told that the Sinopeans
had condemned him to exile beyond the Euxine sea rejoined
' But I condemn them to remain in Pontus (6).')

(*b*)[1]

Such[2] enemies be e'er my pursuers, A hedge-
cricket, Therein is no saltness, Less fruitful than
Adonis (his) gardens, No mere fig but a good mouth-
ful, If hang I must, hang me from strong gallows,
A seer rustic, The poor perforce the rich by persuasion, This plough has no tree to 't, Delian diver's,
A net you 're inflating, Even the gods take bribes,
For Mandron too a ship had—of figwood, The mouse
in trap 's taken, Empedocles' hatred, In summer why
thy overcoat wearest ?, Of one clay founded, Octopus
to rock clinging, Thrice six or three aces, Oaths
in Thrace run not, Than Babys worse player, Than

---

[1] For Πέρδικος καπηλεῖον see on Hippon. **70.**
[2] Greek text corrected by Sauppe.

1839, or in Suid. *s.v.*   [b] *cf.* Suid. ἀπο καλοῦ.   [c] Suid.
[d] Suid. *s.v.* δίκτυον.   [e] χλ. ἐν θ.

FRAGMENTA CHOLIAMBICA

αὐλεῖ, Καλλικυρίων πλείους, Καρικὴ Μοῦσα,
Καρικὸν θῦμα, Κατὰ λίθων σπείρειν, Κατὰ πετρῶν σπείρειν, Κίσσαμις Κῷος, Κρωβύλου ζεῦγος,
Κωδάλου χοῖνιξ, Λίνον λίνῳ κλώθεις, Λυδὸς ἐν
μεσημβρίᾳ παίζει, Λύκου πτερὸν ζητεῖς, Μάρτυς
ἐκ Διὸς δέλτων, Μὴ νεκρῶν θήκας κίνει, Μύωπι
τὸν <τ>ρ<έχ>οντα <πῶλον> ἤγειρας, Ὁδοῦ παρούσης τὴν ἀτ<αρ>πιτὸν ζητεῖς[a]; Οὐ σχολὴ
δούλοις, Παρθένος τὰ πατρῷα, Πρὸς σῆμα μη-
τρυιᾶς κλαίει, Τὰ Σαμίων ὑποπτεύεις, Τὴν ἀπὸ
Σκυθῶν ῥῆσιν, Φάων ὑπάρχεις τῷ κάλλει καὶ
τὸν τρόπον.[b]

[a] Paroem. ἀτραπὸν μὴ ζήτει: Suid. best cod. ἀτραπιτὸν.
[b] e.g. τὸν τρ. καὶ τ. κ.

PROVERBS

Callicurians are more num'rous, Carian music, Carian victim, Seed upon stones sowing, Seed upon rocks sowing, Cissamis Coan, Crobylus' couple, Codalus' pint-pot, Thread with thread spinning, A Lydian at noon playing, As one who seeks a wolf's feather, Witness Zeus' tablets, Let dead men lie quiet, The willing horse whip not, Seek not the by-way when thou hast the highway, Slaves have no leisure, Spends like a virgin, Weeps at the tombstone of his stepmother, The Samians' fate fearing, The Scythian saying, As fair of fame and favour as Phaon.[1]

---

[1] In cod. Urbin. Gr. 125 a fifteenth-century hand gives on the fly-leaf δρυὸς πεσούσης ἀκαμάτως ξυλίζεσθαι, 'small search for fuel when the oak 's fallen.' The alternative version is a pure iambic.

SPURIA

1. αἰσχύνομαι μὰ τὴν φιλότητα γηράσκων
†ἵππος ὑπὸ ζυγὸν θήλειάν τε τροφήν†
ἔχων ὁρᾶσθαι.

(Diog. ii. 53, [Apostol.] i. 67 d, Prov. Bodl. 171.)

2. Χῖος παραστὰς Κῷον οὐκ ἐᾷ †σῷ⌈ζειν†.

(*App. Prov.* v. 28 gives the right form : this is from
Schol. Plat. p. 320 Bekk., Eust. 1397. 39.)

3. ἄρκτου παρούσης ἴχνη μὴ ζήτει.

(Zenobius, ii. 36 ἐπὶ τῶν δειλῶν κυνήγων. *Paroem. Gr.* i. 42.)

4. ὁ τὸν πάτερα εὑρὼν . . . χαλκοῦ χρείᾳ

(Phot. ii. 33 Naber.)

5. ὑπερδεδίσκευκας πονηρίᾳ πάντας.

(Bekk. *An.* 67. 27.   No choliambic writer entirely neglects
the caesura.   It is clearly from an orator.)

6. ἀνθρωποειδὲς θηρίον ὕδατι συζῶν

(See Nauck, *Tr. Gr. Fragm.* p. 11 : attributed to Aeschylus
by Phrynichus, 5. 21.   Read ὕδ. συζ. θηρ. and attribute to
an Attic comedian.)

SPURIOUS

1.   In friendship's name, it shames me to grow old
Like horse in harness and to be seen
Nurtured like woman.

(In the *Proverb-Collections*.)

2.   A Chian speaking may a Coan drown.

(*Ibid.*)

3.   When bear is near seek not his traces.

(*Ibid.*)

4.   Who with no farthing left found his father.

(*Photius' Lexicon.*)

5.   You have o'ershot in villainy all men.

(*Harpocration's Lexicon.*)

6.   A human form living in water

(Concerning Glaucus appearing from the sea.   *Aeschylus* quoted by *Phrynichus* (*Bekk. An.* v. 21).)

---

1. Meineke indicated this : if genuine read $\tau\grave{\eta}\nu$ $\tau\rho$. $\tau\epsilon$ $\theta\acute{\eta}\lambda$. v. 2. But probably in all these seven cases the vague resemblance to metre is *wholly* fortuitous.   2, 3 and 5 Sauppe.   2 is really $\lambda\acute{\epsilon}\gamma\epsilon\iota\nu$.

FRAGMENTA CHOLIAMBICA

7.   πολλά[κι] τοι μῦθος
εἰς καιρὸν ‹ἐλθὼν› ῥᾳδίως κατορθοῖ τι
ὅπερ βιαίως ‹οὐκ ἔπραξεν› ἡ ῥώμη.

(Choricius, p. 15, Graux, *Textes inédites.*)

(Diehl, *fr.* 7)

8.   ἀλλ᾽ ἐμοῦ [τοι] τὸ ἐντὸς [ἔφη] σκοπῶν,
ὦ δικαστά, ποικιλωτέραν με τῆσδ᾽ ὄψει.

(Plut. *Mor.* 500 c ἡ μὲν οὖν Αἰσώπειος ἀλώπηξ περὶ ποικιλίας
δικαζομένη πρὸς τὴν πάρδαλιν . . . (8).)

7. So Weil.   8. is iambic, *e.g.* δικάστ᾽, ἔμ᾽ ὄψει κτλ.
Otherwise omit ὦ and τῆσδ᾽.

SYNESIUS

οἱ πάτταλοι γὰρ παττάλοις ἐκκρούονται.

(*Ep.* 45 Ὀλυμπίῳ· λυποῦσι τὴν ἐκκλησίαν ἀλλότριοι πονηροί.
διάβηθι κατ᾽ αὐτῶν (. . .).)

SPURIOUS

7.   **For persuasion**[1]
   Well timed doth often guide aright business
   Where strength, employing force, achieves nothing.

(*Choricius* in *Graux' Textes inédites.*)

8.   **But look at my inside,**
   Good sir juryman : you 'll find me more spotted.[2]

(The fox of Aesop in his case against the pard. *Plutarch*
on *Mental or Bodily Affliction* (8).)

[1] Conceivably, however, this might be from a lost fable of
Babrius, or from part of the life of Alexander, or even written
in the metre by Choricius. See on Synesius below. ἐλθών
is Graux' suggestion for εἰρημένος.
[2] The word ' spotted ' implied to the Greek both variety
of colour and cunningness of disposition.

SYNESIUS[1]

For wedges must with wedges be knocked out.

(To Olympius.   The church is suffering from evil strangers.
Attack them (. . .).)

[1] Synesius bishop of Cyrene either took this proverb from
a collection in which it was adapted to the choliambic metre
(see below) or so adapted it.

FRAGMENTA CHOLIAMBICA

ARSENIUS

οὕτω σε τανῦν ἑστιῶ τὸν κράτιστον
νηκτοῖς πετεινοῖς, κτήνεσιν ἑρπυστοῖς τε.
αὖθις δέ σοι τράπεζαν, εἰ δοίης, θήσω,
εἰς ἐκτύπωσιν, πορισμὸν τὸν ἀρκοῦντα,
λαμπροῖς στρατηγήμασι τοῦ Πολυαίνου,
οἷς κεῖνος εἱστίασε τῷ βασιλῆε
πάλαι τὸν Οὐῆρόν τε καὶ Ἀντωνῖνον.

Κύων ἐγὼ σὸς καὶ γλυκὺς σὺ δεσπότης·
οὐκοῦν ὑλακτῶ καὶ φαγεῖν ζητῶ βρῶμα.
Ἄναξ λεοντόθυμε τὸν κύνα τρέφε·
θρέμματα γὰρ θηρᾶν σε βλέπω βαρβάρου.

(Phile, p. 1 Didot.   These verses end the dedication.)

ARSENIUS

ARSENIUS [1]

So now most noble one herein find food.
Herein are birds and fishes, beasts, serpents.
If you will pay enough, I 'll get printed
Later a second course, and Your Highness
Regale with Polyaenus his tactics,
Whereon he once feasted the two rulers
Verus and Antoninus of old Rome.

I am thy dog and thou my master art.
So do I bark and wish for my dog-food.
O lion-hearted king feed thou thy dog.
I see thou huntest the barbarian beasts.

[1] Arsenius had lived in Constantinople before its capture and edited his father's collection of proverbs. His choice of metre may be significant.

ADDENDA

P. 46, *fr.* 68. Add the variants: *v.* 1 κατωμόχαιε, καταμόχανε and κακομήχανε: *v.* 6 τὸν τεκνούμενον and τῶν τικείμενον. The verses are also quoted by Tzetzes on his *Antehomerica, v.* 168. For τῶντικείμενον a good case could be made out, but it has little ms. support.

P. 49, *fr.* 70. In order not to confuse the reader I have given what I believe may have been the Lycophron-Tzetzes view of these verses. It has been suggested to me that πυθμένι στοιβῆς may have been taken as a 'bunch of straw.' But I believe the whole to be nonsense and it is superfluous to trouble much over a patent error. στοιβή means a paving, perhaps as Photius, p. 539. 15 (from Eupolis) explains it, an inlaid paving. ὀφέλλω and ὄφελμα are simply used of raising the ground-level or of adorning. πυθμήν has its natural sense of foundation.

> And found a man adorning the mansion,
> Yet unadorned, with an inlaid pavement.

On the word see also Herwerden, *Lex. Suppl.*

P. 91, i. 84 *sqq.* These verses present several unsolved problems: (*a*) why in *v.* 83 is ἔκητι τῶν ἱρῶν unexplained? (*b*) why is there no obvious antecedent to ὅς (*v.* 85), or noun on which σοῦ depends? (*c*) Why is there no note of change of speaker between Γυλλί and τέκνον or ἦλθον and Γυλλί? As to (*a*), traces in 82 are sufficient to show we have no explanatory contrast in ἱρῶν: and as to (*b*), μᾶ τέκνον cannot belong to the same sentence as γένοιτο, so there can be no construction for σοῦ. All these difficulties could be removed by reading, as I should have done, μοι Γρυλλλίων(α) in 84, 'my dear little Gryllos.' The parent ms. probably had Γύλλος at *v.* 50. At *v.* 83 Gyllis says '*I* didn't come or *want* to come,' *e.g.* δεῖξον οὖν ἐπεὶ οὐ σπουδῇ); it was the rites in

354

ADDENDA

respect of which my dear little Gryllos needed you to initiate
him (*e.g.* Γρυλλίωνα ἔχοις μύστην). Then Metriche (not,
as P *pardonably* mistook, Gyllis) says, 'Let him be your
μύστης.' It is much in favour of this view that many other,
and, no doubt, better arrangements of parts and supplements
can be found than these, whereas on the other view nothing
can be done: and that there is far less departure from the
tradition of P that the verses *could* be read consecutively.

P. 104, iii. 20. 21. The transposition of these verses is
unnecessary. The least unsatisfactory interpretation seems
to me to be that given. Not only are they rubbed brighter
than the flask, but their gaudy trappings are contrasted
with the mother's lack of 'vanity bags.' Headlam thought
that the old man was a fisherman. Another suggestion
made to me is that the dibs are left lying at the smithies or
on the foreshore—the low haunts which the boy frequents.
Perhaps φῦσαι and δίκτυα are used ironically, 'puffs and
reticules.'

P. 155, vii. 69, 70. Inexcusably I have failed here to recognize the sequence of thought. We should read in *v.* 69 ὁ τοῦτ'
ἐῶν γὰρ οὔ σε ῥηδίως χηνᾶ (deleting ρ: *cf.* Hesych. χηνῆσαι, to
deride): "he who allows this (so Blass) is not lightly mocking
you." Proceed then, reading τί; in 71: "For of shoes, lady,
the true function you will admit, please, to be—what?
Why, 'pon my head . . . to bring quick profit to tool-pliers:
since if this throw prosper not, O Hermes . . ., I know not
how pot shall thrive better." Those who find this lapse into
the style of Plato difficult should read χρῆναι (χραίνω) ἔοικα·
τούτων οὐκ ἄμεινον εὑρήσειν . . . : but I prefer to translate what
is in the Papyrus. Other accentuations of τι, and divisions
of speakers, are credible.

P. 231. The readings of the Bodleian papyrus not noted
are as follows:
Above υρην in *v.* 13 at distance of one verse is visible (ημο):
certainly not any words in *v.* 11 (Lond). Where εκλιθον
should come (*v.* 9) we have . . . (τα. αν) πολε. . . . In *v.* 13
the τοῦ of ἑαυτοῦ is fairly clear. In *v.* 15 fin. πλωιτηρ is clear.
In *v.* 22 ολλοι is as easy as αλλοι, and in 26 χεις easier than
νεις. In 14 my reading ηθ on which is based Mr. Milne's
clever correction is, I think, certain.

ADDENDA

Pp. 244-5. There are three main points of difficulty associated with this poem.

In the first place the whole story is associated by all other Greek and Latin writers with Sardanapallus, not with Ninos. As to this I suspect that Phoenix is influenced solely by metrical considerations. I do not think it credible that -os is throughout corrupt—'son of Ninos,' 'at Nineveh,' ἶνις Νίνου, κτλ.

Secondly, there are two legends as to the inscription, both given in Athenaeus. According to one, the famous saying, 'Eat, drink, and be merry: the rest is not worth *that*,' is part of an inscription on Sardanapallus' memorial (not tomb) at Anchialé, which, with Tarsus, Sardanapallus built in one day. The other contains the words, 'I drank, I ate, I satisfied my lust.' This was given to Greece by Choerilus. It was once inscribed on a stone pillar on a mound at Nineveh; but the mound was pulled down by Cyrus. In one account Sardanapallus had no regular tomb but burnt himself with his wives and concubines, not at Nineveh (Νίνος). In another, he was murdered in his palace. He was the last of his dynasty. See Mayor's Juvenal, ii. 178.

The decisive point as to which legend Phoenix followed is in v. 12; but unfortunately this ends with a *vox nihili*, αἰδει. Editors have generally read ᾄδει which is precisely the one thing that we cannot read. αἰδές which I give is, in a sense, certain from Hes. *Sc.* 477 τοῦ δὲ τάφον καὶ σῆμ᾽ αἰδὲς ποίησεν Ἄναυρος. We may then either (*a*) regard καὶ . . . αἰδές as an illustrative adscript and read what we will (*e.g.* καὶ τὸ σῆμ᾽ ἵζει), 'for all men writ Where Ninos on his monument doth sit.' The σῆμα might be the Anchialé monument and the quotation given to show that σῆμα is not the same as τάφος. This seems to me all very unlikely. (*b*) We may suppose that Phoenix actually scanned the word ᾄδές and that the diaeresis was put in, as so often in papyrus texts, by editors to call attention to irregularity. (*c*) We may suppose that Phoenix wrote (*e.g.*) ὅκου Νίνος νῦν καὶ τὸ σῆμ᾽ ἀϋστωθέν, and that the adscript gave the same sense as the original. Either (*b*) or (*c*) seems to me certainly right; but it is quite doubtful whether Νίνος is Ninos or Nineveh. I prefer the latter, the destruction of Nineveh (*c*. 600 B.C.) being famous and proverbial. As in the Greek I leave it doubtful in my translation whether ὅκου is locative or not.

P. 249, 3. 9. Malachite—darkish green, rare, beautiful,

ADDENDA

and brittle—would be a suitable extravagance to allege rather than a sober fact. In the grand hundred-marbled church of St. Paul outside the Roman walls it appears only in the altars presented by the Emperor of Russia, Nicholas the First. It is given as a material for a palace floor (πάτος: Sophocles *Lex. Byz.*) in the Septuagint version of Esther.

P. 283. 2. To the Greek humourists appropriate misfortune was an enthralling joke. The Greek book of jests called *Philogelos* says: "A drunkard who had bought a vineyard died before vintage." We are not amused. Or rather we use different forms, 'as unlucky as the man who . . .,' 'Why he couldn't even . . . without . . .,' 'Have you heard about poor old X?'

P. 331, *v.* 329. I am inclined to think the choliambic versifier wrote three poems about Alexander, an "Iliad," a "Thebaid," and a "Dareiad." In editing these verses I have made no attempt to estimate how far the Ionic dialect was employed. The writer of cod. A, otherwise our only good guide, atticizes ruthlessly throughout the history. Slight indications would seem to show that the original was in an Ionic dialect at least as strict as that of the Mimes of Herodes.

P. 350, *Adde* 9. Choliambos Scythini ap. Stob. *Ecl.* i. 8. 43 non recte agnovit Meineke.

CALLIMACHI NOVAE LECTIONES

The following verses of Callimachus have lately been recovered by G. Vitelli (*Bull. Soc. Arch. d'Alex.* No. 24) from scholia. They are verses 99 *sqq.* (see the late Professor Mair's *Callimachus*, p. 272, lines 96 ff.).

They afford an admirable illustration of Callimachus' art in his use of this metre. Essentially lyric in cadence and metre, and strict in their Ionic versification, his verses yet give, as those of no other Greek poet do, the essential illusion of natural speech. A wide and versatile imagination, an use of deft touches to depict the crowd surging round the dead poet Hipponax, who is supposed to be speaking, a breathless but clear and distinct narration—all these mark out the genius of Callimachus as something infinitely higher than that of his rivals.

ADDENDA

ὦ Ἑκάτη πλήθευς!   99
ὁ ψιλοκόρσης τὴν πνοὴν ἀναλώσει 100
φυσέων ὅκως μὴ τὸν τρίβωνα γυμνώσῃ.
σωπὴ γενέσθω καὶ γράφεσθε τὴν ῥῆσιν.
ἀνὴρ Βαθυκλῆς Ἀρκάς—οὐ μακρὴν ἄξω—
ὦ λῷστε, μὴ σίλλαινε, καὶ γὰρ οὐδ᾽ αὐτός
μέγα σχολάζ[ων ε]ἰμί . . ρμεσ(ον) δινεῖν, 105
(ὦ) Ζεῦ Ἀχέροντος!—τῶν πάλαι τις εὐδαίμων
ἐγένετο, πάντα δ᾽ εἶχ᾽ ἐν οἷσιν ἄνθρωποι
θεοί τε λευκὰς ἡμέρας ἐπίστανται.

I translate:

> He'll lose his breath, will my bald-head comrade,
> In panting to keep cloak on his shoulder.
> Let there be silence! write ye my words down!
> In Arcady Bathycles—cease mocking,
> Sirrah! I fly not far: a brief moment
> Have I to spend with you: how stern, great Zeus,
> Is Acheron!—the patriarch thrice blest
> Did live, nor lacked in aught of such riches
> Wherewith endowed men live white days ever.
> (He was about to finish his last lap, etc.)

In v. 108 'white days' are 'days of white-raiment,' 'feast days'; see Hippon. *fr.* 65.

v. 103 αξω P: correxi. v. 105 non fuit παρμεσον. v. 106 num χάξευ . . . !

INDEX I—PROPER NAMES

(References to pages: spelling latinized throughout. In the prose translation I use the Greek forms (excepting y for v) to denote stage characters. In the verse translations I am guided solely by euphony.)

INDEX OF PROPER NAMES

INDEX OF PROPER NAMES

361

INDEX OF PROPER NAMES

[1] Philip was educated at Thebes, but not by Pindar!
[2] Inepte Gerhard legit Cercidea, p. 51 ; ineptius apud Herodis Mimum VIII. inveniunt scholastici.

INDEX OF PROPER NAMES

INDEX II—DOUBTFUL, UNUSUAL, OR CORRUPT WORDS AND USES

INDEX OF DOUBTFUL WORDS

Printed in Great Britain by R. & R. CLARK, LIMITED, *Edinburgh*

(225)

THE LOEB CLASSICAL LIBRARY

VOLUMES ALREADY PUBLISHED

LATIN AUTHORS

THE LOEB CLASSICAL LIBRARY

CICERO: DE OFFICIIS. Walter Miller.

CICERO: DE ORATORE, etc. 2 Vols. Vol. I: DE ORATORE, Books I and II. E. W. Sutton and H. Rackham Vol. II: DE ORATORE, BOOK III; DE FATO; PARADOXA STOICORUM; DE PARTITIONE ORATORIA. H. Rackham.

CICERO: DE REPUBLICA, DE LEGIBUS, SOMNIUM SCIPIONIS. Clinton W. Keyes.

CICERO: DE SENECTUTE, DE AMICITIA, DE DIVINATIONE. W. A. Falconer.

CICERO: IN CATILINAM, PRO MURENA, PRO SULLA, PRO FLACCO. Louis E. Lord.

CICERO: LETTERS TO ATTICUS. E. O. Winstedt. 3 Vols.

CICERO: LETTERS TO HIS FRIENDS. W. Glynn Williams. 3 Vols.

CICERO: PHILIPPICS. W. C. A. Ker.

CICERO: PRO ARCHIA, POST REDITUM, DE DOMO, DE HARUSPICUM RESPONSIS, PRO PLANCIO. N. H. Watts.

CICERO: PRO CAECINA, PRO LEGE MANILIA, PRO CLUENTIO, PRO RABIRIO. H. Grose Hodge.

CICERO: PRO CAELIO, DE PROVINCIIS CONSULARIBUS, PRO BALBO. R. Gardner.

CICERO: PRO MILONE, IN PISONEM, PRO SCAURO, PRO FONTEIO, PRO RABIRIO POSTUMO, PRO MARCELLO, PRO LIGARIO, PRO REGE DEIOTARO. N. H. Watts.

CICERO: PRO QUINCTIO, PRO ROSCIO AMERINO, PRO ROSCIO COMOEDO, CONTRA RULLUM. J. H. Freese.

CICERO: PRO SESTIO, IN VATINIUM. R. Gardner.

[CICERO]: RHETORICA AD HERENNIUM. H. Caplan.

CICERO: TUSCULAN DISPUTATIONS. J. E. King.

CICERO: VERRINE ORATIONS. L. H. G. Greenwood. 2 Vols.

CLAUDIAN. M. Platnauer. 2 Vols.

COLUMELLA: DE RE RUSTICA; DE ARBORIBUS. H. B. Ash, E. S. Forster, E. Heffner. 3 Vols.

CURTIUS, Q.: HISTORY OF ALEXANDER. J. C. Rolfe. 2 Vols.

FLORUS. E. S. Forster; and CORNELIUS NEPOS. J. C. Rolfe.

FRONTINUS: STRATAGEMS AND AQUEDUCTS. C. E. Bennett and M. B. McElwain.

FRONTO: CORRESPONDENCE. C. R. Haines. 2 Vols.

GELLIUS. J. C. Rolfe. 3 Vols.

HORACE: ODES AND EPODES. C. E. Bennett.

HORACE: SATIRES, EPISTLES, ARS POETICA. H. R. Fairclough.

JEROME: SELECT LETTERS. F. A. Wright.

JUVENAL AND PERSIUS. G. G. Ramsay.

2

THE LOEB CLASSICAL LIBRARY

LIVY. B. O. Foster, F. G. Moore, Evan T. Sage, A. C. Schlesinger and R. M. Geer (General Index). 14 Vols.

LUCAN. J. D. Duff.

LUCRETIUS. W. H. D. Rouse.

MARTIAL. W. C. A. Ker. 2 Vols.

MINOR LATIN POETS: from PUBLILIUS SYRUS to RUTILIUS NAMATIANUS, including GRATTIUS, CALPURNIUS SICULUS, NEMESIANUS, AVIANUS, with "Aetna," "Phoenix" and other poems. J. Wight Duff and Arnold M. Duff.

OVID: THE ART OF LOVE AND OTHER POEMS. J. H. Mozley.

OVID: FASTI. Sir James G. Frazer.

OVID: HEROIDES AND AMORES. Grant Showerman.

OVID: METAMORPHOSES. F. J. Miller. 2 Vols.

OVID: TRISTIA AND EX PONTO. A. L. Wheeler.

PETRONIUS. M. Heseltine; SENECA: APOCOLOCYNTOSIS. W. H. D. Rouse.

PLAUTUS. Paul Nixon. 5 Vols.

PLINY: LETTERS. Melmoth's translation revised by W. M. L. Hutchinson. 2 Vols.

PLINY: NATURAL HISTORY. 10 Vols. Vols. I-V and IX. H. Rackham. Vols. VI and VII. W. H. S. Jones.

PROPERTIUS. H. E. Butler.

PRUDENTIUS. H. J. Thomson. 2 Vols.

QUINTILIAN. H. E. Butler. 4 Vols.

REMAINS OF OLD LATIN. E. H. Warmington. 4 Vols. Vol. I (Ennius and Caecilius). Vol. II (Livius, Naevius, Pacuvius, Accius). Vol. III (Lucilius, Laws of the XII Tables). Vol. IV (Archaic Inscriptions).

SALLUST. J. C. Rolfe.

SCRIPTORES HISTORIAE AUGUSTAE. D. Magie. 3 Vols.

SENECA: APOCOLOCYNTOSIS. *Cf.* PETRONIUS.

SENECA: EPISTULAE MORALES. R. M. Gummere. 3 Vols.

SENECA: MORAL ESSAYS. J. W. Basore. 3 Vols.

SENECA: TRAGEDIES. F. J. Miller. 2 Vols.

SIDONIUS: POEMS AND LETTERS. W. B. Anderson. 2 Vols.

SILIUS ITALICUS. J. D. Duff. 2 Vols.

STATIUS. J. H. Mozley. 2 Vols.

SUETONIUS. J. C. Rolfe. 2 Vols.

TACITUS: DIALOGUS. Sir Wm. Peterson; and AGRICOLA AND GERMANIA. Maurice Hutton.

TACITUS: HISTORIES AND ANNALS. C. H. Moore and J. Jackson. 4 Vols.

THE LOEB CLASSICAL LIBRARY

GREEK AUTHORS

THE LOEB CLASSICAL LIBRARY

ARISTOTLE: OECONOMICA AND MAGNA MORALIA. G. C. Armstrong. (With Metaphysics, Vol. II.)

ARISTOTLE: ON THE HEAVENS. W. K. C. Guthrie.

ARISTOTLE: ON THE SOUL, PARVA NATURALIA, ON BREATH. W. S. Hett.

ARISTOTLE: THE CATEGORIES. ON INTERPRETATION. H. P. Cooke; PRIOR ANALYTICS. H. Tredennick.

ARISTOTLE: POSTERIOR ANALYTICS. H. Tredennick; TOPICS. E. S. Forster.

ARISTOTLE: SOPHISTICAL REFUTATIONS. COMING-TO-BE AND PASSING-AWAY. E. S. Forster. ON THE COSMOS. D. J. Furley.

ARISTOTLE: PARTS OF ANIMALS. A. L. Peck; MOTION AND PROGRESSION OF ANIMALS. E. S. Forster.

ARISTOTLE: PHYSICS. Rev. P. Wicksteed and F. M. Cornford. 2 Vols.

ARISTOTLE: POETICS; LONGINUS ON THE SUBLIME. W. Hamilton Fyfe; DEMETRIUS ON STYLE. W. Rhys Roberts.

ARISTOTLE: POLITICS. H. Rackham.

ARISTOTLE: PROBLEMS. W. S. Hett. 2 Vols.

ARISTOTLE: RHETORICA AD ALEXANDRUM. H. Rackham. (With Problems, Vol. II.)

ARRIAN: HISTORY OF ALEXANDER AND INDICA. Rev. E. Iliffe Robson. 2 Vols.

ATHENAEUS: DEIPNOSOPHISTAE. C. B. Gulick. 7 Vols.

ST. BASIL: LETTERS. R. J. Deferrari. 4 Vols.

CALLIMACHUS: FRAGMENTS. C. A. Trypanis.

CALLIMACHUS: HYMNS AND EPIGRAMS, AND LYCOPHRON. A. W. Mair; ARATUS. G. R. Mair.

CLEMENT OF ALEXANDRIA. Rev. G. W. Butterworth.

COLLUTHUS. Cf. OPPIAN.

DAPHNIS AND CHLOE. Cf. LONGUS.

DEMOSTHENES I: OLYNTHIACS, PHILIPPICS AND MINOR ORATIONS: I-XVII AND XX. J. H. Vince.

DEMOSTHENES II: DE CORONA AND DE FALSA LEGATIONE. C. A. Vince and J. H. Vince.

DEMOSTHENES III: MEIDIAS, ANDROTION, ARISTOCRATES, TIMOCRATES, ARISTOGEITON. J. H. Vince.

DEMOSTHENES IV-VI: PRIVATE ORATIONS AND IN NEAERAM. A. T. Murray.

DEMOSTHENES VII: FUNERAL SPEECH, EROTIC ESSAY, EXORDIA AND LETTERS. N. W. and N. J. DeWitt.

DIO CASSIUS: ROMAN HISTORY. E. Cary. 9 Vols.

THE LOEB CLASSICAL LIBRARY

Dio Chrysostom. 5 Vols. Vols. I and II. J. W. Cohoon.
  Vol. III. J. W. Cohoon and H. Lamar Crosby. Vols. IV
  and V. H. Lamar Crosby.
Diodorus Siculus. 12 Vols. Vols. I-VI. C. H. Oldfather.
  Vol. VII. C. L. Sherman. Vols. IX and X. Russel M.
  Geer. Vol. XI. F. R. Walton.
Diogenes Laertius. R. D. Hicks. 2 Vols.
Dionysius of Halicarnassus : Roman Antiquities. Spel-
  man's translation revised by E. Cary. 7 Vols.
Epictetus. W. A. Oldfather. 2 Vols.
Euripides. A. S. Way. 4 Vols. Verse trans.
Eusebius : Ecclesiastical History. Kirsopp Lake and
  J. E. L. Oulton. 2 Vols.
Galen : On the Natural Faculties. A. J. Brock.
The Greek Anthology. W. R. Paton. 5 Vols.
The Greek Bucolic Poets (Theocritus, Bion, Moschus).
  J. M. Edmonds.
Greek Elegy and Iambus with the Anacreontea. J. M.
  Edmonds. 2 Vols.
Greek Mathematical Works. Ivor Thomas. 2 Vols.
Herodes. Cf. Theophrastus : Characters.
Herodotus. A. D. Godley. 4 Vols.
Hesiod and the Homeric Hymns. H. G. Evelyn White.
Hippocrates and the Fragments of Heracleitus. W. H. S.
  Jones and E. T. Withington. 4 Vols.
Homer : Iliad. A. T. Murray. 2 Vols.
Homer : Odyssey. A. T. Murray. 2 Vols.
Isaeus. E. S. Forster.
Isocrates. George Norlin and LaRue Van Hook. 3 Vols.
St. John Damascene : Barlaam and Ioasaph. Rev. G. R.
  Woodward and Harold Mattingly.
Josephus. H. St. J. Thackeray and Ralph Marcus. 9 Vols.
  Vols. I-VII.
Julian. Wilmer Cave Wright. 3 Vols.
Longus : Daphnis and Chloe. Thornley's translation
  revised by J. M. Edmonds; and Parthenius. S. Gaselee.
Lucian. 8 Vols. Vols. I-V. A. M. Harmon; Vol. VI.
  K. Kilburn; Vol. VIII. M. D. Macleod.
Lycophron. Cf. Callimachus.
Lyra Graeca. J. M. Edmonds. 3 Vols.
Lysias. W. R. M. Lamb.
Manetho. W. G. Waddell ; Ptolemy : Tetrabiblos. F. E.
  Robbins.

6

MARCUS AURELIUS. C. R. Haines.

MENANDER. F. G. Allinson.

MINOR ATTIC ORATORS. 2 Vols. K. J. Maidment and J. O. Burtt.

NONNOS: DIONYSIACA. W. H. D. Rouse. 3 Vols.

OPPIAN, COLLUTHUS, TRYPHIODORUS. A. W. Mair.

PAPYRI. NON-LITERARY SELECTIONS. A. S. Hunt and C. C. Edgar. 2 Vols. LITERARY SELECTIONS (Poetry). D. L. Page.

PARTHENIUS. *Cf.* LONGUS.

PAUSANIAS: DESCRIPTION OF GREECE. W. H. S. Jones. 5 Vols. and Companion Vol. arranged by R. E. Wycherley.

PHILO. 10 Vols. Vols. I-V. F. H. Colson and Rev. G. H. Whitaker; Vols. VI-IX. F. H. Colson.
Two Supplementary Vols. Translation only from an Armenian Text. Ralph Marcus.

PHILOSTRATUS: IMAGINES; CALLISTRATUS: DESCRIPTIONS. A. Fairbanks.

PHILOSTRATUS: THE LIFE OF APOLLONIUS OF TYANA. F. C. Conybeare. 2 Vols.

PHILOSTRATUS AND EUNAPIUS: LIVES OF THE SOPHISTS. Wilmer Cave Wright.

PINDAR. Sir J. E. Sandys.

PLATO: CHARMIDES, ALCIBIADES, HIPPARCHUS, THE LOVERS, THEAGES, MINOS AND EPINOMIS. W. R. M. Lamb.

PLATO: CRATYLUS, PARMENIDES, GREATER HIPPIAS, LESSER HIPPIAS. H. N. Fowler.

PLATO: EUTHYPHRO, APOLOGY, CRITO, PHAEDO, PHAEDRUS. H. N. Fowler.

PLATO: LACHES, PROTAGORAS, MENO, EUTHYDEMUS. W. R. M. Lamb.

PLATO: LAWS. Rev. R. G. Bury. 2 Vols.

PLATO: LYSIS, SYMPOSIUM, GORGIAS. W. R. M. Lamb.

PLATO: REPUBLIC. Paul Shorey. 2 Vols.

PLATO: STATESMAN, PHILEBUS. H. N. Fowler; ION. W. R. M. Lamb.

PLATO: THEAETETUS AND SOPHIST. H. N. Fowler.

PLATO: TIMAEUS, CRITIAS, CLITOPHO, MENEXENUS, EPISTULAE. Rev. R. G. Bury.

PLUTARCH: MORALIA. 15 Vols. Vols. I-V. F. C. Babbitt; Vol. VI. W. C. Helmbold; Vol. VII. P. H. De Lacy and B. Einarson; Vol. IX. E. L. Minar, Jr., F. H. Sandbach,

THE LOEB CLASSICAL LIBRARY

W. C. Helmbold; Vol. X. H. N. Fowler; Vol. XII. H.
Cherniss and W. C. Helmbold.
PLUTARCH: THE PARALLEL LIVES. B. Perrin. 11 Vols.
POLYBIUS. W. R. Paton. 6 Vols.
PROCOPIUS: HISTORY OF THE WARS. H. B. Dewing. 7 Vols.
PTOLEMY: TETRABIBLOS. *Cf.* MANETHO.
QUINTUS SMYRNAEUS. A. S. Way. Verse trans.
SEXTUS EMPIRICUS. Rev. R. G. Bury. 4 Vols.
SOPHOCLES. F. Storr. 2 Vols. Verse trans.
STRABO: GEOGRAPHY. Horace L. Jones. 8 Vols.
THEOPHRASTUS: CHARACTERS. J. M. Edmonds: HERODES,
etc. A. D. Knox.
THEOPHRASTUS: ENQUIRY INTO PLANTS. Sir Arthur Hort.
2 Vols.
THUCYDIDES. C. F. Smith. 4 Vols.
TRYPHIODORUS. *Cf.* OPPIAN.
XENOPHON: CYROPAEDIA. Walter Miller. 2 Vols.
XENOPHON: HELLENICA, ANABASIS, APOLOGY, AND SYMPO-
SIUM. C. L. Brownson and O. J. Todd. 3 Vols.
XENOPHON: MEMORABILIA AND OECONOMICUS. E. C. Mar-
chant.
XENOPHON: SCRIPTA MINORA. E. C. Marchant.

VOLUMES IN PREPARATION

GREEK AUTHORS

ARISTOTLE: HISTORY OF ANIMALS. A. L. Peck.
PLOTINUS. A. H. Armstrong.

LATIN AUTHORS

BABRIUS AND PHAEDRUS. B. E. Perry.

DESCRIPTIVE PROSPECTUS ON APPLICATION

CAMBRIDGE, MASS.	LONDON
HARVARD UNIV. PRESS	WILLIAM HEINEMANN LTD